READING'S MUNICIPAL TRANSPORT

1939 – 1950

WAR AND AUSTERITY

Ray Smith & John Whitehead

**A view of Reading in the years of turmoil, adversity and austerity
seen through the operations of Reading Corporation Transport**

There should be a map detailing the routes through the town centre and a network map which accompany this book. Should either be missing, replacements can be requested by visiting our website at www.MillanePublishing.com/maps

Front Cover: *Not quite what it seems – as aeroplane enthusiasts might well have already worked out! The aircraft is in fact a British Bristol Blenheim and the date is Sunday 27th July 1941, during a mock attack designed as a defence exercise – Broad Street was 'bombed' with smoke canisters, and Caversham and Reading Bridges were 'captured' by the 'enemy'. The exercise took place very early in the morning, to avoid inconveniencing the general public! Unfortunately, the identity of the AEC 661T trolleybus is not recorded but, from its adverts, it is one of 121, 122 or 131.*
Reading Standard

Title Page: *AEC Regent 48 (RD 8091) makes about 10 knots as it turns into George Street from Gosbrook Road, Caversham during the floods of March 1947, on a journey from Chalgrove Way to 'Wood Lane Junc.'. During the worst of the floods buses were diverted to use Caversham Bridge rather than Reading Bridge on account of flooding in Lower Caversham.*
© Reading Museum Service (Reading Borough Council); all rights reserved

Above: *A superb lineup of buses outside East Garage, Mill Lane depot circa spring 1943. From left to right they are Guy Arab 28, AEC Regents 9, 56 and 24, Guy Arab 6 and AEC Regents 57 and 47.*
Late W. J. Haynes © Millane Publishing

Back Cover: *The bustle of Broad Street, Reading's main shopping thoroughfare, in summer 1945, with a 1939vintage AEC trolleybus making progress westbound for Oxford Road, Norcot and, ultimately, Kentwood.*
© Reading Museum Service (Reading Borough Council); all rights reserved

---

COPYRIGHT NOTICE

© 2014 R. C. W. Smith, J. R. Whitehead and Millane Publishing

ISBN: 9780992873400

All rights reserved. No part of this publication may be reproduced, stored in a retrieval system, or transmitted in any form or by any means, electronic, mechanical, photocopying, recording, or otherwise, without the prior consent of Millane Publishing, 3 Littlecote Drive, Reading, Berkshire, RG1 6JD, United Kingdom.

Published by Millane Publishing

www.millanepublishing.com

This publication is in no way an official publication of Reading Transport Ltd., or of Reading Borough Council, although due acknowledgement is made of both as sources of official information contained herein.

Typesetting, layout and design by Graham L. Stone, April Cottage, 118 Whitley Wood Lane, Reading, Berkshire, RG2 8PP.

Printed and bound by CPI Group (UK) Ltd, Croydon, CR0 4YY.

MILLANE PUBLISHING exists in support of the READING BUS PRESERVATION GROUP and the research carried out by the READING TRANSPORT HISTORICAL RESEARCH GROUP.

Table of Contents

Introduction .... Page   4
Notes for Guidance .... Page   6

HISTORY OF THE UNDERTAKING 1939 – 1950

The Last Years of Peace 1936 – 1939

| Chapter 1 | Setting the Scene .... Page   9 |
| Chapter 2 | It's a Long, Long Time from May to September .... Page 21 |

Early War Years 1939 – 1940

| Chapter 3 | War is Declared .... Page 29 |
| Chapter 4 | The Calm and the Storm .... Page 37 |

Middle War Years 1940 – 1941

| Chapter 5 | Business as Usual .... Page 45 |
| Chapter 6 | Wartime Specials .... Page 57 |

Later War Years 1942 – 1945

Chapter 7	The Long Years of War, 1942–1945 .... Page 61
Chapter 8	Wartime Rolling Stock .... Page 79
Chapter 9	Getting Better all the Time .... Page 83

The William Little Years 1945 – 1946

Chapter 10	Into Peace – and Austerity .... Page 93
Chapter 11	The Little Year (and a bit!) .... Page 99
Chapter 12	William Little's Rolling Stock Developments .... Page 115

The Early Evans Years 1946 – 1950

Chapter 13	William John Evans Starts his Long Tenure .... Page 125
Chapter 14	Diversions, Snow, Fire, Flood – and Power Cuts! .... Page 131
Chapter 15	Onward Through 1947 .... Page 141
Chapter 16	The Threat of Nationalisation .... Page 151
Chapter 17	1948: Renewal and Expansion .... Page 153
Chapter 18	The 'Bargain Basement' Karriers .... Page 167
Chapter 19	PostWar Specials .... Page 173
Chapter 20	Of Titans and Trolleybuses .... Page 177
Chapter 21	The Light Brightens .... Page 193
Chapter 22	1950: Moving On .... Page 201

APPENDICES

Appendix A	Rolling Stock List (Vehicles Acquired 1939–1950) .... Page 205
Appendix B	Rolling Stock Details (Vehicles Acquired 1939–1950) .... Page 208
Appendix C	Subsequent Disposals of Vehicles .... Page 223
Appendix D	Summary of Route Developments 1939–1950 .... Page 228
Appendix E	The ThirtyNine Stops .... Page 236
Appendix F	Tickets .... Page 237
	Index .... Page 238
	Maps .... *(inside front and back cover)*

Introduction

The corporation's trams, buses and trolleybuses have been, progressively, part of Reading's townscape for more than a century, and this book is the first in an intended series detailing the history of public transport in the town from the nineteenth century to the present day. Between them, the books will record the history of a public service which has been vital to the life of Reading and which, for over sixty years, has been under scrutiny from a band of local transport historians and enthusiasts whose observations and notes have added considerably to the detail of the story.

In this volume the authors record the history of Reading Corporation Transport in the years of war and austerity. It vividly recounts the difficulties of operating a provincial bus fleet during the Second World War in the face of shortages, yet with increasing passenger demand and under the everpresent threat of air raids. Rising postwar demand for its services then stretched the undertaking further as the town expanded and leisure pursuits boomed again.

The authors have built the story upon a brief history of the undertaking which was put together in 1948 by wellknown local enthusiast the late Edgar Jordan, which he constructed from a set of the council's Tramways (and later Transport) Committee Minutes and from his father's own knowledge – for Edgar's father, 'Tim' Jordan, had worked for the corporation from 1906, first as a conductor, then a tramcar motorman and later a trolleybus driver, finally becoming an inspector in 1941. His son's enthusiasm for local transport coupled with his own experiences, notes and memories, provided an invaluable foundation to the text.

The survival of much primary material subsequently made available by the undertaking has caused the story to become so much richer in detail. Indeed, so much has survived, particularly from the wartime and postwar period, that it gave the authors a special appreciation of the operational, managerial and political decisions which were made as the undertaking developed throughout the 1940s, including the real possibility of postwar nationalisation. The book thus offers a unique insight into the operation of a municipal bus fleet in a mediumsized provincial town and sets that operation into the wider national and social context, for we have deliberately told the story alongside the social history of the day. Although the resulting text is longer, the account is surely the richer for telling the story thus, with the pressures of war and subsequent austerity affecting every aspect of life – even the daily operation of a provincial county town's bus services.

The written account has been supplemented by a wealth of contemporary photographs, painstakingly discovered by the authors over a great many years. And here we must record our gratitude to the late W. J. Haynes, a Londoner who visited Reading on several occasions and recorded the years of wartime operation on blackandwhite film, an era seemingly unrecorded by any other enthusiast. His task was a challenging one, constrained not only by the availability of photographic material but by the possible interest of the security forces. Why would anyone be photographing Reading's buses in wartime? Most of Bill Haynes' negative collection of Reading area buses, an extensive local record spanning the 1930s to the 1960s, has found a new home with those involved in the publication of this book.

This view, taken in spring 1939, typifies the doubledeck Reading motorbus fleet at the start of the period covered by this volume. Evidently taken either on a Sunday or a Wednesday afternoon (early closing day – the gates into The Arcade are shut), bus 44 (RD 2944), a Leyland Titan dating from 1931, is bound for Three Tuns. It has evidently fairly recently been repainted, because Gill Sans fleet number transfers were not introduced until December 1937. © Omnibus Society

Our thanks must also go to the Local Studies Section of Reading Central Library, where local newspapers gave additional richness to the historical account, both in word and picture, although the authors crave forgiveness for the sometimes poor reproduction quality of certain pictures photographed direct from newspapers, for these have had to be accepted where original photographic negatives no longer exist; and to Reading Museum Service; to the British Commercial Vehicle Museum; the Omnibus Society; Ian Allan Ltd. (V. C. Jones Collection); and a number of individuals, among them the late C. Carter, A. B. Cross, R. N. Hannay, D. A. Jones, the late H. E. Jordan, M. Manning, J. H. Meredith, A. D. Packer and M. Rooum, all of whom hold negatives relevant to the story; and to the several businesses and individuals who made available prints from their collections, including ACV Ltd; R. V. Fawcett; the late H. G. Hands; D. A. Hall; the late W. J. Haynes; the late H. E. Jordan; D. Lucas; the late R. Marshall; the late G. O. P. Pearce; M. Plunkett; D. Redmond; and A. Stevens. Even so, with around 240 illustrations included in total, the reader may well wonder at the sheer number of images from such a difficult period in the town's history. Each image was scanned by David Hall, to whom we tender our special thanks. Wherever possible, images have subsequently received quality enhancement to the very best standards at our disposal.

This story would not have been as full in detail, either, had it not been for the contributions by some of the older enthusiasts, who kept records and worked through those times – among them the late Edgar Jordan, the late Len Head, Bob Crawley, Dave Embery and the late Nobby Earley, who told of their memories and experiences.

Reading was fortunate to begin the Second World War with almost a third of its fleet less than six months old. The final trams had been withdrawn on 20th May 1939 and, on the following day, twentyfive spanking new trolleybuses had entered service. It was fortunate that these electric vehicles comprised such a high proportion of the fleet, for they shielded the town from the full force of compulsory petrol and diesel rationing – a major reason why Reading did so well.

Fortunately, Reading did not suffer the destruction meted out to certain other British towns and cities, like London, Coventry or Plymouth. As a designated 'safe town', Reading saw its population rise progressively with an influx of evacuees and a number of military establishments and businesses looking for a safer haven, all of which had clear implications for the Transport Department, with correspondingly increased passenger loadings. The extent can be measured by examining the annual passenger statistics, which show that in 1938 Reading Corporation buses and trams carried nearly 20 million passengers, yet by 1945 nearly 41½ million travelled on its services. All this was achieved by a fleet which, during the war, was increased by only six new trolleybuses, while four new motorbuses merely replaced four which were hopelessly obsolete. Evacuation buses, factory specials, and late night munitions specials all add to the story, whilst for a time the engineering staff at Mill Lane depot made parts for aircraft and artillery as part of the war effort.

The war years were also sandwiched into the development of the trolleybus system in Reading – so this book records, too, the planning and processes towards a pollutionfree transport network, decades before such concern about the environmental impact of travel became paramount, for the trolleybuses went on to serve the townspeople until 1968. Also documented are the postwar years of austerity, which serve as a reminder of what is now considered to have been the golden age of bus travel. This history of Reading Corporation Transport reflects those years of high demand for the corporation's services, which further stretched the undertaking as the town expanded in those early years of peace.

This is a book aimed at the local historian as well as the transport historian, but it will also offer much to social historians interested in the impact of war on the infrastructure and patterns of daily living. Of course, it will reawaken memories in those who lived through those times – and it particularly stands as a tribute to the men and women who kept Reading Corporation buses and trolleybuses moving during the war and in the challenging years immediately thereafter.

Finally, may we simply record the division of labour and shared work in putting this volume together? Ray Smith drew together the chronological history of the undertaking from the various diverse sources, a task begun in 1993. John Whitehead wove in the social history, researched the local newspapers, sourced the illustrations and incorporated numerous titbits. Graham Stone had the unenviable task of editing and condensing an end product which was everincreasing in size, arranging the typesetting and page layout, determining the final design – and keeping two headstrong authors in their respective corners!

Ray Smith   John Whitehead   Graham Stone   **June 2014**

During the war, Traffic Areas under the Road Traffic Act, 1930, which controlled passenger transport (but not trolleybuses) were suspended and replaced by Regional Transport Areas wholly within the 'regions' into which the entire country was divided. Each region was answerable to central government, but with a hierarchy for self government in place should the need arise. The regional transport commissioner for the whole of Southern Region was Sir Henry Piggott, who established his offices in Chiltern Court, a mansion in St. Peter's Avenue, Caversham. It still exists, now converted to apartments.

Commercial picture postcard

Notes for Guidance

Trolleybuses – a Technical Overview

Technical terms relating to motor vehicles will be familiar to most readers, but certain terms relating to trolleybuses and their overhead line installations may need explanation. Although this information is presented in the present tense, it relates specifically to trolleybuses of the traditional British type as operated in the UK between 1911 and 1972. Modern (overseas) trolleybus practice is similar but includes new technologies not relevant here.

Trolleybuses are electricallypropelled vehicles which run on rubber tyres and which draw their traction current from two wires (one positive and one negative) suspended above the roadway. In this they differ from trams, which run on rails and which have only one electric wire (the return current passing through the steel rails to earth). The electric motor, mounted under the floor, is controlled through a set of contactors which are switched in and out via the power pedal to supply the required amount of power. Modern trolleybuses use electronics to do this, but that is outside the scope of this book! In Britain, common (though not universal) practice was to mount the power pedal in the leftfoot position, the right foot being used for the brake – which could cause confusion when a driver switched from a motorbus to a trolleybus or vice versa!

Electric vehicles can be fitted with regenerative braking. This uses the principle that, by removing the power feed from an electric motor and using a mechanical force to turn the armature, the motor becomes a generator. On braking, the forward motion of the vehicle is dissipated via the drive shaft and the motor; this generates electricity which is fed back into the system for use by other trolleybuses elsewhere. Reading trolleybuses could not be fitted with full regenerative braking, as this was incompatible with the mercury arc rectifiers used on the Reading system.

Power (at a nominal 550–600 volts DC) is collected from the running wire via the two trolley poles (or trolleybooms), securely mounted on a framework (the trolleybase) on the roof of the vehicle. Large springs each side of each trolley boom provide the tension required to keep the poles in contact with the overhead line. The trolleyhead at the end of each trolleyboom runs along the underside of the running wires to collect the power. Reading, like most operators, initially used brass trolleywheels in their trolleyheads (as per contemporary tramway practice), but from early 1938 they changed to the more modern carbon skids to allow higher speeds.

The overhead line is supported by traction poles – tubular steel poles, usually about 31ft long, set 6ft into the ground at a 5° rake away from the road and surrounded in concrete. Different grades (e.g. light, medium, heavy and extra heavy) are used according to prevailing circumstances. The running wires – the conductor wires along which the trolley heads run – are usually about 20ft above road level, that nearest the centre of the road being positive and that nearest the edge of the road negative polarity. They are typically suspended from span wires erected across the roadway, usually between opposite traction poles (see p165, lower photo) but sometimes from 'wall rosettes' anchored into the fabric of adjacent buildings. In narrow streets, or in streets too wide for span wires to be used, suspension is via bracket arms – horizontal tubular supports fixed at one end to a single traction pole and braced with tie rods (see p150, lower photo). A similar method is the gantry, a tubular support joining two traction poles situated opposite one another (see p132). Whichever method is used to suspend the running wires, insulation is required!

The overhead is divided into electrically isolated sections (in Britain, halfamile is normal). Overhead junctions (like railway 'points') are called frogs. Facing frogs, where one line diverges from another, are springloaded and operated either by hand (the conductor leaving the vehicle and pulling a handle on an adjacent traction pole) or automatically (by the trolleyheads energising, or otherwise, a solenoid fitted to the overhead line a short distance before the frog, depending on whether or not the driver is applying power as the trolley heads pass underneath). Trailing frogs, where two lines converge, are springloaded. Vehicles turn by means of a turning circle, which allows vehicles to execute a Uturn, or via a reverser which (by the use of frogs) allows a vehicle to carry out a 'threepoint turn' into and out of a side turning.

Bodywork Layout

Bus enthusiasts use a threepart code to describe the basic layout and seating capacity of a particular vehicle. The elements of this code that apply to vehicles mentioned in this book are as follows:

First element (alphabetic): Any one of the following:

- L   Doubledeck, lowbridge layout (with offside sunken gangway and bench seats in the upper saloon).
- H   Doubledeck, highbridge layout (with centre gangway on both decks and pairs of seats each side).
- UH As above, but built to wartime utility specification.
- B   Singledeck bus

Second element (numeric): The passenger capacity of the vehicle. A single figure is shown for singledeckers, while doubledeckers are shown with the upper deck capacity 'over' that of the lower deck (e.g. H36/30R). To this may be appended a figure with a plus sign (e.g. H36/30+8R) to indicate the number of standees permitted.

Third element (alphabetic): Any one of the following:

- F   Forwardor frontdoorway position
- R   Rear open platform
- RD   Rear platform fitted with platform doors.
- ROS Rear open platform and open staircase

For example, the Duplebodied Bedford OBs were B30F (singledeck bus with front entrance and 30 seats), and the BUT 9611T trolleybuses were H30/26RD (highbridge double decker with 30 seats upstairs, 26 seats downstairs and a rear platform fitted with doors).

'Normal control' refers to a vehicle in which the driver sits behind the front axle (e.g. the Bedford OBs). On a 'forward control' vehicle the driver sits above or ahead of the front axle, the steering linkage being 'cranked' rather than straight.

Livery

The livery of Reading's buses in this period was crimson and cream, applied in various proportions as described in the text and, more fully, in Appendix B. Sometimes this is described as 'linedout', which means that a thin decorative line of a contrasting colour was painted around the edge of an area of solid colour (e.g. a thin line of cream on the crimson, or a thin line of red on the cream). This was dropped due to the cost, although some subsequent versions of the livery had the horizontal aluminium beading which separated crimson from cream painted black.

Identification Lights

Most corporation doubledeck motorbuses and trolleybuses during the period covered by this book were fitted with a pair of identity lights in the front panel, near the destination blind. Prewar, these were blue for motorbuses and white for trolleybuses. Their purpose was probably to distinguish motorbuses from trolleybuses, and corporation vehicles from those of Thames Valley and other operators, which lacked this feature. They fell out of use with blackout regulations and were not specified for early postwar deliveries, either due to continuing materials shortages or because Transport Manager William Little didn't see their need. Subsequent deliveries, under John Evans, initially included blue lights on both motorbuses and trolleybuses (presumably Mr Evans thought the lights a good idea, but only if all his vehicles had the same identifying colour, viz., blue). Thus, the second batch of AEC Regent IIs and the BUT 9611T trolleybuses had them from new, and the utility trolleybuses had them fitted retrospectively (and, presumably, the AEC 661T trolleybuses were just given blue lamps in place of white). After arrival of the BUTs, it seems that a decision was taken to have all new deliveries fitted with route number blinds in the future, so the need for identification lights evaporated! Henceforth, once the lamps behind the identification lights 'blew' they were not replaced, and were either plated over or the complete panel was replaced when a vehicle fitted with them went in for a body overhaul and/or a repaint.

Abbreviations

A number of specialist abbreviations appear in this book, as follows:

AEC	Associated Equipment Company Ltd.
ARP	Air Raid Precautions – with particular reference to the wardens who patrolled the streets enforcing the blackout etc.
BUT	British United Traction Company Ltd.
DERV	Diesel oil (the acronym stands for Diesel Engined Road Vehicle, and is sometimes presented in lower case).
GEC	General Electric Company Ltd.
LDV	Local Defence Volunteers – later the Home Guard.
MOT	Ministry of Transport (referred to as the Ministry of War Transport (MOWT) from mid1941 until 1945).

Place Names

Reading has changed greatly in 70 years, and many places mentioned in the text no longer exist:

Arcade, The: A shopping arcade linking Broad Street with Friar Street, which subsequently became Market Way and (latterly) Sainsbury's.

Boots: The main local branch of this national chain of chemists was located next to the Broad Street Independent Chapel (now Waterstone's) on the southern side of Broad Street.

Bull Hotel: Located on the corner of Broad Street and Cross Street; the lettering is still visible in the masonry at parapet level.

Coop: Reading's branch of the Cooperative department store was located in West Street, the site now occupied by Primark, with additional entrances in Cheapside and Friar Street.

Cork Street: A *cul de sac* off of Oxford Road (now Broad Street West), buried under today's Broad Street Mall.

J. Samuel Elliott: This highquality joinery company was located in Gosbrook Road, Caversham, almost opposite Westfield Road.

Elm Park: Reading Football Club's former ground, located in the vicinity of Norfolk Road, in the builtup area between Tilehurst Road and Oxford Road.

Engineer's Arms: Located at the junction of Whitley Wood Lane and Whitley Wood Road; demolished 2007.

Four Horse Shoes: Located at the junction of Basingstoke Road and Long Barn Lane; subsequently Eastern Pearl oriental restaurant; empty at time of going to press.

General Post Office (GPO): Located in Friar Street in the building that is currently a Yates's pub.

Grenadier: At the junction of Basingstoke Road and Whitley Wood Lane, now the site of the Holiday Inn.

Heelas: Department store in Broad Street, taken over by the John Lewis Partnership in 1953. The Heelas name was dropped in favour of John Lewis in 2001.

Langston's: This outfitters and country pursuits retailer had two shops in Reading – one in Oxford Road at Cork Street and the other at 'Langston's Corner' at the junction of West Street with Friar Street.

McIlroy's: Department store at the eastern end of Oxford Road (now Broad Street West). The ornate McIlroy's Building is now given over to shops and apartments.

Dorothy Perkins: Ladies' outfitters located on the southern side of Broad Street between Heelas and Chain Street.

Primitive Methodist Chapel: The classicallystyled building in London Street, now the Great Expectations pub.

Ranikhet Camp: Military camp located near the junction of Norcot Road with Church End Lane.

Stations: Reading General, served by the Great Western Railway, forms the main platform area of the current

Reading Station. The Southern Railway's Reading Station (Reading South after nationalisation) was located where today's station concourse stands.

Triangle Car Park: At the junction of Friar Street with Lower Thorn Street and Caversham Road, subsequently obliterated by the Chatham Street roundabout.

Vaudeville Cinema: On the northern side of Broad Street at its junction with Union Street, on the site currently occupied by Boots the Chemist. This was an important bus stop, and a timing point for a number of services as it was adjacent to jeweller H. Samuel's clock.

Vincents: A wellknown motor dealer and bodybuilding business, which had a highprofile showroom opposite Reading Stations, on the site subsequently occupied by the Jolly Porter and Thames Tower at the eastern end of the Western Tower shops.

Wellsteeds: A large department store which occupied the site in Broad Street currently occupied by the entrance to The Oracle. This was an important bus stop and timing point, especially for westbound trolleybus services to Tilehurst and Kentwood.

White Hart: This large public house was located on the corner of St. Mary's Butts and what was then Oxford Road, at the site now occupied by Broad Street Mall.

Currency

Until 15th February 1971, Britain used a currency system in which the pound sterling (£) was divided into 20 shillings (20s or 20/), the shilling itself consisting of 12 pence (12d). £1 therefore consisted of 240d. The shilling was equivalent to 5p in modern money, and one old penny was worth about 0.42p. Of course, a pound in 1940 bought a great deal more than would a pound today!

Coins in circulation at the time were the farthing (¼d), halfpenny (½d, pronounced 'ha'penny'), penny (1d), three pence (3d), sixpence (6d), shilling (1s), florin (2s) and half crown (2s 6d). Banknotes existed for values of 10s, £1, £5 and (until their temporary withdrawal just after the war due to the number of German forgeries in circulation) £10 and £20 – although, as typical fares were only a matter of pence, few people would have offered a banknote in payment! There were also monetary values of a crown (5s) and a guinea (£1 1s, i.e. 21 shillings), although there were no coins in general circulation to represent these units.

Units of Measure

This book uses traditional imperial units of measure. Those which appear within these pages are as follows:

1 inch = 2.54 cm
12 inches = 1 foot (30.5 cm)
3 feet or 36 inches = 1 yard (91.4 cm)
1,760 yards = 1 mile (1.6 km)

1 pound (1 lb) = 0.454 kg
1 stone = 14 lb = 6.35 kg
1 quarter (qtr) = 2 stone = 28 lb (i.e. ¼ cwt)
1 hundredweight (1 cwt) = 112 lb = 50.8 kg
1 ton = 20 cwt = 1,016 kg (1.016 tonne)

1 pint = 0.57 litres
1 gallon = 8 pints (4.54 litres)

Time

The twelvehour clock is used throughout this book.

Another typical Reading bus of the prewar period, in all probability taken on the same day as the view of bus 44 on page 4, this view shows 1936 AEC Regent 50 (RD 8093) on Route N, loading for 'Whitley Estate Callington Road'. This bus, like that on page 4, seems to have had a recent repaint and wears the Gill Sans fleet number transfers introduced in December 1937.

© Omnibus Society

1   Setting the Scene

The accepted origin of the town of Reading is that there was some human habitation on the banks of the River Kennet, near to its confluence with the River Thames, at least as early as the Iron Age – and, most likely, considerably earlier. Doubtless the site of the settlement was chosen because nearby the River Thames was not fordable, whereas the River Kennet was. The settlement had no direct Roman connection but might have expanded in early Saxon times when the former Romano-British town of Silchester, about ten miles to the south-west, became uninhabited for a reason that is so far unknown.

The first documented historical mention of Reading was in the *Anglo Saxon Chronicles* in 871AD, which recorded major skirmishes with Danish invaders in the vicinity while making specific reference to the settlement. After the Norman invasion of 1066 and the subsequent compilation of *The Domesday Book*, a fine Benedictine abbey was founded in 1121. The town was built up around the abbey and became quite an important commercial centre, although there seem to have been regular quarrels between the local merchants and the Abbot for much of the abbey's existence. The abbey, in its day, was of national importance, attracting not only pilgrims, the poor and the sick but also, on regular occasions, royalty together with all its associated retinue.

When the abbey was plundered and left in ruins in 1539 on Henry VIII's instructions, the layout of the town centre as we know it today had already been established, roughly triangular in shape, with what is now known as Friar Street as a northerly base line and roads bounding the east and west meeting at the top of a hill to the south at what is now known as Whitley Street. This is plainly evident from the earliest known map of Reading, published in John Speed's atlas of Great Britain in 1611. The town's population at that time has been estimated as not more than 5,000. With the loss of the abbey the town's fortunes began to waver. However, dominated instead by four ancient churches, all of which still stand, the town had become a trading centre on the major route from London to the west at a point where it was bisected by routes from the south to Oxford, for the Thames had long been bridged just north of the town, at Caversham, and the Kennet by some fairly inadequate structures on both routes into the town from Whitley.

Reading survived a siege in 1643 during the Civil War and subsequently developed new industries. Many of these benefited from the increased use of the River Thames as a haulage route and the subsequent building of the Kennet & Avon Canal, which opened in 1723. As travel became more commonplace, the town also rose in importance as a stopping point on the London to Bath road. Although the town itself had expanded very little in the meantime, it was becoming a little more respectable as new buildings were constructed. A century or so later the Industrial Revolution was beginning to have some effect, the town's population as at the 1801 Census being 9,421.

Expansion of the town beyond its established ancient limits took place mainly along what became known as Oxford Road and along a newly-constructed Kings Road and Queens Road (both opened in 1834). The Royal Berkshire Hospital opened in 1839 and a new cemetery came into use at the end of Kings Road, where it met London Road at the Marquis of Granby, in 1843. When, in 1840, the Great Western Railway reached Reading from London, the town had a population of about 19,000 and thereafter the town and its population expanded, reaching 42,000 in 1881, 60,000 in 1891 and over 72,000 in 1901. A new Reading Union Workhouse (later to become Battle Hospital) in Oxford Road was opened 1867, with market gardens in its immediate vicinity.

As it became obvious that a growing population required local public transport, the innkeepers of the town got together to establish horse bus services from their own premises to certain outlying areas. A horse tramway was established in 1879 between the newly-completed Brock Barracks, headquarters of the Royal Berkshire Regiment (at the westerly extremity of the town at that time) and the aforementioned cemetery at the eastern end of town; traffic soon rose to 14,000 passengers per week.

The various horse bus operators became jealous of the success of the Reading Tramways Company and competition became rife in the quest for passengers. This resulted in accidents, many cases of reckless driving and overloading of vehicles coming before the town's magistrates. The borough council (county borough council from 1888, with the introduction of self-government independent of Berkshire County Council) began to take notice when the Reading Tramways Company's infrastructure began to deteriorate and, in 1898, the borough surveyor was instructed to report on the tramways undertaking and the way in which it was run. He did so in terms of sweeping condemnation. The company, when faced with the report, countered with a proposal to electrify and extend the system. The town council rejected this and resolved to purchase the undertaking (as it was entitled so to do under section 43 of the Tramways Act, 1870) and to electrify and extend the system itself. There followed two years of dispute as to the value of the system, culminating in arbitration, and it was not until October 1901 that the corporation finally purchased the horse tramway company for £11,394, becoming owner of a transport system which by then comprised 13 double-deck tramcars and 85 horses.

The corporation had, meanwhile, sought parliamentary powers to extend and electrify the system and a superb and properly-constructed electric tramway was inaugurated amidst much pomp and civic pride on 22nd July 1903. It was destined to last 36 years, during which time it almost always operated at a profit and gave the town an extremely solid foundation to its public transport undertaking. Postponed from 1914 due to the Great War, the undertaking introduced motor omnibus operation on 6th December 1919 as a start towards meeting the needs of those parts of the town to which the electric tramways did not extend. There had been a boundary revision in 1887–89, which effectively doubled the size of the town, and another in 1911, which brought Caversham and Tilehurst into the borough.

The outer suburbs developed considerably during the 1920s and 1930s and a start was made to clear some of the inner areas of housing in the town, which had degenerated. The motor omnibus network had meanwhile developed to serve the suburbs, but at the same time the electric tramway system was becoming inadequate because it did not reach those suburbs. By the early 1930s the passenger comfort offered by the trams was becoming noticeably inferior to that offered by motor omnibuses which, by now, had become fully-enclosed and fitted with pneumatic tyres. The open top trams in Reading were looking increasingly old-fashioned. There was also a growing national road lobby which saw trams as obstructive to the increasing motor traffic, and dangerous for passengers who boarded and alighted in the centre of the road. The fate of the British tram was finally sealed by a Royal Commission report in 1930 which described them as obsolescent and the cause of *"...much unnecessary congestion and considerable unnecessary danger to the public"*. The report suggested that the tram in British towns and cities should be replaced as soon as possible. Reading's first tramway replacements were the newly-introduced motorbus services which saw the withdrawal of the 'side lines' of the tramway: the Bath Road section ceased after operation on 31st March 1930, and the Erleigh Road section after operation on 7th August 1932. During the 1930s there was also a general expansion of the corporation motorbus services north of the Thames into Caversham, southwards to Whitley and along the Bath Road to Horncastle. At the same time, plans were made to replace the remaining lines of Reading's tramways with a new trolleybus system, which would utilise the electrical infrastructure of the tramway.

In 1934, the Transport Committee's Transport (Future Policy) Sub-Committee recommended a phased conversion programme for the period 1936–42 under which not only would the remaining tramway routes be converted to trolleybus operation but, with only a couple of exceptions, so too would all the existing motorbus routes. This recommendation, the culmination of several years of deliberation by the Transport Committee and the town council, was adopted with minor modifications. If the scheme, as finally agreed, had not been curtailed due to the outbreak of another world war, (which, in itself, resulted in changing the course of history forever), Reading's public transport system would have become almost exclusively trolleybus operated. In the 1930s, trolleybuses were regarded as the pinnacle of municipal transport modernity – and Reading was on that bandwagon!

Phase One of a slightly modified scheme was brought into being on 18th July 1936 with the inauguration of the first trolleybus route, between Caversham Bridge and Whitley Street, using vehicles considered by the undertaking at the time to be experimental.

At that time it was sufficient to define Whitley, at the top of the long hill up from the town centre, as being just that area in the immediate vicinity of Whitley Street. It was dominated, as it still is, by the imposing nineteenth century Christ Church with its very tall steeple. On that side of the hill remote from the town stretched Basingstoke Road, the town's main traffic artery to the south. Nearby was the long, straight Northumberland Avenue, supporting newer middle-class property on both its sides, which petered out as the road went onwards to the south. Although the beginnings of a vast new council housing estate, known as Whitley Estate, was already being established beyond, this was largely the full extent of the locality known as Whitley, although there was also a hamlet some distance down Basingstoke Road, known as Lower Whitley.

Phase One was very quickly deemed a success, so plans went ahead for the abandonment of the two remaining electric tramway routes and implementation of Phase Two of the conversion scheme, which took place on Sunday 21st May 1939, the date which this volume takes as its starting point. It was the day on which a new phase in the history of Reading's municipal transport undertaking commenced. The previous night the town had said a final goodbye to its electric tramway. There was considerable sentiment at the end, it has to be said, despite the anti-tram feeling in the town (so typical of elsewhere in Britain in the 1930s) which was beginning to have an adverse effect on tramway revenue receipts. The service pattern as at early May 1939 is summarised on pages 12 and 13.

It is important to appreciate what it had been like to be living in Reading in the mid-1930s. Times were still hard as the country pulled itself slowly out of the Depression. Reading was largely an industrial and market town, and the principal town in Berkshire. In those days there was still a residual Victorian-type municipal pride and the town was run by an elected yet 'elite' set, with names like McIlroy, Palmer, Simonds and Sutton – from families who had successful and long-established businesses, factories and shops in the town. To put the town's municipal transport undertaking into complete context and for the reader to appreciate sufficient aspects of what was going on at the time, we now need to set the scene as to the way things were.

A few fundamental statistics regarding the County Borough of Reading at the time will be of interest to the reader. At the end of 1935, the town's estimated population was 99,000 (of which roundly 11,400 were children of school age), living in 26,000 dwellings (of which 970 had been newly-built that year). However, it was believed that the town's population increased by around 10,000 during an academic year due to the influx of students to the University of Reading and of boarding pupils and teachers to a sizeable number of private schools which existed in the town at that time. This was about the size of population that the municipal transport undertaking was serving at the beginning of the era which this volume covers. The undertaking's annual report for the financial year 1937/38 records 6,435,541 passengers as being carried on the trams, paying £39,548 in fares, whilst the motor omnibuses carried 11,463,189 passengers, which brought in £90,499; and the experimental trolleybus route had carried 2,091,675 passengers yielding revenue of £9,097.

Times were most definitely 'unsettled'. The United Kingdom had largely pulled through the Depression and there was an

Population and Transport Statistics

These official Transport Dept figures show the dramatic increase in the population of the County Borough of Reading, and the effect on the Department's operations.

Year	Population of Borough	Miles Operated	Passengers Carried
1911	72,217	909,349	7,836,056
1921	92,278	1,069,035	13,886,242
1931	97,149	1,890,490	17,907,093
1935	99,600	2,139,546	17,398,908
1938	100,400	2,296,914	19,990,405
1940	114,600	2,253,908	24,318,420
1941	124,800	2,214,035	31,599,105
1942	117,800	2,603,314	38,697,341
1943	113,000	2,519,312	39,680,551
1944	111,340	2,483,384	39,124,773
1945	108,830	2,612,748	41,385,031
1946		2,761,927	40,729,120
1947		c. 3,196,000	41,753,323
1948	114,500	3,254,109	41,793,878
1949		3,376,533	41,246,239

economic resurgence; however, there was an uneasy political climate. Internationally, and particularly in several parts of Europe, this was certainly the case, with extreme left vying with extreme right, and by the time our story starts, matters had become very worrying. There was a widespread feeling at this time that war was inevitable – there were also vast numbers of pacifists voicing an opinion that confrontation should be avoided at all costs.

In the era with which this volume is concerned, most employees worked a five-and-a-half-day week – Mondays to Fridays and Saturday mornings. Shops, too, were open five-and-a-half days a week – Mondays to Saturdays, but with one mid-week day maintained as an 'early closing day' to compensate for shop assistants having to work on Saturday afternoons. Such matters seem to have been controlled by the local Chamber of Commerce. In Reading, half-day closing was on Wednesdays and, at lunchtime on Wednesdays, all shops shut for the rest of the day – except for newsagents, confectioners and tobacconists, which were allowed to re-open for an hour in the late afternoon, round about 5.00pm to 6.00pm, mainly to sell evening papers. As a rule, lunchtimes during the working week were around an hour-and-a-half long, and in a provincial town the size and layout of Reading, vast numbers of workers reckoned to be able to get home for lunch – after all, in that era, although there were longer distance commuters, the vast majority of persons in employment in the town both lived and worked within the borough or within a short distance.

Motorcars were only just becoming affordable to some sections of the 'middle classes', so that although private car ownership was increasing, most folk in the town were entirely reliant on urban passenger transport, rode bicycles, or walked. There was at that time, however, a proliferation of motorcycles and motorcycle combinations – and increasing numbers of lorries and vans. Urban traffic at that time also comprised a fair proportion of horse-drawn carts and delivery vans, the occasional steam-driven machine, and various barrows and hand-carts. Kerbside parking was just beginning to become 'difficult' in the town's main thoroughfares. There was a cab rank in the middle of Broad Street to the east of Heelas (between the east- and west-bound tram tracks, between Cross Street and The Arcade) and in May 1939, after the final tram had run, it was suggested by one of the local papers that the centre of Broad Street could now be used for car parking! It was at this time, too, that the first one-way street scheme, that of Cross Street, was implemented. Various pedestrian crossing points had already been introduced, together with several sets of traffic signals, the first of which was at the intersection of Friar Street with Station Road and Queen Victoria Street. Most streets were lit by gas, although the first serious attempts to install electric street lighting took place when the new 'main line' trolleybus infrastructure was being put into place, so it was extremely new.

After the end of the Great War – the 'war to end all wars' – the country had entered a new era in which there was a huge shake-up in more-or-less everything, not least lifestyle. Folk became increasingly 'middle-class' and, with significantly fewer employed in domestic service, a typical middle-class housewife was obliged to assume a far more active role. Fortunately, increasing numbers of labour-saving products, both consumables and electrically-powered 'luxury' goods, came to her aid. Gas and electricity steadily became quite normally incorporated utilities in newly-built middle-class housing, bringing with them the cooking stove to supersede the coal-fired kitchen range, various heating devices as alternatives to the open coal fire in the other rooms, and electric light. A good many older houses within the borough, on the other hand, retained gas lighting until well into the 1950s.

The newer houses also had inside toilets and bathrooms, and more compact kitchens, all with cold running water. With instantaneous hot water heaters or a more-basic coke or anthracite boiler and hot water tank, they were considered a luxury when compared with what had gone before! Most households by the start of the period covered by this volume had come to possess a 'wireless', which for many became a focal point in their living room; the whole family would sit together of an evening to listen to the evening's entertainment on the National Programme.

Considerably fewer households had the luxury of a telephone during the era with which we are concerned, relying on the use of public telephone call boxes or coin-box telephones installed in corner shops and sub-post offices – remember the dark blue and white enamel signs reading 'You may Telephone from Here'? On the other hand, there was an extremely efficient postal service, with deliveries throughout the day in urban areas. Newer housing, built post-Great War, became, progressively, more light and airy and more spacious and usually had plenty of garden, front and rear. This allowed occupiers to feel proud and be kings and queens of their 'castles' and their lands, for now as never before, middle-class folk were encouraged to buy their own property (with the inevitable mortgage, of course) rather than renting from a landlord. Alongside this, council housing was also expanding in the suburbs, financed by the local authority; this provided low-cost rented housing to replace life-expired inner-town rented homes.

As a general rule, married women were, first and foremost, full-time housewives and mothers. They spent their time busily keeping house and found it necessary to work to a fairly strict routine, e.g. to be home and have meals ready at 'dinner time'. Shopping, little and often, was slotted in with washing, ironing, baking and housework. There were no domestic refrigerators to speak of, so all perishable food was kept in a cool walk-in cupboard, usually on an outside wall, called a larder (or pantry). There was little food shopping done on a Monday, because without refrigeration perishable food was not left in the shops over the weekend. No wonder that in the home Monday was usually washday and a day for using up perishable food left over from the weekend – cold meat and 'bubble-&-squeak' come to mind! Friday was, traditionally, a fish day.

Corner shops catered for day-to-day shopping in most urban localities, although every item was a penny or tuppence more expensive than 'in town' (or, if you lived in Tilehurst or on Caversham Heights, 'in the village'). The housewife usually had the added benefit of several calling tradesmen, but would still go into town (or to the village) at least once a week for domestic shopping, generally using the municipal transport system to get her there and back.

Leisure time for the working and middle classes, in particular Saturday afternoons and Sundays, was much prized. For the men, going to see Reading F. C. play at Elm Park, or pottering about the garden or on the allotment, was considered relaxation. Saturday night was, traditionally, family bath night and, in the era in which this volume is set, most of the houses in the town still had no inside toilet and no bathroom as such. Indeed, few older houses boasted a hot water supply, so kettles and saucepans full of water had

SUMMARY OF SERVICES AS AT EARLY MAY 1939

The passenger transport services, by tram, trolleybus and motor omnibus, which were in operation as at the final abandonment of tramcar operation – which is the starting point of this volume – were as shown below. The reference numbers given for motorbus services are the Ministry of Transport stage carriage licence numbers allocated by the South Eastern Area Traffic Commissioners, as set up under the Road Traffic Act, 1930.

TRAMS

Route A: Wokingham Road – Oxford Road (from the Terminus Café at the junction of Wokingham Road with St. Peter's Road, via Wokingham Road, Cemetery Junction, Kings Road, King Street, Broad Street and Oxford Road, to the Pond House at the junction of Oxford Road with Grovelands Road). *Mon–Sat and Sun pm*.

Route B: London Road – Barracks (from the Southern Railway overbridge at the borough boundary in London Road, just beyond the junction of London Road with Liverpool Road, via London Road, Cemetery Junction, Kings Road, King Street, Broad Street and Oxford Road, to Barracks, terminating at the cross-over at Wantage Road). *Mon–Sat; also operated London Road – Broad Street only on Sun pm.*

TROLLEYBUSES

Route C: Whitley Street – Caversham (from Whitley Pump, at the junction of Whitley Street with Christchurch Road and Basingstoke Road, via Whitley Street, Southampton Street, Bridge Street, St. Mary's Butts, West Street, Friar Street and Caversham Road to the junction of Caversham Road with Thames Side Promenade, adjacent to Caversham Bridge). *Mon–Sat and Sun pm*.

MOTORBUSES

Route F: Caversham Heights – Shinfield Road (from the junction of Uplands Road with Conisboro' Avenue, via Conisboro' Avenue, Albert Road, The Mount, Priest Hill, St. Anne's Road, Church Road, Bridge Street, Caversham Bridge, Caversham Road, Tudor Road, Station Hill, Stations, Station Road, Queen Victoria Street, Broad Street, King Street, Duke Street, London Street, London Road, Kendrick Road, Christchurch Road and Shinfield Road, to a terminus at the borough boundary at the junction of Shinfield Road with Whitley Wood Lane, and vice versa except returning through town centre between London Road and Broad Street via Crown Street, Southampton Street, Bridge Street and St. Mary's Butts). *Daily* (K55/6); *augmented by a separate Stations – Shinfield Road service via the same route on Weekdays* (K55/4).

Route G: Tilehurst (Plough) – Three Tuns (via School Road, Norcot Road, Oxford Road, Broad Street, King Street, Duke Street, London Street, London Road, Craven Road, Erleigh Road, Crescent Road and Wokingham Road, and vice versa). *Daily, but on Sun am only operated Tilehurst (Plough) – Erleigh Road, to a separate special fare scale.)* (K55/3).

Route H: Emmer Green – Lower Whitley (from the junction of Chalgrove Way with Kidmore End Road, via Kidmore End Road, Peppard Road, Prospect Street, Gosbrook Street, Gosbrook Road, George Street, Reading Bridge, Vastern Road, Blagrave Street, Stations, Station Road, Queen Victoria Street, Broad Street, King Street, Duke Street, London Street, Silver Street, Mount Pleasant, Whitley Street, Basingstoke Road and Whitley Wood Lane to a terminus at the junction of Whitley Wood Lane with Whitley Wood Road, and vice versa). *Daily* (K55/14).

Route I: Lower Caversham – Horncastle (from the junction of Henley Road with Lower Henley Road at the borough boundary, via Henley Road, Donkin Hill, Briants Avenue, Gosbrook Road, George Street, Reading Bridge, Vastern Road, Blagrave Street, Stations, Station Road, Queen Victoria Street, Broad Street, St. Mary's Butts, Castle Street, Castle Hill and Bath Road to the Horncastle public house at the borough boundary, and vice versa except that it was routed through the town centre between Castle Street and Queen Victoria Street via Gun Street, Minster Street and Broad Street). *Daily* (K55/15). Augmented by a separate service Lower Caversham – Broad Street (opposite Vaudeville cinema) by the same route inbound and Broad Street (opposite Cross Street) – Lower Caversham outbound (having turned in the town centre off another service (route K) via Station Road, Friar Street, Market Place, Butter Market and Broad Street. *Sat, Sun and Bank Holidays except Christmas Day.* (K55/9).

Route J: Roebuck – Three Tuns (via Oxford Road, Broad Street, Queen Victoria Street, Station Road, Stations, Station Road, Queen Victoria Street, Broad Street, King Street, Duke Street, London Street, London Road, Craven Road, Erleigh Road, Crescent Road and Wokingham Road, and vice versa). *Mon–Sat and Sun pm*. (K55/10); Operated as **Route A: Roebuck – Three Tuns** (via Oxford Road, Broad Street, King Street, Kings Road and Wokingham Road) *Sun am, to a separate special fare scale* (K55/11).

Route K: Broad Street (Vaudeville) – Woodcote Road (via Queen Victoria Street, Station Road, Stations, Station Hill, Tudor Road, Caversham Road, Caversham Bridge, Bridge Street, Church Road, St. Peter's Hill and Woodcote Road to a terminus at the borough boundary at the junction of Woodcote Road with St. Peter's Avenue, and vice versa to Station Road, thence via Friar Street and West Street to Broad Street). *Mon–Sat. On Sun pm, Good Friday, Boxing Day, and on Easter, Whitsun and August Bank Holiday Mondays, the inbound service operated to Broad Street (opposite Cross Street) to allow the bus to take up service on route I, arriving there from Station Road via Friar Street, Market Place, Butter Market and Broad Street.* (K55/2).

Route L : Berkeley Avenue – Hemdean Road (from a terminus in Littlecote Drive, via Berkeley Avenue, Katesgrove Lane, Southampton Street, Bridge Street, Gun Street, Minster Street, Broad Street, Queen Victoria Street, Station Road, Stations, Blagrave Street, Vastern Road, Reading Bridge, George Street, Gosbrook Road, Gosbrook Street, Church Street and Hemdean Road, to a terminus at the then end of Hemdean Road at its junction with Oakley Road, and vice versa, except between Queen Victoria Street and Bridge Street, via Broad Street and St. Mary's Butts). *Daily.* (K55/1).

Route M: Grovelands Road – Stations (via Grovelands Road, Waverley Road, Tilehurst Road, Russell Street, Castle Hill, Castle Street, St. Mary's Butts, West Street, Friar Street, Greyfriars Road and Station Hill, returning via Station Road, Queen Victoria Street and Broad Street to St. Mary's Butts, then reverse of the inward route). *Daily* (K55/8).

Route N: Broad Street (Arcade) – Whitley Estate (Callington Road or Staverton Road) (via Broad Street, King Street, Duke Street, London Street, Silver Street, Mount Pleasant, Whitley Street, Basingstoke Road and Buckland Road; then either via Cressingham Road to the junction of Cressingham Road with Staverton Road, or via Northumberland Avenue to its junction with Callington Road outwards; and vice versa to Silver Street, then Crown Street, Southampton Street, Bridge Street, St. Mary's Butts and Broad Street). *Mon–Sat and Sun pm.* (K55/21).

Route O: Special factory service: Staverton Road – Queens Road (Wesley Church) (via Cressingham Road, Buckland Road, Basingstoke Road, Christchurch Road, Kendrick Road, London Road and Watlington Street). *Mon–Sat except during biscuit factory holiday periods.* (K55/17).

Broad Street – Blagrave Hospital (via Broad Street, St. Mary's Butts, Castle Street, Castle Hill, Tilehurst Road, Honey End Lane (for Prospect Park Hospital), Cockney Hill, Church Road, Halls Road and Park Lane, and vice versa). *Visiting days only – one journey each way Wed pm, Sat pm and Sun pm.* (K55/7).

There were also separate stage carriage licences held for special purposes, as follows:

Between any two points within the borough, *daily as required, for the conveyance of organised parties, at a minimum fare of 6d per passenger.* (K55/5).

St. Mary's Butts – Tilehurst Road (Waverley Road) (via Castle Street, Castle Hill, Russell Street and Tilehurst Road, returning empty via Liebenrood Road, Bath Road, Castle Hill and Castle Street to St. Mary's Butts); return journey empty via Castle Street, Castle Hill, Bath Road and Liebenrood Road to pick up in Tilehurst Road, returning via Tilehurst Road, Castle Hill and Castle Street to St. Mary's Butts. *Wednesdays and Saturdays throughout the year, and on all other occasions when football matches were played or other sports meetings were held at Elm Park.* (K55/12).

Stations – Reading Stadium (Oxford Road) (via Station Road, Queen Victoria Street, Broad Street and Oxford Road, returning via Oxford Road, Bedford Road, Chatham Street, Friar Street, Greyfriars Road and Station Hill). *On all occasions when greyhound racing, speedway racing or other sports meetings were being held.* (K55/13).

Special services operated to meet excursion trains arranged by the Great Western Railway and Southern Railway returning to Reading, from Stations to any point within the borough, at a minimum fare of 2d. using routes authorised under road service licences held by the undertaking. (K55/16).

Tramway Substitution Service between Oxford Road (Pond House) tram terminus and Wokingham Road tram terminus. *As and when required.* (K55/18).

Tramway Substitution Service between Oxford Road (Pond House) tram terminus and London Road tram terminus. *As and when required.* (K55/19).

Trolley Vehicle Substitution Service between Caversham (trolley vehicle terminus) and Whitley (trolley vehicle terminus). *As and when required.* (K55/20).

In April 1938, the Education Committee requested re-arrangement of the timetable on the Hemdean Road motorbus service, to help schoolchildren who would be attending the new Caversham Council School in that road. It was resolved that a special bus be run on a circuitous route from George Street, Caversham, for a one month trial period, commencing 11th April 1938, via Gosbrook Road, Briants Avenue, Donkin Hill, Henley Road, Lower Henley Road, Donkin Hill, Henley Road, Oxford Street and Hemdean Road. The return journey was the reverse of the foregoing and the service operated before and after school. A further one month trial followed but, following a complaint from the Traffic Commissioners for renewing the temporary licence on a monthly basis, a permanent licence was obtained. Another special service for the same school was introduced from Emmer Green in September 1938. Route details have not survived but it is likely to have been from Chalgrove Way via Kidmore End Road, Peppard Road, Oxford Street and Hemdean Road.

R.C.T. PROFESSIONAL MANAGEMENT as at 21st May 1939

The salaried professional management of the undertaking as at 21st May 1939 was as shown below. There was also, of course, a significant contribution to the undertaking's development by aldermen and councillors serving on the Transport Committee (in particular the chairman) and by the town council as a whole, and this we will acknowledge separately in due course. Let it be said, however, that policy was largely dictated by local authority politics and simply implemented by the salaried professional management of the undertaking.

James McLennan Calder (Transport Manager & Engineer)   **John Fortescue Fardell** (Chief Assistant Engineer)
Albert Gent (Assistant Engineer)   **H. Vincent Lane** (Traffic Superintendent)

to be put on cooking stoves to be boiled for the taking of the family's baths in a galvanised tub on the scullery or living room floor. Newer properties had gas geysers – big cylindrical copper tanks with a gas ring underneath – in bathrooms, usually over the bath (and, sadly the cause of many a death due to carbon monoxide poisoning, the airbricks having been blocked, in ignorance, to counteract draughts). The really up-to-date households had invested in an Ascot instantaneous hot water heater in kitchen and/or bathroom.

Apart from church-goers, Sunday mornings were usually very quiet throughout the borough, with few people about until after about 11.00am. In Reading, there was not much interest in racing pigeons, whippets, ferrets and other like pastimes designed to keep fully-grown men out of mischief but, with the rivers Thames and Kennet near to hand, there always was a particular local interest in angling. Other 'healthy' outdoor activities, such as rambling and belonging to cycle touring clubs were also popular weekend pastimes.

Things certainly woke up a bit after Sunday lunch and the likes of Reading's several large parks and Thames Side Promenade came into their own, particularly during the summer. Alternatively, one might 'window shop' with one's spouse in the town centre, where the tranquillity would be shattered any time after about 4.00pm by outbursts of 'Onward Christian Soldiers', and the like, from the Salvation Army band endeavouring to see to it that Christianity was the essential part of a Sunday.

On occasions, Sunday afternoons were also a time for family visiting, when the parlour would be put into use and all the best china brought out. Church-goers would go to Evensong but, certainly for the middle classes, a winter's Sunday evening was also family time, cosy behind heavy drawn curtains, toasting bread or crumpets over the nice warm coal fire for tea, singing round the piano, playing records on the wind-up gramophone, or listening to the 'wireless' – and finishing up with a nice mug of Ovaltine or Bournvita before retiring to bed, ready to face the week ahead.

Mornings were another matter – with central heating a luxury of the distant future for most people, condensation on windows, walking barefoot on cold lino and lukewarm (or cold) washing water first thing of a morning were an everyday experience. It was much more unpleasant in winter – frosted-up windows and trying to dress under the bedclothes are experiences that our great-grandchildren will probably never have! There were also those prolific fogs and smogs of an urban winter, which were caused by the trapping of smoke and fumes from thousands of domestic open coal-burning fires and industrial chimneys beneath a low cloud-base. Things eventually got so bad that, by the late 1950s, parliament had to bring in the Clean Air Act.

Whilst the 'wireless' had developed some very popular evening entertainment programmes for home consumption, most leisuretime entertainment in this era was outside the home and a couple would go out into town for the evening (by dependable public transport, of course), to the Palace Theatre, in Cheapside, for example. Its rival, the Royal County Theatre, in Friar Street, had been destroyed by fire on 7th January 1937. This was the era, too, where the cinema had come into its own. For many years there had been the Vaudeville, in Broad Street; the Central, in Friar Street; and the Pavilion, along Oxford Road, while in Church Street, Caversham was the Caversham Electric Theatre. The foregoing had been joined by the Granby, at Cemetery Junction, in 1935. Indeed, during the period 1936 to 1939,

the Savoy, in Basingstoke Road (near Buckland Road) had opened in March 1936; the Odeon, Cheapside, in March 1937; the Rex, at Norcot, on 20th September 1937; and the Regal, in Church Street, Caversham, on 3rd October 1938. There was thus an amazing choice of film entertainment to be had within the borough in any one week, Monday to Saturday, for neither theatres nor cinemas were permitted by local by-law to open on Sundays. Ballroom dancing, at several venues in the town centre, was very popular at the time, while various temptations through the week at the Greyhound Stadium, at Norcot, included greyhound racing, grass-track racing and speedway. It was, all-in-all, generally affordable by the masses – and you could be home mid-week (thanks to public transport) by 10.30pm and to bed by 11.00pm, so that you were fit for work early next morning.

Of course there was a 'down side' to life, too, and scanning through the local papers of the era, there were certainly tragedies – deaths in fires, river drownings (often of children), aeroplane crashes, suicides (mainly heads in gas ovens), car crash fatalities (poor roads and lighting, in-effective brakes, steering and lights, and plain inexperience) and a very large number of road accidents involving fatalities to pedestrians and cyclists, often children (mainly due to lack of care and lack of experience in an increasingly dangerous environment). There were murders, too, in spite of the threat of a hanging if caught, tried and being found guilty; babies abandoned; and, surprisingly, quite a lot of bigamy! There were regular epidemics, too, of various nasty illnesses and some, like scarlet fever and diphtheria, were highly contagious. A patient having these, or something even more serious, like smallpox, polio, or tuberculosis, would be sent to Park Isolation Hospital, which was funded by the council. One might also reflect that there was no National Health Service until 1948; doctors were paid per consultation, and chemists stocked all manner of 'patent' remedies – creams, mixtures, powders and potions – most of them claiming wonder cures for all kinds of ailments. There was no penicillin, yet, and no antibiotics. Folk died, sometimes quite young and leaving young families, from conditions like septicaemia and pneumonia, which are so easily diagnosed and treated today. And it was fashionable for adults to smoke…

This, then, is the kind of environment in which the town's municipal public transport undertaking was operating. We cannot possibly relate a definitive background social history of the town in so few pages but the foregoing, hopefully, puts our particular part of the town's social history into context. We now need to recount some recent events in connection with the undertaking's single-deck omnibus fleet and the escalating international crisis onwards from 1938. A summary of the fleet as at 1st May 1939 is shown on pages 16 and 17.

It was decided, during 1938, to recondition existing Guy B 25-seaters 40 and 41 (instead of buying new vehicles), to include an improved engine performance for use up St. Peter's Hill, in Caversham, on the Woodcote Road route. In November 1938 the refurbishment of both was complete. They had each received an AEC four-cylinder oil engine and a self-starter, new gearbox, differential, exhauster, prop shaft (all presumably AEC) and an AEC radiator, together with new seats, additional electrical equipment and a repaint, all at a total cost of £878 6s 6d. Although not an unqualified success, they served their purpose and maintained the Woodcote Road service until it was re-routed and double-decked in 1943. However, it is interesting to note that, in a report on the single-deck fleet from which it was

The somewhat fearsome result of 'modernising' two Guy B single-deckers during 1938 is shown by 41 (RD 2115), now fitted with AEC running units and radiator and seen here in Station Approach sometime in mid-1939. The driver-conductor is at one of the manually-altered time clocks which were a pre-war feature of the undertaking. Note the temporary barriers forming a triangular traffic island at the approach to the King Edward VII statue, at which experiments were being conducted to determine a satisfactory size of roundabout to eventually be constructed there – post-war!

© Omnibus Society

decided that 40 and 41 should be the candidates for refurbishment, older Guys 19 and 20 were stated as having only a further 1¼ years' life. These two vehicles, in fact, pressed on in active service until March 1947!

Guy BA 12 and Guy B 13 were withdrawn on 27th September 1938, followed by Guy Bs 16, 17 and 18 on 1st November 1938, leaving Guy Bs 15, 19 and 20 of the 1926 batch still in service. It is surmised that it had been found possible to 'do without' 1930-vintage Guy Bs 40 and 41 while they were being 'modernised', so that once they re-entered service in November 1938, it was, perhaps, possible to reduce the single deck fleet by two vehicles anyway. This would account for the demise of 12 and 13, being the oldest surviving vehicles in stock. Looked at on a one-for-one basis, there had been an intake of seven new double-deck buses (AEC Regents 55–57 and 21–24) but a corresponding withdrawal of only four (Guy CX three-axle double-deckers 21–24). Thus, the next oldest vehicles, commensurate with carrying capacity and worst condition (and, presumably, expiry of certificates of fitness) were Guy Bs 16–18. It would appear that all five withdrawn Guys (12, 13, 16, 17 and 18) were 'mothballed' and, for whatever reason, no immediate attempt was made to sell any of them, possibly because this all took place at the time of the Munich Crisis and alarm bells were starting to ring.

All the while, the threat of war with Germany edged ever closer. Despite Prime Minister Neville Chamberlain's supposed inability to understand the full danger of Nazi aggression and being seen publicly to be seeking peace, a national plan of preparation was already in place for a likely all-out war with Germany, which had far more vigour than Chamberlain's critics are often prepared to credit and which was already well in hand by 1938, much of it done slowly and quietly to avoid any public panic. In Reading, a civil defence scheme had been published by the council in early 1937.

In February 1938, Germany had marched into and annexed Austria and, during the summer, had threatened to march into Czechoslovakia in order to 'liberate' the German-speaking Sudetenland, resulting in Mr Chamberlain's three famous journeys by air in mid- to late September 1938 to meet Adolf Hitler and to negotiate what became known as the Munich Agreement – the piece of paper held aloft, fluttering in the wind, on his return at Northolt Airport. As a result, this part of Czechoslovakia was ceded to the Reich without bloodshed in return for a promise that there would be no further German advance to the east. The negotiations had been 'touch-and-go', and the Air Raid Precautions Services had been mobilised nationally on 25th September 1938. Even before that, two excavators were digging out 'trench shelters' in Palmer Park...

It is important to appreciate that at this time it was generally assumed that in the event of war with Germany, the first thing that would happen would be that the country would endure more-or-less continuous air-raids on all or any centres of population, with huge devastation and loss of life, until Britain was beaten into submission. This helps to explain the reasoning behind the evacuation from cities of children, expectant mothers and hospital cases, which, in retrospect, and with all its well-documented faults and failings, was well-meaning but somewhat wasted effort. It was also thought, with a good deal of fear, that Germany would ignore the Geneva Convention and resort to gas warfare, which will explain to anyone who is the least puzzled, as to why everyone was issued with a gas mask (respirator) and why there were decontamination squads established throughout the country, to deal with the after-effects of a gas attack.

The Corporation Transport Department had begun its own planning for war in autumn 1938, the transport manager reporting thus to the Transport Committee on 17th October 1938. The basement under the electricity substation at the Mill Lane depot had already been cleared to provide an air-raid shelter for depot staff, the roof of the basement being of concrete and steel girder construction. The department had also purchased 42 civilian-duty respirators and seven suits of protective clothing to be used by the undertaking's decontamination squad. Protection of the depot buildings, particularly the new trolleybus depot, was also discussed, although it was noted that whatever precautions were attempted, the large area of glazed roof made the building vulnerable to air attack. The mercury arc rectifiers in the substation were also considered particularly vulnerable, as the shielding of the glass bulbs was difficult and the equipment was in the middle of the large substation building, which was itself 'exposed'. A large number of sandbags was purchased for the protection of the depot fuel pumps.

Details of vehicle dispersal during air raids were also discussed at the October 1938 meeting, and the vulnerability of

SUMMARY OF ROLLING STOCK AS AT 01.05.39

The following is a record of the undertaking's rolling stock at the start of the period which this volume covers, with the exception of the trams (which were shortly to be withdrawn) and some newly-delivered trolleybuses which had yet to enter service. Full details of vehicles entering service between 1939 and 1950 can be found in Appendices A and B. Information shown *in italics* is unconfirmed.

MOTOR OMNIBUSES: Nos. 1–57, listed in order of age (new buses were given the lowest vacant number)

a) Still in stock but withdrawn from passenger service:

Fleet/Reg. No.	Chassis Make/Type	Chassis No.	Body Make	Layout	Body No.	Licensed	In Service	W'drawn
12	DP 6374	Guy BA	BA2242	Reading C.T.	B20F	–	30.05.25	. .	27.09.38
13	DP 6878	Guy B	B1756	Reading C.T.	B26F	–	19.09.25	03.10.25	27.09.38
15	DP 7253	Guy B	B1896	Reading C.T.	B26F	–	06.03.26	28.03.26	14.02.39
16	DP 7254	Guy B	B1905	Reading C.T.	B26F	–	*01.05.26*	06.03.26	01.11.38
17	DP 7255	Guy B	B1999	Reading C.T.	B26F	–	01.05.26	06.07.26	01.11.38

b) Licensed fleet:

Fleet/Reg. No.	Chassis Make/Type	Chassis No.	Body Make	Layout	Body No.	Licensed	In Service	W'drawn
18	DP 7256	Guy B	B22000	Reading C.T.	B26F	–	01.05.26	06.07.26	c. .07.39
19	DP 7257	Guy B	B22019	Reading C.T.	B26F	–	06.07.26	09.08.26	28.02.47
20	DP 7258	Guy B	B22018	Reading C.T.	B26F	–	06.07.26	09.08.26	30.04.47
27	DP 9708	Guy FCX	FCX22871	Reading C.T.	B32F	–	05.05.28	13.06.28	31.07.39
28	DP 9709	Guy FCX	FCX22821	Reading C.T.	B32F	–	02.07.28	01.07.28	31.07.39
29	DP 9710	Guy FCX	FCX22823	Reading C.T.	B32F	–	04.08.28	03.08.28	31.07.39
30	DP 9711	Guy FCX	FCX22824	Reading C.T.	B32F	–	05.09.28	05.09.28	31.07.39
31	DP 9712	Guy FCX	FCX22830	Reading C.T.	B32F*	–	04.08.28	05.08.28	22.07.43
32	DP 9713	Guy FCX	FCX22962	Reading C.T.	B32F*	–	04.08.28	05.08.28	22.07.43
33	RD 35	Guy B	B22961	Guy	B25F	–	03.11.28	03.11.28	28.02.47
34	RD 36	Guy B	B22963	Guy	B25F	–	01.12.28	01.12.28	25.03.47
35	RD 37	Guy B	B22960	Guy	B25F	–	12.01.29	26.01.29	28.02.47
36	RD 777	Leyland Titan TD1	70729	Leyland	L24/24ROS	?	16.05.29	17.05.29	31.10.48
37	RD 962	Leyland Titan TD1	70727	Leyland	L24/24R	?	13.07.29	.07.29	30.06.49
38	RD 963	Leyland Titan TD1	70728	Leyland	L24/24R	?	13.07.29	16.07.29	30.06.49
39	RD 964	Leyland Titan TD1	70810	Leyland	L24/24R	?	31.08.29	01.09.29	14.07.46
40	RD 2114	Guy B	B23656	Guy	B25F	–	20.09.30	20.09.30	30.11.46
41	RD 2115	Guy B	B23657	Guy	B25F	–	20.09.30	20.09.30	17.07.47
42	RD 2720	Leyland Titan TD1	72100	Leyland	L27/24R	?	15.05.31	.05.31	31.10.48
43	RD 2721	Leyland Titan TD1	72101	Leyland	L27/24R	?	15.05.31	.05.31	30.06.49
44	RD 2944	Leyland Titan TD1	72215	Leyland	L27/24R	?	05.09.31	.09.31	31.10.48
45	RD 2945	Leyland Titan TD1	72216	Leyland	L27/24R	?	05.09.31	.09.31	30.06.49
1	RD 3378	Leyland Titan TD1	923	Leyland	L26/25R	?	23.03.32	. .32	30.06.49
2	RD 3379	Leyland Titan TD1	924	Leyland	L26/25R	?	23.03.32	. .32	30.06.49
3	RD 3676	Leyland Titan TD1A	1335	Leyland	L26/25R	?	07.07.32	.07.32	31.10.48
4	RD 4337	AEC Regent	661.984	Park Royal	L26/25R	*B3348*	07.04.33	.04.33	30.06.49
5	RD 4338	AEC Regent	661.985	Park Royal	L26/25R	*B3349*	13.04.33	.04.33	31.10.50

* These buses had carried Guy B32F bodies from new but, upon the premature withdrawal (in June 1933) of two contemporary Karrier CL6 single-deckers (25 and 26) fitted with Reading Corporation Transport bodies, an exchange of bodies took place. The Guy bodies were disposed of, presumably mounted on the Karrier chassis, with the Reading C. T. bodies being retained, mounted on the Guy FCX chassis of 31 and 32. Colin Morris, in his book *Glory Days: Reading Transport* (Ian Allan, December 2005) suggests that the original bodies on 31 and 32 were not by Guy but by Hall Lewis. Based on subsequent but limited research, we beg to differ!

Fleet/Reg. No.		Chassis Make/Type	Chassis No.	Body Make	Layout	Body No.	Licensed	In Service	W'drawn
6	RD 4339	AEC Regal 4	642.032	Park Royal	B35F	B3350	13.04.33	29.04.33	27.07.40
7	RD 4340	AEC Regal 4	642.033	Park Royal	B35F	B3351	19. 4.33	29.04.33	27.07.40
8	RD 4773	AEC Regent	O661.2152	Park Royal	L26/25R	B3380	06.10.33	.10.33	31.08.49
9	RD 5132	AEC Regent	O661.2296	Park Royal	L26/25R	B3381	12.01.34	.01.34	31.08.49
10	RD 5361	AEC Regent	661.2471	Park Royal	L26/25R	B3389	27.03.34	28.03.34	31.10.50
14	RD 6070	AEC Regent	O661.2895	Park Royal	L26/25R	B3619	03.11.34	.11.34	31.08.49
25	RD 6071	AEC Regent	O661.2896	Park Royal	L26/25R	B3620	03.11.34	.11.34	31.10.50
26	RD 6072	AEC Regent	O661.2897	Park Royal	L26/25R	B3621	03.11.34	.11.34	31.12.49
11	RD 7125	AEC Regent	O661.3645	Park Royal	L26/26R	B3794	05.08.35	06.08.35	30.11.50
46	RD 7126	AEC Regent	O661.3646	Park Royal	L26/26R	B3795	31.07.35	01.08.35	31.10.50
47	RD 7127	AEC Regent	O661.3647	Park Royal	L26/26R	B3796	31.07.35	01.08.35	29.02.56
48	RD 8091	AEC Regent	O661.3772	Park Royal	L26/26R	B4372	11.04.36	01.05.36	29.02.56
49	RD 8092	AEC Regent	O661.3773	Park Royal	L26/26R	B4373	11.04.36	.05.36	31.10.50
50	RD 8093	AEC Regent	O661.3774	Park Royal	L26/26R	B4374	11.04.36	01.05.36	30.11.50
51	RD 8094	AEC Regent	O661.3775	Park Royal	L26/26R	B4375	11.04.36	.05.36	30.11.50
52	RD 8889	AEC Regent	O661.4420	Park Royal	L26/26R	B4461	14.11.36	.11.36	31.10.50
53	RD 8890	AEC Regent	O661.4421	Park Royal	L26/26R	B4462	14.11.36	.11.36	30.11.50
54	RD 8891	AEC Regent	O661.4422	Park Royal	L26/26R	B4463	18.11.36	.11.36	30.11.50
55	ADP 4	AEC Regent	O661.5324	Park Royal	L26/26R	B4881	15.09.37	.09.37	31.12.56
56	ADP 5	AEC Regent	O661.5325	Park Royal	L26/26R	B4882	19.09.37	.09.37	31.12.56
57	ADP 6	AEC Regent	O661.5326	Park Royal	L26/26R	B4883	17.09.37	.09.37	31.12.56
21	ARD 12	AEC Regent	O661.6140	Park Royal	L26/26R	B5103	04.06.38	.06.38	31.12.58
22	ARD 13	AEC Regent	O661.6141	Park Royal	L26/26R	B5104	04.06.38	.06.38	31.12.58
23	ARD 14	AEC Regent	O661.6142	Park Royal	L26/26R	B5105	11.06.38	.06.38	31.12.58
24	ARD 15	AEC Regent	O661.6143	Park Royal	L26/26R	B5106	11.06.38	.06.38	31.12.58

TROLLEYBUSES: Notice that Nos. 102–106 were numbered in alphabetical order of chassis manufacturer!

Fleet/Reg. No.		Chassis Make/Type	Electrics	Chassis No.	Body Make	Layout	Body No.	Licensed	In Service	W'drawn
101	RD 8085	Sunbeam MF2A	BTH202	R13001	Park Royal	L24/26R	B3424	31.03.36	18.07.36*	25.03.49
102	RD 8086	AEC 661T	EE406/A1	661T.078	Park Royal	L26/26R	B4067	11.07.36	18.07.36	31.10.50
103	RD 8087	Guy BT	ECC	BT24188	Park Royal	L26/26R	B4068	13.07.36	18.07.36	25.03.49
104	RD 8088	Leyland TB4	GEC2510D	TB4 8342	Park Royal	L26/26R	B4069	13.07.36.	18.07.36	31.12.49
105	RD 8089	Ransomes	Ransomes	2453	Park Royal	L26/26R	B4070	09.07.36	19.07.36	25.03.49
106	RD 8090	Sunbeam MF2A	BTH202	13054.MF2A	Park Royal	L26/26R	B4071	10.07.36	18.07.36	31.05.50

* Used for driver training on an isolated section of overhead line in Erleigh Road from 18.05.36.

the tramcar fleet from air attack was noted, as dispersal was only possible along the rails. In the event the expected war came after the trams had finished in Reading.

Reading's Air Raid Precautions Committee first met in November 1938. It may have been as part of these preparations for war that the transport manager, in his newly-gained additional capacity as the town's ambulance officer, drew that committee's attention to the existence of the five withdrawn Guy single-deck motorbuses (12, 13, 16, 17 and 18) currently in store. These were immediately available for conversion into 'inter-hospital ambulances', and it seems that the town's medical officer of health was subsequently in consultation with the Ministry of Health on the matter. However, 16 is recorded as having been sold for breaking to local scrap dealers G. R. Jackson & Son in January 1939 – possibly the result of selecting 'the worst of the bunch' as not worth keeping. In spite of this, in February 1939 it was proposed (and an undertaking sought from the Transport Department) that, should the need arise, five buses could be converted at short notice (24 hours) into 8-stretcher ambulances, at an approximate cost of £12 per bus which would be the subject of a Ministry of Health grant.

Guy B single-decker 15 (which was still in service, and thus not one of the five originally proposed for conversion to an ambulance) was withdrawn from service on 14th February

The oldest corporation buses in service in May 1939 were two survivors of a batch of six Guy B 26-seaters from 1926. A sister had already gone for scrap, two others had been withdrawn and stored and the sixth, recently withdrawn from service, was being converted by the town's Air Raid Precautions Committee into a gas mask training vehicle. Bus 20 (DP 7258), seen here in the depot yard sandwiched between a tram and a horse-drawn tower wagon, together with 19 (DP 7257), survived in service throughout the war and were not withdrawn until 1947.

© *A. D. Packer*

1939 and work began next day to convert it for a very special purpose. The Air Raid Precautions Committee was anxious to have a mobile facility in which to train its wardens in the use of respirators and how to deal with gas attacks. It was then realised that training the general public at local level in the correct use of respirators could also be undertaken, rather than expect them to attend on a voluntary basis the lectures and demonstrations being organised at the Respirator Distribution Centre, in Silver Street. Thus, a direct approach had been made to the transport manager & ambulance officer (who, by way of this latter role, became a member of the town council's Emergency Committee), who arranged for 15 to be taken out of service and made available. The idea was to convince the public that they would be quite safe in the event of a gas attack if they wore and used their respirators properly. The vehicle appears to have retained standard bus livery after its conversion and, from photographic evidence, received new-style Gill Sans fleet numbers. The conversion, into a somewhat unfortunately-named 'mobile gas chamber', by all accounts consisted of taking out the bus seating and fitting bench seating down each side, and providing a portable flight of open-riser steps which could be used in connection with the rear emergency door for access. It is quite likely that the driver's cab area was made gas-tight, possibly by either constructing a full-width bulkhead and retaining the existing front access, or by sealing the existing front access, enclosing the cab in 'half-cab' form and providing an offside driver's door. Windows, too, would have been modified to become gas-tight and there was probably also some electrically-driven roof-mounted air extraction device fitted. See also page 25, and photo on page 26.

The transport manager's report to the Transport Committee on 2nd March 1939 clearly indicates that all five vehicles being considered for conversion to inter-hospital ambulances were 26-seaters, that they were free of capital charges, that they were only used occasionally 'for the purpose of relief buses', and that conversion would be carried out 'in our own workshops'. Hence, 12, which was not a 26-seater, did not appear to be part of the equation – and there is nothing, in fact, to suggest that consideration was only being given to currently withdrawn vehicles. At the time the Ministry of Health was first approached, back in November 1938, 15 was still in service and 16 had not been sold for scrap. This did not really matter, because five 26-seater buses could still be found if needs be: 13, 17, 18 were withdrawn and in store, while 19 and 20 were still in service,

Surviving departmental records indicate that 'mothballed' Guy B single-deckers 12 and 13 were hired out for ARP work between 15th and 27th February 1939; it is thought that both were still fitted out as buses at this time. For the record, two pairs of headlamp blackout shields were made for 12 and 13 on 14th April 1939.

A proposal to extend motorbus route L (Hemdean Road – Broad Street) to Berkeley Avenue, was adopted with effect from 1st April 1939. As a result of the introduction of this extended service the undertaking found itself 'one single-deck bus down' and it may be that, to compensate for the withdrawal of 15 for conversion into its new role as the 'mobile gas chamber', bus 18 re-entered service, as it is recorded as having run 10,000 miles in 1939, unlike the other Guys earmarked for ambulance duties, which accrued no additional mileage whatsoever.

Internationally, matters were going from bad to worse. On 14th March 1939, and in direct contravention of the Munich

In May 1939 six Guy FCX six-wheelers, 27–32 (DP 9708–13) were still in stock. 27–30 were on their very last legs and were taken out of service as a result of a reduction in motor-bus route mileage when trolleybuses took over from trams on the 'main line' in May 1939, although they were not officially withdrawn until 31st July 1939. Buses 31 and 32 survived until 1943. Print from J. R. Whitehead's Collection

Bus 33 (RD 35) was one of a trio of Guy Bs new in 1928. Ten years (or so) later, this one is seen basking in the sun while parked in the road outside East Garage. The Gill Sans style of fleet number transfer was introduced in December 1937 to replace the more ornate style seen in the preceding photographs. Note the rather shy Guy FCX inside the depot!
© Omnibus Society

Agreement, Germany invaded Czechoslovakia, thus starting on a new course, one of eventual self-destruction. Prime Minster Neville Chamberlain evidently formed an opinion about these Nazis and fascists and, on 31st March 1939, he assured the Polish government that if Germany threatened their country's sovereignty, Britain and France *"would at once lend them all the support in their power"*. Britain was at that time guarding its own existence as a great imperial power – early in 1939 it had reacted to rumour that Germany had designs on the Low Countries by authorising a major expansion of the army, and developing various precautionary schemes for the protection of civilians. In spite of this, there was still a general hope that there would be no war. To add to the unease, however, on 7th April 1939 the Italians invaded Albania *"because there was a serious danger to the personal safety of Italians living in Albania..."*. At home, on 26th April 1939, six months' compulsory National Service was announced for 20- and 21-year-old males. Meanwhile, the King and Queen set off (by sea) to tour Canada and visit President Roosevelt in the United States. They were building bridges...

In that uneasy spring of 1939, a night-time 'blackout' test was arranged locally, for the night of 5th–6th May 1939. At that time Reading still had its trams, but they did not feature in the exercise, which lasted between 12.00 midnight and 2.15am when all good trams were in bed! There was an elaborate attempt to encourage a complete blackout; all streetlamps, domestic and commercial lighting (including neon signs) and public transport lighting was encouraged to be extinguished. Apparently, Southern Railway trains ran with compartment blinds drawn down, whereas the Great Western Railway was encouraged to run its trains as normal, so that a direct comparison could be made from the air. All private traffic was encouraged to be off the roads for the duration, and ARP vehicles ran with blue cellophane over their headlamps, presumably as a means of identity. Within the borough, all manner of exercises were staged in order to test the efficiency of all the various parts of the Air Raid Precautions network – ambulances, first aid posts, rescue parties, decontamination squads, the Auxiliary Fire Service, and so on. This included the use, at Abbey Mill in Abbey Square, of an inter-hospital ambulance converted from a corporation bus, according to a report in one of the local papers. There was much serious scrutinising and, despite the inevitable mistakes, a great deal was learned. Overall, it was all judged a complete success. In Reading some 3,000 people had volunteered for ARP duties by June 1939.

The undertaking's most modern single-deckers, dating from 1933, were a pair of AEC Regal 4 four-cylinder petrol-engined buses numbered 6 and 7 (RD 4339/40). Bus 7 is seen here in Broad Street at The Arcade, bound for Three Tuns, in the early summer of 1939, with an unidentified inspector modelling his rather uninspiring uniform. © Omnibus Society

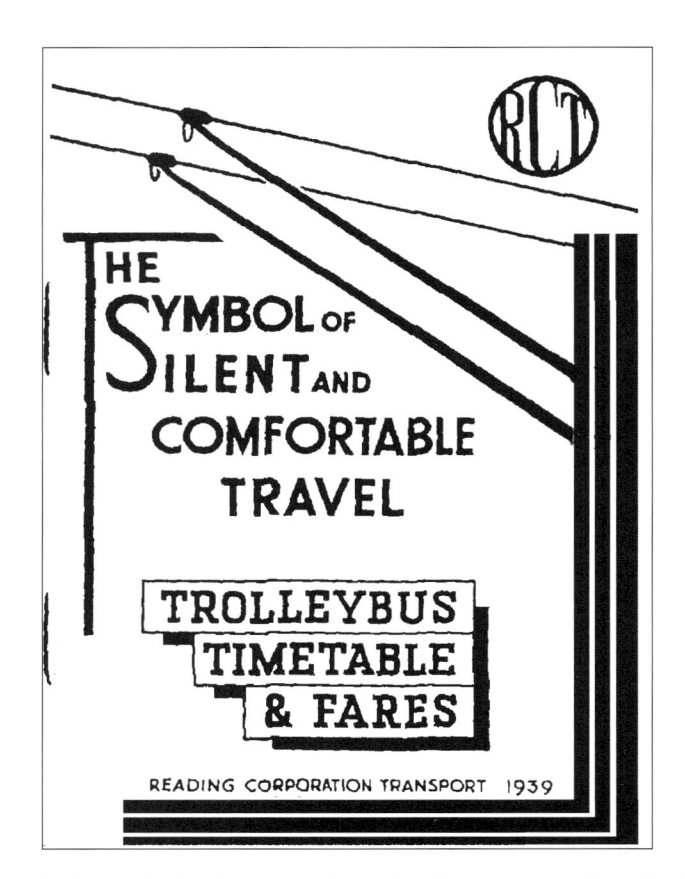

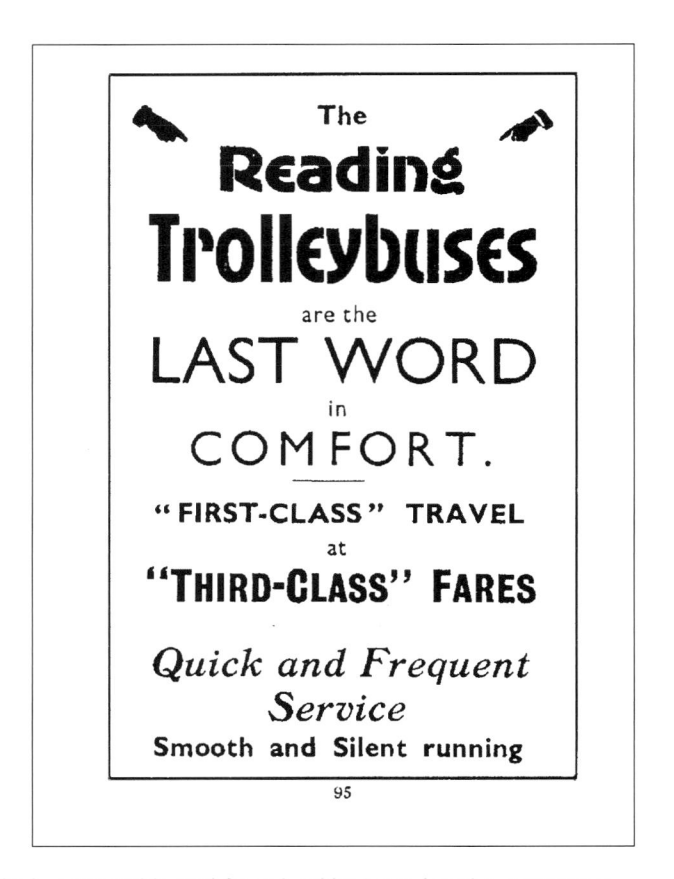

Above: The front cover and an advertisement page from the trolleybus timetable and fares booklet issued at the commencement of trolleybus operation on the Main Line, 21st May 1939.

Below: Brand new AEC trolleybuses (Nos. 120, 112, 129, 113, 114 and two others) lined up westbound in Mill Lane ready to enter service on the 'main line' on the morning of Sunday 21st May 1939 (notwithstanding the blind display on the leading vehicle). While Driver Lewington prepares to enter 120's cab, Transport Manager J. M. Calder (in trilby hat) chats to Inspector Aldworth in the foreground, with Inspector White and Traffic Superintendent H. Vincent Lane adjacent to 112.

Print from Late H. E. Jordan's collection

2 It's a Long, Long Time from May to September

The electric trams were given a final but very fitting farewell on the night of Saturday 20th May 1939. Trolleybus operation of the 'main line' commenced next morning, Sunday 21st May 1939, after a busy night for the overhead linesmen removing final traces of tramway overhead. The line-of-route was considerably extended, with a completely new fare scale and timetable. *"We ask the public,"* the transport manager had said, *"to exercise a little patience and sympathy for the men during the change-over period, until they settle down with their new vehicles. We consider the trolleybus to be the Rolls-Royce of modern public transport. No other vehicle travels so smoothly, quietly, comfortably, and with so little smell of fumes."*

One feature of all six original trolleybuses that certainly had not been popular was the 'lowbridge' bodywork. With a sunken off-side upper-deck gangway and four-abreast bench seating, and the restricted headroom on the off-side of the lower-deck (which resulted in many an unwelcome clout-of-the-head on the ceiling as one rose from one's seat, and associated bad language), these were far from ideal for use on an intensive urban trolleybus service. This layout also adversely affected loading and unloading times. With two exceptions (those in London Road and Caversham Road, which had long been of girder construction) every railway overbridge in the town, both Great Western and Southern Railway, had limited headroom. So far as they affected the town's main traffic arteries, the girder-type overbridges in Vastern Road (particularly the one nearest the town, carrying the Southern Railway) were very tight for headroom, even for lowbridge buses to negotiate. The proximity of the River Thames at this point and the high water table level meant that there was no likelihood that anything could be done to increase headroom, such as lowering the carriageway. In fact, it was not until 1975 that civil engineering technology had advanced sufficiently to permit a major improvement in road width and headroom when the overbridges were replaced. As a result, ever since double-deck buses had become 'roofed in' with the advent of Leyland Titans in Reading in 1929, it had been necessary to buy lowbridge buses, mainly so that they could be used universally on any route in the town. The only exceptions were the four 1927 Guy CX three-axle double-deckers, 21–24. These were of 'normal control' layout (see definition on page 6) and had been delivered as open-toppers; they had been 'enclosed' in 1931 by the addition of a roof, and had subsequently been restricted to route F (Shinfield Road – Caversham Heights); route M (Erleigh Road – Grovelands); and route N (Broad Street – Callington Road or Staverton Road). These latter vehicles had been withdrawn not long before the historical start of this volume.

The twenty-five AEC 661T two-axle trolleybuses for operation of the new installation had been ordered in the spring of 1938 and were delivered over the following winter, certain vehicles being used for driver training once sufficient overhead line had been erected. They carried fleet numbers 107–131 (ARD 670–694). With some adjustment of bridge clearances and a relaxation of standard Ministry of Transport ground clearances, it had been found possible to specify highbridge bodywork, rather than being obliged to fit lowbridge bodywork. The bodies were, in effect, a highbridge version of the Park Royal metal-framed lowbridge bodies, which had been fitted to all the undertaking's new deliveries of motorbuses since 1935. The new trolleybuses were also fitted with English Electric traction equipment, which included an 80hp traction motor and facilities for battery traction for manoeuvring and emergency purposes. The delivery and entry into service dates of the new trolleybuses, together with detailed descriptions, can be found in Appendices A and B.

All went fairly smoothly on the first day, apart from a power failure in the afternoon on the Tilehurst section. Too many vehicles in the section at the same time had caused the Kentwood Hill substation to overload. Having identified the problem, tests were subsequently conducted on the hill in Norcot Road to ascertain how many trolleybuses could draw power in the section at the same time.

Existing trolleybus route C between Caversham and Whitley Street was supplemented by new trolleybus services thus:

Most of the 24 trams which survived to final abandonment on 20th May 1939 were broken up in Middle Garage at Mill Lane depot by an outside contractor. Here are two suffering that fate in mid-June 1939. Looking out towards the road, that nearest the camera is possibly car 22. However, the bodies of up to ten tramcars were not broken up but sold off for use as sheds, etc.

© *Reading Museum Service (Reading Borough Council); all rights reserved*

A (Tilehurst – Norcot Road Junction – Three Tuns)
B (Norcot Road Junction – Three Tuns)
D (Norcot Road Junction – London Road)

The new trolleybus installation comprised a fairly tight turning circle at the very edge of the county borough boundary at the Bear Inn, Tilehurst and, indeed, it was necessary to plant traction poles outside the boundary, in the Newbury Rural District Council area. At the Three Tuns there was also a fairly tight turning circle, into the bell-mouth at the junction of Holmes Road with Wokingham Road, which was already being used by motor omnibuses. At London Road, terminal facilities took the form of a clockwise one-way loop to the left off London Road, just short of the site of the London Road tram terminus, via Manchester Road, turning right into Radstock Road and right again into Liverpool Road to a terminal point before emerging by turning right into London Road to return to town.

Oddly, there was but one short-turning facility provided – at Norcot Road Junction (near Reading Stadium in Oxford Road, just past the Pulsometer Engineering works), in the form of a fully-frogged turning circle. Additionally, however, just past the Plough, at Tilehurst Triangle (which hitherto had been the Tilehurst motor omnibus terminus) a 'reverser' was installed at Westwood Road. This point was never used as a short turn facility until post-war years, however, and seems to have been provided originally solely for driver training purposes. Trolleybuses from town turned into the side road to the right, and then reversed out into the major road on left lock! There were also *new* facilities installed in the town centre, comprising a duo-directional single-wiring depot connection (to, into and around the inside of the new trolleybus depot building) in Mill Lane, via Duke Street, High Bridge and London Street, with a connection from Kings Road and connections in both directions with King Street into the single wiring. There were also curves at West Street Junction as follows: St. Mary's Butts to Oxford Road; West Street to Broad Street; St. Mary's Butts to Broad Street; and Broad Street to St. Mary's Butts. Virtually the whole of the new installation was of span wire construction, whereas virtually the whole of the original Caversham – Whitley Street route employed bracket arms and gantries. Note that there was already a single-wiring depot connection along Mill Lane to Southampton Street, which had been installed in 1936.

Routes A and B had a basic service of every ten minutes, the two combining to give a five minute headway between Norcot Road Junction and the Three Tuns. Route D was operated on a 15-minute headway. On weekdays there were also Factory Specials from the Tilehurst direction to the Huntley & Palmers Ltd. factory in Kings Road. Little is known about them but it is, perhaps, a little odd that a turning facility in the overhead was not provided if regular use was planned. Presumably, the fact that every vehicle except 101 was equipped for battery traction was the main reason. The new trolleybuses carried **FACTORY** on their destination blinds and, having off-loaded, they turned by proceeding beyond the factory and over King's Bridge to Orts Road. Here, they de-poled and reversed on battery into Orts Road, then pulled forward on battery across Kings Road, where they re-poled and headed back towards town.

At the same time as trolleybuses were introduced on the 'main line', a number of alterations were made to the motor omnibus services. From the start it will be noted that the new trolleybus services were operated on Sunday mornings, so that motor omnibus route A (Roebuck – Three Tuns), which had operated over the 'main line' tram route on Sunday mornings at special fares, was withdrawn after 18th May 1939. Similarly operated Sunday morning route G (Tilehurst (Plough) – Erleigh Road) was withdrawn and Monday to Saturday and Sunday afternoon route G (Tilehurst (Plough) – Three Tuns via Erleigh Road) was also discontinued. To replace the eastern section of the latter, route M (Grovelands Road – Stations) was extended to Erleigh Road and onwards, via Crescent Road, to terminate at the old Wokingham Road tram terminus, whilst route J (Roebuck – Three Tuns) was shortened to operate only as far as Erleigh Road. That part of the special hospital service beyond Prospect Park Hospital to Blagrave Hospital was also withdrawn as the new trolleybus terminus at the Bear Inn was in close proximity to Blagrave Hospital. Buses on route M showed **WOKINGHAM ROAD** on destination blinds and terminated in St. Peter's Road, reversing into Brighton Road and pulling forward into St. Peter's Road to wait time. Needless to say, after years of trams showing **WOKINGHAM ROAD** (or a shortened form) the use of the same destination on a motorbus travelling to that location, but via Erleigh Road instead of along the former tram route, caused a great deal of confusion!

That part of route M beyond Erleigh Road terminus, along Crescent Road and up Wokingham Road to the site of the former tram terminus at St. Peter's Road, was soon abandoned. Indeed it last operated on Sunday, 3rd September 1939. Its withdrawal was pre-planned and the fact that war was declared that day was purely coincidental and nothing to do with any wartime restrictions being imposed.

The inauguration of the trolleybuses also saw a new fare table introduced on <u>all</u> motorbus and trolleybus routes. This involved considerable lengthening of fare stages and the removal of the differential in fare scales which had existed between tram and motor omnibus services. This differential had existed since the introduction of motor omnibuses in 1919; higher fares had been charged on the buses both to 'protect' the trams and to recoup the higher operating costs of the motor omnibuses, for the latter ran along more lightly-trafficked routes, had much less passenger capacity than trams, and required more maintenance and administrative support to meet legal requirements. In turn, this policy had also, for good or for bad, forced upon the town a pattern of motor omnibus routes designed to avoid competition over the same roads as the trams. Typical new fares were:

Three Tuns – Cemetery Junction	1d
Three Tuns – Watlington Street	1½d
Three Tuns – Broad Street (Vaudeville)	2d
Three Tuns – Wilson Road	3d
Three Tuns – Church End Lane	4d
Three Tuns – Tilehurst (Park Lane)	5d

Needless to say, not everyone was happy with the new fare scales and a number of approaches were made to the undertaking to have some alterations made. It reached the stage, in June 1939, that Mr Calder had to make the point that no alteration would be considered until the new fare scale had been in operation for six months.

As the new trolleybuses showed their speed and modernity, they soon became an integral part of the daily life of the town. They were an immediate success, with some 175,000 more passengers carried in June 1939 than in the same month the previous year. Indeed, the trolleybuses were described in a *Reading Standard* editorial as the *"quintessence of cosy and speedy travel"*. Evidently, they were perceived by the travelling public as a radical technological move forward from the trams they replaced. Nevertheless, as is often the case, some people were displeased, and there were letters in the local papers bemoaning the fact that vehicles ran full at rush hours and left passengers behind; or that vehicles were stuffy; or there was a tobacco smoke fug on the upper-deck (for in those days people seemed to smoke like chimneys) with no-one bothering to open any windows; or that the new fares and fare stages were unfair to some passengers.

The front destination indicator blinds on the new AECs were similar to those provided on recently delivered motorbuses, in that they not only showed the destination in the usual white letters on a black background but that the outer extremities of the blinds also had the route letter in white on green, e.g.:

> A **TILEHURST** A

The original destination blinds on 107–131 are also worthy of passing mention in that they showed **NORCOT ROAD JUNCTION**. 101–106, however, showed **NORCOT ESTATE**. During the war the location became known as **NORCOT JUNCTION** and finally (as today) simply as **NORCOT**.

The new AECs also had large nearside destination indicators over the platform, with blinds listing intermediate points in addition to the ultimate destination, e.g.:

> **TILEHURST**
> via CEMETERY JUNCTION
> BROAD STREET
> OXFORD ROAD
> NORCOT ROAD
> PARK LANE

There were also subtle changes to the Parcels Express Service. Hitherto, charges for delivery had been made based on the distance away from the line of the tramway. It was henceforth based on distance (as the crow flies) from the Parcels Office at the Broad Street entrance to The Arcade. The trams had stopped outside the Parcels Office and would ring their gongs for a parcels boy to come out and fetch a packet. There was no equivalent facility once the trolleybuses had been introduced, for the parcels travelled under the auspices of the conductor. Finally, the nearest trolleybus stop to the Parcels Office was some distance away along Broad Street, resulting in something of a route-march for a parcels boy detailed to pick up!

With the final conversion from trams to trolleybuses, the new garage at Mill Lane became fully operational and premises rented in Castle Street and Cardiff Road over the past two years (while the new trolleybus depot was being constructed) were given up.

The reduction in motorbus mileage resulting from the introduction of trolleybuses on the 'main line' had enabled Guy FCX six-wheel single-deckers 27–30 to be withdrawn. These three-axle single-deckers were technically withdrawn from service on 31st July 1939 but were retained as 'stand-by' vehicles at the depot. They were considered life expired in all senses, for spare parts were difficult to obtain, they boiled like kettles and, in all probability, although their Road Fund tax and/or certificates of fitness expired on the stated date, they may actually have been withdrawn earlier, as soon as convenient following the 'main line' tram-to-trolleybus conversion.

The reader should, perhaps, reflect that the whole town, has evolved and continues to evolve. Individual buildings, shop fronts, etc., get replaced. So too does street furniture. Road improvements – widenings, straightenings, roundabouts, traffic lights, crossing points and one-way streets, once introduced, change a location's character forever.

It is worth recording, therefore, that in the summer of 1939 Station Hill and Station Approach were being widened. Prior to this, and typical of many a provincial railway station yard, one of the vehicular accesses to the Great Western Railway's Reading station was up an incline from the junction of Greyfriars Road with Tudor Road (presumably built on filling material, and there since the original station was built in 1840, or at least since it was remodelled circa 1868, forming an embankment next to Bay Platform No. 1). This particular road was, possibly until comparatively recently, railway property. Since the late 1920s, considerable congestion was experienced fairly regularly at the arrival times of the more important trains and in the afternoons, particularly, there were serious problems. In 1937/38, the county borough council had implemented a £45,000 scheme to considerably increase the width of the roadway as a

Trolleybus 120 (ARD 683) turns at the Bear Inn, Tilehurst on 13th July 1939. Someone on the nearside front seat upstairs appears to have failed to alight at the terminus! Note the pre-war destination blind display, with route letter at each end of the ultimate destination.

© Late G. O. P. Pearce

This view of West Street Junction looking west from Broad Street into Oxford Road can be fairly accurately dated to the summer of 1939. The tram lines across the junction have been tarred-in, but careful scrutiny of the picture reveals that the lines onward past trolleybus 118 at the Cork Street stop have not! The trolleybus is working short to 'Norcot Rd Jct'. Note the insulated crossovers in the trolleybus overhead, and the thick power 'feeder' cables. Note, too, the Langston's and McIlroy's stores.

Commercial picture postcard

public highway by following the profile of the railway-owned private roadway. Their scheme also included providing a pedestrian subway (as an extension of the railway's inter-platform subway) and public toilets below the roadway, all with a modern ceramic tiled finish to the walls.

Being outside the railway's embankment, the council's scheme was constructed using a reinforced concrete decking on a grid of 219 piles, each 14 inches square and driven a considerable distance into the ground. The resulting roadway was provided with a traffic island down the centre, so forming a dual carriageway, and the original railway-owned roadway was also separated from the public highway by means of a wide footpath. The outer edge of the widened roadway, overlooking a large yard used by Vincents of Reading Ltd., was initially protected with a fence constructed of baulks of timber, although a brick wall was later substituted. The public carriageways in each direction were of sufficient width to allow buses to draw into the kerb without impeding following traffic, so that stops for corporation buses were to be found on both sides of the road near to the flights of subway steps. The Thames Valley Traction Co. Ltd. had several terminal stops in the westbound carriageway down the hill to the junction with Greyfriars Road and, because that company was partly railway-owned, some of the left-hand side of the railway-owned roadway next to bay platform no. 1 was also used as a Thames Valley terminal point. Thames Valley buses otherwise terminated outside the adjacent Southern Railway's Reading station and, when the foregoing scheme was brought into use, a narrow traffic island was constructed to separate the bus terminus from the 'established' public highway. A trial roundabout of road-men's trestles and boards at the King Edward VII statue in Station Square (one of the first roundabouts in Reading – see photo on page 15) had been brought into use in January 1939 in an attempt to regulate the increasing number of traffic movements – buses in particular – across Station Square. The latter, which was railway-owned, was one large expanse of tarmacadam, without any clearly-defined through traffic routes actually marked thereon, so at times and with increasing amounts of traffic, it was all becoming too much of a free-for-all! Thereafter, the area of railway-owned land immediately outside the Great Western Railway station ceased to be a through route and became used for railway parcels (inward and outward), a taxi rank (most taxis in Reading at that time were large saloon cars licensed by the Watch Committee as hackney carriages), and the Post Office.

Everything in this photo of Broad Street looking east from Queen Victoria Street suggests a Sunday during the summer of 1939 – tarred-in tram rail, Watford-type street lamps, the cream roofs of the two eastbound Thames Valley buses and no wartime masks on the headlamps of the corporation-owned AEC Regal 4. The trolleybus overhead line, evidently very faint in the original image, has been drawn-in by hand – the type of twin-line hangers shown were never used in Broad Street!

Commercial picture postcard

Older readers will remember with nostalgia that the Head Post Office, in Friar Street, had a sorting office egress from Wiston Terrace into Blagrave Street, opposite the side of the Southern Railway's Reading station. Battery-powered tugs would pull 'trains' of GPO four-wheeled trailers with 'string' sides, loaded to the gunwhales with mailbags; these were a common sight to behold, as they trundled back-and-forth amongst the buses, taxis and railway parcels vans.

There was, in fact, a protracted delay in completing the project because, with the threat of war looming, the county borough council decided to incorporate air raid shelter facilities beneath the roadway. In fact, the council seems to have been particularly slow in providing air raid shelter facilities throughout the town centre, and it was only through the good offices of some of the larger retailers in the main shopping areas (Broad Street, Friar Street and West Street, for example), even after war was declared, that basement storage facilities were made available to the council for suitable conversion as air raid shelters.

Under the Tramways Act, 1870, a tramway undertaking had a responsibility to maintain that part of the roadway between the pairs of rails and 18in each side, and that area of roadway remained the perpetual responsibility of the undertaking until the rails were removed and the roadway reinstated. Road surfacing had a tendency to break up immediately next to the rails and the resulting voids caused many an accident, to pedestrians and cyclists in particular. Tram track itself was often regarded as something of a hazard to other road users. Yet in Reading, removal of tram track and reinstatement of the highway was not undertaken for years after particular routes were 'abandoned'. Usually, however, work commenced 'filling in' the slot in redundant tram rail with what was intended to be a temporary tarmacadam filling. On 15th June 1939, Mr Calder reported to the Transport Committee that, although work had already been put in hand, particularly at important junctions where there were a number of permanent way crossings, he estimated that the tarmacadam 'filling in' work to disused 'main line' tram track would cost the department £900, which could be drawn out of the reserve fund. Apparently, a report had been received from the inspecting officer of the Ministry of Transport making reference to Reading's street surfaces and instructing that tram track should be 'filled in' with tarmacadam as soon as the tramways ceased operation, pending rail removal in due course. The letter was probably written to ensure that the 'tarring in' was neither ignored nor overlooked; in fact, filling in disused tram rails was well under way by November 1939 – an important task given the difficulties and dangers of the blackout!

'Mobile gas chamber' bus 15 is recorded as first being used in its new guise on Saturday 24th June 1939, on ground near Coley Baths and subsequently at Chaffey's Pits (gravel pits near the top of Berkeley Avenue), for the benefit of residents in ARP Area 'E' (a portion of Oxford Road, Broad Street, Minster Street, Gun Street, Bridge Street, Fobney Street, Temple Place and Berkeley Avenue). The exercise seems to have involved tossing canisters of tear gas into the 'gas chamber', namely the former passenger saloon. Subsequently the vehicle was based at 14 Bath Road (10th–14th July 1939), then at the new Yield Hall car park, off Duke Street (24th–28th July 1939). This use of 'gas bus' 15 continued until late August, when the planned itinerary for 28th–30th August at E. P. Collier School, Swansea Road, was cancelled due to the escalating international situation!

Surviving departmental records indicate that three buses were earmarked for conversion into inter-hospital ambulances on 29th July 1939. Two separate photographs, showing Guy B single-deckers being converted, appeared in the local newspapers, one of bus 17 in the *Reading Evening Gazette* for 25th August 1939 and the other of bus 13, which appeared in the *Reading Standard* for 1st September 1939. That of 17 is captioned to the effect that *"three buses*

The eastern end of Broad Street, looking west, adjacent to The Arcade, perhaps typifies Reading town centre immediately before the outbreak of war on a typical shopping day – kerbside parking, double-parked buses, the C. & G. Ayres Scammell mechanical horse, disused tram track, trolleybus wires and Watford street lamps – and the RCT Parcels Express errand bike.

Commercial picture postcard

This obviously-posed press photograph of the 'mobile gas chamber' converted from bus 15, possibly taken on its inauguration on 24th June 1939, is the only one believed to have been taken to record the vehicle in its new guise. It is interesting to note that it continues to carry its original bus fleet numbers, now in Gill Sans characters.

Reading Evening Gazette

had been withdrawn for conversion into ambulances capable of carrying eight stretchers". These ambulance vehicles had their bus seats removed and the press photographs suggest that a tiered framework for stretchers was fitted down the sides of the vehicles. It is likely, therefore, that the front entrance doorways were sealed shut and, possibly, the nearside front bulkhead removed. The rear elevation of the bus bodywork was also removed, being replaced by a canvas cover, which could be drawn aside or tied shut.

Although a *Reading Evening Gazette* article on 1st August 1939 stated that there were five corporation buses which had been converted into inter-hospital ambulances, some with a capacity for eight stretcher cases, some for six, surviving contemporary official records refer only to vehicles converted to carry eight stretchers. It is surmised that there were, indeed, only three conversions initially, during August 1939, namely 13, 17 and 18 (the latter having again been withdrawn from passenger service), and that the *Reading Evening Gazette* reference to five conversions was in-correctly presented. It seems likely that 15 was withdrawn from its 'mobile gas chamber' duties at the outbreak of war and similarly converted into an inter-hospital ambulance, and this is given added weight by the 1939/40 annual report which makes reference to a fleet of five ambulances, leaving one more to be found to make up the promised five. The only available vehicle was 12, a Guy BA, which was not as long as the others, and there is surviving documentary evidence from 1941 that 12 was, indeed, an inter-hospital ambulance but, being shorter than the others, had only four stretchers. It may even have been 12 which masqueraded as an inter-hospital ambulance during the black-out exercise of 5th and 6th May 1939. All five appear to have been maintained in permanent readiness as emergency transport for patients between hospitals and were intended to be operated using Reading Corporation Transport staff. It is rumoured that, during an exercise, simulated stretcher cases were loaded onto the Guys and when one of the ambulance vehicles bounced over the Mill Lane cobbles, one of the 'stretcher cases' fell out of the back, through the canvas cover and became a real stretcher case!

War is coming closer: stretchers are being delivered to the Broad Street entrance of The Arcade by a recently-withdrawn Guy FCX six-wheeled omnibus, believed to be 27 (DP 9708) in the latter part of August 1939.

© Reading Museum Service (Reading Borough Council); all rights reserved

At first the inter-hospital ambulances were certainly garaged at Mill Lane. On 10th October 1940, during the onset of the Blitz, it was proposed that these vehicles and their fitments should be dispersed, being based or stationed at three premises across the town, the ambulance fittings being stored at Mill Lane depot ready for immediate conversion. Certainly, by the summer of 1941 they had been transferred to Smith's Coaches' premises in Northumberland Avenue, formerly the Silver Grey Coaches depot, partly due to lack of space at Mill Lane and partly due to the need for vehicle dispersal. They were later noted in Mill Lane depot *en masse* in August 1943. Documentation suggests that the regional hospital officer at the Ministry of Health in Reading was billed on a regular basis for the inter-hospital ambulances and for the wages of their drivers. This produced a useful income for the Transport Department which amounted to, for example, £1,044 in the financial year ending 31st March 1940.

Mr Calder, the transport manager, in his capacity as ambulance officer in the town's Air Raid Precautions Service, also took on the responsibility for a collection of 83 cars, vans and lorries which had been gathered together to form an emergency ambulance fleet – these were dispersed throughout the town at various makeshift first aid posts and ambulance stations.

In the summer of 1939 there had been many recruitment campaigns, for police 'specials', for air raid wardens, for St. John Ambulance and British Red Cross Society volunteer first-aiders and nurses, ambulance drivers, the Auxiliary Fire Service, searchlight and anti-aircraft battery reservists, blood donors – and, not least, the armed forces themselves.

Reading had originally been designated as 'non-vulnerable' and, on 18th April 1939, was selected as one of nineteen centres for storage and distribution of the nation's food supply in time of war. However, on 24th August 1939 (the day following that on which the German Foreign Minister unexpectedly went to Moscow to agree an equally unexpected non-aggression pact with Russia, immediately after British and French Ambassadors had met the Soviet Prime Minister), Reading was re-designated a 'vulnerable area', which, at a stroke of a pen, allowed the town additional supplies of materials for public shelters and domestic corrugated iron Anderson shelters. With Reading an important railway junction on both the Southern Railway and Great Western Railway, and with other industrial targets across the town, such vulnerability could not be underestimated.

A second 'blackout' was organised from midnight until 4.00am on Thursday 10th August 1939, covering most of southern England, which was supposed to be part of a defence exercise in which 'Eastland' carried out air raids on 'Westland'. Essentially, this was an RAF exercise but bad weather caused the suspension of much of it and, sadly, there was actual loss of life in air crashes. The blackout across southern England was assessed overall as 'excellent' but in Reading, although a blackout was attempted, the Great Western Railway, with its sidings, sheds and stations, had been exempted from the exercise on this occasion and turned Reading into a beacon of light for any likely 'enemy' raiders! It seems, too, that certain parish councils in the surrounding rural areas found it irksome having to 'go round once again, interfering with street lighting time clocks' and so opted out of the exercise. There was limited 'mobilisation' this time, too, and Reading's Air Raid Precautions Services were reportedly 'fully prepared'.

In Reading, with preparations for war well in hand, the timely replacement of electric trams by a fleet of new trolleybuses just four months beforehand meant that nearly one-third of the undertaking's vehicles were new; this was indeed, as things turned out, very good fortune. Beyond any other preparation, it put the town in an excellent position to face the shortages of war with a greater degree of confidence than might otherwise have been the case. Demands on the municipal undertaking's bus and trolleybus services were going to increase beyond anything that had been envisaged, in order to serve what turned out to be a hugely increased wartime population.

Preparations for a by now inevitable war: Guy B buses 13 (DP 6878), top, and 17 (DP 7255), bottom, are in the process of being converted at Mill Lane depot into inter-hospital ambulances during August 1939. Note the detail differences in the rear treatment of the RCT-built bodywork.

Reading Standard (top) and Reading Evening Gazette (bottom)

Above: *Nearly half of the undertaking's double-deck motorbuses are lined up in London Street after the morning rush hour on Friday 1st September 1939, ready to transport evacuees from the Southern Railway's station to reception centres. Note the reference numbers attached to the radiators. Note, too, the bus stop flag beyond the Morris Series E on the left and the fresh white-painted kerbstones at the junction with Mill Lane on the right.*
© *Reading Museum Service (Reading Borough Council); all rights reserved*

Below: *Evacuee children from south London schools being shepherded aboard Leyland Titan 1 (RD 3378) in Station Square, while Boy Scouts help load luggage into a Guy FCX six-wheel single-decker. Vincents of Reading's motor car showroom is in the background, with a line of buses waiting to turn into the Station Forecourt.* *Reading Evening Gazette*

3   War is Declared

From Friday 1st September 1939, comprehensive plans, which had been put together over many months, for the evacuation of London and 80 other towns and cities considered to be likely targets for German 'blitzkrieg' attacks, were now put to the test. In the overall scheme, 1½ million people – schoolchildren, pregnant women, mothers with very young children, the old and the blind – were evacuated to 1,100 reception centres in England and Wales. This included the evacuation of 80,000 hospital patients and sending home 60,000 others. Various government departments and 20,000–25,000 civil servants had already gone from London, mainly to spa towns and seaside resorts. Objects of national importance were also being trundled away, and a large part of the National Gallery's collection went to the safety of a slate quarry at Blaenau Festiniog, North Wales. The Bank of England went to Overton, near Basingstoke, Hants.

As explained on page 27, Reading had originally been deemed far enough away from London to be a 'safe town', an evacuee haven in that early 'fear-of-attack' era of the war. Secret plans, dated 29th August 1939, show that during this first evacuation scheme, 'Operation Pied Piper', Reading Corporation Transport was required to meet twelve trains a day over three days at Reading Stations. However, before officials were able to rehearse plans for the reception of evacuees, government orders came that the evacuation of half-a-million Londoners would start within 24 hours! This massive exodus took place between 1st and 5th September 1939. The planning of every detail, not least by London Transport and the railway companies, is legendary. However, at the other end of those bewildering and often tear-stained journeys, to what were officially termed 'safe areas' in the provinces, there was similar disruption to bus schedules, for it was the public transport undertakings operating in those provincial towns which provided the vehicles to meet evacuees from the trains to take them to 'reception centres'. A year or so later, once bombs had begun to fall, Reading became a 'reception town' and received refugees, including people who had been 'bombed-out', from London and elsewhere in southern England – individuals, families, businesses large and small, and government departments.

A news item in the *Evening Gazette* for 31st August 1939 warned that after the morning rush hour next day, the town's motorbuses would not be operating for 'several hours' and workers were advised to take sandwiches to work, as lunchtime peak motorbus services would not be operated. Trolleybus services, however, were not affected. Motorbuses were, indeed, withdrawn after 9.30am and a photograph taken in London Street soon afterwards shows a line of about twenty 'evacuation' buses parked down the hill facing town, with number boards on pieces of string hung from radiator filler caps.

Mr J. M. Calder, the transport manager, joined the reception team, which met the first evacuation train to arrive at the Southern Railway's station. As each train arrived, Boy Scouts helped the bewildered evacuee schoolchildren, mostly from the London districts of Vauxhall, Wandsworth, Clapham, Battersea, Barnes and Putney, onto the corporation buses and loaded their luggage onto what were described in the local papers as 'luggage vans'. Three convoys, each of twelve corporation transport double-deck buses, together with the 'luggage vans', went to schools acting as reception centres in various parts of the town, from where the children were distributed to their lodgings. That day the anticipated 12 train-loads (slotted in between the normally-timetabled Southern Electric services), carrying 5,771 children with 767 teachers, were safely received, together with three hospital trains, together carrying 384 patients. The latter were distributed, presumably by newly-converted inter-hospital ambulance, to local hospitals.

It will be noted that as at 1st September 1939, the Transport Department happened to have a fleet of 36 double-deck motorbuses (1–5, 8–11, 14, 21–26, 36–39 and 42–57), so three convoys of twelve buses could just be achieved! The 'luggage vans' are thought to have been the previously withdrawn Guy FCX six-wheel single-deckers, 27–30.

In addition to providing these convoys when required, there were further requirements, on each of the three evacuation days, for vehicles to take evacuees from the reception centres to their final destinations in the homes of people around Reading, thus:

- Railway Station: 2 single-deck buses for conveyance of expectant mothers to reserved billets.

- Battle School, Cranbury Road: 2 single-deck buses or one double-deck bus for conveyance to Horncastle, Burghfield Road and outlying districts.

- Katesgrove School, Dorothy Street: 1 single-deck bus for transport to outlying parts of the area.

- St John's School, Montague Street, Caversham: 1 single-deck bus for transport to outlying parts of the area.

- St. Peter's Hill School, Caversham: 2 single-deck buses or 1 double-deck bus for transport to outlying parts of the area.

- St Mary Magdalen Church Hall, Weald Rise, Kentwood: 1 single-deck bus for transport to outlying parts of the area.

If only single-deck buses were allocated for this purpose, as seems likely in view of the full deployment of the double-deck fleet on convoy duties from the railway station, it will be seen that nine were required out of eleven in stock (numbers 6–7, 19–20, 31–35 and 40–41) if one discounts 27–30 as withdrawn from passenger-carrying but on 'luggage van' duties and 12, 13, 15, 17 and 18 in use already as ambulances. Thus, virtually every corporation motorbus was required for use in the evacuation scheme!

Since requirements appear to have exceeded the undertaking's own motorbus fleet strength, other operators must have assisted, it being suggested that vehicles from Smith's Coaches were used from the GWR's Reading station. The Thames Valley Traction Company declared to the press that across its network 86 single-deck vehicles were used for evacuation purposes, disrupting most of their single-deck services; some of these vehicles may have assisted in Reading.

Not all evacuees travelled to 'safe areas' by train; a local Reading enthusiast observed on 9th September 1939 that there was still heavy evacuation traffic to be seen through the town, including 'several' London buses.

As is so well documented, Britain declared war on Germany on the morning of Sunday 3rd September 1939, and the population, particularly those in towns and cities, immediately prepared itself for air attack, anticipating either gas or high explosive. It was predicted that 700 tons of bombs would be dropped daily on British cities, causing 600,000 deaths in the first two months of war. Furthermore, following its use against civilians by the Italians in their war against Abyssinia in 1935, poisonous gas attacks from the air were considered a real possibility, to the extent that everyone had been issued with a gas mask. Indeed, it was generally expected and feared at the beginning of the war that this kind of attack was inevitable. Government orders putting the country on a war footing had gone out forty-eight hours beforehand, when all the railway companies were brought under government control. In Reading, the town clerk, in his capacity as ARP controller, received telegrams from the Home Office directing him to carry out 'the provisional local war instructions', which had been issued as early as 22nd March 1939. The town's Emergency Committee for Civil Defence therefore met for the first time on 1st September 1939. The transport manager, Mr Calder, in his capacity as ambulance officer, was also a member of that committee and served thus for the duration of the war.

That evening, with a total blackout imposed, Reading's bus drivers found themselves under immense pressure, trying both to find their way and maintain schedules in almost total darkness. Thereafter, temporary schedules were prepared for what became known as 'blackout slow running', which gave longer journey times during the hours of darkness. Blackout slow running was subsequently introduced into the published timetables, there being an official reduction in service speed from 9.78 mph to 7.8 mph. It seems, however, that allowances for 'slow running' applied only to the evening blackout, as there were complaints at meetings of the undertaking's Works Committee in August 1941, and again in December 1941, that the timetable was not amended to take account of the necessary speed reduction in the early morning darkness.

The completely unlit street became a very dangerous place and, nationally, the number of people killed and injured on the roads rose sharply. Vehicle lighting restrictions in the blackout were relaxed within a few weeks but not before there had been a number of fatalities locally. During September 1939 there were 112 blackout accidents in the borough, resulting in 4 fatalities and 52 injured, whereas in the same month in 1938 there had been 55 accidents resulting in one fatality and 29 injured. At about 10.20pm on the evening of Sunday 10th September 1939, just a week after the declaration of war, two women wheeling a pram were killed, yet the infant escaped with no injury whatever, when they were hit by a Thames Valley bus at the junction of Broad Street with Minster Street. The following day a man was killed by a corporation bus outside the Prince of Wales at the top of Prospect Street, in Caversham.

Reading's first air raid warning was given at 7.32am on 6th September 1939, at the start of the morning peak period. People were directed to remain in air raid shelters in central Reading until the 'all-clear' siren sounded, at 9.02am. It had proved to be a false alarm. It was not until 3rd December 1939 that the sirens were heard again – and then only as a test. Thereafter, within the borough it became the practice throughout the war (and for some years afterwards) to test air raid sirens each first Sunday of the month at 1.00pm.

In accordance with government instructions relating to all motor vehicles, work was put in hand to mask the headlamps and sidelights of buses and trolleybuses, initially with white paint. The masking on vehicle lights, which, in those early days of the war, was simply a semi-circle of white paint on the lens to reduce glow, found little favour with corporation bus drivers. Some of them attempted to improve the illumination during the blackout, prompting a circular from Mr Calder as early as 6th September 1939, threatening drivers who scratched off the white paint with severe consequences! All vehicles were subsequently fitted with headlamp masks, giving minimal illumination of the road in front. Saloon lamps were initially painted with blue lacquer; later, they were fitted with shades to cast the ordinary light to the gangway floor. It has to be assumed that the ownership identification lights on the fronts of vehicles – white on trolleybuses, blue on motorbuses – were also victims of the blackout.

In order to aid their visibility in the blackout, the bottom 6ft of items of street furniture, e.g. lamp standards and trolleybus traction poles and other hazards, like trees adjacent to the highway, were painted white or given white bands (see photo on page 36). Alternate kerbstones in urban areas at

AEC trolleybus 118, still pristine, having turned at the Three Tuns for another trip to Tilehurst circa December 1939. Note the pre-war destination blind, headlamp mask to the nearside only (presumably the bulb was removed from the offside headlamp), masked side-lamps and the striped base to the traction pole in Holmes Road. © Omnibus Society

road junctions and kerbs to traffic islands, roundabouts, etc., were also painted white. Traffic light lenses were fitted with covers incorporating a small cut-out cross. Fire hydrant covers were painted yellow. Vehicles, too, were encouraged to have white painted wings, fenders and edges of running boards. White tips to front wings, white lifeguard rails or white to the edges of wings were not part of Reading Corporation Transport's wartime livery as it was elsewhere. In fact the corporation motorbuses had very little white paint applied – only to the rearmost section of the rear wings and to the rear bumper (where fitted), relying more, perhaps, on the cream bands of the existing livery to show up in blackout conditions. Trolleybuses did not even have the rearmost section of the rear wings painted white – only the rear bumper, so, presumably, this was a way in which corporation drivers were able to differentiate that a vehicle they were overtaking was a motorbus or a trolleybus! Perhaps this further helped drivers to differentiate between corporation and Thames Valley vehicles. Neither was it considered necessary to apply anti-blast netting to saloon windows. Reading, after all, was supposed to be a 'safe town'.

A report, which appeared in the *Evening Gazette* on 15th September 1939, is a useful illustration of the extreme conditions of the original blackout arrangements: *"...coming up St Mary's Butts towards Gun Street traffic lights, we saw a red gleam ahead and started to slow down. Our surprise was great when the red traffic light moved off, apparently into mid-air, and it was only when we were about four yards away from it that we realised it was a bus in front of us. Buses are almost completely invisible and they have a disturbing habit of looming up out of a mass of utter darkness. We have always admired bus drivers. Under present conditions, that admiration has increased a thousand-fold"*. It is difficult to comprehend, well over 70 years later, what it was like to live with total blackout. Even pedestrians collided with each other and there were many fatal road traffic accidents, two of Reading's more serious serving as examples. At 10.25pm on 19th September 1940, two soldiers were killed and 13 seriously injured when a westbound army lorry carrying 17 Royal Engineers overturned after swerving and hitting a brick wall a glancing blow at the junction of Chatham Street with Bedford Road, the driver realising all too late that he was not, as he had thought, in Oxford Road. Some years later, a man died in the blackout near to the Whitley Street trolleybus terminus after starting to cross the road immediately after a lorry had passed – not aware that the lorry was towing a long pole trailer of the type used to haul huge tree trunks. When fog was added to the blackout conditions, operation of bus services was virtually impossible. Conductors and inspectors were issued with hooded torches, often used by conductors to lead vehicles through thick fog and smog.

Another report, published in the *Evening Gazette* on 19th September 1939, told of an 'invisible lighting system' demonstrated to the Transport Department's management at Thames Valley's Lower Thorn Street Garage, in Reading, the previous day. Using ultra-violet rays and radium (which is, of course, radioactive) it was claimed to be the answer to the blackout, it being suggested that radium paint could be applied to every fifth white line on the roadway and on signposts and obstructions. Vehicles fitted with an 'ultra-violet ray bulb' in just one headlight could, it was claimed, see far enough ahead to travel at 40 to 50 mph! A bus fitted with such a bulb was demonstrated and was described as *"seeing without being seen"*. That was one side of the problem, because as applied to road vehicles, pedestrians would be unable to see an approaching vehicle even if they could hear it and would thus be unable to estimate its speed when crossing the road. The idea had come from Professor Alan Rhead, of Oxford University, and it was claimed that radium paint applied to ceilings of houses and factories and up-lit by ultra-violet lamps would facilitate ordinary tasks being carried out in blackout conditions, as no visible light could be seen from above. Thankfully, apart from the use of radium paint for exit signs and other small applications, this serious threat to public health and the environment seems not to have been implemented!

In blackout conditions, conductors had problems checking the coinage tendered, giving change, counting their takings and 'bagging-up', let alone working out where they were along the route. Passengers, too, found that getting off buses could be hazardous. This was especially so from the quieter trolleybuses, as it was sometimes difficult to know when they had actually stopped! There was also considerable concern in the local press that passengers were missing their stops in the darkness. Trolleybuses were also affected rather seriously if they happened to de-wire from the overhead line in the blackout. To assist crews at termini and other strategic points where de-wiring was more likely (such as at the inbound stop at Norcot, where it was frequently necessary to de-pole in order to allow another vehicle to pass), screened lamps were installed just above the overhead, from where they took their current.

In the early weeks of the war, public shelters in Reading were few and far between. Some of the first were slit trenches in Palmer Park. Attention then turned to building communal shelters in the town centre, in Broad Street, Oxford Road, West Street, King's Bridge[*], High Street, Queen Victoria Street, Station Road and Market Place, and subsequently at other locations, such as Caversham Bridge and Coley Park. Those in the town centre made extensive use of shop basements. Reading's largest public shelter was constructed next to the new Station subway, still being built at the time under Station Hill, which could accommodate 1,200 people. By early 1940, some 12,000 people could be accommodated in town centre public shelters. Gradually thereafter, other shelters were constructed in the areas beyond the town centre. These would come to be used throughout the war by passengers of corporation buses and trolleybuses as air raid sirens wailed the 'alert'.

During September 1939, the disruptions of war began to make an impact on ordinary home and family life as the government implemented the powers it had obtained under its Emergency Powers (Defence) Act 1939, which had been rushed through parliament on 24th August 1939. This gave a direct and draconian state control to virtually every aspect of daily life by bringing supreme power to the War Cabinet for the control of the war effort. Hence, the government could seize any property or undertaking; take over any invention or patent; commit anyone to prison without trial; compel an individual to grow specific crops or fell specific trees; do anything with any manufactured article of any description – and control the price; and control the behaviour of individuals under pain of prison (e.g. for refusing to take an evacuee, for not carrying a gas mask, storing more than a week's supply of food, or refusing entry of a warden into a dwelling to put out a light). Later, as will be seen, it could direct labour, male or female, wherever it was required to support the war effort. As E. S. Turner put it,

---

[*] The bridge in Kings Road, outside Huntley & Palmers, was rebuilt in 1935/36 and renamed 'King's Bridge' – but the name never stuck and it continued to be known locally as Factory Bridge.

> **READING CORPORATION TRANSPORT**
>
> **POSTPONEMENT OF PETROL RATIONING**
>
> Owing to the postponement of the rationing of Petrol and Diesel Oil, the Motor-Omnibus Services will continue to run unaltered until Sunday, September 24, inclusive.
>
> The curtailment of Motor-Omnibus Services already advertised will, therefore, not come into force until Monday, September 25.
>
> J. M. CALDER,
> Transport Manager.
>
> Corporation Transport Offices,
> Mill Lane, Reading.
> September 16, 1939.

"One day sufficed to turn Britain into a totalitarian state". The country was divided into 'regions', each answerable to central government, with a hierarchy for self-government in place and able to be brought into operation if the need arose. From 29th September 1939, National Registration was set up, resulting in the issue of identity cards.

Leaflets, booklets and posters began to appear in profusion; even milk bottle tops eventually carried slogans like *"Carry your gas mask at all times"*, *"Careless talk costs lives"*, *"Keep Mum – She's not so dumb"*, and *"Coughs and sneezes spread diseases"*. Every part of life took on the mantle of war. The wireless became a focal point both for family entertainment and latest news. In due course patriotic and morale-boosting songs against the Blitz, bombing, shortages, salvage, queues, separation, etc., and lampooning the enemy and its leaders, became the norm as the war wore on.

In the area of public transport regulation, on 26th September 1939 one of the first Orders under the new Act, in addition to giving powers to requisition vehicles and equipment, relaxed the number of standing passengers permitted on two-man-operated motorbuses from 5 to 8. A contemporary report in the *Berkshire Chronicle* tells of the provision of additional ceiling straps for standing passengers. The Transport Committee appears to have agreed that at the same time the standing capacity on trolleybuses be increased from 8 to 12. An article in the same paper on 6th October 1939, incidentally, suggested that destination 'signs' on the buses were to be given more illumination in the blackout, although how this was to be achieved remains something of a mystery! Under the new Act also, regional transport commissioners (who replaced the area traffic commissioners established under the Road Traffic Act 1930, for the duration of the war) were given powers to modify routes and to introduce temporary services for up to one week without the usual lengthy procedures or conditions. Under the same regulations, in the coming months the minister of transport was to issue further orders on a wide range of subjects. These included orders regulating queues at bus stops, the regulation and control of vehicle manufacture and the control of vehicle disposal.

The government also very soon announced road fuel rationing measures to achieve a 60% cut in consumption, originally intended to come into effect from 17th September 1939 but later deferred until 23rd September 1939. This drastic reduction in fuel allocation, especially petrol, forced the Transport Department to perform juggling acts with the vehicle allocations to routes in favour of 'oilers' (diesel buses). As we shall see, this urgent fuel saving pressure was present throughout the war and constantly prompting management to be extremely economical with fuel. Every last drop had to be accounted for but, specifically in Reading, it had to be carefully balanced against an ever-increasing demand for passenger transport because of the town's ever-increasing population.

A surviving memo, dated 22nd September 1939, shows the pattern of vehicle allocations prior to fuel rationing being introduced, both for the bulk of the daytime service and for the various 'specials' (used on school runs and as 'extras'):

	Service buses	Specials
Double-deck buses	16 diesel	2 diesel
Double-deck buses	4 petrol	5 petrol
Single-deck buses	1 diesel	0 diesel
Single-deck buses	2 petrol	2 petrol

Following the introduction of fuel rationing, and a curtailment of services, an internal memo was issued on 25th September 1939. Fewer buses were to be used and the allocation was balanced to use allowances of petrol and diesel efficiently and to minimise use of single-deckers which, with fewer seats, used the fuel allowance less efficiently. The allocation was listed thus:

	Service buses	Specials
Double-deck buses	12 diesel	2 diesel
Double-deck buses	6 petrol	4 petrol
Single-deck buses	1 diesel	0 diesel
Single-deck buses	2 petrol	1 petrol

From 27th October 1939, the double-deck special allocation was changed to 4 diesel and 3 petrol, thus increasing the allocation by one vehicle.

Trolleybuses were free from fuel rationing – and, initially at least, from the regional transport commissioner's control. As far the man-in-the-street was concerned, trolleybuses was simply electric buses – but they were operated under completely different legislation from motorbuses and in ordinary times, unlike motorbuses, they were not controlled by the Road Traffic Act 1930. Thus, the peacetime traffic commissioners, who were authorised under that Act, had no jurisdiction over trolleybuses. Instead, each trolleybus route was authorised by Act of Parliament, and each complete trolleybus system was overseen by the Railway Inspectorate of the Ministry of Transport. Trolleybuses were otherwise controlled by a town's transport committee, which vested responsibility for the day-to-day running in the transport manager. Trolleybuses in Reading, like the trams before them, were always operated in parallel with the motorbuses, more-or-less as two separate businesses, and strenuous efforts were made to keep separate accounts and to avoid one mode being in direct competition with the other. That, in a nutshell, rather defines why the town and its transport services have developed in the way they have.

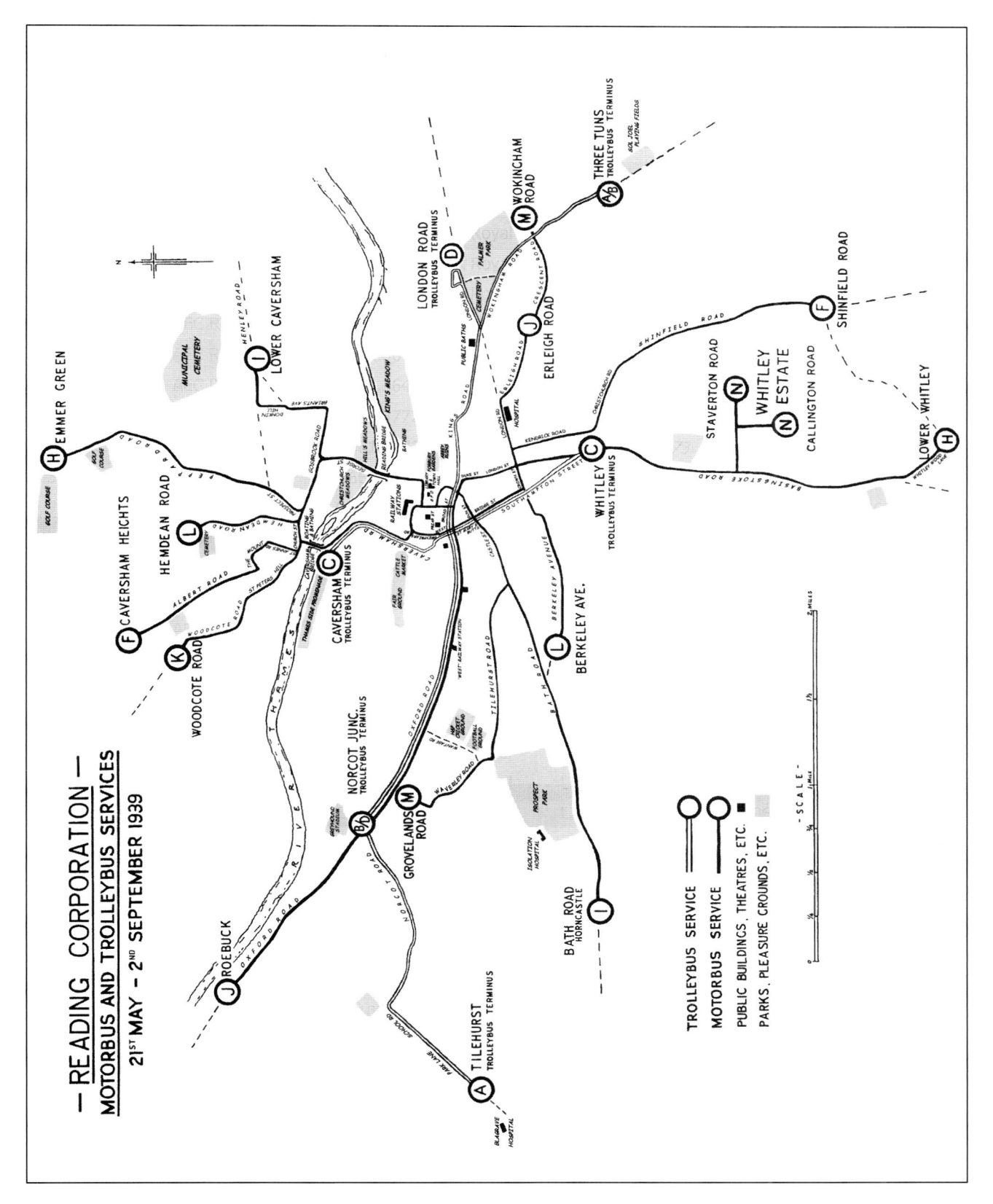

This map is based on a map contained in the November 1938 timetable booklet, suitably updated to show the routes in operation from 21st May 1939. Motorbus routes are shown as thick black lines, while trolleybus routes are shown by parallel thin black lines. Special services (e.g. for schools, hospitals and factories) are not shown; neither is trolleybus wiring used solely for 'not in service' depot journeys or driver training. Refer also to the maps inside the front and back covers. The last two tram routes, withdrawn on 20th May 1939 and not shown here, were as follows:

A: Oxford Road (Pond House, at the bottom of Grovelands Road) via Oxford Road, Broad Street, Kings Road and Wokingham Road to a terminus at the junction of Wokingham Road and St. Peter's Road (at the site currently occupied by a motoring shop).

B: Barracks (junction of Oxford Road with Wantage Road) via Oxford Road, Broad Street, Kings Road and London Road to a terminus at the railway overbridge.

Trolleybus services thus remained unaltered, but revised omnibus services to meet the impending 60% fuel reduction were approved by the Transport Committee at its meeting on 13th September 1939. With effect from Saturday 23rd September 1939, up to 9.00am services ran as normal during the morning peak; between 9.00am and 12.00 noon services were reduced; from 12.00 noon to 2.30pm, services were again run as normal over the lunchtime period; between 2.30pm and 5.00pm services were again reduced; the evening peak, from 5.00pm to 7.00pm, was also operated as normal; and thereafter, from 7.00pm until 'the last bus', there was again a reduced service. Revised schedules were also introduced on Sunday motorbus services.

Further, it had been announced initially that route L (Hemdean Road – Berkeley Avenue), which had only been introduced on 1st April 1939, would be suspended entirely after Sunday 24th September 1939, but on 20th September 1939, newspaper advertisements announced that a restricted service would be retained from Monday 25th September 1939, with both route K (Woodcote Road – St. Mary's Butts) and route L (Hemdean Road – Berkeley Avenue) curtailed from the same date to operate during the morning and evening peak hours only.

At the Transport Committee meeting held on 20th July 1939, the transport manager had been authorised to vary any motorbus route where it operated over a trolleybus route. Thus, also from 25th September 1939, route J (Roebuck – Erleigh Road) was cut back to operate between Roebuck and Norcot Road Junction only (Pond House from 20th November 1939), evidently to save the vital fuel used by single-deckers 6 and 7, the pair of four-cylinder petrol-engined AEC Regal 4s dedicated to this route. However, in order to make up for the reduction on the Erleigh Road section, route M was altered from 20- to 15-minute head-way, resulting in the Grovelands Road section getting an improved service brought about by fuel rationing!

These initial restrictions on fuel supplies had a serious effect on the town's motorbus services. In short, they were unsustainable, given the influx of evacuees and the move-ment of a large number of businesses, government offices and military establishments into the town. The resulting increase in passenger traffic onto the town's transport system was therefore very soon met by additional fuel supplies as agreed with the regional transport commissioner – but not before letters had appeared in local newspapers complaining about reductions in service at the same time as increased loadings brought about by an influx of 25,000 evacuees. As one correspondent noted *"... the management still provide a few football specials"*. Notices were posted on the buses and trolleybuses discouraging short journeys. However, in this 'Phoney War' period, when nothing seemed to be happening, such advice tended to be ignored by the masses. The increases in passenger traffic, in fact, brought forth a flood of letters to the local papers complaining about overcrowded buses, 'crowding out' by short distance passengers and demands for a minimum fare on the Tilehurst trolleybuses. In mid-November 1939, the story was being reported in the local papers of an obstreperous passenger who refused to leave an already full bus. Without more ado, the driver took his bus off route, to Valpy Street Police Station, where a Reading Borough Police constable induced the offending passenger to change his mind! It was a theme destined to continue for the duration of the war.

In contrast with pressures of daytime and peak loadings, evening passenger traffic was at an all-time low due to the blackout. At the very start of the war, cinemas and theatres had been closed by government edict for fear of heavy loss of life in the expected air raids, resulting in a further loss of passenger traffic, but by Saturday 9th September 1939, it was agreed that cinemas could reopen provided they closed by 10pm. Cinemas and theatres reopened in Reading from 18th September 1939, resulting in a modest increase in passengers.

By the end of September 1939, the rush to put the nation on a war footing was gradually slowing down and transport operators were able to take stock of the new operating conditions. One problem having to be faced was that some platform staff decided to 'join up'. The deputy manager, Mr J. F. Fardell, was an officer in the Territorial Army and had been required to report for army service at the declaration of war. He was away for the whole of the war and Alfred Gent, the engineering assistant, 'temporarily' deputised.

At Mill Lane depot, an air raid shelter had been constructed in the basement under the substation. The depot later had its own Home Guard unit, as a result of which rifles, ammunition and other equipment were stored on the premises. The trolleybus substation at the depot was guarded each night, between 9.00pm and 6.00am, initially by armed Local Defence Volunteers.

In October 1939, the Transport Committee requested the borough surveyor to camouflage the roof of the newly-built trolley vehicle depot, at a cost of £165, to make it less evident from the air and this was done at the end of 1939. The Transport Committee, at its meeting on 12th October 1939, also approved a decontamination scheme at the depot, at a cost of £850, for use in the event of a gas attack. The Emergency Committee for Civil Defence was informed subsequently that the foregoing facility would be available as a general vehicle decontamination centre.

The construction of workshop accommodation was now urgent, no progress (apart from demolition) having been made since the agreement to proceed with the work had been given in 1937. After seeking competitive tenders, A. J. Main Ltd was successful in securing the contract for the supply and erection of structural steelwork to join the workshop with the new depot. Its tender, of £3,351 6s 1d, was second-lowest, although a request to increase the amount by £75 6s 0d and insert new clauses in the contract to cover increased costs and insurance against damage to materials by enemy action was also agreed. However, it was still over a year before work could commence, as authority from the Ministry of War Transport, now necessary because of wartime conditions, was not immediately forthcoming.

The initial pressures of war, particularly the influx of large numbers of people into Reading, made the Transport Committee unwilling to grant a cheap fares concession to members of His Majesty's Forces, nor to provide free transport for evacuated schoolchildren to visit the surround-ing countryside. The department did, however, provide free transport for local and evacuated children to halls and cinemas for Christmas entertainment in 1939. Amongst other demands on the department's vehicles was a request, in February 1940, to provide transport for bedding and mattresses from the Friar Street YMCA to the Public Health Fumigation Facility at Woodley…!

Even though the trams had gone, under the provisions of the Tramways Act 1870 the Transport Department retained responsibility for the maintenance of the track – and the roadway between the rails and 18 inches either side – for as long as rails remained in place, although it was the Borough Surveyor's Department that actually undertook the work. To assess the costs of removal of rails, sections were completely removed from the road in April 1940 from outside the Primitive Methodist Chapel in London Street (nearly opposite the end of Mill Lane), where the road surface was reinstated using granite sett paving, and in Erleigh Road at the former tram terminus, where wood block paving was reinstated. The rails in parts of Mill Lane were also removed in April 1940. Further rails in London Street were lifted in September 1940 although the task was not completed until spring 1947, when the centre of London Street was being suggested as a possible car parking area.

From 1st December 1939, parking a vehicle on the offside of the road at night was made illegal, in order to remove any confusion with vehicle reflectors in the blackout. As far as it affected omnibuses in Reading, the Caversham Heights terminal arrangement, whereby buses turned right into Uplands Road to drop off, reversed to the left into the 'unmade' section of Conisboro' Avenue, then pulled forward clear of the Uplands Road junction to wait time on the offside of the road, was altered so that buses now pulled up on the nearside. Presumably, this resulted in a bus stop post being planted, but the omnibus indicator clock would have been left where it was, on the opposite side of the road. The same piece of legislation is thought to have also put paid to the long-established cab rank in the centre of Broad Street at the end of Cross Street.

In a letter published in the *Reading Standard* on 22nd December 1939, it was suggested that if a loudspeaker system operated by the driver could be fitted to corporation buses, it would be helpful during the blackout. Much later, possibly not until mid-1941, the idea was adopted by the department, when bus 51 was experimentally fitted with a microphone in the driver's cab, connected to a loudspeaker on the platform. Also provided was a 'Bus Moving' illuminated sign on the platform, which extinguished when the vehicle reached a stop. The experiment was not extended to other vehicles, perhaps because of wartime shortages rather than the failure of the experiment, although drivers are also understood to have been 'mike shy', so the experiment never reached its full potential. Passengers and anyone who has not actually been in the cab of a bus of the type in use at the time will not be able to appreciate the comparative engine noise levels when a bus is being driven, or, indeed, when the vehicle is stationary and the engine is 'ticking over', so there is every chance that the driver could not hear what he was saying, and the passengers could not actually hear what the driver was saying because of the engine noise!

The government evacuation schemes had originally been conceived as an emergency measure during times of attack, but emergency was not evident in the uneasy calm of what became known as the Phoney War of 1939 and early 1940. The long-term imposed billeting of evacuees caused friction and the enforced separation endured by both children and parents was traumatic. While there had been occasional German air attacks in the early months of war, these were largely 'testing the defences' and there was no immediate emergency. This resulted in a slow drift back to London of the evacuees towards Christmas 1939 and in early 1940.

Whilst the British people were beginning to adjust to new patterns of leisure, to the daily difficulties caused by the blackout and to government interference in their lives, little else seemed to be happening. The British Expeditionary Force had gone off to France and, in April 1940, Norway and Denmark had fallen. In the midst of the daily inconveniences at home, observers were struck by a strange phenomenon: Angus Calder (no relation to the transport manager, so far as is known), in *The People's War*, tells how *"... in the buses, the trains and the pubs of Britain, strangers were speaking to one another!"*

A token section of tram track being removed from London Street in April 1940 to assess the cost of reclamation. The government was keen to buy clean new or used high-quality steel tram rail, but their standard buying price per ton was less than the borough's costs for removal and cleaning. Therefore, although on the face of it somewhat unpatriotic, the borough left its disused rail in place for the duration of the war. © *Reading Museum Service (Reading Borough Council); all rights reserved*

Ransomes trolleybus 105 (RD 8089) was known by staff as 'The Lawnmower' on account of its manufacturer's other stock-in-trade – agricultural machinery. It is seen here standing at the Whit-Pump terminus of the town's original trolleybus route awaiting departure for Promenade (as these termini became known for wartime security reasons in August 1940) one day the following winter. Note the already-fading white bands round trees and traction poles, also the fading kerb stripes. Other points of interest are the short-lived RCT Trolleybus Fare Stage stop flag (and the interesting way it is mounted on the traction pole) and the original non-illuminated pre-war belisha beacons – the flashing type were introduced with zebra crossings in 1952. Novel idea though it could have been, the paraffin road lamp at the stopping point was not standard blackout practice!

Late W. J. Haynes © Maiwand Photographic Archive

4   The Calm and the Storm

A departmental review of trolleybus mileage showed that the weekly mileage for the pre-war week ending 2nd September 1939 was 19,684 miles, and that this had increased by 8.8% to 21,412 miles for the week ending 9th December 1939. This represented a passenger mile capacity in December 1939 of 1,456,074, allowing for 12 standing passengers. There followed an interesting calculation which showed that, had motorbuses been used on the trolleybus services (or, indeed, had motorbuses had been used instead of trolleybuses to replace Reading's trams), and were then subjected to a 60% cut in fuel to allow for rationing, then only 708,644 passenger miles would have been available. This reduction allowed also for the 60-passenger limit on motorbuses (52 seated plus 8 standing) as compared with the trolleybuses with a 68-passenger limit (56 seated plus 12 standing). The report went on to explain that had motor-buses been operating on the routes worked by trolleybuses, then the service would have been under 49% of the total trolleybus service actually provided. It was also stated that, taken across the whole day, only 34% of the available seats on trolleybuses were in use although, of course, this use would have varied greatly between peak and off-peak. Already, therefore, the new trolleybus fleet was proving itself to be an invaluable asset to the town as wartime difficulties began to bite. This, after all, turned out to be just the beginning...!

Due to the war, British Summer Time was extended beyond 8th October 1939 until Saturday 18th November 1939. To make additional fuel savings, from Monday 20th November 1939, the times of last buses and trolleybuses (any day of the week) from Broad Street were cut back to run at 10.30pm instead of 11.00pm, although on certain routes last journeys from the town centre left even earlier – 10.24pm to London Road; 10.12pm to Grovelands Road; 10.20pm to Erleigh Road; 10.20pm to Lower Caversham (10.30pm on Saturdays); and 10.07pm to Berkeley Avenue.

Reading Corporation Transport

FURTHER CURTAILMENT OF MOTORBUS AND TROLLEYBUS SERVICES

On and after **Monday, 20th November, 1939**, the **LAST** Motorbuses and Trolleybuses will leave **BROAD STREET** for the various outer termini every day (including Sundays) approximately **30 MINS. EARLIER** than at present.

Time-tables may be had free of charge from the Conductors.

Corporation Transport Offices,
Mill Lane, Reading.
18th November, 1939.

J. M. CALDER,
Transport Manager and Engineer

The last bus for Roebuck departed Grovelands Road at 10.40pm. The Berkeley Avenue service was, thereafter, withdrawn on Sundays. In the circumstances, there is little wonder that nothing could be done at this time to respond to a petition to provide a bus service along the upper part of Northumberland Avenue!

In spite of using an unrestricted source of energy, at some point during the earlier stages of the war (but not necessarily as early as 20th November 1939 – we have been unable to trace more precise details), trolleybus operation was withdrawn on route D (Norcot Road Junction – London Road) in the evenings, possibly every day of the week, after 7.00pm and, instead, every third vehicle from Tilehurst was diverted to London Road instead of Three Tuns. This had the effect of providing a new Tilehurst – London Road service, but also resulted in an irregular 5 and 10 minute headway to the Three Tuns.

The rectifier plant at the trolleybus substations serving Oxford Road had been re-deployed just prior to the war, and additional equipment ordered for installation at Crescent Road substation. In spite of this, the dramatic increase in traffic on the main line trolleybus route brought on by the war was now causing severe overloading of the substation equipment at Mill Lane. This may have had something to do with the aforementioned unpublicised alteration to trolleybus services. At its meeting on 23rd November 1939, the Transport Committee was, therefore, rather obliged to agree to the purchase of yet another mercury arc rectifier from the Hewittic Electric Company. The purchase of 30 additional TIM ticket machines was agreed at the same meeting, to cover for failures and servicing of the existing machines, which were already receiving heavy use under wartime conditions.

Within a few months of their introduction the previous May, the new trolleybuses had been beset by leaf spring failures, resulting in frequent and ongoing contact with AEC at Southall for the rest of 1939 and throughout 1940. Trolleybus 119 was fitted with strengthened rear springs on 30th December 1939 as a trial, but these were, in turn, replaced by springs with an improved camber on 30th January 1940 in an attempt to increase the road clearance at the rear; the earlier springs were returned to Southall. It appears, from surviving correspondence, that AEC did not agree with the undertaking's efforts to increase the rear clearance by fitting harder springs and, on 29th February 1940, a letter from AEC set out the company's opinion, that the front mountings of the rear springs were two inches higher than the rear mountings. AEC suggested that pack-ing the rear mountings would overcome the clearance problem at the rear, rather than fitting springs of a new specification. The Transport Department remained un-convinced and rear springs continued to fail throughout 1940 and into 1941, Reading's engineers continuing to replace them using the model with improved camber. In January 1940, AEC and the undertaking had agreed to replace springs as they failed, rather than refit the fleet as a whole in one programme. Replacement was carried out in pairs, any unbroken spring of a removed pair being re-used on other vehicles when their old springs failed. Both measures were calculated to take account of wartime production shortages and the need to use materials efficiently. By December 1940, more than half the springs had been replaced and every vehicle had been affected at least once. After prolonged negotiation with AEC over an extension of the guarantee period, it was agreed that the last 37 of 100 springs would be delivered to the undertaking on beneficial financial terms in 1941.

8th January 1940 saw the beginning of food rationing – ham, bacon, sugar and butter, followed by meat in March. January and February 1940 were also the coldest winter months in Britain for 45 years. The Thames froze hard for eight miles through Reading and people were able to skate or walk across the frozen water at Caversham. Huge falls of snow then added new dangers to the blackout, with outlying villages cut off. Troops were used to keep the railways open, yet main line trains were sometimes a day late arriving at their destinations. There was also some acute staff sickness, resulting in a serious staff shortage, with over 100 absentees at one period. To avoid cancelling timetabled services, the Transport Department was, for two months, loaned a team of drivers from Smith's Coaches, Reading.

Local enthusiast Bob Crawley witnessed the start of this period of harsh weather and its effects on Reading's public transport. He writes *"... on Sunday afternoon, 28th January 1940, after a period of really freezing temperatures, it began to rain heavily. Within minutes everything was covered in ice. A Thames Valley Leyland TS7 single-decker came from Wokingham Road across Cemetery Junction at about 2 mph and slithered in the gutter down Kings Road. This was followed by a trolleybus doing the same and making an amazing display of blue-green sparks off the overhead, which were reaching the road accompanied by loud cracklings"*.

No more buses ran that day; even the Southern Railway's electric trains gave up, reappearing two days later coupled to steam locomotives as their motive power. By the time darkness fell, the ice was three-quarters of an inch thick, breaking trees and flattening bushes. Overnight, the situation worsened, as 10 to 12 inches of snow fell on top of the ice. On the Monday morning, Bob Crawley recorded a Thames Valley Leyland TD1 double-decker running in from Ascot along Wokingham Road and a few corporation motorbuses running a restricted service in place of the trolleybuses, which were off the road for three or four days. The annual report for 1939/40 tells of *"...the cancellation of all our services on several occasions. After several attempts to run, it was found desirable to withdraw the vehicles before they became stranded along the routes. During the history of this undertaking... no such drastic action has ever before been taken"*. It was also noted that the damage to road surfaces from the weather had caused some deterioration to the department's vehicles. Greyfriars Road had to be completely re-laid after the thaw – the freeze had destroyed the thin tarmacadam surface and the inadequate foundation of chalk and loam was replaced with a new concrete base. This was reputedly the worst ice storm in southern England and Wales since records began!

The conversion of the 'main line' to trolleybuses and the increased traffic generated due to the war resulted in the undertaking more-or-less doubling net profit in the financial year ended 31st March 1940 compared with the previous financial year. Because of the final changeover from trams and the associated changes to motorbus operation during rather than at the beginning of the financial year, the usual comparisons and comments would not mean very much. That the trolleybus conversion was well-received is borne out by statistics for the months of June, July and August 1939 (between the conversion from trams and the declaration of war) compared with the same months the previous year: 1,153,426 more passengers, a £4,944 increase in revenue and an extra 40,153 miles operated. Overall during the financial year, operation of the new trolleybus fleet helped produce a net profit for the undertaking of £15,544; this included a small contribution from the Parcels Express Service, albeit reduced from the previous year's £205 to £62. The extra passenger loadings of wartime produced profits throughout the war, which were held in a reserve fund and used after the war to help meet the cost of replacing rolling stock.

At the start of the war there had been two fairly modern, well-appointed 35-seat AEC Regal 4 four-cylinder petrol-engined single-deckers in the fleet, numbered 6 and 7 (RD 4339/40). Having been purchased in April 1933, they were used as crew-operated buses, latterly almost exclusively on route J (Roebuck – Three Tuns). Enthusiasts' records suggest that both were 'withdrawn', probably following the shortening of route J as a result of petrol rationing towards the end of September 1939. Departmental mileage records for the first quarter of 1940 show that neither 6 nor 7 were used in the early months of 1940, adding weight to an autumn 1939 withdrawal date. However, it seems that 6 covered a further 78 miles before being 'officially withdrawn' from stock on 27th July 1940. Both were then requisitioned by the War Department (Southern Command) in those weeks following the fall of France. In short, we surmise that both buses were stored from autumn 1939 but only deleted from stock when commandeered. Where they went with the army must remain something of a mystery, at least for the time being. When both were 'de-requisitioned' late in 1942, Reading Corporation Transport appears to have elected not to buy them back into stock, presumably because as petrol-engined single-deckers they were an unattractive proposition. Through sheer coincidence, though, they still managed to return to Reading, in deplorable condition and in camouflage livery, for they were offered by Arlingtons, the coach dealer, and taken into stock by Smith's Coaches, of Reading. RD 4339 (formerly bus 6) was first noted in service in Smith's livery on 10th November 1942, although we understand that of the two this particular vehicle was acquired in a 'stripped out' state. Smith's used both of them, mostly for transporting prisoners-of-war.

Still in stock but withdrawn were buses 27–30 (DP 9708–11), four 1928-vintage 32-seat Guy FCX three-axle single-deckers. No attempt at disposal seems to have been made, and the four buses appear to have been retained in case they were needed for some sort of emergency. At least one of them is believed to have been converted later into a mobile enquiry office, as on 20th August 1940, for example, while there was a reference in one of the local papers to a vehicle described as *"the mobile enquiry office"*, it is also referred to as a bus. Similar buses 31 and 32 were described in a contemporary document as *"out of service in September 1939 – ARP Transport and used as relief buses on occasions"*, and they did indeed see irregular passenger use at peak hours and as 'spare' vehicles. They also seem to have been used to deliver civilian respirators around the town in the early stages of war preparation. Whilst, mercifully, gas attacks never materialised, it seems that at least one Guy FCX was used from 23rd July 1941 in a similar role as a mobile gas chamber to that for which Guy B 15 had originally been converted. By a process of elimination it was probably bus 32; it was hired as a 'mobile respirator-testing chamber', visiting schools during much of the rest of the war for this very purpose. The bus was filled with tear gas and children, wearing their gas masks,

Two of the withdrawn Guy FCX three-axle single-deckers were used during Reading's War Weapons Week, 9th–16th November 1940, to promote National Savings. The £450,000 target (the cost, at the time, of a naval destroyer) was exceeded, with £851,319 actually raised! This local newspaper photo shows that at least one of the two vehicles was in a non-standard livery, possibly grey, with darker beading, but retaining its original crimson roof. It is likely that one of these four vehicles (27–30) was the 'mobile enquiry office' referred to in local press reports and used at various events in the early years of the war, and that others may have seen similar use.

© *Reading Museum Service (Reading Borough Council); all rights reserved*

entered the front door and walked to the rear emergency exit. Children had to put a finger under the rubber nosepiece to get a whiff of tear gas, to dissuade them from behaving similarly during a real gas attack. Just imagine the furore there would be from today's parents!

An unusual and rather unexpected decree introduced under Defence Regulations, was that clocks should be put forward another hour with effect from Sunday 6th March 1940, to give 'Double Summer Time'. This was thus two hours ahead of Greenwich Mean Time and because, for the duration of the war, there was no reversion from British Summer Time to Greenwich Mean Time each autumn, darkness did not impinge on normal activities at all during the summer months. Britain was thus a land of midnight sun, and buses and trolleybuses made their last journeys each evening in daylight, sometimes in blazing sunshine. These 'extra' hours of daylight, of course, fuelled demands for later running!

From the same date, trolleybuses were restored to operate last journeys from Broad Street at 11.00pm. This change, which was agreed subsequently at the Transport Committee meeting of 14th March 1940, was decided by the transport manager using the discretion given to him at the beginning of the war. A decision was taken at the same meeting to extend motorbus services by half an hour, with last buses at 11.00pm from Broad Street, in order to take account of the lighter evenings. This was implemented from 27th April 1940, following the agreement of the regional transport commissioner. Locally, amidst a great deal of protest, the town council had agreed to permit cinemas to open on Sundays, with effect from Sunday 7th April 1940.

Rapidly increasing passenger loadings were by this time causing chaos at certain bus stops, particularly in Broad Street, and measures were necessary to relieve the pressure. In fact, as early as September 1939, an approach had been made to the department by a Mrs G. E. Gumm, of Harrogate Road, Caversham, to introduce some form of properly-regulated system of boarding buses and trolley-buses, viz., queuing. In connection with the 'de-congestion' of Broad Street – of both bus queues and buses terminating – the Transport Committee recommended in February 1940 that two services should be re-routed and the loading points for certain other services relocated and provided with suitably-designated stop flags.

Part of the original plan was to alter the town centre terminal arrangements of route K (Broad Street – Woodcote Road) from a route from Stations anticlockwise via Station Road, Friar Street (with a stop opposite the Central Cinema) and West Street to terminate in Broad Street outside the Vaudeville Cinema to a clockwise loop via Station Road, Queen Victoria Street, Broad Street, West Street and Friar Street, with a terminal stop outside the Central Cinema. This was re-thought and, instead, with effect from Saturday 27th April 1940, the terminus became St. Mary's Butts, buses approaching via Friar Street and West Street and returning via Broad Street and Queen Victoria Street. This helped ease congestion at the Vaudeville, with passengers now queuing at one stop for the two Caversham Heights services; a separate one for Emmer Green and Lower Caversham passengers outside Fergusons; and the eastbound stop for trolleybuses on the 'main line'. The newspaper advertisement publicising the changes (see page 40) contained an error in suggesting that buses returned to Station Road via West Street and Friar Street…

A town centre re-routing of route M (Erleigh Road – Grovelands Road) was also proposed, to traverse Broad Street, Queen Victoria Street and Station Road to reach Stations from Erleigh Road, thence proceeding to Grovelands Road via Station Road, Friar Street and West Street to St. Mary's Butts, instead of via Queen Victoria Street and Broad Street. Indeed, a bus stop post was erected outside A. H. Bull Ltd's Friar Street entrance to meet this change. Erleigh Road-bound buses would travel from St. Mary's Butts, via West Street, Friar Street and Greyfriars Road to Stations, and thence via Station Road and Queen Victoria Street to Broad Street. Route M was not, in the event, re-routed.

The Broad Street stop for motorbuses southbound on route H (Emmer Green – Lower Whitley) and the terminus of route N (Broad Street – Callington Road or Staverton Road) was relocated from outside The Arcade to King Street, between Butter Market and High Street, which allowed more room at The Arcade for route M (Grovelands Road – Erleigh Road), and a second eastbound stop in Broad Street for eastbound main line trolleybuses was introduced. On the south side of Broad Street, it was also found possible to provide a separate stop for Horncastle passengers at the end of Chain Street.

Having re-sited the stops as described, a by-law to regulate queues was drafted, being agreed on 1st June 1940, which stated that when more than six people gathered at a stop, they must queue in twos. The by-law was inaugurated on Friday 9th August 1940 and the *Reading Standard* reported how a lady "… *anxious to make up for lost time, made for the head of the queue instead of the rear, and was*

READING CORPORATION TRANSPORT

Later Motor-Omnibus Services from Broad Street

On and after Saturday, 27th April, 1940, the LAST MOTOR-OMNIBUSES will leave Broad Street for the undermentioned termini approximately 30 mins. later than at present

Departure Times from Broad Street will be as follows:—

	MONDAYS to SATURDAYS. Last 'Bus from Broad St.	SUNDAYS. Last 'Bus from Broad St.
For BERKELEY AVENUE	10.7 p.m.	No Sunday Service.
„ GROVELANDS ROAD	10.40 „	10.40 p.m.
„ ERLEIGH ROAD	10.50 „	10.40 „
„ "HORN CASTLE," BATH ROAD	10.50 „	10.45 „
„ CAVERSHAM HEIGHTS	11.0 „	10.45 „
„ EMMER GREEN	11.0 „	10.45 „
„ LOWER CAVERSHAM	11.0 „	10.40 „
„ SHINFIELD ROAD	11.0 „	10.45 „
„ LOWER WHITLEY	11.0 „	10.45 „
„ WHITLEY ESTATE	11.0 „	10.45 „
The LAST 'Bus will leave Grovelands Road (Pond House) for the "Roebuck" at	11.15 „	11.0 „

Woodcote Road and St. Mary's Butts

On and after Saturday, 27th April, 1940, the town terminus for the Woodcote Road 'Buses will be in St. Mary's Butts instead of Broad Street. These 'buses will run along the same route as at present except that they will run via West Street to St. Mary's Butts and vice versa instead of via West Street to Broad Street and vice versa. Two extra journeys will be run daily on Mondays to Saturdays, namely:—
At 3.7 p.m. from St. Mary's Butts to Woodcote Road, returning at 3.22 p.m. from Woodcote Rd.
At 7.15 p.m. „ „ „ „ „ „ „ „ 7.30 p.m. „ „ „

Hemdean Road and Berkeley Avenue Route

Commencing on Saturday, 27th April, 1940, One extra journey will be run daily (Mons. to Sats.) from Broad Street to Hemdean Road, viz., at 7.15 p.m. from Broad Street to Hemdean Road, returning at 7.30 p.m. from Hemdean Road to Broad Street.
The 7.25 a.m. 'Bus from Berkeley Avenue to Broad Street will run as usual, but the 'Buses NOW LEAVING at 7.55, 8.25, 8.55 and 9.25 a.m. WILL DEPART at 7.45, 8.15, 8.45 and 9.15 a.m.
The Berkeley Avenue terminus will be moved to a point about 300 yards nearer Bath Road.

Grovelands Road and Erleigh Road Route

The Service on this route will be improved between Grovelands Road and Railway Stations.

Reading Corporation Transport Offices. 23rd April, 1940.   J. M. CALDER, Transport Manager and Engineer.

---

courteously rebuked: 'No, no, madam!' the conductor told her, when the bus arrived, 'the last mustn't be first. The queue system is in operation now'. The lady seemed not to know what to make of it 'How curious', she muttered, as she reluctantly joined the end of the procession". Subsequently, in Reading from July 1941, queue regulators were employed to educate the public on the art of queuing for and boarding buses in an orderly manner; their title was boldly displayed on their uniform caps. Would-be passengers who refused to wait their turn found themselves in the Reading Borough Police Court! 'Queue plates' were erected at the Broad Street stops and yellow lines were painted on the pavements at Stations and Broad Street, and at other stops where queuing was a problem. Curiously, at this stage it was decided that railings at the pavement edge were not to be encouraged and that any barrier rails in the middle of pavements would be a blackout hazard to other pedestrians. Queue lines were also painted at stops in Caversham, at the Highmoor Road stop in Albert Road and in Briants Avenue near Gosbrook Road.

Much later, the 'Battle of the Queue' was recognised nationally, when the Minister of War Transport promulgated yet another government directive under Defence Regulations. The Regulation of Traffic (Formation of Queues) Order 1942 came into force on 12th April 1942 and required that where six or more people were waiting, an orderly queue should be formed, two abreast, on pain of legal penalty.

At the Transport Committee meeting on 22nd May 1940 an unusual proposal from Church Ward Labour Association was considered — that of fitting postal boxes to evening motor-buses, as done in some other towns, allowing later posting times, especially in outlying areas. It did not find favour in Reading and, at the next full council meeting, it was commented that postal boxes (which, it had been intended, would be restricted to motorbuses) would result in accidents and would 'disfigure' the vehicles. Councillor Palmer suggested that perhaps after the war the idea might be reconsidered. It was not!

Despite the restrictions of war, the Transport Department was still planning for the daily needs of Reading in peacetime. It was clear that building new housing in South Whitley would inevitably produce a growth in traffic. The pressures of wartime operating conditions proved without doubt that the new trolleybuses had been an obvious success in terms of cost, loadings and revenue. It was hoped that this success could be built upon and so, early in 1940, informal discussions took place between the transport manager, the deputy town clerk, the regional transport commissioner and the Ministry of Transport, which looked at the extension of the trolleybus system over four additional sections of route:

(a) From Whitley Street roundabout, along Whitley Street, Basingstoke Road and Whitley Wood Lane, to the existing motorbus terminus at Whitley Wood Road.

(b) Along Buckland Road, Northumberland Avenue and Callington Road.

(c) Along Mill Lane, London Street, Silver Street and Mount Pleasant to its junction with Southampton Street.

(d) From Norcot Road Junction, along Oxford Road to the Roebuck.

The regional transport commissioner agreed, at the end of April 1940, that the Ministry of Transport had no objection to the first three routes and the town clerk was told that the corporation would be able to obtain the appropriate raw materials and agreements. Discussions had not been concluded a month later when the war suddenly became far too real. In May 1940 Germany invaded the Low Countries, the blitzkrieg tore through France, and the Phoney War period drew to a close. Now, rather all too suddenly, there was a serious threat. Already, the vulnerable coastal areas of Kent, Sussex and East Anglia were subjected to a second evacuation scheme and some Kentish evacuee schoolchildren arrived in Reading on 19th May 1940. The fortunes of war in Europe had turned against Great Britain and France and the British forces were driven back towards the French coast. The evacuation of the British Expeditionary Force from the Dunkirk beaches took place between 30th May and 14th June 1940. France, Britain's ally in this conflict, finally fell on 27th June 1940, leaving Britain to stand alone to fight an enemy which had occupied much of Europe.

Following the Dunkirk evacuation, much of British industry's production and raw materials had to be directed towards the building of arms and military vehicles. Of necessity, proposals for trolleybus extensions in Reading were postponed, with no further progress on the Whitley extensions until after the war. That from Norcot Road Junction was introduced in part during 1944, as we shall see later.

Now it really was time to put on a brave face. Prime Minister Neville Chamberlain had stood aside on 10th May 1940 and, in our darkest hour, Winston Churchill took over and formed a National Government to lead the country forward. As threats of an extensive bombing of British cities loomed larger than they had ever been, nearly a hundred thousand London schoolchildren were evacuated again, between 13th and 18th June 1940, and it was reported in the *Berkshire Chronicle* that 2,000 of them were being evacuated to Reading (using E. P. Collier and Alfred Sutton schools as reception centres) between Sunday 16th and Tuesday 18th June 1940. Civilian evacuation from the Channel Islands came <u>after</u> Dunkirk, between 20th and 29th June 1940.

Thereafter, the threat of a German invasion of the British Isles became very real – although it now appears that preparations by the Germans for their 'Operation Sealion' were not even launched until 16th July 1940. A sense of common purpose was harnessed against the perceived threat of an airborne invasion. In the country, old and rusting vehicles and farm machinery were moved into large fields as obstructions and iron hoops were fixed across long stretches of main roads to discourage aircraft or airborne assault forces from landing. In truth, the chances of a successful airborne landing by German parachutists were somewhat exaggerated and the threat of invasion by sea was in fact greater from a reluctant German Navy. The Local Defence Volunteers, established on 14th May 1940, were very soon renamed the Home Guard. Defence lines were drawn and fortifications were built with great haste. Special groups were trained in subversive warfare. The country did what it could to be 'ready'.

As part of these anti-invasion preparations, the government issued the Removal of Direction Signs Order on 30th May 1940, by which steps were taken to confuse any parachutist invaders by the removal of all road signs, street names, distance posts, milestones and railway station names. Largely for the remainder of the war, travel in an unfamiliar area became something of an adventure. In Reading, it was reported to the ARP Emergency Committee on 8th June 1940 that the removal of all direction signs and milestones in the County Borough of Reading had been completed. A little later, Reading Corporation Transport introduced its own way of confusing the enemy by renaming the termini on the destination blinds of its buses and trolleybuses – often using the name of a nearby side-road or public house which would be understood by the local inhabitants but which would be meaningless to a stranger. There was one notable exception, especially for the benefit of the residents of the hamlet of Lower Whitley – their bus terminus came to be known by the completely fictitious name of 'Wood Lane Junction'. The destination 'Promenade' related to Thames Side Promenade, adjacent to Caversham Bridge, which had been laid out in Edwardian times following its purchase in 1907 by the borough council; it might just have suggested to an unwary parachutist that he could have landed in a seaside town! Downright despicable, however, was the use of 'Liverpool Road', which would have deceived any enemy parachutists quite nicely! The new blinds were fitted from 3rd August 1940 and showed the following changes:

TILEHURST	became	**BEAR INN**
CAVERSHAM	became	**PROMENADE**
WHITLEY STREET	became	**WHIT-PUMP**
LONDON ROAD	became	**LIVERPOOL ROAD**
SHINFIELD ROAD	became	**MERRY MAIDENS**
CAVERSHAM HEIGHTS	became	**UPLANDS ROAD**
LOWER WHITLEY	became	**WOOD LANE JUNC**
EMMER GREEN	became	**CHALGROVE WAY**
LOWER CAVERSHAM	became	**DONKIN HILL**
NORCOT ROAD JUNCTION	became	**NORCOT JUNC.**

The indications **FACTORY**, **STADIUM**, **FOOTBALL**, and **STATIONS** were omitted, probably more as an economy measure than for security reasons, but **TROLLEY BUS RELIEF** was added to motorbus blinds for use when motorbuses were used on trolleybus services as reliefs or replacements. Of course, Three Tuns had already been adopted as the name for the new Wokingham Road trolleybus terminus, and was therefore <u>not</u> a wartime change. With the introduction of the new blinds, the route letters which had been included on front destination blinds fitted to all trolleybuses apart from 101 and to motorbuses 48–57 and 21–24, disappeared, never to be replaced. At the same time, the quarter-inch-high word 'Reading' was painted out from below the county borough crest on the vehicle sides and from the legal ownership panel. Other corporation vehicles, such as vans, lorries and dustcarts, also had references to Reading removed. When the threat of invasion had subsided, circa 1943, the ribbon which incorporated the word 'Reading' under the crest was reinstated.

Old-style enamel bus stop flags carrying the word 'Reading' were also removed, although some did turn up back in use later in the war and afterwards. Many, however, were re-used during the war by being painted over and made into fire hydrant or air raid shelter direction signs and the like. In addition, photographic evidence suggests that paper notices with legends such as *"Bus Fare Stage"* were pasted at slightly above eye level both sides of lamp posts, traction poles etc. as temporary replacements, which may have lasted longer than originally intended before permanent stop flags without the word 'Reading' became available. Printed timetables issued by the undertaking during the war simply stated 'Corporation Transport', with no specific reference to Reading, although with the RCT motif. Anywhere else, such as in public notices in the local paper, the undertaking's full name was used quite openly for the complete duration of the war.

At Mill Lane depot, the Edwardian cast stone plaque, which declared 'Reading Corporation Tramways Power Station' high over the street, was boarded over. This boarding remained in place until the 1960s, when it chose to fall off, revealing a piece of Reading's transport history! Following the demolition of Mill Lane depot in 1998, this same stone now graces the wall of the new Oracle retail/leisure development facing onto the dual carriageway which was once the narrow Mill Lane.

Traders throughout the town were also encouraged to obliterate the word 'Reading' from shop fascias, delivery vehicles, etc. But in spite of all these precautions being taken to the 'nth degree' and at some considerable cost, it would have been very unlikely that any invaders would have been completely bewildered if they had dropped in on Reading; the Thames Valley Traction Company continued to

AEC Regent 9 (RD 5132) bides its time between duties, standing on the cobbles outside Mill Lane depot sometime circa 1943. The view somehow typifies a Reading Corporation motorbus in the mid-war period: both headlamps masked, white blackout markings on the rearward half of the rear mudguards only and, of course, no anti-splinter netting. Although not yet 'down at heel', there is an air of heavy use – and almost a whiff of hot diesel fuel wafting from under the bonnet!

Late W. J. Haynes © Millane Publishing

operate their vehicles into the town with the destination **READING** firmly in place!

On Sunday 2nd June 1940, the entrances and exits to the borough were being guarded by police and the Local Defence Volunteers for the first time. A week later, on 7th June 1940, the Transport Department supplied labour and materials to the borough surveyor for constructing roadblocks within the town as part of anti-invasion preparations, placed under instructions issued by the military authorities. In the early stages a certain amount of tram rail was supplied, which may have come from unused stock. There was a roadblock in Basingstoke Road near the Four Horse Shoes consisting of four concrete blocks set in a line across the road, with three lengths of tram rail set horizontally into slots, thus barring all passage except through the middle gap. Traffic in each direction passed between each pair of blocks alternately and further lengths of rail could be inserted to bar the middle gap, the slots running straight through the blocks to allow the rails to slide through.

Another roadblock, using three concrete blocks, was at the Merry Maidens in Shinfield Road, with tram rail available but not fitted, the traffic passing on both sides of the central concrete block. Further roadblocks were sited in the side roads of Whitley Estate, in Tavistock Road and Yelverton Road, near to their junctions with Buckland Road. These light roadblocks were constructed with four vertical tram rails with hawser wire used to form the barricade, which could be drawn through to seal the centre access section. Other concrete block and tram rail roadblocks were situated in Buckland Road and in Northumberland Avenue near the Community Centre. The RCT job book records this or similar work being undertaken on 8th July 1940, whilst the Emergency Committee minutes of 10th June 1940 record that a total of seven roadblocks were to be sited within the county borough – presumably on roads leading to/from the south of England. One certainly existed in Henley Road at the borough boundary at All Hallows Road, where, sadly, it was the root cause of a fatality on Sunday 24th October 1943, involving a 4-year-old boy and a bus making its terminal reversing manoeuvre. It had been intended that the road blocks be removed by March 1943, but in some cases the concrete blocks were left in situ.

The nation's scrap metal campaign was also getting into full swing by this stage of the war, with railings and saucepans being sacrificed for the nation's need for steel and aluminium. In reality, this campaign had more purpose as a morale boosting exercise than as a serious attempt to provide metal for the war effort. The demand for steel from the Ministry of Supply provoked an annoyed response from Dr Neville Smith, a member of Bradfield Rural District Council, at its meeting on Tuesday 11th June 1940, who, referring to disused tram rail, complained that there was more scrap steel in the roads of Reading than in the whole of the rest of Berkshire!

At the Transport Committee meeting of 8th August 1940, following receipt of a letter from the Ministry of Transport, it was agreed that tram rail recovered from Reading's roads would be made available to the War Department rather than being sent for scrap, because it could be used for roadblocks and other defence purposes. It was decided, however, that no pro-active removal programme of the 1,500 tons of rail available from Reading's roads would be undertaken as a response to this letter. Systematic removal of tram rail was considered to be uneconomic, as the War Department was offering £6 per ton rather than the £12 per ton that the removal work and the temporary repair of the carriageway would actually cost. The rails were clearly seen by the War Department as a recyclable asset, and it is even possible that they could have been reused in towns where repairs to tramways were necessary following air raids. Certainly, in Reading some rails were lifted, cut and supplied to other towns for defence purposes. The borough surveyor at Slough was supplied with tram rail in August 1940 and Oxfordshire County Council (Henley Division) was supplied with six 9-foot lengths of tram rail early in 1941.

The effect of German U-boats sinking British merchant ships began to bite. In July 1940, more foodstuffs became rationed – tea, margarine, cooking fat and cheese – and a worsening fuel shortage resulted in further demands for savings. A departmental memo dated 13th June 1940 indicates a further move towards diesel-engined vehicles, with a corresponding further reduction in petrol-engined vehicle usage. The Leyland Titans and the petrol-engined AEC Regents were, therefore, out of use other than at peak times, in favour of the oil-engined AEC Regents.

In June 1940 it was decided to defer conversion to direct injection of the last two indirect injection 7.7-litre oil engines (in buses 52 and 54) as a wartime economy measure. In a letter from AEC Ltd dated 7th November 1940, a crankcase, which had been returned to AEC for overhaul, was reported as having been destroyed when the AEC service station received a direct hit during an air raid on Southall on the night of 24th September 1940.

Two new 1,500 gallon fuel tanks were installed at the depot in 1940 at a cost of £120, thus doubling the undertaking's diesel fuel storage capacity from 3,000 to 6,000 gallons. This allowed for some reserves to be held as a contingency should the supply of fuel be interrupted by enemy action. A fuel pump test bench was also purchased, at a cost of £232.

The expected invasion of the British Isles never materialised, of course. Instead, between August and October 1940, there was an air war as the Battle of Britain raged over south-east England. At first the Luftwaffe focused its attacks on the Royal Air Force – its fighters and its bases. The first bombs fell on mainland Britain near Canterbury on the night of 9th May 1940 and the first bombs fell near London – onto a ploughed field near Addington, in Surrey – on 18th June 1940. Thereafter, the Luftwaffe prepared for the forthcoming battle for air supremacy over Britain by utilising its newly-won bases in France and reconnoitring its bombing routes to Britain's industrial towns. The initial phase of the Battle of Britain commenced on 10th July 1940 with the first large air raids and culminated in a week of all-out raids in mid-August 1940 – and the famous Churchill speech *"Never in the field of human conflict…"*.

Germany then adopted a new strategy and, as a prelude, the first bombs were dropped on London on the night of 24th/25th August 1940. From 31st August 1940, the Luftwaffe began to concentrate its bombers on British shipyards, gasworks, oil refineries and other industrial targets, rather than focusing on British airfields. Saturday 7th September 1940 saw the first major aerial assault on London, as waves of bombers set fire to London's docks and the East End. While London burned as a result of nightly air raids during October 1940, RAF Fighter Command was given the breathing space it needed to repair and re-group. From 5th October 1940, provincial towns, cities and ports began to endure months of bombing, which devastated their townscapes and infrastructure. Reading was subjected to almost nightly air raid warnings as enemy bombers flew overhead, but the town itself was spared any intensive bombing. Evidently, Reading was not on the Luftwaffe's list, although there were visits, usually by a lone aircraft, with bombs dropped in Henley Road, Caversham on 1st October 1940, Berkeley Avenue two days later and Emmer Green on 9th October 1940. Bombs also destroyed four houses in Cardiff Road, next to the railway, on 26th November 1940, when the railway also received some damage. As a precaution against explosions, 'splinternet' was applied to the windows of the inter-hospital ambulances on 2nd October 1940.

The devastation of towns and cities meant that plans for a further evacuation were put into operation. From September 1940, with the onset of the Blitz on London, women and children were evacuated, some of them to Reading, although far fewer than a year earlier. A letter dated 6th March 1940 from the regional transport commissioner (southern region) had informed the Transport Department of its responsibilities under the Government Evacuation Scheme for Schoolchildren, which would be brought into operation in the event of intensive air raids. The undertaking was required to give assurances that, if and when such an evacuation scheme was implemented, the facility would remain available, using either their own or hired vehicles. This would entail meeting children on three consecutive days at 11.17am from Reading's Southern Railway station for transport to reception areas within the borough. 700 children could be expected on the first two days and 600 on the third and it was calculated that eight buses would be required per day.

A surviving vehicle list dated 1st October 1940, detailing mileage and driver hours – and used, presumably, for billing purposes – shows in detail the vehicles deployed for this latest evacuation into Reading. It began four days after the Blitz on the East End of London commenced, so it is almost inevitable that the evacuees and refugees arriving in the town were fleeing the terror of the London bombing. Some of the buses carried passengers, others luggage, and a number of vehicles were simply on stand-by. Two vehicles carried blankets and beds.

Date	Quantity	Fleet Nos.
11 Sept.	19 buses	2, 5, 8, 9, 12, 20, 25, 27, 28, 31, 32, 36, 37, 38, 39, 40, 48, 49, 51
12 Sept.	13 buses	1, 4, 20, 25, 27, 30, 32, 33, 36, 49, 50, 55, 56
13 Sept.	8 buses	25, 27, 28, 29, 32, 39, 46, 48
14 Sept.	2 buses	38 and one unknown
15 Sept.	4 buses	3, 40 and two unknown
16 Sept.	1 bus	20
17 Sept.	4 buses	19, 20, 28 and one unknown
18 Sept.	3 buses	5, 19, 34 (and one 30 cwt lorry for luggage*)
19 Sept.	2 buses	19, 34
20 Sept.	2 buses	33, 34
21 Sept.	2 buses	19, 33
23 Sept.	3 buses	19, 33, 34
24 Sept.	2 buses	32, 38

* This was probably the 1931 Morris-Commercial departmental lorry, RD 4696.

It is known that Smith's Coaches hired vehicles to RCT during some of the evacuation schemes, so the 'unknown' buses in the list may well have been hired from Smith's. It will be noted that one of the inter-hospital ambulances, former bus 12, was used in this evacuation, together with 27–30 which, we have recorded, had been withdrawn from passenger service in July 1939. These Guy vehicles, used as luggage carriers, were probably licensed temporarily under the G or H certificates issued for untaxed vehicles used 'On His Majesty's Service' or local authority duties relating to transporting the sick and injured during air raids. One earlier such carriage was also recorded, of 26 children and their luggage in a single-decker on 6th August 1940.

From 26th August 1940, a school special was operated between the junction of Cressingham Road with Northumberland Avenue and the junction of Queens Road with Sidmouth Street. The route was 1.6 miles in length and ran via Long Barn Lane, Basingstoke Road, Christchurch Road, Kendrick Road and London Road. Two inward journeys were operated, at 8.55am and 1.35pm, together with two outward journeys to Whitley, operated at 12 noon and 4.20pm. These journeys carried a large number of evacuated school children from the South Lambeth Road Schools and were provided at a cost of 13s per day, which was charged to Reading Education Committee. This was raised to 19s per day from 4th November 1940, on the understanding that a double-decker would be used instead of the existing single-deck vehicle. Other school specials were, of course, still operating from pre-war days, one from George Street and Donkin Hill to Hemdean Road School; and the other to Whitley School (later Whitley Special School).

The Dunkirk evacuation had not included any of the army's heavy equipment, neither tanks nor lorries nor guns. Britain might have saved its fighting force, but it was without the equipment of war. Much of British industry was therefore geared up through the summer of 1940 to produce arms and military vehicles to make good the deficit. Local engineering companies started to divert some of their production to 'war work'. This not only included heavy engineering companies like the Pulsometer Engineering Co. Ltd., at Norcot but also firms like Vincents of Reading, the coachbuilders opposite Reading station, who became involved in building Spitfires after the dispersal of Spitfire production in August 1940. J. Samuel Elliott Ltd, at Caversham, produced parts for Halifax bombers and later built landing craft for the Royal Navy; and John I. Thornycroft Ltd, based alongside the Thames at Caversham, on Christchurch Meadows, became involved in producing motor torpedo boats and landing craft.

Reading Corporation Transport also diverted some of its time to the war effort. In May 1940, the repair shop at the depot undertook some war work for the Air Ministry, boring gun turrets for Cope & Cope and using the heavy turning lathe to produce trunnion blocks for artillery guns for Phillips & Powis, the Woodley aircraft factory. In September 1940, the workshops produced 20 anti-aircraft gun mountings and 81 Lewis gun fittings. A more unusual task for the department's paint shop was painting 25 steel helmets for the Berkshire Constabulary in October 1940 and stencilling the word 'POLICE' thereon, followed in November 1940 with painting 24 similar helmets for the Reading Borough Police. There was also an arrangement with the Reading Borough Police from 22nd December 1939 that they should always have a single-decker available *"at a minute's' notice as a 'Police Emergency Bus'"* One of the Guy B buses, either 40 or 41, were the vehicles selected to be available and there is a record of a vehicle being used thus on 25th June 1940 for a confidential journey which was *"... not beyond the Borough boundary!"* Will we ever find out what that was about?

Nearly 9,000 Reading householders had received billeting notices during the 1939 and 1940 evacuations and about 25,000 evacuees and refugees were brought to the town under official schemes. Thousands more came unofficially, to friends and family or fending for themselves. In addition, a number of businesses were transferred to Reading, some of them bombed out of their offices, bringing hundreds of employees with them. Reading was becoming overcrowded – a town of 100,000 in 1939 had grown to 140,000 in 1942. In October 1941, Reading had to be declared a 'closed town', with the local authority being given powers to control the influx of new inhabitants.

All of this, of course, had serious implications for the Transport Department. In fact it coped in the face of overwhelming odds – of ever more severe fuel cuts, earlier and earlier 'last buses', labour shortages and insufficient vehicles – against a continuous tirade of unrelenting criticism from the public to the undertaking itself, to town councillors, and to the editors of the local papers. Statistics contained in the undertaking's annual returns show that Reading's municipal transport undertaking carried 19,990,405 passengers in 1938. This actually doubled, to 38,697,341 in 1942. It rose even more, to 41,385,031 in 1945. The reader might just care to reflect, therefore, on just how many extra pennies were collected, carried, counted, bagged, checked and banked – daily. Somebody had to do it!

The school population too, was inflated by almost 55%, which meant that the 44 Reading schools were over-crowded and were having to run additional classes in church halls and other large buildings. Some schools were operating a shift system, with Reading children attending morning classes and evacuees attending in the afternoon. Once again, this had implications for the Transport Department, for it had to run lunchtime school services.

As 1940 progressed, the war was really beginning to colour every circumstance of ordinary life. School life was disrupted, heavy industry was diverting its output to war work and even Reading's municipal transport undertaking was finding its engineers' skills and its workshops were being used to further the war effort.

The band of the Royal Berkshire Regiment beating retreat in St. Mary's Butts during War Weapons Week (9th–16th November 1940). The double-decker, an AEC Regent, appears to be 49 (RD 8092), whilst the single-decker in the distance is a 1928/29 Guy B, one of the batch 33–35 (RD 35–37).
Reading Standard

5   Business as Usual

To 'gain' an extra hour of daylight later in the day and to ease blackout problems during peak periods, clocks did not revert to Greenwich Mean Time for the winter of 1940/41 and, in fact, always remained at least one hour ahead of Greenwich Mean Time for the duration of the war.

With the onset of the Blitz on London and bombing raids on provincial towns, Reading was, as mentioned, subjected to frequent air raid warnings during the late summer of 1940. At the start of the war, instructions had been issued to bus and trolleybus crews in Reading regarding the action they were to take in the event of an air raid warning, namely to continue driving to the nearest public shelter, provided that this was not more than five minutes' running time away, and to then disembark passengers as quickly as possible. The driver was required to bring his vehicle to a stop tightly into the kerbside, although vehicles in narrow main streets were to be driven to a wider part or to side streets to leave ARP rescue vehicles a clear run in the main streets. Vehicles travelling closely together in service were to be parked 50 yards apart in order to reduce the risk of more than one vehicle at a time being damaged by a bomb. Only then could the crew themselves proceed to shelter. Vehicles were to remain stationary on the roads and streets of the town throughout an air raid, whilst passengers and crews sheltered in public air raid shelters along the routes. When the 'all clear' was sounded, bus services could be resumed. It is recorded that on one Sunday evening, sirens sounded the 'alert' between 8.00pm and 9.00pm and the service was eventually resumed in the early hours of the Monday morning. In September 1940, following Ministry of Transport advice which noted that 'maintenance of output' in industry was dependent on public transport services, it was decided that services should *"continue to operate until such time as bombs were being dropped in the vicinity"*, rather than ceasing when the air raid warning was first sounded.

> **Don't wait until the Last Bus, it may be full.**

Complaints were being received about the failure of conductors to alter the times on the omnibus indicator clocks along the routes during the blackout – and the use of torches if they did so. Regrettably, this caused abandonment of the intermediate clocks in October 1940. These devices were used to indicate the departure time of the following bus, and their abandonment provoked concern in the local newspapers that the decision completely ignored their usefulness in the daytime. The *Reading Standard* for 31st January 1941, while reporting that the Transport Committee refused to reconsider its earlier decision, commented that with the clocks in place but unused *"they fib shamelessly"*, as Councillor Evans had told the council when he asked that the clocks should, in the hours of daylight, *"tell the truth and nothing but the truth"*. All the indicator clocks, including those at outlying termini, were thereafter removed *"for the duration of the war"* in the autumn of 1941. Although initially it was intended to retain the clocks at the termini, they never re-appeared.

The influx of a large number of evacuees into Reading, the frequent evening air raid warnings and the earlier blackout hours of winter, meant that new patterns of travel were developing. This was especially so amongst shoppers, who were crowding into Reading during the middle of the day, when there was a less-frequent bus service, yet trying to avoid the lunchtime peak when workers returned home for 'dinner'. To meet this new operating context, a report dated 23rd October 1940 proposed the augmentation of a number of services, as follows:

(a) Route F (Merry Maidens – Uplands Road) improved to operate a 15 minute service all day until 8.30pm, thereafter every 20 minutes.

(b) Route N (Callington Road or Staverton Road – Broad Street) doubled in frequency, from 30 to 15 minutes, between 9.00am and 12 noon. A fifteen minute service was, in fact, introduced throughout the day, until 8.08pm.

(c) Route J (Roebuck – Grovelands Road) extended to Stations during the day which, although requiring an extra bus, cancelled the need for passengers to transfer to/from trolleybuses at Norcot Junction. Inbound, trolleybuses were often already filled to capacity coming down from the Bear Inn.

(d) Route I (Donkin Hill – Horncastle) provided with duplicate workings between 4.00pm and 6.00pm.

(e) Route H (Chalgrove Way – Wood Lane Junc.) extended experimentally from Chalgrove Way to Courtenay Drive and operated every 15 minutes until 8.30pm and, thereafter, every 20 minutes. This was proposed after conducting a survey of residents' needs on Rosehill Estate, off Peppard Road, following requests to the regional transport commissioner that the protective fare on Thames Valley's service 7 (Reading – Peppard – Nettlebed) be removed on this section, thus allowing cheaper fares into Reading on a route not served by the corporation. Out of 81 people in 24 houses on Rosehill Estate, the survey revealed that only 20 return journeys a day would be made, making an extension to the estate uneconomic. Instead, the extension to Courtenay

Drive was proposed, both to serve the new Links Estate and to be within walking distance of Rosehill Estate.

The foregoing changes were adopted, effective from 4th November 1940. From the same date, resulting from petitions and complaints about the restrictions put on them a year earlier, route K (Woodcote Road – St. Mary's Butts), and route L (Hemdean Road – Berkeley Avenue) were 'improved', to run at lunchtimes (between 12.30pm and 2.30pm), to cater for workers returning home for mid-day 'dinner'. It will be recalled that as an initial economy, when petrol and diesel rationing was first imposed in late September 1939, both routes had been curtailed to operate during the morning (7.00pm–9.30am) and evening (5.00pm–7.30pm) peak hours only. On the same date, last motorbus journeys from Broad Street were cut back, to leave Broad Street generally at 10.15pm instead of 11.00pm, although the last on route L (Hemdean Road – Berkeley Avenue) left the town centre at 10.07pm. The last bus on route J (Roebuck – Grovelands Road) left the Pond House at 10.15pm. Despite the original proposals to run last trolleybuses at 10.15pm, the last trolleybus journeys were left as before, with last departures from town at 11.00pm.

Although the extension of route H, from Chalgrove Way to Courtenay Drive also came into effect on 4th November 1940, the lengthening of the route using the same allocation of four vehicles on this 1½-minute extension meant that the route could no longer run to time and the timetable became completely *"disorganised through late running"*. An extra vehicle was out of the question in these times of fuel restrictions and so, on and after 7th November 1940, the route had to be cut back again, to Chalgrove Way. The Courtenay Drive extension had thus been operated for just three days. The transport manager later informed the Transport Committee that further consideration would be given to the matter in the New Year.

So that the reader is able to relate these local events to the national scene, it was at this time that the devastating air raid on Coventry took place, on 14th November 1940, followed by raids on Southampton on 23rd and 30th November and 1st December 1940.

At the Transport Committee meeting on 21st November 1940, it was proposed that both route K (Woodcote Road – St. Mary's Butts) and route L (Hemdean Road – Berkeley Avenue) should be further improved – but in the event only route K was changed, in December 1940, to run throughout the day until after the evening peak. A surviving memo dated 12th December 1940 asks that the notice board in St. Mary's Butts, at the route K terminus, should be rewritten to show new departure times at 7.47am, 8.17am, 8.47am and 9.37am, with a half-hourly service until 6.37pm and a last bus at 7.15pm.

At the November 1940 Transport Committee meeting also, it was decided to withdraw trolleybuses from route C (Promenade – Whit Pump) between 10.00am and 8.00pm over the Christmas period 16th–26th December 1940, and to use the trolleybuses so released to relieve pressure on the overcrowded 'main line' trolleybus routes. According to newspaper publicity issued by the Transport Department, on 18th, 19th, 20th, 21st, 23rd and 24th December 1940, route C was operated instead by coaches hired from Smith's Coaches of Reading, driven by Smith's drivers but with corporation conductors. Trolleybuses continued to operate the service between 5.30am and 10.00am and between 8.00pm and 11.00pm and also all day on Sunday 22nd

---

READING CORPORATION TRANSPORT.

Whit-Pump and Promenade Route.

On DECEMBER 18th, 19th, 20th, 21st, 23rd & 24th, Trolleybuses will be withdrawn from this route each day between 10.0 a.m. and 8.0 p.m., and will be used to augment the service on the Main Line during that interval.

The service on the Whit-Pump and Promenade route will therefore be operated as follows, on the above mentioned six days:

Up to 10.0 a.m. by TROLLEYBUSES.
From 10.0 a.m. to 8.0 p.m. by SMITH'S COACHES (on hire to Corporation).
From 8.0 p.m. to finish by TROLLEYBUSES.

On SUNDAY, 22nd DECEMBER, TROLLEYBUSES ONLY will run on Whit-Pump and Promenade route.

Intending passengers are asked to queue-up at stopping-places, and all are advised to

T R A V E L   E A R L Y

J. M. CALDER,
Transport Manager and Engineer.

CORPORATION TRANSPORT OFFICES,
5th December, 1940.

December 1940. Up to six hired vehicles were said to have been required, but the timetables for route C indicate requirements of four vehicles on Monday–Friday and five on Saturday. The *Berkshire Chronicle* reported that the replacement service was *"much more expeditious than the trolley bus service in ordinary use, a service which is much complained of for its infrequence and inconvenient running"*.

Bus 47 was fitted with experimental anti-splinter window protection on Monday 27th November 1940, consisting of a thin cellophane film, but this wrinkled on application and was worn away and picked off by passengers, making the windows look unsightly. By 12th December 1940, the cellophane was reapplied more evenly and, on two windows, a thicker gauge of cellophane was used in a further trial. Printed slips were applied to the windows with the message *"This material is put up for your protection. Do not remove or damage it"*. It seems that this trial was deemed unsuccessful, or considered unnecessary, as it was not applied across the fleet.

In December 1940, a GPO mobile telephone repeater station, about the same size as a bus, was installed in Mill Lane depot. It increased the opportunity for telephone facilities in Reading, where demand had grown from the start of the war (including some 200% growth in demand during the first week of war) as official messages, new ARP posts and evacuated businesses demanded lines. Heavy usage in any case caused disconnection of domestic telephone lines at certain peak periods of use.

For the first time since early tramway days, in 1940 it was decided that the undertaking should operate Christmas Day services, running to the Sunday timetable. Additionally, it was also arranged to operate two motorbuses as workmen's specials, carrying staff from the Huntley, Boorne & Stevens tin box factory, in London Street, to various parts of the town. Workman tickets were issued, and provision was made for other passengers to be carried if space was available. The vehicles ran from London Street at 7.00am and it is recorded that one vehicle ran to Wood Lane Junction (21 passengers) and Donkin Hill (9 passengers), whilst the other ran to Three Tuns (6 passengers) and Bear Inn (20 passengers).

This Christmas Day operation caused some protest, with a 203-name petition from Transport Department employees being handed to management, for whilst crews had no objection to running a service for servicemen, they were very much against having to work a normal service for the public. At the council meeting on Tuesday 7th January 1941, there were allegations from Alderman Mrs Jenkins of wasteful use of fuel and inadequate notice given to those staff required to work on Christmas Day. A number of councillors felt that Transport Department staff should have been given a holiday with their families. It was also alleged that these services, which were stated to be important to munitions workers, were simply in place to carry football supporters to Elm Park for the Christmas Day match against Aldershot (which, incidentally, Reading F. C. won!). In his response, Councillor Palmer, Transport Committee chairman, declared that the situation had been forced upon the Transport Committee by the regional transport commissioner and that, as well as munitions workers, the services had carried postal and railway workers and soldiers. No services were operated on subsequent Christmas Days during the war, apart from those special services for war workers operated as contracted services. Even so, in subsequent years there were persistent complaints about staff absenteeism on Boxing Day, which inevitably caused cancellation of timetabled bus and trolleybus journeys.

An invitation was made by AEC circa Christmas 1940 asking if the department wished to be added to the priority list for the supply of chassis after the war, and this was accepted.

1941 started with the issue of new ration books. With the war now gaining momentum, more foodstuffs went 'on ration' or became scarcer (although there was a thriving – albeit illegal – 'black market') and, in some cases, rations had to be cut. Shop queues, like bus queues, grew longer, the latter to the extent that R. Watts & Co., the Oxford Road cycle shop, advertised in the local press with the slogan *"Don't wait for a 'bus! Ride a bicycle!!"* Newspapers and women's magazines carried recipes and good ideas as to how to stretch the ration. Reading's Food Advice Centre was opened in Cross Street in March 1941 just as the 'Dig for Victory' campaign started, and there was a Reading Food Week from 31st March to 5th April 1941, opened at Palmer Hall, West Street, by popular novelist J. B. Priestley. In fact for the next few years there was scarcely a week that went by without it being dedicated to some war-oriented scheme or other, linked with the inevitable Sunday procession, or something-or-other on exhibition, or a well-known figure of royalty or the aristocracy or from the world of politics or entertainment visiting the town to promote a 'good cause'.

Home life became a bit mundane, relieved, perhaps, by morale-boosting radio humour, which became exceedingly popular – the likes of Tommy Handley *(ITMA – It's That Man Again)*, Arthur Askey *(Band Wagon)* and Vic Oliver, Ben Lyon and wife Bebe Daniels *(Hi Gang!)*, whilst cinema-goers enjoyed *Pinocchio* and *Fantasia* (new from Walt Disney), and Charlie Chaplin in *The Great Dictator*. Evacuated mothers were at a particular disadvantage and, from June 1941, the Oxford Halls became a venue for a Rest & Community Centre for them.

Off-duty forces personnel needed entertainment, too. By March 1941 there were regular Sunday concerts at the Palace Theatre in Cheapside, and Welfare Command had arranged more-or-less weekly dances at the Olympia, London Street. Later the Jacobean Restaurant in McIlroy's department store became a well-known dance venue for Canadian forces in the area, while the recently-closed London Street Methodist Church soon became Reading Services Club.

The drive to recycle more-or-less everything was also in full swing by this period of the war, with legal penalties in force for wasteful disposal, for we must not forget that as a result of U-boat successes in the Atlantic, Britain was now very much under siege. Commencing in March 1941, waste paper, including office waste and used tickets, was collected by the Borough Surveyor's Department for recycling. At the Transport Department, a notice to employees was issued with regard to avoiding waste and unnecessary disposal. Indeed, Reading aspired to be a model in the National Waste Paper Salvage Campaign held between 21st April and 3rd May 1941! In such an environment it is not surprising that there was austerity packaging of nearly everything – smaller labels, poorer quality board and less ink; and a shortage of glass, soap, saucepans and toothbrushes, to name a few; and a general having to make-do-and-mend literally everything. Ladies resorted to Silktona 'liquid silk stockings' (for painting their legs). In March 1941 more foodstuffs went on ration – jam, marmalade, treacle and syrup.

A local by-law, effective from 9th August 1940, stated that where six or more people were gathered at a bus stop they should queue two abreast. In early April 1941 this long, ramshackle queue (with backs to oncoming traffic) waits to board Reading's unique open-staircase Leyland Titan, 36 (RD 777), which appears to have been brought from the depot to help out. The government recognised the nationwide bus queuing problem and the Regulation of Traffic (Formation of Queues) Order 1942 took effect on 12th April 1942.
      Reading Standard

The driver of Guy B 40 (RD 2114), having arrived at Woodcote Road terminus, appears to have made something of a ham-fisted attempt at reversing into St. Peter's Avenue ready to return to town, probably during the winter of 1941/42. On the 'stink pipe', above the litter bin and the black-and-white stripes, there appears to be pasted a somewhat faded paper label reading 'Bus Fare Stage'.

Late W. J. Haynes © Millane Publishing

In the early months of 1941, the undertaking faced a growing shortage of platform staff as increasing numbers of employees were called up to serve in the armed forces. There was also a large amount of sickness due to an influenza epidemic. As a temporary measure, once again six drivers from Smith's Coaches were hired, officially to drive single-deck motorbuses so that corporation drivers could be released for double-deck work. In reality, these single-deck drivers were often used to drive double-deckers during the three months they worked from Mill Lane, thanks to the relaxed PSV regulations of wartime.

Sporadic air raids in the Reading area continued, usually involving just one aircraft, and on the afternoon of 30th January 1941, there was an incendiary raid on Caversham, in the shopping and residential areas in the vicinity of Hemdean Road and Priory Avenue. Generally speaking, householders were well-versed and equipped to deal with incendiaries, so damage to housing was limited – but a furniture store was burnt out. This sort of raid prompted the introduction, not long afterwards, of a further Order under Defence Regulations. The Fire Prevention (Business Premises) Order, 1941, required 'fire watching' on all business premises 24 hours a day, meaning every employee of a business had to take turns on a rota, day and night, for virtually the rest of the war. One such was set up for the depot and its offices. The undertaking also participated in an area scheme at the Parcels Express Office in the Covered Market in Broad Street and with the Electricity Department on rotas at the four trolleybus substations, at Crescent Road, Catherine Street, Oxford Road (Rex) and Kentwood Hill. At the depot, the penalty was that overtime previously spent on munitions work had to be cut back and a 33% fall in output on external 'war work' was recorded.

At its meeting on 13th February 1941, the Transport Committee was asked to consider whether the department should render assistance (the loan of vehicles, crews and engineering assistance) to other undertakings, in towns where intensive bombing had caused such major disruption and devastation that there was a need to re-establish public transport and carry workers evacuated to outlying towns and villages to their workplaces. Mr Calder was not in favour, due to overwhelming demand for public transport which already existed in Reading and the *"...almost continuous complaining"* from residents pleading for better services. Further, there was the possible demand on the undertaking by the public assistance officer in the event of a serious air raid on Reading. The Transport Committee, however, did not agree, so there followed a meeting between the regional transport commissioner, the transport manager and the chairman of the Transport Committee. At the next Transport Committee meeting, on 13th March 1941, it was agreed to provide mutual help amongst operators in line with *"...every other undertaking"*.

On 11th March 1941, bus 46 was used on an evacuation task, carrying 11 mothers and 25 children from Reading station to Battle Hospital, and a charge was made to the Ministry of Health. There may have been some connection with Portsmouth, which had received its heaviest air raid to date the previous night; or with London, which received one of its last large-scale raids (although one of the worst, with 1,436 killed, 1,792 injured, a string of important public buildings and famous churches hit and the House of Commons chamber destroyed).

A Reading ARP anti-gas exercise took place on the morning of Thursday 20th March 1941, between Argyle Street and Bedford Road, on each side of Oxford Road, using tear gas canisters. At the sound of rattles, ARP and police officers put on their gas masks (respirators) and passing pedestrians, motorists and cyclists were requested to do the same. Instructions were given to the public by means of a loudspeaker van and the *Berkshire Chronicle* reported that *"...this was not a success owing to the fact that the announcements were so blurred as to be practically useless ...due to the fact that (the announcer) had to speak through a microphone attached to his respirator"*. The ringing of hand bells, which was the regulation method, was used to give the 'all clear' signal. The *Berkshire Chronicle* also happened to comment that there was no interruption to the bus services along Oxford Road, and that the drivers and conductors carried out their duties wearing their respirators, as did most of the passengers! This raises the question of what happened to those passengers who had forgotten to have their gas masks with them and who had to ride through a cloud of tear gas? Some 70 years later, it also conjures up some wonderful imagination: of a crowded trolleybus, bursting at the seams, everyone wearing a gas mask, and a 'rookie' conductor, gas mask steamed up inside, rushing to 'get all the fares in' before McIlroy's, saying an inaudible *"Fares Please!"* and trying to interpret equally inaudible fares requests from the passengers!

Two RAF impressment officers are known to have visited the depot late in March 1941, to secure vehicles for RAF use. The transport manager argued a strong case that Reading had no spare operational vehicles that could be released. However, he was willing to release for sale the four withdrawn Guy FCX six-wheel single-deck buses, 27–30, which had been officially withdrawn for some time but which had been retained as stand-by vehicles. It seems that the RAF officers could not believe their luck and, before departure, some work was done in connection with the batteries and lights in order to put the buses into normal working order. The sale included some spares, but a spare engine was retained for 31–32. We have so far been unable to trace the RAF history of any of the four but are confident that records do exist. In post-war years, bus 29 was seen in use with a showman in September 1945, and was noted at a Northampton fair still in use as such in October 1949.

In March 1941, a request from the southern divisional office of the Ministry of Food to provide five bus drivers on stand-by to drive food lorries, canteen lorries, and mobile canteens in their new Emergency Feeding Scheme mobile convoy had to be declined. Given existing commitments for bus drivers to drive ambulances and give mutual help to bus undertakings in other towns, there were limits to the assistance which could be given!

In March 1941, too, certain improvements to the movement and stopping of buses on Station Approach were planned for introduction following the imminent completion, at last, of the £50,000 joint Great Western Railway/County Borough of Reading project, started in December 1937 and protracted because of the war. This comprised roadway improvements and the construction of a new pedestrian subway extension from the station to the south side of the roadway, including subterranean toilets, etc. The roadway alongside the station itself was owned by the Great Western Railway and its use by corporation buses was by agreement with the railway, the council paying for any additional maintenance costs. To maintain its claim to the whole site by using the new facilities, various bus route diversions were proposed for implementation upon the civic opening of Station Approach, Station Hill and the new subway on Wednesday 16th April 1941:

(a) Route J (Roebuck – Stations) altered so that it approached Stations via Greyfriars Road instead of via Friar Street and Station Road, thus avoiding having to make a U-turn on Station Hill.

(b) Route M (Grovelands Road – Erleigh Road) altered so that it operated via Friar Street and West Street, as originally sanctioned by the Transport Committee a year previously, in February 1940.

Once again nothing changed; route M continued to share a stop in Broad Street with route L (Hemdean Road – Berkeley Avenue), still labelled as a 'temporary stop' for the Grovelands Road route.

Also at this time, two large notice boards were proposed for the new station subway, giving information about bus services, thus:

i) USE THIS STAIRCASE FOR BUSES TO Uplands Road, Woodcote Road, and Trolley Vehicles in Broad Street.

ii) USE THIS STAIRCASE FOR BUSES TO Erleigh Road, Merry Maidens, Grovelands Road, Roebuck.

A general notice board was also proposed, giving a summary of the corporation transport services, to be fixed to the wall overlooking Vincents yard, south of the station (the site of the subsequent Western Tower and Thames Tower buildings).

On 15th May 1941, the transport manager reported to the Transport Committee that the undertaking had been registered in the Schedule of Reserved Occupations and Protected Work. This provided a degree of protection for any more of the department's workforce from being called up into the armed forces as a result of new legislation. The Essential Work (General Provisions) Order 1941, (which had become law on 5th March 1941) was something else. Broadly, male or female, everyone had to be either in the armed forces or, if excused from military service, the Ministry of Labour and National Service put them to employment in support of the war effort, unless there was a very good reason to excuse them from this too (e.g. being an expectant mother, a mother with very young offspring, or someone employed in a reserved occupation). It was also able to 'direct' labour into a particular occupation, where, for example, there was a shortage. But it had a down side, as it gave powers to the National Service officer to enforce workers to work stated hours and to control their ability to resign without the permission of the Ministry of Labour. The Essential Work Order also controlled the ability of employers to sack employees when no replacement was available. Managers complained that the Essential Work Order had destroyed discipline, but the truth was that, in any case, full employment gave little room for manoeuvring when it came to sacking incompetent workers. Thus, both employees and management had their decisions controlled by state regulations – and neither group was pleased!

Workshop employees at the depot were frequently used for traffic work – usually as conductors – and great use had always been made of this flexibility, although it resulted in complaints from some employees who were concerned that such work was being allocated unfairly. Depot men were also used as drivers, sometimes in service, and on the night dispersal runs referred to later in this chapter. Under the Essential Work Order, however, the occupations of certain individuals were not regarded by Ministry of Labour officials as 'essential' and certainly, in their opinion, not beneficial to the war effort. A visit to Mill Lane by a labour supply inspector from the Ministry of Labour on 1st January 1942 reveals how the 'direction of labour', as it was called, could affect staff availability. A review of male employees meant that thirteen night cleaners, one parcels porter, twenty-five conductors, four queue regulators and three traffic inspectors were earmarked for transfer to munitions work or other vital services related to the war effort. Despite pleadings for their retention, not all of them could be retained and it was stated at the Transport Committee meeting on 15th January 1942 that women, some part time, would have to be recruited to fill the vacancies.

The Transport Department undertook the training of driver-mechanics for the Royal Army Ordnance Corps in the summer of 1941 but, earlier than that, Reading Corporation Transport also trained some of its own conductors as drivers. The problem here was finding an instructor with the necessary time – and the necessary gallon or two of fuel, which had been saved from somewhere else!

There was, however, always a shortage of conductors, so at the meeting of the Transport Committee held on 13th February 1941 it had been agreed that between 10 and 12 women conductors should be employed. Certainly, within a month there were some women already so employed, one of the earliest recruits having done the same job on the trams during the Great War. By June 1941 there were 60 women conductors and this had doubled by December 1941. Their pay scale was 90% of male conductors' rates for the first six months of service and, thereafter, the same rate. One of the first to be trained, in the first days of March 1941, was Mrs Lucy Jones, who was soon appointed 'Inspector of the Conductresses'. In those days of sexual inequality, the 'conductresses', as they were known, were not always well received by the men. The appointment of 'inspectresses' in 1942 caused further disquiet and the issues of seniority and promotion were discussed by the Works Committee. Management, too, was concerned that conversations between drivers and conductresses, using the communication window between cab and saloon of a bus whilst in motion, was discouraging proper supervision of the platform, losing fares and distracting drivers, so bulkhead windows were screwed up in the summer of 1942.

There was further concern that absenteeism amongst married conductresses made it difficult to maintain services, especially when, for example, a husband was home on leave from the forces. Somehow or other, it seemed that the Ministry of Labour had a policy of turning a blind eye to such absenteeism amongst married women, although it was difficult for management to comprehend, and alien to the smooth running of a bus service. The reader will appreciate that up to this time the employment of married women was rare; and women who were managing a home and had what were sometimes termed 'domestic difficulties', with children and a job, had an unusual and challenging task. It should also be remembered that many of Reading's conductresses were evacuees, or were 'directed labour' billeted in Reading. Nevertheless, uncontrolled, absenteeism by both male and female employees was seen as likely to pose a serious threat to Reading's bus and trolleybus services and, in turn, was seen as a threat to the efficiency of wartime industries in and around Reading. On a number of occasions in the winter of 1942/43, some journeys did not operate purely because of such absenteeism, as a result of which Regional Transport Commissioner Sir Henry Piggott was asked to raise the problem with the Ministry of Labour & National Service and to request that ministry to direct 'a more responsible and suitable type of female employee for conducting work'.

To assist with this combination of work and home pressure on working women, from February 1941 several nursery schools were planned for establishment around the town, to supplement the existing Reading Nursery School. These additional nursery facilities opened across Reading between 1941 and 1943, offering nursery education and afternoon sleeping facilities for pre-school children whose mothers were employed on 'war work'. Those nurseries at Whitley Park, Norcot, Victoria Square, Holybrook House, Gosbrook Road, Torrington Road, Recreation Road and Bridge Street were retained after the war, but those at Denmark Hall, Bul-

In March 1941, Mrs Lucy Jones (left) was one of the first conductresses to be recruited and trained and was soon appointed 'Inspector of Conductresses' (but with no superiority over existing male platform staff). Mrs Muriel Fawcett (right), recruited a little later in 1941, is wearing the original conductress's uniform. Previously a nurse, she later became the welfare officer responsible for chasing-up absentee conductresses – a particular problem after 'directed labour' was introduced by the Ministry of Labour & National Service and totally unsuitable persons were 'directed' into the job. Naturally, new uniforms had to be ordered for the ladies, which originally included skirts, although these were soon superseded by 'slacks'.

Left: © Reading Museum Service (Reading Borough Council); all rights reserved   Right: Print from R. V. Fawcett's family collection

mershe Road, and London Road were closed. Their establishment across the town during the war gave Reading a very high level of local authority-funded post-war nursery provision that has lasted into the twenty-first century.

Letters to local newspapers showed, however, that the conductresses were well received by the public. They were also discussed in the Council Chamber, the deputy mayor, Alderman Mrs Jenkins, expressing her concern that *"...some of them were carrying out their duties with their nails adorned."* Others, however, described *"...the ladies...as neat as they are efficient"*. And the mayor gave his own support to what were described in the *Berkshire Chronicle* of 26th September 1941 as 'conductorettes'. *"They were"*, he said *"...a very satisfactory type of woman"* and, amidst laughter, he noted that *"...one advantage was that if one was on the platform when the bus started away, the 'conductorette' would put her arm around the passenger to steady him"*. The newspaper noted that *"His Worship did not give his authority for the experience"*!

The increased loadings, especially during peak hours, and the larger number of standing passengers, often all day, meant that fare collection became an increasingly difficult task. In late November 1941, in an attempt to recoup an increasing number of unpaid fares, which the platform staff were having difficulty in collecting, uncollected fares boxes were fitted on the platforms of most, but not all, of the department's vehicles. These 'honesty' boxes, which became a standard fitment on corporation buses and trolleybuses, lasted until late January 1973 on crewed buses. The keyholes to empty them were covered with paper labels to prevent tampering, yet these were a source of concern in January 1942, when many vehicles were returning to the depot with the labels removed – and some of the boxes emptied of their contents.

Mr Calder had written to all municipal undertakings in southern England early in January 1941 enquiring whether they had surplus motorbuses or trolleybuses, which could be hired or purchased. Nothing suitable to Reading's requirements was forthcoming and, in the case of trolleybuses, it was probably because any that were offered had regenerative braking, which could not be used with a current supplied through mercury arc rectifiers. Mr Calder was therefore authorised to begin negotiations with the Ministry of Transport for the purchase of six new trolleybuses and six new motorbuses. We understand, although we have seen no source material, that in 1939 it had been planned to order four further AEC Regent double-deck motorbuses, but that the decision had been deferred due to the war.

A questionnaire from the Municipal Passenger Transport Association, which was sent to the department on 2nd April 1941, sought to establish the demand for new trolleybuses during the following twelve months. The transport manager's reply referred to a requirement for six new motorbuses and six new trolleybuses, which would 'liberate' motorbus usage on trolleybus routes and would allow the withdrawal of the two remaining Guy FCX six-wheel single-deck buses, 31 and 32. Mr Calder contacted the regional transport commissioner and subsequently met with Colonel Trench, an officer at the Ministry of Transport in Reading, and was informed that Reading was the only undertaking in the country to have made an independent application for additional trolley vehicles. In consequence, Reading was promised six new vehicles once a decision had been made regarding a national trolleybus-building programme. In fact, presumably as a result of the poor response, the Ministry of Supply decided not to permit the building of any new trolleybuses during 1941 and early 1942, relying instead on meeting any demand by redirecting trolleybuses already built for export to South African fleets, the delivery of which had been halted by the attacks on shipping. The announcement that 'outsize trolleybuses' were available was made public in the issue of *Passenger Transport Journal* dated 30th May 1941, in which an accompanying article stated that bodies had not yet been manufactured.

Accordingly, the Ministry of Supply offered Reading Corporation Transport six Sunbeam trolleybuses – part of a 1939 order of 25 two-axle vehicles for Johannesburg Municipal Transport – the chassis of which were already constructed and stored at Sunbeam's Wolverhampton Works. They were 8ft wide, six inches wider than the maximum width of vehicle permitted on the roads of the United Kingdom. Mr Calder was no doubt shown the original MCCW bodywork arrangement drawings featuring an additional front exit door. This seemed to cause him some concern, even though the bodies had not yet been built.

Unlike Reading's latest AEC trolleybuses, with their lower floor-line to facilitate operation under the town's railway bridges, these chassis would have had a higher floor-line and, for operation in Reading, would have meant a reversion to lowbridge bodywork with a side gangway and four-abreast bench seating on the upper deck. Mr Calder had no wish to take any more lowbridge trolleybuses, like 101–106, into stock, and also noted that, as a non-standard batch, it would have meant having to maintain a separate stock of spares. He pointed out, too, that the BTH control equipment was manufactured to operate the opposite way round to standard British practice (wherein the right foot operated the brake pedal while the left operated the power pedal), resulting in a non-standard feature in the fleet which could prove an operational hazard. These concerns were apparently enough to render such vehicles unsuitable for use in Reading and the minutes of the Transport Committee meeting of 9th June 1941 record that *"...no action be taken in regard to the acquisition of certain trolley vehicles now offered to the Corporation on the ground that such vehicles are not and cannot be made suitable for use in Reading."* This minute was immediately followed by a resolution that Mr Calder should continue negotiations for six new AEC trolleybuses similar to the 1938/39 specification.

It is of note that all 43 of the available three-axle South African vehicles, which were delivered to London Transport, were fitted with bodywork built to the original South African design. The batch of 25 two-axle Sunbeam MF2 chassis which had been offered to Reading, however, were eventually fitted with early austerity bodywork, not with their originally-specified MCCW bodies. All 25 vehicles were delivered in 1942 – five to Nottingham Corporation as their 447–451 (GTV 47–51) with Weymann bodywork; ten to Bradford Corporation as their 693–702 (DKW 993–999 and DKY 2–4), also with bodywork by Weymann; and ten to St. Helens Corporation, with lowbridge Massey bodywork as their 157–166 (DJ 9005–9014). The latter were to become the only 8ft wide lowbridge trolleybuses in Britain.

With hindsight, we could be surprised that with all the exceptional wartime pressures on Reading's trolleybus fleet, the transport manager felt able to refuse an offer of six new trolleybuses, a decision which could be said to have delayed fleet expansion for almost two years and which, in fact, was instrumental in stunting the intended expansion of the town's trolleybus system. We may note too, that despite Mr

Calder's insistence that only 'standard Reading trolleybuses' should be taken into stock, some non-standard (albeit highbridge) utility Sunbeam vehicles did enter the fleet, in 1943, as the only type of trolleybuses available under wartime supply conditions. The point is that lowbridge vehicles were slower to load, unload and collect fares, which would have caused serious timekeeping problems in a 'mixed operation' situation on an intensive service. Given the wartime passenger loadings of the 'main line' and for sometime afterwards, not to wantonly buy a perceived 'nuisance' was probably the correct decision.

On 5th June 1941, it was reported that some concern had been voiced by the highways officer that reversing buses at the junction of Whitley Wood Lane with Whitley Wood Road (alias Wood Lane Junction) were causing damage to the footpath. The deputy transport manager was also concerned that the reversing procedure was especially dangerous during the blackout and it was suggested that the schedules should be arranged to ensure that two buses were never there together. On 20th June 1941, it was decided that all relief buses would terminate at the Grenadier (the site of the present Holiday Inn hotel), whilst school bus journeys were altered to no longer use the location as a terminus.

The undertaking's returns for the financial year ending 31st March 1941 were published in mid-June 1941. Net profit had increased only marginally, from £15,554 (the highest previously attained in the history of the undertaking) to £16,387, mainly due to heavy increases in working expenses – £12,200 attributed to wages and roundly £6,000 to fuel and tyres. Whilst passengers carried on the 44 motorbuses (35 double-deck and 9 single-deck) had increased by 2,284,295 to 13,369,679, they had operated 42,371 fewer miles, due to the reduced service and earlier daily finishing brought about by wartime fuel restrictions. The 31 trolleybuses, on the other hand, carried a total of 18,229,426 passengers, compared with the 12,382,774 carried in the 7 month period the previous year following final tramway abandonment, and operated an additional 282,105 miles. Overall, therefore, there were 7,280,685 extra passengers carried, of which almost six million were carried on the trolleybuses. Mr Calder, in attaching his report, observed that the number of residents requiring transport facilities in the borough was now far in excess of the accommodation which could be provided by the normal services, even if they were wholly available for this purpose.

June 1941 saw the last and most difficult period of the Blitz and the worst period thus far in the Battle of the Atlantic, with particularly large shipping losses – both tankers and cargo ships – caused mainly by U-boat attacks. This resulted in an even greater shortage of fuel and materials which, in turn, led to further demands for cuts and even a proposal to stagger working hours, in order to make best use of vehicles running in the off-peak period. Basic fuel rationing was abolished from 19th September 1941, as there was, after all, no private motoring permitted – only essential users, government and civil defence users, the military, taxis, haulage businesses and passenger transport undertakings. Thereafter, road fuel was allocated to users by the regional transport commissioner according to need.

On 3rd July 1941, the regional transport commissioner had drawn Mr Calder's attention to government instructions calling for the further fuel reductions. Independently, the Transport Department had received notice that the supplementary road fuel allowance would have to be reduced by 500 units per fortnight from 26th July 1941, which would have resulted in having to cut total weekly bus mileage by between 1,500 and 1,600 miles. At the Transport Committee meeting on 17th July 1941, various proposals were discussed as to how to achieve this, which centred around severely curtailing the usual targets – routes J, K and L – and introducing still earlier timings for 'last buses'. After some special pleading from the transport manager, given Reading's special wartime conditions, the regional transport commissioner agreed to reduce the targeted mileage savings required to around 700 or 800 miles a week – but he was still of the opinion that as a 'reception area', late journeys in Reading catered purely for amusement and relaxation, and should be cut out.

The Transport Committee agreed to once again reduce the service on routes J, K and L together with cutting some 'duplicate' journeys on other routes. Effective Monday 28th July 1941, routes K and L again became morning, lunchtime and evening peak services only; and route J (Roebuck – Stations) was withdrawn entirely on Sundays and on weekdays between the morning and lunchtime peaks (9.20am to 11.40am), when a Roebuck – Pond House shuttle service was again substituted.

These reductions together produced a weekly saving of 820 miles and therefore met in full the required demand for fuel savings. It was agreed that this reduction in mileage in the middle of the day could delay the demanded evening reductions until Monday 6th October 1941, when the departure times of 'last motorbuses' on services from Broad Street were to be brought forward from 10.15pm to 9.30pm. The departure time for 'last trolleybuses' remained unaffected: 11.00pm on weekdays, 10:45pm on Sundays.

At the same Transport Committee meeting, on 17th July 1941, it was agreed to purchase 40 new TIM ticket machines. These were required to replace worn-out machines from the 1934 batch and to take advantage of the new situation with the employment of conductresses, who could be 'doubled-up' on busy journeys.

On Sunday 27th July 1941, an early morning defence exercise took place on the streets of Reading town centre, involving the Home Guard and regular troops staging a 'mock attack'. It started at 5.45am and, according to the *Reading Standard*, a corporation trolleybus was *"bombed by teargas in the main thorough-fare"* by low-flying aircraft (as shown in the illustration on the front cover) and both Caversham Bridge and Reading Bridge were 'captured' by the 'enemy' before their attention was turned to the railway stations at around 8.00am. This early morning exercise was no doubt timed to cause minimum disruption to the town.

During the winter months of 1940/41, disused tram track had continued to cause problems. Heavy rains caused the wood block road surfacing in a part of Oxford Road, near Cheapside, to lift, producing large potholes in the road. This made the road unusable, particularly during the blackout and it had to be closed, traffic being diverted up Cheapside while repairs took place. Tram rail removal also began at the Pond House in early May 1941 and in Oxford Road, between Valentia Road and Bedford Road, at the end of July 1941, when the road also had to be closed for repairs. Presumably, bus and trolleybus services were maintained.

The disused tram track and the road surface in Kings Road, between Duke Street and Cemetery Junction, also seriously deteriorated during the summer of 1941, accentuated, perhaps, by a severe and prolonged thunderstorm on Saturday

> **READING CORPORATION, TRANSPORT**
>
> ## IMPORTANT NOTICE
> ### MOTOR OMNIBUS SERVICES
>
> In view of the Government's instructions that a substantial reduction must be effected in the consumption of motor fuel, the following alterations in the motor omnibus services will be in force on and after MONDAY, 28th JULY, 1941.
>
> **Woodcote Road & St. Mary's Butts**
> The service will be suspended between 9.15 a.m. and 12.7 p.m. and between 3.37 p.m. and 4.37 p.m.
>
> **Hemdean Road & Berkeley Avenue**
> The service will be suspended between 9.22 a.m. and 12.8 p.m. and between 3.8 p.m. and 4.38 p.m.
>
> **"Roebuck" & Railway Stations**
> On WEEKDAYS (Mondays to Saturdays) the usual service, as at present, will be run on this route **except that from 9.40 a.m. to 11.40 a.m. buses will not run all the way** between "Roebuck" and Railway Stations, but will run only between "Roebuck" and "Pond House."
>
> On SUNDAYS there will be no through service between "Roebuck" and Railway Stations, but a shuttle service between "Roebuck" and "Pond House" will be operated throughout the day.
>
> Corporation Transport Offices.   J. M. CALDER,
> 17th July 1941.   Transport Manager and Engineer.

> ## Important Notice
> ### MOTOR-OMNIBUS SERVICES
>
> In consequence of the Government's instructions for a further reduction to be made in the consumption of motor fuel, the motor-omnibus service will be
>
> **CURTAILED on & after OCT. 6, 1941**
> as follows, viz. :—
>
> LAST MOTORBUSES will depart from BROAD ST. at 9.30 p.m. for the termini, *INSTEAD of at 10.15 p.m. as at present.*
>
> ### TROLLEY - VEHICLE SERVICES
> Trolleybuses will continue to run as at present.
> **LAST TROLLEYBUSES from BROAD STREET :**
> WEEKDAYS (Mon. to Sat.) 11.0 p.m.
> SUNDAYS - - - - 10.45 p.m.
>
> Corporation Transport Offices.   BY ORDER — J. M. CALDER,
> 12th August, 1941.   Transport Manager and Engineer.

26th July 1941. Wood blocks were lifting and, for a time, traffic was suspended between Eldon Road and Cemetery Junction, although presumably trolleybus operation was maintained. Subsequently, some rails along this section were removed and others covered over by the Highways Department and the Transport Department's permanent way engineers. The Ministry of Supply was again concerned around this time that all redundant tram rails should be made available for scrap as they were of high-grade steel. It was especially concerned about *"...the considerable tonnage of rails still laying in the streets of Reading"*. The ministry was also anxious to recover rail used for defence purposes at roadblocks and these were replaced with rolled steel joists. The scrap price offered, of £8 a ton, was still not enough to encourage the council to begin proactive removal on those sections where the tram track and roadway was sound, calculations suggesting an actual cost of £15 16s 0d for removing and cleaning each ton of rail.

The so-far unused trolleybus operating powers, which had been granted for implementation within five years under the 1936 Provisional Order, expired in 1941. The town clerk sought to renew them, but the Ministry of War Transport was unwilling to grant renewal, due to shortage of materials to construct any extensions to the trolleybus system, let alone provide help in obtaining any new vehicles. The town was therefore obliged to continue with its existing trolleybus system in a situation of a growing population but with increasing shortages of fuel and rubber.

Concerns about electrical flashes from trolleybus overhead in the blackout were expressed by the employees' representative at the Works Committee meeting on 19th August 1941, when it was also agreed that trolleybooms would receive additional white paint *"to enhance their visibility during the blackout"*.

In August 1941, the regional transport commissioners were given powers to grant dispensation permitting a larger standing capacity on single-deck buses equal to the number of seats fitted — up to a maximum of 30 standees. This meant that seating had to be refitted around the perimeter, in order to create a large central standing area. These changes were designed to make better use of single-deckers, which used similar quantities of fuel to double-deckers but carried far fewer passengers. During the late summer of 1941, the seating in three of the undertaking's single-deck Guy Bs, 33–35, was re-arranged to 22 perimeter seats, so these vehicles were thereafter able to carry 22 standing passengers. All three are thought to have retained perimeter seating for 22 until the end of their service lives. The new seating was trimmed in a moquette similar to that used in the subsequently-delivered wartime utility vehicles. Older Guy Bs 19 and 20, which were 26-seaters, had a 'smoking compartment' bulkhead in the saloon, which may have made them unsuitable to be 'rearranged', so they retained their original seating and layout throughout the war and afterwards, until disposal. Guy 40 was rearranged with perimeter seating for 24 but reverted to normal layout after the war and certainly had 24

Guy B 35 (RD 37), seen here during the late summer of 1941 outside the depot, was one of the single-deckers to have its seating re-arranged around the perimeter to accommodate 22 passengers but having the effect of increasing the area available for standing an equal number of passengers.

Late W. J. Haynes
© Millane Publishing

seats when sold in 1947. It is not clear whether bus 41 was rearranged but post-war it had 24 seats of normal layout, although it was sold minus seats in 1947. Buses 40 and 41 were both new as 25-seaters. There is, however, surviving official documentation quoting both as having only 22 perimeter seats during war, bus 40 being recorded as a *"20 seater plus 20 standing"* in surviving disposal notes, which have been amended to *"24 seats"* in pencil. The two surviving Guy FCX six-wheel single-deckers, 31 and 32, were also converted, from 32-seaters, to 28 seated and 28 standing. Surviving post-war disposal notes for the pair refer to *"converted under wartime dispensation to 30 seated, 30 standing"* but a pencil note amends it to *"28 each"* (presumably seating and standing).

In August 1941, Guy FCX 32 was used as a mobile enquiry office for Reading Women's War Work Week (as similar buses 27–30, one or more of which had been converted as a mobile enquiry office, had by now been disposed of to the RAF). 32 may well have been used thus after its seating was stripped out ready to be re-fixed round the perimeter. This event, which proved to be very beneficial, included a street parade on Sunday 10th August 1941, in which the undertaking's conductresses took part, together with AEC Regent 47.

Trolleybuses and motorbuses were, at this time, dispersed around the town overnight to minimise losses should the depot be hit during an air raid. Dispersal of vehicles had begun in the autumn of 1940, when the risk of air raids was at its peak. At that time, motorbuses were parked in side streets and about 12 trolleybuses were parked in the streets around Liverpool Road terminus. Severe weather in the winter of 1940/41 froze radiators, and caused two watchmen to quit in one week, and the dispersal soon ended. In June 1941, the regional transport commissioner instructed that collections of more than fifty public service or goods vehicles should be dispersed to avoid total loss in the event of an air attack. In consultation with the chief constable, about one third of the undertaking's fleet was dispersed around the town. Trolleybuses were again parked around the turning loop at Liverpool Road terminus, whilst motorbuses were parked at dispersal sites in South Street, in Eldon Square (7 buses), Christchurch Gardens (9 buses), in Battle Street, off Bedford Road (7–11 buses); and in Sidmouth Street (12 buses). Most were dispersed immediately from service and brought back to the depot after 4.00am next morning for cleaning, fuelling and servicing. Watchmen were again employed at each site. In connection with this scheme, it was at this time that the ARP inter-hospital ambulances were moved to Smith's Coaches' premises (the former Silver Grey garage) in Northumberland Avenue, at 5 shillings per vehicle per week. There were again frozen motorbus radiators – and trolleybus air compressors – in the winter of 1941/42, when the scheme had to be temporarily abandoned. By January 1942, however, with a reduction in the threat from air raids, the transport manager was able to cancel the nightly dispersal of the fleet altogether.

Throughout the war there were frequent parades around the town, usually at weekends, for the purposes of recruitment, fund-raising, morale-building or expressions of support for one cause or another. On Sunday 10th August 1941 the feature was Reading Women's War Work Week. A contingent of post women (one of them out-of-step) precedes AEC Regent 47 (RD 7127) carrying conductresses recruited by Reading Corporation Transport – a total of 60 had been recruited by June 1941. The number of onlookers is quite remarkable in this Blagrave Street scene. The edifice in the background behind the bus is Friar Street Chambers, which, in 18 months time, will receive a direct hit during an air raid which killed 41 people.

© *Reading Museum Service (Reading Borough Council); all rights reserved*

On 23rd July 1941 a complaint was received from the ARP rescue service about buses using the Sidmouth Street dispersal site, it being claimed that the rescue service was prevented from being able to disperse its own rescue party vehicles into the same street from The Dell Rescue Depot, at the council yard in Boult Street. Mr Calder was not open to persuasion that his buses should move and in September 1941 the buses were still in Sidmouth Street. A memo dated 4th September 1941 shows that during the short period of operation of the Reading West station specials, (see next chapter) vehicles were actually booked out for service from the Sidmouth Street dispersal site rather than from the depot itself. Presumably, this was to avoid congestion at the depot, as the ten buses were required to be booked out at around the same time. The duties booked out from Sidmouth Street, together with their reporting times were:

FA	(6.00am)	**HC**	(6.15am)	**MA**	(6.30am)
FB	(6.30am)	**FC**	(6.40am)	**IA**	(6.45am)
MD	(6.50am)	**FD**	(6.50am)	**JB**	(6.50am)
MB	(6.53am)	**H Rlf.4** Hemdean School Special (6.54am)			
IB	(7.00am)				

So that the reader might understand the foregoing (and similar references in this book), it is worth explaining the system used in Reading to identify individual vehicle duties. It is believed that this originated in early horse tram days, and it is still used in a modified form a century-and-a-quarter later. The first letter of each pair refers to the route and the second to the particular duty on that route. In the simplest case, once all the duties (bus, driver and conductor, and, indeed, ticket machine) are in place on, say, Route F, duty **FA** is chased round and round all day by **FB**, followed by **FC**, followed by **FD**, etc, etc. Note, however, that at the start of a duty, not every bus enters 'the loop' in the same direction. Because both ends of an urban route need to start at more-or-less the same time, each bus is slipped into its eventual correct place as soon as possible, so that the headway (the time between two buses) is established with the least possible delay. Of course, the duty may, indeed, do 'something else' before, during or after its allocated main duty on a route (in our case, route F).

On 6th August 1941, Ransomes trolleybus 105 chanced to shoot across Southampton Street from Mill Lane as it was entering service – and very nearly plunged into Mill Stream! It was towed back to the depot and eventually repaired.

Construction of new workshops for repair and maintenance of the fleet was eventually started in the summer of 1941, in the area vacated by the old power station equipment, in the building alongside the new trolleybus depot. Following Ministry of War Transport approval, arrangements were now made to convert the former boiler house to a further light workshop. Contracts were awarded to Francis Brothers Ltd, Tilehurst, for construction of inspection pits, sunken workshop, drainage and concreting of the workshop floor, at a cost of £2,897 13s 1d; to H. C. Goodman Ltd for installation of a heating system and boiler plant, at a cost of £4,900; and to the Franki Compressed Pile Company Ltd, for the construction of four concrete piles in connection with the erection of a boiler house for the heating system, at a cost of £125. It was not until the war was nearly over that the whole workshop area was completed, at a total cost of £26,920.

At this time, to comply with a Government Order made through the Petroleum Board in August 1941, the fuel

Ransomes trolleybus 105 (RD 8089) will forever be remembered as something of a 'jinxed' vehicle! On 6th August 1941 it suffered an accident when the driver, who had just changed over from driving a motorbus, depressed the power pedal (which was in the same position as the clutch on a motorbus), thus accelerating instead of braking when approaching the junction of Mill Lane with Southampton Street. The vehicle shot across the road, crashed through the parapet of the bridge over Mill Stream (a backwater of the River Kennet) and stopped with the front nearside wheel in mid-air over the water! It is seen here in the process of being retrieved from the brink.

© *Reading Museum Service (Reading Borough Council); all rights reserved*

pumps at the depot had to be rendered incapable of manual use. Although a handle was held in reserve, for use during a power cut, this somewhat conflicted with the concern that *"...fuel is not available to the enemy if he arrives..."*. There was a delicate balance to be struck between sealing supplies to prevent use by the enemy and making supplies accessible during a raid if there was an electrical failure!

At the Transport Committee meeting on 17th November 1941, it was finally decided to abandon any plans to operate route M (Grovelands Road – Erleigh Road) via Friar Street and West Street, a proposal which had been under consideration since February 1940. Thus, route M continued to serve Broad Street and the bus stop post planted outside A. H. Bull Ltd's shop in Friar Street was finally removed, having never been used. At the same meeting, it was agreed to cease locking bus shelters overnight, as had been standard practice, and to remove the doors. Many conductors had mislaid their pass keys and there was irritation from the public regarding shelters being left locked up during the day.

Changes were made under Defence Regulations, which permitted more standing room on buses and coaches in the extreme conditions of wartime loadings. From November 1941, twelve rather than eight standing passengers were allowed on double-deck motorbuses. As stated on page 32, Reading's trolleybuses had already been authorised by the Transport Committee to carry 12 standing passengers from September 1939, because trolleybuses operated under different legislation to motorbuses. Throughout the war and in spite of operating grossly overloaded for most of the time, but with minimum maintenance or servicing, the whole fleet performed excellently.

During December 1941, the Transport Department was involved in transporting Civil Defence Casualty Services personnel by omnibus on a day visit to Southampton, to view the serious air raid damage inflicted on that town. The personnel were drawn from the Foxley Ambulance Depot in Redlands Road and Castle Ambulance Depot, at Hewens Garage in Castle Street. The most serious air raids on Southampton took place on 23rd November, 30th November and 1st December 1941.

The war was now about to expand into a new arena, for early on the morning of 7th December 1941, without any warning, the Japanese bombed the United States naval base at Pearl Harbour, in Hawaii, sinking five battleships and killing 2,344 men. Predictably, the USA declared war on Japan the following day. In support of its ally, Germany declared war on the USA on 11th December and U-boat operations moved closer to the east coast of America, causing further losses of ships, men and cargo during the following year. Somehow or other Britain, too, found that it was at war with Japan for, on 9th December 1941, the Japanese sank two British capital ships – HMS Repulse and HMS Prince of Wales – off the coast of Malaya and, as 1941 drew to a close, the Japanese invaded the British colony of Hong Kong on Christmas Day.

Even though Britain and her empire were being attacked and battered on all fronts and the grip would tighten rather more, RAF air raids on Germany were beginning to build up. Germany suffered its problems too, like the sinking of her proud battleship Bismarck on 27th May 1941, and her miscalculated invasion of the Soviet Union from 22nd June 1941. The American eagle had had its feathers ruffled – and that was something it just would not stand for! At a local level, however, in Reading the threat of nightly air raids was diminishing and the threat from Japan was not something of immediate concern. The Transport Department's most pressing problems as 1941 drew to a close continued to be shortages of all sorts – crews, buses, fuel and materials – and vehicle overloading.

Guy B 33 (RD 35) takes its layover in the specially-constructed lay-by at the Berkeley Avenue terminus of route L (Hemdean Road – Berkeley Avenue), which was brought into use on 27th April 1940 (and which, indeed, still exists). Evidence suggests that the photograph dates to autumn 1941 or spring 1942: the bus stop post is minus a flag, the bus appears to have perimeter seating – and grass seeding has only just been carried out!   Late W. J. Haynes © Millane Publishing

6 Wartime Specials

Reading became an important administrative centre during the war as a number of government departments and private firms were evacuated from London, and large houses were taken over in and around Reading to accommodate them. The armed forces, too, required similar premises.

To help the reader appreciate why the corporation transport department had such difficulty coping with demand for its services, it is worth providing an idea of some of the administrative departments that were attracted to the Reading district during the war, many bringing with them a sizeable workforce. The Regional Commandant for the Women's Mechanical Transport Corps became established at 25 Craven Road, with further offices at Rotherfield Grange, 61 Bath Road, together with the Women's Voluntary Service (which, after all, had been founded by the Marchioness of Reading). The wartime headquarters of the British Institute in Paris was newly opened in Reading in March 1941. Two months later the War Damage Commission (Southern Region) set up in Coley Park; and in June 1941 the Ministry of Health established a regional headquarters at 17 Bath Road. The National Fire Service set up its regional headquarters in Reading, too, at the Mansion House in Prospect Park. Brock Barracks, in Oxford Road, home of the Royal Berkshire Regiment, was obviously in use by the army during the war but, in October 1943, it was partly occupied by American troops. The Royal Army Pay Corps was based at offices and church halls all over Reading, but their headquarters was a large number of Nissen huts at Balmore House, in Balmore Drive, Caversham and, at one time, the whole of Ranikhet Camp, in Church End Lane, Tilehurst, was also occupied by the Royal Army Pay Corps. Later, there were Americans at Ranikhet as well as at Aldermaston, at a huge supply dump on Newbury racecourse, and in the woods between Highmoor and Nettlebed. The Royal Engineers were at Arborfield and there was a Royal Army Service Corps camp at Heckfield. An Auxiliary Territorial Service training centre was set up at Aldermaston Court, some miles outside Reading. The RAF had a recruitment office at the old St. Giles' School. Raw recruits to the RAF reported to Sylvesters, a large house in Berkeley Avenue. The Ministry of Transport had moved to Reading, to offices in Minster Street and the regional transport commissioner (southern region) and his staff went into Chiltern Court, a mansion in St. Peter's Avenue, Caversham. The Salvation Army moved their national headquarters out of London, to Rosehill House, virtually on the borough boundary at Emmer Green, which they had bought after it had ceased to be the preparatory school for The Oratory in 1938. The Great Western Railway established its headquarters at Goring. For most of the war Reading Gaol was not used as a prison but as the headquarters of the Censor's Office. The southern regional office of the Ministry of Information was in Broad Street and the Army Comforts Depot, which serviced the whole of the British army, was based in St. Mary's Butts.

In August 1939, the BBC had moved into Caversham Park, a large mansion in Peppard Road, Emmer Green, which since 1922 had been home to The Oratory School. There, the BBC and the Ministry of Information set up a 'listening unit', to intercept, record and translate radio broadcasts from enemy and neutral countries. In 1943, Caversham Park became the permanent home of a newly-established BBC Overseas Monitoring Service which, under the supervision of the Ministry of Information, played an important role in the interception of enemy broadcasts for the rest of the war and which continues (in much modified form) to the present day. It was at Caversham Park in May 1945 that the first news of Germany's surrender was received. Although this site was served by route H (Chalgrove Way – Wood Lane Junction), once the Monitoring Service was established, the BBC chose to provide its own staff transport (possibly for security reasons); two ex-LPTB open-staircase Tilling STs were noted on 13th April 1943, operating between Stations and Caversham Park on what was probably a daily staff service. One was former ST1014 and both were painted flat green and unlettered. London Transport records show that four such vehicles, all similar, were sold to the BBC on 10th May 1940, namely ST841 (GJ 2017), ST909 (GJ 2084) and ST1013/14 (GK 6289/90). Another empty house, Basildon Park, on the main road between Pangbourne and Streatley, was requisitioned by the Ministry of Works in 1939. At first the British Army used the grounds for practicing tank warfare. Later, two units of the 101st Airborne Division of the American Army completed their training for D-Day there and subsequently returned to prepare for the invasion of Holland in September 1944. Later, the Nissen huts in the grounds became a prisoner-of-war camp, the house itself being used by the officers-in-charge. The house was de-requisitioned in 1952.

Special relief buses and late specials often ran to meet the needs of those who worked at these scattered premises, and these demands caused additional pressure on the Transport Department's fuel allowance, which was finely balanced and tightly controlled. Detailed records of the mileage run and the fuel used show how firm the controls were; but they also provide detailed historical records of the services that were operated.

One of the most interesting operations was the provision of Royal Ordnance Factory specials. Initially, this was a very large and complicated operation involving the transport of building workers employed by Sir Robert McAlpine & Sons, to and from the Burghfield site (at this time, extensive building work was being undertaken on a site which, in post-war years, became central to Britain's nuclear weapons programme). Some 50 buses (not corporation vehicles, but probably those of local independent operators such as Smith's, Spratley, Venture and the like) were used daily to carry construction workers to site, so it was proposed that by running a train direct onto the private sidings already installed, there would be a considerable saving in fuel. The co-ordinated operation involved transporting some 1,000 workers per day by bus and train via Reading West station. Another 464 workers had still to be carried by some 20 buses, from Wokingham, Alton, Slough, Basingstoke, Newbury and Fleet. Other workers used their own bicycles, whilst some 700 workers lived in a camp on site. Initial planning for these services took place in the Mill Lane offices of Reading Corporation Transport on 2nd September 1941, at a meeting attended by the Burghfield ROF co-ordinating engineer, the regional transport commissioner, and representatives from the Ministry of Supply, the Ministry of Transport, the Great Western Railway, and Reading Corporation Transport, when it was provisionally agreed that the new arrangements would be implemented from Monday 15th September 1941 (although the start was subsequently delayed a month, until Monday 13th October 1941). The heart of the operation was a special Monday to

Saturday workmen's train, running from Pangbourne, via Tilehurst and Reading West, thence onto the private sidings at ROF Burghfield, where it remained stabled during the day for the evening return journey.

The Transport Department's responsibility was to meet the train, which departed Reading West station at 7.05am, by operating 14 special motorbus journeys from St. Mary's Butts to Reading West station via Oxford Road, turning via Beresford Road, Catherine Street and Salisbury Road, to return to St. Mary's Butts or to otherwise take up the rest of their duties. Five buses left the depot at 6.30am, four of them running two journeys each, whilst another five left at 6.35am, each running a single journey. All the relevant duties were garaged overnight in Middle Garage, all being rostered for later use, namely on duties **JB**, **MC**, **MD** and **IB** (2 journeys each); and **FD**, **IA**, **MB**, **FE**, **H Rlf 3** and **H Rlf 5** (single journeys). The reader is referred to page 55 for an explanation of the method by which individual duties were identified; **Rlf** is short for 'relief'. These motorbus specials were supplemented by three trolleybus journeys between St. Mary's Butts and Reading West station between 6.30am and 7.00am as they took up service on the main line, ROF workers being permitted to use these journeys as well. No fares were taken and no tickets were issued, but all workers were issued with a workman's six-day weekly ticket to 'Burghfield Factory Junction', which was purchased by Messrs McAlpine from the stationmaster at Mortimer station at a cost of 5s 3d from Pangbourne, 4s 3d from Tilehurst, or 2s 3d from Reading West.

Return journeys meeting the train were also organised, the train arriving at Reading West station at 7.40pm on Mondays to Thursdays, 6.44pm on Fridays and 4.30pm on Saturdays. The Friday arrival time caused some problems with vehicle availability and it was stated in the planning document that relief buses on route F (Uplands Road – Merry Maidens) and route H (Wood Lane Junction – Chalgrove Way) would specifically have to be withdrawn to meet the demand for vehicles working as ROF workers' specials. Buses awaiting service from Reading West station in the evenings were parked in Salisbury Road.

Originally, this arrangement was intended to operate for just one month, until 8th November 1941, when new train timetables were expected to be introduced, but after only one day of operation new plans were drawn up to make best use of winter daylight hours. The morning train was re-scheduled to arrive at Reading West station at 7.35am every day, including (for the first time) Sunday, with a return journey arrival at Reading West station at 6.04pm on Monday to Friday and 4.29pm on Saturday and Sunday. This pattern was operated from Friday 31st October 1941 to Thursday 27th November 1941.

Between Friday 28th November 1941 and Thursday 5th February 1942, the morning train left Reading West station at 8.05am, with the evening return journey arriving at 5.44pm on Monday to Friday, and 4.29pm on Saturday and Sunday. These new timings made it impossible for the undertaking to continue to run the morning specials between St. Mary's Butts and Reading West station, as all their buses were required for service use at this time. The morning shuttle service thus lasted only until 30th October 1941 – just over two weeks of operation! It was considered that the existing trolleybus service was sufficient to serve the needs of workers living in Tilehurst and from the eastern end of Reading and, whilst Mr Calder recognised the needs of workers living on the Whitley Estate, he suggested that Smith's Coaches could provide a shuttle service to/from St. Mary's Butts at both ends of the day. How long this later pattern of service continued beyond 5th February 1942 is unknown but, as the building work was completed and fewer workers were required, the service was gradually cut back.

There then arose a new demand – for transport of munitions workers to ROF Burghfield. This was a different kind of service, which was planned to carry shift workers in the early mornings (from 5.00am, before the start of the daily timetabled services) and at 11.00pm (after the last service buses had operated). These munitions workers' specials met the trains at the GWR's Reading General station and at Reading West station (trolleybuses) on Monday to Friday evenings, with reduced services on Saturday and Sunday evenings. Trolleybuses had yet to reach Reading Stations, of course, so the pick-up point would have been in Caversham Road at Subway Road, opposite the Fire Station. The services were reported as 'starting shortly' at the Works Committee meeting of 27th July 1942 and they were certainly in operation by the first days of January 1943, although by then only evening journeys were listed.

The journeys were actually chartered by The Burghfield Agency for their munitions workers and in the late evenings they ran setting down passengers only. An operating chart with the vehicle arrangements from 4th January 1943, shows that on Monday to Fridays at 10.40pm, four trolley-buses (**CD**, **B**, **BA** and **DE**) and five motorbuses (**MB**, **HC**, **FC**, **FA** and **IC**) were operated to various parts of the town from 'the Stations'. Sunday operation used only eight vehicles – three trolleybuses (**CD**, **B** and **BA**) and five motorbuses (**MB**, **IA**, **FA**, **FC** and **HC**). Saturday operation was much reduced, probably due to an earlier shift pattern, which allowed munitions workers to use normal service buses. In the January 1943 chart, it seems that no motor-buses were used on Saturdays and only two trolleybuses (**DG** and **DA**) were required, the crews to report to the inspector for instructions at 7.30pm and 8.12pm. Motor-buses were used subsequently, as shown by the surviving record of Saturday mileage used on these services from November 1944, which shows 9.86 miles as against 44.60 miles on weekdays. The timings of these munitions specials were later changed, according to a chart dated 20th October 1944 and showing daily vehicle usage. Nine vehicles were still used but at later timings, between 11.20pm and 00.40am.

These specials followed established service routes and, certainly, one of these Burghfield Agency journeys went through to Uplands Road, for it was the subject to a police complaint in April 1943, it being alleged that on some nights the bus waited time at an unofficial stop in Conisboro' Avenue at 11.00pm and picked up passengers from the end of a footpath (where Kelvedon Way now is) leading to the Grosvenor House Hotel in Kidmore Road. The bus concerned was the 11.10 p.m. return journey from Uplands Road and, as a journey chartered by The Burghfield Agency, it was, strictly speaking, for war workers only, and was being used by previous arrangement. The police were informed that no official arrangement had been made to stop at the back of the Grosvenor House Hotel and that proper bus stops existed at Uplands Road and Richmond Road. It seems however that some drivers were unofficially *"...obliging parties from The Grosvenor, by stopping if hailed"*. As chartered services, the public were not permitted to use them but it seems that military personnel could be carried, which led Mr Gent, the deputy manager, to comment that *"...it would appear that local inhabitants are at a disadvantage compared with people who are temporarily resident in Reading."* Despite his observations, it was firmly stated that *"Army Pay Soldiers"* only would be carried on the return journey from Uplands Road terminus.

With definite changes in the fortunes of war becoming obvious by the beginning of 1945, late working at ROF Burghfield was no longer necessary and the munitions workers' specials were discontinued on 11th March 1945. Other specials, for service personnel, were, however, still running in August 1945, late in the evenings, after the times of last service buses.

Another wartime special to be operated was a contract service to the Auxiliary Territorial Service Training Centre at Aldermaston Court, which was running Monday–Saturday in November 1944, but no further details appear to survive. For the record, the ATS later became the Women's Royal Army Corps.

The existence of a Pay Corps special is revealed by a surviving record, from January 1943, of a complaint about damage to a private road on the Balmore Estate (caused by the reversing of special buses for the Pay Corps) and the danger to residents of buses reversing during the blackout. Again, no further details appear to have survived.

Staff specials were introduced originally as conductresses' transport, operating in the early mornings to carry conductresses to Mill Lane for the early shift. Three routes are shown on a plan dated 8th January 1943; these were revised in August 1943 with the facility being made available to male staff if space was available. A further revision to route 3 was proposed on 6th December 1943, with the aim of saving some pool car mileage. The three routes also ran at Sunday lunchtimes, with an arrival time at Mill Lane of 12.45pm. The three routes ran as follows:

Route 1: SOUTH READING
4.20am Four Horse Shoes
4.23am Callington Road
4.25am Lower Whitley then return to Hartland Road,
 Shinfield Road and Wilderness Road
4.40am Three Tuns
4.45am Cemetery Junction
4.50am Mill Lane depot

Route 2: WEST READING
4.30am Tilehurst
 via Norcot Road, Blundells Road
 Recreation Road and School Road
4.35am Norcot Junction
4.40am Kentwood Circle via Oxford Road –
 then return via Oxford Road
4.50am Mill Lane depot

Route 3: CAVERSHAM
 via Reading Bridge
4.40am Gosbrook Road
 via Lower Henley Road
4.45am Lower Caversham
 via Caversham Bridge
 Caversham Road & West Street
4.50am Mill Lane depot

These staff specials became an established part of operations in the post war years and, indeed, they still continue (in modified form, of course) to this day.

Other specials operated during the war were to established industries in the town. There was a Monday–Saturday jam factory special to the Co-operative Wholesale Society Preserve Works at Coley from 'Wood Lane Junction', via Whitley Wood Lane, Basingstoke Road, Callington Road, Northumberland Avenue, Buckland Road, Basingstoke Road, Elgar Road and into Berkeley Avenue, which was listed in November 1944 schedules. The Huntley & Palmer's biscuit factory, in Kings Road, also had a number of factory specials to carry employees to their work. There were trolleybus and motorbus factory specials, the motorbuses operating originally from Staverton Road. The trolleybus specials listed on 17th October 1940 show that they were used to supplement the normal service at lunchtime and in the evening peak, with no apparent demand in the morning peak. The duties were listed as **Fac.Sp.1**, **Fac.Sp.2** and **Fac.Sp.3**, which operated at midday, while **Fac.Sp.3** and **Fac.Sp.4** were operated in the evening. The motorbus service as listed on 19th September 1940 shows the duties and timings from Whitley as follows:

Stav Fact 1: Staverton Rd – Queens Rd (ex depot 7.22am)
Stav Fact 2: Staverton Rd – Queens Rd (ex depot 7.22am)
Stav Fact 3: Queens Rd – Staverton Rd (ex depot 12.45pm)

Also listed as a Saturday special on 20th July 1940 was a 'Pulso' special, from The Pulsometer Engineering Co. Ltd. at Norcot, to Tilehurst.

School specials, as already documented, continued to operate, for Caversham Primary School and Whitley School. For example, on 19th September 1940 the Caversham Primary School specials required two buses, with provision for a relief bus ex depot at 12.50pm. The Whitley School specials on the same date were:

Whit Spec 1. ex depot 8.30am
Whit Spec 2. ex depot 8.30am
School Spec 3. ex depot 11.55am for Queens Road

Whit Spec 1. ex depot 3.30pm
Whit Spec 2. ex depot 3.30pm

Another special which is known to have operated was to and from Watlington House, in Watlington Street, on Tuesday to Fridays. Only 9 miles a day was run for this duty and two vehicles were used (4 miles and 5 miles respectively per day) with the duty listed as at November 1944. It has not yet been established why and to where these specials operated but it is possible that it was in connection with a school evacuated from London.

Schools 'swim specials' were also operated and were still listed on 19th September 1940 as shown below, although it is unlikely that they survived the rigours of fuel rationing.

Swim Spec Kings Mdw Rd Tuesdays (ex depot 9.54am)
Swim Spec Whit Pump Fridays (ex depot 1.50pm)
Swim Spec Cav'm Primary Tuesdays (ex depot 2.40pm)
Swim Spec G. Palmer Sch Thursdays (ex depot 2.55pm)

In October 1943, a Kentwood Hill School bus was also listed, serving the primary school at the bottom of the hill. Finally, there was also still a Park Hospital special on Wednesday afternoons, from Broad Street at 1.40pm.

The Jam Factory special and the journeys to Huntley & Palmer's and Park Hospital continued to operate long after the war ended, as shall be seen in Chapter 19.

Left: A 'full-frontal' view of AEC 661T trolleybus 123 (ARD 686) taken circa July 1943 at the Bear Inn terminus, Tilehurst, ready for a departure to Three Tuns. The black-and-white striped poles behind the trolleybus suggest that they are what remains of a wartime roadblock erected in summer 1940 but declared obsolete in March 1943.

Late W. J. Haynes © Maiwand Photographic Archive

Below: Leyland Titan motorbus 38 (RD 963), in all its wartime glory, is at the Erleigh Road terminus of Route M, at the junction of Addington Road with Erleigh Road, having decanted its passengers. It will now U-turn and depart for Grovelands Road. The pole is a traction pole for the ½-mile disused trolleybus driver training line (the overhead remaining aloft until removed in 1955). Also of interest is the tower in the background, which was used for hose drying at the wartime Auxiliary Fire Station, fire watching and as an aircraft observation post.

Late W. J. Haynes © Millane Publishing

7 The Long Years of War, 1942–1945

The early months of 1942 marked the lowest point of the war for Britain and its allies. The British colony of Singapore fell to the Japanese on 15th February 1942, followed by Rangoon on 7th March 1942. With German U-boat successes in the Atlantic and off the east coast of America, the pain of war became even more intense. In fact, the loss of so much shipping off the American eastern seaboard saw a temporary suspension of all tanker traffic across the Atlantic; the resulting increased fuel shortages meant additional rationing, which forced further reductions in motorbus services across Britain. In Reading, the effects were at least reduced, because the town had a local coal-fired power station and much of its municipal transport system was served by trolleybuses.

By the beginning of 1942, the town really was bulging at the seams, its population having increased by 40,000 to about 140,000 in two years. With no additional vehicles added to stock, no wonder the town's transport services were under considerable strain! Over the next two-and-a-half years, however, matters would continue to get worse, with Reading becoming host to some of the ever increasing numbers of our new allies. The Yanks were coming – in total, not far short of 1½ million of them! They first hit British soil on 26th January 1942.

The Transport Committee, at its meeting on 12th February 1942, endorsed Mr Calder's suggestion that a bus shelter, formerly at Buckland Road and currently in store at the depot, should be re-erected at the inbound stop at Norcot Junction, with part of it adapted for use as an office for Billy Dew, the traffic regulator at this point. At the same meeting, Mr Calder advised that, following an approach to the town clerk by the Berkshire Printing Company, an outbound request stop had been provided in Oxford Road, between the Pond House and Norcot Junction. In addition, two outbound stops in Kendrick Road, at Abbey School and at Morgan Road, had been 'combined'. Two months later, Mr Calder reported that at other locations where bus shelters were provided, in particular at the Merry Maidens terminus and outbound at the Pond House, broken seats and broken window glass, attributed to 'blackout boredom', was becoming a problem and he proposed to remove glass and seats from shelters for the duration of the war.

Heavy passenger loadings in Reading prompted the regional transport commissioner to request that, to make best use of available bus services, passengers making journeys wholly within the borough should be able to travel on Thames Valley Traction Company buses at corporation fares. Effectively, this was a request that the 'protective' higher fares charged by Thames Valley to passengers riding on their buses on journeys entirely within the borough should be removed. Any loss of that 'protection' was of major concern to the municipal undertaking. The precursors of the company had come onto the scene in Reading during the Great War, before municipal motorbus operation had commenced, and arrangements had very soon been made that company buses would not run in competition with the corporation trams and that this would be facilitated by charging more than the tram fare to passengers carried wholly within the borough. Usually, this was around 1d extra per ride. This might seem a trivial amount when viewed from the 21st century but, considering bus and tram fares levels in relation to wages and the cost of living at the time, this 'premium' was a considerable extra cost per ride – and, thus, a discouragement as intended.

At their meeting on 19th March 1942, the Transport Committee reluctantly agreed to the regional transport commissioner's suggestion and Thames Valley commenced charging the corporation fare scale <u>on inward journeys only</u> from Easter Monday, 6th April 1942 (Double Summer Time having commenced the previous day). It had been agreed that the arrangement would last initially for 12 months but be periodically extended for the duration of the war. In fact it ended on 13th February 1947. Outbound Thames Valley buses did not adopt the corporation fare scale – presumably to prevent long-distance passengers from being crowded out by those travelling wholly within the borough. The division of income between the two operators from fares taken by Thames Valley was not settled immediately, the takings being paid into a joint suspense account with a promise that, after the war, a proportion should pass to the corporation. In 1947 it was agreed that this should be split 60/40 in favour of Thames Valley. In the first nine months of the scheme, 30,172 'local' passengers were carried on Thames Valley buses, raising £226 5s 3d.

The regional transport commissioner also requested that there should be a serious attempt to establish co-ordinated timetables and services within the borough, initially for the duration of war but also in the hope that the arrangement would continue in peacetime. In fact, they sought implementation of a co-ordination scheme similar to those already in use in Brighton and Portsmouth. A meeting called by the regional transport commissioner was attended by Alderman Bale, the transport manager, the deputy town clerk, and representatives of the Tilling Group to which Thames Valley belonged. This meeting considered the possible establishment of a joint committee to plan all transport matters in Reading and the surrounding area. Effectively, this plan would have removed the county borough boundary as the limit of the municipal undertaking's operation, and proposed a sharing of services and a pooling of receipts that would be proportionately divided between the two operators in relation to the mileage that each of them operated.

THE
THAMES • VALLEY
TRACTION COMPANY, LIMITED.

BEGS to announce that, with the approval of the Regional Transport Commissioner, arrangements have been made with Reading Corporation Transport that as from Monday, April 6th, incoming Thames Valley omnibuses (excluding London Express Services A and B) which have seats available shall pick up passengers in the Borough at Corporation 'bus stops at the fares charged by Reading Corporation Transport.

Prepaid tickets issued by the Corporation, i.e. Discount and Scholars' Tickets will not be accepted, neither will Workmen's Tickets be issued or accepted.

The transport manager, meanwhile, had conducted his own survey of the corporation's services, in order to clarify both the discussion and decision of the Future Policy Sub-Committee. A departmental map, dated 8th April 1942, shows the frequencies of the routes of both Thames Valley and RCT and obviously formed part of the assessment. Mr Calder noted that six of the corporation's eight motorbus routes were wholly or partly duplicated by Thames Valley routes. He noted also that where there was a combined service, it far exceeded traffic requirements, so that some rearrangement of services would benefit fuel economy and the war effort. It was obvious, too, that the corporation's motorbus route I, along Bath Road to Horncastle, was particularly vulnerable to the removal of protected fares and to any future co-ordination, as Thames Valley's services along Bath Road were more frequent than those of Reading Corporation.

All trolleybus routes were affected by Thames Valley services picking up on inward journeys. Mr Calder was unwilling to consider any additional sharing of traffic or reduction of service on these routes, especially the 'main line', which was the mainstay of all the corporation's services and, therefore, its income. He also noted that *"...any form of transport service other than that using electricity as a motive power should be discouraged and, having regard to present day conditions, vehicles using petrol or fuel oil along this route ... should be regarded as being redundant."*

Mr Calder also looked further at the implications of co-ordination beyond the borough boundary, with the possible extension of existing services from the outskirts of the borough to the nearest important population centre at around six miles beyond the existing termini in mind (the distance discussed at the initial conference) and listed the routes and their extensions as follows:

Destination	Extend to:
Bath Road omnibus route:	Theale
Oxford Road trolley/omnibus route:	Pangbourne
Emmer Green omnibus route:	Peppard
Lower Caversham omnibus route:	Harpsden
London Road trolley vehicle route:	Twyford
Three Tuns trolley vehicle route:	Wokingham
Shinfield Road omnibus route:	Eversley
Lower Whitley omnibus route:	Swallowfield/Riseley

Mr Calder concluded that only extensions to Theale and Wokingham were viable, and that little additional traffic would be gained from extending the other routes to serve the small villages and country districts that surrounded Reading. He also came to the conclusion that Thames Valley would hardly agree to sharing their best routes; and by any estimation it would be Thames Valley who gained the financial benefit from implementation of any co-ordination plan which shared the carriage of short-distance passengers within the borough. Thus, he concluded that the corporation would lose control of its undertaking and would lose out financially.

On 16th April 1942, therefore, the Future Policy Sub-Committee recommended to the Transport Committee that *"the Regional Transport Commissioner be informed that the Corporation are not prepared to consider any co-ordination on the lines suggested at the conference"*. The Transport Committee was, however, prepared to consider any wartime co-ordination the commissioner considered practical in the interests of saving fuel and avoiding duplication, provided that *"...the rights, powers and privileges of the Corporation were not prejudiced in any way"*. Despite several later attempts, another half-century was to pass before 'co-ordination' became a reality. By then the 'boot was on the other foot' and eventually, in 1992, it was the municipal undertaking that took over many (but not all) of the rural services operated by a Thames Valley successor.

At administration level, Chief Clerk Mr R. J. Fardell, (father of Deputy Manager Mr J. F. Fardell, who was away on war service), was retained beyond normal retirement age because younger clerks were being 'called up'. In view of the continued development of the undertaking and resulting increased workload, Costing Clerk Mr Ernest H. Warrell was appointed assistant chief clerk, taking up his new position on 1st April 1942.

Meanwhile, with continually increasing loadings on all forms of public transport throughout the country, the boarding of buses at peak times was becoming an increasingly unruly affair, which prompted the government to introduce another directive under Defence Regulations. The Regulation of Traffic (Formation of Queues) Order 1942 came into force on 12th April 1942 and 'queue jumpers' and those who refused to queue in an orderly fashion were often taken to court and usually fined. This, of course, simply reinforced the local by-law, which had been introduced in Reading from 1st June 1940. Increased loadings also put a strain on 'last buses' at 9.30pm, which resulted in having, where necessary, to operate relief vehicles – which rather defeated the object of stopping services early to conserve fuel!

Notwithstanding the employment, now, of around 120 women conductors, 70% of them evacuees living on the edge of or outside the borough, it had become difficult for bus crews to take their meal breaks at home as had hitherto been common practice, so a canteen was set up at the depot. First mooted at the Transport Committee meeting on 17th December 1941, it opened on Monday 13th April 1942, offering light refreshments and snacks. It continued after the war, providing subsidised meals for the office personnel, bus crews and depot staff. During the war, the Transport Department also operated a van during the evenings and on Sundays, which visited Broad Street, Norcot and St. Mary's Butts with an urn full of tea, which was sold to traffic employees at a nominal charge. During the severe winter of 1944/45, the service additionally provided free tea to late shift bus crews during the evenings from 8.00pm. The tea van service was eventually discontinued in October 1949, the facility thereafter being provided only in an emergency.

Early on Sunday morning, 3rd May 1942, Tilehurst was the scene of an 'invasion' by the 'enemy', with their attack resisted by a company of the Reading Battalion of the Home Guard. A surviving photograph shows a trolleybus continuing to operate serenely through the hand-to-hand street 'fighting'!

The accounts for the financial year ended 31st March 1942, published in June 1942, were deliberately incomplete in accordance with government guidelines, should information find its way to and be used by the enemy. However, the town's trolleybuses had carried 22,509,208 passengers (an increase of 4,279,782 over the previous year) and run 1,330,156 miles (an increase of 101,763 miles). Motorbuses carried 16,188,133 passengers (an increase of 2,818,454) and, at 1,273,158, had run 83,517 more miles. All this was achieved with no additional rolling stock whatsoever! In presenting the report to the Transport Committee, Mr Calder said he was concerned that fuel consumption on motorbuses had increased by 2.390d per bus mile in the past year, no doubt due to continued excessive wear-and-tear and the restricted ability for better maintenance. Of trolleybuses, he said *"There may be a diversity of opinion as to the relative advantages and disadvantages of this form of passenger transport, but this much can be said of the trolley vehicle system in Reading: The services rendered to members of the travelling public in these days has proved to be of in-estimable value by reason of the accommodation on the vehicles, the acceleration provided by means of the powerful driving unit, and the smoothness of its riding qualities."*

The profitability of the undertaking's Parcels Express Service suffered particularly during the early years of war and, during the financial year 1941/42 it lost £98 compared with a profit of £91 the previous financial year. Because blackout restrictions had shortened the working day and rationing had caused a general reduction in trade, it was perhaps inevitable that the number of parcels carried had decreased.

The overcrowding of vehicles, including permitting an increase in standing load capacity, brought about a situation whereby peak periods now seemed to last all day! As a result, fare collection was becoming increasingly difficult. Conductors, while expected not to 'miss' any fares, had to issue correct value tickets, give correct change, and lug around an increasingly heavy cash bag containing mainly bronze coinage – and keep the bus moving. A suggestion was made during a meeting of the Transport Committee at this time that queue conductors should be introduced, to assist with the 'pre-collection of fares'. This prompted Mr Calder to visit Bournemouth (where such a system was already in use) with the traffic superintendent and Transport Committee chairman, and they were able to observe conductresses collecting fares and issuing tickets at busy stops in that town's central area. Mr Calder noted that more fares were apparently being collected and, on crowded vehicles, the conductor was able to spend more time on the platform supervising boarding and alighting, thus reducing platform accidents (of which a disturbing number had lately occurred in Reading, some of them with fatal results). In Reading, queue conductors were first used in Broad Street during evening peak periods, commencing in early September 1942. They issued TIM tickets using coloured ticket rolls, rather than white, for ease of distinction.

The successes of the German U-boat attacks on Allied shipping increased still further during 1942, due to improved refuelling facilities from large, newly-launched U-boat supply submarines in the Atlantic Ocean. Over the whole of 1942, some 1,100 Allied ships were sunk, the U-boat fleet meanwhile increasing in size from 57 at the

The morning of Sunday 3rd May 1942: Tilehurst was 'held' by A Company 7th Berks Home Guard in the face of a strong three hour onslaught from a 'Panzer division' of the Army's Infantry Training Centre. The street-to-street 'fighting' wasn't enough to stop the trolleybus service operating on route A (Bear Inn – Three Tuns) and an AEC trolleybus can be seen sailing down from Park Lane into School Road – and a Home Guard ambush at the junction with Westwood Road! Note the bands round the traction pole and 'S – Shelter' sign made from a bus stop flag.
Berkshire Chronicle

beginning of 1942 to a staggering 393 a year later. In June 1942 alone, 173 Allied ships were sunk but, from July 1942 the tide began to turn, thanks to vastly-improved radar equipment being fitted to Royal Navy ships protecting the Atlantic convoys. The Atlantic supply routes grew more secure as U-boats became the hunted as well as the hunter. Despite this growing advantage, by early autumn 1942 Atlantic shipping losses had reached a critical point and, as fuel shortages became yet more severe, there was again a demand for further fuel savings by bus operators.

The growing crisis also saw various organisations 'mucking in' to help with the war effort – for example, from March to September 1942, heavy machining tasks were undertaken at the depot for local firms, to make up for their loss of skilled workers to His Majesty's Forces.

In summer 1942 the Ministry of War Transport had decreed, in the interests of bringing about further economies in fuel consumption, tyres and brake linings, that local authorities should switch off all 'unnecessary' traffic lights and had advised passenger transport undertakings that bus and trolleybus stops should be not more than four per mile (this latter subsequently becoming post-war Ministry of Transport passenger transport planning criteria). In Reading, even before this edict, certain stops had already been either eliminated or combined. Nevertheless, a schedule, dated 14th September 1942, was drafted, with 39 further proposals, and subsequently public notices dated 1st October 1942 appeared in local newspapers, advising passengers to look for and read the notices posted at the stops henceforth declared redundant. The list of 39 proposals has been reproduced in Appendix E.

Following on from a voluntary scheme, introduced in May 1942, which encouraged bus operators with over 50 vehicles to convert to producer gas operation, the Ministry of War Transport, on 1st October 1942, issued a directive that all passenger transport undertakings operating more than 150 motorbuses should convert 10% of their fleets thus. Reading, with a fleet of less than 50 motorbuses, was not subject to either directive and was thus spared being obliged to operate gas-powered buses, with their notoriously sluggish performance, let alone the need to have to both garage and maintain the coke-burning trailers, find storage space for the anthracite and work out ways of replenishing trailers during a days' operation.

On the 'home front', 1942 had seen hardship really beginning to bite. This was the era of utility clothing and furniture, the rationing of soap and sweets, the unpopular 'National Loaf', tinned dried egg, blended chocolate and improvised cosmetics – and it was still 'Dig for Victory', 'Make-do-and-Mend' and 'Mrs. Sew-and-Sew'. Consumers' local van deliveries were already pooled, as were milk deliveries on overlapping rounds – even by horse-and-cart! Council-run 'British Restaurants' made their first appearance in Reading. The individual consumer did his/her bit by saving all manner of salvage, and the 'Holidays at Home' scheme (5th June to 5th September 1942) was launched. By the end of October 1942, too, American forces had become more evident in the Reading locality; in fact, they became increasingly prolific thereafter. On a national basis, wooing British girls with smooth talk (and packets of nylon stockings!) eventually won them 75,000 'GI Brides'.

AEC trolleybus 114 was noted in Whitley Street at 7.45am on 6th October 1942 by a local enthusiast, the point being that route C (Promenade – Whit Pump) was the exclusive preserve of experimental (lowbridge) trolleybuses 101–106; the allocation of a 1939 AEC was very rare. If more than one of 101–106 was off the road it is more likely that a 1939 AEC trolleybus would be the next choice, in preference to a motorbus – provided that one could be spared from the 'main line', of course, and in spite of the tight fit under Caversham Road railway bridge.

In the autumn of 1942, with well over 100 conductresses now employed by the undertaking, a great many of them 'placed' by the Ministry of Labour & National Service under the Essential Work Order rather than hand-picked as suitable by the undertaking, the problem of absenteeism and persistent lateness in reporting for duty became increasingly apparent. This seriously affected operations and, in turn, directly caused essential war workers to arrive late for work, thus affecting the war effort. A bus which did not leave the depot for want of a conductress could inconvenience innumerable would-be passengers during the course of the 'missed' duty. The problem was not unique to Reading, yet it had to be addressed before getting out-of-hand. A well-qualified welfare officer was appointed, whose job it was to visit absentees fairly promptly, to establish the exact reason for not attending work, medical or otherwise.

From 2nd November 1942, Thames Valley buses inbound from the east were re-routed from Kings Road to Stations via Forbury Road rather than via Broad Street. New fare scales had also been approved, in line with those of the corporation, although none of the corporation's services operated via Forbury Road:

Between Cemetery Junction and Streeters' premises (Kennet Street):	Fare 1d
Between Streeters' premises (Kennet Street) and the Railway Stations:	Fare 1½d
Between Cemetery Junction and the Railway Stations:	Fare 2½d

On 30th October 1942, the regional transport commissioner had written to the undertaking enquiring whether trolleybuses were operating to a later hour than motorbuses – a matter which, thus far, had not needed his approval and which had been left to the transport manager's discretion by the Transport Committee. The commissioner was concerned about tyre wear, for there was now an extremely urgent need to conserve rubber as new supplies were affected by continuing losses from Atlantic shipping convoys and, not least, by the Japanese occupation of Malaya and other rubber-producing countries in Southeast Asia. There had been a demand from the Ministry of War Transport itself that, across the country, bus services should cease daily at between 8.00pm and 10.00pm. The commissioner now required that if 'last journeys' by trolleybuses and motorbuses were not already synchronised, that they should be by 15th November 1942, suggesting also that there was little need, in a concentrated urban environment, for a Sunday morning bus service, so that ordinary Sunday bus services need not begin before 1.00pm and should end at 9.00pm. He also suggested that it might be desirable to *"lay buses off during the quieter hours"* on weekdays. In Reading, as we have seen, quieter hours simply did not exist!

At a conference held in the Nisi Prius Court at Berkshire County Court, in Reading's Forbury, on 10th November 1942, the regional transport commissioner, Sir Henry Piggott,

Top: *A nice wartime rear-end study of AEC 661T trolleybus 108 (ARD 671) waiting time at Three Tuns for departure to Norcot Junc. Note the fairly minimal application of white paint for safety reasons when operating in the blackout. The fact that the undertaking's standard livery included fairly broad cream bands at lower levels probably had much to do with the fact that only the bumpers required additional emphasis.*

Late W. J. Haynes © Maiwand Photographic Archive

Centre: *Bus 52 (RD 8889), new in November 1936, is an oil-engined AEC Regent with 52-seat 'all-metal' Park Royal lowbridge body; this was Reading Corporation Transport's latest standard of double-deck motorbus at the time the war started. It is seen here well loaded in Crown Street in early 1944 operating on route N (Broad Street – Callington Road/Staverton Road). 'Callington Road' is shown on the destination blind, probably because the driver committed the cardinal sin of forgetting to change it at the terminus, or changed it before the end of the journey, ready for another outward trip – he would gain a severe reprimand from any inspector who caught him! To gain the correct side of Broad Street for departure to Whitley Estate the inward journey from Silver Street was via Crown Street, Southampton Street, etc. Note the kerb guide on the nearside front wing – not a particularly common feature in the fleet.*

Late W. J. Haynes © Millane Publishing

Bottom: *1931 petrol-engined Leyland Titan TD1 42 (RD 2720) is seen here outside the GWR Station working on route M bound for Grovelands Road. Note that the bus is in service without a radiator grille – the radiator cooling tubes being exposed. The glass rain deflectors over the saloon opening windows on both decks were retained throughout the war (and afterwards in most cases). The rearward-hinged driver's cab door was a typical Leyland trait, as was the 'push-on' handbrake. The bus in the background belongs to Thames Valley.*

Late W. J. Haynes © Millane Publishing

65

London Street Miscellany 1

Top: *Outbound in London Street having ascended the hill (and without a radiator grille), Leyland Titan 45 (RD 2945), heading for Erleigh Road, has reached the cluster of shops at the top, popular at the time with housewives for domestic shopping. Emerson & Chanin was a well-known Reading dairy, which also had a shop in Caversham at the junction of Hemdean Road and Priest Hill. Note that in this and the following view there are as yet no cast iron water mains laid in the gutter to charge static water tanks*

Centre: *1935-vintage 'oiler' AEC Regent 46 (RD 7126), in this case on route N bound for Staverton Road, has reached the traffic lights at the top of London Street, outside Frank Eyles, the pawnbroker. By this stage certain national (as opposed to local) advertisements on corporation buses had become paper posters for the duration of the war rather than being signwritten. With no cream lining out, it suggests the picture dates from after April 1943. Traffic lights – a comparatively recent invention – were still rather uncommon at this time; those which incorporated a belisha beacon in the design, as seen here, were particularly unusual.*

Bottom: *Wooden-bodied bus 10 (RD 5361) was the last petrol-engined AEC Regent to enter service, in March 1934. It is seen here around 10 years later, at the top of London Street; note the cast iron water main which by this time has been laid in the gutter to keep large static water tanks full for immediate use by the fire service should the town centre receive attention from the Luftwaffe. The little girl is probably waiting for her mother to alight from what appears to be a fairly heavily-laden bus bound for Merry Maidens. H. Lee & Sons were cobblers, while Miss A. E. Spencer was a draper.*

Top: Bus 23 (ARD 14), from the last batch of AEC Regents to be delivered (in June 1938), seen on route H, bound for the highly fictitious Wood Lane Junc. (Lower Whitley in happier days). When new, this batch, 21–24, had longer radiators but 23 had already gained an older, shorter one by the time of this photograph, which is thought to have been taken sometime between June 1943 and September 1944. Note the signwritten advert for Reed's of Broad Street – one of a handful of local businesses whose ads often appeared in this position.

Centre: ……and the next bus along (because it is numerically the next on the film), heading for Merry Maidens, was 55 (ADP 4), the first of a batch of three AEC Regents new in September 1937, packed to the gunwales and not intending to stop – it is out in the road, the driver having evidently received 'three bells'. Only with the building of this batch and 21–24 in 1938 (and trolleybuses 107–131 in 1938/39) were opening windows fitted to the front of the upper deck; they were to be locked shut for most of their time post-war, and eventually replaced by fixed panes on motorbus 22 and trolleybuses 107, 109–15, 120–25 and 127–31.

Bottom: Finally, 1933 woodenbodied petrol-engined AEC Regent 5 (RD 4338) bound for Erleigh Road – also full. Note the badly-dented front wing! This bus was later rebuilt – compare this with the views shown on pages 120/121.

All photos on this and the previous page were taken by W. J. Haynes, at that time of south-east London. His wartime photos of Reading buses and trolleybuses, virtually the only ones ever taken by a private individual, have been used extensively in this volume. Unique views though they are, it is a matter of regret that so many depict offside views of different buses – but in the same location! Perhaps, however, we are not acknowledging the constraints that were heaped upon Mr Haynes. Film was difficult for the private individual to obtain anyway, and private photography in a public place could result in the film (and camera) being confiscated………

All photos Late W. J. Haynes
© Millane Publishing

67

was insistent that the current times of last motorbuses and trolleybuses from Reading town centre *"could not continue"*, yet Mr Calder fought hard to retain a later service. However, the commissioner was against operation of any service that was *"not essential to the war effort"*, insisting that his demands should be placed before the corporation's Transport Committee. Mr Calder was concerned that, with a number of industrial establishments engaged on war work in and around Reading, there was a demand for later services to run in order to transport late-shift workers home after a taxing day, or make connection with train services to and from outlying villages. He was adamant, therefore, that the evening services provided by his undertaking were not primarily for leisure and that certainly no reduction to finish before 9.30pm (Broad Street departure time) could be entertained.

At its meeting on 1st December 1942, however, the Transport Committee reluctantly agreed to some curtailment of service and this was implemented from 4th January 1943. Last trolleybuses were cut back to leave the town centre at 9.30pm, in line with the existing motorbus pattern – although the motorbus services themselves were cut back to leave town a half-hour earlier still, at 9.00pm! On Sundays, all services were changed to operate only between 1.00pm and 9.00pm, although it was noted that this would affect churchgoers. Indeed, there were complaints, both direct to the regional transport commissioner, and in letters to the local press, including one from the Rural Dean of Reading, the Revd R. E. T. Bell, jointly with leaders of some of the other denominations. The only Sunday morning services to remain were workmen's specials operated by trolleybuses. Withdrawal of Sunday morning motorbus services was especially unpopular with local firms, such as Huntley & Palmers, whose workers required early morning transport home after Fire Watching and Home Guard duties, both of which were now required of employees by law. Late evening buses for essential war workers continued to be operated as before but these services were never available to the general public.

A detailed analysis of all 'unallocated' road fuel was sought of all corporation departments by the Finance & General Purposes Committee just after Christmas 1942, an immediate 10% cut being demanded. Although the transport manager was able to reduce his department's use of auxiliary vehicles, cutting fuel requirements immediately from 342 to 308 gallons per month, he pointed out that departmental vans and cars were of necessity in regular use *"to keep the wheels turning"* – whether, for example, as conductresses' transport in the early mornings and late evenings, or because a light van or car was often, of necessity, needed to be sent to London (to AEC at Southall) to collect the spare parts to keep the bus and trolleybus fleet on the road.

With a continuing build-up of British, Commonwealth and American troops in the area, there was considerable progress locally in establishing entertainment and relaxation facilities. Even prior to Christmas 1942, the Services Entertainments Committee had arranged concerts for troops at the Palace Theatre, in Cheapside, while Wellsteeds' Restaurant was turned over to an Allied Services Club. The Wellington Services Club was established in Station Road in April 1943, and hospitality arrangements for forces personnel included an increasing number of local dances – at the Town Hall; at various ballrooms which already existed in the town (such as the Olympia in London Street); and plenty more which were arranged in various church halls. The Palace Theatre was popular with the troops and was especially loved by local inhabitants, who liked to see entertainers who had hailed from Reading and had reached stardom – like comedian 'Chips' Sanders and the singing and dancing twins Joan and Evelyn Eacott, who were quite famous at the time. It was during this era, too, that 'Carroll Levis Talent Shows' at the Palace became popular. Carroll Levis was a Canadian, who 'discovered' several entertainers of later note.

The arrangements made by the undertaking for Christmas Day 1942 were, predictably, that ordinary bus and trolleybus services would be suspended but that *"such special services as may be required for workers engaged on work of national importance"* would be provided. There was, however, a problem on Boxing Day, when 43 employees failed to report for morning duty, causing a number of timetabled buses not to operate.

In spite of very positive progress with offending conductresses by the recently-appointed welfare officer, absenteeism and persistent lateness was still an acute problem. The undertaking was receiving admonishing letters from local employers whose war production was being affected. At the Transport Committee meeting on 14th January 1943, Mr Calder reported that the Employees' Works Committee had become involved and that any failure on their part to address the problem would have to be referred to the Ministry of Labour & National Service for prosecution of offenders in the courts. The Ministry of Labour & National Service appeared to pay no attention particularly to the suitability or otherwise of the labour they were 'directing' into bus work, and both the ministry officials and many of the women would have been completely ignorant that the bus industry was arduous, involved working irregular hours and required considerable dedication for a very small reward.

The problem persisted. The Transport (Employment) Sub-Committee reported to the Transport Committee on 8th October 1943 that the Works' Absenteeism Committee had met on six occasions between 4th January and 15th September 1943, dealing with 74 cases of absenteeism and

---

READING CORPORATION TRANSPORT

IMPORTANT NOTICE

Curtailment of Motor Bus and Trolley Bus Services on Weekdays and Sundays on and after Monday, 4th January 1943

OWING to the urgent and vital need for economy in the use of Rubber and Fuel, REDUCED SERVICES of Motor Buses and Trolley Buses will be in operation as shown below, commencing on 4th January, 1943:

LAST BUSES	Weekdays	Sundays
Last Motor Buses from Centre of Town ...	9.0 p.m.	9.0 p.m.
Last Trolley Buses from Centre of Town ...	9.30 p.m.	9.0 p.m.

SUNDAY MORNINGS

On Sundays, Motor Buses and Trolley Buses will not run before 1.0 p.m., excepting those which are run specially for War Workers before 8.0 a.m.

In order that adequate but only strictly necessary transport may be provided for War Workers, employers of such workers are asked to send particulars of their transport requirements to the undersigned.

Corporation Transport Offices,   J. M. CALDER,
Mill Lane, Reading.   Transport Manager & Engineer.

persistent lateness, resulting in 34 warning letters. In several instances matters had gone further and culprits had been suspended from duty, and nine employees had actually been dismissed because of inefficiency and irregular attendance. Between 24th March and 30th September 1943, 314 vehicles were between five minutes and nearly four hours late leaving depot for want of a crew and, more importantly, between 12th June and 30th September 1943, 21 buses did not go out at all on certain days. There were, also, roundly 20 staff away sick on any one day during the summer. Whilst there were always genuine cases of sickness, all council employees in Reading received sick pay after nine months' service and management were well aware that there was much 'lead-swinging' – in spite of the usual *"Don't you know there's a war on!"*

In November 1942, the undertaking had issued new traffic arrangements to staff as to what to do in the event of an air raid on Reading. Previously, from September 1940, bus crews had been instructed to continue in service after an air raid warning had been given and to stop only when an aerial attack was developing in the immediate vicinity. New regulations now gave clearer instructions as to what to do. Motorbus drivers were instructed to pull into a side street and take local shelter and were specifically told to avoid running their vehicles into the centre of town. After the 'all clear', drivers were required to proceed to Mill Lane where they would be instructed where to park their vehicle and to await further instructions. The west sides of London Street and Sidmouth Street were available for parking and crews were required to stand by with their vehicles until instructed for further duty. No motorbuses would be returned to public service until the public assistance officer had confirmed that (a) buses would not be required for the transport of air raid casualties; and (b) that bus routes were open for general traffic.

Trolley vehicles, being wire-bound, were not required to be available to the public assistance officer. Trolleybus crews were instructed to park their vehicles in a side street using battery power immediately an air raid started and, similarly, to avoid the town centre. After the 'all clear' had sounded, trolleybus drivers were required to manoeuvre their vehicles back into the main road, into the direction in which they were originally travelling, again using battery traction, and to wait with the booms off the wires until instructed by messenger how to proceed into service. In the event of an air raid, inspectors, both on and off duty, were required to report to Mill Lane in order to act as messengers.

These air raid arrangements had seldom to be implemented, for Reading was undoubtedly fortunate to be spared the general devastation meted out on so many other British towns and cities. However, it was on a dull and drizzly afternoon on Wednesday 10th February 1943, that Reading was destined to receive its most serious air raid. A solitary Dornier Do217 twin-engined German bomber approached from the south-west at low level, looped clockwise over Coley and Katesgrove, just short of the town centre, then at 4.34pm commenced a bombing run, strafing as it went, almost as if intending to fly a straight line between the steeple of St. Giles' Church, in Southampton Street and the tower of St. Laurence's Church, at the head of the Market Place, and proceeded to drop a stick of four 500kg bombs. The first hit Fuller's paint stores and wrecked the Heelas garage and furniture repository on the south side of Minster Street. The second extensively damaged the Minster Street end of Wellsteeds' department store and Wellman's Wine Vaults, mercifully missing Reading

---

IF YOU ARE A STRONG GIRL

AND LIKE

an open air life,
plenty of people,
movement;

THEN HERE IS YOUR CHANCE

You can volunteer as a bus conductress.

If you are working in a hospital, laundry, or similar organisation, or are doing a really skilled job, please don't volunteer.

Otherwise—all you have to do is to

ENQUIRE AT YOUR NEAREST EMPLOYMENT EXCHANGE

---

telephone exchange, but killing three, two of them children sheltering in a shop doorway. The third bomb, which caused the most damage and loss of life, hit the Friar Street end of the Market Arcade, where a British Restaurant known as The People's Pantry was situated, killing 35 people. The fourth bomb demolished one end of the Town Hall and the adjoining offices of Blandy & Blandy, a well-known Reading solicitors' practice, and seriously damaged St. Laurence's Church. The raider went on to machine-gun three or four streets and an elementary school in Caversham as it made its getaway. Fortunately, being a Wednesday, it was early closing day but, even so, in total the raid resulted in 41 deaths and 151 injured, 49 of them seriously. The search for survivors went on through the night and into the next day.

For many years it was assumed that the pilot had simply picked Reading town centre at random as a civilian target, but an article in the *Reading Chronicle* in 1993 suggests that the target was a secret broadcasting facility installed in the Market Arcade, which was, in fact, destroyed in the bombing. This facility, known as 'Station 19', was one of 61 such stations built in towns with a population in excess of 50,000 in a project codenamed Group H. Each radio station operated a low-powered transmitter broadcasting the BBC Home Service on 1474 kHz to confuse and hinder enemy aircraft, which were using the larger BBC regional transmitters as radio navigational aids. It is further alleged that the Reading facility was afterwards re-sited in the Sutton's Seeds glass gazebo in Earley, and that it operated there until closedown on 28th July 1945. The aerial of this latter facility was apparently still in evidence in the early 1970s, and some of these Group H transmitters were subsequently used in connection with local radio stations.

Alongside the town centre 'target' there were also several local firms whose workshops were contributing materially to production of war machines and which were, in the crazy

The 'Experimental' Trolleybuses

Reading's first trolleybus, 101, was bought as a 'means-to-an-end' – to train drivers and to gain experience of trolleybuses and their operation before the five experimental vehicles arrived. The experimental trolleybuses (102–106) were ordered from different chassis manufacturers for use on the trial route (Caversham to Whitley Street), opened on 18th July 1936. The termini of this route had been renamed 'Promenade' and 'Whit-Pump' respectively in 1940 to confuse any invading enemy. These photos were taken in November 1943.

All photos Late W. J. Haynes
© Maiwand Photographic Archive

Top: 101 (RD 8085) was a Sunbeam MF2A, which had been built in 1933 as a lowbridge demonstrator. It was the only trolleybus in the fleet without a battery traction facility, and so tended to be used in passenger service as a last resort! It is seen at Promenade terminus awaiting departure for Whit-Pump.

Centre: 102 (RD 8086) was an AEC 661T with an 'all-metal' Park Royal lowbridge body. It is seen here also having turned at Promenade ready to journey back to Whit-Pump. This bus gave an excellent account of itself, resulting in the order for 25 tramway-replacement trolleybuses being awarded to AEC and Park Royal for delivery in 1938/39. 102 differed from the subsequent AEC trolleybuses in that the traction motor was mounted over the front axle rather than amidships, while the bodywork was of six bay lowbridge rather than five-bay highbridge construction.

Bottom: With a Park Royal 'all-metal' lowbridge body similar in nearly all respects to 102, trolleybus 103 (RD 8087) was a Guy BT. It was photographed having turned at Promenade ready to return to Whit-Pump. One tiny visual difference between 103 and the four other experimental trolleybuses (102/4/5/6) was that the sidelamps at the front of 103 were partly in the lower cream band, rather than wholly within the crimson front dash panel. Note the tea hut at the end of the advertising hoarding.

Top: Also carrying a Park Royal 'all-metal' lowbridge body, identical in nearly all respects to 102 and 103, was Leyland TB4 trolleybus 104 (RD 8088), seen here southbound in Southampton Street at its junction with Mill Lane (notwithstanding that its front destination blind is showing 'Promenade'). Note the roof-mounted radio suppression coils as compared to the type apparent on trolleybus 103 and barely apparent on trolleybus 102.

Centre: Ransomes trolleybus 105 (RD 8089) seen at the Promenade terminus of route C – at a time when it was 'on the road' having not recently tried to self-destruct! This one carries a Park Royal timber-framed body. Notice the slightly 'set back' front axle, 'square' rather than radiused bottom corners to the windows and the square top to the cab door (both sides, as it happens). There are also roof-mounted radio suppression coils similar to those on trolleybus 104 – and a roof-mounted 'shield' to the trolley gantry (each side of the vehicle).

Bottom: Also carrying a Park Royal timber-framed lowbridge body was Sunbeam MF2A trolleybus 106 (RD 8090), seen at the Promenade terminus of route C. In addition to the observations made in respect of the bodywork of trolleybus 105, note the very distinctive shallower windscreens and consequent 'make-up piece' between the bottom edge of windscreen and the top of lower cream band, making the vehicle appear rather different! Roof-mounted radio suppression coils are barely apparent and, as on 105, the vehicle is fitted with a roof-mounted 'shield' to the trolley gantry.

Comparison of these photos with the 25 trolleybuses ordered for the conversion of the 'Main Line' from trams reveals that in all cases the front upper-deck windows were fixed panes; that no rear two-tier spring steel bumper bars were fitted; and that only trolleybuses 102 and 105 had fluted removable front towing panels. One assumes that these little differences were intentional, to determine the best design features under service conditions, for incorporation into the specification for the tram replacement vehicles.

logic of war, 'legitimate targets' – firms such as Vincents of Reading Ltd., opposite the Stations, and even Reading Corporation Transport's Mill Lane depot which, in this raid, so narrowly avoided destruction.

Inevitably, the town centre must have been considerably disrupted, with bus and trolleybus services seriously affected, although we have been unable to discover any precise details as to exactly how extensively the bus and trolleybus routes were affected. The reader will appreciate, however, that the narrow Minster Street, which was not only an important thoroughfare but also carried certain bus routes to Broad Street, was totally impassable, and the eastern end of Broad Street itself must also have been closed in one or both directions, for it was covered in shards of glass from blown out windows. One can only surmise that trolleybuses were turned short using battery traction either side of the obstruction. The only corporation transport vehicle believed to have been involved in the incident was trolleybus 119, which was standing in Broad Street, near Wellsteeds, at the time of the attack. It suffered shrapnel damage to the rear emergency window, was showered with dust and debris giving it a new livery of sand yellow, and was surrounded by shoes which had been blown out of Mansfields' shoe shop, which at that time was on the corner of Broad Street and Minster Street. The bomb-damaged buildings were boarded-up, and unsafe structures demolished over the ensuing year – but a facade on the south side of Minster Street (which included the Reading Trade Union Club and Institute), and the Friar Street facade of the shuttered ruin of the Market Arcade, remained as an ugly reminder of the raid well into the 1950s, the latter until Bristol & West Arcade, the Friar Street end of Marks & Spencer and the parade of shops opposite the erstwhile General Post Office (now Yates's) were built.

Further economy of fuel and materials, especially rubber, was a priority and an internal circular dated 18th February 1943 urged further savings, particularly of fuel. The undertaking had already felt the effects of the rubber shortage the previous November, when Dunlop had refused to supply any rubber platform mats for the trolleybuses and had pointed out that even London Transport had been refused. A note in the traffic arrangements file, dated 19th April 1943, shows that trolleybus operation was also subject to cutbacks in order to save on tyre wear. The following trolleybus journeys were not run from Liverpool Road on Mondays to Fridays: 9.56am; 10.26am; 10.56am; 11.26am; 11.56am; 3.26pm; 3.56pm; 4.26pm and 4.56pm.

During 1943, the earlier 'last buses' caused a particular problem in the training of part-time ARP volunteers and, at the Emergency & Invasion Committee meeting of 17th March 1943, it was decided that ARP rescue tenders should be used for transport home. Of the volunteers, it was noted that *"...very few of them can attend before 20.00 hours and if they rely upon public transport to get them to their homes they must leave the [ARP] depot or lecture room not later than 20.50 hours. The time they receive for training is therefore very much curtailed"*. Perhaps this answers the regional transport commissioner's belief that evening bus services were only being used for leisure purposes! In short, insisting that 'last buses' be operated so early was extremely counter-productive.

In early 1943, it was proposed that the separate ARP rescue service, ambulance and first aid parties should be combined into an enlarged ARP rescue service. This duly took place, the southern regional commissioner recommending that, where possible, this should prove "*a suitable opportunity for centralising the supervision of all whole-time Civil Defence Vehicles*". At a meeting of the Emergency & Invasion Committee on 23rd June 1943, however, the transport manager, in his role as transport & ambulance officer, submitted a report on the maintenance and repair of ARP vehicles. It was decided that the most economic option was to continue the existing practice, whereby the borough surveyor remained responsible for servicing 'rescue vehicles', while the transport & ambulance officer continued to maintain all whole-time 'casualty service vehicles' at Mill Lane depot. In addition, the transport & ambulance officer became responsible for supervising all rescue vehicles. In addition, the Transport Department became responsible for registration, licensing and insurance of all ARP and civil defence vehicles. This may account for the Transport Department finding itself responsible for the post-war disposal of non-departmental vehicles in its care.

Double Summer Time commenced on 4th April 1943 in advance of a rather late Easter, which was actually on Sunday 26th April 1943 and celebrated by church bells being rung in thanksgiving for the Allied armies' triumphs in Tunisia. As well as this final Axis defeat in North Africa, which led to an Allied invasion of Italy a few months later and the toppling

AEC Regent 50 (RD 8093) is full to bursting, inbound at Norcot from Roebuck (which the front destination still shows), circa November 1943. Evidently it is quite cold – witness the winter clothing! Note, too, the passenger shelter, the fading white blackout paint on the trolleybus section box, the 'tired' road surface and the lined-out livery of the bus itself. Compare this with the view of the same bus in pristine condition on page 8!

Late W. J. Haynes
© Millane Publishing

of Benito Mussolini, the German successes in Russia were also being reversed; the Allies had started bombing Berlin; and Japanese advances in the Pacific were also in check.

Unauthorised use of fuel was a serious offence during the war, which could result in prosecution and a heavy fine. It is clear from surviving documentation that the Transport Department was especially concerned that they should not meet such a fate! A memo dated 16th April 1943 to Mr Calder from the acting deputy transport manager refers to a complaint from Reading Borough Police concerning an investigation of "...alleged waste of fuel and tyres by buses running beyond the Chalgrove Way terminus on the Emmer Green route". It appears that this 'extension' was being operated by a relief bus between 5.05pm and 5.20pm each weekday evening, to pick up staff from the evacuated London office of the Salvation Army Insurance Department from Courtenay Drive, to safeguard the normal service bus leaving full from Chalgrove Way terminus and thus being unable to pick up anyone along the route into town. Although an extension to Courtenay Drive had been operated for just three days, between 4th and 7th November 1940, no approval had actually been given by the chief constable for this latest circumstance and, following the current investigation, approval was quickly sought – on 19th April 1943!

Concern was also expressed, on 4th June 1943, that vehicles used as auxiliary transport were not properly authorised in a written form but arranged over the telephone or by word-of-mouth, which, it was said "... could be distorted in all kinds of ways in a Court of Law". It seems that the department was providing vehicles for many different reasons – for example, transport of a band for 'Wings for Victory Week' (5th–12th June 1943); or carting of furniture and crockery for the British Restaurant at Northumberland Avenue. Mr Calder seemed unconcerned, responding to the acting deputy transport manager to the effect that "... these vehicles are being used by the local authority for work of national importance".

The steady build-up of American forces continued and an American Services Club had been established at St. Laurence's Hall, being officially opened on Independence Day, 4th July 1943. 'Holidays at Home' were again promoted, together with an alternative recommendation – of spending the family holiday in the country at a Harvest Camp to help on a farm. Double Summer Time 1943, in fact, ended on 15th August 1943.

Letters were being received by the Ministry of War Transport complaining of overcrowding on two routes during the peak hour periods they were being operated. On route J (Stations – Roebuck), longer-distance passengers were being excluded by short-distance passengers who could have used a trolleybus on any journey as far as Norcot Junction; and on route K (St. Mary's Butts – Woodcote Road), the demand from Woodcote Road in the morning peak far exceeded the vehicle's passenger carrying capacity. This led to two letters being received at Mill Lane from the regional transport commissioner in April 1943 offering solutions in each case. His proposals were discussed at the Transport Committee meeting on 20th May 1943.

The commissioner proposed two options for route J:

- A limited stop service, with the first setting down stop at the Greyhound Stadium at Norcot; or

- A minimum 3d fare being charged on outward journeys from the Railway Stations to Reading West station, whilst the usual fare scales applied into town.

The second option was adopted for a three-month experimental period from 8th July 1943. At the Transport Committee meeting prior to this, on 17th June 1943, an extension of the trolleybus system to serve Kentwood had been proposed and, as we shall see, this went forward to fruition. Consequently, after its three-month trial, the minimum fare arrangements continued until the trolleybus extension was in place and route J withdrawn.

Regarding overcrowding on route K (St. Mary's Butts – Woodcote Road), it will be recalled that this route was operated by Guy B single-deckers 40 and 41, which had been refurbished in 1938 and given AEC four-cylinder oil engines for the climb up the steep St. Peter's Hill. How much of a coincidence was it, one wonders, that the regional transport commissioner and his staff were resident in a large mansion in St. Peter's Avenue, Caversham, so that this was the bus service they would use?

In order to ease the overcrowding, the regional transport commissioner suggested that route K should be wholly or

Widening Station Hill using pre-cast concrete decking on concrete supports and construction of a pedestrian subway started in 1937, but was not completed until the summer of 1941 – largely due to the onset of the war and subsequent incorporation of a large air raid shelter. AEC Regent 48 (RD 8091), bound for Erleigh Road, takes a break 'waiting time' sometime circa 1943. The view gives a fairly good indication of the uninviting wilderness that was to be found here for a good many years by anyone arriving in Reading by train, until Western Tower was built and shops began to appear at street level. Bearing in mind this was around the middle of the war, the number of private cars in use is surprising.

© *Omnibus Society*

Guy B 20 (DP 7258) takes a Sunday afternoon nap in Mill Lane outside the former power station in the company of her surviving sister, 19 (DP 7257) in May 1943. The departmental van in between is dispensing tea to crews coming on/going off duty.
Late W. J. Haynes © Millane Publishing

partially operated by double-deckers. Accordingly, on Wednesday 20th May 1943 (the day of a Transport Committee meeting), a test run took place using bus 46 with the certifying officer, the transport manager and the traffic superintendent on board. It was agreed that if double-deckers were to operate the service it should be re-routed, to avoid both the low trees and the incline on the steep and (at the time) narrow St. Peter's Hill. On the test run over an alternative route, via St. Anne's Road, Priest Hill, The Mount, Albert Road and Highmoor Road (i.e. largely over existing route F), it was found that retaining the existing timings would prove fairly tight. It was even suggested that two stops – at Caversham Road Fire Station (alias Subway Road) and at Darrell Road – or alternatively all the stops between St. Anne's Road and Woodcote Road – should be abandoned! However, the service was retimed and three new stops were sited, one in Woodcote Road between Harrogate Road and Ilkley Road; one in Highmoor Road near the Methodist Church; and one in Highmoor Road at the end of Darrell Road. For the remainder of the modified route, the existing stops for route F were used. In connection with the re-routeing, the Chief Constable recommended that the borough surveyor should install a 'Halt! Major Road Ahead' sign at the junction of Highmoor Road with Woodcote Road. The revised service, using double-deckers, commenced on 8th July 1943, although still operated only during the morning, lunch-time and evening peaks. Guy Bs 40 and 41 were released for use on route L (Hemdean Road – Berkeley Avenue).

Following a petition to the transport commissioner, however, a service via the original route up St. Peter's Hill was very soon reinstated, primarily for the benefit of children attending the private St. Peter's Hill School near the summit of St. Peter's Hill, possibly from the start of the new academic year sometime in September 1943. This avoided the children having to cross a dangerous road on their way into school. Single-deckers were used, on two return journeys per day, recorded in the regional transport commissioner's letter of 6th July 1943 (i.e. two days <u>before</u> introduction of double-deckers) as:

Ex-St. Mary's Butts	8.47am and 12.37pm
Ex-Woodcote Road	9.02am and 1.52pm

Early concern over timekeeping on the modified route proved correct and, in early September 1943, one proposal to improve timekeeping was to omit four stops – at Tudor Road, Subway Road (Caversham Road Fire Station), Promenade, and Priest Hill. However, this idea was rejected as impracticable (bearing in mind that much of the modified route was superimposed on route F) and, instead, from early October 1943, (precise date not recorded, but thought to have been sometime between 8th and 14th) the route was shortened to terminate in Friar Street (opposite the General Post Office) instead of St. Mary's Butts, being routed from Stations via Blagrave Street and returning via Friar Street and Station Road. It is on record, once again from a trusted enthusiast source, that bus 48, driven by the deputy traffic superintendent, was seen on tests one day prior to the change, going clockwise round and round the Queen Victoria statue situated on a traffic island outside the bombed-out end of the Town Hall. It is reasonable to suppose that it was the original option for buses to proceed from Stations via Station Road and Friar Street, terminate outside the GPO, then U-turn round the statue to pick up by the bomb-site opposite the GPO. Evidently, turning around the statue was found not to be entirely satisfactory.

The regional transport commissioner subsequently suggested that route K (Friar Street (GPO) – Woodcote Road) could be withdrawn if route F (Merry Maidens – Uplands Road) were bifurcated to provide alternate buses to Woodcote Road and Uplands Road. This would co-ordinate services, save mileage and improve the enforced restricted morning, lunchtime and evening peak service still in operation on route K. The transport manager, however, presented a firm defence that the Woodcote Road route did not warrant a better whole day service to the detriment of that to Uplands Road, pointing out that on weekdays there were 55 trips per day to Uplands Road but only 18 to Woodcote Road and also that every journey into town from Uplands Road between 8.00am and 9.00am was duplicated, to cope with the heavy loadings. The regional transport commissioner's suggestion was thus firmly rejected by the Transport Committee at its meeting on 17th February 1944.

Meanwhile, the annual report of the undertaking for the financial year ended 31st March 1943 was presented to the Transport Committee at its meeting on 17th June 1943, again in an abridged form. Compared with the previous financial year, trolleybuses had carried 23,555,651 passengers (an increase of 1,046,443, again with no additional rolling stock) but had run only an extra 856 miles! The motorbuses, at 1,188,300, had operated 84,858 fewer miles and at 16,124,690, had carried 63,443 fewer passengers. The Parcels Express Service returned an increased loss, from £98 the previous year to £278, again put down to a severe reduction in the number of parcels carried, possibly due to rationing and shortage of supplies

Guy FCX 31 (DP 9712), serving as a mobile promotional vehicle on 10th June 1943 at the Erleigh Road terminus of route M during 'Wings for Victory Week' (5th–12th June 1943). It is now very near the end of its service life, being used in service for the very last time on 22nd July 1943 on route H (Chalgrove Way – Wood Lane Junc.)

Late W. J. Haynes © Millane Publishing

of most commodities. In making his usual comments Mr Calder again made reference to the good fortune still being derived for choosing trolleybuses rather than motorbuses to replace the trams. He also pointed out that the severe operating restrictions imposed by government policy, again because of drastic rationing and short supplies, was entirely responsible for an overall reduction in passengers carried and miles operated by the motorbuses. After the January 1943 cuts, motorbus services were operating 7½ and trolleybus services 15 fewer hours per week than before.

Throughout the war it was a continuous battle trying to keep ageing vehicles on the road. The Leyland Titans, with their timber-framed bodies, were literally falling apart through lack of maintenance and appalling road conditions. Bus 37 was declared unsafe on 4th June 1943 and sent for repair in the carpenters' shop, and a memo dated 5th August 1943 indicates how bus 1 was subject to excessive movement due to the bodywork flexing, although wartime pressures meant that the PSV examiner did not go so far as to suggest that its certificate of fitness should be withdrawn. Messrs. Markham, a local firm of coachbuilders and vehicle repair specialists, of Caversham Road, were contracted to renovate bus 1, this contract following on from some work already carried out by them on AEC Regent 10. Continual overloading was also causing excessive wear on all the undertaking's buses and trolleybuses, but a considerable reserve fund was being built up from the operating profits of the war years, which was earmarked for purchasing replacement vehicles once the opportunity arose.

Both remaining Guy FCX three-axle single-deckers, 31 and 32, were used during Reading's 'Wings For Victory Week', from 5th–12th June 1943, which aimed to raise one million pounds to build 25 Lancaster bombers. There were displays in the Town Hall, parades, and a Spitfire in the town centre – and the target was comfortably exceeded, to raise a magnificent £1,390,106. Buses 31 and 32 were never popular with the drivers, for as well as being petrol-driven, they were difficult to handle and only made rare appearances, usually during rush hours. Indeed, in surviving departmental records they are listed as unlicensed in February 1940. 32 had been noted in public service on route H (Chalgrove Way – Wood Lane Junction) by a local enthusiast on 12th April 1943 and both 31 and 32 were last noted in public service by the same enthusiast on 22nd July 1943, bus 31 operating route H (Chalgrove Way – Wood Lane Junc) and 32 on route I (Donkin Hill – Horncastle). However, records suggest that 31 was finally withdrawn on 31st July 1944 (mileage is recorded for 1944) and 32 on 30th June 1944 (again with mileage in 1944), so after their last recorded use in passenger service, it is likely that they continued to be available for use on a variety of duties for a further year. They were rarely (if ever) required for passenger service after the arrival of Guy Arab utility motorbuses 27 and 28, the purchase of which we will relate in due course.

From 18th July 1943, Sunday services, both trolleybus and motorbus, were altered to commence at 1.30pm instead of

Guy FCX 31 (DP 9712) lurks in the shade of the depot on a sunny Sunday afternoon in May 1943 in the twilight of its career. This view was taken shortly before the vehicle's transformation for use in a non-PSV capacity during 'Wings for Victory Week' (5th–12th June 1943) as shown above.

Late W. J. Haynes © Millane Publishing

1:00pm and to finish at 9.30pm rather than 9:00pm (Broad Street departure times). This followed concern that late-finishing crews on Saturday evenings did not have a sufficient break before reporting before 1:00pm for their Sunday duties. The extra half-hour also allowed those crews working on a Sunday to have Sunday lunch with their families before their shift!

To counter losses made by the Parcels Express Service over the previous two years, charges were increased from 1st November 1943, although the transport manager's proposals to increase the internal charge for corporation letters from 1d to 2d and to raise the charge for carrying parcels of library books between branches were resisted by the Transport Committee at its meeting of 16th October 1943.

Trolleybus 102 was used as wedding transport between St. Mary-the-Virgin church in St. Mary's Butts and the reception at Caversham Bridge Hotel at 3.00pm on 4th December 1943. The vehicle was actually hired by Cllr. Bennet Palmer, chairman of the Transport Committee – for ten shillings.

By the end of 1943, the war had turned decisively in favour of the Allies, but probably most importantly for bus operators, Atlantic shipping losses had been dramatically reduced by the ongoing development of radar technology, leading to increasing U-boat losses. As a result, a small increase was made in the fuel allowance during 1944 – with explicit instructions from the regional transport commissioner that it should be used for *"...the elimination of queues for workers, and ... shopping facilities outside peak hours for housewives"*. In response to this offer, Mr Calder proposed the following additional services at the Transport Committee meeting of 18th November 1943:

1 single-deck bus between Broad Street and Callington Road from 6.45am to 9.00am.

1 single-deck bus between Callington Road and Broad Street between 1.38pm and 2.38pm.

1 bus between the Grenadier and Broad Street at 2.30pm.

1 bus from Broad Street at 6.15pm to the Merry Maidens.

1 bus between Stations and the Roebuck from 5.00pm to 7.00pm.

1 bus from Prospect Street, Caversham to Wood Lane Junction at 5.30pm (for employees of J. Samuel Elliott Ltd.).

Staff sickness over the 1943/44 winter resulted in none of these proposals being followed up until early spring when, on Monday 3rd April 1944, route I (Donkin Hill – Horncastle) had its Monday–Friday frequency increased to one of 15 minutes all day rather than an alternate 15 and 20 minute service, whilst on Sundays route F (Uplands Road – Merry Maidens), route H (Chalgrove Way – Wood Lane Junction) and route I (Donkin Hill – Horncastle) were given increased frequencies of 15 minutes rather than 20 minutes.

Needless to say, whereas war workers' services were again required, none of the regular services were operated on Christmas Day 1943. Managerial attempts were made to try to prevent the Boxing Day absenteeism problems of the previous year recurring and these were largely successful. Just before Christmas, however, there was a serious influenza epidemic which, although it inevitably took its toll on staff, also had the effect of making the rest of them realise that this was not an occasion to make circumstances unnecessarily worse than they were! Between 15th November and 4th December 1943, a total of only 330 miles were lost out of a combined weekly 45,000 miles. Christmastide 1943 was otherwise a time when much was made of American Red Cross parties for local children and, in particular, orphaned evacuees.

Despite enquiries, Reading had been unable to borrow vehicles from other municipalities throughout the war but, on 28th December 1943, two Bournemouth Corporation Sunbeam MS2 trolleybuses with Park Royal bodies, 77 (AEL 405) and 123 (ALJ 997), were seen on tow through Reading *en route* to the Llanelly & District Traction Company. Both remained on loan there until 29th June 1945, when they were again seen passing through Reading, heading home.

AEC Regent 54 (RD 8891) 'waits time' at the Grovelands Road terminus of route M circa November 1943. Although still quite smart with cream lining-out after four years of war, something has scored three of the offside lower panels which in peacetime would have soon been replaced.

Late W. J. Haynes
© Millane Publishing

In July 1942, there had been a request from the Royal Ordnance Factory at Theale *(sic)* that workman tickets should be available throughout the day for use by those war workers on night shift or working staggered hours. This was deemed unworkable, as conductors would be unable to differentiate between Ordnance Factory workers and ordinary passengers and unequal fares would be seen as unfair.

Further discussions took place with the regional transport commissioner and, at its December 1942 meeting, the Transport Committee considered the commissioner's suggestion that local industrial companies engaged on war work should be able to purchase bulk supplies of pre-paid workman tickets for use outside normal hours of availability. Mr Calder noted that the undertaking's income had already fallen due to earlier last departure times and that this measure would cause a further decrease in revenue. Against the wishes of the regional transport commissioner, the Transport Committee therefore declined to adopt the suggestion. It seems that, following extensive discussions between the ministry and the operator's associations, some other undertakings had not adopted the proposal either.

Reading's refusal was, nevertheless, badly received by the regional transport commissioner, the Ministry of War Transport and the Municipal Passenger Transport Association, who were beginning to speak about compelling Reading to observe the agreed formula. A letter from Mr C. B. Clapham, the MPTA general secretary, dated 29th December 1943, demanded an urgent meeting with Mr Calder, who travelled to London in January 1944. Mr Calder expressed the firm opinion that Reading had been let down by the MPTA and insisted that the enhanced wages paid to war workers for night shift work did not necessitate reduced fares; and that the perceived wisdom of many operators was *"...that workmen's fares ought not to be encouraged but should be abolished"*. He asked the MPTA to write to its members for their views and, from the replies, Mr Calder discovered that of 71 replies, only 11 granted workmen's fares to shift workers. The problem was not resolved and negotiations were left with the Ministry of War Transport in London. No further detail on this issue has been discovered. However, it was noted in 1946, by Mr Calder's successor, that special prepaid workman tickets had been made available under Defence Regulations (Statutory Rule & Order No. 1109) but that they had fallen from use after the war. Maybe that Defence Regulation relates to this issue.

The undertaking's printed timetable of 1st April 1944 (Double Summer Time 1944 commenced the following day) lists seven special workmen's motorbus routes, described as 'temporary services', using seven vehicles, which operated on Sunday mornings for war workers. Although their date of introduction is not recorded, these services were quite possibly introduced in response to the outcry which followed the withdrawal of Sunday morning motorbus services in January 1943.

War Emergency. **Temporary Services.** Buses.
Special Workmen's Buses for War-workers only.
SUNDAY MORNINGS ONLY.

LEAVE.		a.m.	a.m.	a.m.	a.m.	a.m.	a.m.	a.m.	a.m.
Wood Lane Junction	(for Broad Street)	5 45	6 15	6 30	6 45	7 0		7 15	7 40	8 0
Whitley Estate	(for Broad Street)	5 37	6 15			7 8	7 36		
Merry Maidens	(for Broad Street)	6 30	7 30						
Donkin Hill	(for Broad Street)	6 10	6 30		7 0	7 30			8 5
Chalgrove Way	(for Broad Street)	7 30							
" "	(for Wood Lane Junction)	7 30							
Roebuck	(for Pond House)	6 0	6 30	6 48	7 40				
LEAVE.									
Broad Street	(for Wood Lane Junction)	5 33	6 0	6 15	6 30	6 43	7 0	7 28	7 45
" "	(for Whitley Estate)	5 23	5 53	6 30	7 23				
" "	(for Merry Maidens)	6 15	7 15						
" "	(for Donkin Hill)	6 0	6 20	6 45	7 15		7 50		
" "	(for Chalgrove Way)	7 15							
" "	(for Roebuck)	5 45							
Pond House	(for Roebuck)	6 10	6 40	6 56					

NOTE:—Above are temporary Bus Services, subject to alteration or withdrawal at short notice.

In the spring of 1944, shipbuilders and engineering firms, including firms like J. Samuel Elliott Ltd., in Caversham, were directing their energies towards the construction of landing craft in preparation for the invasion of Europe. The influx of troops and equipment from the USA had turned the southern counties of England into such a vast holding area that jokes were made about the country tilting and sinking beneath the weight! On the streets of London, every known Allied military uniform could be seen and, by the last days of May 1944, the invasion force was ready – delayed only by bad weather in the English Channel.

Few photographs seem to exist of trolleybuses showing 'Liverpool Rd' as opposed to 'Liverpool Road'. A rare exception, therefore, is this mid-war view of 128 (ARD 691) inbound at Norcot.

Late W. J. Haynes
© Maiwand Photographic Archive

Above: *Guy Arab motorbus 6 (BRD 754), powered by a Gardner 5LW engine, seen when new in Blagrave Street next to the Southern Railway station. It is working on route I bound for Donkin Hill, and is about to pull round one of three Bedford OWB utility vehicles that Kemp's Bus Service put into service about the same time. The livery is lined-out with fine cream lines in the traditional manner – it was probably the very last to be outshopped thus. The lowbridge 55-seat body-work was by Strachan, with only one opening window per side per deck and unglazed rear upper-deck emergency door – all soon altered. No nearside wing mirror is fitted – something else to make life difficult for drivers in the blackout!*

Print from Late R. Marshall's Collection

Below: *First of a batch of six Park Royal-bodied Sunbeam W utility trolleybuses put into service earlier in 1943, heavily-loaded 132 (BRD 797) is seen here town-bound circa November 1943, having joined Oxford Road at Norcot Junc.*

Late W. J. Haynes © Maiwand Photographic Archive

8 Wartime Rolling Stock

At the start of the war, production of new motorbuses and trolleybuses had continued as manufacturers met outstanding pre-war orders. These vehicles, built to pre-war specification, were delivered into the early months of 1940, after which bus production rapidly dried up as war production took precedence. Meanwhile, of course, most of the army's equipment (including some 600 tanks) had been abandoned in France as a result of the British retreat through Dunkirk, and full-scale manufacture of new military equipment was of the utmost priority under the threat of an invasion. As a stop-gap, vast numbers of buses and coaches were 'commandeered' – compulsorily acquired – by the War Department in order to give the armed forces some mobility. Thus, by the summer of 1940, the manufacture of civilian motor vehicles of any sort was mostly suspended as the British engineering industry set itself to re-equip the army. Even this priority was set aside late in the summer of 1940, when aircraft production had to be stepped up to meet the demands of the Royal Air Force when it was desperate to replace aircraft lost during the Battle of Britain.

In July 1940, vehicle manufacturing restrictions following the Dunkirk evacuation had prompted the Minister of Transport to issue an Order under Defence Regulations controlling the sale of new goods and public service vehicles. Another came into effect in July 1941, which controlled the sale of buses second-hand. Subsequently these were superseded by the Acquisition and Disposal of Motor Vehicles Order 1942. Effectively, the purchase and disposal of vehicles was forbidden without a licence.

This 'marking time' could not be allowed to go on. The Ministry of Supply became responsible for the strict control and allocation of new vehicles from the total it determined should be built which, for the period July 1941 to the end of 1942, was intended to be 1,500 double-deck motorbuses. The first 415 of these were, in fact, constructed by manufacturers from partly-built vehicles and spare parts, on which work had been frozen because of wartime restrictions. These vehicles were termed 'unfrozen' and differed from the later 'utility' vehicles in being built to the originally intended peacetime specification, although delivered where they were urgently wanted, not to their originally-intended customers. Twenty-five motorbuses originally built for export were also released for use in Britain.

The 1,000 utility chassis in the 1941/42 programme were originally intended to be equally split between Guy and Leyland, with bodies being supplied by several body-builders to an extremely basic standard design drawn up by the National Federation of Vehicle Trades using timber frames and steel (rather than aluminium) panels and with a minimum of internal trim – essentially spartan and functional and with 'no frills' whatsoever.

Bus operators were somewhat concerned about the ministry's choice of Guy Motors as the chassis supplier. Transport managers with not-too-long a memory were able to recall that Guy had ended bus production in 1936 following the unpopularity of their original Arab bus chassis and, in 1938, had completely abandoned the civilian market to concentrate on military vehicle manufacture and the design of armour plate. Bus operators would have preferred that all 1,000 buses be built by Leyland, whose reputation was well-regarded. Leyland built none of them, however, being too heavily committed to war work and with no spare production capacity.

Guy Motors thus took on the responsibility of designing their version of a double-deck bus chassis based on the utility specification they were given and this resulted in a new version of the Arab. Consequently, only the 500 vehicles from Guy of the originally intended total of 1,000 were actually built in this first programme.

A single-deck half-cab utility body was also designed and the Bedford OWB lightweight single-decker also became available, mainly to suit small, rural operators, with production commencing in January 1942.

We have already noted how it had been decided that no new trolleybuses would be built during this 1941/42 period. Instead, 'over-width' trolleybuses originally destined for South Africa were made available in early 1942, with the first new Sunbeam W trolleybuses being built from the end of that year. Sunbeam was chosen as the sole trolleybus chassis manufacturer during the war, although for some unknown reason some of its production was 'badge-engineered' as Karrier. Further batches of vehicles, motorbuses (not all of them by Guy) and trolleybuses, were sanctioned for building in following yearly programmes during and after the war, the allocation of new vehicles between operators being under the strict control of the Ministry of War Transport. Competition for an allocation of new buses from across the country always resulted in far more vehicles being sought than were actually made available; as a result, applications were invariably cut back.

In Reading, motorbus breakdowns were increasing. Harsh winter conditions had weighed heavily on the overnight dispersal of vehicles across the town, as a result of which dispersal had been suspended in January 1942. There was also a difficulty in obtaining spare parts, because they were frequently diverted for military purposes. With vehicles becoming unusable, bus services had to be maintained using fewer spare vehicles. In turn, regular servicing of each vehicle became postponed, resulting, in the long run, in even more vehicle failures. Addressing these difficulties, the Transport Department introduced special arrangements whereby repairs and servicing took place during the night.

It was in this operating context that the Transport Committee, at its meeting on 2nd February 1942, agreed

The Utility Shortfall – Double-deck Motorbuses	
Requirement July 1941 – December 1942:	1,500
Less: Vehicles supplied 'unfrozen':	- 415
Vehicles originally built for export:	- 25
Outstanding requirement:	1,060
1941/42 Utility Programme:	1,000
Original requirement omitted from Programme:	+ **60**
Total:	1,060
Built by Guy:	500
Allocated to Leyland; not built:	**500**
Overall shortfall (60 omitted plus 500 not built):	**560**

A crew change eastbound on one of the new Sunbeam W utility trolleybuses in Broad Street, outside The Arcade, sometime circa the autumn of 1943. Meanwhile there is something of a clamour at the 'back end' as an otherwise orderly queue fragments to board. The lack of passengers already aboard suggests that the vehicle has been brought up from depot for a 'change-off'.

Print from J. R. Whitehead's collection

that the undertaking should make an application to the regional transport commissioner for a licence to purchase three new motorbuses. As a result of the restrictions on production outlined earlier, only two licences were granted, for Guy Arab double-deckers; and because they were required to be fitted with lowbridge bodies, they were to be bodied by Strachan, of Acton, West London, the designated builders of this type of body. These 55-seat vehicles (three more seats than most of Reading's existing motorbuses), built to Ministry of Supply specification, were supplied fitted with Gardner 5LW engines. Buses fitted with the more-powerful 6LW engine were, at this stage, only available to undertakings operating routes having steep gradients to contend with, mainly in the north of England and the Midlands, and comprised only about 5% of total production. The first utility bus to be delivered to Reading, number 6 (BRD 754), arrived on 17th November 1942. The second, 7 (BRD 755), arrived on 1st February 1943. Other details will be found in Appendices A and B. Note the significance of the fleet numbers, for they in-filled the two numbers left vacant, now that the two 'commandeered' AEC Regal 4 single-deckers were not rejoining the fleet. Both were delivered in grey primer and were painted into fleet livery at Mill Lane. From photographic evidence, bus 6 was out-shopped in lined-out livery. Bus 7 may have been dealt with similarly, but it would have been one of the last to have been lined-out. The Gardner 5LW engines fitted to these two vehicles caused them to be somewhat underpowered for use in Reading. As a result, their performance was sluggish and they very soon became unpopular with the travelling public – and particularly with the drivers, especially when allocated to some of Reading's hillier routes! For the most part, therefore, it was agreed with the union that they would be restricted to route I (Horncastle – Donkin Hill) and route M (Grovelands Road – Erleigh Road), both of which were being operated as a 15-minute service.

With regard to their unpopularity with crews, an oft-quoted anecdote is that, once the war was over and things were returning to normal, it was standard practice to park the 'spare' buses (which were used to change-off any vehicle which became defective during the day) outside the depot. Buses 6 and 7 were favourites for this role, as their unpopularity meant that drivers would think twice before defecting the bus they were currently driving!

Shortly after the Guy Arabs arrived, in April 1942, the undertaking received authorisation to order six Sunbeam W

Assumedly taken just after the crew change illustrated above, the utility trolleybus is revealed to be 132 (BRD 797), whilst the two AECs following can be identified as 120 (ARD 683) followed by 108 (ARD 671). Evidently 132 has just 'taken off' eastbound from The Arcade stop in Broad Street, presumably on route B bound for Liverpool Road, although still showing 'Norcot Junc.' With headlamps masked and at a time during the war when all unnecessary 'frills' would have been deleted, it is odd that these vehicles, the very first batch of double-deck Sunbeam W trolleybuses to have been built, were equipped with fog lamps – which could not be used!

© R. N. Hannay

Sunbeam W utility trolleybus 135 (BRD 800) seen at the Three Tuns terminus of the 'main line'. A 'shelter' sign has been attached to the traction pole, and the brick pillar in the entrance to the Three Tuns public house has dabs of white paint to aid visibility in the blackout. Note the 'hop leaf' emblem of the local brewer, Simonds, on the pub sign. Milwards, the local chain of shoe shops, advertised on buses in the Reading area for many years.

Late W. J. Haynes
© Maiwand Photographic Archive

utility trolleybuses to Ministry of Supply specification. Reading was the only transport undertaking in the country to receive its full quota of requested trolleybuses without the Ministry reducing the number. They were in fact, apart from obviously special batches of single-deck trolleybuses for Darlington Corporation and Mexborough & Swinton Traction, the very first utility trolleybuses to be ordered and delivered. The chassis cost £1,745 each. These two-axle vehicles, fitted with Park Royal 56-seat bodies, which cost £1,350 each, were duly delivered between March and August 1943 numbered 132–137 (BRD 797–801/14). Other details will be found in Appendices A and B. Each arrived in grey primer and was painted into fleet livery in the Mill Lane paint shop, although cream lining-out was not included. 132 was seen by a local enthusiast in the depot in otherwise full Reading livery on 31st March 1943 (although it was another three weeks before it entered service – presumably awaiting Ministry inspection). 135 was seen on test in Whitley Street in grey primer, and was still in the depot in grey on 5th June 1943, as were 136 and 137 on 8th July 1943. None ever ran in service in this condition, however. Like the two Guy motorbuses, the Sunbeam trolleybuses were fitted from new with upholstered seats rather than wooden-slat seats as fitted to buses constructed from later in 1943.

It was more usual for Sunbeam to favour British Thomson-Houston for traction motors and electrical equipment, so these trolleybuses were also a little non-standard in being fitted with English Electric traction motors and electrical equipment, which was as in line with the undertaking's preferred choice as one was ever likely to get in wartime – <u>and</u> the vehicles were equipped for battery traction. In practice, however, nothing was actually interchangeable with earlier vehicles – except, apparently, the prop shaft!

Sadly, so it would seem, the omission of cream lining-out from the fleet livery had, indeed, been adopted as standard practice. Motorbus 47 was the first of the existing fleet to receive a repaint without this embellishment, re-entering service on 17th April 1943.

In June 1942, application was made for a licence to obtain a further new motorbus which, together with the outstanding third vehicle of the previous application, prompted the granting in October 1942 of another two licences by the regional transport commissioner. Two more Guy Arab vehicles, again to be fitted with Strachans 55-seat low-bridge utility bodies, were duly ordered and were delivered in June 1943. The Ministry of Supply had, meanwhile, relaxed the specification, so that the larger Gardner 6LW

A fairly new utility trolleybus, Sunbeam W 133 (BRD 798), town-bound from Bear Inn, has arrived at Norcot Junction and is preparing to overtake AEC trolleybus 114, as soon as both the latter's trolleybooms have been taken off the overhead line and hooked down. Note the screened lamps just ahead of trolleybus 133's trolleybooms. These lamps were of considerable assistance to crews trying to re-pole trolleybuses in black-out conditions. Note too the unmasked offside headlamp suggesting the early spring of 1945.

Late W. J. Haynes
© Maiwand Photographic Archive

81

A nice atmospheric view of the 'face' of Reading Corporation utility trolleybus 135 (BRD 800) 'waiting time' at the Three Tuns before departure to Norcot Junc. With headlamp masks and the murk of a cold, damp, foggy morning, most probably circa November 1943, the view somehow conjures the mental picture of a dependable municipal public transport system whatever the weather and whatever the circumstances, in the days when, for most people, owning a private motorcar was but a very distant pipe dream.

Late W. J. Haynes © Maiwand Photographic Archive

engine could be authorised for any operator, not just those with hilly routes. Reading, therefore specified 6LW engines in these two vehicles, which was expected to give them a much livelier performance than the 5LW engines fitted to the previous two Guy Arabs, buses 6 and 7.

Once again the vehicles were delivered in grey primer and painted into fleet livery (no cream lining-out) at the depot. Bus 28 (BRD 816) entered service on 2nd June 1943, but both vehicles were noted in the depot on 5th June 1943 each carrying fleet number 28 and registration number BRD 816, one obviously in full livery, the other in grey primer with white hand-painted fleet numbers! The wrongly numbered bus (the grey one) was soon painted in crimson fleet livery and given the correct fleet number 27 and registration BRD 815; it entered service on 8th July 1943. Other details will be found in Appendices A and B. Note, once again, the significance of the in-fill fleet numbers re-used from sold vehicles – in this case, Guy FCX three-axle single-deckers 27 and 28 which had been requisitioned two years previously.

Towards the end of 1942, the undertaking had been asked by the Ministry of War Transport to submit its application for new motorbus requirements for the 1943 national allocation programme. No application was made, for it was felt that the four buses already received, or on order, would fulfil Reading's need for spare vehicles to facilitate the necessary repair and maintenance work on the motorbus fleet. Further, at its meeting in January 1943, the Transport Committee was also advised that the earlier ending of services each night and revised Sunday running, brought about by the need to reduce total mileage operated, had made any further fleet expansion at that time unnecessary.

The austere construction of all the utility vehicles meant that there were frequent passenger complaints about lack of opening windows in the summer heat, while conductors complained of a lack of bell pushes which, with only one on each deck, caused more work for the conductor and delayed the bus at stops.

Probably in the summer of 1943 when new, bus 27 (BRD 815) climbs the hill in London Street bound for Erleigh Road. This second batch of two utility Guy Arab motorbuses were fitted with Gardner 6LW engines rather than the 5LW type fitted to the first two, Nos. 6 and 7. Note the protruding radiator and outswept front wings to accommodate the extra length of the six-cylinder engine. Even so, performance failed to compare with the AEC Regent 'oilers' and they were not particularly liked by crews as they were difficult to keep to time!

Late W. J. Haynes © Millane Publishing

9 Getting Better all the Time

Reading held a 'Salute the Soldier Week' commencing 3rd June 1944. The Week was well in hand when on the following Tuesday, 6th June 1944, Operation Overlord – the long-awaited invasion of Europe by Allied forces – was finally launched in the minutes after midnight. The landings on the beaches of Normandy saw the beginning of the liberation of Europe from German oppression. Months of preparation were now tested, and the military vehicles and equipment that had been stockpiled more or less everywhere in England's southern counties were now transported across the English Channel.

D-Day had arrived, incidentally only ten days short of the first anniversary of the first GIs arriving in Reading at the American Red Cross Services Club. One has to record, however, that the American forces also brought their own troubles with them to Reading, including racial discrimination in the ranks. One GI also met a very tragic end on Tuesday 8th August 1944 in Oxford Road at Elm Lodge Avenue. Driving a jeep in wet conditions, his foot slipped off the throttle pedal and jammed underneath it. The jeep skidded, crashed into an oncoming lorry and burst into a 15ft wall of flame.

The annual report of the undertaking for the financial year ended 31st March 1944, as presented to the Transport Committee at its meeting on 15th June 1944, was again in abridged form, supposedly to confuse the enemy – although on this occasion Germany had other matters with which to concern itself, rather than the trading affairs of a municipal transport undertaking in a town around 40 miles west of London! The town's trolleybuses had carried 23,555,651 passengers (a decrease of 855,203 on the previous year) and ran 1,252,614 miles (a decrease of 78,398 miles). The motorbuses carried 16,424,325 passengers (an increase of 299,635) and ran 1,230,770 miles (an extra 42,470). This turn-down in the undertaking's results – in spite of putting six extra trolleybuses and four new motorbuses into service during the year – was put down, officially, solely to the Ministry of War Transport's enforced restrictions. Despite an increase in the carrying rates during the year, the Parcels Express Service also returned some disappointing results – 3,800 fewer parcels and only a marginal improvement in the year's trading, represented by a loss of £222 instead of £278. In his comment on the year, the transport manager said: *"During the year under review the motor omnibuses have been very fully employed. In addition to the regular services which are provided, numerous duplicates, specials and reliefs are constantly being run, particularly for the convenience of passengers whose hours of duty are staggered, and as a result, the services of these vehicles are called on at all hours between 5am and 1am the following morning. I think it will be conceded that this is a very long day, and calls for many broken hours of duty, as well as an extraordinary amount of work from an administrative point of view, in order that such a long period of time might be covered by vehicles which, in addition to providing a regular service, have to again turn out for special work such as that to which I have referred. Such conditions undoubtedly tell on the repair and maintenance of the fleet as a whole, and much credit is due to the staff whose duty it is to maintain these vehicles in a roadworthy condition, in order that they may be regularly employed to meet the requirements of the travelling public".*

We have noted already on page 73 that, before the introduction of the peak hour 3d minimum fare on route J (Stations – Roebuck) on 8th July 1943 to ease the overcrowding of buses to Roebuck, a report had been submitted to the Transport Committee meeting on 17th June 1943, arguing that a permanent solution to the problem would be to extend the trolleybus system from Norcot Junction as far as Kentwood, along the 'wide avenue' section of Oxford Road. Powers to operate trolleybuses on this section had lapsed in 1941, but informal discussions with the Ministry of War Transport now indicated a favourable response if it could be satisfied *"that the extension of the trolleybus route was needed in connection with the maintenance of a service essential to the life of the community"*.

The area to the north of Oxford Road beyond Norcot Junction was largely adjacent to railway tracks, but that to the south had become a housing development in the 1930s. It included what was known as Norcot Estate and the semi-detached development at Kentwood (or Lower Tilehurst, as it is now known). An estimated 6,000 people lived between Norcot Road and Kentwood Hill and it was argued that the existing motorbus service was inadequate to meet the

AEC 661T trolleybus 117 (ARD 680) 'takes off' westbound from the 'Pulso' stop at Norcot Junc. before wending its way up Norcot Road to Tilehurst circa early spring 1945. Note the unmasked offside headlamp in readiness for the return to peace and the white hoops on the traction pole. An air-raid siren is mounted on top of the pole behind the bus. The shop window (behind the disused cigarette vending machine) appears to have been boarded up, incorporating a smaller, temporary sheet of glass – quite a common occurrence when shop windows were broken, or damaged in air raids, as prompt replacement was often impossible!

Late W. J. Haynes
© Maiwand Photographic Archive

It is autumn 1944 and, having arrived at the Three Tuns terminus and disembarked her passengers, AEC 661T trolleybus 107 (ARD 670) prepares to turn ready for a journey back to Norcot Junc. Note the two American soldiers walking past. By September 1944, only three months after D-Day, it was already apparent that the Reich would crumble and there was thereafter a steady relaxation of wartime regulations as became appropriate, hence the removal of offside headlamp masks in readiness for a return to peace – although at this time the offside headlamp would have had the bulb removed!

Late W. J. Haynes
© Maiwand Photographic Archive

demand, yet under wartime restrictions no improvement was possible. If a trolleybus route could be implemented, withdrawal of motorbuses could save over 20,000 gallons of petrol or 9,500 gallons of diesel fuel per year. Operation of trolleybuses further west than Norcot Junction was also expected to solve a 'bunching' problem, which frequently occurred in the town centre.

As no labour was available to excavate and construct a turning facility at the Roebuck, the roundabout at Kentwood was seen to provide a ready-made turning circle without any roadworks or additional labour being necessary. In making the terminus at Kentwood Circle, a 620-yard stretch of the Oxford Road, from Kentwood to the Roebuck, would no longer be served by Reading Corporation Transport. This stretch of road would not be left without a bus service, however, as Thames Valley operated its routes 5 (Reading – Oxford, jointly with City of Oxford Motor Services route 34), 5A (Reading – Wantage) and 5B (Reading – Yattendon), together giving an hourly service.

Following informal discussions between the transport manager, the deputy town clerk and officials of the Ministry of War Transport, the case was put to the Minister personally, based on the foregoing reasons. As a result, powers to operate trolleybuses to Kentwood were approved under wartime emergency legislation on 29th November 1943 by the issue of the Reading Corporation (Trolley Vehicles) Order 1943. 6,000 yards of trolley wire, together with fittings and other overhead equipment were authorised by the Ministry of Supply and purchased from British Insulated Cables Ltd., of Prescot, Lancashire, and 92 traction poles were purchased from Stewarts & Lloyds Ltd., Glasgow, although not delivered until the following April. Clough, Smith & Company did not have labour available to undertake the erection work, so it was decided that the Transport Department itself should carry it out using its internal labour force – presumably, also, at lower cost. Pole planting began on 8th April 1944. The overhead had been erected by 13th July 1944 and was connected to the main line (for which purpose the current was switched off) on two consecutive Sunday mornings, 23rd and 30th July 1944, when motorbuses substituted for trolley vehicles on the Sunday morning workmen's special services.

Provided at a total cost of £3,709, the Kentwood trolleybus extension opened for public service on Monday 31st July 1944. For operational purposes it was made an extension of

Seemingly during the winter of 1944/45 (as the offside headlamp is unmasked), AEC 661T trolleybus 113 (ARD 676) is at the Three Tuns having turned and is awaiting departure to the Bear Inn. The adverts on the hoarding are decidedly tatty – but there is one on the extreme left hinting that a general election cannot be far away!

Late W. J. Haynes
© Maiwand Photographic Archive

existing route D (Liverpool Road – Norcot Junction), which thus became route D (Liverpool Road – Norcot Junction – Kentwood). Operated to a ten-minute headway, quite remarkably the extension was implemented without the need for any additional trolleybuses. It is interesting to note, incidentally, that before inauguration a fare table was also drafted for a Wokingham Road – Norcot Junction – Kentwood service, suggesting that it was at quite a late stage that consideration was given as to how a service over the new extension would be incorporated into the existing trolleybus network. It was always the intention to extend the Kentwood trolleybus route after the war to the Roebuck, the originally intended terminus. Indeed, plans for the construction of a turning circle at the Roebuck were drawn up subsequently, but circumstances changed as will be recounted in due course.

Motorbus route J (Stations – Roebuck) was, of course, withdrawn as a result. However, according to a subsequent borough council meeting report, a very limited shuttle service of motorbuses was re-introduced between Pond House and Roebuck for a short time, but was soon withdrawn. Nothing more precise has been found regarding this service, which has led us to believe that it was probably the Sunday morning war-workers' feeder service referred to on page 77.

From Sunday 3rd September 1944, some trolleybus-operated workmen's special journeys were diverted from the Bear Inn to serve Kentwood Circle instead. This arrangement was sanctioned by the regional transport commissioner for an experimental period on condition that the abovementioned Sunday morning feeder service, operated by motorbuses between the Roebuck and Pond House to link with the workmen's trolleybus-operated specials from the Bear Inn, could be withdrawn. The trolleybus journey times from Kentwood were given as 6.50am, 8.00am and 9.10am. Thus the proposed fare charts for a Kentwood – Three Tuns service, as already commented upon, came in for some good use after all! In September 1944, passenger traffic on the Kentwood extension was described as *"...very good, and so far quite up to expectations"*.

By October 1944, however, the old issue of short-distance passengers crowding out the Kentwood service was again concerning local residents, and the matter was brought up at the Transport Committee meeting of 12th October 1944. The transport manager showed convincingly from the experience of other bus routes that it was the short distance traveller who sustained the financial base of any service. He commented, with some feeling, that *"...the residents in the Kentwood area would like a bus reserved for traffic between Norcot Junction and Kentwood terminus"*. This he was not prepared to grant, and he proved his case by an experiment, which, effectively, would remove the political pressure from the department.

Mr Calder noted that when the route was opened, the town centre stops towards Kentwood were:

At Wellsteeds: joint stop for Norcot Junction and Kentwood
At Boots: joint stop for Norcot Junction and Kentwood
At Cork Street (White Hart): special stop for Kentwood only

An experiment was undertaken to separate the short-distance travellers by encouraging them to board Bear Inn trolleybuses. An additional stop was set up in Broad Street and it should be noted that there was already an additional stop for Bear Inn trolleybuses at Cork Street. The new arrangements were:

At Wellsteeds: stop for Norcot Junction only
At Dorothy Perkins: stop for Kentwood only
At Boots: joint stop for Norcot Junction and Kentwood
At Cork Street (White Hart): stop for Kentwood only
At Cork Street (White Hart): stop for Norcot Junction and Bear Inn only

These stops were subjected to detailed observation and the report on one of them on 5th October 1944 showed that at 6.00pm a half-full trolleybus bound for Kentwood passed twenty passengers waiting at the Cork Street stop for Norcot Junction and Bear Inn, in order to pick up a single passenger at the Kentwood stop. A number of people ran from the other stop and boarded the Kentwood-bound trolleybus, presumably to travel to somewhere between West Street and Norcot Junction. The case was seemingly proven – protection for Kentwood passengers would result in a loss of passengers and therefore a loss of revenue.

Complaints continued to reach the regional transport commissioner from the residents of the cluster of housing around Tilehurst Station and from the Vicar of Purley (whose parish was, in any case, beyond the borough boundary), expressing their concern about the loss of 'their' bus service to and from the Roebuck. At some unknown

Seen inbound at Kentwood terminus in autumn 1944, soon after the Kentwood extension opened, AEC 661T trolleybus 122 (ARD 685) has lost its cream lining-out on repaint. Note, too, the unmasked offside headlamp, provision of foglamp and destination blind showing 'Liverpool Rd.' The brick-built ARP post is also of note.

Late W. J. Haynes
© Maiwand Photographic Archive

date, presumably following the October 1944 Transport Committee meeting, a Pond House – Roebuck motorbus service was re-introduced, running only in the early morning and in the evening, specifically for war workers and to test its viability. The service was reviewed at the Transport Committee meeting on 15th February 1945, when it was shown that fares receipts were low, resulting in it being withdrawn on 16th April 1945.

Throughout the summer of 1944 intense military activity continued throughout southern England, as the invasion forces were supplied and reinforced. Military vehicles were on the move across the land. In Reading, a tank collided with a trolleybus traction pole in Wokingham Road in 1944, and on 20th January 1945, bus 47 was damaged in an accident with an army lorry.

Much blood was spilt and many lives lost in fighting fierce battles across Normandy but, happily, it resulted in an Allied breakout into the rest of France and the victorious liberation of Paris on 25th August 1944. By September 1944, most of France was free and the theatre of war moved towards Germany. Those three months had been decisive and it is interesting to note that, on the Home Front, vast amounts of expensive home defence infrastructure were already being dismantled with amazing haste. So soon after D-Day, there was no shadow of doubt as to the eventual outcome of this long-fought war. The loss to Germany of its U-boat bases in France ended much of the threat to Britain's Atlantic supply routes. The tide of war had now turned decisively in favour of Great Britain and her Allies.

At the depot, the new workshops alongside the trolley vehicle garage, in the old power station area, had been commissioned in April 1944, which, in turn, released some space in Middle Garage and East Garage. In September 1944 it was decided to spend £220 so that the overhead department, their vehicles and equipment, could be moved from the body shop to their own newly-created partitioned area of the former carpenters' shop, between Middle Garage and East Garage.

By early 1945, when we believe these pictures to have been taken, utility Guy Arab 6 (BRD 754), seen here at the Grovelands Road terminus of route M, was just over two years old and definitely worthy of comparison with the view on page 78 taken when the bus was new. There is no cream lining-out, so it has evidently received a repaint already – and the lower cream band extends across the dash panel to the radiator. The rear upper-deck emergency door is now glazed; the cab door has had its glazing modified; there are changes to the layout of the opening windows on the upper deck; and the offside head-lamp mask has been removed, together, presumably, with the offside headlamp bulb. So why is it sitting at Grovelands Road terminus advertising that it is going to Donkin Hill? Quite possibly the driver accidentally turned the handle the right number of turns – but in the wrong direction! And please do appreciate the pre-war type of bus stop flag in the upper view, which has made a welcome re-appearance.

Late W. J. Haynes © Millane Publishing

Also in September 1944, consideration was given by the Transport Committee to a plea from a Lower Caversham resident to provide a link between residential Lower Caversham and the shopping area of Caversham (referred to in those days as 'the village') – but it was still inopportune to contemplate such a service at that time.

On 15th November 1944, a meeting of the National Joint Industrial Council resolved that buses and trolleybuses should be run *"on the day on which hostilities with Germany cease"*. The transport manager was, however, concerned that, at the end of the First World War, the high spirits of street crowds in Reading (as elsewhere) had caused some damage to the tramcars and that *"...for some time the Tramways Department were short of vehicles, whilst the tramcars were being repaired"*. It seems that 'lager louts' (or, at least, their loutish 'light-and-bitter' ancestors) were nothing new, and Mr Calder gave notice that he would not hesitate to withdraw all vehicles from service if necessary!

Meanwhile, of course, the war had been going well for the Allies. True, there had been a German counter-attack, which had been repulsed at the 'Battle of the Bulge'; and the onslaught of V1 flying bombs, mainly on London and south-east England, had caused much fear on the Home Front. This was followed by the Allied failure at Arnhem and the launching by Germany of V2 rockets, mainly against London. Nonetheless, Allied forces were at the German border soon afterwards and the Soviets reached Prussia. Victory was at last coming into sight. On the Home Front some most welcome news had been a promised relaxation of blackout regulations, under which a certain amount of street lighting would be permitted, although all lights were still required to be shielded from above. Note again the confidence that existed, only three months after D-Day, even though the war in Europe turned out still to have eight more months to run.

Under these 'relaxed' regulations, some of the first of Reading's street lights were restored at 7.45pm on the night of Sunday 17th September 1944, with the ending of Double Summer Time, when clock-controlled gas lamps were lit in Forbury Road, Cheapside, Blagrave Street, and some streets off Oxford Road. At the same time Home Guard recruitment ceased, the Home Guard itself being finally 'stood down' on 14th November 1944, with a final parade taking place in Reading on Sunday 3rd December 1944. At the same time, too, fire watching was largely eliminated.

Until the conversion of the 'main line' tram route to trolleybuses in 1939 there had been very little electric street lighting in the town. It was now intended to equip important cross-roads and road junctions with electric light once fittings which complied with the new regulations had been delivered. The first electric street lighting to return was on the Caversham approach to Reading Bridge – which happened to be directly above the council's street lighting depot! Despite the relaxations, however, in Reading full street lighting was still some way off, as new fittings had to be obtained and old fittings adapted. In the town centre, the new fittings were often box-shaped lamps, known as Watford lamps, usually attached to trolleybus traction poles. For many years the illumination of Reading's main streets and arteries came to be by distinctive mercury vapour lamps, whose eerie blue-white light eventually gave way to the yellow sodium vapour lamps we know today. This was partly because the latter proved cheaper to run, and partly because their illumination was softer and lacked the deep shadows cast by mercury vapour lamps – a big improvement to safety as traffic increased so dramatically.

In connection with blackout relaxation, vehicle side-lamps needed simply to be covered by a sheet of tissue paper to diffuse the light. Soon, however, from January 1945 (i.e. still well before the war ended), all remaining side and tail lamp restrictions were abolished. Advance notice was also given that, from 29th March 1945, rear registration number plates would have to be illuminated again, just as they had been in peacetime. Although the necessary work was put in hand, such was the extent of the national task that the date was deferred to 30th June 1945. Wartime austerity vehicles, not built with the facility, had to have a number plate fabricated in the rear external wall of the vehicle. The rear registration number on utility buses and trolleybuses was usually painted in the top nearside corner on the inside of the rear platform window glass (or sometimes on the rear nearside bulkhead window glass) where, in blackout conditions, it was hoped that a very dim glimmer of light would shine through from the saloon in order to give the vehicle an identity.

In December 1944, as the end of the war in Europe approached, the Home Guard was 'stood down'. Transport Manager Jimmy Calder, very shortly to retire himself, is seen here with members of the Reading Corporation Transport platoon, 'X' Detachment 7th Berks Home Guard.

Print from J. R. Whitehead's collection

London Street Miscellany 2

In late 1944/early 1945, as he did two years previously (see pages 66/67), Bill Haynes chose London Street to record a succession of motorbuses a few weeks prior to the end of the war in Europe. Headlamp restrictions have been modified, with only the nearside headlamp needing to be masked, although that on the offside needs to be completely inoperative for the time being. Note the cast iron water main in the gutter for charging static water tanks as an air raid precaution. Note also how full the buses are!

Top Left: Reading's Leyland Titans had still to put in a few more years' work before they were replaced. Bus 44 (RD 2944) of 1931, bound for Merry Maidens, isn't stopping at Emerson & Chanin's dairy. Still lined-out, it has lost its radiator grille, exposing the fairly delicate cooling fins.

Left: AEC Regent 8, bound for Callington Road and not stopping at Emerson & Chanin's dairy either, was the undertaking's first to be fitted with an oil engine. It was also fitted with the very first Park Royal 'all metal' body.

Lower Left: AEC Regent 11 (RD 7125), bound for Merry Maidens and still looking quite tidy, isn't going to stop outbound at the top of the hill

Bottom Left: Not stopping is metal-bodied AEC Regent 47 (RD 7127), bound for Merry Maidens, looking fairly tidy whilst passing Miss Spencer's drapery shop (still with anti-blast sticky tape on the shop windows).

Below: This time bound for Wood Lane Junc. (Lower Whitley in peacetime), AEC Regent 22 (ARD 13), of 1938 vintage, has already gained a 'short' pre-1938 radiator (and a gouged panel!).

All photos Late W. J. Haynes © Millane Publishing

Seen heavily loaded southbound on Route F (Uplands Road – Merry Maidens) outside the Great Western Railway station circa early 1945 is petrol-engined bus 4 (RD 4337), the undertaking's very first AEC Regent, new in 1933

Late W. J. Haynes © Millane Publishing

Headlight restrictions were not relaxed until they were abolished completely on 27th December 1944, although photographic evidence indicates that the undertaking's vehicles ran for a while, presumably the period 1st September to 27th December 1944, with the offside head-lamp masks removed but the nearside masks in position. All remaining vehicle blackout lighting restrictions were finally removed with effect from 5th May 1945.

There then appears to have been a period when certain of the undertaking's motorbuses were in operation with only an offside headlamp fitted. Indeed, the undertaking's first batch of motorbuses to enter service after the war, early in 1947, were not fitted originally with a nearside headlamp. The 20mph maximum speed limit after dark continued until 26th September 1945. One might speculate that at that time, with the undertaking's buses restricted to an urban area, there was no need for twin headlamps in order to give a 'high beam', for in those far-off days, and, indeed, right up until the late 1960s, headlamps on buses and lorries were 'dipped' by extinguishing the offside headlamp.

During the closing months of the war in Europe, the slow progress towards normal life produced increasing demands for improved bus services. Rubber and fuel supplies were still restricted (although petrol became available for sale to the public – albeit rationed – from 1st November 1944) and shortage of staff (and sometimes vehicles) made improvements difficult. Despite these difficulties, the Ministry of War Transport was anxious that bus services were improved and the regional transport commissioner asked bus operators for information about possible service improvements under five headings:

a) strengthening of peak hour services
b) strengthening of off-peak services
c) strengthening of services on Saturdays and Sunday afternoons and evenings
d) later services in the evening
e) reinstatement of Sunday morning services

It was made clear that, while the regional transport commissioner was not in favour, just yet, of restoring Sunday morning services, an increase in the fuel allowance of around 5% was likely. At another conference held in the County Court building, in Reading, bus operators gathered from across the Southern Region to discuss the issues. Mr Calder was in favour of later evening services as a priority.

In Reading, during the weekday evening peak, at the cost of three additional bus crews, duplicate journeys were suggested on route F between Broad Street and Merry Maidens, between 4.30pm and 7.30pm. Additional school specials were also proposed. In the 'off peak' it was suggested that route K (Woodcote Road – Friar Street (GPO)) should operate all day, from 7.30am to 8.30pm, instead of only during the morning, noon and evening peaks. Although this would require an additional crew, it would help strengthen the service in Caversham up to Highmoor Road and relieve the congestion on route F for passengers bound for Uplands Road. On Saturdays, four additional motorbuses were proposed as football and stadium specials, to augment the trolleybus services. From Monday 6th November 1944, therefore, route K (Woodcote Road – Friar Street (GPO)) was strengthened to operate throughout the day on Monday–Saturday, but there was still no Sunday service. None of the other foregoing suggestions were implemented at this time, but timings of last buses and trolleybuses from Broad Street on Mondays to Saturdays were improved, to depart at 10:00pm – an hour later than hitherto for motorbuses and half-an-hour later for trolley-buses.

In early December 1944, over a two week period, the undertaking's motorbuses were used to transport *"within the borough, evacuated mothers and children and escorts"*, who were returning to their homes in Kent. These evacuees were en route from the West Country and, over a number of evenings, were arriving in Reading by train at around 6.00pm, to stay overnight at schools in the town. On the morning following, they were returned to the station, to special trains taking them to their destination. This operation required between ten and twelve double-deck motorbuses each time. In fact the Reading area's evacuee children were not far behind. Many of them were home for Christmas.

On the operating front, bus stop lines on the road were approved on 6th December 1944, for the inward stop at Highmoor Road for both routes F and K.

In December 1944, with hopes for peace in Europe growing, there was increasing fuel availability and signs of an improvement in recruitment of staff of the right calibre. Partly as a result of a petition, the transport manager sought improvements to motorbus route L (Hemdean Road – Berkeley Avenue), which had continued to be operated only during the morning, noon and evening peaks, and also to route M (Erleigh Road – Grovelands Road). However, matters still had to be deferred until sufficient new staff were available.

Mr R. J. Fardell, the Transport Department's chief clerk, was at last 'allowed to retire' on 10th December 1944, having worked in the department since the electrification of the tramway, in 1903. He was originally supposed to have retired on 10th June 1941, his 65th birthday. The assistant chief clerk, 'Ernie' Warrell, and, indeed, several other staff

James McLennan Calder had been the undertaking's transport manager & engineer since 1920 and was largely responsible for developing the undertaking into a successful and a worthwhile asset to the borough. He also dealt with all manner of problems in keeping the wheels turning during the war, and finally retired in March 1945. He is seen here with some of the management, inspectors and senior drivers of the undertaking – key support staff, whose faces would have been very familiar to nearly everybody in the borough who used corporation transport.

Print from J. R. Whitehead's collection

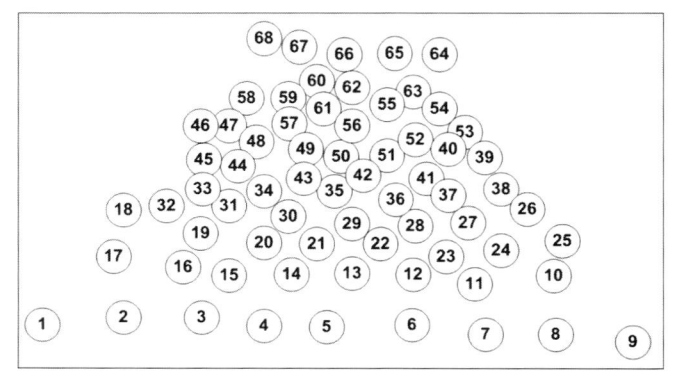

We enlisted the help of the late Edgar Jordan, whose dad was in the employ of the undertaking from 1906 through to retirement early in 1947, to put names to the faces in the above photograph. He managed 38 out of the 68 persons appearing in the photograph. We would certainly like to hear from any reader able to expand on this, or who can name the female staff on page 92, so that a permanent record can be maintained:

2 Don Courtnage (Union Rep)	26 Inspector Ernest Aldworth	45 Inspector Leonard Stone
3 T. Lewendon (Traffic Office)	29 Driver Bert Walker	46 Inspector Alfred Scearce
4 A. Gent (Deputy Manager)	32 Inspector William Jackson	47 Inspector Frederick Probyn
5 James McLennan Calder (Manager)	33 Inspector 'Tim' Jordan	50 Driver Bert Willoughby
6 William Benham (Cashier)	34 Driver Jack Rodgers	52 Driver Frederick Rogers
7 William Foster (Traffic Office)	(later Inspector)	53 Driver Walter Wells
8 Driver Richard Dowling*	35 Driver Ernest White	(later Inspector)
10 Driver J. E. McGuirk	36 Driver Jack Munday	54 Driver Bullpitt
11 Driver Phillips	(later Inspector)	56 Driver Edward Banks
12 Driver 'Midge' Cunningham	37 Driver Hawkins	57 Driver Walter Hinton
21 Driver Burroughs	38 Inspector Horace Walker	62 Driver de Gruchy
22 Driver Les Chandler	39 Inspector George Green	64 Driver Hensley
25 Inspector George Fuller	40 Driver Morrison	65 Driver Beet
42 Driver Les Batty	43 Driver Day	

*   'Dick' Dowling was formerly the driver of the departmental Foden steam wagon, M 9619.

90

in the same department (including one Ron Butler), had recently been 'called up', leaving it hopelessly under-staffed, so Mr Wilfred B. Hill was made up to acting chief clerk. Also, John Trustrum, assistant traffic superintendent, was going to be another loss of vast experience when he too retired in the following June on his 65th birthday.

Only war workers' special services were operated on Christmas Day 1944, which actually, turned out to be a white one – in full measure – so much so that corporation buses had to be 'taken off' on Boxing Night and late home-comers from parties, pictures and public houses were obliged to walk to their destinations. Once again, however, the undertaking suffered mass absenteeism in the run-up to and over the festive period. Between 22nd and 31st December 1944 there were between 50 and 80 staff absent per day, as a result of which 10 trolleybuses were unable to operate!

For the country at large the new year started with immense optimism that there was soon to be a new beginning. It was intensely cold, with snow, icy gales and up to 20 degrees of frost (and all in the middle of a coal shortage) – and the Thames froze over again at Caversham. However, it was recorded in the *Berkshire Chronicle* that *"In Reading the trolley 'bus and omnibus services have kept good schedule, and any slight curtailments that there may have been have been more due to an abnormal amount of illness amongst employees rather than the effect of the weather conditions"*.

On 15th February 1945, Mr Calder reported to the Transport Committee that the Municipal Passenger Transport Association had requested an indication of new trolley vehicle requirements to the end of 1946, for forwarding to the Ministry of War Transport. At a meeting at the ministry, Mr Calder learned from Col. Trench that none would be allocated for system expansion, only as replacement vehicles or to meet increases in demand on existing services. Mr Calder said that in Reading six vehicles would be required before the end of 1946, presumably to replace the 1936 vehicles. Once again, he said he was anxious that they should be to the same specification as the undertaking's 1939 AEC/Park Royal trolleybuses and, having had operating experience of six utility Sunbeam Ws, he was not willing to receive any more of them. After discussions with the ministry, the Transport Committee did not pursue the matter further – presumably because the standard utility vehicle was not acceptable to the department, yet nothing else was available. The requirement for low-height vehicles fitted with traction batteries, together with Mr Calder's insistence on the AEC/Park Royal/English Electric combination, once again delayed Reading's trolleybus fleet expansion and probably led to the trolleybus shortages which prompted the temporary withdrawal of trolleybus route C (Promenade – Whit Pump) in the austerity period of the late 1940s.

In March 1945, an urgently-required new Fordson 10cwt departmental van, BRD 957, suitable as a runabout for conveying conductresses and for longer journeys (e.g. to fetch urgent spares from AEC, at Southall), was delivered via Gowrings Ltd., at that time of London Road, Reading. Its purchase had been authorised in May 1944.

Mr Calder finally retired at the end of March 1945. On Tuesday 27th February 1945, he had addressed Reading Round Table on his forty years of service with the Transport Department in Reading – twenty-five of them as transport manager. Curiously, he was reported by the *Reading Standard* as commenting that he did not recommend trolleybuses in urban areas – surely a very unfortunate misquote!

In April 1945, his successor, another Scotsman, Mr William Morison Little, was appointed as transport manager. Reading, incidentally, also gained a new town clerk and a new chief constable at roundly the same time.

Unfortunately, after giving such long service to the town, Mr Calder was destined to have but a very brief retirement. He and his wife moved away, to Felpham, Bognor Regis. However, already in poor health, doubtless due to the extraordinary pressures under which he had had to work during the war, he fell ill again and died in a Reading nursing home on 30th November 1945, aged 68. His funeral, which took place at St. Laurence's Church, Reading, on Wednesday 5th December 1945, was extremely well attended and included, needless to say, a very large number of his former employees. What better tribute! More than half a century on, Reading has much to thank him for. He spent his life working for the town and in his time he gave the town's municipal transport undertaking a thoroughly sound foundation. Men rarely come like that any more.

On 23rd March 1945 the British Eighth Army, Montgomery's men, crossed the Rhine, following American forces in their drive towards Berlin. The war in Europe was at last coming to an end. Reading had been unscathed by them, but the last V2 rocket fell on Orpington, in Kent, on 27th March 1945 and the last V1 flying bomb was launched two days later. The menace of air attack on London and south-east England was at last at an end.

William Morison Little was only 35 years old when he took over the reins as transport manager & engineer in April 1945. He hailed from Edinburgh and after university he gained all of his transport training with Edinburgh Corporation Transport, becoming maintenance engineer in 1937. In 1941, at age 31, he took up the position of general manager & engineer with St. Helens Corporation Transport and was, at the time, the youngest general manager of a public transport undertaking in the country.

Print from J. R. Whitehead's Collection

Above: Sixty of the undertaking's wartime conductresses photographed with Jimmy Calder at his retirement in March 1945.

Print from J. R. Whitehead's collection

Bottom: Jubilation in Broad Street on VE Day. This scene, photographed from a first floor window of the Midland Bank (now HSBC) on the corner of Broad Street and Queen Victoria Street, shows elated soldiers and townsfolk milling about around a static water tank (for firefighting purposes) in the centre of Broad Street – indeed, some of them seem to be dancing the conga – while AEC Regent 46 (RD 7126) takes on passengers bound for Chalgrove Way. © Late H. G. Hands

10   Into Peace – and Austerity

War in Europe ended with a cease-fire on the evening of Monday 7th May 1945 and unconditional surrender by all German forces next morning. The end had, of course, been anticipated and plans laid some weeks beforehand as to how (and when) Victory was to be declared and celebrated, but when the time came it was all a bit of a muddle. There had been a wireless newsflash at 9.00pm that Monday evening and, with the news spreading like wildfire, most folk went to bed knowing more-or-less what to expect next day – except that they had not been told whether or not a public holiday had been declared or if they were expected to go to work as usual. In Reading, VE Day was actually heralded by scores of railway engine steam whistles reminiscent of New Year's Day in peacetime. Apparently, a thunderstorm broke at the same time, adding a touch of natural grandeur. Later, church bells were rung what seemed like incessantly and there were Services of Thanksgiving continually throughout the day, more-or-less hourly, or so it seemed, with thousands paying a visit to church to pray privately. Food shops opened for a brief two hours. Winston Churchill's radio broadcast to the nation was not made until 3.00pm, and in central Reading this was relayed to the public by loudspeaker from a specially-erected rostrum in front of the Queen Victoria statue outside the Town Hall: *"We may allow ourselves a brief period of rejoicing"*, he said – and, more famously – *"Advance, Britannia! Long live the cause of freedom! God save the King!"* At the same spot at 6.45pm, postponed because of the delayed Churchill speech, another large crowd gathered to hear the mayor, Alderman W. M. Newham, officially announce the end of hostilities, followed by a rendition of the National Anthem – although no band had been arranged – before heading the corporation in a procession into St. Laurence's Church for a Civic Service of Thanksgiving. Later, H. M. The King broadcast to the nation, and this was relayed to a floodlit Forbury Gardens, where dancing went on into the early hours to gramophone records amplified over a public address system. There were street bonfires all over the town, including one in Broad Street, and the merriment went on unabated. In the meantime and as planned, Reading Corporation Transport buses and trolleybuses operated a full service throughout the day.

Also as planned, the following day, Wednesday 9th May 1945, having been declared a public holiday, the undertaking operated services to a normal weekday timetable, commencing at 9.00am. This, too, had been planned, the Transport Department having posted window notices in all vehicles some days earlier announcing that on whichever day was proclaimed a public holiday, *"Omnibus and Trolleybus Services would commence at approximately 8.00am* [sic] *from the outer termini"*.

It was a day, generally, of street parties and merriment. Although flags and bunting had begun to appear the previous weekend (many of the Union flags, as usual, being flown 'wrong way up'), the decoration of municipal buildings was a long time coming and no-one seemed to have thought about floodlighting for the celebrations after dark.

On the following Sunday, 13th May 1945, known at the time as Thanksgiving Sunday, there was a victory parade through the town of service units, the erstwhile Home Guard and Civil Defence services and other organisations, commencing 2.50pm prompt from Kings Meadow Recreation Ground. It was routed via Vastern Road, Caversham Road, Chatham Street, Bedford Road, Oxford Road, Howard Street, Hosier Street, St. Mary's Butts, Broad Street, High Street and Market Place, passing the mayor's rostrum outside the Town Hall 40 minutes later. A remarkable list of detachments took part, taking half-an-hour to pass the saluting base, and thousands lined the route. It must have played havoc with the town's passenger transport services!

Just prior to an interdenominational Civic Thanksgiving service in Forbury Gardens at 8.00pm, led by the Bishop of Reading and with a Salvation Army band accompanying the hymn-singing, there happened to be a quite spectacular fly-past of hundreds of aircraft in formation. However, there was a municipal debacle over reserved seating, which spoilt the occasion for many of the general public who attended!

Over the following weeks there were innumerable VE parties. One was for the children of Reading Corporation Transport staff. On Thursday 24th May 1945, 250 of them were given tea and entertained – and went home with a shiny sixpence, a book, a novelty and a bag of cake! The following month, Reading Corporation Transport Athletic and Social Club revived a summer outing tradition, 200 members and their wives and children going on a river trip to Goring-on-Thames on Friday 29th June 1945 and a similar number a week later.

There was more jollification on 'VE2 Day', a day deemed by the government to be a public holiday but left to individual local authorities to decide which particular

---

READING CORPORATION TRANSPORT.

VE DAY ANNOUNCEMENT

As the day following the above announcement will be a public holiday, **OMNIBUS** and **TROLLEYBUS SERVICES** will operate as on a Bank Holiday, commencing at approximately 8 a.m. from the outer termini.

Corporation Transport Offices,
Mill Lane,
Reading.

W. M. LITTLE,
B.Sc., Assoc.M.Inst.C.E.
Transport Manager and Engineer.

Parasin The Printers, Ltd., Reading

Summer 1945; the war is over. Leyland Titan 3 (RD 3676) is at rest for the afternoon, out on the cobbles in Mill Lane, showing off well the lines of her Leyland bodywork. She's proper worn out, with faded lined out livery, and even has white paint still applied to the rear half of her rear wings. But she still has to work three more summers, poor thing! Evidently on light duties – witness the bald offside front tyre, and the missing radiator grille exposing the delicate bank of cooling fins. Both headlamp masks have gone.

Bus 3 was the last Titan to be purchased. As a 'one-off' it differed in minor ways to those which preceded it. The front destination indicator in the canopy fairing and the projecting box in the centre cream band at the rear were specific distinguishing features.

The Titan era lasted in Reading for around 20 years, their lives having been extended due to the war and the short supply of new vehicles in its aftermath.

Centre:© Late W. J. Haynes
Top & Bottom: Late W. J. Haynes © Millane Publishing

> **READING CORPORATION TRANSPORT.**
>
> ## LOCAL HOLIDAY—
> ## Monday, 25th June, 1945
>
> Normal Monday Motorbus and Trolleybus Services will operate on this day.
>
> ## LATER MOTORBUSES AND TROLLEYBUSES
>
> Commencing Monday, 25th June, 1945, and until further notice, weekday services will be extended, and **LAST MOTORBUSES and TROLLEYBUSES** will leave the town centre at **11.0 p.m.** for the termini of main routes. Services will terminate on Sundays at **9.30 p.m.** as at present.
>
> Corporation Transport Offices,　　　**W. M. LITTLE,**
> Mill Lane, Reading.　　　B.Sc., Assoc.M.Inst.C.E.,
> 　　　Transport Manager & Engineer.

day suited their area. In Reading, Monday 25th June 1945 was adopted. The weather turned out to be pleasantly fine and hot. An attractive programme of events was devised, centred on Palmer Park and opened by the mayor at 2.20pm. It was preceded by a parade of decorated vehicles, which assembled in Kings Meadow, moving off at 1.30pm by way of Vastern Road, Caversham Road, West Street, Broad Street, Kings Road and London Road, to Palmer Park. Once again, one can reflect on the disruption this had to passenger transport services. The local papers reported that not one motor vehicle was entered – presumably on account of petrol shortages; horse-drawn vehicles and bicycles were used instead!

One group of people, who had been in Reading throughout the war, nevertheless missed all this excitement. 212 evacuee children (and 20 parents and old people) were collected from assembly points within the borough by seven corporation buses and returned to their homes in London from the Southern Railway's Reading station on Wednesday 20th June 1945. This still left 900 evacuees still in the town – some of whom had no homes to return to...

On 1st May 1945, shortly before the end of the war in Europe, all remaining ARP members were given a month's notice. Ever since the previous September, only three months after D-Day, there had been a steady flow of government instructions for a progressive run-down of all those sections of the Home Defence and Civil Defence organisation no longer required. It culminated nationally on Sunday 17th June 1945 with a Civil Defence 'Farewell Parade', held in Hyde Park, London, before H. M. The King. In fact there were many organisations, established purely on account of the war, which were now 'stood down'. The part-time personnel of the National Fire Service in the those counties comprising the southern region were 'stood down' during a parade in Hill's Meadow, Reading, on Saturday 18th August 1945.

The wartime coalition government, its function now achieved, 'stood down' too, an interim caretaker government led by Winston Churchill taking over until a general election could be organised and held. This took place on 5th July 1945, but final results were not known for nearly three weeks as members of H. M. Forces serving at the farthest ends of the Earth had a right to vote. Contrary to expectations, Churchill and the National Party were rejected in favour of a Labour government under the leadership of Clement Attlee, with a declared policy of establishing a 'welfare state' and of nationalising gas, electricity, steel, coal, railways, road haulage, ports and civil aviation. It had a singularly unenviable task ahead of it. A country almost bankrupted under the pressures of six years of war urgently needed to manufacture to export in order to pay its debts. To do this, the country's own people were going to have to 'do without', having already 'done without' for so long. There were shortages of most commodities for other reasons, too, and there were other serious problems to overcome. At a local level, the electorate in Reading, communists amongst them, rejected having Councillor William McIlroy, the Conservative candidate, as their MP, in favour of a vociferous socialist from the south coast, Ian Mikardo by name.

The Pacific War ended with the surrender of Japan on Tuesday 14th August 1945, the very day on which the new Parliament was opened. There was an even greater foul-up in pronouncing the Second World War at an end than there had been at VE Day! Mr Atlee made his announcement at midnight when, in those days, all good people had retired to bed. Many therefore went to work next morning as usual, only to find their firms closed in celebration of VJ Day! Once again, food shops opened for only a couple of hours or so. There was something of a scramble by housewives, all with empty larders since the preceding weekend, who were obliged to join food queues, some even before the shops opened. Fortunately, Reading was without the queue violence suffered in other towns and cities in Britain! Again, there were victory celebrations (mostly street parties), although there was no civic recognition in Reading until the evening. However, on Sunday afternoon, 19th August 1945, the mayor and corporation went in civic state to Forbury Gardens for an open-air Service of Thanksgiving.

A nation which had lived with 'make-do-and-mend' through nearly six years of war now began planning a post-war rebuilding programme, for as well as repairing war damage, much of the nation's infrastructure itself was worn out and dilapidated through delays, shortages and lack of maintenance created by war and needed replacement.

With peace, too, came new hope from everyone for a better future. But, despite this, shortages of more-or-less everything remained severe. Rationing continued, and there were longer-than-ever food queues. In essence, merchant shipping was needed to return the armed forces and their equipment to Britain for demobilisation. The American food that Britain had been receiving had, as a matter of urgency, to be diverted to feed the starving millions in the war-torn former Axis-conquered countries of the world.

Civilian life did, however, become more relaxed. As well as the journey to and from school or work, there was increased demand for travel to entertainment and leisure facilities, for people had more spare time than many could remember for a long while; evening entertainment outside the home was particularly enjoyed. In those balmy days, when private cars were all but unavailable to the ordinary person and television was still in its infancy, leisure use of public transport put great pressure on all Britain's transport undertakings. This applied particularly in the evenings and on Saturdays, as people visited football and greyhound stadiums, speedway and other sports grounds, theatres and cinemas and dance halls to enjoy their new-found freedom. What is rather surprising, bearing in mind the huge use put to public transport in Reading during the war and in the years immediately following, is that no attempt was made to provide any queue barriers at town centre stops (as in some other towns and cities), either for protecting waiting passengers from oncoming traffic or for segregating queues waiting for buses on different routes.

Towards the end of June 1945, even before the war against Japan had been concluded, a start was made to 'de-mob' conscripted members of the armed forces, with the promise that one million of them would be back in 'civvy street' by December 1945. Some 162 members of the Reading Corporation Transport staff had joined the armed forces during the war, five of whom had lost their lives. A million civilian workers would also by then have been released from munitions manufacture. Stockpiles of all manner of military plant and equipment had to be dispersed to secure storage, while land and property which had been commandeered (and which was costing the taxpayer money) had to be released.

Men (and women) being 'de-mobbed' with all due speed had to find themselves not only employment but also somewhere to live. Six years of war meant six years of housing not built to replace both slums and war losses, or, indeed, to provide family homes for a backlog of six years of marriages. Huge numbers of refugees also made their home in Britain. Housing never could be built at the flick of a finger, of course, but the problem was now exacerbated by the fact that the materials to build them were on ration. There was also no immediate source of skilled labour to make the components, let alone build the houses themselves. Indeed, for a wartime-married couple, if one or other set of parents were unable to give them a room, matters were very serious. Therefore it should have come as no real surprise that as hutted army camps closed, squatters took them over. Such was their desperation for somewhere to call home that they fought tooth-and-nail to avoid eviction and prevent demolition, even if their accommodation was damp, dirty, unsanitary, or anything else. One of the first to close within the borough and attract squatters was Ranikhet Camp, in Tilehurst; others were situated in the vicinity of Hartland Road and Basingstoke Road in Whitley, one of which had served for a time as a prisoner-of-war camp. At least one corporation bus conductor was a squatter, whose first married home was in an underground air-raid shelter in one of Reading's parks.

By mid-July 1945, a start had been made on the groundworks at several sites within the borough for the erection of 200 'pre-fabs' – the name by which factory-prefabricated bungalows came to be known – in Whitley Wood Road and Shirley Avenue (Whitley Wood), Barnsdale Road and Windermere Road (off Northcourt Avenue), Green Road and Bulmershe Road (Oliver Dixon's Field), and Grove Road (Emmer Green). There were, at that time, advanced plans for building 600 permanent homes on the Whitley Estate and tentative plans for 600 council houses on a site on Bath Road opposite Prospect Park – eventually to become the Southcote Estate.

The capitulation of Japan had, of course, been very sudden, with the dropping of two atomic bombs. The return to peace, and the consequent cessation of Lend-Lease, by which Britain was supplied by Canada and the United States of America, was a sudden jolt, putting the United Kingdom into a very serious financial position. Having to pay-on-the-nail for imports meant that items which were pure extravagance could no longer be afforded. The United Kingdom was a debtor to the world. The way forward was to export in order to pay for imports. That meant limiting both imported and home-produced goods to the consumer, resulting in commodities being in short supply and rationing continuing for a few years to come. In the shadow of final victory to the Allies, the austerity era had arrived for this particular ally.

Factories were released for peacetime production, and government control of labour was phased out. Transport undertakings were released from the control of the Essential Work Orders on 15th May 1946. Slowly but surely everything would eventually get back to normal...!

Compulsory use of blackout curtains had been eased even before the war in Europe had concluded, and blacking out of windows, etc., ended completely on 23rd April 1945 (except along the coast), together with full lighting being permitted in trains and buses.

Having endeavoured to paint as true a picture as possible of what life was like in Reading and, indeed, in Britain, in those first weeks and months following a return to peace, the fortunes of the town's municipal transport undertaking over the same period can now be related in a more fitting context.

READING CORPORATION TRANSPORT.

SUNDAY MORNING WORKMEN'S MOTOR-BUS SERVICES.

DEPARTURE TIMES.

Revised Time-Table commencing SUNDAY, 12th AUGUST, 1945.

LEAVE		a.m.	a.m.	a.m.	a.m.	a.m.	a.m.	a.m.
✯Wood Lane Junction	(for Broad Street)	5 40	6 15	6 55	7 30	8 10	8 50	9 30
✯Whitley Estate (Callington Road)	(for Broad Street)	5 45	6 20	7 0	7 35	8 15	8 55	9 35
Donkin Hill	(for Broad Street)					8 5	8 35	
Chalgrove Way	(for Broad Street)				7 30			9 15

LEAVE		a.m.	a.m.	a.m.	a.m.	a.m.	a.m.
✯Broad Street	(for Wood Lane Junction via Whitley Estate)	6 0	6 35	7 15	7 50	8 30	9 10
Broad Street	(for Donkin Hill)				7 45	8 20	
Broad Street	(for Chalgrove Way)			7 15			9 0

✯WOOD LANE JUNCTION AND WHITLEY ESTATE ROUTE.

Buses will proceed inward from Wood Lane Junction via Basingstoke Road, Hartland Road into Whitley Estate, Northumberland Avenue, Buckland Road, Basingstoke Road, Southampton Street, St. Mary's Butts to Broad Street.

Buses will proceed outward from Broad Street via London Street, Basingstoke Road, Buckland Road, Northumberland Avenue, Hartland Road, thence to Wood Lane Junction.

W. M. LITTLE, B.Sc., Assoc.M.Inst.C.E.
Transport Manager and Engineer.

NOTE.—The above are temporary Bus Services, subject to alteration or withdrawal at short notice.

Parnells The Printers, Ltd., Reading.

Above: *Keeping the wheels turning, circa summer 1945 – AEC trolleybus 123 (ARD 686 – identified from the removable towing panel propped against the end wall of the low-level working area) and AEC Regent motorbus 46 (RD 7126) over the pits – to the right of the main depot entrance – for a 'heavy dock'. The motorbus has had its engine and gearbox removed and both units are receiving separate attention.*

© Reading Museum Service (Reading Borough Council); all rights reserved

Below: *A scene in the crew canteen at Mill Lane depot sometime in 1945. A conductress is evidently being distracted whilst trying to 'cash up' having worked duty BB – vehicle B on trolleybus route B (at that time Three Tuns – Norcot Junc.). From surviving paperwork to hand, duty BB commenced by departing eastbound from Broad Street at 06:49. Bus crews have their own particular brand of good-natured banter and the general atmosphere captured in this view is rather typical! Note the very serious young Parcels Express lad enjoying a bun on the left.*

© Reading Museum Service (Reading Borough Council); all rights reserved

Above: Tram rail being lifted from Oxford Road, near Brock Barracks, in late February 1946 by Fitzpatrick & Son. It is interesting to note the state of the carriageway after six years of war – disintegrating cobbles and tarmac etc. – and the complete absence of barrier rails, red lamps, warning signs and so on, between traffic and road works. AEC trolleybus 128 (ARD 691) negotiates the uneven surface at a fairly wide deviation from the overhead line as it proceeds towards Norcot Junc. and thence Bear Inn.

© Reading Museum Service (Reading Borough Council); all rights reserved

Below: 1937-vintage AEC Regent 56 (ADP 5) southbound in St. Mary's Butts on route M, ready to turn right at the traffic lights into Castle Street, en route to Grovelands Road. It is a sunny day in spring 1946, a year before cobbles and tram rail are lifted from St. Mary's Butts and new destination blinds are fitted using the post-war choice of names for terminal points. Note, particularly, that the bus still has white paint applied to the rear half of its rear wings for blackout purposes!

Late W. J. Haynes © Millane Publishing

11   The Little Year (and a bit!)

In April 1945, motorbus route F (Uplands Road – Merry Maidens) was causing some concern, and there was a request from staff to loosen running times to allow for longer layover time, thus presenting an opportunity to make up time. The new transport manager, Mr Little, responded, saying that although schedules were tight, overloading was slowing the service, which, in turn required more time to load and unload. He agreed that an increased service allocation would help relieve pressure and commented that *"...in order to cope with peak traffic, we are already duplicating to the extent that we have as many relief buses as service buses"*.

A proposal that conductors could be trained as drivers was difficult to implement because fuel was neither allocated nor allowed for tuition duties. Essentially, training runs had to be achieved out of small fuel surpluses resulting from vehicle juggling to gain some fuel consumption advantage, or by lost service journeys.

A departmental memo dated as late as 11th April 1945 gave the schedule speed for normal running as 9.78mph, and for blackout slow running as 7.8mph. In Reading, there was a particular saga over a return to full street lighting. Sunday 15th July 1945 marked the end of Double Summer Time for 1945, the country returning to British Summer Time (although Double Summer Time was to return in summer 1947 to facilitate the staggering of factory working hours). The above date is significant, however, because it was also supposed to see the re-introduction in Reading of full street lighting – but this did not happen! Even 'dim-out' (the very limited street lighting, which had replaced the wartime complete blackout) was replaced – with complete blackout again! The Highways Committee was to blame, for it had decided, at its meeting the previous Friday, to be patriotic and respond to a government request to save fuel (rather than money), as a result of which the street lights would stay out until 1st September 1945. There was an outcry, not least from the town's busmen and the town council, at its meeting on 6th August 1945, overturned the Highways Committee's economy measure with immediate effect. Full all-night street lighting went on the following night, Wednesday 7th August 1945. A month later, on Tuesday 4th September 1945, the town council overturned a subsequent Highways Committee decision (brought about as a result of a Ministry of Fuel & Power plea to save fuel to help alleviate shortages in the coming winter), that street lighting should be extinguished at midnight.

In cold and snowy conditions, the Great Western Railway carried out major maintenance work to the railway bridges in Caversham Road on Saturday and Sunday, 28th and 29th April 1945, which required the roadway underneath to be closed for part of the weekend. Early in 1939, work had been carried out (at the undertaking's expense), to lower the roadway under these bridges in order to provide adequate headroom for the operation of tramway-replacement 'highbridge' trolleybuses on route C (Promenade – Whit-Pump). It seems, however, that the provision of 'troughing' for the overhead and the slewing of the overhead line was never carried out at that time and, with the other events of 1939 preoccupying thoughts, nothing had been done. There are certainly very few recorded instances of 1939 AEC trolleybuses ever being used on route C up to this time. A surviving departmental drawing shows that in April 1945, while the GWR was carrying out its work, there were certainly intended to be some changes, involving troughing and overhead suspension under the bridges, and it specifically shows new headroom clearances relating to the utility trolleybuses, which were higher than the AECs, so it is likely that in connection with the bridge closure there was also some preliminary work to further reduce the road level. However, the alterations themselves are more likely to have been carried out in June 1946, as mentioned on page 111. Utility trolleybuses never seem to have been used on route C up to this time either, and no photographs are known to exist to prove otherwise.

On the Saturday, there was a need for the current to be off under the bridges, effectively cutting the trolleybus service in two. Trolleybuses operated until 1.30pm, when a single motorbus operated a shuttle service between Stanshawe Road and Promenade. At first, as a trolleybus arrived on route C from Whit-Pump, it was turned by pulling across Caversham Road and reversing on battery into Stanshawe Road. Thereafter, trolleybuses were gradually 'changed off' at Whit-Pump terminus, until a full motorbus service was in place using five Leyland Titans (numbers 1, 38, 39, 42 and 44) and through-running under the bridges was established. On the Sunday, Caversham Road under the railway bridges

Scene at Kentwood with AEC trolleybuses 113 (ARD 676) and 120 (ARD 683), circa spring 1946, after the introduction in October/November 1945 of a 6½-minute service operated as route B (Kentwood – Three Tuns) instead of the original 10-minute service (Kentwood – Liverpool Road) – but before introduction of new terminal names in April 1947. Note also the black and white terminal bus stop post

Print from Late H. E. Jordan's collection

was closed to all traffic and route C was operated by motorbuses diverted via Stations and Vastern Road. Motorbus route F, to and from Uplands Road, was similarly diverted via Vastern Road. This motorbus substitution, together with the diversion, meant that an additional 675 miles was run over the weekend, thus using more of the undertaking's precious fuel allocation.

The annual report for the financial year ended 31st March 1945, published in May 1945, was again in the statistical form the undertaking was obliged to use during the war. After all, although the war with Germany might almost have concluded, there was still a war being fought against Japan. The town's trolleybuses had carried 24,608,854 passengers (an increase of 1,908,406 over the previous year) and ran 1,341,841 miles (an increase of 89,227 miles over the previous year), making a net profit of £60,978 compared with £42,940 the previous year. The motorbuses made a net profit of £29,455 compared with £31,999 the previous year, carrying 16,776,177 passengers (an increase of 351,852 over the previous year) and, at 1,270,907 miles, ran 40,137 more miles. At 55,993, Parcels Express carried 9,880 fewer parcels than the preceding year but reduced a trading loss of £222 during the previous year to one of £156, mainly on account of a full year having been worked at the increased charges introduced on 1st November 1943. Based on the foregoing, the net profit on the undertaking taken as a whole was therefore roundly £90,250, compared with roundly £74,750 in the financial year 1943/44, which reflected the first full year's effect of the addition to the fleet of all the utility vehicles and the opening of the Kentwood trolleybus extension, together with the more recent relaxation of controls permitting later running.

There was a gradual easing of restrictions on everything which had been in short supply or on ration to the civilian population. Fuel oil and petrol restrictions were eased slowly, with a basic petrol ration being introduced for private motorists from 1st June 1945 which, for example, allowed the transport manager's car to be 'restored'. Petrol was not completely free of rationing until May 1950. For motorbus operators, increased fuel supplies meant that services could be improved – but within the parameters of an increase in mileage which did not exceed 10%. In Reading, with effect from Monday 25th June 1945 (which was also the day deemed by the council to be the local 'VE2 Day' public holiday), last buses from the town centre, as well as trolleybuses, were restored to leave at 11.00pm instead of 10.00pm on Mondays to Saturdays. They departed each night on the blast of the duty inspector's Acme 'Thunderer' pea-whistle – a legacy from early in tramway days and a ritual which was carried on for almost the next half-century. It was impossible at this stage to improve Sunday services.

As already mentioned, Double Summer Time ended on Sunday 15th July 1945, reverting to British Summer Time (i.e. one hour ahead of Greenwich Mean Time), at which it had always remained for the winter months for most of the war. British Summer Time itself ended (for 1945) on Sunday 7th October 1945, reverting to GMT for the first time since 25th February 1940.

Lt. Col. J. F. Fardell's return from war service was delayed by seven weeks; he resumed his duties as deputy transport manager from 22nd October 1945, although word got out almost immediately that he was seeking a position elsewhere. Meanwhile, Mr Trustrum, assistant traffic superintendent, retired during June 1945 and Mr H. V. Lane, the traffic superintendent, who was due to retire on 31st July 1945, agreed to stay on for an extra month to help facilitate a re-organisation of the undertaking's crumbling management structure. On 20th November 1945, Mr Fardell reaffirmed his intention to stay with the undertaking as deputy manager, as a result of which Mr Gent, who had 'acted up' in Mr Fardell's position during the latter's wartime absence, became traffic superintendent as a matter of some urgency, from 3rd December 1945. In April 1946, when it had already become most essential to do so, the appointments of a new assistant traffic superintendent and of a chief inspector were hampered. Because of a delay in being 'de-mobbed', several experienced members of staff who might have been considered were still in the armed forces. In his new position, Mr Gent was inexperienced in knowing the abilities of existing staff sufficiently for selection as candidates; and it was morally incorrect, under such circumstances, to advertise the posts outside the undertaking.

At its meeting of 14th June 1945, the Transport Committee had requested the transport manager to *"bring into effect such improvements in the services as could be made from time-to-time as the staff position allowed"*. As a result and following agreement at the Transport Committee meeting of 11th October 1945, the trolleybus services on the 'main line' were re-arranged and strengthened with effect from a still so far unrecorded date in late October/early November 1945:

Wartime arrangements:

Route	Description	Av. Frequency
A	Three Tuns – Bear Inn	6½ minutes
B	Three Tuns – Norcot Junction	6½ minutes
D	Liverpool Road – Kentwood	10 minutes

Revised arrangements:

Route	Description	Av. Frequency
A	Three Tuns – Bear Inn	6½ minutes
B	Three Tuns – Kentwood	6½ minutes
D	Liverpool Road – Norcot Junction	10 minutes

It will be seen that this allowed for an alternate service from the Three Tuns to Kentwood or the Bear Inn, and also increased the frequency of the service to Kentwood to 6½ minutes rather than 10 minutes. At the same time, the service beyond Norcot Junction up to the Bear Inn retained its 6½-minute headway and that beyond Cemetery Junction to Liverpool Road maintained its 10-minute headway. On Sunday evenings, last trolleybus journeys left Broad Street at 10.30pm rather than 10.00pm as hitherto. On Sundays, too, route D operated as Liverpool Road – Kentwood and there was no service operated as Three Tuns – Kentwood.

The south of England experienced a prolonged fog on 20th–22nd October 1945 but, while bus and rail public transport was seriously disrupted elsewhere, the local papers reported that Reading Corporation Transport ran its services to schedule. However, there was disruption to the town's trolleybus system on Tuesday 23rd October 1945, for at around 10.00am there was a 'flash-over' on the high-tension switchboard at the Reading Electricity Works, causing a widespread 90-minute power cut. Traffic lights failed, factories were without power and offices were without lighting. More to the point, trolleybus services had to be suspended, *"a fact which caused great inconvenience to women shoppers and others"*, according to one local paper. That somewhat contemporary word 'tiresome' also springs to mind!

Cemetery Junction, with AEC trolleybuses, cobbles, tarred in tram track and police box controlled traffic lights. Of interest is the notice between London Road and Kings Road advising town centre traffic diversions during extensive tram rail removal and road reconstruction, dating the photograph to early summer 1946. The double electric Watford street lamp is also worthy of note!
Commercial picture postcard

At the last Transport Committee meeting of 1945, on 20th December, the transport manager proposed that motorbus route K (Woodcote Road – Friar Street) and route L (Hemdean Road – Berkeley Avenue) should be combined. Both were still part-day routes following wartime curtailments and Mr Little proposed that the new route should operate along the line of route L, from Berkeley Avenue to Hemdean Road, then via Oakley Road, Kidmore Road and Highmoor Road, and thence down the existing line of route K to Woodcote Road terminus. By this proposal, he considered, new links to Caversham Primary School would be made available to children living on Caversham Heights. At the same time, he pointed out that the existing routing through Katesgrove Lane would be unsuitable for double-deck operation, suggesting a diversion via Southampton Street and Pell Street. If the proposal was adopted, the existing allocation of one double-deck bus on route K and two single-deckers on route L would be replaced by only two double-deckers, following delivery of the new buses on order, thus saving the cost of one crew. The one single-deck journey on route K, which ran during the morning rush hour via St. Peter's Hill to Woodcote Road terminus in order to serve St. Peter's Hill School, was also destined for withdrawal, as the service was under-used, and *"...used a crew wastefully at a most important time of the day"*. Evidently, the other return journey, at lunchtime, had by now been withdrawn. Unfortunately, it has proved impossible to determine when this actually took place but is assumed to have been at the end of the Christmas term – so that it simply did not re-appear at the start of the Lent term. Although the idea of the combined route K/L surfaced at Transport Committee meetings a number of times during 1946, it was quietly dropped after Mr Little left the undertaking at the end of that year.

One of the worst fogs experienced for years descended on Reading during the afternoon of Sunday 30th December 1945, persisting into the evening in freezing conditions, to such an extent that by 9.00pm all corporation bus and trolleybus services were abandoned. Although disruption was initially slight in the daylight of the following morning, the fog thickened considerably as the day progressed before it began to dissipate from mid-afternoon.

Reading's roads, never good at the best of times, had suffered further from a lack of maintenance during the war. Tarred surfaces had broken up and pot-holes had become manifest because nothing much could be done to repair wear-and-tear for six years. Plenty of heavy rubber-tyred over-laden military vehicles, both multi-axled and articulated, to say nothing of track-laying vehicles, light and heavy, had helped to chew up the surfaces of the town's through routes, while granite and jarrah teak setts and disused and tarred-in tram track still made driving, and certainly cycling, hazardous. Caversham Road was particularly bad, according to a note in the 'Reading Week by Week' column in the *Berkshire Chronicle* for 24th August 1945 asking for something to be done. The buses, which bumped and jolted over indifferent surfaces, were only making things worse, of course, and they were also rattling themselves to bits into the bargain!

Under the Reading Corporation Act 1935, the corporation had been empowered to raise a loan of £64,500 for the removal of tramway tracks and to reconstruct the roads affected. This sum was intended to cover the cost of a thorough job resurfacing the whole width of road, not just those parts of the roadway deemed the responsibility of the Transport Department to reinstate under the provisions of the Tramways Act 1870. Plans were therefore made in late 1945 for the removal of tram rails in and the reconstruction of King Street, Broad Street and Oxford Road; work appears to have commenced circa mid-February 1946. Notices advising the public of the coming disruption to routes and stopping places were posted in corporation buses and trolleybuses from 15th January 1946. During the works, through traffic would be diverted at approaches to the town and local traffic around the town centre diverted via a one-

Mid-April 1946, with a start being made to remove tram rail from Broad Street and King Street prior to reconstructing the carriageway.

Reading Standard

way scheme. Westbound motorbus services were diverted via Friar Street, and westbound trolleybus services via Duke Street, London Street, Mill Lane, Bridge Street and St. Mary's Butts. All eastbound buses and trolleybuses continued to use Broad Street, where they manoeuvred around the road works. The works were undertaken by contractors, and a charge was made by the council to the Transport Department under the Tramways Act, 1870, to cover the latter's responsibility for the cost of reinstating the carriageway.

On 11th January 1946, before work commenced to alleviate the Broad Street and King Street tram-rail hazards, the road actually collapsed in Broad Street, opposite The Arcade. It is quite likely that this was brought on by the after-effects of the air raid of February 1943, the bombs which were dropped nearby probably having had a detrimental effect on the culverted watercourses in that vicinity. While the collapse was repaired, which, by all accounts, was over a period of two or three days, westbound trolleybuses on the 'main line' were diverted via Duke Street, London Street, Mill Lane, Bridge Street and St. Mary's Butts, as planned for implementation during the forthcoming road works, regaining their usual route by turning left into Oxford Road. As there were no through wires in Mill Lane past the depot entrance, trolleybuses had to de-pole and run on battery traction over the unwired section. It is said that the crews of the first few buses to be diverted took the easy way out, taking passengers on a depot tour!

In autumn 1945, the new chief constable of the borough police drew the new transport manager's attention to what he considered were badly-placed bus stops in King Street, serving route H (Wood Lane Junction) and the terminal point for route N (Whitley Estate), because he considered them too near to the traffic signals at Jackson's Corner. Mr Little heartily agreed, and foresaw that the offending stops would be eliminated within a greater scheme which was in the process of being developed for fairly early implementation, in order to start accustoming the public to a change in the pattern of services which was inevitably going to result when the next phase of the expansion of the trolleybus system took place. Although, as it happened, the trolleybuses would serve the very same destinations referred to on the offending stops in King Street, they would be doing so by being operated via St. Mary's Butts, Bridge Street and Southampton Street. The transport manager had it in mind, therefore, to start a 'gradual transition' of services so that when trolleybuses were eventually substituted, it would be a simple change-over, in the eyes of the public, from one type of vehicle to another.

If the transport manager's original concept related just to the routes serving Whitley, it all very quickly snowballed, on the basis, presumably, that if there was going to be an upheaval it might as well be a big one – to be 'got over' in one go! Firstly, it was considered necessary to group all routes passing along the same corridors to the suburbs, so that they used the same stops in the town centre. It was also considered advantageous to eliminate all those confusing situations where the outward routing of a specific service traversed different streets from the routing in the opposite direction of travel (remember that in 1946, one-way streets had hardly been thought of!). The town's bus routes were routed along different streets in each direction more due to a historical quirk than for any other reason! Further, it was considered desirable – if there were to be major changes to the routing of services – that there should be a fairly even spread of bus services using the different traffic arteries they always had used. Finally, it was desirable, in any case, to rationalise town centre stopping places and to eliminate stops wherever possible in order to release 'pavement space'. This had become a major problem in Broad Street, particularly during the war, as we have seen. If passenger numbers had doubled, so had queues waiting for buses, to the extent that the kerb line of virtually the whole length of both sides of Broad Street was taken up with bus queues waiting for either Thames Valley or Reading Corporation services!

The foregoing considerations were investigated and reported upon, and recommendations made by the Transport (Future Policy) Sub-Committee. In general these were adopted, and subsequently endorsed by the town council. Many of the changes turned out to be somewhat fortuitous (and others turned out to be only 'nominal' for a long while), because the town was about to embark on a progressive scheme to rid itself of redundant tram rail and to reconstruct most of the town centre thoroughfares. Whilst this was taking place, it would result in extensive and prolonged diversions of bus routes coupled with temporarily altered stopping places. The overall scheme (irrespective of any temporary change brought about by roadworks) involved major revisions to a number of motorbus routes. The changes were originally intended to have taken effect from

The driver of AEC 661T trolleybus 126 (ARD 689) pauses to have a word with Inspector Jackson as he leaves the depot to enter service on the 'Main Line' in this 1945 view. Female cleaners, typically in dungarees and headscarves, are hard at work on some motorbuses in the background, AEC Regent 22 and Leyland Titan 3 with two others. The trolleybuses are Nos. 115 and 129.

© *Reading Museum Service (Reading Borough Council); all rights reserved*

Construction of Whitley Estate started shortly before the war and resumed in the postwar years. Utility Guy Arab motorbus 28 (BRD 816) townbound in Buckland Road (notwithstanding the destination reading 'Callington Road' – which is in the opposite direction) seen from the roof of the Savoy Cinema at the corner with Basingstoke Road, circa summer 1946.

Print from J. R. Whitehead's collection

Bus 25 (RD 6071), photographed at the GWR Station in spring 1946, was a 'wooden bodied' AEC Regent, one of several fitted from new with AEC 8.8 oil engines. Note the slight slope to the radiator and its protrusion forward of the dash panel. This one had a replacement AEC 7.7 oil engine fitted in September 1946 and lost this 'snout'. Once again, it is well after the war, yet white paint as used for blackout markings is still to be seen on the rear half of the rear wings.

Late W. J. Haynes
© *Millane Publishing*

> **Reading Corporation Transport.**
>
> **NOTICE**
>
> **Trolley Bus & Omnibus Routes & Stops during Road Work in Broad Street**
>
> *The attention of passengers is drawn to the following :—*
>
> During the progress of the roadwork in Broad Street the exigencies of the work, may from time to time, make it necessary to **ALTER**
>
> (1) the routeing of omnibuses through Broad Street
>
> (2) the position of stopping places in Broad Street.
>
> As and when necessary, notification of intended alterations will be detailed on temporary notice boards affixed to poles at existing stopping places.
>
> Mill Lane, Reading
> 15/1/1946
>
> W. M. LITTLE, B.Sc., Assoc.M.Inst.C.E.
> Transport Manager and Engineer.
>
> Parnells The Printers, Ltd. Reading.

11th February 1946, but were postponed for a week, being introduced from 18th February 1946.

Route F had, for many years, run into town from Shinfield Road via Crown Street, Southampton Street, Bridge Street and St. Mary's Butts and thence into Broad Street to load outside the Vaudeville cinema. It was now changed to run into town over the same roads as its outward journey, i.e. via London Street, Duke Street and King Street. Routes I and L, running in from Horncastle and Berkeley Avenue respectively, had until this time reached Broad Street via Gun Street and Minster Street, but they were now diverted to run in the reverse direction of their outward routes, i.e. into Broad Street via St. Mary's Butts.

Until this time routes H and N, serving Wood Lane Junction and Callington Road or Staverton Road respectively, ran inbound via Silver Street. Route H continued via London Street, Duke Street and King Street to Broad Street, while route N turned left into Crown Street and ran via Southampton Street, Bridge Street, St. Mary's Butts and Broad Street to reach the offending terminal stop in King Street. Both routes departed southbound via Duke Street and London Street, thence via Silver Street. From 18th February 1946, however, routes H and N were both altered to run inbound from Whitley Street via the full length of Southampton Street, Bridge Street and St. Mary's Butts. Route H then proceeded via Broad Street, Queen Victoria Street, Station Road and Stations and onward to Chalgrove Way as before, whilst route N henceforth terminated at 'The Butts', turning empty via Oxford Road, Cheapside, Friar Street and West Street and returning to Whitley via the reverse of the inbound route. The northbound stop, outside The Vaudeville, was shared with route I to Donkin Hill and adjacent to the separate Hemdean Road stop. The resulting seemingly-permanent melée of passengers for the three services via Reading Bridge had, by all accounts, to be seen to be believed! There was, intentionally, no southbound stop in Broad Street for route H; southbound buses stopped in Station Road and then at St. Mary's Butts, before continuing south via Bridge Street and Southampton Street. It is worth noting that the changes to routes H and N removed buses from Silver Street and Crown Street altogether.

Also from 18th February 1946, there were alterations to three town centre trolleybus stops. The Three Tuns stop at Butter Market was combined with the Liverpool Road stop further west; the northbound stop in West Street was eliminated; and two separate westbound stops in Oxford Road at Cork Street, for Bear Inn and for Kentwood, were combined at a new location west of Cork Street – although very soon made two again, for it seems that the single stop encouraged short distance riders to crowd out trolleybuses bound for Kentwood. At rush hours, queues at the original location had been too large for the available pavement area, being too near to both St. Mary's Butts and Cork Street!

The foregoing route changes resulted in some new bus stop flags being set in place around the town centre. Certain stops at the Minster Street end of Broad Street had to be temporarily taken out of use anyway, due to the roadworks, and, indeed, a number of other temporary bus stop alterations had to be made during this period of reconstruction of Reading's main thoroughfare.

The changes to bus services to and from the Whitley area proved extremely unpopular with shop-keepers at the upper

Tram rail removal and road reconstruction in Broad Street/ King Street in spring 1946. Whilst buses and trolleybuses were still able to use these streets in an eastbound direction, as per trolleybus 137 (BRD 814) as shown, westbound trolleybuses were diverted via Duke Street, London Street, Mill Lane, Bridge Street and St. Mary's Butts to regain their normal route along Oxford Road. Motorbuses used Friar Street and West Street as appropriate.

Reading Standard

end of London Street, which, at that time was a thriving little centre for domestic shopping. They complained bitterly of a loss of trade, and the Chamber of Commerce sent a letter to the transport manager expressing its concern and asking whether the diversion was a temporary one. They received the response *"...that the change is a permanent one and is in line with the policy of extending the existing Caversham – Whitley trolleybus service to serve the Whitley Estate"*. A public meeting held at South Reading Community Centre on 14th March 1946 showed more public concern about the change of route into town and formally demanded that the council should *"...facilitate a service of buses to the centre of the town and Stations"*. This seemed to be an attempt to press for an extension of route N from St. Mary's Butts to the Stations along the line of route H, via Broad Street. The transport manager, whilst agreeing that such an extension was possible at that time using motorbuses, said that it would run against the gradual process of changes which were preparing the way for extending the Whitley – Caversham trolleybus route, where access to the Station would be via Tudor Road only. No route modifications were therefore undertaken. The public, on the other hand, griped in the local papers about buses to Lower Whitley being crowded-out at the St. Mary's Butts stop by short-distance passengers who could have used a trolleybus working only as far as Whit-Pump.

Commencing on 15th March 1946, further work (additional to the subsidence repairs) was undertaken on the south side of Broad Street, from opposite Queen Victoria Street to West Street Junction, which involved re-kerbing and removing the escape manholes from the subterranean air raid shelters created from the basements of shops fronting Broad Street. The memo reveals something of the network of tunnels under Broad Street when it says *"...the tunnel is to be blanked off near the kerb edge in each case"*.

Yet more work, this time in the Oxford Road from 19th March 1946 by Post Office Telephones engineers, meant the temporary removal of the stops near McIlroys. This work subsequently prevented access to Cheapside, too, which meant that buses working route N, to Whitley Estate, which turned empty by using Oxford Road, Cheapside, Friar Street and West Street, to reach the new terminus in St. Mary's Butts, were temporarily made to turn (until 1st April 1946) by circumnavigating The Triangle car park, via West Street, Friar Street, Caversham Road, Lower Thorn Street and Friar Street back to West Street.

Operation of bus and trolleybus services then became something of a nightmare due to extensive removal of tram track and road reconstruction. It took place initially in Oxford Road and, by 27th March 1946, work on that section from Kensington Road to Elm Lodge Avenue resulted in single alternate lane working for all traffic, whilst on 1st April 1946, a surviving memo details further road works at Argyle Street and at Kensington Road and the associated bus stop changes which were required. In April 1946, too, there was a suggestion that the centre of London Street, a street which was not otherwise due for reconstruction, might be used for public car parking, so the transport manager arranged for the lifting of what remained of the disused tram track rather than effect a temporary repair.

A further notice appeared in corporation buses and trolleybuses from 5th April 1946 regarding the final stage of the reconstruction in Broad Street (the north side), due to commence on Monday 8th April 1946. This, as already outlined, demanded one-way traffic through Broad Street, with the westbound trolleybuses again being diverted via Mill Lane and motorbuses via High Street, Market Place and Friar Street, as had occurred after the subsidence incident, eastbound transport fighting its way past the roadworks.

The *Reading Standard* for Friday 12th April 1946, had this to say under a heading of *"Two Miles of Roadwork – Reading's Big Scheme in Progress"*:

"Hundreds of tons of steel, which would have been of great value to Britain's war effort, but which was too costly in labour and time to remove, is now being prised out of its setting in Broad Street and Oxford Road, Reading. It is the old tram track, last used in May 1939, before the advent of the trolleybuses on the main route. Now it will be melted

---

Reading Corporation Transport.

Trolleybus & Omnibus Routes and Stops during Road Work in King St., Broad St. & Oxford Rd.

During the progress of the road work in King Street, Broad Street and Oxford Road, it may be necessary to alter from time to time the routeing of omnibuses and the position of stopping places.

As and when necessary, notification of intended alterations will be detailed on temporary notice boards affixed to poles at existing stopping places.

Mill Lane, Reading
18/3/1946

W. M. LITTLE, B.Sc., Assoc.M.Inst.C.E.
Transport Manager and Engineer

Reading Corporation Transport

Reconstruction of Broad St.

One Way Traffic

TROLLEY BUS SERVICE. From 8th April, 1946, during completion of reconstruction of Broad Street, Trolley Buses travelling westwards from **Duke Street Stop** to **Cork Street Stop** will be diverted via Duke Street, Mill Lane and St. Mary's Butts.

OMNIBUS SERVICES. The Buses normally running through Broad Street in an East to West direction will be diverted to **Friar Street** stopping at the following positions:

Merry Maidens to Uplands Road ⎫ in **Friar Street**, opposite
Erleigh Road to Stations ⎭ G.P.O. (Woodcote Rd. stop)

Donkin Hill to Horncastle ⎫
Hemdean Road to Berkeley Avenue ⎬ in **Friar Street**
Stations to Grovelands Road ⎭ East of Greyfriars Road

Mill Lane, Reading
5th April, 1946

W. M. LITTLE, B.Sc., Assoc.M.Inst.C.E.
Transport Manager and Engineer

down to make fresh steel for Britain's export trade, and to help in reconstruction.

"The job of reconstructing two miles of Reading's main thoroughfare will take a long time. Broad Street itself, at an optimistic estimate, will be "up" for two or three months. The whole road is worn out and long overdue for repair. It is being completely dug up, new concrete foundations put in and a new asphalt non-skid surface laid down.

"The task of planning the reorganisation of traffic routes has been no small one, but the arrangements are on the whole working well. Traffic to and from London and Oxford is being diverted at the approaches to the town and local traffic, by means of one-way notices, is being shepherded around the by-streets. Petrol buses going west are picking up their passengers in Friar Street and trolleybuses going west are using the London Street – Mill Lane route.

"A star turn for the public 'gallery' which watches road worker teams every day is the mechanical shovel, operated from a caterpillar cabin.

"It is estimated that the total amount of steel rails available for smelting will be 550 tons."

Comparison of passenger figures for the month of February in 1945 and in 1946 showed little or no reduction in traffic on any of the town's bus routes, the wartime level of loadings having been maintained. At its meeting of 21st February 1946, the Transport Committee was advised that in order to ease the pressures on the department just a little, arrangements had been made to hire four coaches from 'Messrs. Smith's Coaches & Cars, Mill Lane, Reading' during Monday to Friday morning and evening peaks. These hired vehicles were to be used primarily on contract services provided to transport army personnel. In turn, the corporation double-deckers previously used would be released to permit strengthening of other town services at peak times, when overall passenger demand was high. The committee was informed that, although the replacement of double-deck buses by hired (single-deck) coaches would result in an actual financial loss to the department due to the reduced passenger capacity, the effect of strengthening other services made the decision a viable one.

The hired Smith's coaches operated eight duties, which are listed in a surviving document dated 4th February 1946 (a Monday) and which may suggest that this was the date on which the hire commenced. They were certainly recorded as being in operation a month later. The Transport Committee had been told that the coaches were for the transport of army personnel, but the schedules show a much more general use on the town's bus routes and rush hour specials to schools and factories as well as to military establishments. The Royal Army Pay Corps (RAPC), based at Balmore House, off Peppard Road, in Caversham, was served by these duties. Auxiliary Territorial Service (ATS) staff, who were lodged at Aldermaston Court, some miles out of Reading, helped staff Balmore House and, presumably, they were conveyed to and from Aldermaston by a separate contract service operated by the likes of the Thames Valley Traction Co. Ltd., or by Smith's Coaches. The Corporation Transport Department's duties were listed as S "A" Duty to S "H" Duty – four morning duties, and four evening duties, from which it will be noted that there appears to have been a transfer point in the mornings in Bath Road near the top of Castle Hill for ATS personnel coming in from Aldermaston. Smith's Coaches provided the drivers and the conductors were picked up at Mill Lane depot. The duties were as follows:

Morning duties – Smith's Coaches

S "A" Duty   Leave depot 6.50am   Return 10.05am
Callington Road to CWS Jam Factory; run empty; Callington Road to Elliotts – Westfield Junction; run empty; Hartland Road to Balmore Drive for RAPC Personnel only; run empty to depot to exchange conductor for school attendant for school specials from East & South Districts for Whitley Special School and then from South District for Watlington House.

S "B" Duty   Leave depot 6.50am   Return 9.45am
Callington Road to CWS Jam Factory; run empty; Callington Road to Elliotts – Westfield Junction; run empty; Hartland Road to Balmore Drive for RAPC Personnel only. In service route I to Broad Street and depot to exchange conductor for school attendant for School Specials from West & North Districts for Whitley Special School.

S "C" Duty   Leave depot 8.05am   Return 9.05am
Hartland Road to depot (pick up conductor) and continue to Balmore Drive in service; run empty to George Street; stage carriage service from Donkin Hill, Hemdean Road School; thence via Henley Road to Donkin Hill, Broad Street and depot.

S "D" Duty   Leave depot 7.55am   Return 9.10am
Southcote Road and Coley Avenue to pick up ATS personnel; via St. Mary's Butts to pick up conductress for stage carriage service N to Balmore Drive; run empty to George Street; stage carriage service from Donkin Hill, Hemdean Road School, thence via Henley Road to Donkin Hill, Broad Street and depot.

Evening Duties – Smith's Coaches

S "E" Duty   Leave depot 5.15pm.   Return 6.45pm
Run empty to Balmore Drive to pick up RAPC personnel only to Hartland Road; run empty to Queens Road to take up stage carriage service N to Staverton Road and in service to depot.

S "F" Duty   Leave depot 5.15pm   Return 6.45pm
Run empty to Balmore Drive to pick up RAPC personnel only to Hartland Road; run empty to Queens Road to take up stage carriage service N to Staverton Road and in service to depot.

S "G" Duty   Leave depot 5.15pm   Return 6.45pm
Run empty to Balmore Drive to pick up RAPC personnel only to Hartland Road; run in service to London Street (Huntley, Boorne & Stevens) to take up stage carriage service N to Callington Road and return via Hartland Road, Wood Lane and depot.

S "H" Duty   Leave depot 5.15pm   Return 6.45pm
Run empty to Balmore Drive to pick up ATS personnel only to Coley Avenue and Tilehurst Road; run empty to depot 5.50pm. Wait until 6.15pm to take up stage carriage service N from London Street Top (H. B. & S) to Callington Road and return to depot via Wood Lane.

On the parts of these duties serving the ATS and RAPC, no fares were taken as the services were contracted. How long this operation continued is not known, although rush-hour operation using Smith's Coaches vehicles was still reported in 1947 and into 1948. Presumably, a number of RAPC personnel were billeted in the wartime hutted camp which existed at the junction of Northumberland Avenue with Hartland Road. Smith's Coaches were hiring vehicles to London Transport at this time, to help them through an acute shortage of serviceable vehicles, and many of Smith's Coaches vehicles were to be seen in Reading complete with London Transport radiator 'bulls-eyes' and London Transport route numbers! Usually, the Smith's vehicles used were drawn from a sizeable fleet of ex-Scottish Motor Traction 1936-vintage petrol-engined Leyland Cheetahs, which Smith's had only recently acquired, overhauled and put into service.

It was clear that for the Transport Department, the financial year 1946/47 was likely to show a deficit. A report prepared by Mr Little in February 1946 suggested that a number of changes be made to fares and charges, proposals he repeated to a meeting of the Transport (Future Policy) Sub-Committee in May 1946, although, in the event, not one of his proposals was adopted. Firstly, he proposed that discount tickets be withdrawn and replaced by tokens – a sort of internal transport currency, which could be sold at full price. Discount tickets had cost the department £1,668 18s 8d in 'lost revenue' during the year ending 31st March 1945. As at February 1946, the 3d, 4d and 5d values were still available. Tokens could be used like cash and 'paid in' by conductors like cash. Indeed, using tokens would obviate the need to issue 'NVX' tickets (NVX = No Value Exchange). Workmen's fares were another area where the department lost revenue and Mr Little demonstrated that, if they were withdrawn completely, some £20,000 could be raised in a financial year. However, around three million workmen's fares would be issued in the financial year 1945/46. He proposed the abolition of the 1d, 1½d and 2d workmen's fares, together with the hardly-used 5d value (only 487 tickets in the whole financial year 1945/46), leaving only the 3d and 4d fares in place. This, it was estimated, would raise £15,000 for the department in a financial year. Finally, he proposed increasing the minimum ordinary fare from 1d to 1½d (which would raise another £12,000 in a financial year) and an overhaul of the fare stage structure. After all the hard work which had been undertaken in the latter direction in 1939, the wartime restriction of stopping places, in particular, had created a number of anomalies.

At a meeting of the Education Committee's Schools Sub-Committee on 4th April 1946, it was proposed to ask the Transport Department to run a school bus service from the junction of Oxford Road with Kentwood Hill (Kentwood Circle) to Park Lane School, via Armour Hill. Although around 70 children required transport, most of them lived less than the three mile minimum distance ('as the crow flies') from the school to entitle them to free travel which, under the new Education Acts, was at the expense of the Education Committee. Income could not therefore be guaranteed and the cost of running a bus full of children at normal 'half-fare' scales was deemed by the Transport Department to be uneconomic, so although it was stated that there was no 'technical difficulty' in running the service, the request was refused. Over the next few years, there were a number of requests by both parents and the Education Committee for the Transport Department to provide school bus services across the town. The Transport Department consistently resisted these demands because of the financial loss which would be incurred. Indeed, it was suggested to the Education Committee that it should carry the costs of educational reorganisation itself, by contracting a school bus service at its own expense. The Education Committee's response, however, was merely to stagger school hours to alleviate the difficulties of peak loadings on public transport – but no special school services were provided. Mr Little noted that, although special school bus services would not cover their costs if funded only by charging children's fares, provisions under the Education Act, 1944 for pupils living beyond the three mile limit to travel to and from school free of charge led him to propose that a flat rate, pre-paid ticket be issued for all children travelling by bus, and that the existing scholar's tickets, which allowed half fare travel up to 17 years of age, be withdrawn. School season tickets were actually issued in the autumn term of 1946, at a cost to the Education Department of ten shillings per term per pupil. Pre-paid scholar's tickets remained in use.

Another report by Mr Little to the Transport (Future Policy) Sub-Committee, dated 28th June 1945, had set out a three to five year plan for the extension of trolleybus services, which resulted in obtaining a 1946 Provisional Order for route extensions. The report separately examined a number of routes for conversion to trolleybuses, for it will be recalled that before war had interrupted its phased development, the future policy of the undertaking was the introduction of a grand scheme in which all major motorbus routes would be eventually converted to trolleybus operation. Mr Little was simply taking the project forward.

One route now projected for conversion to trolleybus operation was that between Erleigh Road and Stations. It was noted that there was already overhead line installed, virtually from Stations to Mill Lane, and that traction poles from tramway days were still in place along London Street, London Road and Erleigh Road. Strangely, Mr Little seemed to ignore the fact that the trolleybus overhead line erected along Erleigh Road for the long-disused training route was still in place. Perhaps in the three months he had been transport manager, he had not found the time to learn about things like that!

Powers already existed for the construction of trolleybus overhead across Caversham Bridge and in Caversham along Bridge Street, Church Road, St. Anne's Road, Priest Hill, The Mount and Albert Road, to its junction with Harrogate Road (the site of the original motorbus terminus). Mr Little proposed an extension of these existing powers further along Albert Road, and along Conisboro' Avenue to its junction with Uplands Road as an indication of the anticipated trend of traffic in future years. He also proposed an extension to serve the actual 'village' (as the shopping area of Caversham was referred to at that time), with overhead along Church Street and round a terminal loop comprising Hemdean Road, Oxford Street and Prospect Street. Even though powers had already been obtained to extend the trolleybus system across Caversham Bridge (a rather pleasing ferro-concrete structure opened in 1926, of which the council was justly proud), some undercurrents could already be detected which were completely opposed, on aesthetic grounds, to having trolleybus poles and overhead wiring across the bridge. No-one dared pipe up to say that Kingston Bridge, linking Middlesex with Surrey, quite successfully carried London Transport trolleybuses across the River Thames and, half-a-century later, no-one dared criticise the tatty bits of plastic which were strung across Caversham Bridge to dissuade swans from landing amongst the traffic!

Trolleybus operation in Lower Caversham was also considered, with a suggested conversion of the Donkin Hill motorbus route. At the time, this area of Caversham presented the most important housing estate development on the north side of the town, although the low railway bridges in Vastern Road (which were the sole reason for all of the undertaking's motorbuses being of the lowbridge type), were a particular problem when it came to substituting trolleybuses. If a trolleybus route to Lower Caversham via Reading Bridge and George Street, Caversham, was operated under Vastern Road railway bridges, it would require single-deck trolley vehicles. Mr Little was quick to point out that, although this might seem undesirable at first, it could have a positive effect on the motorbus fleet, provided that the Emmer Green motorbus route was diverted to operate via Caversham Bridge instead of Reading Bridge, because henceforth all double-deck motorbuses could be of the much-preferred 'highbridge' type. The alternative, of course, was for the proposed trolleybus service to Donkin Hill to be operated via the proposed wiring across Caversham Bridge and through Caversham 'village', in which case double-deck trolleybuses could be used.

Although all these suggestions were no doubt discussed at the meeting of the Transport Committee on 19th July 1945, the committee's more modest decisions were, perhaps, reflected in the subsequent application to the Ministry of War Transport, for a Provisional Order to be obtained during the parliamentary session 1945/46 with a view to an extension of trolleybus services being implemented in spring 1947. This largely comprised the renewal and modification of authorisations contained in the 1936 Provisional Order, the unexercised powers of which had lapsed after five years, in 1941. Of these, the Whitley Estate and Whitley Wood trolleybus extensions were, perhaps, the most important issues, although Mr Little also convinced the committee that, to provide maximum flexibility for trolleybus routes in the town centre, certain links should also be provided, by wiring Crown Street, Friar Street, Tudor Road and the Station approaches. An application for an extension beyond Kentwood to the Roebuck was also included, as was authorisation for routes to serve Caversham village which enhanced those already contained in the 1914 Act (which was still operative). In May 1946, therefore, the resulting authorisation, known as the Reading Corporation (Trolley Vehicles) Provisional Order, 1946, contained proposals for ten trolleybus route extensions, as follows:

Route 1:   Hemdean Road, Oxford Street and Prospect Street, in Caversham.

Route 2:   Caversham Bridge to Church Street, Caversham.

Route 3:   Tudor Road, Station Hill and Station Approach.

Route 4:   Friar Street, between West St and Blagrave St.

Route 5:   London Street, London Road and Erleigh Road.

Route 6:   Crown Street.

Route 7:   Christchurch Road*, Basingstoke Road and Whitley Wood Lane.

Route 8:   Buckland Road and Northumberland Avenue.

Route 9:   Norcot Junction to Kentwood Hill (already authorised by wartime Statutory Rules & Orders, 1943 and already in operation; this was an application for permanent authorisation).

Route 10: Kentwood Hill to Elsley Road.

Christchurch Road (marked * above) would have been something of a simple technicality in that traffic proceeding, for example, from Whitley Street into Basingstoke Road at that time did so by running a few yards in Christchurch Road. Certain undated departmental plans survive from this period, some bearing rubber stamps reading 'Ministry of War Transport', which show the proposed layout of overhead and the positioning of traction poles in Caversham, including detailed plans showing the layout over Caversham Bridge; in Bridge Street and Church Street; and between Hemdean Road and Prospect Street.

A meeting of the Future Policy Sub-Committee the following year, on 2nd July 1946, received a report from the transport manager, which again considered future trolleybus extensions in anticipation of a further application being made in the 1946/47 parliamentary session for a Provisional Order for additional powers. Trolleybus links within the town centre were examined in two areas. The first was along Greyfriars Road, linking Friar Street with Tudor Road, which was rejected due to the need for road improvements at the Friar Street end. The second was in Silver Street and Mount Pleasant which, again, was rejected due to the need for road improvements at the Crown Street/London Street junction and in Duke Street, all of which were some way off. The proposed trolleybus route to Donkin Hill was again considered in view of the partly completed housing estates in the Donkin Hill area, together with another route, to Emmer Green to serve a new council housing estate being proposed in that district. The latter could not be discussed in detail, however, because some of the roads along which the trolleybuses were likely to run had not even been designed, let alone built!

At the following Transport Committee meeting, on 18th July 1946, it was decided to follow the transport manager's advice that no further applications should be made until those powers already obtained in the 1946 parliamentary session had been progressed. It seems that, effectively, this decision killed off once and for all plans to extend the trolleybus network north of the River Thames, as no further discussion appears to have taken place within the Transport Committee, even though departmental drawings existed, some of which dated from 1936. Five surviving detailed overhead and traction pole plans show the proposed layout along Peppard Road at various locations – Kidmore End Road; Emmer Green Pond; Oratory School (BBC Caversham); near Horse Close; and Surley Row. Whilst many of these ideas were not pursued (presumably because, by 1946, the main road layout in Emmer Green along Peppard Road was planned to be replaced by a new 'by-pass' road, subsequently known as Buckingham Drive) Mr Little's report is significant in that this seems to be the last time that any large-scale trolleybus route developments were seriously considered. This is reinforced by the statement from the subsequent transport manager, in 1950, that he *"...did not anticipate any large extensions of our trolleybus system within the next few years"*. And indeed, as he predicted, apart from route extensions, not one additional and complete trolleybus route was constructed thereafter!

For the moment, however, the most important task was to serve the expanding Whitley Estate which, in the immediate post-war years, was being extended progressively southwards towards Whitley Wood Lane. With the 1946 Provisional Order virtually in place, 510 traction poles were ordered in April 1946 from Stewart & Lloyds Ltd., of Glasgow, at a cost of £9,939 12s 6d, together with the necessary feeder cables from Standard Telephones &

Cables Ltd., of London, at a cost of £540. Some two months earlier, on 6th February 1946, yellow spots were appearing on the pavements in Basingstoke Road to mark the future positions of traction poles. Despite plans to construct the infrastructure, trolleybus operation to Lower Whitley and into the Whitley Estate was still some way off, for although the Transport Committee had, in May 1946, requested AEC Ltd. to quote for twenty new trolleybus chassis, as noted elsewhere, Park Royal Vehicles Ltd. was unable to undertake the building of any trolleybus bodies until late 1947. The 'knock-on' effect of this, of course, was that it would be necessary to retain certain already old and life-expired motorbuses in service for even longer...

A completely new timetable was introduced from Sunday 12th May 1946 for motorbus routes F, H, I and M and on the Staverton Road leg of route N, all of which considerably improved the frequencies of many of the town's bus services:

Route	Old Service	New Service
F	15 mins	7½ /10 mins
H	15 mins	10 mins
I	15/20 mins	15 mins
M	15/30 mins	15 mins
N (Callington Rd.)	30 mins	10 mins
N (Staverton Rd.)	30 mins	20/30 mins

All of the above (with the exception of the service to Staverton Road) were further augmented by short workings on Mondays–Fridays at peak hours and on Saturdays.

The greatest improvement, it will be seen, was on the Basingstoke Road group of routes (H and N) which, between them, now provided a 5-minute frequency on Mondays–Fridays and a 2½-minute service on Saturdays between the town and Buckland Road (Savoy Cinema).

It had not been possible to improve Sunday motorbus services until now, due to acute staff shortage, and they had continued to operate only between 1.30pm and 9.30pm. The Transport Committee had subsequently been informed, at its meeting on 17th October 1945, that an improved situation with regard to both fuel supplies and labour meant that further improvements to services could be considered. It was proposed that, commencing early in the New Year, a double shift system could be introduced on Sundays. Thus, first buses on all routes operating a Sunday service could commence at 9.00am, and thereafter provide a half-hourly service until 1.30pm. It was also proposed that last evening departures from Broad Street could also be extended, from 9.30pm to 10.30pm.

Letters appearing in the *Reading Standard* for 12th April 1946 and 3rd May 1946, complaining that the promised Sunday morning operations were still not a reality, turned out to be a shade premature for, from Sunday 12th May 1946, Sunday morning operation was reintroduced, quarter-hourly from 9.00am on the 'main line' trolleybus routes and half-hourly from 9.30am on most of the motorbus routes. At the same time, last town centre (Broad Street) motorbus departures on Sunday evenings were extended to 10.30pm, bringing them into line with the trolleybuses.

So pressing was the need for public transport to adequately serve the housing development at Whitley that, also from 12th May 1946, another route change and increase in frequency was made to improve facilities. Trolleybus route C (Whit-Pump – Promenade) was reduced to run during peak hours only and, as such, it became a supplementary service to an extension of the Callington Road (rather than Staverton Road) branch of motorbus route N, which was extended from St. Mary's Butts to Promenade, via West Street, Friar Street and Caversham Road. These changes met some of the concerns of Whitley Estate residents expressed earlier in the year for a more frequent service, although Stations continued to be unserved by either leg of route N. The reduction in service of trolleybus route C also had the effect of releasing more trolleybuses to work the hard-pressed 'main line' routes during the day, for even the trolleybuses were finding it hard to cope. Initially, not all motorbuses had **PROMENADE** on their destination blinds and after a few days only those with the correct blinds were rostered. Considerably improved frequencies were also brought in on motorbus route H (Wood Lane Junction – Chalgrove Way), route I (Horncastle – Donkin Hill) and route M (Erleigh Road – Grovelands Road).

St. Mary's Butts, looking south, spring 1946, just before tram rail and cobbles were lifted and the carriageway reconstructed. Notice the Watford-type street lamps on the traction poles, also the single bracket arm type of trolleybus overhead construction. The railings had been removed from St. Mary's Churchyard during the war. *Print from A. Stevens' Collection*

The work on the north side of Broad Street was completed, apparently with all speed. Queen Victoria Street, which had been closed as part of the Broad Street reconstruction, was re-opened from Wednesday 29th May 1946 and Broad Street itself for two-way traffic from Friday 31st May 1946, with bus and trolleybus services being restored to 'normal' from Monday 3rd June 1946. It was stated at the town council meeting the following day that as soon as work in King Street and Oxford Road was complete, work would start on the reconstruction and surfacing on Whitley Street, Southampton Street, Bridge Street and St. Mary's Butts.

Further reconstruction work in two stages then started on the intersections with the surrounding streets and roads. Duke Street and West Street themselves were closed from Monday 3rd June 1946 for about three weeks through to about 22nd June 1946, followed by the High Street/King Street intersection from Monday 24th June 1946, while St. Mary's Butts was closed completely at its West Street end from the following day, Tuesday 25th June 1946. These works necessarily caused a number of temporary route changes and variations, all as agreed on 27th May 1946.

During the West Street and Duke Street closures (from 3rd June 1946), trolleybuses operating on peak hour route C (Whit-Pump – Promenade) were suspended entirely, motor-buses being substituted. Additional (relief) motorbuses were operated on route N between Whit-Pump and Promenade, route N itself necessarily being diverted to run via Oxford Road and Cheapside instead of via West Street and Friar Street. At the same time, with Duke Street closed, motor-buses on route F (to and from the Merry Maidens) and route M (to and from Erleigh Road) were diverted to run in both directions between Broad Street and London Street via Minster Street, Gun Street, Bridge Street and Mill Lane. Similarly, due to the closure of West Street, route M (to and from Grovelands Road) was diverted in both directions between Stations and St. Mary's Butts, via Oxford Road, Cheapside and Friar Street to Greyfriars Road. The factory special service, route O (Staverton Road – Queens Road) – the normal route of which evidently had been altered at some time from that described on page 13 to run via the town centre – was run into St. Mary's Butts, where it U-turned, to run to Watlington Street via Bridge Street and Mill Lane and across London Street into Queens Road. When work in Duke Street had been completed, motorbus route F (Shinfield Road – Uplands Road) was able to revert to its usual route.

Temporary loss of use of the depot wiring connection via Duke Street put trolleybuses running in off service on routes A, B and D into depot from either direction to considerable inconvenience, for they had to make their approach via Broad Street, St. Mary's Butts and Bridge Street, all vehicles having to travel to the Three Tuns to turn for a correct approach! As it was impossible without the use of the Duke Street wiring for westbound trolleybuses to take up service from Broad Street, they had to be content to use Bridge Street and St. Mary's Butts and enter service at Cork Street. For some unexplained reason, too (presumably an encroachment of roadworks at West Street Junction), trolleybuses entering service eastbound on the 'main line' at Broad Street had first to run out to Norcot Junction to turn for a correct approach. These arrangements seem rather odd in view of the fact that every trolleybus (except 101) was fitted with traction batteries as a matter of policy. It is tempting to speculate that these batteries had not always been maintained or replaced when necessary, due to on-going shortages – and thus could no longer be relied upon!

In the midst of all this reconstruction and the continuing shortages of more-or-less everything, the whole nation paused for its Celebration of Victory Day. Saturday 8th June 1946 was a public holiday, and a huge Victory Day celebration parade closed much of central London from the early hours, where there were two processions and a firework display on the River Thames. To Reading Corporation Transport fell a particular honour, because trolleybus driver John Edward McGuirk was chosen to take part in the London parade past Their Majesties The King and Queen, being one of several representative provincial busmen selected in recognition of the part they played during the six-year conflict.

It was also 'Whit Weekend', with Bank Holiday Monday on 10th June. Reading Corporation Transport did not operate any early morning services on either 8th or 10th June, with services not starting on either day until after 7.00am, departures from the outer termini being as follows:

Trolleybus Driver J. E. McGuirk, who was chosen as a representative of provincial busmen in the Victory Parade in London on Victory Day, Saturday 8th June 1946. Driver McGuirk was a veteran of the Great War and holder of the Military Medal, the 1914 War Medal, the 1914–15 Star, the General Service Medal, the Iraq Medal and the Long Service Territorial Medal. In 1940 he was enrolled in the first batch of Local Defence Volunteers, becoming an NCO in the Home Guard. He was stated by the undertaking to "have a reputation for regularity and for working exceptional overtime when required" and was described as "a model for others to follow".

© *Reading Museum Service (Reading Borough Council); all rights reserved*

TROLLEYBUS SERVICES		OMNIBUS SERVICES	
from Bear Inn	7.30am	from Uplands Rd	7.45am
from Kentwood	7.37am	from Merry Maidens	7.40am
from Three Tuns	7.40am	from Chalgrove Way	7.40am
from Liverpool Rd	7.40am	from Wood Lane Junc.	7.40am
		from Donkin Hill	7.45am
		from Horncastle	7.45am
		from Woodcote Rd	10.22am
		from Hemdean Rd	7.50am
		from Berkeley Ave	7.45am
		from Grovelands Rd	7.35am
		from Erleigh Rd	7.45am
		from Callington Rd	7.45am
		from Promenade	7.45am
		from Staverton Rd	7.53am

Late buses were operated on all routes from Stations on 8th June 1946, to meet the London trains, and ran after midnight. Perhaps as compensation, there were no early morning services on Sunday 9th June 1946, normal Sunday services being operated from 9.00am until the last buses at 10.30pm. The undertaking's publicity also shows that the parcels service was closed on 8th and 10th June 1946.

On Celebration of Victory Day itself, Reading held its own festivities, most of them arranged by the town council's Victory Celebrations Committee, and the Transport Department was asked to supply six buses for the transport of bands. There were events held on the river at Thames Side Promenade, in Palmer Park and in Forbury Gardens, and yet more street parties in various parts of the town. Unfortunately, that afternoon was marred by rain.

Finally, in connection with this momentous weekend, it might just be appropriate to mention another occasion worthy of note. On the Friday evening, 7th June 1946, the BBC recommenced television transmissions from studios at Alexandra Palace, in north London, after a forced curtailment at the start of the war. It was, initially, a severely limited service, with reception in the London area only, by only 10,000 receiving sets – but it caught the public's imagination, went from strength to strength, and changed our lives for ever. It proved to be a turning point for the public transport industry, too, just as it was for the film and cinema industries – and almost every other leisure-time pursuit that there was – for it was no longer necessary to be entertained outside of home. Reading was no exception, of course, and the use of public transport to attend centres of entertainment slowly but surely started to go into decline, particularly in the evenings. So, was this the start of a demise in the actual need for public transport – perhaps a first nail in the coffin?

The Great Western Railway contributed its own disruption to another of Reading's roads later the same month, over three successive weekends. On 15th/16th June, 22nd/23rd June, and 29th/30th June 1946, they undertook painting and maintenance work on their bridges over Caversham Road, for which purpose the current was switched off on that section of trolleybus overhead from midnight on each Saturday through to 1.00pm each Sunday (although, as trolleybus operation on route C had been suspended, it is interesting to speculate why the wires remained energised in the first place!). It is likely that some work was also undertaken on the trolleybus overhead under the bridges at this time, as a drawing dated 4th June 1946 survives showing the overhead slewed over the pavement and held in troughing fixed to the underside of the bridges, with the clearances shown relating to the utility trolleybuses. The utility vehicles were higher than the AECs, for which the road had been lowered in 1938/39 (but without the wire slung in troughing). In order to get the utilities (and the Karriers and subsequent types) to Caversham Bridge, the road would need lowering again – but this happened at a later date, after the troughing had been installed.

The annual report for the financial year ended 31st March 1946, as presented to the Transport Committee on 13th June 1946, was once again in the statistical form the undertaking had been obliged to use during the war. The town's trolleybuses carried 24,283,799 passengers (a decrease of 325,055 over the previous year) but ran 1,425,805 miles (an increase of 83,962 miles over the previous year), making a net profit of £56,635 compared with £60,978 the previous year. The motorbuses made a net profit of £22,142 compared with £29,455 the previous year, carrying 16,445,321 passengers (a decrease of 330,856 over the previous year) and, at 1,336,122 miles, ran 65,215 more miles. At 49,375, Parcels Express carried 6,618 fewer parcels than the preceding year and increased the trading loss of £156 the previous year to one of £328. The net profit of the undertaking, taken as a whole, was therefore roundly £78,500 compared with roundly £90,250 in the financial year 1944/45. This was seen to reflect a satisfactory transition from wartime to peacetime, with the wartime inflation of the town's population now substantially reduced and an enhanced service being operated on all routes as a result of fuel restrictions being eased. However, with no new vehicles joining the fleet, the cost of maintaining an ageing fleet was rising.

Notices dated 17th June 1946 were posted in corporation buses and trolleybuses describing the disruption to services during what was described as the *"Reconstruction of Broad Street at West Street and Duke Street Junctions"*. When work commenced at the junction of High Street with King Street at Jackson's Corner on Monday 24th June 1946 (presumably with half the roadway being closed at a time), there appears to have been no effect on motorbus services, although the trolleybus depot connection might still have been affected. With St. Mary's Butts closed at the West Street end from the following day, trolleybus route C remained suspended and the Staverton Road operation of route N remained unaffected, continuing to terminate in St. Mary's Butts. Earlier plans to divert the other leg of motorbus route N (Callington Road – Promenade) in both directions, via Mill Lane, London Street, Duke Street and Broad Street, were laid aside in favour of a split service. Buses from Callington Road terminated in St. Mary's Butts, whilst the other section, from Promenade, ran to West Street and turned via Oxford Road and Cheapside. Coloured transfer tickets were issued to link these services, the tickets showing the stage boarded on the first bus. Motorbuses on route H (Chalgrove Way – Wood Lane Junction), route L (Berkeley Avenue – Hemdean Road) and route I (Horncastle – Donkin Hill), unable to use the full length of St. Mary's Butts, were diverted via Gun Street and Minster Street to Broad Street in both directions. Route M (Grovelands Road – Erleigh Road) was split into two sections, with buses running Erleigh Road – Stations and Grovelands Road – St. Mary's Butts only, with passengers able to transfer to the Donkin Hill service in Castle Street to reach Stations.

Trolleybuses were re-introduced on peak hour route C, and motorbus routes M and N reverted to their normal routes, with effect from Wednesday 10th July 1946; this was followed by the remaining services with effect from 11th July 1946.

Route I (Donkin Hill – Horncastle) was still being operated to a 15 minute frequency, as a result of which the Transport Committee came in for some criticism at the town council meeting of 1st October 1946 for not having improved it to one of 10 minutes when timetable revisions had been introduced on 12th May 1946. It was explained that the undertaking was very hard-pressed to provide a better level of service to meet demand, mainly because it simply did not have enough buses – and, what is more, could not get additional or replacement buses any faster than it was already doing. In reporting this, the chairman of the Transport Committee, Alderman H. V. Kersley, observed that the undertaking was finding the evening peak particularly difficult to cover, since all manner of businesses seemed to want to conclude the working day at around the same time. He appealed to housewives who went out shopp-

The undertaking's forty remaining conductresses and some former colleagues exchanged their uniforms for party frocks on Thursday 3rd October 1946, having accepted an invitation to a 'Farewell and Appreciation Dinner' at the Town Hall, given by the Works Committee and the Transport & General Workers Union. It is recorded that amongst those attending was Mrs. Jose Johnson (who was still serving) who, in March 1940, had been the first to join the undertaking.   *Reading Standard*

ing in town in the afternoons to be sure to make their way home before the rush hour began, rather than add to it.

Initially, the general attitude to women in employment, particularly married women, reverted to pre-war values after the war. There was also the perception that they were in occupations which they should be obliged to relinquish in favour of males returning to 'civvy street' from the armed forces. There was always, in any case, a promise made to men who had volunteered for the armed forces, that they would be entitled to be reinstated in their old employment when hostilities were over. Thus, on 1st August 1946, those conductresses who had chosen to remain in the employ of the undertaking were given advance warning of the termination of their services. A total of 270 women had rallied to the call and worked as conductresses during the war years, with the highest number employed at any one time being 180. There were still 40 conductresses employed at the end of September 1946, and a 'Farewell and Appreciation Dinner' was given on 3rd October 1946 *"for the women who had worked the buses"* throughout the war. Looking back from our own perspective, this seems a minimal acknowledgement and appreciation of the important task which they had fulfilled under the extreme pressures of wartime in Reading. Seventeen of the remaining 40 received compulsory redundancy notices in mid-October 1946, and none of them were still employed by the Transport Department after the end of November 1946. The others, 23 of them, were employed in their own right, rather than as wartime cover for male conductors who had been called up for military service. It was not so very many months later that it was found necessary to again recruit conductresses upon an ever-increasing shortage of suitable men for the job!

Even before the war, when there was considerably less vehicular traffic than one cares to remember, with few private cars, there was an atrocious record of street accidents. Pedestrians, young and old, had not mastered some of the basic techniques of personal safety and most individuals simply were not vehicle-oriented. The original *Highway Code*, which followed the Road Traffic Act, 1930, was a start but it was not compulsory reading and unlikely to find its way into houses other than those in which lived drivers of motor vehicles. There had been driving tests since 1935 but vehicles did not have particularly good lighting, steering or braking capability by today's standards. Drivers, perhaps, still had a lot to learn about the speed of their reactions and the capabilities of their vehicles. There was still much to be learned, too, about road surfaces,

Bus 35 (RD 37) was decorated with coloured lights (fed from the nearby lamp-post or the trolleybus traction supply) and posters, etc., to promote Reading Safety Week (14th to 21st September 1946) and, in particular, the road safety exhibition at the Town Hall. It is seen here outside Jackson's Outfitters, in Kings Road. Afterwards, it returned to service for the few remaining months of its working life, having already had a stay of execution, such was the critical need for buses at that time. It was finally withdrawn on 28th February 1947.

Late W. J. Haynes © Millane Publishing

Some of the forty remaining conductresses in the employ of the undertaking at the end of September 1946. There had been three distinct types of female labour – those taken on for the duration and who would vacate the job when men from the undertaking returned from the services; a handful who took up the job in their own right; and those who were later 'directed' into the job by the Ministry of Labour & National Service. By the time only a handful remained of those who had taken up the job in their own right, it became obvious that there was a chronic shortage of conductors and women were again recruited – they remained a familiar sight until crew operation ceased some 30 years later. Reading Standard

street lighting, road layouts, signs and notices and all the rest. The *Reading Standard* made a point each week of drawing the attention of its readers to various matters of road safety and recorded the number of road accidents and fatalities which had occurred within the borough during the preceding week. In Reading, prompted by a national campaign sponsored by the government, a local Road Safety Committee had been formed during the spring of 1946, which included amongst its number the chairman of the Transport Committee and the transport manager. Plans were laid to hold Reading Safety Week in the town from 14th to 21st September 1946, with a number of local activities including a road safety exhibition in the Town Hall, supported by the Royal Society for the Prevention of Accidents. Permission was sought of the Transport Committee to allow a bus to be used for display purposes during the week in question and, accordingly, bus 35, one of three Guy B single-deckers (which had, in fact, been put back into service in May 1946 having been withdrawn) was the one chosen, for which purpose it was decorated with posters and coloured lamps and fitted with a large roof-mounted loudspeaker. The Transport Department also conveyed 3,300 schoolchildren to the Town Hall exhibition.

Notices were posted on 4th November 1946 warning of yet further disruption, as road reconstruction and tram rail removal work moved on to Southampton Street, Bridge Street and the southern section of St. Mary's Butts. Large parts of the cost of these works fell on the Transport Department, which was still responsible, under the Tramways Act, 1870, for the maintenance of the carriageway while tram track remained in place. These costs were met out of the department's reserve fund and from the salvage of the steel rails. However, £7,500 voted by the Highways Committee to spend on temporary repairs to the two bridges over Mill Stream in Bridge Street, would not be any part of the Transport Department's liability and, in spite of the repairs, the Ministry of Transport could not be persuaded to revise the weight limit of eight tons they had imposed on the bridge to one of twelve tons.

1945 and 1946 were years of gradual and obvious but painfully slow improvements to the quality of life. Food rationing, in fact, had become even more stringent for some commodities – but clementines appeared for the first time, bananas (much missed during the war) re-appeared, and poultry became available as something of a luxury. Jam came in tins because of the shortage of glass – and Boy Scouts raised funds by collecting old jars to sell back to the jam makers! There were the beginnings of London Airport, now Heathrow; Laszlo Biro's revolutionary ball-point pen became publicly available (at 55s each); enter, too, Rev. Awdry's *Thomas the Tank Engine*, Birds Eye Frozen Foods and the new dance craze called the 'Jitterbug'. The BBC re-organised its wireless programmes from National and Regional into the Home Service and the Light Programme – and the Third Programme was launched. One cooked and ate one's breakfast, for example, listening to five minutes each of *The Radio Doctor* (Dr. Charles Hill) and *Lift up your Hearts* (having a religious connection), then two or three minutes of the Weather, any SOS messages (the police, for example, trying to contact relatives who were away from home when some poor unfortunate was in hospital, seriously ill or had died), then there was a 'makeweight' of pealing church bells, before 'the pips' from Greenwich Mean Time on the hour, followed by ten minutes of *The News* (the official version). Housewives were helped through the drudgery of household chores with *Housewife's Choice*, and morning and afternoon sessions of *Music While You Work* and *Mrs. Dale's Diary* and in October 1946 *Woman's Hour* was launched.

Above: *Summer 1945, and the war is over. Commuters clamber aboard 1937-vintage AEC Regent motorbus 57 (ADP 6) in Albert Road, Caversham at the Highmoor Road stop for a ten-minute journey into town. Trilby and Homberg hats on the gents and a headscarf on one of the ladies is very typical of the era, while the attaché cases are also worthy of note. With the rears of buses so rarely photographed, it is interesting to note the two-tier rear bumper painted blackout white, the Clayton Dewandre offside corner advert and the positioning of the rear registration and fleet number. The rear lamps were thus nowhere near indicative of the width of the vehicle! The wartime destination and the rings around the tree further epitomise the era.*

© Reading Museum Service (Reading Borough Council); all rights reserved

Below: *A reminder of the way things used to be, certainly up until the mid-1960s. It was a frequent occurrence for cattle to be driven from the railway cattle pens, down the roadway between the railway and fire station and under Caversham Road railway bridge, thence to the abattoirs (along the road to the right, immediately past the bridge) or to the cattle market in Great Knolly's Street. In this 1945 view, the progress of a Bedford OWL army lorry (on L-plates) and Guy BT trolleybus 103 (RD 8087) is being impeded while the drovers bring country into town past the Duke of Edinburgh (demolished around the turn of the 20th/21st century) and the Corn Exchange (later a roller-skating rink and, subsequently, the Majestic dance hall – and, much later, a bingo hall and more recently a night club before demolition in 2005 to make way for apartments).*

© Reading Museum Service (Reading Borough Council); all rights reserved

12   William Little's Rolling Stock Developments

At the end of the War in Europe, many bus operators were running vehicles in extremely poor condition and Reading Corporation Transport was no exception. Buses that in normal circumstances would have been well beyond the end of their working lives were still in everyday and all-day service. For many bus fleets a renewal programme was long overdue. The cost of the war, however, and the enormous task of reconstruction at home and across Europe meant that shortages and rationing would continue for several years yet. It was the Age of Austerity, with little in the way of luxuries or consumer goods. The country had been almost bankrupted by the six years of war, and the government kept a firm control on the production of more or less everything, including buses, right through to the early 1950s.

It had been Reading's good fortune, at the start of the war, to have only just put into service 25 new trolleybuses, and these made up over one third of its overall fleet. Even these trolleybuses were by now six years old and therefore one third life-expired, and with the shortages of war and the pressures there had been on maintenance, they were now in need of attention. A spare English Electric traction motor was purchased at the end of 1944 and this, together with a spare motor already held by the department, allowed an overhaul programme to begin. The department had also struggled on through the war years with an ageing motorbus fleet and, in 1945, the oldest vehicles in stock were a single-deck fleet of seven Guy Bs dating from 1926 to 1930 and eleven double-deck Leyland Titan TD1s dating from 1929 to 1932, all of which were petrol-engined. By the end of the war these were all life-expired, this showing most clearly in the bodywork where age and insufficient maintenance had caused the wooden framework to sag. The Titans were, in fact, beginning to give rise to some concern and, due to very high maintenance costs, were having to be used where possible only on very light duties.

Post-war shortages being what they were, however, the Leyland Titans were destined to have to continue in service on Reading's streets for a few more years yet. Obtaining spare parts was a particular problem, and an enquiry to Leyland Motors Ltd. on 1st May 1945 asking about the availability of spare parts and service exchange units for the Titans met with a negative response. This led the deputy transport manager to request that bus 38 be taken out of service and cannibalised to provide a pool of spares. He commented that if the spares situation did not improve from Leyland Motors Ltd. within twelve months, then *"...the time is right for the abandoning of this type of vehicle"*. In fact it was not bus 38 but 39 which was withdrawn the following year, after service on 14th July 1946. 39 was broken up at Mill Lane to provide spares for the rest of the fleet, many of which, as it turned out, remained in service with the undertaking until the end of June 1949.

Also in May 1945, soon after taking up his new appointment, the new transport manager asked that the department's immediate post-war demands, for ten new AEC double-deck motorbuses, should be registered with the regional transport commissioner. In this era of austerity, new Ministry of War Transport procedures demanded that a first and second choice of manufacturer should be registered. In Reading's case, however, possibly on account of already having placed a 'reservation' with AEC early in the war, the regional transport commissioner agreed to accept an application for ten AECs, for delivery once peacetime delivery schedules were restored, possibly early in 1946. Although they were intended to replace, as a matter of extreme urgency, the 11 Leyland Titan TD1 double-deckers, it was hinted that it was unlikely that all ten would be supplied in one batch.

Normal commercial vehicle manufacture re-started in the last months of 1945; at first, this was mainly to meet export opportunities to help satisfy Britain's need for foreign exchange. Nevertheless, the Ministry of Transport (as it had been re-named following the end of the war) continued to exercise considerable control and new vehicles were still

Leyland Titan 36 (RD 777) was one of the best remembered of corporation motorbuses in this era by ordinary passengers, because it was the only one with an enclosed top deck but outside staircase. By all accounts it was a regular performer on route F (Uplands Road – Merry Maidens). On this occasion the bus seems to have turned 'short' at Stations and is preparing, perhaps, to return to the Merry Maidens, for which there was a separately licensed superimposed service – note the driver 'twiddling the handle' to change the front destination blind.
Late W. J. Haynes © Millane Publishing

rationed, which meant that on a national scale there was still considerable delay in replacing worn-out vehicles.

Park Royal Vehicles Ltd. were providing some assistance to the Transport Department in May 1945, too, undertaking some work on AEC Regent 26. They were also at this time discussing the repair of trolleybus 105, which had been seriously damaged in a second major accident on the morning of Thursday 19th April 1945, less than three weeks after Mr Little had taken over as transport manager and engineer. On emerging from the depot, it had careered across the road and embedded itself into the front wall of Charles Elsbury & Son's printing works, a corner of the building being completely demolished. 105 had never been a very popular vehicle and, indeed, there had been an 'inquest' on one occasion in February 1941 after a driver had refused point blank to take over the bus. A very tangible reason for this latest saga was that there had been frequent trouble with the vehicle's control equipment, the power supply to the traction motor reportedly being not always consistent. If this caused 'unpredictable' acceleration, it would certainly explain both its accident at the Southampton Street end of Mill Lane in August 1941 (see page 55) and this latest accident opposite the depot entrance. 105 was reputedly out of action for a full seventeen months and did not officially return to service until 3rd September 1946 (although there is evidence to suggest that it was in service for some of the time but also spent long periods off the road with defects). During that period, the Allen West electrical control equipment was replaced by English Electric Series Dynamic control equipment; the two two-seater rearward-facing bench seats at the front of the lower deck were replaced by two pairs of forward-facing seats, thus providing a more conventional seating arrangement; and all the road springs were reconditioned. Trolleybus 104 is also understood to have been out of service for much of the summer of 1945 requiring, presumably, motorbus substitution on trolleybus route C.

Commencing at the end of May 1945, all bell pushes were gradually eliminated from the upper decks of motorbuses and trolleybuses, except for that at the head of the staircase. This was done to ensure that conductors only signalled for the bus to proceed if they had sight of the platform (directly or by means of the staircase mirror). Evidently, there had been some concern within the Transport Committee regarding platform accidents. With many thousands of extra passengers carried during the war, in often overloaded vehicles and in blackout conditions, and with conductors – often novices – usually working under extreme pressure, such an increase is hardly surprising.

The departmental van, a one-ton lorry and a three-ton lorry were all life-expired and needed replacing, according to a report the transport manager placed before the Transport Committee at its meeting of 17th May 1945. It so happened that, following its disbanding, a number of redundant civil defence vehicles were about to be offered for sale by the council. The Transport Committee therefore agreed to purchase three of them, the vehicles having in any case been in the care of the Transport Department throughout the war.

The minutes of the Emergency Committee confirm that one was a Commer 8hp Supervan (GX 2472), which was transferred in June 1945. The second was a Crown-owned Commer 5-ton lorry (BRD 838), which had been stored with another lorry at Mill Lane depot for some years before being registered in May 1943. Reference to this vehicle first appears in the Emergency Committee minutes for 12th May 1943, when the Ministry of Home Security directed that the town's two mobile gas cleansing units, at that time mounted on elderly Austin chassis, should be remounted onto the chassis of these two ex-army vehicles in store at the depot. One of these two was given civilian registration BRD 838, whilst the second (civilian registration unknown), which became the other gas cleansing unit, was transferred to H. M. Dockyard, Portsmouth, in June 1944. On 8th June 1945, the transport and ambulance officer (now, of course, Mr Little) was authorised to make application to acquire BRD 838 for the undertaking, the original intention being that it would be converted to provide an additional tower wagon. In the event, costs were reviewed and the purchase of a new tower wagon was authorised instead, on 17th September 1945. Tenders were invited for the supply of a chassis, and a Commer Superpoise was subsequently delivered circa April 1946. This was soon dispatched to the Eagle Engineering Co. Ltd., of Warwick, for a body and tower to be fitted. The completed tower wagon was delivered at the beginning of July 1946, and was registered CDP 583 on 12th July 1946. It duly entered service in the auxiliary fleet as No. 33, and was to remain in departmental service until February 1969. BRD 838, having already been purchased, had its gas cleansing unit body removed and replaced with a sided lorry body and lifting crane. It was mainly used as a pole carrier, entering service on 1st July 1946. It remained in stock until around late 1965.

A third ex-ARP vehicle taken into stock following the Transport Committee's decision of 17th May 1945, was a Commer 2-ton lorry (GXO 662), which was one of five vehicles to be collected together into a newly-formed 'dinner wagon' fleet, to be run by the transport manager & engineer from the bus depot on behalf of the Education Committee. In these early days of the Education Act, 1944, and the arrival on the scene of 'school dinners', its primary purpose was to transport bulk food containers from school meals kitchens to the schools. It was joined by another ex-ARP Rescue Service vehicle, a Bedford 2-ton lorry (FKT 154), the purchase of which was authorised on 17th September 1945. GXO 662 and FKT 154 were joined by another Bedford 2-ton lorry (BMO 451), a Bedford 30-cwt Van (JB 2090), and a Morris 25-cwt van (BDP 542). It is worth pointing out that no fleet numbers were carried on ancillary vehicles at this time.

A surviving schedule dated 5th May 1945 indicates that the 1925/26-vintage Guy B single-deckers, 12, 13, and 17, which had been used as ARP inter-hospital ambulances throughout the war, were withdrawn at this time and prepared for sale, together with the two surviving Guy FCX six-wheelers, 31 and 32, which had been withdrawn and held in reserve since July 1943. It is not known when the two other Guy B inter-hospital ambulances – former buses 15 and 18 – were withdrawn. A surviving memo dated 5th June 1942 suggested that 'an ambulance' (which we take to mean either 15 or 18) be withdrawn and its gearbox used to replace the unit in a failed service bus (Guy 35). This would seem to be a false lead, however: local enthusiast Edgar Jordan's diary records Guy 15 in Mill Lane depot on 22nd July 1943 still fitted out as an ambulance. Furthermore, 15 is known to have survived the war as Mr Jordan records it in Reading on 6th April 1946, evidently sold on and painted in all-over flat maroon, apparently in use as a mobile workshop. Although only four ambulances were recorded in Mill Lane depot on 7th August 1943, with bus 18 not being one of them, 18 was still being recorded in the annual record of mileages dated 31st March 1945 and must therefore have still been active towards the end of the war.

For some totally unexplained reason, the wartime destination blinds fitted to AEC Regent 49 (RD 8092) in August 1940 contained the destination 'Wood Lane' rather than that which had been approved for the wartime renaming of 'Lower Whitley', viz., 'Wood Lane Junc'. The bus, showing the said destination, is depicted here outside the Great Western Hotel on arrival at Stations from Chalgrove Way one day in September 1946. By this time it had lost the blackout markings to the rear wings that so many other corporation buses seem to have retained until at least this time.

Late W. J. Haynes © Millane Publishing

The sale of the ARP inter-hospital ambulances did not, however, relieve the transport manager of his care of an ambulance fleet, for the Reading borough-owned hospital ambulances had also found their way into his care for maintenance purposes during the war years. With the demise of the civil defence organisations after the war in Europe had drawn to a close, responsibility for the town's ambulances had remained with the council. It was soon confirmed, at the Transport Committee meeting of 14th June 1945, that the ambulances (and also the borough's fleet of pool cars) would remain with the Transport Department. Those ambulances based at Battle Hospital and Prospect Park Hospital (both at that time, in those pre-National Health service days, run by the County Borough of Reading), would continue to be based there, but the remainder would be based at the Mill Lane bus depot. All of the town's ambulances at that time (and for many years to come) were operated in emergencies on the nationally-accepted 'scoop-and-run' principle by two-man crews with a knowledge of first aid, who aimed simply at getting patients to hospital as quickly as possible. On 11th September 1946, in another change, it was confirmed that the operation of the town's ambulance service would remain with the Transport Department, who would run it henceforth on behalf of the Ministry of Health.

As expected, the Transport Department received a licence, dated 13th October 1945, to obtain only five new AEC double-deckers out of the ten required. An order was therefore placed with AEC within the month for five Regent II chassis, at a cost of £1,450 each. They were still under 'wartime' government control and described as *"...a proprietary article"*, being supplied by AEC Ltd. *"under their standard terms of contract under wartime conditions"*. They were further described at the Transport Committee meeting of 22nd November 1945 as *"...the same as those supplied in 1938"*. It was also reported that the chassis *"...are now delivered to our Works"*, effectively for storage, namely:

Delivered	Chassis No.	Fleet No.
09.11.45	O661.7532	59
09.11.45	O661.7533	60
13.11.45	O661.7541	61
13.11.45	O661.7542	62
16.11.45	O661.7531	58

To speed the process of delivery, the Transport Committee, at its meeting on 22nd November 1945, agreed to place orders for bodywork direct with Park Royal Vehicles Ltd. (thus avoiding any delay caused by the usual tendering procedures) at an estimated cost of £1,520 each. The chassis were added to the corporation's own fire insurance policy and were expected to be delivered early in the new year to Park Royal Vehicles Ltd. for bodying to a 'relaxed utility' design. The five chassis were still at Mill Lane depot on 14th January 1946, provoking an enquiry from the insurers – the Liverpool & London Globe Insurance Co. Ltd. – as to whether they had been moved. It seems that the corporation was also responsible for insuring the chassis whilst the bodies were being constructed at Park Royal.

Meanwhile, with a delay in the delivery of new AEC double-deckers, it had become obvious that existing vehicles would have to sustain services for some time to come. It was therefore decided, at the Transport Committee meeting of 11th October 1945, to refurbish the three remaining petrol-engined AEC Regent buses (4, 5 and 10) dating from 1933/34, and to fit them with direct injection oil engines. This, it was claimed, would modernise them *"...to a condition nearly equivalent to new"*. This work involved the major overhaul of the chassis and the rebuilding of the bodywork, the latter to be carried out by Vincents of Reading Ltd., who were, apparently, engaged in similar work for other undertakings. The work on bus 5 was listed in the undertaking's job book on 1st October 1945, some ten days before the aforementioned agreement of the Transport Committee, when it was reported that one vehicle (presumably 5) was *"already with Vincents for preliminary inspection"*. Indeed, it was observed at their premises by a local enthusiast on 13th October 1945. The body of 5 was, thereafter, extensively rebuilt on an 'actual cost' basis, which was cheaper *"...than laying down a completely new body"*. There is a suggestion that the body was actually removed from the chassis, in which case the overhaul of the chassis and running units and the conversion to diesel is quite likely to have been carried out at Mill Lane.

For the moment, however, Reading Corporation Transport found itself in late 1945 left with a mixture of older vehicles to meet a rapidly rising travel demand. People were returning to peacetime employment and leisure patterns – especially so as servicemen and women were being 'demobbed' at unprecedented rates. Delayed maintenance from the war years meant that vehicles were frequently off the road, adding further to the department's problems. The Transport Department therefore looked around for additional vehicles. An interesting enquiry was made of the Thames Valley Traction Co. Ltd. on 6th November 1945 exploring the possibility of hiring vehicles. The department was informed that no double-deckers were available but was offered the loan of eight Tilling-Stevens 32-seat single-deckers, previously used on a wartime contract transporting GWR staff to and from Aldermaston. If they were wanted by Reading Corporation Transport, they were requested to collect them by 12th or 13th November 1945, as they had already been offered to the European Inland organisation, which was providing transport facilities in war-damaged European cities where the transport infrastructure had been destroyed. With reference to the fleet details in Paul Lacey's *A History of the Thames Valley Traction Co. Ltd. 1920–1930*, it is certain that the vehicles referred to were Tilling Stevens B9As with Brush bodywork, of which only eight remained in the Thames Valley fleet by November 1945, as follows:

Fleet No.	Reg. No.	Layout	Date New	Disposal
144	MO 9316	B32R	.05.27	.12.45
149	MO 9321	B32R	.05.27	.12.45
150	MO 9322	B32R	.06.27	.12.45
152	MO 9324	B32R	.06.27	.02.46
153	MO 9325	B32R	.05.27	.01.46
156	MO 9328	B32R	.05.27	.01.46
159	RX 1394	C28F	.05.28	.11.45
160	RX 1395	C28F	.05.28	.11.45

No-one recalls these vehicles being used by Reading Corporation Transport and it is unlikely that any of them were either hired or purchased. It is equally unlikely that any of them ended their long service lives helping to re-establish transport services in the shattered cities of war-damaged Europe, especially as one of these vehicles, 152, was subsequently discovered serving as a shed in Ash, near Aldershot and is now preserved at Amberley Working Museum, near Arundel, West Sussex.

On 9th November 1945 a single-deck bus was loaned to the London Passenger Transport Board to complete a journey being undertaken by a failed Green Line coach which had been converted to an emergency sitting-case ambulance. London Transport was charged 18s 9d for the loan of the vehicle for the 12 miles operated. It is interesting to speculate what the passengers might have thought of the very elderly Guy B supplied as a replacement.

During 1945, utility trolleybus 134 was rebuilt at the front end, reducing the depth of the windscreen to bring it in line with the side windows. A 'square'-type side destination box was also fitted over the platform and the front registration number plate was repositioned to the bottom of the removable towing panel. It re-entered service thus modified on 7th November 1945. None of the other utility trolley-buses were similarly treated.

Under an Order of the Road Traffic Act, 1930, all motor-buses were required to be fitted with a device which would give warning of an impending failure of brake vacuum. During the war, under Defence Regulations, this Order had been relaxed year-by-year, but in view of the end of the war, it was not safe to assume that this would continue for a further year when due for reconsideration in January 1946. Thus, the transport manager sought authority to buy and fit suitable gauges to vehicles devoid of them but likely to be retained for the foreseeable future, it being considered unlikely that the Order would be enforced on vehicles earmarked for early withdrawal!

The transport manager had reported to the Transport Committee meeting of 22nd November 1945 that the seven Guy B vehicles remaining in service (19, 20, 33–35, 40 and 41) were proving difficult to maintain, with spares only available on the second-hand market and, like the Leyland Titan double-deckers, it would be expedient to retire them before the Ministry of Transport vehicle examiners brought pressure to bear. It was agreed, therefore, as a temporary measure and because a minimum delay in delivery was promised, that six petrol-engined Bedford OB single-deckers be ordered for use on lightly-trafficked routes and schools work. They were ordered through and supplied by Great Western Motors Ltd, the local Vauxhall and Bedford dealer, at a cost of £1,045 each. These vehicles, developed from the wartime utility OWB model, were built to a less austere specification, with rounded bodylines and Rexene upholstered seats. The six chassis were delivered to Duple for bodying during February 1946, three on 15th and three on 18th, and insurance was arranged through the borough treasurer's office. The completed vehicles arrived in Reading in late April and early May 1946. As delivered they carried 30-seat bodies (re-seated to 28 soon after delivery) and were numbered 12, 13, 15, 16, 17 and 18 (CDP 231–236). These fleet numbers had previously been carried by those Guy B vehicles which had been withdrawn from passenger service immediately before the war (most of which had subsequently become ARP inter-hospital ambulances) – the policy of the undertaking at this time still being to infill vacant fleet numbers. Initially, at least, these buses were regularly in use on route L (Hemdean Road – Berkeley Avenue). For further details see Appendices A and B.

Reading Corporation Transport's first post-war buses were six Duple-bodied Bedford OB single-deckers. These were obtained purely as a stop-gap because the availability of new double-deckers in the short term was nil and certain of the undertaking's older double-deckers were in an advanced state of decrepitude and approaching the point where, under peacetime standards, they would probably be banned from use. Buses 12, 13, 15, 16, 17 and 18 (CDP 231–6) are lined up next to the railway embankment in Palmer Park for the picture.

© Millane Publishing

The Duple-bodied Bedford OBs

Top: The Callington Road branch of route N had been extended from St. Mary's Butts to Promenade as a result of a curtailment (initially intended as temporary) of trolley-bus operation on route C (Whit-Pump – Promenade). Bus 16 (CDP 234) is seen here loading for Promenade at the stop in Friar Street, by the Co-op department store.

Centre: Duple-bodied Bedford OB 17 (CDP 235), still fairly new, was photographed in September 1946 loading at the Berkeley Avenue stop in St. Mary's Butts on route L. Mr W. M. Little, the new transport manager & engineer, was evidently keen on adopting a much simplified livery, with cream restricted to some mouldings, so eliminating black lining between colours.

Bottom: Bus 18 (CDP 236), the last of the six Duple-bodied Bedford OBs delivered in summer 1946, is seen in West Street heading southbound, en route for Callington Road. This view was probably taken on the same dismal day in September 1946 as a number of other views on nearby pages.

All photos Late W. J. Haynes
© Millane Publishing

119

The five AEC Regent II chassis delivered in November 1945 were still at Mill Lane on 30th January 1946 but, on 13th February 1946, chassis O661.7531 was the first to be delivered to Park Royal Vehicles Ltd's factory for bodying. When built, this became bus 58 in the Reading fleet and seems to have been completed much earlier than its sister vehicles. The completed bus 58 was sent to London Transport's Chiswick Works for a tilt-test, where it was photographed on trade-plates prior to its registration. The early delivery of 58's chassis to Park Royal suggests that the bus was the trial vehicle for the whole order and that the vehicle was used for tests prior to completion of the order. An interesting observation is that the method of construction of the bodies for this batch is not altogether typical of post-war Park Royal design and detail. Indeed, at a time when there was little opportunity to develop a design other than one which could be regarded as standard, it is quite surprising that the design of these buses was absolutely unique to Reading! It might have something to do with the fact that these buses were 'lowbridge', so that much use had to be made of pre-war construction techniques, resulting in the framework being something of a 'mixture'. As a result of the extra interest having to be taken by the Park Royal drawing office, there was thus an opportunity to develop a special outward appearance. What is not explained is the fact that, at a time when seating capacity was very important, these vehicles were fitted-out with only 24 instead of 26 seats on the upper deck.

Despite assurances from Park Royal in May 1946 that the five completed AEC Regent II vehicles would be delivered in June and July 1946, the remaining four chassis stayed in store at Mill Lane depot until the middle of July. Thereafter, one chassis was sent to London each day, on 10th, 11th, 16th and 17th July. Before these last four of the initial delivery of five chassis had left for Park Royal, another five AEC Regent II chassis were sanctioned, in May 1946, bringing the order to the original requirement for ten vehicles. The Transport Committee, at its meeting on 16th May 1946, was only too pleased to agree to purchase these vehicles! Again, the chassis, when built, found a temporary residence at Mill Lane in the summer and autumn of 1946, awaiting bodying, insured for £1,575 each. The complete batch of ten vehicles was collected from Park Royal Vehicles Ltd. by corporation drivers on various dates in January 1947.

Delivered	Chassis No.	Fleet No.	Left Mill Lane
09.08.46	O661.7940	65	05.11.46
10.08.46	O661.7938	63	07.11.46
10.08.46	O661.7939	64	06.11.46
10.08.46	O661.7941	66	02.11.46
23.08.46	O661.7942	67	04.11.46

Also on 16th May 1946, Mr Little informed the Transport Committee that his enquiries regarding the supply of new trolley vehicles had revealed that Park Royal Vehicles Ltd. would not be undertaking any trolleybus work until August or September 1947 and that, therefore, nothing would be lost in advertising for tenders for twenty trolleybus bodies. It was also agreed to ask AEC to quote for twenty trolleybus chassis and equipment, with a view to maintaining some standardisation in the trolleybus fleet. However, in September 1946, following a visit by Mr Little to the Park Royal works at Harlesden, and in consultation with Mr Evans, the prospective new transport manager, a provisional order for twenty trolleybus bodies was placed with Park Royal upon the promise of priority delivery dates.

The arrival of the Bedford OBs did little to ease the vehicle shortage. Only three of the seven remaining Guy Bs had been withdrawn upon the arrival of the OBs (33, 34 and 35 on 30th April 1946) – and these were re-licensed from 16th May 1946 and returned to service! Guy 35, as mentioned in the previous chapter, was subsequently decorated for Reading Road Safety Week (14th–21st September 1946); it was thereafter repainted and had something of a revival, operating on school services and rush hour journeys.

On 12th July 1946, bus 5 emerged from Vincents of Reading Ltd. fitted with a later-style 'long' radiator and with a completely restyled body. It had retained its six-bay frame but in many other respects looked very similar to the AEC Regent IIs, which were at that time being bodied by Park Royal. To the public, 5 was a new vehicle – but for all Vincents' hard work, it lasted in service only until 31st October 1950. Neither of the two other Regents earmarked for the same treatment (4 and 10) were similarly rebuilt, although 10 is listed in the undertaking's job book as receiving a diesel engine sometime during the period March to May 1947, its type A162 six-cylinder petrol engine being replaced by an indirect injection type A173 six cylinder 7.7-

In early 1946, AEC Regent 5 (RD 4338) had its timber-framed Park Royal body completely rebuilt by Vincents of Reading Ltd., returning to service on 12th July 1946. The original six-bay frame was retained, as were the roof panels, rear platform and domes and the single pane rear upper-deck emergency door but a new curved front, with larger windscreen and almost flush dash replaced the original. Quarter-turn (instead of straight) stairs, a sliding cab door, new half-drop windows and new seating for 50 gave the impression of a new bus. External livery was unchanged except that there was no black beading between the colours. A view of the bus in its original form appears on page 67.

*Late W. J. Haynes © Millane Publishing (left)
Copied from* AEC Gazette *(right)*

FAR FROM FINISHED

Just one of the many Southall-built machines in the Reading Corporation fleet, this "Regent" is daily enhancing A.E.C. reputation for longevity.

It is one of three purchased in 1933 and ran 432,232 miles with its original petrol engine until fitted with a 7.7 litre oil engine in August last. Now the body has been reconditioned by Vincents of Reading, provided with new seats and windows and modernised by the inclusion of a sliding cab door.

No fulsome praise is needed for a vehicle which can begin a new life when over 13 years old. Its special qualities are apparent to any transport engineer.

litre oil engine. It was possibly at this stage (as per photographic evidence) that it was fitted with a post-1937 'long' AEC radiator, although a 'short' radiator was reinstated some time before it was eventually withdrawn. Bus 4 was never 'modernised', and it now became the only petrol-engined Regent in the fleet. It was eventually withdrawn on 30th June 1949.

Back in March 1946, in an interesting engineering exercise, utility Guy Arab 27 had received an AEC type A173 oil engine in place of its Gardner 6LW unit. It re-entered service on 23rd May 1946, with its Guy wording filed off the radiator top tank and replaced by cream-painted lettering on maroon to read *"Reading Transport"*. Apparently, Gardner engines were unpopular with the undertaking's drivers because they were responsible for a very slow gear-change. The engine change was considered successful, and it is rumoured that 27 was often used thereafter as the early morning staff bus, so that the distinctive throb of the AEC 7.7-litre oil engine would have warned employees living on the Whitley Estate well in advance of its arrival! In September 1946, five 7.7-litre AEC type A173 oil engines, complete with clutches, flywheels and other equipment, were ordered at a cost of £554 10s 0d. each, with a view to replacing the Gardner engines in the other three Guy Arabs and to provide two replacement float engines for the two previous floats now used in buses 5 and 27. In the event, and probably due to a different attitude by the incoming transport manager, no further Guy Arabs received AEC engines, although one of the new engines was fitted to AEC Regent 10 as detailed above. Oil-engined Regent 25 received a new engine at this time, too, swapping its 8.8-litre type A165 oil engine for a 7.7-litre type A173 oil engine. When the old engine was taken out, the bus lost its protruding radiator, which had marked it out in the fleet as 'different'.

Meanwhile, the *Berkshire Chronicle* for 27th September 1946 carried the following reference in its editorial column 'Reading Week by Week', by 'Chronicler': *"Fumes in 'Buses: Recently, complaints have reached me about the fumes which are apparently escaping from the engines from some of the Reading Corporation omnibuses amongst the passengers. Regular riders have spoken of the choking sensation experienced when riding in these vehicles, and of the great relief it has been to get out into the fresh air at their destination. I know that the answer is likely to be that replacements of worn parts are extremely difficult to come by nowadays. But surely some sort of temporary repair can be effected to prevent fumes escaping inside the 'bus, where they almost overcome the passengers".*

It had become something of a tradition within the municipal transport industry that, soon after a new transport manager was appointed to an undertaking, there would be an attempt to change (or at least modify) the livery. It should have come as no surprise, therefore, when Guy Arab 27, at the time of its engine change, was given an experimental livery of 'all-over' maroon but retaining the centre cream band and with the other two bands reduced in depth, and with no black beading (see page 122). Trolleybus 123 was similarly out-shopped on 7th June 1946 in a livery of 'all-over' maroon (or crimson as it was officially called) with a reduced depth of centre cream band and the horizontal moulding beneath the lower-deck windows picked out in cream but with no black beading (also illustrated on page 122). This was not considered a success and the vehicle last ran thus on 23rd November 1946, the normal cream bands and black beading being reinstated. As already recorded, AEC Regent 5 re-entered service in July 1946 after re-building by Vincents. It did so in standard livery but without the beading being picked-out in black.

As early as October 1943, a report to the transport manager, which was related specifically to future trolleybus purchases, had looked forward to an age when new materials, processes and technologies, which had been developed as a result of the demands of war, would contribute to the peacetime environment. It predicted, with some accuracy, the post-war attempts at a reduction in vehicle unladen weight by the use of new alloys, and of an increased use of 'easy-to-clean' synthetic materials internally for seats, floors and fittings. It was, in fact, remarkably far-sighted, discussing issues which were to be important principles behind bus design through the early 1950s, at a time when staff costs rose and passenger loadings increased, and when the need for high-capacity and light-weight vehicles taxed the best minds in the industry. There were also national campaigns to increase maximum vehicle dimensions, from 7ft 6in to 8ft wide and from 26ft to 30ft in overall length, targeting, initially, the new intake of MPs after the 1945 general election. In February 1946 it was announced that a width increase to 8 feet had been granted,

Mr Little's Livery Experiments

In the twenty months that William Morison Little was transport manager & engineer, he tried a number of innovations, not least of which was a modified livery. The Duple-bodied Bedford OBs (see pages 118/119) were first to appear in a simplified livery using much less cream and no black beading. It was then a case of experimenting with an existing trolleybus and double-deck motorbus.

Top and Centre: AEC trolleybus 123 (ARD 686) ran in its simplified livery between 7th June and 23rd November 1946, literally days before Mr Little's time as manager drew to a close. As modified, the upper cream band was eliminated; the lower cream band was replaced by cream-painted horizontal strapping immediately below the lower-deck windows; and the centre cream band was greatly reduced at upper-deck floor level. All horizontal black lining-out of beading between colours was also eliminated and the fleet numbers were repositioned in the now-maroon waist rail area. In the top view, 123 is followed by 121 (ARD 684) in 'normal' livery.

Both Late W. J. Haynes © Maiwand Photographic Archive

Bottom: Guy Arab 27 (BRD 815) was selected for painting slightly differently from the trolleybus. Both upper and lower cream bands were replaced by cream-painted horizontal strapping immediately below both upper- and lower-deck windows, but the centre cream band was retained; indeed, it was widened to include the horizontal strapping both sides. All black paintwork separating cream and maroon areas was eliminated and fleet number positions were raised to the now-maroon waist rail. It appears that the lower panels of the bus were replaced before painting and the opportunity was taken to dispense with the horizontal strapping originally used to delineate the lower edge of the lower cream band. The dates during which the bus ran in this livery are not recorded, but may have commenced on 23rd May 1946, on which date the bus was returned to service after being fitted with an AEC engine.

Late W. J. Haynes © Millane Publishing

but the existing limit in overall length for two-axle buses remained, for the time being, at 26 feet. In Reading, it was anticipated that when trolleybuses for use on the Whitley extensions came to be ordered, they would be built to whatever maximum dimensions were permitted at the time.

The delay in delivery of new trolleybuses, and the knock-on effect of delaying the introduction of the proposed Whitley trolleybus services, caused more problems for the existing motorbus fleet. It had been intended that introduction of trolleybus services in Whitley in 1947 would have released around eighteen motorbuses for use on services elsewhere in the borough, which would have permitted the withdrawal of the Leyland Titans. Notwithstanding the return home to London and the south coast of the town's wartime evacuees, an anticipated reduction in passenger traffic to pre-war levels was a bit naive and never took place. Instead, it was necessary to increase the basic service provision on route F (Merry Maidens – Uplands Road) and route M (Erleigh Road – Grovelands Road), each by two buses. There was also a general need to meet increased requirements at peak times.

Mr Little was able to demonstrate the existing shortfall and projected future requirements of the undertaking over the next few years, until the Whitley trolleybus route extensions were in operation. This, in turn, indicated the future of the undertaking's motorbus rolling stock. It went without saying that all 11 Leyland Titans and the five surviving Guy B single-deckers would be the first to go, it being said that *"there is very little doubt that the PSV examiner would refuse to certify the use of these vehicles if times were normal"*. The Guy Arabs, it was stated, would be kept *"only if they could be made to operate as efficiently as the remainder of the fleet or there is some special work for which they are suitable"*. All AEC Regents still with petrol engines or 8.8-litre oil engines were to be converted to indirect injection 7.7-litre oil engines which, as we have already seen, largely came to pass.

So it was that the Transport Committee was informed at their meeting in November 1946, that a provisional order for ten AEC Regent III chassis, at an estimated cost of £1,643 each, had been placed during the previous month. The delivery dates for new bus bodies was critical, and a survey of body builders revealed a general inability to provide early delivery, one bodybuilder – Duple – even quoting early 1950! Park Royal, the preferred supplier, was unable to provide lowbridge bodies to Reading's specification on AEC Regent III chassis before the middle of 1948, due, apparently, both to a shortage of skilled draughtsmen to produce new drawings and the non-availability from AEC of Regent III chassis drawings showing the body mounting points for lowbridge bodies. However, Mr Little had been told that if the ten bodies were replicas of the ten currently being constructed on AEC Regent II chassis, then Park Royal Vehicles Ltd. would be able to offer delivery of ten bodies during 1947 – but it was Park Royal's understanding that AEC had ceased production of Regent II chassis. Mr Little pressed Park Royal to adapt their drawings of standard double-deck bodies fitted to Regent III chassis and on the promise of delivery in 1947, an order was placed with Park Royal Vehicles Ltd. for ten bodies similar to those currently under construction on Regent II chassis but to be fitted to Regent III chassis.

At the same Transport Committee meeting, on 21st November 1946, and with the delay in obtaining double-deck motorbuses in mind, it was reported that Bedford OBs were still available on fairly short delivery dates and that the manufacturers had indicated that they were able to supply ten buses, commencing in March 1947, at the rate of one per month. However, only six further new petrol-engined Bedford OBs were ordered, more-or-less immediately, this time to be fitted with 32-seat Mulliner bodies, at an overall cost of £1,144 4s 6d each. They were purchased purely as a temporary solution to the delivery delays of double-deckers, and it was made perfectly clear that *"...it must be borne in mind that D/D buses are what we wanted, and such S/D as you may decide to obtain would have to go to make room for D/D buses when these are available"*.

The transport manager, Mr W. M. Little, and the deputy transport manager, Lt. Col. J. F. Fardell, had both tendered their resignations to the Transport Committee on 25th July 1946 to take up new posts elsewhere, Mr Fardell going to the newly-formed Christchurch Tramways Board, in New Zealand, as general manager. He was succeeded by Mr A. Gent, who had been acting deputy manager while Mr Fardell was away during the war. Mr Little took a post as deputy transport manager back with Edinburgh Corporation Transport, where he had received all his training and basic experience before moving to St. Helens Corporation Transport as general manager in 1941. Subsequently, he went on to even greater heights in his career, becoming transport manager at Edinburgh, sooner rather than later, upon the sudden death, in September 1948, of the incumbent transport manager, Mr Robert McLeod. He later held senior positions in the Scottish Bus Group and, in 1974, his career reached its peak when he became president of the Chartered Institute of Transport.

When Mr Little left Reading at the end of November 1946, he did so after just twenty months. During his brief but very busy stay in Reading, he had presented a number of reports containing several interesting ideas for the development of the Transport Department, including changes to routes, vehicle policy and fares policy – yet none of these seemed to find acceptance with the Transport Committee. He had to work in the most difficult of circumstances during his incumbency, with town centre streets being reconstructed and bus route diversions having to be implemented during virtually the whole period of his tenure. He did his best, too, to obtain replacement motorbus rolling stock and to get the pre-war trolleybus system expansion plans rolling again. He also had to follow a rather well-respected and admired predecessor, of some 25 years' standing, in James McLennan Calder. Could it be that his short period of office in Reading and his departure was provoked by frustration?

Three candidates had been interviewed to fill the vacancy of transport manager and engineer:

Mr R. E. Cox, rolling stock engineer, Newcastle upon Tyne Corporation Transport and Electricity Department.

Mr W. J. Evans, chief engineer and joint manager, Cardiff Corporation Transport Department.

Mr E. J. Robertson, electrical engineer, Manchester Corporation Transport Department.

Mr Little's successor was selected as Mr William John Evans, who had previously been interviewed for the same post when Mr Calder retired, and who had been a key figure in Cardiff when trolleybuses were introduced there in 1942. He started his new job as transport manager and engineer with Reading Corporation Transport on 2nd December 1946 and a new – and long – era began...

All the surviving Guy B single-deckers were already in the twilight of their lives. Fitted with AEC running units in 1938 (as was her sister, bus 41), bus 40 (RD 2114) is seen here on a dismal day in September 1946 loading southbound in the upper part of St. Mary's Butts while operating on route N to Callington Road. Leyland Titan 45 (RD 2945) is behind, loading for Wood Lane Junc.

Late W. J. Haynes
© Millane Publishing

It seems in this view that Guy B 34 (RD 36) has just arrived in Broad Street empty from depot, as Duty Inspector 'Tim' Jordan is giving the driver new instructions for parking as a 'spare' on the same damp and dismal September day as the view above. The bus obviously cannot be left double-parked, as it is here, in this part of Broad Street! Its passenger-carrying days will be over next spring and it will be sold off, to eventually become a caravan. The clock on the wall of H. Samuel, jeweller, was used by the Transport Department for timing purposes.

Late W. J. Haynes
© Millane Publishing

The official Park Royal Vehicles Ltd. photograph of AEC Regent II 58 (CRD 252) undergoing its tilt test, probably at London Transport's Chiswick Works, in spring 1946. This view, from William Little's era, shows a new livery with more cream. A few months later, livery experiments using bus 27 and trolleybus 123 featured reduced cream in the existing 'three cream bands' double-deck livery (see page 122); while bus 5 returned to service extensively rebuilt and wearing the standard three cream bands without the black lining between the colours (see pages 120/1). This suggests that liveries carried by buses 5 and 58 were also part of the livery experiments.

Print from J. R. Whitehead's collection

124

13   William John Evans starts his Long Tenure

On 10th December 1946, just days after Mr W. J. Evans had taken up his new task as transport manager he visited AEC at Southall with the chairman of the Transport Committee, Alderman Kersley, and Councillor A. E. Smith. The problems in fitting lowbridge Park Royal bodies to the proposed Regent III chassis ordered in November 1946 were clearly causing delay and so discussions on that day produced a promise of a further ten Regent II chassis for delivery from February 1947 – even though the type was no longer in production! Park Royal Vehicles was immediately contacted to discuss a programme of construction for bodies similar to the ten on Regent II chassis already in the Reading fleet. So it was that Reading Corporation Transport lost its chance to take new AEC Regent IIIs into the fleet, instead to receive the very last O661 Regent II chassis built by AEC, some months after Regent II chassis production had officially ended. Regent IIIs did not arrive in the Reading fleet for another ten years – and when a second batch of Regent IIIs was ordered in 1956, these were to be the very last of that model too!

Two days later, on 12th December 1946, Ministry of Transport authority was received for Reading Corporation Transport to operate newly-permitted 8ft-wide buses and trolleybuses on all routes. Work thus proceeded to design the new trolleybuses to these dimensions.

From the same date, in an attempt to discourage short-distance passengers from using that service when buses on other routes were available, a 2d minimum fare was introduced from St. Mary's Butts on the Staverton Road section of route N on evening peak journeys, which were suffering from overcrowding.

Also in December 1946, purchase of a replacement departmental car was authorised, in exchange for BPC 391, the 1934 Morris Cowley.

Walter Kershaw, formerly with Nottingham City Transport, had been selected as traffic superintendent and took up his appointment with effect from 1st January 1947.

The reader will get some idea of the sort of town and transport undertaking that William John Evans and Walter Kershaw had moved to, from a report under the heading *"Transport Services Criticised – 'No punctuality, no regularity'"* published in the *Reading Standard* on Friday 10th January 1947, of matters discussed when the town council had met the previous Tuesday evening:

"Strong criticism of Reading's transport services on the Shinfield Road route were made in a debate arising from a question to the Transport Committee chairman (Alderman H. V. Kersley) by Alderman A. F. Clark at Tuesday's meeting of the Town Council.

"Alderman Clark asked if the delivery of new omnibuses would enable the department to provide a more efficient service on the main routes of the town, and if so, when such a service would become operative.

"Alderman Kersley said that the new buses might be delivered in the early days of 1948, but the ten trolley [sic] buses ordered some eight or nine months ago might be delivered in the next few days. He was not in a position to promise what was going to be done with them, but he would promise that consideration would be given to all routes where there was hardship.

"Alderman Kersley, referring to queues outside the Bull Hotel in Broad Street, said that intending passengers seemed to be adopting a policy of walking to the stations to ensure getting on a vehicle, with the result that the buses were loaded before coming into Broad Street.

"Alderman Kersley went on to give the following figures of passengers carried by the department. In February 1939, a total of 1,444,975 were carried. In February 1946, a total of 2,936,787 were carried – an increase of over 100 per cent in passenger loading.

"Since May, 1946, the total weekly mileage operated on all routes had increased by 10,277 miles – an increase of approximately 20 per cent.

"Due to the general adoption in the area of a 44-hour (five-day) week by engineering and other industries, several works had changed their starting and finishing times, so that the latter now coincided with the evening peak period.

William John Evans succeeded William Morison Little as transport manager & engineer, taking up his duties on 6th December 1946. He was, like the late Jimmy Calder, destined to spend many years in the position, in the process putting his own stamp on the development and financial stability of the undertaking. He had previously been chief engineer of the municipal undertaking in Cardiff, having been rolling stock & overhead line engineer at Rotherham and formerly in the Traction Department at GEC, and so was well versed in trolleybus operation.

Passenger Transport

Typical of retirement ceremonies over the years, Inspector 'Tim' Jordan receives a presentation on his retirement in January 1947 from Mr W. J. Evans, the new transport manager & engineer. Those present are, from left to right, Driver Don Courtnage (T&GWU representative); Driver Dick Dowling; W. John Evans (transport manager), Insp. Jack Rodgers; Insp. Alf Scearce, Driver Chris King; Insp. Bert Walker; Insp. 'Tim' Jordan; unidentified; Walter Kershaw (traffic superintendent); and Albert Gent (deputy manager). 'Tim' Jordan, the father of H. Edgar Jordan, the local tramway historian, is indirectly responsible for the tome you have in your hands! He had joined the undertaking as a tram conductor in October 1906, becoming a motorman in November 1910, a trolleybus driver in 1936 and an inspector in 1941.

© Reading Museum Service (Reading Borough Council); all rights reserved

"Alderman Kersley said that the position would be appreciably improved when delivery was obtained during the next four to eight weeks of ten new double-decker buses. Those vehicles would be used on routes where they were most required.

"Alderman Clark said that he used the 'Merry Maidens' service many times a day, and he thought that it was absolutely the worst service in the town (A voice: "Try Caversham"), and he thought it was time something was done. From The Green, said Alderman Clark, it took half an hour to get to the town. There was, he complained, no punctuality or regularity in the service.

"The Transport Committee chairman, Alderman Clark observed, lived outside the borough and did not have to use the 'Merry Maidens' service. If he were to travel on this service he would hear some of the very uncomplimentary remarks that are made, he said.

"Councillor C. F. V. Baker asked Alderman Clark whether it was the people who went to work or people who went to offices who were complaining.

"Councillor A. Lockwood said he had a lot of sympathy both with Alderman Clark and with the Transport Committee chairman. He had noticed in these days that there was nothing like certainty in time-keeping. It was due, he thought, to the condition of the vehicles, to the roads, and to many other things not within the control of the chairman of the Committee. At the same time, he believed that the operatives were not entirely blameless and he hoped that something could be done by them to keep better time.

"Councillor Lockwood said that the Corporation had received many more complaints from passengers during the short period towards the end of last year and ending about November. He suspected that people had been encouraged to make these complaints because there was certain political capital in them.[*]

"Councillor E. Russell Jackson also spoke of what he described as the irregularity of the 'Merry Maidens' service.

"Alderman F. G. Sainsbury suggested that the Transport Committee chairman might consider restoring clocks at the stages so that people would know if the bus had gone.

"After the Mayor had intervened to ask: 'Has not anyone seen any bouquets thrown at the transport undertaking?' Councillor Gower spoke of complaints he had heard from people living in Tilehurst, not of the lack of buses, but regarding the fact that although there were many trolley buses it was almost impossible to get on them!

"Replying to the debate, Alderman Kersley said: 'Bus services will always be subject to criticism, but there are answers to the critical. Providing the questions are asked in

---

[*] At that time (and until 1949) municipal elections took place each November, not in May. The difficulties Cllr Lockwood emphasised were not peculiar to Reading.

the way they have been asked this evening, we shall welcome them. Everything is being done, and more will be done.'

"Alderman Kersley concluded with a warning regarding an increase of fares. 'We are determined to give as good a public service as is possible, but figures relating to the department show that it will not be long before we have to consider increased fares,' he said. The Thames Valley Co. and other privately owned services always got a system operating with a full a load per vehicle as possible. When the Corporation received their new buses, overheads would be increased if they had to run them with only part loads – and obviously someone had got to pay for this."

The following week, incidentally, Alderman H. V. Kersley, who had been a Reading town councillor since 1932 and who had taken over the chairmanship of the Transport Committee in November 1945, was appointed deputy transport commissioner for the South Eastern Traffic Area, which was being revived following its suspension during the war.

Within the first five weeks of assuming his new position, Mr Evans presented a report to the Transport (Future Policy) Sub-Committee, dated 6th January 1947, taking up the concerns of the previous manager with particular regard to declining revenue. The report, incidentally, made passing reference to the 23 conductresses and also two female inspectors still employed in their own right by the undertaking, rather than as replacements for men away on war service.

Quite obviously, the financial state of the undertaking required some urgent attention in the light of a predicted loss of £11,500 in the financial year ending 31st March 1947. Put in simple terms, Mr Evans reported that he could quite easily justify a substantial fares increase, because at the time of the tram-to-trolleybus conversion in 1939 there had actually been a fares reduction of roundly 13½%. Not only had these lower fares levels been maintained throughout the war, the additional operating costs had been met out of increased revenue generated by the vast increase in the number of passengers – and the opportunity had also been taken to pay off the outstanding charges on the operating fleet in a far shorter period than originally intended. Consequently, there was now only a modest reserve of £45,000.

As well as having to meet future running costs, Mr Evans had to be able to find the capital cost required to replace obsolete buses and trolleybuses and employ the additional staff required to meet an anticipated increase in demand in the post-war period. He therefore proposed a new set of fare stages, which retained the 1d minimum fare (but for a shorter distance of ½ mile), and to introduce a new 1½d fare. He also proposed that the ¾d scholar's ticket should be withdrawn and that scholar's ticket rates should be revised so that the highest rate became 3d instead of 2d. He further proposed that term passes (issued via the Education Committee under the Education Act, 1944, to scholars living over three miles from their school) should be increased from 10s to 12s 6d, to take account of the proposed increase in scholars' fares. Finally, he proposed that the minimum workmen's fare should be increased to 2d; that the wartime concession of issuing workman tickets on Sundays should be discontinued; and that discounted prepaid tickets should be withdrawn. Most of these changes were implemented later in the year, having received approval from the traffic commissioners during the summer. Mr Evans' original intention was that, as the matter was urgent, the new fares should be effective from as early as Sunday 30th March 1947. Perhaps, however, matters were left while some fairly substantial pay and conditions improvements for virtually all employees of the undertaking had come into effect and had settled down. The subject was publicly advertised in the local papers on 23rd May 1947, inviting objections to be lodged by 7th June 1947.

Mr Evans was also keen to discourage works specials, which, he said, encouraged a demand for 'immediate buses' and were always 'one-way loading', which did not cover operating costs. A policy he intended to implement, anyway, was that the frequency of service on any route at any time of the day would be closely related to the fares taken.

Following on from the above, at the Transport Committee meeting of 13th February 1947, Mr Evans broached the subject of school specials and two requests he had recently received to run more of them. The chief education officer had made an approach for the transport of an estimated 43 children aged between 5 and 14 between 'Southcote Estate' (junction of Monks Way with Southcote Lane) and Battle and Wilson schools (off Oxford Road). There had also been a personal approach by some mothers on the Greenfields Estate, in Whitley, to run a single-decker from the junction of Hartland Road with Basingstoke Road, via Whitley Wood Lane and Whitley Wood Road, to a footpath which necessitated only a short walk up to Ridgeway Primary

In early 1947 (and maybe a little earlier, as mentioned on page 89), certain AEC Regents – including 23 (ARD 14), seen here outside the GWR station – 'lost' their nearside headlamps. We surmise that delivery of new buses was being impeded partly because headlamps of the correct specification were not available, so some were 'borrowed' from the nearsides of existing buses to fit to the offsides of the new AEC Regent IIs (see page 136). At the time, obligatory vehicle lighting did not include headlamps, much less a pair – witness the single headlamps on most trams, the 60 'Diddler' trolleybuses in London and numerous local Shelvoke & Drewry municipal vehicles! © M. Rooum

School (off Shinfield Road). The reader should appreciate, of course, that at this time the development of the Southcote council estate, with schools and shops, etc., was five years into the future; also, while much further advanced as a council estate, new schools had yet to appear in Whitley. The Transport Department was at this time operating a seemingly little-used stage carriage school bus service (which apparently, had been re-introduced sometime in 1946) from Wood Lane Junction terminus to the Hartland Road end of the same footpath. The top end of Hartland Road was, at that time, an unfinished 'dead end' into scrubland. There were also, apparently, *"a number of other school specials as stage carriage vehicles"*, although no record of these seems to have survived. Operating school services under a stage carriage licence was an expensive option, especially with the Transport Department's limited resources. Mr Evans suggested that school transport could be far better provided under a contract hire arrangement, particularly if schools could be persuaded to delay their morning start time by 15 to 20 minutes. The matter was referred to the Education Department for further consideration and, from 21st April 1947, Katesgrove Senior Boys' School and Caversham Primary School altered their morning start from 8.50am to 9.20am – apparently with notable good effect as far as the Transport Department was concerned. Nearly a year later, in January 1948, there was an approach to run a school bus between Baydon Drive (off Berkeley Avenue, one stop back from the terminus of route L) and Battle School but all the points previously made were just as valid and thus nothing transpired.

From 10th March 1947, pink ticket rolls were introduced for use during the issuing period of workman return tickets (up until 7.45am), which of course meant that *all* tickets issued during the period were pink. A notice to conductors describes the procedure to be followed after this period, when the pink rolls were to be removed from the machines and the normal white roll substituted. When a 'WR' (workman return) ticket was proffered on a return journey, the 'WR' ticket was torn in two, one half being retained by the conductor and the other returned to the passenger with a newly-issued 'NVX' (no value exchange) ticket.

Evidently, too, the new transport manager had a different perception to that of his predecessors regarding the petitions from Whitley residents for a bus service to Stations. With effect from Thursday 9th January 1947 (and, presumably, upon completion of the reconstruction of St. Mary's Butts) the Staverton Road branch of route N was extended from St. Mary's Butts to Stations. It operated inwards via West Street, Friar Street, Greyfriars Road and Station Hill, but was routed outwards via Station Road, Friar Street and West Street. Equally interesting is that, as requested in previous petitions, the route was also diverted to operate via Christchurch Gardens and Northumberland Avenue instead of via Basingstoke Road and Buckland Road. As such it became a separate route, designated route P, operated every 30 minutes throughout the day, generally by Bedford OBs. The 2d minimum fare in operation during the Monday to Friday evening peak was retained. Presumably from the same date, the Callington Road branch of route N was reinstated to operate Callington Road – Promenade (and reverting to double-deck operation); this service had been operated during the St. Mary's Butts reconstruction in two halves (Callington Road – St. Mary's Butts and West Street – Promenade), invariably by Bedford OBs.

Guy B 20 (DP 7258) had celebrated her 20th birthday a couple of months before this picture was taken in West Street, whilst on layover on that same grey September day in 1946 that we have encountered in previous photographs! It would not be reasonably expected for a bus new in 1926 to have lasted quite so long – she was in front line service for almost twice as long as she was built for, this and similar bus 19 (DP 7257) lasting through to the spring of 1947. The Allies Restaurant was well-known in the town, although in 1944 it had been known as The Criterion. Henry Playfair were bootmakers.

Late W. J. Haynes © Millane Publishing

Routes N and P were immediately disrupted the other side of the weekend, however, with effect from Sunday 12th January 1947, in connection with the start of the reconstruction of Bridge Street and Southampton Street, a scheme estimated to cost £42,000. Once again, this work included the removal of tram rails and the Transport Committee met 60% of the cost of resurfacing the Bridge Street bridges. The detailed effects of this work will be related in the next chapter.

Nationwide, in the immediate post-war period there were problems of overloading public transport during peak hours, for there simply were not enough buses to meet passenger demand. This was further exacerbated by the need to provide factory specials at the very same times as this peak demand occurred. In Reading it was mooted that a letter should be sent to the town's employers, seeking to gather passenger transport demand data, including starting and finishing times of offices and factories. Nationally, the need to maintain and renew bus fleets which were larger than really necessary, because some units were used for only part of the day, was draining in terms of local resources. It also put added pressure on the vehicle builders, who were finding great difficulty in meeting, nation-wide, the post-war demand for new vehicles.

The difficulties of peak hour travel were further highlighted in the following extract, taken from *Passenger Transport* of 3rd January 1947. The piece, entitled 'What Staggered Hours Means to You', in fact used the first letter of each line to spell out the message STAGGERED HOURS. It seems to have originated from Coventry Corporation, indeed being described by Mr Evans as *"... clever Coventry Propaganda":*

"**S**preading the loading will create additional facilities.
Transport to serve you when you want it.
Automatically more buses available to and from the factories.
Greater freedom on the roads will result.
Give the worker more leisure time in the evening.
Earnings greater, no lost time waiting in queues.
Roads will be safer for you and yours.
Everyone travelling at peak times will benefit.
Delays through traffic congestion reduced.
Hours of production will be increased.
Only co-operation will overcome transport difficulties.
Unless staggered hours are adopted the transport position will deteriorate as no more buses are available.
Recommend staggered hours to your fellow workers.
Start the good work today."

Some minor alterations (presumably improvements) to the Sunday service on motorbus route F (Uplands Road – Merry Maidens), route M (Erleigh Road – Grovelands Road) and route N (Promenade – Callington Road) were introduced with effect from Sunday 2nd February 1947. There was also a minor alteration made to the Monday – Friday service provided on route H (Chalgrove Way – Wood Lane Junction) which took effect the following day.

In the early post-war years Reading expanded rapidly, large housing estates being built at Whitley, Tilehurst and Emmer Green, with more being planned at Southcote and Tilehurst Church End. At a meeting of the town council on Tuesday 4th February 1947, it was announced that during 1946 a total of 334 families had been found accommodation and no less than 488 dwellings were in course of construction.

A number of new and revised bus routes were being considered to serve to these new developments and it

---

READING CORPORATION TRANSPORT.

ALTERATION to MOTORBUS SERVICES

Commencing on Sunday, 2nd February, 1947 and until further notice the following Alterations will come into Operation.

Route F. Shinfield (Merry Maidens) to Uplands Road. Sunday Service

The normal 30 minutes service will remain in operation until 2.05 p.m. Uplands Road and 2.05 p.m. Shinfield, after which a 15 minute service will operate until 10.50 p.m.

Last through vehicle 10.20 p.m. from each terminus.

Route M. Erleigh Road to Grovelands (Grovelands Road). Sunday Service

A 20 minute service will operate from 1.50 p.m. Erleigh Road and 2.05 p.m. from Grovelands Road until 10.40 p.m.

Last through vehicle 10.15 p.m. from Erleigh Road and 10.20 p.m. from Grovelands.

Route N. Callington Road to Caversham (Promenade). Sunday Service

The normal 30 minutes service Callington Road to St. Mary's Butts will operate until 1.30 p.m. Callington Road, after which a 10 minutes service will be in operation until 10.35 p.m. commencing at 1.55 p.m. from Callington Road and 2.05 p.m. from Caversham.

Last through vehicle 10.15 p.m. from Callington Road and 10.25 p.m. from Caversham.

Commencing Monday, 3rd February, 1947.

Route H. Emmer Green (Chalgrove Way) to Whitley Wood (Wood Lane Junc.) Monday to Friday Service

The normal Monday to Friday service will operate until 7.0 p.m. from each terminus, then a 15 minute service will be in operation until 11.0 p.m.

Transport Offices, Mill Lane, Reading.
W. J. EVANS, M.I.E.E., M.Inst.T., Transport Manager and Engineer.

---

became obvious to Mr Evans that Mill Lane depot would not be large enough to house the additional vehicles that would be required. Depot accommodation was already tight and was destined to be increasingly so over the next twenty years as the fleet strength and vehicle dimensions increased. To release more garaging space at Mill Lane, Mr Evans proposed that the heavy maintenance workshops be moved to another location. One such site, which the borough surveyor had suggested, was at Home Farm, between Northumberland Avenue and Basingstoke Road. Mr Evans considered this unsuitable, however, as the new building would have to be on three levels on a sloping site; in any case, it was too small. However, Mr Evans was also adamant that as an operational depot, the Mill Lane premises was ideally sited, both to keep dead mileage to an absolute minimum and to avoid the enormous costs that would result if, for crew changes, crews had to be paid travelling time to and from the town centre and an out-of-town site. The matter was discussed at some length by the Transport Committee at its meeting on 18th March 1947, when it was agreed that a second depot would, indeed, have to be provided.

A serious fire at Mill Lane depot on 18th January 1947, which will be recounted in more detail in the next chapter, had also shown how vulnerable the main trolleybus depot and its vehicular content would be in the event of an even more serious conflagration – and how the existing single exit increased that vulnerability to a risk described as 'very high'. At the same Transport Committee meeting, therefore, agreement was reached to deck over the Mill Stream at Tan Lock, immediately to the west of the trolleybus depot, and to provide a continuous vehicular link alongside the River Kennet, extending from the trolleybus depot through into Middle Garage. When the second depot, at Bennet Road, was opened in the early 1950s, the pressure for vehicle space at Mill Lane was considerably reduced and the improvement plans

> **READING CORPORATION TRANSPORT**
>
> ## Alteration to Trolley-Bus Services
>
> Until further notice, the following alterations will come into operation.
>
> **MONDAYS TO FRIDAYS**
>
> The Service between 9.0 a.m. and 12.0 noon, and from 7.0 p.m. until 11.0 p.m. will be reduced to :—
>
> | | | |
> |---|---|---|
> | Three Tuns and Bear Inn | - | 10 Minutes Service |
> | Three Tuns and Kentwood | - | 10 Minutes Service |
> | Liverpool Road and Norcot | - | 12 Minutes Service |
>
> **SATURDAYS**
>
> No alteration to Services.
>
> **SUNDAYS**
>
> The Early Morning Service will operate as usual :—
> From 9.0 a.m. to 2.0 p.m. the following Service will operate.
>
> | | | | | |
> |---|---|---|---|---|
> | Between | Three Tuns and Bear Inn | 9.0 a.m. | and every | 20 minutes |
> | ,, | Three Tuns and Kentwood | 8.50 a.m. | ,, ,, | 20 minutes |
> | ,, | Bear Inn and Three Tuns | 9.15 a.m. | ,, ,, | 20 minutes |
> | ,, | Kentwood and Three Tuns | 9.10 a.m. | ,, ,, | 20 minutes |
>
> From 2.0 p.m. onwards :—   Last Through Trolley Vehicle
>
> | | | | | |
> |---|---|---|---|---|
> | Between | Three Tuns and Bear Inn | 2.0 p.m. & every | 6 min. | 10.17 p.m. |
> | ,, | Bear Inn and Three Tuns | 1.54 p.m. ,, | 6 min. | 10.11 p.m. |
> | ,, | Liverpool Rd. and Kentwood | 1.54 p.m. ,, | 12 min. | 10.18 p.m. |
> | ,, | Kentwood and Liverpool Rd. | 2.0 p.m. ,, | 12 min. | 10.12 p.m. |
>
> Last Trolley-Buses from Broad Street, in either direction - 10.30 p.m.
>
> Transport Offices,
> Mill Lane, Reading.   W. J. EVANS, M.I.E.E., M.Inst.T.

were shelved — although the fire risk had certainly not diminished! It was not until 1968, some 21 years later, that Tan Lock was eventually decked over and the connecting section (known by depot staff as the 'Khyber Pass' on account of the wind which whistled through it) was built.

It had been agreed by mutual consent at a joint meeting on 13th February 1947, that the wartime arrangement with the Thames Valley Traction Co. Ltd. whereby its vehicles were permitted to pick up passengers on inward journeys to Reading charging only the corporation's fares, should now be discontinued. Things were not that simple, and at a public inquiry during the summer, the traffic commissioners refused to cancel the concession because it had been granted to Thames Valley, not to the corporation, saying that it would have to be argued whenever Thames Valley next applied to renew their stage carriage licences. At a meeting held between Mr Evans and his opposite number at the Thames Valley Traction Company on 16th October 1947, it was agreed that the wartime fares held in the joint suspense account (approx. £700) should be split 60/40 in favour of Thames Valley. The wartime arrangement was finally withdrawn with effect from 1st January 1948.

From 18th February 1947, the off-peak frequency of trolleybus services operating over the 'main line' was reduced.

During the financial year ended 31st March 1947, the undertaking's trolleybuses carried 2,024,159 fewer passengers than in the previous year but operated almost 67,000 more miles. The motorbuses carried 3,448,362 additional passengers and operated roundly 387,000 more miles than the previous year. In financial terms there was a reduction in revenue on the trolleybuses of £2,854 but a corresponding increase in revenue on the motorbuses of £21,648. Expenditure amounted to an increase of £17,123 on the trolleybuses and £36,292 on motorbuses. Parcels Express made a net loss of £466 compared with one of £328 the previous year. In short, almost 16½% more miles were operated for an increase of roundly 3½% more passengers.

Very soon after becoming the new transport manager, Mr Evans had arranged that, for the first time in the department's history, tyres would be hired rather than purchased, and this came into effect in May 1947. The original tyre contract was won by the Dunlop Rubber Company, who retained it for many years and, in the years following implementation of this scheme, considerable savings were made.

> **READING CORPORATION TRANSPORT.**
>
> ## STAVERTON ROAD OMNIBUS SERVICE–VARIATIONS
>
> Commencing Thursday, January 9th, 1947, the above route will be operated from the **RAILWAY STATIONS** and will divert via Christchurch Gardens and Northumberland Avenue instead of Basingstoke Road and Buckland Road.
>
> Stopping on the **OUTWARDS JOURNEY** at :—
>   Stations.
>   Friar Street (Nr. Central Cinema).
>   West Street.
>   St. Mary's Butts.
>   and all Bus Stops to
>   Whitley Street (Christchurch Road)
>   Newcastle Road.
>   Buckland Road Circle.
>   Staverton Road.
>
> Stopping on the **INWARDS JOURNEY** at :—
>   Staverton Road.
>   Buckland Road Circle.
>   Newcastle Road.
>   and all Bus Stops to
>   St. Mary's Butts.
>   Greyfriars Road, (top).
>   Stations.
>
> Leaving the **STATIONS** at the following times :—
> **Weekdays.** Mondays—Saturdays   6.25 a.m.
>   6.53 ,,
>   7.27 ,,
>   7.57 ,,
>   and every 30 mins. until 10.57 p.m.
> **SUNDAYS.** 1.57 p.m. and every 30 mins. until 10.27 p.m.
>
> Leaving **STAVERTON ROAD** at the following times :-
> **Weekdays.** Mondays—Saturdays   6.40 a.m.
>   7.15 ,,
>   7.45 ,,
>   and every 30 mins. until 11.15 p.m.
> **SUNDAYS.** 2.15 p.m. and every 30 mins. until 10.45 p.m.
>
> **Minimum Fare at Peak Traffic Periods.** On Mondays to Fridays inclusive on the 4.57, 5.27, 5.57, 6.27, and 6.57 p.m. journeys from the Stations to Staverton Road the fare for any passenger who boards before Whitley Street will be 2d, and no workman's return tickets of less value than 2d. will be accepted.
>
> Transport Offices,
>   Mill Lane, Reading.
> 6th January, 1947.
>   **W. J. EVANS**, M.I.E.E., M.Inst.T.,
>   Transport Manager and Engineer.

14   Diversions, Snow, Fire, Flood – and Power Cuts!

The disruption to those services which used Bridge Street and Southampton Street was severe while these thoroughfares were being reconstructed. From Sunday 12th January 1947, in readiness for work to commence, changes were made to motorbus routes H, L, N and P. These services were normally routed from Broad Street via St. Mary's Butts (but at this time had already been routed temporarily via Minster Street and Gun Street) and thence via Bridge Street and the lower section of Southampton Street. From 12th January, these routes were diverted (outbound only) via Broad Street, King Street, Duke Street and London Street. Routes H, N and P continued via Silver Street and Mount Pleasant to Whitley Street, while route L ran via Crown Street and Pell Street to regain its usual route into and along Berkeley Avenue. Once again, temporary stopping places were established.

It had been intended, originally, that during reconstruction of Bridge Street, operation of peak hour trolleybus route C (Promenade – Whit Pump) would be northbound (as usual) via Bridge Street and St. Mary's Butts to West Street, but southbound via Broad Street, Duke Street and Mill Lane, to regain its normal route in Southampton Street. There was, of course, no direct wiring across the depot entrance and, had this been implemented, it would also have caused chaos because the wiring in London Street and Duke Street was used duo-directionally for depot access. This plan was therefore rejected, possibly by Mr Evans, and operation of route C was 'temporarily' suspended with effect from 12th January 1947. In fact, this 'temporary suspension' of trolleybus operation of route C was far more long-lasting – it turned out to be permanent! Trolleybuses did not return to service under the 'side road' wires until the introduction of trolleybuses to serve Northumberland Avenue in June 1949. The short-term by-product of this decision, however, was that the pressures on peak trolleybus allocation were considerably eased, for it had become increasingly difficult to cope with the peak hour loadings on the 'main line'.

Commencing sometime around the end of March 1947, route L (to and from Berkeley Avenue) is believed to have been altered from being operated outbound via Duke Street, London Street, Crown Street and Pell Street and inbound via Katesgrove Lane, Southampton Street, Bridge Street and St. Mary's Butts to being operated between Katesgrove Lane and Queen Victoria Street in both directions via Mill Lane, London Street, Duke Street, King Street and Broad Street. In spite of this, the Transport Department decided subsequently that, to avoid causing confusion amongst the public using their services during the Bridge Street and Southampton Street road works, they would implement a 'loop' arrangement whereby all motorbus routes serving the south of the town used the same roads on inward and on outward journeys. Thus, with effect from Monday 5th May 1947, motorbus route F (Merry Maidens – Uplands Road) and route M (Erleigh Road – Grovelands Road), whose normal routes in both directions had recently become via London Street and Duke Street (and not, therefore, directly affected by these road works), were temporarily re-routed inwards via London Street, Mill Lane and Bridge Street. After work in the lower section of Southampton Street was completed, both were restored to normal, via London Street and Duke Street in both directions, with effect from Monday 29th September 1947.

From Monday 5th May 1947 also, the narrow upper part of Southampton Street (between Whitley Street and Crown Street/Pell Street) was closed completely for reconstruction, including the removal of disused tram lines and wooden paving blocks. This turned out to be a very protracted affair, and work stopped for a while at the end of May 1947 because it was not possible to make cement available for projects of this nature to the exclusion of house-building. During this phase of the works, the diversion of motorbuses operating routes C, H, N and P was altered so that they worked inwards (between Whitley Street and the town centre) via Mount Pleasant, Silver Street and Crown Street, to rejoin their normal inbound route in the now re-constructed lower section of Southampton Street. Routes H, N and P (now joined by route C, albeit operated by motorbuses), continued to run outbound from the town centre via Duke Street and London Street because continuing work in Bridge Street meant that it remained closed to all southbound traffic until the end of November 1947.

Unconnected with the reconstruction of the Bridge Street roadway, the bridges in Bridge Street had also been found to need extensive repair – to the extent that it had been deemed 'inadvisable' to take out the disused tram track from over the bridges – and some urgent temporary work had had to be put in hand. Being located on one of the traffic arteries linking from the south of the town, these bridges are likely to have deteriorated significantly during the war from being grossly overloaded by war transport and from an enforced lack of maintenance. As permanent repair work, at least six months away, would again restrict traffic in Bridge Street, it was decided, as far as Reading Corporation Transport services were concerned, that it would save confusion for bus passengers if operations were left as they were until after permanent bridge repair works were complete. Thus, instead of buses working routes H, L, N and P reverting to their original routing in both directions

---

READING CORPORATION TRANSPORT

Reconstruction of Southampton Street and St. Mary's Butts

It is expected that the reconstruction of the above-mentioned roads will commence shortly, and it will be necessary from time to time to alter stopping places temporarily, and occasionally divert 'buses from the normal routes.

As much notice as possible will be given to the public by posting notices at each stopping place affected by any change.

In the event of the necessity of operating ONE WAY TRAFFIC, buses proceeding towards the town will keep to their normal routes, and buses leaving the town will be diverted for part of their journey by way of Duke Street, when the main boarding point in the town centre will be in Broad Street near the Arcade.

Transport Manager and Engineer.

4th November 1946.

Transport Offices,
Mill Lane, Reading.

via Bridge Street and St. Mary's Butts, they continued to operate outbound via Duke Street and London Street. This did not please everyone, of course, for there were residents in Southampton Street who complained about the continued lack of buses outbound from town. As already recorded, buses on routes F and M had at this stage reverted to operating via London Street in both directions. The Thames Valley Traction Co. Ltd., on the other hand, had reverted immediately to two-way operation in Bridge Street.

By mid-March 1948, it had become obvious that there was going to be difficulty in obtaining loan sanction from the Ministry of Transport to proceed with permanent repairs to the Bridge Street bridges, so it was decided to simply resurface the roadway in the interim. More importantly, a 12 ton laden weight limit was imposed. The Transport Department had to bear a considerable proportion of the cost because, under the Tramways Act, 1870, until it was lifted, the old tram track, the road area between the rails and eighteen inches either side, remained that department's responsibility. Once the resurfacing was done, traffic was able to resume travelling southbound in Bridge Street.

The upper part of Southampton Street (between Pell Street and Whitley Street) was completely closed to traffic from 5th May 1947 while tram rail and cobble stones were removed and the carriageway was reconstructed. In those days of acute shortages of more-or-less everything, it was quickly found that licences for cement were not as easy to obtain as first thought because redressing a huge national housing shortage was taking precedence. Although the carriageway was eventually re-opened in two phases, northbound then southbound, trolleybuses remained suspended from the route and were not restored until two major extensions to serve Whitley Estate were introduced, in June and August 1949.

Reading Standard

Meanwhile, with the re-opening of half the road width for use by northbound traffic down the upper (narrow) part of Southampton Street, journeys inbound from Whitley Street on the now motorbus-operated route C and on motorbus routes H, N and P had reverted to their proper inbound route, commencing Monday 18th August 1947. With re-construction of the southbound carriageway continuing, however, outbound journeys on these routes had continued to be operated from the town centre via Duke Street, London Street, Silver Street and Mount Pleasant. It should be mentioned that Whitley Street was also reconstructed during summer 1947, during which time southbound traffic was diverted from Mount Pleasant via Highgrove Street and Christchurch Road, to re-join the normal route at Whitley Pump. The dates of this diversion have eluded us, however! The reconstruction of 'upper' Southampton Street was still proving to be a very protracted affair because of the continued difficulty in securing permits for the allocation of building materials, but work was eventually completed and the road re-opened southbound from Easter Monday, 29th March 1948. With effect from the same date, motorbuses on routes H, N and P reverted to operating in both directions via Southampton Street and Bridge Street. Route C, latterly motorbus-operated and extensively diverted, appears to have been withdrawn permanently henceforth. From the latter date also, motorbus route L (Hemdean Road – Berkeley Avenue) was restored to operate in both directions via St. Mary's Butts, Bridge Street and Southampton Street; however, from the same date it also became permanently routed in both directions via Pell Street instead of Katesgrove Lane, in the process becoming double-deck operated.

Reading's overworked public transport system was now being subjected to extra pressure, especially during the evening rush hour, by having suddenly to cope with around 1,500 extra passengers finishing work earlier than hitherto with the advent of the 44-hour week. This was an era of misery, too, in so many other directions – in particular, there had been a staggering 12% increase in a year in the demand for electricity. On a national basis, there simply was not, at that time, the capacity to generate the extra amount of electricity demanded – and neither was there likely to be in the foreseeable future, notwithstanding any shortage of coal that also happened to exist at that time. The short-term result was an all too regular occurrence during the winters of those austerity years – power cuts!

But, then, absolutely everything was in short supply. There were still queues at most food shops, for there was still food rationing – in fact, even worse than during the war years. In the aftermath of the war, the country was heading for bankruptcy. Desperate measures were being taken by the government to steer a course finely balanced between trying to put the country itself back on an even keel, earning money abroad from exports in a very competitive market, and helping feed the starving populations of parts of war-torn Europe. The government was also honour-bound to introduce the improvements promised when it was voted into office in 1945 – nationalisation of fuel and power, haulage and public transport and introduction of the National Health Service amongst them.

New housing was unable to be built anything like fast enough. In Reading, although considerable numbers of new houses were being built, there were simply not enough trained building operatives and tradesmen to get on with the job. As a result, 'desperation housing' brought about by the takeover of former army camps as squats, like the one at Ranikhet Camp, on the slopes of Tilehurst, had had to become official temporary council housing. The labour market was, in any case, extremely fluid, and the Corporation Transport Department was just one of many employers where staff were continually changing in very large numbers. It was little wonder, therefore, that with a large section of comparatively inexperienced labour, the public perception of the municipal transport undertaking being run erratically was not too far from the truth! Take, for example, the reference by 'Chronicler' in his 'Reading Week by Week' column in the *Berkshire Chronicle* on 24th January 1947:

"Push Chairs and 'Buses – Can I make a plea on behalf of mothers in the town for a little more consideration from 'bus conductors? Normally cheerful and co-operative, some conductors become almost truculent when confronted with push-chairs. 'No room for that', I heard one young man declare brusquely to a mother who was trying to get a push-chair, two children and herself on a 'bus recently. Conductresses, no doubt more understanding of the difficulties, invariably go out of their way to make things easier for harassed mothers, and some of the men might take the example from them. It is no joke for a woman with children and a push-chair to be met with non-sympathetic unhelpfulness from a public servant."

But it is necessary to back-track. Snow had begun falling during December 1946 – and continued to fall during the early part of January 1947. It then got very cold! Temperatures recorded at the University of Reading during the week commencing Sunday 26th January 1947 were all well below freezing, the lowest being recorded on Wednesday 29th January 1947 at 8°F (−13°C). Whiteknights Lake froze over enough for skating and there were ice floes in the River Thames between Caversham Bridge and Reading Bridge. Lumps of ice floating in the River Kennet fouled the turbines for pumping the fresh water supply at Fobney Pumping Station and there was a continual need, too, to have to break ice on the filter beds.

By the end of that month the whole country was paralysed. Snow drifts in some places were some fourteen feet deep. Whilst this 'big freeze' gripped the country, there was also a national fuel crisis and, in an effort to conserve coal stocks, Defence Regulations were again implemented, which forbade the use of domestic electric heaters when factories were working. Electricity supplies were forcibly reduced, in any case, by 'load shedding' of up to 25%, with all the resultant problems of no heating and spoiled cooking at a time when many foodstuffs were still rationed. Street lighting was once again turned off and working hours staggered. Domestic coal was in extremely short supply and it was said that in many homes the coal bunkers were scraped clean of even the coal dust!

In Reading the freezing weather continued, although it must have become slightly warmer as the six more inches of snow, to which the town had woken up on Sunday 9th February 1947, had thawed three days later. Meanwhile, fuel shortages locally had reached crisis levels, forcing factories to close down; over 6,000 workers were 'laid off'. Power cuts commenced on 10th February 1947. Things gradually got better the following week and were generally back to normal from 3rd March 1947 but, on the domestic front, coal was still very much in short supply and folk found themselves trekking down to the gas works with barrows and old prams for half-a-bag of 'off-ration' coke. It is somewhat remarkable, therefore, that trolleybus services do not appear to have been affected during this particular crisis! As an aside, it is of interest to reflect that generations have grown up in recent decades with no knowledge of anthracite and what various other grades of coal there were, or who know anything about coke being a by-product of the town gas works, or, indeed, what it was or what it looked like!

The severe winter weather also took its toll on vehicles, which were already weakened by years of inadequate maintenance. Radiators are known to have frozen while a bus was running in service! A failed bus – and every other sort of vehicle – drawn up at the side of the road, became commonplace throughout the country. During the period 19th January to 10th March 1947, therefore, it is rather remarkable that Reading Corporation Transport lost only 327 bus miles (0.13%) and 550 trolleybus miles (0.24%), of which 370 miles were attributed to fog and the remainder to icy road conditions. It was therefore rather pleasing that the public noticed. A letter from 'Agriotes', which was published in the *Reading Standard* for 28th February 1947 under the heading 'Tribute to Bus Services', read:

Two of the undertaking's six Sunbeam W utility trolleybuses proceeding eastwards in Broad Street during severely cold weather in the last week of January 1947. The coach travelling westbound is a 'half-cab' likely to be a second-hand pre-war Dennis Lancet II operated by Smith's Coaches.

Berkshire Chronicle

"Sir – The thanks of the travelling public are due to all concerned for the efficient way in which the Reading Corporation passenger transport services have been carried on during the recent wintry spells. Not only have the services been maintained, they have also been regular and punctual, no small feat in the conditions which prevailed."

A very similar letter written under the same *nom de plume* appeared in the *Berkshire Chronicle* the following week.

During January 1947, in the midst of the bitter weather and the travel difficulties, Reading Corporation Transport took delivery of its ten long-awaited new AEC Regent II double-deckers, 58–67 (CRD 252–261) which, collected by corporation drivers either singly or two-at-a-time, trickled down from the Park Royal factory into Mill Lane depot. Finer details will be found in Appendices A and B.

Only five of the batch had arrived, when, at around 1.00pm on Saturday 18th January 1947, a serious fire broke out in the fitting & machine shop in the depot. It turned out that Mr Evans was lunching with his wife at the Ship Hotel in Duke Street at the time, when a fire engine, bell clanging furiously, rushed down Duke Street and over High Bridge. The *Berkshire Chronicle* in reporting the event mentioned with, perhaps, a shade of licence, that Mrs Evans had said, jokingly, *"That's your transport depot going up in flames!"* and Mr Evans had omitted to touch wood. Five minutes later he was called to the telephone...

The fire grew from a comparatively small outbreak to something of quite serious proportions in a matter of minutes but prompt action by those on the spot, followed by the quick arrival of the fire brigade, localised the damage. Buses were being prepared for service as football specials when smoke was seen curling out from the machine shop, and this had sent one man running to raise the alarm. Fortunately, Mr Gent, the deputy transport manager, had not left the premises for the weekend (remember that, at that time, most persons in employment worked on Saturdays at least until lunchtime) and was able to direct operations. A general call put out to technicians and key officials who had already left work for the weekend had them returning 'at the double' to render assistance in a number of invaluable ways. The football specials remained where they were, while every available man concentrated on getting vehicles, including newly-delivered buses 58–61, away from the danger zone and tackling the fire as best they could before the fire brigade arrived. Two pumps were sent from Caversham Road Fire Station, augmented by the one from the 'retained' fire station at Sonning, whereupon Fire Force Commander B. M. Taylor took charge. At the height of the fire, the machine shop roof collapsed and dense smoke spread over the town's shopping centre. The fire was under control within an hour and completely out at 3.26pm. Only slight dislocation of services resulted, although the football specials did not operate. This caused a number of fans to miss the start of the match at Elm Park – and a few to grumble!

The fire resulted in extensive damage to the building and machinery. It also caused secondary damage to the adjoining stores and to the Staff Social Club premises. More importantly, however, it completely destroyed the body of bus 62, one of the much-needed and long-awaited brand-new double-deckers, delivered only two days previously and not yet in service. At the same time, a 1932 Commer 8hp departmental van (GX 2472) was totally destroyed, together with the body of the Battle Hospital Austin ambulance (BRD 346). The latter was salvaged, the chassis and engine overhauled, and it was then re-bodied. The departmental van, however, was written off. In due course, the chassis of bus 62 was sent to the AEC factory at Southall for rectification work, at a cost of £333 2s 5d, and a replacement body was subsequently ordered from Park Royal. The latter was, in fact, built as part of the second batch of AEC Regent IIs and, as such, the body was of a different design to that of the original batch. It is worth pointing out that, for many years, it was thought that no photographs existed of 62 with its original body – until the discovery of that shown opposite, in the aftermath of the blaze!

The damaged machinery, all using the archaic system of line-shafting and belts, was beyond economic repair and was written off. It was duly replaced, fortunately with government-backed priority, with modern machines with self-contained electric drives. These were sourced by Mr Evans, and they were not all new – indeed, many were war surplus. In the interim, arrangements were made for work to be carried out at other corporation-owned workshops, such as those of the borough electrical engineer, the borough surveyor and the borough water engineer.

The cost of repairing the burnt-out machine shop was originally estimated at £12,000. When carried out, the

Leyland Titan 2 (RD 3379), on Route K (Woodcote Road – Friar Street (GPO)), is just leaving the GWR station for Friar Street, hence the reason for not being very full. However, there are a lot of soggy passengers waiting for the next bus to Shinfield Road! Although it is March 1949, only three months before withdrawal, it is interesting to note that, while the external paintwork is past its prime, the vehicle is still fully lined-out in pre-war livery, with black beading between maroon and cream, cream lining below the upper and lower cream bands and fine red lining inside the cream bands. There is also still a hint of white blackout paint on the rear wing!

© Late W. J. Haynes

FIRE!

The serious fire which started in the machine shop on 18th January 1947 very quickly took a hold. This major incident on a Saturday lunchtime caused great quantities of smoke and debris to be blown down onto shoppers!

Top Right: The scene in the machine shop itself, with what appears to be the remains of an old departmental van. One gets the impression that it is a bit hot!

Reading Standard

Centre Right: The scene from the other side of the River Kennet. The workshop roof has collapsed, the fire crew is still actively fighting the fire – and men in suits look on!

© *Millane Publishing*

Below Right: The only known photos of AEC Regent II 62 (CRD 256) with its original body turned up just as we were going to press! The burnt-out bus is alongside what is probably the chassis of the Battle Hospital ambulance, whose body was also destroyed in the blaze.

© *Millane Publishing*

Below: A sure-footed fireman tackling the fire from a new angle.

Reading Standard

repairs, which were substantial, also involved extending the building nearer to the riverside and up to the boiler house, with a view to linking up in the future with further modifications to the paint shop, body shop and East Garage.

A surviving memo to the traffic office dated 1st February 1947 (a Saturday) heralded the entry into service of many of the batch of recently-delivered AEC Regent IIs. It also gives details of the temporary short-length destination blinds initially fitted in these vehicles – only four destinations were shown on each blind, so that each vehicle could only be rostered to operate on either of two routes! The memo specifically refers to these as 'temporary' destination blinds, so they were clearly meant as a stop-gap until the already planned renaming of terminal points, which subsequently took place on 13th April 1947, on which occasion the whole fleet received new blinds. In such times of austerity, it was certainly out of the question to provide new full-length blinds which would have seen only ten weeks' use. For just that period, therefore, the brand new buses could be seen operating with such wartime destinations as **PROMENADE, MERRY MAIDENS, WOOD LANE JUNC, GROVELANDS RD.** and **CHALGROVE WAY**. Sadly, no-one seems to have photographed the buses actually in service during those ten weeks. It is most likely that the 'temporary' blinds were assembled by breaking up spare existing blinds, one full-size blind producing two short 'temporary' blinds – this would also account for the lack of such intermediate points on the 'temporary' short blinds as **STATIONS, BROAD STREET, RELIEF** and **DEPOT**, which, of course, would have appeared only once on a full-size wartime blind. The dates on which the nine Regent IIs entered service, and the routes to which they were temporarily dedicated, were as follows:

Bus	In Service	Routes	Bus	In Service	Routes
58	01.02.47	H M	64	06.02.47	F N
59	17.02.47	H I	65	01.03.47	H I
60	01.02.47	H I	66	01.02.47	H M
61	06.02.47	F N	67	01.03.47	F N
63	01.03.47	F N			

Three new experimental liveries were carried. Buses 58–61 were maroon with cream window surround areas to the front and sides but not to the rear and, on these four vehicles only, the cream was 'streamlined' on the lower deck staircase panel to echo the shape of the upper-deck 'D'-window above. Buses 63 and 66 (and probably 62, although there is no surviving documentation to confirm) were maroon with cream window surrounds to the front, sides and rear, including the upper-deck rear corner pillars. Buses 64, 65 and 67 carried the livery which was finally adopted as the post-war standard for motorbuses, according to a surviving coloured-up drawing dated Sunday 29th August 1948, and confirmed to Park Royal Vehicles Ltd. on 31st August for the second batch of AEC Regent IIs. This livery featured all windows with cream surrounds but without the cream carrying across the upper-deck rear corner pillars. All nine vehicles had black beading and wings and subsquently carried signwritten Simonds Beer adverts on both sides. It is said that the directors of H. & G. Simonds Ltd, the local brewers (who were quite well-known, particularly in south and south-west England, for their hop leaf logo) were politically against the Labour Party's nationalisation policies, so they ceased advertising on Thames Valley buses, which were part of the Tilling Group (which was in favour of nationalisation) and transferred their local bus advertising to Reading Corporation Transport. In a short time the brewery presumably reviewed its advertising policies and ceased bus advertising in the Reading area completely!

These new buses were delivered and entered service fitted with only an offside headlamp. Certain of the pre-war motorbus rolling stock, invariably the AEC Regents, also 'lost' their nearside headlamps for a time during the early post-war years (see page 89 and photo on page 127). It is thought that new headlamps were in short supply, so nearside headlamps on existing buses were 'borrowed' for a few months and fitted to the offside of the new buses. In those days, double-filament bulbs were not yet in common use, and one method adopted for 'dipping' headlamps was simply to turn one of them (albeit normally that on the <u>offside</u>) off. A bus permanently at work in an urban environment would never need to use headlamps on 'high beam', so in an urban area only one headlamp was ever required. Within a few months, nearside headlamps were fitted/re-fitted as required, presumably as soon as the supply situation improved.

Bus 67 (CRD 261), the last of a batch of ten new AEC Regent IIs (the body of one of which was, of course, lost in the depot fire) was shown to the public in this photograph published in one of the local weekly newspapers on 7th February 1947. It wears the version of the livery finally adopted as standard. Note the absence of a nearside headlamp, for reasons described in the text above. Note also the use of a wartime destination blind for the first few weeks, before certain destinations were re-named on 14th April 1947 when the whole fleet was equipped with new blinds.

© Millane Publishing

Regent II Livery Styles

Top: A pre-delivery photo of bus 66 (CRD 260) in a livery in which it was never seen in Reading. The panels directly above the lower deck windows and the platform valance are maroon rather than cream; there is no black beading separating the two colours; the fleet number has moved from the rear to the front bulkhead; and the front registration number is above the driver's cab. These may have been part of Mr Little's plans for livery and other detail changes which did not meet Mr Evans' approval. Note the new-style blind, which was not used in service until 13th April 1947.

ACV Limited

Centre: Bus 60 (CRD 254), on route F bound for Shinfield Road, is double-parked at the GWR station – evidently with a spot of bother! Its experimental livery featured a completely maroon rear elevation, the resulting treatment of the lower-deck cream window surround areas being as shown.

Print from J. R. Whitehead's collection

Bottom: Bus 63 (CRD 257), seen on Sunday 6th March 1949 in the experimental livery in which it was delivered, with cream rear upper-deck corners, rather than maroon. It has acquired its nearside head-lamp in the interim. Note the revised trolleybus wiring layout across the front of the depot in the background (see page 157).

Late W. J. Haynes © Millane Publishing

137

AEC Regent IIs 63 and 67 in Mill Lane, by the gates into East Yard, when fairly new: no adverts or near-side headlamps, and clean wheels. 63 has a step ring on the offside front wheel, a feature which was not retained. Ambulance SHX 264 sits in East Garage. The transport manager, who had the additional job of ambulance officer from 1939, was in 1946 given the police ambulance as well – and in 1948, with the advent of the National Health Service, all the local hospital ambulances too! Only in 1974, with local authority boundary and status changes, was a separate ambulance service established.

© *Omnibus Society*

The introduction of the Regent IIs finally saw the withdrawal of the seven aged Guy B single-deckers (19, 20, 33, 34, 35, 40 and 41). These should have been withdrawn upon the arrival of the Bedford OBs in spring 1946 (and, indeed, buses 33–35 had been withdrawn at this time, only to be reinstated after a couple of weeks due to a shortage of vehicles). From December 1933 these buses had often been used as driver-operated vehicles (i.e. without conductors).

19	DP 7257		withdrawn 28.02.47
20	DP 7258	last operated 30.04.47	withdrawn 30.04.47

19 was transferred to the Reading Corporation Catering Department, which still traded as 'The People's Pantry', and was converted for its new task in the body shop at Mill Lane depot in May 1947. It served as a mobile tea stall at Thames Side Promenade from June 1947 until 1949, being stored over winter months in the yard at Caversham Court (it was towed from the Promenade across to Caversham Court on 29th September 1948, for example). Conversion work also started on bus 20 but, after storage at Caversham Court during the winter of 1947/48, it was sold due to the winding-up of the People's Pantry. Note that 19 and 20 were not <u>officially</u> transferred to the Catering Department until October 1947.

33	RD 35		withdrawn 28.02.47
34	RD 36	last operated 25.03.47	withdrawn 30.04.47
35	RD 37		withdrawn 28.02.47

33–35 were recorded at withdrawal as having had a capacity of 22 seated with 22 standing, indicating that the wartime perimeter seating with which they had been fitted had been retained. It seems that it was originally intended that bus 33 would join 19 and 20 with the People's Pantry, but this was not to be. Bus 34 is known to have had its seats removed before disposal. All three subsequently became caravans, 35 lasting until May 1961 at Mill Green, Caversham, where it was broken up on site.

40	RD 2114		withdrawn .09.46
41	RD 2115	last operated 17.07.47	withdrawn 17.07.47

Bus 40 had been withdrawn due to shortage of spares and was sold minus engine and gearbox. Remembering that this was an oil-engined vehicle, it was thus survived by older petrol-engined vehicles! Evidently, its withdrawal enabled bus 41 to be kept running for a few more months, but 41 was offered for sale *"after 30th July 1947, with the seating removed and with a spare engine"*. Records suggest a spare gearbox was also available, presumably the units which had been retained as a contingency from bus 40. 41 was noted at the back of the depot in the company of withdrawn bus 20 on 6th October 1947. It is also interesting to note that, on 28th October 1947, two redundant Guy bus engines were delivered to the Metalwork Department at Leighton Park School. Presumably, in those days of shortages, this provided suitable material for teaching the techniques of turning, milling, etc.

Meanwhile, the freezing weather continued. As already recounted, there was more snow in the middle of February, followed by a short-term thaw (bringing with it the usual problem of burst pipes) and the continuing misery of coal shortages, lay-offs and power cuts. During the week commencing Sunday 9th February 1947, there was a slight curtailment of trolleybus services as a minor repercussion of the power cuts. Because of factory lay-offs, there was also a reduction in the number of works services and relief buses operated, while, on Sunday 16th February 1947, no service was operated on route N (Promenade – Callington Road).

On 6th March 1947, another heavy snowfall again disrupted the bus services and it took three snow ploughs, a broom and six lorries to clear Broad Street! In their last weeks of service, Guys 20 and 34 were to be seen pressed into service on the Liverpool Road trolleybus route, while new AEC Regent II 63, which had entered service only days earlier, was noted working the Wokingham Road trolleybus route – seemingly with a trolleybus blind temporarily fitted.

After the snow and freezing conditions of the 1946/47 winter came the thaw – and with it the worst floods in Reading for more than fifty years. During the night of Friday 14th March 1947, the River Thames rose by fifteen inches, flooding twenty streets in Lower Caversham and some 1,600 houses, many being submerged in three feet of water. The roads through the railway under-bridges in Caversham Road and Vastern Road were both flooded, effectively severing transport links between Reading and Caversham. Although not generally deep, the floods, which stretched from Lower Caversham to Great Knollys Street, were deemed the most serious since those of 1894 and a state of emergency was declared. A ferry service was established through the bridges using dinghies and high-wheeled lorries and, on Tuesday 18th March 1947, two amphibious DUKWs were loaned by the War Office. Fobney Pumping Station on the River Kennet was put out of action and water for drinking could not be filtered; Reading's population was told over the wireless to boil all drinking water.

It was a week before the floods subsided and, although photographic evidence confirms that buses continued to pass under both Caversham Road and Vastern Road railway bridges in about fifteen inches of water, the flooding disrupted bus services along Caversham Road (to Promenade, Uplands Road and Woodcote Road) and in Vastern Road (to Emmer Green, Hemdean Road and Lower Caversham). George Street, Caversham became impassable during the worst of the floods and those services normally routed via Reading Bridge were therefore diverted via Vastern Road, Caversham Road, Caversham Bridge and through Caversham village. Because the flooding in Lower Caversham extended to an area bounded by Westfield Road, Star Road and South View Avenue, buses to Donkin Hill had to be routed in Caversham via Prospect Street and Henley Road. Trolleybuses were not affected, of course, because, as previously mentioned, route C (Promenade – Whit Pump) was suspended for other reasons. The Transport Department is understood to have provided transport and other services in connection with the flooding but the details are not known. Mr Evans recorded in the department's annual report for 1946/47 that *"...the unusual climatic conditions, with severe and prolonged periods of frost, snow and floods, plus the fire in the Depot, was a real test of co-operation..."*. 'Chronicler', in his 'Reading Week by Week' column in the *Berkshire Chronicle* for 21st March 1947 wrote:

"Buses Did Not Stop – During the floods this week the Corporation 'buses to and from Emmer Green and Lower Caversham have been diverted via Vastern Road, Caversham Road and Bridge Street. The employees on all the Caversham routes are to be congratulated on having maintained so excellent a service. But instructions have apparently been given that no passengers are to be picked up unless they are on the normal route of the 'buses. Thus people waiting at the Bridge Street stop have been somewhat annoyed to see buses from the East Caversham area go quickly by even when they are only half full, leaving them to be picked up by the Uplands Road and Woodcote Road vehicles, which are often crowded when they reach this spot. One could understand it if the 'buses not normally on this route were filled before reaching this stop but one cannot imagine any really sane reason for vehicles not picking up here – a regular fare stage for other 'buses – when there has been plenty of room in them."

The reason, of course, is never as obvious to the man in the street as it is to the 'informed'. These buses were on an enforced diversion of separately-licensed routes granted within the workings of the Road Traffic Act, 1930, where each and every licensed journey was accountable in regard to mileage operated, passengers carried, revenue generated, the resulting statistical information, insurance cover, and the like, so that picking up passengers to the detriment of other licensed services operating as normal along the diversionary route would generate false information and could also, under the terms implied by the Act, invalidate insurance cover on any particular journey!

The River Thames burst its banks in mid-March 1947 as a result of a rapid thaw following a sustained period of freezing weather with copious quantities of snow. The flood waters were not deep, just extensive and muddy – and inconvenient! Here, Leyland Titan 45 (RD 2945) makes about three knots as it negotiates the Great Western Railway bridges in Vastern Road on its way to Stations. It was not so much these bridges that compelled Reading to specify lowbridge double-deck motorbuses as that for the Southern Railway, on which the photographer is standing, which was extra low at 13ft 6in.

Berkshire Chronicle

Above: *A flooded Caversham Road looking towards Caversham Bridge from outside Wall's Carnival Stores, with a Leyland Titan making gallant progress northbound. In the distance is an oncoming corporation bus, seemingly one of the AEC Regent II buses recently put into service and possibly working route N (Promenade – Callington Road). Note the trolleybus overhead, in particular its 'gantry' construction and the feeder point. Trolleybus operation of route C was suspended at the time because of extensive road reconstruction works elsewhere along the route following removal of disused tram rail.*

Print from M. Plunkett's collection

Below: *A busy afternoon scene in 1947 looking from Queen Victoria Street down towards the western end of Broad Street after its reconstruction. The AEC trolleybus, identified as 121 (ARD 684), has just set off eastbound from the stop outside the Vaudeville cinema. Private cars are increasing in number and there is a fair amount of 'bustling about' by pedestrians – and mothers pushing prams in the roadway!*

Commercial picture postcard

15   Onward Through 1947

It has already been mentioned that ten further AEC Regent II double-deck chassis were ordered in October 1946, just before Mr Evans took over as transport manager. The order for the bodies had not yet been placed, so once again the chassis were delivered to Mill Lane for storage before bodying. They were noted in Mill Lane depot by local enthusiast Len Head, each carrying a plate attached to a chassis cross-member with the vehicle's future fleet number painted on it in white.

Delivered	Chassis No.	Fleet No.
26.02.47	O661.8089	77
26.02.47	O661.8095	83
19.03.47	O661.8086	74
19.03.47	O661.8094	82
16.04.47	O661.8087	75
16.04.47	O661.8088	76
13.05.47	O661.8090	78
13.05.47	O661.8091	79
04.06.47	O661.8092	80
04.06.47	O661.8093	81

The order for the bodies was not placed with Park Royal Vehicles until March 1947, at a cost of £1,995 each, together with a new body to replace the burnt-out body of 62 at a cost of £2,347 10s 0d. The chassis of buses 74–83 remained in store at Mill Lane until the following year, during which time Park Royal were building large numbers of London Transport RT bodies. Eventually, Reading Corporation Transport informed Park Royal Vehicles that they would be sending *"one chassis on Tuesday 25th May 1948; one chassis on Tuesday 1st June 1948; two chassis on Tuesday 8th June 1948; and two chassis on each Tuesday following until all are delivered"*. As the letter refers to eleven chassis, it is likely that the chassis of 62 had found its way back to Reading after reconditioning and recertification at AEC's Southall Works at a cost of £333 2s 5d. Having been recertified, it was to all intents and purposes a new chassis, identical to the other ten – so the additional cost of 62's new body over that of the other ten buses cannot be explained other than, perhaps, by the inclusion of a sum for the removal of the old body, and any extra ferrying costs incurred.

On Sunday 13th April 1947 the titles of many of the terminal points which had been changed during the war were re-named, some of them reverting to their pre-war titles. Some, which had been changed in 1940, were left as they were, e.g. Donkin Hill, Uplands Road and Liverpool Road. Others, such as Erleigh Road, Horncastle, Kentwood, Staverton Road, Callington Road, etc., were retained as they always had been. This had been agreed eleven months earlier by the Transport Committee on 16th May 1946, when it was stated that *"the purpose of the (Wartime) Order was to conceal the true destination and avoid giving an indication of districts"*, with the observation that *"... this is, of course, not normally a desirable practice for public transport operation!"*

MERRY MAIDENS	reverted to	SHINFIELD ROAD
CHALGROVE WAY	reverted to	EMMER GREEN
WOOD LANE JUNC.	became	WHITLEY WOOD
BEAR INN	reverted to	TILEHURST
NORCOT JUNC.	became	NORCOT
THREE TUNS	became	WOKINGHAM ROAD
PROMENADE	reverted to	CAVERSHAM
WHIT-PUMP	reverted to	WHITLEY STREET
GROVELANDS RD	became	GROVELANDS

Over the weekend of 12th/13th April 1947, the huge task of fitting the whole fleet, both motorbuses and trolleybuses, with new blinds was undertaken. The layout of the motorbus blinds (as fitted to the AEC Regent IIs) is shown on the left, and that of the trolleybuses (as fitted to the utility Sunbeams) on the right. The blinds on other vehicle types would have been similar, but adapted to fit various differently-sized blind boxes.

Motorbus blinds	Trolleybus blinds
SHINFIELD ROAD	TILEHURST
UPLANDS ROAD	NORCOT
EMMER GREEN	WOKINGHAM ROAD
WHITLEY WOOD	KENTWOOD
CALLINGTON ROAD	LIVERPOOL ROAD
STAVERTON ROAD	RELIEF
ST MARY'S BUTTS	DEPOT
HARTLAND ROAD	RESERVED
CAVERSHAM	BROAD STREET
WHITLEY STREET	STATIONS
HORNCASTLE	SPECIAL
DONKIN HILL	WHITLEY STREET
STATIONS	WHITLEY WOOD
GROVELANDS	CAVERSHAM
ERLEIGH ROAD	HARTLAND ROAD
WOODCOTE ROAD	ORTS ROAD
HEMDEAN ROAD	
BERKELEY AVENUE	
TILEHURST	
NORCOT	
WOKINGHAM ROAD	
KENTWOOD	
LIVERPOOL ROAD	
ORTS ROAD	
RELIEF	
DEPOT	
RESERVED	

It is particularly interesting to note from the above that (a) both motorbus and trolleybus blinds carried **STATIONS**, **WHITLEY WOOD** and **HARTLAND ROAD** (and note also that at this stage the intended trolleybus terminus in Northumberland Avenue was being referred to as Hartland Road well in advance of trolleybuses serving these locations); (b) motorbus blinds did not carry **BROAD STREET** or **FRIAR STREET** (which seems particularly odd) or **SPECIAL**; and (c) blinds carried that wonderfully evocative display from those balmy days of bus travel – **RELIEF** – which gave so little information to intending passengers! An equally vague term used in other towns was 'duplicate'.

With effect from the following day, Monday 14th April 1947, the weekday frequency of motorbus route N (Stations – Staverton Road) was increased to 20 minutes. It was recorded also, by 'Chronicler' in his 'Reading Week by Week' column in the *Berkshire Chronicle* on 18th April 1947 that *"bright new bus and trolleybus stop signs"* had also appeared in the streets during the previous week. While this most probably referred to those stop flags in the town centre upon which the revised terminal destination names appeared, it might just have referred also to a regularisation and/or change in the type of stop flag used at ordinary and fare stage stops elsewhere on the network, which would have included replacement of any non-standard and surviving pre-war examples. The latter would have included the 'home made' stop flags along the original trolleybus route, between Caversham Bridge and Whitley Street, and all surviving pre-war red background 'Bus Fare Stage' plates. It was probably at this time that 'Trolleybus Fare Stage'

AEC trolleybus 123 (ARD 686) at the Three Tuns in the winter of 1946/47. The road is completely empty apart from one lady cyclist; the picture is, conceivably, one of Sunday morning solitude, such as was to be had in those days. Whilst still retaining chromed front wheel nut guard rings, the trolleybus had been repainted out of its experimental livery (see page 122) in November 1946, which was presumably when its rear registration plate was re-located. New destination blinds with revised terminal names are due into use on 13th April 1947.

Late W. J. Haynes
© Maiwand Photographic Archive

flags (red on an off-white ground surmounted by a brown RCT monogram) were replaced by the well-remembered buff background flags with 'Trolley Bus Stop' in green and the RCT monogram and 'Fare Stage' in brown.

At the Works Committee on 17th April 1947 it was suggested that the new destination blinds should be 'back-stamped' (marked on the back) to ensure correct positioning from the inside of the vehicle. On trolleybuses the front destination blinds were wound from inside the cab by the driver (and, without 'back-stamping', the driver would have relied on his conductor standing in front of the vehicle to indicate correct positioning). Those on most (if not all) of the pre-war motorbuses were altered by the conductor turning a handle under the front canopy whilst standing, somewhat precariously, on a step which doubled as a fog lamp bracket. After the war, in Reading the front blinds on motorbuses became altered by the driver from inside the cab. Rear blinds (and, where fitted, side blinds over the platform) were altered by the conductor winding handles from inside the bus, originally while hanging on and leaning out to observe that the correct display was being shown. This, of course, was an extremely dangerous practice if carried out 'on the move', particularly in regard to the side blind, and elsewhere in the country a number of bus conductors were killed as the bus passed trees, lamp posts, parked vehicles, etc. Conductor safety may have been a major reason why, commencing with the subsequent batch of AEC Regent IIs (the first vehicles over which Mr Evans had any control), the side blind displays were relocated over the rearmost nearside lower-deck window, and thus had to be altered from inside the lower saloon. The practice of altering destination blinds 'on the move' for the return journey as a bus approached a terminus probably came into vogue either during the black-out or in the balmy days of bus use in the years immediately after the war, when running to time was particularly difficult to achieve due to heavy passenger loadings on all journeys, so that there was invariably little or no layover time to be had at termini.

The front blinds on the four Guy Arab utility motorbuses appear to have been altered by the driver from inside the cab. This may account for the reason behind two well-known photographs of bus 6 taken at Grovelands Road terminus during the war with the blind turned to 'Donkin Hill' instead of 'Erleigh Road' (see page 86), because these were either side of the **GROVELANDS RD** display. The driver had probably learned that the blind could be correctly altered, without the conductor out in the road in front of the bus, by so many turns on the winding handle – but had happened, on this occasion, to have turned the handle the wrong way!

Following Transport Committee agreement in April 1947 and costing £241, blackout shuttering to the roof of the main repair shop, put up in 1942/43, was replaced by patent glazing to maximise the amount of daylight in which

This evocative view of AEC Regent 24 (ARD 15) opposite the GWR station circa 1947 on route F bound for Uplands Road is worthy of comment for several reasons. It is not only minus a nearside headlamp, it also appears to be equipped with a side or rear destination blind at the front, with the ends of the box blacked out, which suggests 'making do' in the weeks preceding the introduction of new blinds having the new place names introduced on 13th April 1947. The kerb guide on the nearside front wing is also worthy of note, a nice half-forgotten period feature not common in Reading. Finally, although delivered new with a 'long' radiator, the bus has subsequently acquired a pre-1938 'short' one.

Late V. C. Jones © Ian Allan Library

to work. At the same time, authorisation was sought to renew the depot heating system's coke-fired boiler with an oil-burning one, which would also be more efficient with regard to labour and space.

Meanwhile, two possible sites for the new depot and overhaul works had been investigated. The first was in Long Barn Lane, off Basingstoke Road, at the Four Horse Shoes public house, while the second was at Bennet Road, a turning off Basingstoke Road serving a new industrial estate, a mile further south. At the Transport Committee meeting of 14th April 1947, it was agreed to reserve the Bennet Road site.

The reader will have noted the interest held in travelling by corporation transport by 'Chronicler' in his column 'Reading Week by Week' in the *Berkshire Chronicle*. The edition on 16th May 1947 carried the following, which is included here simply to 'flavour the times', both in the way it was written and to bring out the prevailing circumstances relevant to bus travel:

"'Bus Queue Embarrassments – Inconvenience and ill-feeling are often caused at stopping-places on the Reading Corporation 'bus routes through queues forming on the wrong side of the electric standard to which the "trolley 'bus stop" notice is attached. Many people seem still to be unaware that queues should, from the commonsense point of view, face the direction from which the 'bus they hope to board is approaching, i.e., that the first arrival should take up his position, for example, on the east side of the standard while awaiting an east-bound 'bus, others forming up behind him. Unfortunately, the opposite procedure often takes place, with the result that the second or third arrival has to choose between deliberately lengthening a queue which he knows to be facing in the wrong direction, or making a minority of one on the other side of the notice, thereby risking the odium attaching to the suspicion that he intends to 'jump' the queue, as well as causing embarrassment when a crowded 'bus arrives and his position in the waiting list may have to be hastily determined by a harassed conductor faced with two 'heads' to his queue. I understand that the police, on whom the duty of the regulation of traffic devolves, do not invariably favour traffic-facing queues, but reserve the right to institute the opposite method on special occasions, such as the dispersal of football and greyhound racing crowds. Nevertheless, I fail to see any insuperable objection to establishing a rule merely because it may have to be set aside in one case out of a hundred, and the more general employment of the sign, 'Queue this side' would, in the opinion of most of the travelling public, go a long way towards solving the difficulty." And then……

"The Humorous Side – Incidentally, the history of the problem in Reading is not without its humorous side. Queuing for 'buses may be said to have commenced during the war, and it was decided that in Reading the queues should form with backs to the approaching traffic (that is, if the passengers stood behind one another, as directed). After some considerable experience it was noted that the queues in other towns usually formed facing the traffic, and that many passengers in Reading did not know which way to turn (or on which side of the notice to commence queuing). London people queued the London way and Reading people the Reading way, and at one particular stopping-place at a certain time of day the conductors knew that it was a 'London' queue, while all the rest of the day the queues at the same spot were 'Reading' queues! Obviously, it was a case in which uniformity was desirable, and with what may be briefly described as war-travel conditions (a term involving a variety of circumstances) still with us, I contend that the need not only for uniformity but also for the education of the public on the matter, is as desirable as ever it was. Surely that education in correct queuing can best be provided by the simple sign, 'Queue this side' affixed at every halting-place and acted upon at all times except in special emergencies."

In May 1947, the first of the new batch of six Bedford OBs arrived – one being delivered each month as agreed the previous December. Their Mulliner bodies actually seated 31 rather than 32 as intended at the time they were ordered. They were delivered to the undertaking via Great Western Motors Ltd, of Station Road, as 68–73 (CRD 591–596). Further details will be found in Appendices A and B. Bus 68

Ascot Week, June 1947. Duple-bodied Bedford OB 12 (CDP 231) is loading up on route L for Hemdean Road at the Broad Street stop outside H. Samuel, Jewellers, while three AEC trolleybuses, which have 'bunched' on their way into town and are now in a slow-moving traffic queue, discharge large numbers of impatient passengers not content to wait until arrival at the Vaudeville stop. Note the two different styles of bus stop flags and the canvas awnings over the shop fronts.

© *Millane Publishing*

Love on the buses because of the war, July 1947. Actually, both of these individuals were married – but not to each other! Mrs. Fennechien Blacquiere, who was Dutch, had been an Amsterdam waitress and met her future husband, a Canadian soldier, when the Allies liberated Holland. They came to England and settled in Reading, he working in a factory, she on the buses. Warren K. Collins, from Great Falls, Montana, had been with the 343rd American Army Engineers, at one time camped at Nettlebed. He became engaged to a local girl, who went out to America to marry him after the war but they later decided to settle in England. He became a conductor with Reading Corporation Transport.

Reading Standard

was used as a test vehicle and was duly weighed and certified.

The Mulliner delivery notes to Great Western Motors Ltd show that all six vehicles were delivered to the dealer in red primer. They were transferred to Mill Lane within a day or so and painted by the operator into a revised fleet livery, which was similar to the AEC Regent II scheme in having cream window surrounds. 68 was noted standing in the depot, fully painted, on 6th June 1947.

During the summer of 1947 (and that summer was a hot one – temperatures of 87°F on 31st May 1947 and 92°F on 3rd June 1947), the department found itself with a surplus of single-deckers at off-peak periods and weekends and the Transport Committee agreed to hire out some of the Bedfords to Smith's Luxury Coaches (Reading) Ltd. This caused some consternation at the town council meeting on Tuesday 3rd June 1947 when it was sought to ratify this decision and, after nearly an hour's debate, it was approved by a vote of 25 to 13. The undertaking took on the task of providing standby cover on Sundays for Smith's Coaches during the 1947 summer season. Thus, a vehicle was available with a corporation driver to cover for coach failures between 9.00am and 12.00 noon and between 6.00pm and 10.00pm, at a charge of £1 for each period and 2/- per mile for any mileage run. During the summer of 1947, some of the OBs were actually hired (with drivers) to Smith's Coaches on Sundays and on 15th June 1947 and again during July 1947, one of them is known to have made a trip to Whipsnade Zoo. Another hire to Smith's Coaches took place on Sunday 6th July 1947, when bus 15 went to Swindon and 16 went to Brighton. On the same date, 68 was on standby as a spare vehicle. It would seem that a single seat was replaced by a twin to up-seat the Mulliner-bodied vehicles to 32 when on hire to Smith's, as a memo dated 22nd August 1947 warned that this seat should not be fitted to the first batch of vehicles (12, 13, 15, 16, 17 and 18), which were only licensed for 30 passengers. At this stage only 68, 69 and 70 had been delivered and they were licensed as 32-seaters, although they ran as 31-seat vehicles on stage carriage service. The complete batch, 68–73, was re-seated permanently to 29 in 1950, due partially to 'seating pitch' requirements imposed by the certifying officers. Smith's Coaches were obviously stretched to their full vehicle capacity in trying to meet the demand in the booming leisure industry of post-war Britain. Day trips to the coast, the zoo or to other tourist attractions, such as castles and palaces, were common and, in the absence of private cars, these journeys were invariably made by coach or by train. The 'arrangement' with Smith's Coaches lasted for one season only, that of the summer of 1947. It was reported to the Transport Committee at their meeting on 11th December 1947 that the total distance travelled by hired vehicles was 3,424 miles, at a cost of £128 and an income to the Department of £317. In spite of this surplus, the transport manager was instructed to discontinue the hiring out of the undertaking's vehicles to other operators – presumably a political decision to *"...preserve the life of the bus fleet for the only business for which it is licensed – work within the borough"*. This certainly seems to have taken Mr Evans by surprise, causing work to be turned away during the summer of 1948. Except for departmental outings such as the staff outing to the bi-annual Commercial Motor Show, at Earls Court, London, the undertaking's vehicles were not again privately hired for trips outside the borough until after the 1974 local government reorganisation.

A fire at Norcot (Rex) substation on the evening of Friday 30th May 1947 damaged secondary cables to the transformer. Mr Evans was of the opinion that the fire had been caused because wartime blackout coverings to the ventilation openings had impaired the ventilation of the transformer, which was, in any case, frequently overloaded and therefore inadequate. At the Transport Committee on 11th June 1947, a quotation of £3,345 was accepted from the Hewettic Electric Company Ltd. for new 300kW rectifying equipment to augment the existing transformer. The £150 estimated cost of modifying the substation building itself, including improvements to ventilation arrangements, was also agreed, using the council's own building department. This cost subsequently increased to £290, but the substation's capacity effectively doubled.

At the same Transport Committee meeting, it was also agreed that in connection with the established policy of expanding the existing system, trolleybuses would replace motorbuses on route H (to Whitley Wood) and route N (to Callington Road) by proceeding with the construction of Routes 1 and 2 of the Reading Corporation (Trolley Vehicles) Provisional Order, 1946. In this connection, sites for two new substations needed to be identified. One possible site was identified as an extension of the Reading Corporation Electricity Department's substation at the junction of Basingstoke Road with Christchurch Gardens, only a short distance from Whitley Street. It was announced that the complete infrastructure for the extension would be carried out by Transport Department direct labour.

On the Whitley trolleybus extension, traction pole planting began in Basingstoke Road on 6th July 1947, although progress was slow. The turning circle at Whitley Street was altered in October 1947, in connection with a new roundabout being constructed at the site of the existing terminus, which was completed by the end of the following month. The Whitley Pump traffic island (where buses waited their departure time before returning to town) was demolished and the pump, which gave the location its name, sadly vanished when the roundabout was constructed (a non-functioning replica was provided when the roundabout was tidied-up in the early 1990s). The new arrangement incorporated the necessary leading and trailing frogs for the extension, for the existing terminal arrangement at Whitley Street was destined to be retained as a short-turn facility. The sites for the two intended substations had, by now, been agreed, in Christchurch Gardens at its junction with Basingstoke Road and on corporation-owned land between 305 and 313 Basingstoke Road, to the south of Buckland Road, near the Savoy cinema (which stood just on the town side of the junction with Buckland Road).

On the morning of Sunday 27th July 1947, there was, according to a surviving memo, motorbus substitution for trolleybuses running the workmen's special services whilst the street lighting was cleaned in Norcot Road and Park Lane, for which purpose the traction current had to be turned off. Presumably this was a reasonably common occurrence but was not often reported. Double Summer Time, re-introduced by the Attlee government on 13th April 1947 as an aid to increasing factory production to increase exports, came to an end on Sunday 10th August 1947, when clocks were 'put back' an hour. The usual British Summer Time, one hour ahead of Greenwich Mean Time, continued until 2nd November 1947.

At the meeting of the Transport Committee on 17th July 1947, quotations were accepted for the supply of twenty British United Traction two-axle trolleybus chassis at £2,370 8s 6d each, to be fitted with Park Royal bodywork at a cost of £2,630 each. These vehicles were the first in the Home Counties to take advantage of the new regulations permitting an overall width of 8 feet instead of 7ft 6in.

Mr Evans was always very keen to incorporate innovative features on the undertaking's vehicles, which would encourage safer operation. Thus, he had been impressed with the platform doors fitted to a motorbus operated by the Manchester Corporation Passenger Transport Department and arranged for the bus to be inspected by the Transport Committee (possibly in Manchester, as there is no evidence of a Manchester bus visiting Reading at this time – but see also pages 165/6 and 183). A vehicle fitted with folding platform doors was expected to reduce platform accidents, which were, in any case, more common on trolleybuses than on motorbuses *"...due to their better acceleration and retardation"*. He noted in his report that *"...if the experiment is a failure, the sliding* [sic] *doors can be removed and the only difference from our present type of vehicle will be the platform step on leaving the vehicle, instead of the platform step from the lower saloon onto the rear platform"*.

During that summer the concept of folding platform doors being fitted was further developed, with safety in mind. One suggestion was that an interlock should be incorporated with the driver's controls, so that the vehicle could not move unless the doors were closed. Another was that a small window should be incorporated high in the front bulkhead, with a rear-view mirror placed in the cab in front of the driver in such a position that he could see through to the rear of the vehicle to check whether it was safe to open or close the doors. Both were incorporated into the new trolleybus specification. Other modifications included deeper windscreens and cab side windows to give the driver the best possible all-round visibility; and a wider staircase that passengers would find easier to negotiate, with a quarter-turn landing just two steps up from the platform. This latter was able to be incorporated principally due to the vehicle being six inches wider than hitherto, but also because the staircase flight had one tread less, since the platform was at a level one step higher than usual. However, some influence was also apparent from the 'patent safety staircase' designed by the bodybuilders Charles H. Roe (1923)

This view, taken at Cemetery Junction in July 1947, actually depicts a sad scene, a labourer having thrown himself under the unidentified Kentwood-bound utility trolleybus in a successful suicide attempt. The corporation ambulance, SHX 364, is an ex-Royal Navy Morris Commercial LC. It was obtained in September 1946 to join the police ambulance when a separate service was set up. With the advent of the National Health Service in August 1948, the various local hospital ambulances joined the fleet and numbers were allocated, SHX 364 becoming fleet number 2.

Berkshire Chronicle

145

Ltd., of Leeds, which turned 180 degrees and incorporated two quarter-turn landings. Bus staircases, otherwise, had developed very little beyond the quarter-turn spiral staircases fitted to trams and open-top buses – indeed, they had become even less safe, with the use of two or three tapered treads to achieve the quarter-turn.

All of these design proposals were agreed at the Transport Committee meeting of 11th September 1947. During late 1947, an industrial exhibition was held at the Town Hall, where one of the exhibits was a mock-up of the rear platform of a BUT trolleybus incorporating the proposed platform doors. The outside of the mock-up was painted in the new livery incorporating cream window surrounds, introduced with the AEC Regent II motorbuses at the beginning of the year. Presumably, the decision to perpetuate the older livery style (crimson with three cream bands) on trolleybuses had not yet been taken. It may be that the old livery was retained as a simple means by which the driver of a trolleybus could recognise the type of vehicle he was following or passing – the reader will appreciate that one trolleybus attempting to overtake another which had its booms still on the wires was an error which could have some disruptive and expensive consequences! The mock-up was seemingly used to illustrate that it was safer to have doors to the rear platform of a bus than an open rear platform, and that Reading would be the first town to place into service a batch of buses with automatic folding rear doors. It may have been included as a prelude to the town's Road Safety Week the following week

Also at the Transport Committee meeting of 11th September 1947, it was agreed that the Great Western Railway should be informed, ahead of its being absorbed into British Railways as part of the Labour government's nationalisation policy, of the corporation's intention to operate trolleybuses along Station Road, Station Approach, Station Hill and Tudor Road and, therefore, over railway property at the Station. It had been agreed with the GWR in 1937, at the time when the extensive road improvements in front of the station were being planned, that the corporation would have priority of use for trolleybuses over the private lay-by adjacent to Platform 1. In any case, Mr Evans was of the opinion that trolleybuses should serve Stations and also deemed it advisable to have some form of town centre turn-back facility. Again, plans exist showing the proposed trolleybus overhead layout for this scheme.

There was, at least until fairly recently, a situation at Stations where some of the roadway was not, strictly speaking, a public thoroughfare but on railway-owned property. It is interesting to note that in 1947, particularly Station Road, and to a lesser extent Tudor Road, were referred to in this context. When the Great Western Railway arrived in Reading, in 1840, the approach to the station from the town was along an obviously railway-owned gated road running north from Friar Street, which subsequently developed into Station Road, and it would be interesting to research into when that road ceased to be railway property. At some stage – possibly after the later re-modelling of the station building, c. 1893, and the arrival on the scene of the South Eastern Railway in 1899 – ramped accesses were provided to the Stations from both east and west on the southern (town-ward) side of the railway, using surplus spoil from the railway construction. In each case, this access ran from embankment railway bridges over the two roads leading to Caversham Bridge, i.e. Vastern Lane (as it was originally) to the east and Caversham Road (as it became) to the west. Note also that there was no Reading Bridge over the River Thames until 1923.

At the same meeting, the transport manager was authorised to prepare a specification for twelve further new trolleybuses, together with a specification for six new motorbuses, for delivery in 1949/50. The trolleybuses were partly in anticipation of the withdrawal of the six original experimental trolleybuses, 101–106, but mainly to improve fleet strength in order to serve an anticipated increase in the population of the borough during the 1950s. The six motorbuses would have been regarded at this time purely as 'fleet replacements'.

In September 1947, work was about to commence to have 'camp sheathing' (close sheet piling) executed to 110ft of river frontage to the depot, having been authorised in June 1946. Only 149ft would then remain as not yet dealt with (in a project which dated back to 1930), so it was considered sensible to authorise the new transport manager to

Ooops! This altercation in Castle Street in late October 1947, involving AEC Regent II 63 (CRD 257), saw the demise up against a lamp post (or was it a former tram standard?) of what was probably a perfectly good Ford Prefect – no match for some 7 tons of bus!

Reading Standard

> **READING CORPORATION TRANSPORT**
>
> ## FARES and STAGES
>
> Commencing on SUNDAY, 2nd NOVEMBER, 1947, Revised Fares and Stages will come into operation on all Trolleybus and Motorbus Routes.
>
> Booklets showing the New Fares and Stages may be obtained from the Transport Offices, Mill Lane, Reading, The Parcels and Lost Property Offices, Arcade, Broad Street, Reading, or from any Conductor or Inspector.
>
> READING CORPORATION TRANSPORT,
> Mill Lane, Reading.
> 24th October, 1947.
>
> W. J. EVANS, M.I.E.E., M.Inst.T.,
> Transport Manager and Engineer.

have this final length done as an extension to this present contract rather than carried out at a later date.

A request had been received in May 1947 to again provide and decorate a vehicle for the town's 1947 Road Safety Week, which took place during the week commencing Saturday 4th October 1947. On this occasion no suitable vehicle was considered available on which to provide extensive decoration, so a somewhat restricted display was provided, comprising illuminated slogans in the lower-deck rearmost windows of no less than two trolleybuses, 105 and 106. It was common practice for the undertaking to display notices on its vehicles during such a campaign. How curious, however, that accident-prone 105 should have been one of the vehicles selected! In 1948 and on subsequent occasions, trolleybuses were again chosen for this role.

October 1947 saw a revision to certain bus and trolleybus stopping places, moving them away from road junctions and from opposite one another, possibly as a response to the post-war increase in motor traffic. However, rather unfortunately, no advisory notices appear to have been given, either to the public or to bus crews! 'Chronicler', in his 'Reading Week by Week' column in the *Berkshire Chronicle*, cited one particular example relating to the inbound stop in Kings Road at Cemetery Junction, which had been relocated nearer to the town and resulted in trolleybuses sailing past the location of the old stop (at which some intending passengers were queuing, none the wiser) and taking off again from the new stop location before the intending passengers had 'twigged' what was happening!

A new fare scale was implemented on Sunday 2nd November 1947 – mainly to offset an anticipated deficit in the coming years, due to the cost of catching up on the maintenance arrears of the existing fleet resulting from the war, together with the cost of essential fleet renewals. This involved revised fare scales, together with new fare stages and re-sited bus stops. It followed on from Mr Evans' report to the Transport (Future Policy) Sub-Committee at the start of the year. In effect, fares were increased by 2%, producing a new 1½d fare and a shorter 1d fare stage. The new fare scales also saw the withdrawal of Reading's lowest value fare – the three-farthing scholar's fare. The prices of workman tickets, now issued up to 7.45am, were increased and prepaid tickets became available only in packets of six – at 3d, 4d and 5d prices. For the time being, however, discount arrangements had to remain on prepaid tickets. In 1944, the Ministry of Transport had made an Order under Defence Regulations, which had the effect that the corporation would be obliged to issue workman tickets in bulk to such employers as may be designated by the commissioner, these employers then selling the tickets to their shift workers, which would allow travel at any time of day at workmen's fares. The undertaking's application for the fares increase had included a request to the commissioner to make recommendations to the Minister of Transport to rescind the Order. The undertaking had received a formal letter from the Minister of Transport in this connection in which they were told that *"the present is not an opportune time to cancel this Order"* – but the wartime measure whereby workmen's fares were granted on Sundays was repealed. The sale of discounted prepaid tickets and three-farthing prepaid scholar's tickets was eventually discontinued with effect from Thursday 18th March 1948, which turns out to have been the Thursday prior to Maundy Thursday and possibly, therefore, the day on which the schools broke up for the Easter Holidays.

The fares increase produced an increase in revenue of £1,058 in the first week and £1,083 in the second, when compared with the same weeks in 1946, although there was a slight reduction in passengers carried. Mr Evans' final statement in his report on the increases has a whiff of the modern day about it, when he states *"...I am fully conscious of the requirements of the public, who, it must be appreciated, are our customers and every endeavour ... is being made to give them the best possible service"*. However, the new fare tables issued to the public for these changes take us firmly back to the austerity of the 1940s, for it states *"Owing to paper restrictions only a limited number of copies of this Fare Table can be printed and the public are therefore requested to share copies wherever possible"*.

From the same date, Sunday 2nd November 1947, and as sanctioned by the traffic commissioners at the two-day hearing, which had taken place in Reading on 15th/16th July 1947, motorbus route N was extended to run beyond Callington Road, further along Northumberland Avenue to Hartland Road. Effectively, this was implemented not only because there was an immediate need, but as a prelude to the planned introduction of a trolleybus route as far as this point. Rush-hour extras continued to work short to Callington Road. There was already a roundabout at the crossing of Hartland Road with Northumberland Avenue, constructed pre-war (and one of the first in Reading), and near which, during the war, there had been an anti-aircraft gun emplacement adjacent to an army camp on the site of what became Ashmead School (and, decades later, the John Madejski Academy). Later, the camp became a prisoner-of-war camp for Italians and when it was vacated it was taken over for a while by squatters having nowhere else to live. Buses turned at Hartland Road terminus simply by circum-navigating the roundabout.

It would seem, also, that from the same date, Sunday 2nd November 1947, regular use began to be made of motorbuses as trolleybus reliefs, according to a diary entry made by a local enthusiast. Trolleybuses in Reading were, indeed, a commodity in great demand at this time!

A new feature of trolleybus operation in Reading was brought into use on 7th November 1947, when fog guiding-lights, to aid trolleybus drivers in foggy weather, particularly at night-time, were installed on the trolleybus overhead at the 'fork' junction of Queens Road with Kings Road. In thick fog, it had not been unusual for westbound trolleybuses to stray into Queens Road. These 'fairy lights' consisted of what looked to be a string of domestic 'pearl' lamp bulbs between the 'up' and 'down' lines and could be switched on as required. In the era with which we are concerned, street lighting was much less effective than in more recent times and winter fogs were much more common. Particularly in

A reconstructed Broad Street looking east from Cross Street (possibly very soon after the work was completed, as there are no traffic islands), with Thames Valley buses ahead of utility trolleybus 136 (BRD 801), lots of 'jay-walkers' (including mums with prams) and private cars badly parked on bus stops.
Commercial picture postcard

urban areas, too, there was widespread use of open coal fires, which often resulted in some dense urban fogs. In such conditions, 'fairy lights' gave some idea to a trolleybus driver as to where to drive his vehicle without losing contact with the overhead wires (with trams, which were track-bound, of course, 'fairy lights' had been unnecessary). Sets of 'fairy lights' were subsequently installed at other locations on trolleybus routes, usually on the outside of a curve or between the two sets of overhead wires, where the road changed direction or the route of the overhead line made a sharp deviation.

The Ministry of Transport was working with the borough surveyor regarding proposals to improve the road layout at Cemetery Junction, an oblique crossroads where, for many years, traffic had been controlled by traffic lights, which were manually operated by a policeman sitting in a raised cabin. Plans for constructing a bone-shaped roundabout, which were made public at the town council meeting of 3rd June 1947, would affect trolleybus operation as it would prove necessary to alter the overhead wiring layout. An entirely new layout was designed, having through-running in an easterly direction, from King's Road to London Road, with a branch connection outbound for Wokingham Road; and through-running in a westerly direction from Wokingham Road to Kings Road with a 'trailing connection' from London Road. At the same time, a short-turn facility would be incorporated at the eastern end of the roundabout, to allow trolleybuses to terminate short at Cemetery Junction and return towards the town centre. No contribution towards the cost of the alterations was available and the Transport Department was saddled with having to find an estimated £2,000 from its own resources to meet the cost of this work. An order was placed with Stewarts & Lloyds at this time for the supply of 110 trolleybus traction poles, at a cost of £2,447 10s 0d in connection with the foregoing modification at Cemetery Junction, the new roundabout at Whitley Street and the new extension along Tudor Road to serve Stations.

At the Transport Committee meeting on 11th December 1947, it was once again agreed to hire in vehicles for peak hour use to cope with pre-Christmas traffic and Saturday football extras. In fact, coaches were already being hired-in from Smith's Luxury Coaches from late November 1947. The vehicles used were often some of the 1936-vintage petrol-engined Leyland Cheetahs which Smith's Coaches had acquired ex-Scottish Motor Traction. Whilst in use with Reading Corporation Transport, these vehicles invariably still carried London Transport 'bullseye' motifs on their radiators and London Transport 'slip boards' in the front windscreens, having been at work during the previous week on hire in London to help alleviate the vehicle shortage then prevalent in the capital. Indeed, the further need to carry statutory 'On Hire' notices for Reading Corporation Transport must have resulted in a somewhat cosmopolitan combination!

The post-war boom in travelling by public transport meant that many operators, including Reading Corporation Transport, were finding that they had more passengers than their existing fleet could cope with. At the end of 1947, for example, the department had 37 trolleybuses, of which 36 were rostered at peak duty times. Thus, only one trolleybus could be off the road for maintenance or repair at

In all probability the last Saturday in October 1948, this is the eastern end of Broad Street looking west, with utility trolleybus 135 (BRD 800) westbound in a traffic queue and much going on. Traffic islands have appeared down the middle of Broad Street and the rear registration number on the trolleybus has been transferred from being painted on the rear platform window to a position on the offside of the rear lower panel.

Reading Standard

any one time before there was a major problem. Despite the excellent reliability of trolleybuses, it was still a difficult target to meet, and, with the motorbus fleet equally stretched, there were only occasional opportunities to use motorbuses to make up the numbers should the occasion demand. The bonanza in the use of public transport at this time was enough to suggest that even the twenty BUT trolleybuses on order for the Whitley routes might not be enough and, although it had been agreed in September 1947 to purchase twelve additional trolleybuses, the specification for them (as required for Ministry of Transport approval) was only just being drawn up. Even when a definite order could be placed, such was the nationwide demand for new vehicles that delivery could not be expected for up to two years after the signing of contracts. The search was on for some second-hand vehicles.

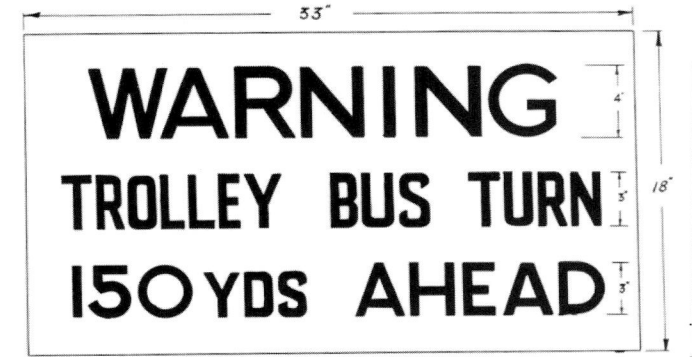

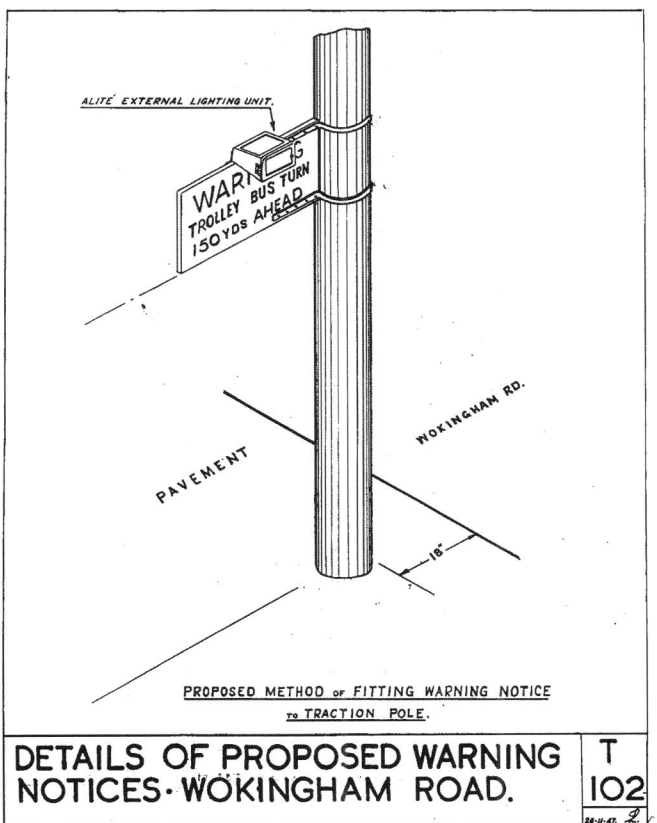

WARNING TROLLEY BUS TURN 150 YDS AHEAD

PROPOSED WARNING NOTICE.

DETAILS OF PROPOSED WARNING NOTICES · WOKINGHAM ROAD. T 102

In late November 1947 there was a proposal to site a notice on Wokingham Road to warn approaching motorists that they might meet a trolleybus turning across the road. The Three Tuns turning circle where trolleybuses turned across a main thoroughfare was never popular with the borough police, and there were always concerns about safety. The drawings were prepared but it seems unlikely that the notice was in fact sited as nobody can remember it! Buses on route 17 make the same 'unsafe' turn across Wokingham Road today, but in the year 2014 they are Alexander-Dennis diesel-electric hybrid motorbuses rather than trolleybuses!

Silver Lining Savings Exhibition

These three photographs were taken, presumably towards the end of 1947, as publicity photographs in connection with the undertaking's display at the 'Silver Lining Savings Exhibition' at the Town Hall during the first week of February 1948. However, they are obviously posed, and appear to have been taken on a Sunday morning by C. E. May, a well-known London Street photographer who was also contracted to supply press photographs to the Reading Standard.

Top: *AEC Regent II 60 (CRD 254) is nicely posed in Broad Street outside The Arcade – which is nowhere near the stop for Shinfield Road! Note the missing nearside headlamp but, particularly, that the platform valance is maroon rather than cream, showing how a completely maroon rear elevation was achieved (see also the picture of the same bus at the GWR station depicting the offside (page 137)); and that the bus has fleet numbers on the nearside at both front and rear. Both variations are thought to have been part of Mr Little's livery experiments.*

Centre: *AEC trolleybus 123 (ARD 686) parked in the middle of the road, playing at being a tram. The vehicle is working inbound in Wokingham Road at the Melrose Avenue stop, with a posed group of intending passengers – and a nosey bystander. This is the trolleybus used for livery experiments the previous year, but it now wears standard livery.*

Bottom: *123 again, in the middle of Mill Lane, seemingly heading west past the departmental offices, whereas it is actually posed – where is the crew? No public services ran along Mill Lane – and, in any case, Wokingham Road is in precisely the opposite direction!*

All photos © Late C. E. May

16 The Threat of Nationalisation

In early post-war Britain, nationalisation was centre stage. At the Labour Party Conference held in December 1944, a resolution by Reading's prospective Labour parliamentary candidate (and later MP) Ian Mikardo, which was passed on a clear show of hands, called for nationalisation to be the central plank of Labour's post-war election manifesto. This intended public ownership, which was based around efficiency and central planning rather than pure Socialist dogma, was at that time to embrace heavy industry, building, banking, transport, fuel and power.

At a meeting on 19th July 1945, the Municipal Passenger Transport Association (MPTA) refused to run a national campaign emphasising the achievements and advantages of municipal control of public service vehicles. It did, however, provide posters and logos for local campaigns – perhaps deciding that sitting on the fence was the safest option for the moment!

Following the Labour Party's post-war general election victory in July 1945 (and with it Ian Mikardo's election as Reading's MP), nationalisation moved to the top of the political agenda. The railways, docks, coal mines, steelworks, canals, buses and road haulage were to be drawn into public control, together with the utilities of water, electricity and gas, which were most usually to be transferred from local authority control. Despite firm opposition from the Conservative Party and its supporters, the transition to state control had a relatively easy path in Britain in peacetime. Peace had brought new hopes and high expectations for full employment and state funded health care and education, which caught the mood of the time and found a ready acceptance by the British public. This political mindset and a softening of public attitudes had occurred because of the experiences of controls and restrictions by wartime regulations, for in wartime Britain these regulations had been almost as severe as in those countries suffering from the strictures of totalitarian government.

It took a couple of years to get round to nationalising transport. The Transport Bill, 1947, proposed the nationalisation of many of the nation's bus companies and it was planned that Area Boards would eventually be set up to operate all passenger transport. The bill aimed for a degree of co-ordination and control in matters of service frequency and shared routes with municipal undertakings, including joint purchase of rolling stock and pooling of workshop facilities. The MPTA, at a meeting on 13th March 1947 as part of its campaign to retain local authority control and influence on these Area Boards, declared that this responsibility should be a statutory obligation on local authorities, which should themselves appoint the Joint Area Committees. However, under Section 63 of the resulting Transport Act, it was the British Transport Commission (which was founded in 1948 to control the railways, docks and inland waterways), and not local authorities, that was eventually charged with preparing Area Schemes. The Act did, however, preserve the interests of the local authorities by a protective clause that ensured consultation with them.

In April 1947, with the Transport Act, 1947, looming, Reading's Transport Manager was granted permission by the borough council to aid the Ministry of Transport in valuing road haulage fleets for nationalisation, although he does not appear to have become actively involved until he was approached again in spring 1949.

The scope of the new Act became more apparent and, not unnaturally, the Transport Committee, at its meeting on 16th October 1947, voiced its strong resentment to the proposal that bus services should subsidise the railways and that municipal bus services should cease to remain under municipal control. It was resolved *"that the Transport (Future Policy) Sub-Committee be requested to consider and report to the Committee on the matter insofar as the road passenger transport undertaking may be affected by the Act"*.

John Evans, the Reading undertaking's transport manager, had greater expectations than simply absorption of Reading's municipal transport undertaking into what he perceived as a Berkshire-wide Area Committee. On 21st January 1948, which is after the Transport Act had become law, he presented a report to the Transport (Future Policy) Sub-Committee. In it he argued that as Reading was *"...a commercial and social centre for a large area"*, the corporation was the natural and obvious body to control and develop local and long-distance services in Reading and the surrounding area under any Area Road Transport Scheme established under the Act. He also had visions of the planned building of a new workshop and depot, to be followed by an administrative centre, ideally in the Basingstoke Road area, which would provide a ready-made centralised area headquarters for the newly-nationalised and co-ordinated road passenger transport and road haulage industries. Thus, he saw new opportunities for the stabling and maintenance of lorries as well as buses.

This extension of the borough's control would, he argued, have a considerable effect on the prosperity of Reading and he went on to describe the possibilities. The area of deployment of the department's motorbus services could be extended to Kidmore End, Chazey Heath, Purley, Pangbourne, Theale, Grazeley, Spencers Wood, Arborfield, Winnersh, Wokingham and Sonning, while the trolleybus services might be extended to Woodley and Loddon Bridge. After trolleybuses were introduced to serve Whitley Wood, they could, perhaps, be extended beyond, to Shinfield village. In short, he was proposing that the Thames Valley Traction Company's services from Reading should be co-ordinated and pooled with the Transport Department's services under one authority – a vision which, in fact, finally became a reality 44 years later, in 1992, when the Bee Line services in the area were purchased by Reading Transport – but all due to very different circumstances! But there was more. Mr Evans proposed that the Administrative Area, with headquarters based in Reading, could extend to the edges of the London Passenger Transport Board area and take in Henley, Marlow, High Wycombe, Maidenhead, Ascot, Guildford and Aldershot and, in the other direction, Thame, Wheatley, Oxford, Wantage, Hungerford, Newbury and Basingstoke. Some pipe-dream – with John Evans sitting pretty in the middle of it all, of course – or, preferably, somewhere near the top!

As matters stood, the Transport Commission would determine the areas of regional control. Mr Evans had already noted that the Tilling Group, which owned the Thames Valley Traction Company, was a long-time supporter of nationalisation and already in negotiation with the Transport Commission – perhaps positioning its undertakings for future influence. He warned that unless the corporation had *"...definite and constructive proposals* for Reading as a main junction of National Transport, we may find ourselves left with only operating our trolleybus routes, while the Administrative centre for any regional Transport Board for this area may be located elsewhere". Without some firm planning and new vision, he thus painted a gloomy picture – of the Transport Department stripped of its motorbus services; with its town bus routes controlled by a distant body; and the corporation's civic pride diminished, with only a trolleybus system left in its control.

This suggests that trolleybuses would possibly have been excluded from the grasp of the 1947 Transport Act. Whilst most British trolleybus systems were municipally-owned, there were several which were not. That in Llanelli (or Llanelly, as it was then), West Wales, for example, was one such which, indeed, was operated by the local private electricity company. When the electricity industry was nationalised under the Electricity Act, 1947, the Llanelly trolleybus system became, technically, nationalised – but seems to have been sold-off almost immediately, although, surprisingly, not within the Tilling Group but to a British Electric Traction Group subsidiary. Mr Evans later wrote a joint report with the borough treasurer, on 12th February 1948, in which he presented his concern "...that an efficient and economical organisation, which will be a credit to Reading, shall be handed over to the National Authority".

In 1948, the Tilling Group holdings were, indeed, nationalised, together with Bristol Commercial Vehicles Ltd and Eastern Coach Works Ltd, which set the die for the future vehicle purchasing policy of the nationalised bus companies until the 1980s. London Transport was also nationalised from 1st January 1948 and the Scottish Motor Traction Group followed in 1949. They were all formed into Executives and brought under control of the British Transport Commission. Nearly 4,000 road haulage concerns, with responsibility for 40,000 vehicles, were also absorbed, between 1948 and 1951 under the name 'British Road Services'.

In spring 1949, Mr Evans was again approached to carry out duties over a period expected to exceed 12 months, on behalf of the Road Transport Executive, in connection with the valuation of privately-owned fleets of road haulage vehicles. The Finance & General Purposes Committee of the town council, now Conservative-controlled and therefore not a supporter of Labour's nationalisation plans (especially with the threat of its municipal transport undertaking being whisked out of its control), this time refused to grant him permission to take on this work. The work involved was estimated to take two days a week, so the reason for the refusal was that with his existing workload, let alone the future developments, it was considered that he already had sufficient work to occupy him full time. It was added, somewhat disingenuously, that the refusal had nothing to do with the council's political views on nationalisation...!

Views from a number of municipal operators were sent to the Municipal Passenger Transport Association, which in turn passed resolutions that were sent to the Road Passenger Executive. In particular, the MPTA sought to influence the structure of the Area Boards, being concerned that ownership and control of bus services should be firmly in the hands of local authorities, with Area Boards consisting of elected representatives. There was, indeed, considerable concern expressed at the implications. In Reading, for example, a special meeting of the Transport Committee on 24th October 1949 considered the proposed Passenger Road Transport Northern Area Scheme – under the Transport Act 1947: Part IV – in order to be aware of what could be 'just round the corner'.

In 1949, in an article entitled *Progress in Municipal Transport* in the Ian Allan book *Buses and Trams*, Mr Evans stated that co-ordination (he avoided the 'N' word!) could be used to combine the best of company and municipal undertakings, suggesting that the interchange of staff between urban, rural and private hire work could relieve the monotony of driving the same routes day after day. He also pointed out "a definite case for simplifying ticket systems and unifying the transfer of passengers between the long-distance and local services". He did, however, offer a cautionary note that "whilst co-ordination and standardisation have their advantages in many directions, they must be pursued with caution if transport is to fulfil its proper function in the life of the whole community".

In the event, the ongoing and lengthy process of consultation with local authorities changed as the political climate altered following the February 1950 general election, in which Labour – after nearly five years in office – was returned to power with a reduced majority. Another general election, in 1951, returned a Conservative government to power; the previous administration's nationalisation policies were halted, and the British Electric Traction Group and the municipally-owned passenger transport undertakings 'escaped' completely from being involved any further. In the case of road haulage, the new parliament decided to de-nationalise a large part of British Road Services. Nationalisation and Area Committees did not figure again in the political agenda of government until the Labour Party returned to power in 1964 and the bus industry subsequently entered the era of the National Bus Company and Passenger Transport Executives.

Route N was extended beyond Callington Road to Hartland Road from 2nd November 1947. AEC Regent II 64 (CRD 258) is seen at the terminal stop, probably in spring 1948. Note the absence of a footpath and the remains of the army camp on the John Rabson Recreation Ground, which had latterly become a squat due to inadequate supplies of housing being available after six years of war. As recounted on page 136, the directors of H. & G. Simonds Ltd. were politically against the Labour Party's nationalisation policies, so they transferred their advertising from Thames Valley (which was part of the pro-nationalisation Tilling Group) to Reading Corporation Transport.

W. J. Haynes © Millane Publishing

17   1948: Renewal and Expansion

By 1948, the public demand for bus services was beyond the imagination of any modern bus operator. The joy of operating in such a strong context was tempered, however, by the irritating delays in delivery of new vehicles and the ongoing difficulties experienced in trying to keep elderly vehicles not only running, but up to a minimum standard.

From 14th January 1948, following an agreement with the employees' representative, it was decided that utility Guy Arab motorbuses 6 and 7, which had already been restricted to routes I and M (see p.80), should now be restricted to route I (Horncastle – Donkin Hill), on duties **IB** and **ID** only. The allegedly underpowered Gardner 5LW engines with which these buses were fitted made them slow, making them unpopular with the drivers as they were unable to maintain schedules, particularly during peak hours.

At the Transport Committee meeting of 15th January 1948, the old chestnut of operating a connecting bus service from Kentwood to the Roebuck (and beyond) was again raised – considerable fuss over a distance of only 620 yards that no longer had a corporation bus service! Councillors Woodrow and Barrett (the two gentlemen, who, incidentally, formed the erstwhile Chiltern Queens company seven years later) had received a petition from 150 people. Analysis revealed, however, that whilst many petitioners did live east of the Roebuck, many others lived beyond the county borough boundary, in Thames Valley territory, which already had a half-hourly bus service. Mr Evans undertook a census, which showed that very few people walked to or from the Roebuck, and that an imbalance inwards in the early morning was because people were connecting with the trains at nearby Tilehurst Station. Mr Evans commented that the traffic commissioner had agreed to the discontinuation of the service in March 1945 *"...owing to poor demand"* and observed that *"...it can be assumed that the same people are petitioning today as petitioned in 1944"*. He was disinclined to provide either a trolleybus extension or a motorbus service, given the shortage of supplies, the shortage of vehicles, the shortage of platform staff and the energy difficulties at the time – which, in 1948, were proving very similar to wartime problems.

Nevertheless, in spite of his obvious reluctance to provide a service, the Transport Committee asked him to prepare a report on extending the trolleybus system beyond Kentwood to the Roebuck and overhead layout drawings were made for construction of a trolleybus turning circle on the site at the borough boundary, opposite the Roebuck, which had been given to the corporation by Mr Arthur Newbery some time previously for that specific purpose. Mr Evans reported to the committee again on 14th April 1948, re-iterating that he was unwilling to provide a service over the short distance in question and the Transport (Future Policy) Sub-Committee was asked to consider the matter. The land in Oxford Road given by Mr Newbery was on a bend, so that any bus terminus at this point was considered dangerous by the chief constable. As the cost of construction of the necessary trolleybus turning facilities was also considered excessive, the matter was once again dismissed.

A civic and industrial exhibition, part of what was known as The Silver Lining Campaign – to encourage people to buy savings stamps and certificates and open Post Office Savings Accounts to raise government funds – was planned to be held in the Town Hall from 31st January to 7th February 1948. The Transport Department was expected to contribute a display stand, the transport manager being given authority by the Transport Committee chairman to incur such reasonable expenditure as was deemed necessary. The end result comprised the mock-up of the platform of a bus fitted with folding platform doors (as shown at an exhibition the previous year, but now carrying fleet number 138), together with a simulated trolleybus chassis with a cab fitted with a full set of controls, so that small (and not-so-small) boys could experience 'driving' a trolleybus. The backboard to the display depicted the aims of the department and was illustrated with a number of superb large-format photographs, which happily still survive, now in the ownership of a local enthusiast.

From 60 applicants short-listed to five, Mr John Perry, senior traffic assistant at Stockport Corporation Transport, was appointed assistant traffic superintendent and took up his position on Monday 2nd February 1948.

The Silver Lining Savings Exhibition at the Town Hall in early February 1948 was part of a government scheme to persuade people to invest in National Savings. In Reading, various committees of the borough council, e.g. police, fire brigade, transport, water, electricity, gas, etc., were encouraged to put on a display. The Transport Department's contribution included a mock-up of a trolleybus driving cab. The photo of a trolleybus on the wall behind, and several others which were used, still exist; some have been reproduced in this book (see page 150).

© *Reading Museum Service (Reading Borough Council); all rights reserved*

Mr Evans had already stated, in January 1947, that he was not satisfied with the existing TIM ticketing, the speed of which he said was "... *easily offset by their inadequate printing of vital information on the tickets, particularly when return tickets are available*". This may explain why five or six experimental Bell Punch 'Ultimate' ticket machines were trialled for a few weeks from 20th October 1947, as part of research organised by the Bell Punch Company and the Municipal Passenger Transport Association. The Ultimate was designed for town services where a speedy issue of a limited range of tickets was required. These pre-production prototypes were equipped with four containers holding four different values of square, pre-printed coloured tickets (see Appendix F); additional fare values could be achieved by issuing combinations of tickets. They were used by conductors on a variety of routes, issuing tickets from a stock provided by the manufacturer and headed "BLANK CORPN". The latest TIM machine was also inspected – this now had the option of twelve fare values and up to six classes of ticket (ordinary, workman, child, parcel, dog, etc.) as opposed to the Ultimate's three (single, return and child).

Mr Evans approved of the Ultimate's coloured tickets to aid inspection, but noted the need for extra storage space for the various pre-printed ticket rolls, and additional office staff to issue these to the conductors. He would have preferred five rather than four ticket containers (and, when it eventually went into production, it did indeed have five containers). The Ultimate was a new machine, which would not come into full production until July 1948. There was a 2½-year waiting list, and machines were available only on rental at £6 a year. In contrast, TIM promised delivery in 12 to 15 months, and machines could be purchased outright at a cost of £30.

Mr Evans reported in January 1948 that nearly 80% of the department's stock of over 200 TIMs was worn out and needing replacement and that (in spite of his earlier reservations) the model had given every satisfaction. The committee agreed to purchase 120 new TIM machines on 15th January 1948 and, in September 1948, authorised the withdrawal and sale of the worst of the worn-out pre-war machines. The new machines were delivered from January 1949, and were put into service on a rolling basis

Information came to hand that Huddersfield Corporation Transport was offering for disposal twelve Karrier E6 three-axle trolleybuses dating from 1934, with Metropolitan Vickers traction equipment and Brush 64-seat bodywork. This came to Mr Evans' attention as he beat his breast in frustration over his own shortage of trolleybus rolling stock, for at peak times, it will be recalled, he needed to use 36 of the 37 trolleybuses in the fleet. Needless to say, he brought the matter to the immediate attention of the Transport Committee. Although the Huddersfield trolleybuses were two to three inches higher than any in the existing fleet and would therefore have to be restricted in operation to south of Caversham Road railway bridge, they were, in Mr Evans' opinion, attractive financially and likely to give Reading around five years of good service. At the Transport Committee meeting of 12th February 1948, Mr Evans was authorised to purchase five, or alternatively ten, of the twelve vehicles available. The saga of their acquisition, rebuilding and entry into service is told in the next chapter. At the same meeting, authority was given to replace the four wooden-slat roller shutters to East Garage, which had fallen into a bad state of repair, with steel shutters at a cost of £1,219. Authority was also sought to have an additional maintenance pit provided in the repair workshops at an estimated £350.

Whilst the extensive town centre tram track removal and road reconstruction was taking place, there had been further deterioration of the road surface elsewhere, largely due to the presence of disused tram track, which meant yet more repairs at the Transport Department's expense. In particular, this included the junction of Craven Road with Erleigh Road and, at its meeting of 11th March 1948, the Transport Committee agreed to fund the immediate removal of tram track at this location. It was not, in any case, removed until the autumn of 1948, during which, for about three weeks Eldon Road had to be closed and Craven Road temporarily became a one-way street. No other sections of tram track were removed during the financial year 1948/49.

Provision of the new Christchurch Gardens substation became seriously delayed at this time, and it was reported at the Transport Committee meeting of 11th March 1948 that this was likely to hold up the introduction of trolleybuses to Whitley Wood. Purchase of three 300/500kW Hackbridge & Hewettic Electric Company rectifier units and switchgear was authorised at the same meeting, one for Christchurch Gardens and two for Savoy substations.

The town was honoured with a royal visit on Wednesday 7th April 1948 by H. M. The King, who was Colonel-in-Chief of the Royal Berkshire Regiment and who visited Brock Barracks in the late morning and Forbury Gardens after lunch, to see the Maiwand Memorial. With his inward route via London Road, Kings Road, Broad Street and Oxford Road and a return via the same route but with a diversion via Buttermarket to Market Place and The Forbury, returning via High Street, there was an inevitable dislocation of bus and trolleybus services on the day. From information derived from the *Berkshire Chronicle*, the King was due to arrive at Brock Barracks at 11.45am, so last 'through' trolleybuses westbound left Wokingham Road at 11.10am and Liverpool Road at 11.15am, before the road was closed, whilst eastbound the last for Liverpool Road was timed to leave Norcot at 10.55am and that for Wokingham Road at 11.00am, all others from Norcot up to 11.10am running to depot. Motorbus services crossing the Royal route after 11.15am were held at Stations or St. Mary's Butts as appropriate until after the royal visitor had cleared the town centre section. Similarly, in the afternoon, with the King due to arrive at Forbury Gardens at 2.30pm, services crossing the royal route after 2.01pm were held at Duke Street, St.Mary's Butts, West Street and Stations. Last eastbound <u>omnibuses</u> *(sic)* departed Norcot for Liverpool Road and Wokingham Road at 1.45pm, resuming at about 2.25pm for Broad Street only. The last westbound <u>'bus</u> *(sic)* passed through Cemetery Junction at 2.30pm arriving at Duke Street for depot at 2.35pm, all buses from the east having run into depot since 1.40pm. One must assume from the foregoing, therefore, that there was probably an almost complete motorbus substitution on the 'main line' between the first and second 'run-ins' to depot and that, while His Majesty was at Forbury Gardens, there was another substitution going on at the depot, with trolleybuses re-entering service via Mill Lane, Bridge Street and St. Mary's Butts – almost all, presumably, working west along Oxford Road with some turning short at Norcot to pick up the eastbound service at the correct times.

With its acute shortage of rolling stock, the logistics of operating the foregoing will have been quite trying for the Transport Department, but the fact that the King was in town during the middle of an early closing day probably helped. Together with an anticipation that most folk ordinarily requiring to travel at lunchtime would stay in

AEC Regent 10 (RD 5361) at Whitley Wood terminus of route H (formerly Wood Lane Junc. and known pre-war as Lower Whitley). It has reversed into Whitley Wood Road and will pull forward to the departure stop in Whitley Wood Lane before setting off for Emmer Green. The photograph is thought to have been taken circa spring 1948, for there is no sign of any trolleybus infrastructure beginning to appear. The destination blind is a two line exposure which reads 'Whitley Wood Basingstoke Road'.

Late L. G. Head © Millane Publishing

town to see the King, a temporary shortage of motorbuses on motorbus routes, which were disrupted anyway, would probably not have caused too much of a problem either.

Meanwhile, a strike, the first to affect the undertaking since the General Strike of May 1926, took place between 2nd and 27th April 1948, when staff in the body shop and paint shop, who were members of the National Union of Vehicle Builders, withdrew their labour. It was recorded by a local enthusiast, incidentally, that AEC trolleybus 114 was put back into service in undercoat during the strike. Indeed, a news snippet in the *Reading Standard* for 16th April 1948 states that *"many buses are appearing in service with windows patched with plywood, while others are being used partly painted, just as they stood when the men stopped work"*. Sadly, no-one seems to have taken any photographs!

All was not gloom at this time, however. With effect from Monday 26th April 1948, improved evening frequencies were introduced on the motorbus routes F (Shinfield Road – Uplands Road); H (Emmer Green – Whitley Wood); K (Friar Street – Woodcote Road); L (Hemdean Road – Berkeley Avenue); and P (Hartland Road – Caversham). The supplementary operation of route I between Broad Street and Donkin Hill was also improved in the evenings and on Sundays between 1.53pm and 6.08pm. Effectively, a 7½-minute service was provided on that section of route I between Donkin Hill and Broad Street when the supplementary service was in operation. These changes prompted 'Chronicler' to write the following lines in his 'Reading Week by Week' column in the *Berkshire Chronicle* on 4th June 1948:

"The Last 'Bus – The recent additions to the Reading Corporation Transport's evening services have been greatly appreciated by the public, and it is a great boon to those attending the theatres and cinemas to know that, should one 'bus be full, they have a comparatively short time to wait for the next one. It is the last 'bus, however, which gives cause for so much concern. Why is it that in nearly every case the drivers of the 11pm 'bus or trolley 'bus endeavour to break all speed records? Their anxiety to finish their duties is understandable, but the few minutes so gained are hardly worth it when the safety and comfort of the travelling public are concerned. Or is it that this does not matter?"

Once again, work on the Caversham Road railway bridges caused the closure of Caversham Road from 10.30am on Saturday 5th June 1948, and all traffic, including the bus services, was diverted via Vastern Road. The road under the railway bridges was re-opened the following day.

Alongside the refurbishment of the second-hand Karriers, the Transport Department was still battling with the massive demands made on its services and vehicles by the people of Reading for both work and leisure. Such demand is exemplified by the Easter Weekend traffic of 1948. Over the four days of Good Friday, Holy Saturday, Easter Sunday and Bank Holiday Monday (26th–29th March inclusive), over 425,700 passengers were carried, exceeding those carried over Easter the previous year by 42,000. Receipts for the four days totalled £3,899 – a new record in the history of the undertaking. It seemed that wherever people were spending their leisure time, Reading Corporation Transport was running buses! Possibly because of this nationwide demand for public transport, it was reported in May 1948 that the Minister of Transport had issued a new Regulation. The Standing Passenger Order, 1948, permitted an increase in the number of standing passengers allowed to travel in the lower saloons of buses and trolleybuses from five (the level to which it had reverted sometime after the return to peace) to eight.

The garage accommodation at Mill Lane was becoming increasingly overcrowded, for it now housed dinner wagons and ambulances as well as increasing numbers of buses and trolleybuses. With all this jostling for increasingly limited space, some twenty vehicles were now having to stand in Mill Lane overnight. In a report to the Transport Committee on 21st January 1948, Mr Evans urged that a site for a second depot and workshops, which had been talked about the previous April, should now be secured as soon as possible. A further report, submitted to the Transport Committee on 3rd March 1948, requested that about fifteen acres of land owned by the Drainage and Sewage Disposal Committee on the new Bennet Road Industrial Estate, should be placed at the disposal of the Transport Department. This land, just behind the last factory site on Basingstoke Road, was considered adequate for the construction of a machine shop, heavy workshops and additional garage accommodation.

Because of difficulties in obtaining steelwork at the time, it was decided to try to obtain a surplus wartime aircraft hangar to form the main part of the new depot building. Mr Evans estimated that a second-hand hangar would have a 25-year life and would accommodate 70 to 80 vehicles – exactly the right size to relieve the worsening congestion situation at Mill Lane. Ministry of Transport permission was nevertheless obtained for an allocation of reinforcement steel needed in the construction of the new facility, and the regional disposals officer at the Ministry of Supply was informed of the department's need of a second-hand hangar. Initially, various hangars were located but rejected, either due to their inadequate size or to their excessive distance from Reading and the associated costs of transport. Matters seemed desperate when the only four offered

A typical outer terminus scene in the late 1940s – 1935-vintage AEC Regent 46 (RD 7126) is on layover at Chalgrove Way, Emmer Green, with the crew having a chat before 'sallying forth' into town and onward to Whitley Wood. On every route the running time between outer terminus and town centre was between 10 and 15 minutes, so that a 'trip' was about 25 minutes and a 'round trip' was allocated one hour, which was fairly easily achieved given the traffic levels of the time. Note the 'long' 1938-vintage radiator and the lack of blue identification lights.

Late L. G. Head © Millane Publishing

which did comply with requirements, particularly regarding size, were in the north of Scotland or the Shetlands! Eventually, council approval was sought to erect a new building instead – a wildly expensive alternative.

By the Transport Committee meeting of 11th June 1948, formal approval had been received from the various ministries regarding (a) the purchase of a hangar-type depot building for the Bennet Road site; (b) the covering of Mill Stream next to the trolleybus garage at Mill Lane with provision for a secondary means of exit; and (c) the rebuilding of the burnt out repair shop. The estimated cost of decking over Tan Lock (which included an estimated 40 tons of steel reinforcement), the necessary relocation of the sluice gates, and the alterations to the adjoining garage buildings (including the provision of new roller shutter doors) was put at £15,000. Having negotiated this first hurdle, real progress had yet to take place.

The annual report for the financial year ended 31st March 1948 records that the undertaking made a profit on the year's working which amounted to £13,609, compared with a loss of £9,734 in the financial year 1946/47. This improvement was due partly to the fare increase effective from 2nd November 1947. Rolling stock comprised 37 trolleybuses (with another 20 on order) and 60 motorbuses, of which 23 were petrol-engined and the remainder oil-engined (with 11 new ones on order). 48 vehicles had received repaints, compared with 40 the previous financial year.

At the Transport Committee meeting on 14th April 1948, the Transport (Future Policy) Sub-Committee had been asked to consider, as part of Whitley trolleybus conversion scheme, a further extension of the trolleybus system, comprising a town centre loop. This would also serve Stations, by erecting wiring along Friar Street, Station Road, Blagrave Street and Station Approach to link with the already authorised wiring in Station Hill and Tudor Road to Caversham Road. This idea was abandoned the following month.

Final agreement as to the turning arrangements at the new Northumberland Avenue trolleybus terminus was also the focus of some discussion at this meeting. The original intention, as contained in the Reading Corporation (Trolley Vehicles) Confirmation Order 1946, had been that the new trolleybus route should terminate at the roundabout where Hartland Road crossed Northumberland Avenue, which was already being used as a terminus by motorbuses on route N. However, council housing was already being built beyond that point, southwards on the eastern side of Northumberland Avenue and it was thought that the authorised trolleybus route ought to be further extended at this stage. Following discussions with the Ministry of Transport, it was decided that the terminus could be relocated on the west side of Northumberland Avenue, in a purpose-built lay-by

Route N (Caversham – Callington Road) was extended to Hartland Road from 2nd November 1947 as a prelude to a conversion to trolleybuses. AEC Regent 57 (ADP 6) 'waits time' at the inward stop at Hartland Road terminus shortly before the introduction of trolleybuses along Northumberland Avenue in mid-1949. Note the two blue lights just below the front upper-deck windows – these were used pre-war and half-heartedly post-war after dark to distinguish corporation buses from those of other operators.

Late L. G. Head © Millane Publishing

The trolleybus nearest the camera leaving the Cork Street stop westbound as a 'relief' is experimental lowbridge AEC 661T 102 (RD 8086). It is working on the 'main line' to help relieve the pressure while it has been ousted (theoretically temporarily) from the 'side road' due to the extensive road reconstruction programme, circa 1947/48. Compare with the similar view on page 24, and note that the tarred-in tram tracks have now been removed.

Commercial picture postcard

opposite some shops, approximately 300 yards south of Hartland Road roundabout. Ministry of Transport approval to this arrangement was notified at the Transport Committee meeting of 11th June 1948. It was, presumably, at this stage, once it was defined as not at the Hartland Road roundabout, that the terminus was re-designated 'Northumberland Avenue'. At that same meeting, incidentally, it was suggested that as further new council housing was already proposed which would extend along the rest of Northumberland Avenue to its junction with Whitley Wood Road, the authorised terminus should again be revised, with a purpose-built lay-by and turning circle at that location. No action was taken at this stage – however, it was eventually implemented 15 years later! On a practical note, it seems that some difficulty was experienced in constructing the Northumberland Avenue turning circle, because the traction poles had a tendency to move in the ground when the overhead wiring was tensioned.

At the same meeting, on 11th June 1948, the Transport Committee also agreed to the provision of a duplicate set of trolleybus wires along Mill Lane, between Bridge Street/ Southampton Street and the depot, in order to provide connection in both directions to the extended 'side road'; together with the provision of duplicate wiring from the depot via Mill Lane, London Street, High Bridge and Duke Street to the junction of Duke Street with Kings Road (Jackson's Corner). This latter was also a logical development in view of the pending increase in the size of the trolleybus fleet, which would inevitably lead to an increase in the use of the depot connection wiring. There was no direct line of sight between the depot and Jackson's Corner (and vice versa), so duo-directional use of single wiring would become even less appropriate than hitherto. A local enthusiast has recorded that work on the foregoing was 'in progress' on 13th October 1948. Having this double-wiring facility must have been nothing less than a boon, yet it seems that in the early stages it was all to easily open to error. On 1st January 1949, for example, the same local enthusiast managed to avert a disaster when he noticed 137 leaving the depot via Duke Street on the wrong wires and was able to run after and stop the vehicle and point out the fact to the crew!

It was further proposed that at the same time the wiring layout inside the depot should be revised to incorporate some parking roads, presumably to make life easier when parking the ex-Huddersfield Karriers, as they were not fitted with a battery traction facility. When this work was done, the opportunity was also taken to bridge the gap outside the depot entrance (see photo on page 137) to allow through running in Mill Lane without having to de-pole (or alternatively make a circuit of the depot). When frogs were inserted, the latter were set for the depot entrance and through-running involved having to pull a handle on the adjacent traction pole in order to change the frog setting.

Yet again, at the same Transport Committee meeting, it was reported that some attention was being given within the department to future vehicle requirements, taking into account a need for extra football specials. Eleven AEC Regent II motorbuses (including 62, being rebodied after the depot fire) were due for delivery at the end of August 1948, and twenty BUT 9611T two-axle trolleybuses were expected by the following Christmas. Also on the horizon were the anticipated ten ex-Huddersfield Karrier three-axle trolleybuses (none of which was expected to enter service until refurbished). All the above meant that a number of motorbuses would become surplus to requirements. Mr Evans also asked about the future of six single-deck buses, the first batch of Bedford OBs – these, he said, would be difficult to justify keeping without that special type of contract work which had been specifically denied to the department by the confirmed policy of the Transport Committee. The normal daily service allocation and vehicle availability at this time was given thus:

NORMAL DAILY SERVICE ALLOCATION

	Motorbuses				Trolleybuses	
	Peak		All-day		Peak	All-day
	D/D	S/D	D/D	S/D	D/D	D/D
Weekday	41	10	30	2	31	23
Saturday	42	2	31	2	31	28
Max Specials (football)			13		6	

VEHICLE AVAILABILITY

	Motorbuses		Trolleybuses
	D/D	S/D	D/D
Existing fleet	48	12	37
On order	11	0	30

As from 12th June 1948, a new Saturday short-working was introduced on route H (Emmer Green – Whitley Wood) on Saturdays, between Stations and the junction of Hartland Road with Basingstoke Road, a new two-line destination, **BASINGSTOKE RD / HARTLAND ROAD**, being added to the destination blinds of the remaining Leyland Titans – even though their days were very much numbered! As might be imagined, with the size of destination apertures on the Leylands, the print size was miniscule. After four of the Titans were withdrawn at the end of October 1948, a

Saturday short-workings between Stations and 'Basingstoke Road Hartland Road Junc' were introduced in June 1948 on Route H (Emmer Green – Whitley Wood), operating until trolleybus route D (Stations – St. Mary's Butts – Whitley Wood) was introduced on 7th August 1949. It was initially operated by Leyland Titans and later Guy Arabs, which received a new two-line destination on their blinds, as seen here on Guy 7 (BRD 755) waiting in St. Mary's Butts. The bus has been rebuilt with a standard Reading-style front destination box and has even had a pair of blue identification lights fitted under the front upper-deck windows.

Print from Late H. E. Jordan collection

similar destination, **BASINGSTOKE RD / HARTLAND RD JUNC** – again in two lines – was added to the destination blinds of utility Guy Arabs 6, 7 and 28, all by now rebuilt with the latest standard size of 'slit' destination aperture instead of the squarer type with which they had been delivered. When similar bus 27 emerged from the workshops in December 1949 following rebuilding, it too was fitted with the new-style blinds.

Buses operating this short-working turned at Stations by proceeding down Blagrave Street and The Forbury to use Forbury 'roundabout', outside Valpy Street police station, in order to turn back and start from outside the Great Western Hotel. Forbury 'roundabout', was not, at this time, a roundabout in the true sense, whereby all approaching traffic negotiated it one-way clockwise. Rather, it was a large tarmacadam area of irregular shape, on which were a number of mature trees, with a little-used roadway through the centre linking Valpy Street to Forbury Road. Traffic movements to or from Valpy Street (other than that previously mentioned) or to or from that section of The Forbury skirting Forbury Gardens, used the highway as a roundabout. Traffic movements involving that section of The Forbury leading to Stations to or from Vastern Road under the railway bridges, treated the intersection as a simple T-junction. At a later date, as the roads became much busier, traffic from Forbury Road (which, at that time included all incoming Thames Valley bus services from the east, apart from those from London) became directed round the island as at a roundabout. However, traffic from Vastern Road bound for Stations was always still permitted to make a right turn into The Forbury and up to Blagrave Street – just another of those little Reading foibles!

Another short-working appears to have been introduced in or around June 1948, on route N (Caversham – Hartland Road), which was operated to Buckland Road Circle. On 31st July 1948, Bedford OB 70 was noted by an enthusiast working the service with a painted destination board (known as a 'slip board') propped in the nearside windscreen.

Mr G. Mackay, senior engineering assistant, left the undertaking in June 1948. The position remained vacant for a full year, the matter of advertising for a replacement and making an appointment not being addressed until the Transport Committee meeting of 23rd June 1949.

Ooooops!! For readers too young to actually remember seeing something like this happen, one or other (or both) of the spring-loaded booms on top of a trolleybus might very occasionally part company with the overhead wiring infrastructure, the vehicle would be forced to a standstill and the crew would have to extricate a long bamboo pole with a hook on the end, usually from a tube under the vehicle, to 'fish' down each boom and replace it on the correct wire. Conductresses were usually excused from having to perform this task! At the end of each boom was a swivelling trolleyhead with a groove in the top in which was bolted a renewable carbon insert which made contact with a cable which ran down the inside of the boom and down the vehicle to the traction motor. A well-maintained overhead line installation and collector equipment on each vehicle – and a correct driving technique – would avoid most of the causes of a dewirement. AEC trolleybus 117 (ARD 680) is seen here 'wiv both of 'em 'orf' at Norcot on 8th August 1948. Note that a new policy of applying the fleet number to the front nearside lower panel had been implemented.

© J. H. Meredith

East Garage, Mill Lane depot, summer 1948. The first of the second-hand six-wheeler trolleybuses have arrived from Huddersfield as can be seen on the right. An AEC motorbus is out of service at the back, with departmental lorry RD 4696 (which was advertised for sale in the autumn) parked in front. AEC 661T trolleybus 127 (ARD 690) would be in for running repairs to bodywork. Note the residue of blackout paint on the garage's 'north-lights'.

Late W. J. Haynes
© Maiwand Photographic Archive

A reminder of how things used to be was contained in 'Townsman's' 'Talk of the Town' column in the *Reading Standard* for 30th July 1948:

"School children seldom fail to offer their bus seat to a woman whether she be elderly or not. Girls and boys are equally considerate in this. They do it readily, sometimes with a shy but engaging little smile. The schools, one may therefore hope, will leave their mark on the manners of the rising generation."

Sadly, when a lot of the children themselves grew up and became middle-aged, they forgot the common courtesy of saying *"Thank you!"* to the child who, in turn, had given up his or her seat. And so that child had grown to ponder *"Why bother?"* Not helped, of course, by the mother heard to chastise her offspring thus: *"Never mind about that! Just sit down, I've paid for your seat!"*

Certain replacements to the ancillary fleet were sanctioned in July 1948 and two 10–12cwt Bedford vans (DRD 423 and GRD 362) were subsequently taken into stock in 1949 at a cost of £305 each, effectively replacing DP 8189 (a Morris 1-ton lorry of 1926) and JB 602 (a Commer 2-ton open lorry of 1932), although the latter was initially retained *"for training purposes and as a spare"*. Two Bedford 2-ton long-wheelbase lorries (DRD 285 and DRD 696) were also taken into stock in 1949, at a cost of £485 each. These were intended to replace Guy 2½-ton open lorry DP 6373 (formerly bus 11) of 1925 and Morris 30cwt open lorry RD 4696 of 1933. RD 4696 was advertised for sale by tender in October 1948 and DP 6373 in March 1949.

After a week of fine weather (during which, incidentally, the Olympic torch was carried through Reading en route for the 1948 Games at Wembley), August Bank Holiday Monday, 2nd August 1948, also dawned bright and sunny. Vast crowds 'went out for the day' to enjoy a number of attractions in the locality – fetes, shows, regattas and the like. But they were all caught by a very sudden change in the weather – and most of them were without their 'macs'. Those that had hired skiffs and punts for an hour or two on the river at Caversham, in true Bank Holiday tradition, found themselves drenched to the skin and several thousand were caught in the persistent downpour while attending the massive Blue Coat School Fete in Hills Meadow. But, rising to the occasion (as recounted in the *Reading Standard* the following Friday), the transport undertaking soon had buses at 'the Meadows' to take people home. According to the same report, Oxford Road was flooded between Weald Rise and Kentwood roundabout for about two hours, resulting in trolleybuses to Kentwood being turned short at Norcot. A substitute motorbus shuttle service was hastily implemented 'round the houses' to get passengers to Kentwood. Presumably, this was a novel operation via Weald Rise, Grasmere Avenue and Rodway Road.

So that the reader might appreciate how the Reading suburbs were being developed at this time, we must record that at a meeting of the town council on 5th August 1948, it was announced that there was currently a commitment to providing a total of 602 new dwellings in the borough, including 200 'prefabs'. At Emmer Green, road and sewer construction was reaching completion, the building of the first ten houses was about to commence and, by the end of the year, some 120 dwellings were expected to be 'in build'. In Whitley, roundly eight houses a week were being completed and handed over.

The first ever tour of the Reading trolleybus system by enthusiasts took place on Sunday 8th August 1948, when trolleybus 111 was hired by the Southern Counties Touring Society. Apart from, perhaps, in London, at this time most road passenger transport enthusiasts pursued their hobby as individuals rather than in organised clubs or societies. For the record, the complete itinerary comprised Depot – St. Mary's Butts – Kentwood – Liverpool Road – Duke Street – Mill Lane – Whitley Street – St. Mary's Butts – Tilehurst – Wokingham Road – Depot. Included in the itinerary was the use for the first time in well over a year of the Southampton Street – Whitley Street section of trolleybus overhead; one can just imagine the amount of arcing as the trolleyheads progressed along the long-disused wiring!

In August 1948, a letter was sent to Reading County Borough Council to inform the clerk to the council that the Ministry of Fuel and Power was working towards an organised plan for reducing peak hour electrical demand during the forthcoming winter. There was still a national shortage of generating capacity and the post-war industrial boom meant that demand for electricity was still soaring. This demand unfortunately meant that during the winter of 1948/49 there were, once again, frequent power cuts – 'load-shedding'. The aim was a 20% reduction in commercial and industrial demand for electricity between 8.00am and 12.00 noon, and between 4.00pm and 5.30pm in the months of December, January and February. In the months of October, November and March, the regional boards were to be responsible for local plans based on their local conditions. Clearly, the intention was that the Transport

AEC trolleybus 111 (ARD 674) was used by the Southern Counties Touring Society for the first ever private tour of the town's trolleybus system, on 8th August 1948. It is seen here having turned round the new roundabout at the junction of Whitley Street and Christchurch Road (which had seen the demise of Whitley Pump). Because of the continuing curtailment of route C, originally due to removal of tram rail and extensive road reconstruction, this was, presumably, the first trolleybus to venture thither since January 1947. Note the traction poles already 'planted' down Basingstoke Road for the major trolleybus extensions to Whitley Wood and Northumberland Avenue, which were opened in the summer of 1949.

© J. H. Meredith

Department should work towards such cuts in its offices and maybe in its use of trolley vehicles.

On the motorbus front, the deputy manager, Mr Gent, and the undertaking's bodyshop foreman, Mr W. G. Calver, visited Park Royal Vehicles on 7th September 1948 and reported back on the progress in bodying the Reading order of eleven AEC Regent IIs. The replacement body on bus 62 was almost finished and the bus was in the paint shop but the inside finishings and seats were not fitted. The platform seems to have been fitted with a mixture of timber and steel platform slats, which was unacceptable and needed to be replaced by wooden slats up to the rubber platform edging. It was delivered ten days later. Two other buses were completely panelled and glazed and awaiting entry into the paint shop. One bus was *"...completely panelled and glazed and stood in the water spray frame, awaiting the paint shop"*. Three chassis were in the body shop with the *"...framework of lower saloon well advanced"* whilst nearby three upper saloons were *"...framed up and almost ready for mounting"* onto the lower decks. Three buses were in the building line and panelling was being fitted, and windows glazed, and one bus was in the building line simply as a framework.

At the same time, three of the BUT 9611T trolleybus chassis were also on site – 9611T.063, 9611T.064 and 9611T.065 – later to be Nos. 138, 139 and 140, but no work had started on them. It was hoped that work on the prototype would begin in October and that it would be ready in January 1949, with the whole batch complete in mid-April 1949. In the event, 138 entered service on 21st March 1949 and the last vehicle, 156, was delivered on 10th June 1949.

The eleven AEC Regent IIs were delivered in late September and October 1948, as 62 (CRD 256) and 74–83 (CRD 863–872). Further details are given in Appendices A and B. Bus 83, which was collected from Park Royal using Reading Corporation Transport's trade plate RD 086, was the highest-numbered chassis in AEC's 661 Regent series, which had been commenced in 1929. Like all other Reading Corporation double-deckers, they were lowbridge vehicles with a sunken gangway on the upper-deck offside to allow them to operate under Vastern Road railway bridge. By February 1949, a stiff steering problem was affecting the whole batch, which was rectified by the attendance of an AEC engineer. On the same day as bus 62 entered service, so also did trolleybus 158 (VH 6757), the first of the ex-Huddersfield Karrier three-axle trolleybuses, fully refurbished.

A second batch of AEC Regent IIs, 74–83 (CRD 863–72), was delivered in September 1948, together with the re-bodied 62 (CRD 256), the original body of which had been lost in the fire in January 1947. 82 (CRD 871) is seen here at the AEC works, at Southall, prior to delivery. The Park Royal lowbridge body was aesthetically more pleasing than the design used for the 58–67 batch – and had a distinct similarity to the design of body supplied to several other operators.

ACV Limited

160

Brand new AEC Regent II 75 (CRD 864) is seen here in the first two weeks of October 1948, at Whitley Wood terminus during 'layover'. Note the driver holding a white enamelled tea can – and the two cups of tea on the nearside wing! Note also that this batch of buses was equipped from new with blue identification lights above the front destination indicator.

Late L. G. Head © Millane Publishing

During July 1948, approval had been given to withdraw and sell three of the remaining Titans, although, in fact, four of the type were subsequently withdrawn, on 31st October 1948, upon the arrival of the Regent IIs. On 23rd October 1948 the deputy manager selected Titans 42, 44 and 3 for disposal, together with the open-staircase bus, 36, which was deemed no longer fit for service *"because of safety considerations"*. He suggested also that AEC Regents 8 and 9 would *"...run the life of another body"*. Running pre-war AEC Regents in Reading into the 1960s is an attractive thought, but nothing came of it. The four Titans were offered for sale, in *Commercial Motor* on 5th November 1948 and in the local press on 17th November 1948, and they were subsequently purchased on 3rd December 1948 by George Dunaway, of Sutcliffe Avenue, Earley, Reading, for £448 for all four. Bus 3 was noted partly broken up in his yard on 5th May 1949, on which date 36, 42 and 44 were still extant.

The six Duple-bodied Bedford OBs of 1946 were also withdrawn at this time. They had been offered for sale by tender during September 1948, whilst they were still in service, and a number of offers were received, including two from Kemp's Motor Services Ltd., of Woodcote, the forerunner of Chiltern Queens. However, the successful tenderer was Great Western Motors Ltd., who had originally supplied them, and they took delivery of 13 and 15 on the day they were withdrawn, 14th October 1948. 16 followed on 15th October 1948, with 12, 17 and 18 remaining in service until 31st October 1948, all three being collected later the same day. At £1,576 for each vehicle, the undertaking made a profit of £3,165 on the sale, notwithstanding eighteen months in service! 18 was, for a while, displayed in Great Western Motors Ltd's showroom in Station Road.

Over the years some ideas and subjects recurred, but few lasted longer than that which exercised council officers for more than 15 years. It had started at the Transport Committee meeting on 16th September 1948, when the possibility of erecting a turning circle in St. Mary's Butts was discussed. This would enable trolleybuses from Whitley to turn short when required, allowing extra trolleybuses to start from the town centre in peak periods. More to the point, by having the facility in St. Mary's Butts, it would preclude vehicles working 'short' having to cross the 'main line', which was also the main east – west thoroughfare, in order to turn. Reading Borough Police were strongly against the idea, because in their view heavy traffic in St. Mary's Butts

Leyland Titan 44 (RD 2944), seen at least seven months before final withdrawal, opposite Mill Lane at the foot of London Street, while working route N (Caversham – Hartland Road). The outward southbound journey to Hartland Road reverted to traversing St. Mary's Butts, Bridge Street and Southampton Street upon completion of the reconstruction of the southbound carriageway in the upper section of the latter as from 29th March 1948. The trolleybus wiring in the background is the curve into Mill Lane for access to the depot. Note the Civil Defence office to the right of the picture.

Late H. E. Jordan © Millane Publishing

AEC Regent 51 (RD 8094) had an altercation with a street lighting column in Blagrave Street early in the war. It was rebuilt with a deeper windscreen, which was brought forward from its previous position, and the valance across the front carrying the central cream band was dispensed with. Note the painted radiator shell and otherwise superb paint condition of the vehicle shortly before withdrawal in 1950.

© A. B. Cross

would make the turning of trolleybuses dangerous. Eventually, a meeting was arranged between members of the Highways and Transport Committees, the police, the transport manager and his deputy and, on 18th November 1948, a vehicle was used to test the feasibility of just such a turning circle. The Highways Committee, apparently, was not keen for this plan to succeed either, but left the decision to the Transport Committee. Following further tests in the first days of 1949, as we shall recount in due course, the turning circle was duly constructed in time for the inauguration of the Whitley trolleybus route extensions later that year. The subject was raised originally because the rapid development of the Whitley council estate had already caused the Transport Department to have to run large numbers of special and duplicate motorbuses from St. Mary's Butts on the existing routes in order to cope with demand.

At the same Transport Committee meeting, on 16th September 1948, two proposals were put forward to provide a town terminal point for route H (Emmer Green – Whitley Wood) after the Whitley Wood section was converted to trolleybus operation. One was to run via Vastern Road, Blagrave Street and Friar Street, terminating with route K opposite the GPO and returning via Friar Street, Station Road and Stations. The other, which was subsequently adopted, was to run via Vastern Road, Blagrave Street and Friar Street, setting down opposite Greyfriars Road outside Langston's shop and turning empty via Caversham Road and Lower Thorn Street to reach a terminal point in Friar Street adjacent to The Triangle car park[*], then return by the same route.

'Chronicler', by his piece in 'Reading Week by Week' in the 15th October 1948 issue of the *Berkshire Chronicle* added a bit more colour to the contemporary bus scene we are looking back upon more than sixty years later:

"Speedy 'Buses – Why is it that Reading's 'buses and trolley-'buses appear to go at a faster speed than other 'buses? Travelling by Corporation Transport and later by Thames Valley Traction Co. vehicles the other day I was very much struck by the contrast. The journey in one seemed a race against time – no sooner was I on the vehicle than it dashed away before I had time to get into my seat, and later it braked so hard that I was nearly thrown out. On the other vehicle, acceleration was quiet and the whole ride was pleasant and smooth. Lest it be thought that I have singled out one incident, I may add that I have travelled on a number of Corporation 'bus and trolley-'bus routes, and in regard to the 'buses particularly, the same state of affairs existed in nearly every case. Is it that the schedules are so finely drawn that the 'buses have to be driven in this manner to keep to the timetable, or is it that the drivers and conductors take just that shade too long at the terminus? The public should know the reason, for they are paying plenty now for their rides and are entitled to a little comfort in the bargain, not to mention the question of safety."

The foregoing inspired one Robert F. Albon to write a letter, which was published the following week:

"Sir – I was much interested in 'Chronicler's' remarks on Corporation transport under the heading 'Speedy 'Buses' in the Berkshire Chronicle of October 15th.

"Having now been resident in Reading for 16 months, I feel able to express opinions on our public transport; opinions formed very early in my acquaintance with Reading, and alas, confirmed almost daily. I travel about the country a good deal and use public vehicles in many towns and cities, but in none is discourtesy of drivers and conductors so general as in Reading. Here, in fact, I find civility the exception rather than the rule.

"Nor elsewhere are the flying starts, which 'Chronicler' remarks noticeable, with their obvious danger to the aged and to women carrying young children. If these are indeed due to the timing of services, no doubt the authorities concerned will be interested in making alterations or, at the worst, explaining to the public why the existing timings are necessary.

"If, as I suppose, the root of the trouble lies in the disinterestedness of the drivers and conductors, any disciplinary action to improve matters should, in the public interest, be taken most rigorously."

But, then, Don Courtnage, the undertaking's Transport & General Workers Union representative had this to say:

"Sir – ...The drivers and conductors of the Reading Corporation Transport Dept greatly resent the remarks made and, as a

---

[*] Lower Thorn Street is now known as Thorn Walk; the car park was bounded by the three streets mentioned and was situated roughly on the north side of the present-day Chatham Street roundabout.

union representative and a member of the Safety-First Committee, I can give the fullest assurance to the public that the schedules and running times of all Corporation vehicles have been fully tested out with Trade Union agreements. During the past 18 months there has been an increase of the time allowed on many of the routes and the frequency of the services has been increased.

"The Reading Corporation Transport are proud to say that no driver from this department has been prosecuted for speeding on any of the routes, and we ask for an apology from the writer of the above article, to be published in the next edition of your paper."

Only three weeks later, in the 12th November 1948 issue of the same paper, Henry L. G. Heath had the following letter published:

"We all know what transport conditions are like on the 'buses during rush hours, and how grimly we take our places dutifully in the queues where the 'buses are alleged to stop and pick us up.

"What a difference there is at other times! At 10am yesterday morning (November 10th) I was in a 'bus which stopped just over the Pell Street crossing going town-wards. It picked up a few passengers and got under way again, but the conductor spotted an old gentleman just arriving at the stop. Without further ado the 'bus was put into reverse and went back for him!

"This does demonstrate that your 'bus conductors are possessed of an innate sense of courtesy, but seldom, because of overcrowding, can they exercise it so effectively."

In the late 1940s, another sign of the changing times was the post-war growth of television ownership, which was now gaining momentum. On 9th November 1948, the Transport Department received a delivery of suppressors, which were for fitting into the ignition circuits on all petrol-driven vehicles in their care, in order to prevent television interference, which had become something of a problem. However, it seems that, possibly due to their planned early demise, none of the Leyland Titans were so fitted. Despite these alterations, complaints continued to be received and there is a surviving note that on 8th February 1949, Bedford OB 68 was used for tests in Mayfield Drive, off Henley Road, with the ignition and windscreen wipers being used to test levels of interference.

Towards the end of 1948, overhead construction on the Whitley routes was progressing somewhat faster, the first lengths of running wire being run out between Whitley Street and Long Barn Lane on 12th November 1948. By 21st January 1949, it had been run out along Basingstoke Road as far as Hartland Road. It was only at this fairly late stage, however, that the building contracts for the construction of the two substations were let, that at Christchurch Gardens being undertaken by Crosby and Co Ltd for £1,139 and that at the Savoy by F. Newberry & Son Ltd for £1,670.

A spartan offside view of Strachan-bodied lowbridge utility Guy Arab 28 (BRD 816), seen at the Caversham Bridge terminus of route N (Caversham – Hartland Road) on cobble stones and tarred-in tram track. Note the 'snout' effect of the projecting bonnet and radiator beyond the driver's dash and the up-swept edges to the front wings, together with the opening windscreen. Note, too, the subsequent modifications carried out by the department, such as the increase in the number of half-drop windows on each deck. Also of interest is the hoarding advert for the Palestine Police Force, which had been established on 1st July 1920 as part of the British Mandate for Palestine, and which was disbanded on 15th May 1948 upon Britain's termination of the mandate and the establishment of the independent state of Israel.

Late W. J. Haynes © Millane Publishing

As at early 1949 Whitley Pump has been consigned to scrap and the junction with Christchurch Road at the top of Whitley Street has a newly constructed roundabout. As a result, while trolleybus operation to Whitley Street was suspended due to tram rail removal and road reconstruction on the route into town, the turning circle has been re-modelled very neatly and wiring connections made ready for the major extensions of the trolleybus system to serve Whitley.

Print from J. R. Whitehead's collection

Between 26th November and 1st December 1948, the town was shrouded in a continuous fog, during which all transport was disorganised. It is recorded as having been of record duration. Corporation transport was exceptionally well maintained throughout, with no services suspended, and the *Reading Standard* commented specifically that *"drivers and conductors on bus and trolleybus routes worked magnificently as a team under conditions that were sometimes verging on hopeless, particularly on Wednesday night"*. In an unconnected incident, Norcot-bound trolleybus 108 ran into and demolished the front garden wall of 570 Oxford Road, near Brock Barracks, at 5.55pm on Friday 26th November 1948. Its driver had collapsed at the wheel and had to be taken to hospital. The *Reading Standard* records that no-one was injured and that, when the breakdown van arrived with a replacement driver, the vehicle carried on along its journey, which implies that the vehicle was undamaged. This seems extremely unlikely – passengers would have been transferred to following trolleybuses before the van arrived and, bearing in mind the circumstances, 108 would have been taken out of service, taken to Norcot to turn, and returned to depot to be checked and repaired.

At about this time the specification was finalised for the 12 additional trolleybuses it had been agreed to purchase in September 1947. Tenders were invited by public advertisement for both standard two-axle double-deckers and also for three-axle vehicles with bodywork accommodating 68/70 seats, both types of vehicle to be 8ft wide. On receiving tenders, Mr Evans prepared a report to the Transport Committee, which he presented at its meeting on 16th December 1948. Five quotations had been received for chassis and three for 56-seat and 68/70-seat bodies. The report continued thus:

"Having regard to the heavy loading on our trolleybus routes, which is now occurring over longer periods than what might be termed "peak load" traffic, I have to seriously consider whether this traffic could be handled better by a larger vehicle, or by an increased frequency.

"In my opinion, having regard to the present problem of congestion in the town centre, a larger vehicle (only 3–4 feet longer) is the best way of dealing with this problem. Our present 2-axle trolleybuses have 56 seats whereas the 3-axle trolleybuses can have 70 seats, viz., an increase of 14 on 56, or 25%.

"I would, therefore, ask the Committee to authorise the purchase of 12 three-axle trolleybuses. This proposal has been discussed with the Chief Constable, and he is raising no objection, except that the turning circle at the Bear Inn Tilehurst, might be enlarged."

Fog was a regular winter visitor in the Thames Valley, in the days when thousands of homes and businesses were heated by coal fires. Fogs could be thick and were often persistent, such as that illustrated here which lasted from 26th November to 1st December 1948. The transport undertaking nearly always managed to maintain services. Insp. Bert Willoughby is duty regulator in Broad Street, with AEC Regent II 59 (CRD 253) outside Wellsteeds about to set off in the murk to Emmer Green, while AEC trolleybus 119 (ARD 682) feels its way up to the Tilehurst and Kentwood stops further up. Perhaps because he was late at Liverpool Road terminus, the driver has forgotten to alter the destination blind to Kentwood – something the inspector will miss!

Reading Standard

A pre-war 'metal-bodied' AEC Regent belts southwards, down a traffic-free Basingstoke Road, between Hartland Road and the Grenadier in autumn 1948, en route to Whitley Wood. Traction poles for the forthcoming conversion of the route to trolleybuses have been planted, ready for the installation of the overhead line. Note the five degree rake out of plumb away from the road to counteract the tension that will be put on the line when 'strung'.

Late W. J. Haynes
© Millane Publishing

The report went on to give details of tenders received. Regarding three-axle chassis, the Sunbeam quotation, for its S7-type vehicle, was the lowest at £3,029 per vehicle and £48 15s 0d extra per vehicle for automatic acceleration equipment; this was accepted (although the latter equipment was never installed). Quotations were also received from Guy Motors Ltd, British United Traction Ltd, Transport Vehicles (Daimler) Ltd, and also Crossley Motors Ltd, who tendered for building complete vehicles. Loan sanction for the 'six-wheelers' was obtained from the Ministry of Transport on 23rd April 1949.

As well as Crossley Motors Ltd, the three tenders received for 68-seat 'all-metal' bodies of six-bay construction and including platform doors were from Chas. Roberts Ltd, Park Royal Vehicles Ltd, and Metro-Cammell-Weymann Ltd. The last two named both quoted the lowest price, of £3,095 each, but because Park Royal had bodied all previous trolleybuses for the undertaking, it was decided to accept its quotation. Delivery was promised in 1950. After much correspondence with the Ministry of Transport regarding loan payments, final ministerial approval was given to proceed with the order on 18th July 1949.

The Transport Committee meeting of 16th December 1948 also considered tenders for new motorbuses. For a period of three or four days from 26th October 1948, open-platform Manchester Corporation Transport 8ft wide Crossley double-decker 2132 (JND 773) had been in Reading for test and inspection. The original intention, in the capital estimates of January 1947, was for six buses. A year later this had been increased to ten, and Mr Evans now pointed out to the committee that, in order to meet present requirements, it was now necessary to obtain twelve. Three tenders had therefore been received for the supply of twelve chassis, together with nine tenders for the supply of bodies to be fitted to them. The lowest tenders for bodies, from Barnards Ltd of Norwich and from Mann Egerton, also of Norwich, were for using light alloy structures, which Mr Evans considered as *"still experimental structures"* and urged acceptance of *"all steel-framed"* bodies. Mr Evans recommended that the Transport Committee should favour the placing of an order for twelve complete buses – chassis and double-deck lowbridge bodies – from Crossley Motors Ltd., of Errwood Park, Stockport, at £4,167 per vehicle. At that time, Crossley Motors had just become part of Associated Commercial Vehicles, formed by the amalgamation of the AEC, Crossley and Maudslay companies with effect from 1st October 1948, which may have eased the breakaway from, traditionally, Park Royal-bodied AEC vehicles. The Transport Committee concurred, and twelve Crossley lowbridge double-deck motorbuses were ordered, originally with open rear platforms. A suggestion that platform doors should be fitted, as per the BUT trolleybuses on order, was deferred.

For some years a traffic regulator had been posted at Wokingham Road (Three Tuns) trolleybus terminus. Indeed he had a little timekeeper's hut there and, during and immediately after the war, when the protective fares scheme was suspended, one of his functions was to ensure that trolleybuses were sent off towards town immediately a Thames Valley bus was seen in the distance, approaching from the east! With the imminent construction of the new 'roundabout' at Cemetery Junction, Mr Evans thought that it

Early 1949 in Basingstoke Road just south of Hartland Road, with not one item of traffic in sight (and precious little in the way of road markings for such a wide road). A very neat job has been made of 'stringing up' the trolleybus overhead line but, on account of delays in completing and commissioning substations, the conversion of this route to trolleybuses cannot take place until August 1949.

Print from J. R. Whitehead's collection

At the end of October 1948, Manchester Corporation 2132 (JND 773), a Crossley-bodied Crossley DD42/8 built to the newly-permitted 8ft width, was borrowed and is seen here on Reading Corporation Transport's trade plates (086 RD), it is thought in Bath Road near Liebenrood Road, close to Prospect Park. It spent three or four days in Reading, during which time it was taken to various points in the borough, in particular Tilehurst Road railway bridge, to prove that the six inches extra width would not be an operational problem in the town.

Print from D. Lucas' collection

might be more advantageous to re-locate him to Cemetery Junction. He had, by December 1948, started to make enquiries locally with a view to finding a site for a traffic regulator's and timekeeper's office and had received a favourable response from the Gladstone Club, whose premises adjoined the inbound stop in Kings Road.

Special Christmas peak services were in operation on Christmas Eve 1948, with 'shorts' noted being operated to Cressingham Road on route F; Tilehurst Road (Prospect Park) on route M; and Buckland Road Circle on route P.

Extra trolleybuses were being run to Tilehurst from Broad Street, these being turned in the depot on their return to town.

1948 thus ended with a partially-renewed motorbus fleet but with a large section of trolleybus overhead line, between Caversham Bridge and Whitley Street, still unused. However, even larger new sections of overhead were under construction along Basingstoke Road to Whitley Wood, with a branch down Buckland Road and along Northumberland Avenue. 1949 was destined to be the year of the trolleybus!

In this scene in Whitley Wood Lane, probably taken in the early spring of 1949, the planting of traction poles to receive the overhead line installation for the forthcoming major trolleybus extension has reached the Whitley Wood terminus. Meanwhile, 1934-vintage wooden-bodied AEC Regent 26 (RD 6072), still retaining its AEC 8.8-litre oil engine, spends a few minutes on layover before returning to Emmer Green.

Late W. J. Haynes © Millane Publishing

18   The 'Bargain Basement' Karriers

It will be recalled that early in 1948 the demand for trolleybuses in Reading had become critical, with only one spare vehicle available at the peak period, which was on those winter Saturdays when Reading F. C. was playing at home and football extras were required. Although new trolleybuses were on order, delivery was many months away and the need for additional vehicles was urgent. Reading was not the only town suffering such shortages, and there were few second-hand trolleybuses on the market at the beginning of 1948. Those which were available were ancient vehicles dating from 1930 or earlier, so the sudden availability of twelve three-axle Karrier E6 vehicles in Huddersfield, built in 1934 with 64-seat Brush bodywork caused some interest – and not only in Reading. They were being replaced in Huddersfield some five or six years earlier than originally intended because the Ministry of Transport had demanded that, on account of that town's steep gradients, all the trolleybuses in operation there should be fitted with a 'run-back' braking mechanism as a safety measure. New vehicles incorporating this requirement had therefore been ordered instead of fitting some of the older vehicles with the necessary equipment retrospectively, so the twelve 14-year old trolleybuses, which were fitted with Metropolitan Vickers traction equipment, were being withdrawn before their time.

At the Transport Committee meeting on 12th February 1948, Mr Evans was given authority to purchase five, or alternatively ten, of the twelve vehicles available, at a cost of £400 each, with an additional budget set aside for towing charges, modifications, and repainting. Nottingham City Transport was also considering the purchase of five of the vehicles at this time. Representatives from Reading, which certainly included the body shop foreman, Mr W. G. Calver, visited Huddersfield and even travelled on some of the Karrier E6s, which were still in service. In the end, Nottingham City Transport decided otherwise and Reading Corporation Transport purchased all twelve of the available vehicles, Huddersfield Corporation Nos 407–418 (VH 6750–61), at a cost of only £200 per vehicle. Bargain – or pup?

Most of the twelve vehicles were in service in Huddersfield until February 1948, although Nos. 409 and 410 were not withdrawn until March, while 413, 415 and 416 were not withdrawn until the end of May 1948, as it was necessary to retain them in service until the replacements arrived. This delay was caused by the strike by members of the National Union of Vehicle Builders at Park Royal and Sunbeam, which affected the collection and delivery of any new vehicles during much of April 1948. This was, of course, the same strike that was also affecting the Reading undertaking's body shop and paint shop as already mentioned.

Huddersfield 414 was the first to arrive in Reading, on 25th March 1948, and thus became the town's first three-axle trolleybus. The Karriers were collected by Sunbeam Commercial Vehicles Ltd from Huddersfield Corporation's John William Street depot. As Sunbeam delivered one of their new Sunbeam MS2 trolleybuses to Huddersfield, they took one of the Karriers back to their Moorfield Works at Wolverhampton on the return journey. Here, the vehicle was inspected and then towed to Reading by the Sunbeam Commercial Vehicles towing crew who were en route to Park Royal Vehicles, in west London, to collect the next newly-bodied trolleybus bound for Huddersfield. A quantity of parts and spares was also collected. This towing arrange-

Some of the Huddersfield Corporation trolleybuses purchased in 1948 looked to be in good condition when received, such as this one (VH 6758), seen here outside East Garage upon arrival; perhaps three or four of them came into this category. It had been hoped that six, if not ten of the batch of twelve, could be refurbished economically for continued use in Reading. In practice it proved difficult in managing to get six on the road in four years – by which time the undertaking's circumstances had changed.   © *Reading Museum Service (Reading Borough Council); all rights reserved*

ment was rather neat and allowed for conservation of fuel and lack of wasted mileage at a time of fuel shortages.

The list shown below gives the dates of collection of the Karriers from Huddersfield, and the dates of delivery to Mill Lane depot. The list, derived from surviving documentation originating in the Transport Department, is substantial yet incomplete.

Hudds. Fleet No.	Reg'n Number	Chassis Number	Date ex-Huddersfield	Date ex-Sunbeam
407	VH 6750	54088	. .	19.05.48
408	VH 6751	54085	07.04.48	19.04.48
409	VH 6752	54086	. .	31.05.48
410	VH 6753	54087	. .	08.04.48
411	VH 6754	54089	. .	07.06.48
412	VH 6755	54090	26.04.48	.04.48*
413	VH 6756	54091	09.06.48	17.06.48
414	VH 6757	54092	24.03.48	25.03.48*
415	VH 6758	54093	. .	17.06.48
416	VH 6759	54094	. .	23.06.48
417	VH 6760	54095	13.04.48	21.04.48
418	VH 6761	54096	. .	24.05.48

* One enthusiast's diary records the first ex-Huddersfield as being delivered to Reading on 19.03.48. If this was Huddersfield 414 (later Reading 158), this is a week earlier than the date given above! The same diary notes, by inference, 412 delivered possibly on 24.04.48.

It soon became clear that these timber-framed vehicles were in a worse state than expected – most were good illustrations of how timber-framed bodies deteriorated after years of unavoidable wartime neglect. Plans to put them into service quickly were soon abandoned and, instead, it was decided to extensively rebuild each vehicle before putting it into service, at an estimated total cost for each vehicle of £1,000 inclusive of its acquisition cost. Each trolleybus was stripped down to the chassis and body shell and all mechanical and electrical parts cleaned and overhauled, the chassis being silver-painted. The Brush body was then rebuilt using the original parts where possible, although some minor changes were made to the design. According to a brief article, which appeared in *Modern Transport* circa April 1949, overhaul of the bodies particularly involved attention to the lower-saloon pillars, the floor bearers and the front and rear ends, but the most noticeable modification was the revision to the styling of the front lower panels and to the front destination blind apertures. With regard to the refurbishment, another local enthusiast records Mr W. G. Calver, the body shop foreman at the time, saying in his retirement a good many years later that *"....Reading had no experience of Brush bodies, 'Mae West' fronts, or humps in floors. The new floor was laid flat but by the next morning had sunk. It was re-laid again but the same thing happened, so eventually the hump was retained! Furthermore, although you want to get these vehicles into service, you have a bigger fleet than ever before and the existing fleet needs the same kind of attention after years of bodging but you don't have any extra workshop space"*. The Karriers were, evidently, refurbished as workshop space and time permitted, but eventually the supply of new vehicles and reduction in passenger numbers made further rebuilds unnecessary.

The first Karrier, numbered 158, was noted 'ready' in the depot on 8th September 1948 but did not enter service until 18th September. By then only ten vehicles were earmarked for service, with two to be set aside for cannibalisation for spares, a fact recorded in a memo dated 11th June 1948 listing future fleet strength before all the vehicles had been received from Huddersfield. It had probably become clear by this time that there would not be enough re-useable mechanical and electrical parts without some cannibalisation.

It is virtually certain that all the Karriers were allocated their original Reading fleet numbers in the order in which they arrived in Reading. During an official visit to the depot a local enthusiast was told that at this time the Karriers were all numbered from 158 in the order in which they arrived, and that they had to carry an identification number for insurance purposes. The first four Karriers to be refurbished seemingly retained their allocated fleet numbers, and it seems highly probable that the original intention was to work through the whole batch (of ten or twelve), more-or-less in the order of delivery, with the first two or three vehicles being worked on together, on an occasional basis, in the Mill Lane body shop.

It seems likely, however, that the original 161 (VH 6760) was found to be in such poor condition that it was passed over and that 162 (VH 6755) was worked on instead, during 1949 – and that this was before a decision was made to refurbish only six vehicles. Thereafter, it seems that the two best vehicles of the remaining eight were selected for refurbishment and renumbered back into the 158–163 series.

This speculative account of the renumbering would appear to explain the reason for an 'internal' fleet list, which records chassis 54095 (registration VH 6760) as trolleybus 161 rather than 165. The likely original numbering is shown in the list on page 170, and there are photographic indications that the allocated numbers were chalked on or roughly painted onto the Huddersfield livery as they arrived.

If the foregoing 'renumbering' theory is correct, it is also interesting that it was 167 (VH 6756), which turned up at Mill Lane in early 1950, because the vehicle which eventually became 167, VH 6750, was originally allocated fleet number 163. This original 163 might well have been examined at Mill Lane as a possible 'runner' as the next-in-line numerically for refurbishment after 162 but, once again, was found to be in a poor condition, resulting in the vehicle being 'dumped' in East Yard, rather than being returned to where the others were stored.

With two of the first six found to be unsuitable for rebuilding, it seems that there was then some further thought about the wisdom of refurbishing even ten of the ex-Huddersfield vehicles. If this was so, then the date of the decision to refurbish only six Karriers can be more accurately pinpointed to early 1950, and might well have been taken due to (a) a significant reduction in the fortunes of public transport at that time; and (b) a worrying prediction that the Transport Department would be making increasing losses. The reason for VH 6756, the original 167, becoming 169, fits uneasily into the theory. Possibly, the original 167 (VH 6756), delivered on 19th June 1948, was seen to be in such poor condition when it arrived, that it was considered fit only for breaking for spares, resulting in it being renumbered as 169, and making it the last in the series. Perhaps, also, it was this decision which provoked the earlier 1948 plan to refurbish only ten vehicles (possibly to be numbered as a complete block from 158 to 167). This would make sense, as the original 169 (VH 6759) was one of the last three of the batch to operate in Huddersfield; was the last to be delivered, on either 23rd or 24th June 1948; and was last to be refurbished – as 161. It is also record-

The quality of workmanship emanating from the undertaking's body shop and, indeed, its paint shop in those days is to be marvelled at – a throwback to pre-war days long past, when replacement tramcar bodies were fashioned from new and the first thirty bus bodies were built from scratch too.

Top: Former Huddersfield Corporation Karrier E6 trolleybus 160 (VH 6751) is newly into service in Reading, and seen here at Kentwood ready for a trip to Wokingham Road. It was the first vehicle to be outshopped with a fleet number instead of the RCT emblem on the front panel. It entered service thus on 18th February 1949. (from H. E. Jordan collection)

Right: A rear end study of trolleybus 160 (VH 6751) newly into service on 18th February 1949. The knob in the lower cream band on the platform side of the rear bulkhead was, in fact, the end of the trolley-boom retriever pole, which went down the inside of the lower-deck rather than in a tube underneath the vehicle. A design quirk of Huddersfield trolleybuses was that, instead of the platform being a step down from the lower saloon, it was on the same level, so that there were two steps up to the platform from pavement level on boarding and alighting. This was, apparently, seen as one way of strengthening a bus platform. Some care was needed when using the stairs on these buses, as the staircase was effectively two treads longer, descending straight down to pavement level, with the bottom stair very close to the platform edge. This design may have contributed significantly to the death of a young woman passenger visiting Reading who, on Sunday 17th April 1949, descended the stairs of the moving vehicle and fell off the back of 160 as it was ascending the hill in Norcot Road.

Both from Late H. E. Jordan's collection

169

ed as having been stored at Mill Lane from an early date, perhaps being perceived as one of the best of the batch. As a theory, this story hangs together, but the originally-allocated fleet numbers upon delivery to Reading, although almost certain, must remain speculative, as no complete official list (which shows the numbering of the whole batch upon delivery) has yet been found. Fleet numbers 164–169 were never 'officially' carried by any vehicle in service, of course, so the foregoing 'renumbering' theory is of academic interest only. At best it is based on delivery dates, some imagination and a 'rogue' chassis number on an internal departmental list, which has been taken at face value rather than as a typing error!

Fleet No. Delivered	Final Fleet No.	Ex-Hudds Fleet No.	Reg'n Number	Entered Service
158	158	414	VH 6757	18.09.48
159	159	410	VH 6753	01.04.49
160	160	408	VH 6751	18.02.49
169	161	416	VH 6759	01.02.51
162	162	412	VH 6755	13.12.49
165	163	409	VH 6752	01.06.50

The first three must have overlapped in the workshops and it is suggested that the next three delivered – and, potentially, the next in line for refurbishment – were stored under cover at Mill Lane in East Garage. Six unrefurbished Karriers were stored in the open at a corporation-owned yard in Crescent Road from late in 1948 (we suggest that these vehicles may have changed from time to time as their condition was assessed). As they deteriorated, they provoked complaints from local residents about them being eyesores and there was pressure to have them removed. In early 1950, five of them – 164, 165, 166, 168, 169 (final numbers!) – were moved to outside storage at the Bennet Road depot site, which was at that time under construction. They were all dismantled at this location and then scrapped – 168 on 24th September 1951, and the remainder in April 1952, after which, on 21st April 1952, the four remaining hulks were burnt on site. As we have noted already, 167 (probably the previously rejected and renumbered 163) was dumped at the back of East Yard at Mill Lane, where it was used as a source of spares until it was broken up there in May 1952.

Fleet No. Delivered	Final Fleet No.	Ex-Hudds Fleet No.	Reg'n Number	Date Scrapped
164	164	418	VH 6761	21.04.52
161	165	417	VH 6760	21.04.52
166	166	411	VH 6754	21.04.52
163	167	407	VH 6750	.05.52
168	168	415	VH 6758	24.09.51
167	169	413	VH 6756	21.04.52

Trolleybus 160 (VH 6751), the second of the batch to be refurbished, was the first vehicle in the trolleybus fleet to be outshopped without the 'RCT emblem' (the letters RCT within a circle) on the front panel. Thus, by February 1949, two of the ex-Huddersfield Karriers, 158 and 160, were out on the streets of Reading – the first three-axle trolleybuses in the town and able to carry 64 seated passengers, more than any other corporation bus or trolleybus at that time. A surviving memo from the deputy manager, dated 28th February 1949, shows the list of duties that were regarded as suitable for Karrier allocation:

Weekdays: **B** (6.54am to 8.39pm) **BA** (6.37am to 11.10pm)
BE (6.39am to 11.20pm)

Sundays: **D** (8.58am to 10.39pm) **DB** (8.15am to 10.55pm)

Karriers were also available for use on any 'specials' – but with the exception of those duties which required the use of batteries for turning round. Their one big drawback, which became immediately apparent, was that they did not have battery traction, unlike every other Reading trolleybus apart from 101. Equipping a trolleybus for battery traction is not simply a matter of connecting a crate of batteries to the motor – the motor itself has to be compatible and a different master controller is required. In those days of austerity, this expenditure on such old vehicles would have been deemed 'unnecessary'. Factory specials to Orts Road, for example, were therefore outside the Karriers' domain.

On three axles, the Karriers appeared to give a smoother ride, much appreciated by the passengers, over Reading's indifferent road surfaces, which were more atrocious then than they are now! The conductors, initially, liked them for

158 (VH 6757), the first of the ex-Huddersfield Karrier E6 trolleybuses to be refurbished and enter service, had done so on 18th September 1948. It is seen here at the Bear Inn, Tilehurst, soon to depart for Wokingham Road, in the slushy snow of the morning of 6th March 1949.
Late W. J. Haynes © Maiwand Photographic Archive

Top: On a Wednesday afternoon (early closing day) in late August 1949, ex-Huddersfield Karrier E6 trolleybus 159 (VH 6753), smartly refurbished and recently into service, waits time eastbound at the Vaudeville stop in Broad Street.

Late W. J. Haynes © Maiwand Photographic Archive

Centre: Karrier 167 (VH 6750), one of those which were destined never to see service in Reading, was dumped at the back of East Yard at Mill Lane depot as a source of spares. It was broken-up on site in May 1952.

© J. H. Meredith

Bottom: Karriers 164–6 and 168/9 were also destined never to run in Reading, and were dumped at Bennet Road depot. Three of them (including 169 (VH 6756) closest to the camera, and 164 (VH 6751)) are visible in this view.

© J. H. Meredith

171

the extra room that was available for collecting fares, particularly at peak times when the vehicle was full. There were, however, a number of disadvantages which soon became manifest. The vehicles had 'high tension' lighting circuits, with current being taken direct from the overhead line, so that the saloon lighting flickered on and off as the trolleyheads passed under 'dead sections', such as at section insulators and at frogs and crossings. Their lack of battery traction was certainly not appreciated by the crews. Conductors, usually with the enlisted help of some passengers, literally had to get out and push if a vehicle got stuck on a 'dead section'! Drivers also came to detest the Karriers because their steering and braking came to be regarded as 'unpredictable'. Thus, applying the brakes could result in either an immediate stop or a pause, which seemed like eternity before the brakes began to bite, both extremes being something of an embarrassment. With the steering, the road wheels seemed to turn by delayed action, making it important for drivers to 'straighten up' a few seconds before they wished the vehicle to follow. Meanwhile, conductors discovered that they had to go mountaineering in order to alter destination screens at the rear and over the platform! As a result, they quickly became unpopular with the crews and, like the utility Guy Arabs, a number of ruses came to be employed in trying to have a Karrier changed off. 'Accidentally' spilling the contents of one's tea can into the contactor box was a good one!

The regenerative braking system created surges of current, too. Although the Mill Lane substation was capable of absorbing current surges by trolleybuses regenerating whilst descending Southampton Street, the newer 'main line' equipment was not (regenerative braking cannot be used with mercury-arc rectifiers, as used in all the other substations on the system). There were a few embarrassing incidents. On one memorable occasion, a Karrier trolleybus descending Norcot Road (and thus using its regenerative braking) blew all the saloon lamp bulbs on another Karrier ascending the hill! Regenerative braking was finally deemed unsuitable for use in Reading, so the electric braking arrangements on the Karriers were soon modified accordingly.

162 and 163 were the subject of a paint comparison test in December 1949 when paint supplier Hadfields was consulted over an apparent darkening of the maroon enamel. There was some dispute over this allegation which, it was suggested, was due to the lighting conditions and the age and general appearance of the paintwork. However, it was suggested that a brighter tone of undercoat, called 'special bright crimson', should be tested on 163 with 'coach enamel crimson' topcoat, which was also a new colour. This 'coach enamel crimson' had already been applied to 162 over the old shade of undercoat. The result of the experiment was not reported, but the impression of 'darkening' may account for the reports in some contemporary enthusiast publications that the Reading fleet colour was chocolate!

The prolonged suspension of trolleybus route C must have made the immediate need for additional trolleybuses less critical, which may account for a more leisurely attitude to the rebuilding of the remaining two vehicles. The sixth vehicle to enter service, 161 (VH 6759), did not do so until 1st February 1951, almost three years after the first ex-Huddersfield Karrier had arrived in Reading!

The Karriers are often thought not to have been the immediate bargain that had been hoped for – especially since it took three years to get just half the batch on to the road. The published (average) cost of each rebuild was £1,971. There is no indication as to whether or not this includes the purchase price of the vehicle from Huddersfield (£200), or whether an allowance of £200 was included to cover the cost of each non-runner (which could be thought of as a 'donor' vehicle on a one-to-one basis), so the 'real' cost could have been as high as £2,171 or even £2,371 per vehicle. However, the cost of each new BUT two-axle trolleybus delivered in 1949 was £5,309, and each Sunbeam S7 three-axle trolleybus delivered in 1950 cost £6,010. So in fact, each three-axle Karrier actually cost well under half the price of a new two-axle trolleybus! Three of the vehicles (161, 162 and 163) remained in service until 31st December 1956 and most of the six managed between six and seven years' service in Reading before withdrawal. The first two happen to have been vital in increasing the trolleybus fleet strength at a difficult time. So maybe Reading Corporation did get a bargain after all! However, the fact that they only managed to get six out of the twelve on the road – and this at roundly twice the £1,000 per bus originally sanctioned for the project – must have been the cause of some embarrassment to the department.

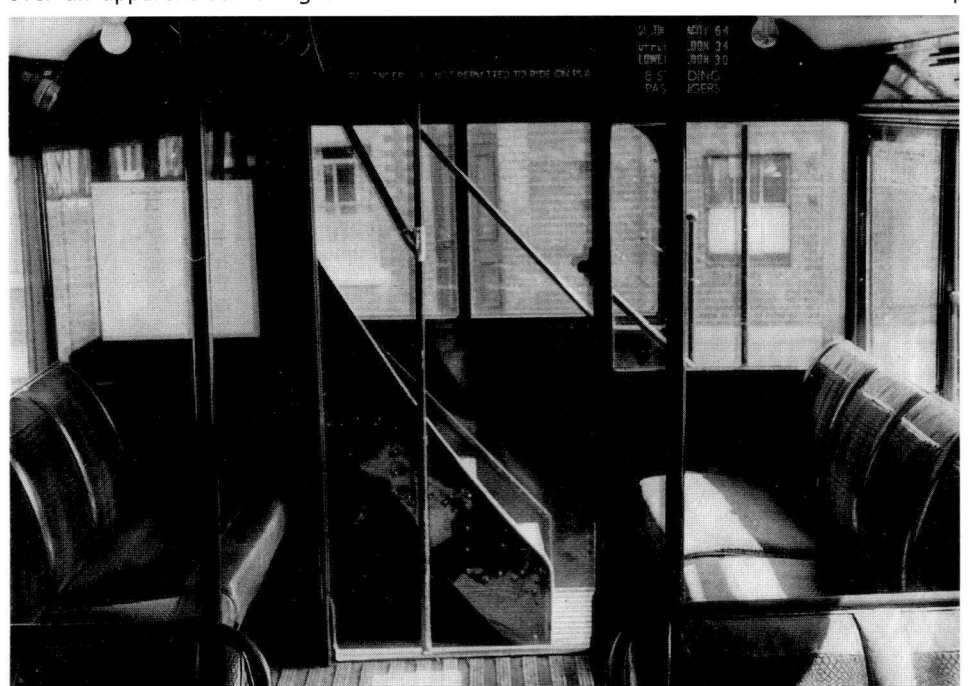

The Karriers' larger seating capacity, for 64 passengers, provided eight more seats than on one of Reading's standard two-axle trolleybuses, which made the Karriers popular with passengers. The unusual 'Huddersfield platform' on these buses, however, made descending the stairs somewhat of a challenge – and potentially dangerous!

Print from D. L. Lucas' collection

19   Post-War Specials

As we saw in Chapter 6, various special services were operated during the war – some in direct support of the war effort, others to serve various established industries in the town, and local schools. One such was the Monday – Saturday 'jam factory special' to the Co-operative Wholesale Society Preserve Works at Coley from 'Wood Lane Junction' via Whitley Wood Lane, Basingstoke Road, Callington Road, Northumberland Avenue, Buckland Road, Basingstoke Road, Elgar Road and into Berkeley Avenue. This service was still operating to the same route in mid-November 1946, but it is thought that, at about this time, it was cut back to operate only from the junction of Callington Road with Northumberland Avenue. Then, around April/May 1947, it was modified to Hartland Road. A post-war timetable dated 1st February 1948 shows the following:

Motorbus Service					Mondays to Fridays
C.W.S. PRESERVE WORKS (Coley)					HARTLAND ROAD

	a.m.	a.m.	p.m.	p.m.						
Hartland Road	7 10	7 12	1 14	1 15	...	...	...	...	...	...
C.W.S. Preserve Works (Coley)	7 25	7 27	1 25	1 26	...	...	...	...	...	...

	p.m.	p.m.	p.m.	p.m. NF	p.m. FO					
C.W.S. Preserve Works (Coley)	12 35	12 35	5 5	6 15	5 30	...	...	...	...	...
Hartland Road	12 50	12 50	5 20	6 30	5 45	...	...	...	...	...

NF—Not Fridays   FO—Fridays Only

Saturdays

	a.m.	a.m.								
Hartland Road	7 10	7 12	...	...	...	...	...	...	...	...
C.W.S. Preserve Works (Coley)	7 25	7 27	...	...	...	...	...	...	...	...

	noon	p.m.								
C.W.S. Preserve Works (Coley)	12 0	12 30	...	...	...	...	...	...	...	...
Hartland Road	12 15	12 45	...	...	...	...	...	...	...	...

This service is for the purpose of conveying employees and others to and from the Preserve Works, coincident with the working hours of the Factory.

Huntley & Palmer's biscuit factory, in Kings Road, had a number of trolleybus and motorbus factory specials, the motorbuses operating originally from Staverton Road. The trolleybus specials listed on 17th October 1940 show that they were used to supplement the normal service at lunchtime and in the evening peak, with no apparent demand in the morning peak. The duties were listed as **Fac.Sp.1**, **Fac.Sp.2** and **Fac.Sp.3**, which operated at midday, while **Fac.Sp.3** and **Fac.Sp.4** were operated in the evening. The motorbus service as listed on 19th September 1940 shows the duties and timings from Whitley as follows:

Stav Fact 1: Staverton Road – Queens Road (ex depot 7.22am)
Stav Fact 2: Staverton Road – Queens Road (ex depot 7.22am)
Stav Fact 3: Queens Rd – Staverton Road (ex depot 12.45pm)

The motorbus service was retained for many years after the end of the war, when it was known as route O. The times shown in the 1st February 1948 timetable are as follows:

Motorbus Service	Route O			Mondays to Fridays
STAVERTON RD. & HARTLAND RD.		QUEEN'S RD. (Junc. of Watlington Street)		

	a.m.	a.m.	p.m.						
Staverton Road	7 7	7 37	1 25	...	...	...	...	...	...
Queen's Road (Junction of Watlington Street)	7 20	7 46	1 40	...	...	...	...	...	...

	p.m.	p.m.							
Queen's Road (Junction of Watlington Street)	12 38	5 48	...	...	...	...	...	...	...
Staverton Road	12 50	6 0	...	...	...	...	...	...	...

	p.m.								
Queen's Road (Junction of Watlington Street)	5 55	...	...	...	...	...	...	...	...
Hartland Road	6 8	...	...	...	...	...	...	...	...

This service is for the purpose of conveying employees and others to and from the Biscuit Factory, coincident with the working hours of the Factory.

There were plans in April/May 1947 to alter the terminus in the Whitley Estate from Staverton Road to Hartland Road.

There was still at this time a 'Park Hospital special' on Wednesday afternoons, from Broad Street at 1.40pm. In later years, this service also operated on Sundays, as shown by the February 1948 timetable reproduced below:

Motorbus Service	Park Hospital (Prospect Park)		Visiting Days Only

Wednesdays

	p.m.		p.m.
Broad Street (Opposite Vaudeville)	1 40	Park Hospital (Prospect Park)	3 15
Park Hospital (Prospect Park)	1 55	Broad Street (Vaudeville)	3 30

Sundays

	p.m.		p.m.
Broad Street (Opposite Vaudeville)	2 10	Park Hospital (Prospect Park)	3 45
Park Hospital (Prospect Park)	2 25	Broad Street (Vaudeville)	4 0

On 5th July 1947, seven double-deck buses were provided after 11.00pm to run a special late-night service meeting trains from Henley Regatta. They operated from Stations to various parts of the town under the special licence held by the department (K55/16) to operate such services.

Both motorbus and trolleybus football specials were a common feature of post-war corporation transport operation when Reading F. C. were playing at home, at Elm Park. At its maximum operation these extra journeys took the trolleybus service allocation beyond the peak hour weekday totals. As no turning facilities existed in Oxford Road, the special trolleybus duties had to be operated through to Norcot. Saturday was the busiest day of the week for the Transport Department anyway, and every possible vehicle had to be 'cleared for service' on a Friday night, with the transport manager requiring a very good reason for a bus or trolleybus not being available.

A typical example was an F. A. Cup tie on Saturday 11th January 1947 (Reading v Grimsby Town); the undertaking ran special motorbus services from 12.30pm with an 'all-through' fare of 6d charged from the outside termini and special services operating from Stations and St. Mary's Butts, the single fare from these points being 2d.

On 22nd November 1947, heavy football traffic for a cup-tie had seen six Smith's Coaches augment buses 7, 37, 48, 51 and 54 working the St. Mary's Butts – Elm Park Football Ground special service, together with, for the first time, some of the undertaking's own Bedford OBs (13, 18, 70 and 71), which augmented 'main line' trolleybuses on workings between Cemetery Junction and Wantage Road before the match. The 'main line' trolleybuses were, in fact, themselves enhanced by specials comprising 102–106 and 109. A week later, on 29th November 1947, some of Smith's ex-Scottish Motor Traction Leyland Cheetahs were noted on Football Specials, still showing **LPTB RELIEF** and stickers reading **6 HACKNEY WICK** and the like, for at the time these vehicles were being hired to London Transport during Mondays to Fridays to help alleviate a huge vehicle shortage in the capital.

On another memorable day, 3rd April 1948, when Reading F. C. was playing Port Vale at Elm Park, there was also the International Cross-Country Championship being held at Leighton Park School, in Shinfield Road and both required

173

vehicles to operate specials. Twenty-one motorbus specials were operated and small identification boards, cream-painted with crimson numerals, were hung from the radiator filler caps of the vehicles, numbered 1 to 21. There were fourteen specials to take the football traffic to the Tilehurst Road entrance of Elm Park, and these returned empty to St. Mary's Butts, apparently via Wantage Road. As usual there were queue conductors taking the fares on both outward and, later, the return journeys, issuing TIM tickets on coloured paper. Specials 1 and 2 were two hired Thames Valley 1931 Leyland Titans, 233/4 (RX 8166/7); specials 3 to 8 were hired from Smith's Coaches; and the department itself provided specials 9 to 14, of which four (9–12) were single-deckers. Corporation conductors were on all the vehicles.

The remaining seven specials were operated to serve the cross-country event. Specials 15–18 operated via the normal Shinfield Road service as far as Pepper Lane, returning to Stations empty via Wellington Avenue, Northcourt Avenue and Christchurch Road. Special 19 was a journey from the Town Hall. Specials 20 and 21 were single-deck operated, being used to carry the competing international teams. Later in the afternoon, the seven specials were parked in Wellington Avenue until required for the return journeys. Transport for the competitors and officials was supplied gratis.

Two weeks later, on Saturday 17th April 1948, Reading F. C. played Torquay United. The match must have drawn a large crowd, for the traffic arrangements record a full turnout of trolleybus specials and motorbus specials. For the student of transport history, the survival of a complete and detailed record of this provision (which was so typical of the late 1940s and early 1950s, before the attractions of television began to keep people at home) is of immense interest. Six short-working trolleybus specials were run to Norcot before the match (most working two journeys):

No.1   2.50pm from Liverpool Road
No.2   2.10pm from Liverpool Rd; 2.50pm from Orts Rd
No.3   2.25pm from Tilehurst to Broad St; 2.50pm from Broad St
No.4   2.20pm from Cemetery Junc; 3.00pm from Liverpool Rd
No.5   2.20pm from Liverpool Rd; 3.05pm from Orts Rd
No.6   2.20pm from Orts Rd; 2.55pm from Broad Street

After the match the specials were run as follows:

No. 1   4.20pm to Norcot for Reading Stadium
         4.55pm Wantage Road to Wokingham Road
No. 2   4.50pm Wantage Road to Broad Street
         5.10pm Wantage Road to Tilehurst
No. 3   4.55pm Wantage Road to Wokingham Road
No. 4   5.00pm Wantage Road to Liverpool Road
No. 5   5.05pm Wantage Road to Wokingham Road
No. 6   5.00pm Wantage Road to Kentwood
         5.10pm Kentwood to Wokingham Road

It seems that this was the 'standard' timetable pattern for the six trolleybus-operated football specials; it was repeated on 1st May 1948 and probably on other days. The only change on 1st May was that after the match, special No.2 served Kentwood whilst special No.6 ran to Tilehurst, removing the working between Kentwood and Wokingham Road.

Thirteen motorbus specials were also listed to run on 17th April 1948, to operate from St. Mary's Butts to Tilehurst Road between 2.00pm and 3.11pm. They also operated back to town after the match. Seven of them operated extra service journeys to the town centre before running the football specials:

No. 1	2.00pm	St. Mary's Butts to Tilehurst Road
No. 2	2.00pm	St. Mary's Butts to Tilehurst Road
No. 3	2.00pm	St. Mary's Butts to Tilehurst Road
No. 4	2.15pm	St. Mary's Butts to Tilehurst Road
No. 5	2.15pm	St. Mary's Butts to Tilehurst Road
No. 6	2.17pm	from Donkin Hill
	2.32pm	St. Mary's Butts to Tilehurst Road
No. 7	2.20pm	St. Mary's Butts to Tilehurst Road
No. 8	2.15pm	from Whitley Wood
	2.30pm	St. Mary's Butts to Tilehurst Road
No. 9	2.15pm	from Callington Road
	2.28pm	St. Mary's Butts to Tilehurst Road
No. 10	2.15pm	from Cressingham Road
	2.30pm	St. Mary's Butts to Tilehurst Road
No. 11	2.25pm	from Buckland Road Circle
	2.37pm	St. Mary's Butts to Tilehurst Road
No. 12	2.13pm	Erleigh Road to Grovelands
	2.55pm	St. Mary's Butts to Tilehurst Road
No. 13	2.28pm	Erleigh Road to Grovelands
	3.11pm	St. Mary's Butts to Tilehurst Road

On the return journeys, the football specials were run from Tilehurst Road to St. Mary's Butts as follows:

Nos. 1–6	4.40pm	Tilehurst Road
Nos. 7–11	4.45pm	Tilehurst Road
No. 12	4.50pm	Tilehurst Road
No. 13	4.55pm	Tilehurst Road

The football special schedule of six trolleybuses and thirteen motorbuses was a standard pattern, but was dependent upon the expected crowds. Upon that assessment only, the appropriate number of specials were run – but always with the associated service journeys beforehand. As an example, on 1st May 1948, only specials 1, 3, 4, 7, 8, 9, 11 and 13 were operated.

It was not only football specials that were operated, however. Others, such as to Reading Stadium (which was at Norcot) – usually using trolleybuses – were provided for those attending greyhound racing or dirt-track events, usually on weekday evenings.

Any event which drew a crowd, such as a show in one of the parks or on Thames Side Promenade, would often result in the operation of a special service. For example, on 17th April 1948, football specials 12 and 13 (see above) were used while the game was being played to run Circus Specials to Prospect Park, as follows:

No. 12	4.15pm	George Street to St. Mary's Butts,
then	4.50pm	at Tilehurst Road

No. 13	4.15pm	George Street to Whitley Wood,
then	4.55pm	at Tilehurst Road

The eight vehicles used for football specials on 1st May 1948 (see above), together with four stadium specials, were later used to carry passengers from a grass track motorcycle meeting at Denton's Field, Bath Road (the site on which Blessed Hugh Faringdon R. C. Comprehensive School was subsequently built), to St. Mary's Butts.

Other specials were operated on school journeys and, on 14th May 1948, the only open-staircase bus in the fleet, Leyland Titan 36, was the subject of a complaint from the

Leyland Titan 38 (RD 963), now in the twilight of its working life, stands in St. Mary's Butts outside St. Mary's Parish Church, working a special, presumably to football at Elm Park, circa spring 1948.

Print from J. R. Whitehead's collection

Headmistress of Caversham Primary School, who was concerned that the vehicle's open staircase was dangerous. Thereafter, 36 was not used on school specials.

As the only vehicle in the fleet with an outside staircase, the thoughts of intending passengers on dark, wet, rush hours can only be imagined as 36 drew up to the stop! But 36 obviously did leave an impression, for it is amazing just how many persons who have been interviewed over the years have singled out this bus as 'different'! Despite its open staircase, no attempt was made to dispose of 36 before its time. In fact, it was out-shopped after its last repaint on 21st March 1947. From 15th May 1948, it was intended that AEC Regents 50, 52, 55 and 22 should not be used on regular service but on reliefs and specials only. However, the specific reason for this edict has been lost in the mists of time. The reader might be surprised, if not already aware, that within the industry it is common for management to issue 'traffic notices' to staff instructing all manner of matters, large or small, for the proper regulation of the undertaking and sometimes to ensure working within technical parameters of the law. Thus, for any number of good reasons, management saw fit to limit the use of these particular buses.

When the new football season started, buses on football specials continued to use the crimson-on-cream numbered duty boards hung from vehicle radiators. This was certainly the case on 4th September 1948 but it is uncertain just how long they remained in active use.

An approach by Reading Football Club for the undertaking to operate football specials to their match on Christmas morning 1948 was rejected as likely to cause more problems than it solved. It was standard practice not to operate any Christmas Day services at all, and pay scales and holiday entitlement to operatives at all levels was geared to complete shut-down.

AEC Regent 10 (RD 5361) is operating a football special from St. Mary's Butts; surviving documentation suggests that this view was taken between 31st October 1948 (when the Barnes & Avis advert was applied) and final withdrawal exactly two years later. Note the 'short' radiator compared with the 'long' one this bus carries in the photo on page 199. Note, too, the duty number '7' on the radiator, indicating that this was the 2.20pm departure to Tilehurst Road (see previous page).

Print from J. R. Whitehead's collection

175

Above: *The scene at Norcot sometime during the 'austerity years', showing little traffic along Oxford Road, a queue of passengers waiting to board AEC trolleybus 118 (ARD 681), the distinctive pitched-roofed bus shelter, the advert on the hoarding for Reading-brewed Simonds Beer (complete with hop leaf trade mark), and the Rex Cinema. Out of shot to the left is the Pulsometer Engineering Company (opposite the trolleybus) and the Berkshire Printing Company, nearer the camera.*

Commercial picture postcard

Below: *Wooden-bodied AEC Regent 26, which retained its AEC 8.8-litre oil engine to the end of its days in Reading, stands in the sunshine at Grovelands terminus awaiting departure to Erleigh Road, probably in spring 1949, the driver not having yet changed the destination blind. Note the open engine side cover, propped against the nearside wing, an extensively-used method of keeping bus engines a degree or two (Fahrenheit, of course!) cooler than would otherwise have been the case. It is nice to see that the glass rainshields over the lower-deck opening windows have managed to survive to the last few months of service life left in the old girl.*

Late L. G. Head © Millane Publishing

20   Of Titans and Trolleybuses

1949 began with the resolution of a long-discussed problem: the turning of trolleybuses in St. Mary's Butts. An on-site demonstration to the Highways Committee, the Transport Committee and the borough police was set up on 3rd January 1949, the turn being demonstrated by AEC trolleybus 118 using traction batteries to demonstrate the proposed turning procedure using the neck of Hosier Street and then turning across the road to outside the church of St. Mary-the-Virgin. On completion of the manoeuvre, it was found that there was at least 9ft to spare between the nearside of the vehicle and the kerb edge. The vehicle then returned to the same starting position but this time a car was parked hard into the kerb at the entrance to Hosier Street. It was proved that even if an obstruction prevented using the entrance to that street, a trolleybus could still turn within the available road width so long as the driver was quick to achieve full right lock. The ability to turn a three-axle vehicle was also considered, this requiring two or three feet more than a two-axle vehicle. The turning manoeuvre had, in any case, always been resisted by the borough police, who considered it dangerous, and had opposed its implementation over many years. However, after this successful demonstration of a two-axle vehicle and sub-sequent discussions with the chairman and vice-chairman of the Highways Committee, who were most reluctant to agree to the proposal, it was agreed that a turning circle could be erected for a *trial period of six months* from commencement of services to Whitley Wood, and a turning circle was duly constructed for trolley vehicles travelling inwards from the south to be turned short. Thereafter, the turning circle drifted into permanence, the borough police raising no further official objections to the turn, although the chief constable had a continuing dislike of the turning facility on safety grounds and his opinion was made only too well-known to Mr Evans over the following years! In spite of the temporary nature of the arrangement, no action was taken either to make the scheme permanent or to remove the facility, and one can imagine that Mr Evans would not wish to risk losing the turn by raising the matter.

It had also been intended to discuss the question of turning trolleybuses from the north side of Oxford Road into St. Mary's Butts but, at Mr Evans' request, that matter was dropped – presumably to avoid raking up the matter of the 'temporary' turning circle in St. Mary's Butts.

Times were hard for the Labour government. Electrical 'load shedding' was causing turmoil in industry, and workers were having to work outside normal working hours. Thus, the Reading Trades Council made an approach via the town clerk to see if anything could be done regarding the issue of workman tickets on corporation buses outside the usual hours. There had been a recent announcement by the Minister of Transport that employers had to make approaches to a transport undertaking for a card of identity, which entitled the holder to workmen's fares. However, as Mr Evans pointed out, Statutory Rule & Order No. 1109 of 1944 was still operative in regard to workmen's fares in Reading and, as far as he was aware, no applications for such tickets had been received!

Another thick fog descended on the town on 26th January 1949 and all services ceased at 5.00pm. Fortunately, it was a Wednesday, and, therefore, early closing day. Slow running due to the fog caused the resistances of a newly-repainted 102 to overheat and scorch the new paint on the cabinet in the cab. It is recorded that it took an hour (instead of the usual 25 minutes) to run from Broad Street to Norcot and back. Both 114 and 119 were damaged in accidents, one of which occurred at the junction of Constitution Road with Oxford Road on Friday 28th January 1949, when a trolleybus ran into the back of a removal lorry. The fog persisted in the town itself (although many of the surrounding country areas were fog-free), and became so bad at dusk on Saturday 29th January 1949 that all corporation motorbuses were recalled to depot, the crews being placed on standby until the fog lifted a little around 9.00pm, when a skeleton service was put into operation. Trolleybus operation on the 'main line' does not appear to have been so much of a problem, for the service carried on.

As already recorded, when the second ex-Huddersfield Karrier to enter service did so as 160 on 18th February 1949, it was the first trolleybus to carry a fleet number in the centre of the front dash panel instead of the RCT emblem. Next day, AEC trolleybus 119 re-entered service after a repaint similarly treated. Thereafter, trolleybuses lost the emblem at their next repaint. In fact, this marked the start of the demise in the use of this RCT logo, although there is an archived Transport Department drawing dated January 1949, which shows trolleybus stop and bus stop

A faithful servant as the end of its working life looms. 1931-vintage Leyland Titan 1 (RD 3378) reflects on life while parked in the road outside the depot, in the days leading up to its final withdrawal on 30th June 1949.

Late W. J. Haynes
© Millane Publishing

The Southern Counties Touring Society paid their second visit to the town within a year on Sunday 6th March 1949, to tour the bus and trolleybus routes using AEC Regent II 83 (CRD 872), the undertaking's latest, delivered six months previously. The morning turned out to be one of slushy snow. Some of the party are seen here with the bus for the customary 'record shot' at the Bear Inn, Tilehurst. Note the Tower Café in the background, much frequented by trolleybus crews; it was demolished circa 1963 to make way for Boundary Close.

Late W. J. Haynes © Millane Publishing

flags incorporating the device, which had its origins in 1936 on trolleybus dash panels when these vehicles were being introduced to the town. The idea was similar to the situation just before the war in London, with the extensive promotion of trolleybuses to replace trams using the famous London Transport bullseye motif on the front dash panels of their trolleybuses. The Reading motif was subsequently used as a marketing device on the front covers of timetables and other literature as well as on stop flags. However, in February 1949 there was no rash decision to paint out the emblem on the trolleybuses; rather, it remained on the vehicles until repaint. It remained much longer on the stove-enamelled stop flags, of course, some even surviving into the early years of the 1970s until replacement.

At the town council meeting on Tuesday 1st March 1949, in the midst of considerable protest, the council voted that £12,000 from the Transport Department's profits should be used to subsidise the general rate for the town for the financial year 1949/50, representing a 3d rate. This was part of the £14,666 profit made by the undertaking during the financial year ending 31st March 1948 and an anticipated profit of £22,000 for the financial year ending 31st March 1949, brought about largely due to the fares increase introduced on 2nd November 1947. Pointing out that in due time the undertaking would be going out of the control of the corporation (due to nationalisation), Councillor A. Lockwood regarded it as wrong to take £12,000 out of an undertaking whose position might become very precarious before very long. *"The trading balances are not as substantial as all that"*, he said, *"and there is actually a decline in revenue. That is sheer madness from the financial angle and I can only assume that it has been done for political reasons"*. The users of the undertaking were, he argued, largely working-class people who had been spread over a wider area in the past few years, which meant increased use of the service. Councillor C. R. Evans complained on behalf of Caversham residents (as usual) that people who lived outside the borough got preference on the buses. *"They crowd the buses out and the ratepayers cannot get a seat"*, he said. *"The £12,000 could very well have been used to improve the transport facilities in the Caversham area"*.

Use of Transport Department profits for the relief of rates rather concerned Reading Trades Council and, at their February 1949 meeting, it was urged that such surpluses should be used to improve bus services and the wages and conditions of service of Transport Department employees. The real motivation for the transfer of the Transport Department's profits was revealed a year later by Alderman Bennet Palmer, formerly chairman of the Transport Committee, in February 1950, at the time of a fairly ill-timed general election in which the Labour majority was substantially reduced, resulting in their nationalisation policies having to be scaled down, too. The £12,000 was used for rate relief, he declared, *"...rather than give it up to nationalisation"*.

On 5th March 1949, the first two of the twenty new British United Traction trolleybuses were delivered to Mill Lane. Numbered 138 and 139 (DRD 124/5), they were very

The first of the twenty new BUT 9611T two-axle Park Royal-bodied 8ft wide trolleybuses were being delivered during March 1949. Trolleybus 138 (DRD 124) peers out of Middle Garage with two others behind, in company with 1947 Mulliner-bodied Bedford OBs 69 and 70 (CRD 592/3) and two of a growing number of ambulances, which had become stabled in this particular building as standard practice. Both of the ambulances in this view are of the Morris Commercial LC type, that at the front being No. 2 (SHX 364).

Late W. J. Haynes © Maiwand Photographic Archive

Thought to have been 13th March 1949, with trolleybus 120 (ARD 683) on its test run of both major trolleybus extensions in Whitley. It seems that the wiring in Northumberland Avenue stopped just short of Hartland Road roundabout at that time, pending deliberations regarding turning there (as originally intended), or via a purpose-built loop 300 yards further on. The trolleybus, indeed, appears to have been driven on battery beyond Hartland Road roundabout and reversed into what became Brayford Road, just short of the proposed lay-by. The persons present included Albert Gent (deputy manager) (extreme left) and W. John Evans (transport manager) and Ernie Worrell (extreme right); Eddie Beats (dark overcoat, light trousers) and to his immediate right a member of the Overhead Line Department.

Print from D. Redmond's collection

different from anything else that had gone before, with an 8ft overall width, deep windscreens and folding platform doors, the first such vehicles in the country. The delivery of these vehicles was well-timed, for the following day, Sunday 6th March 1949, the Southern Counties Touring Society used AEC Regent II motorbus 83 on a tour of the town's bus and trolleybus routes on what turned out to be a damp snowy day, and participants had an opportunity to inspect the two new deliveries during a depot visit.

At that time the new Northumberland Avenue and Whitley Wood trolleybus routes were still being prepared for service, with the wiring at the junction of Buckland Road with Basingstoke Road awaiting connection and erection of overhead also still in progress between Caversham Road and Stations. At the Transport Committee meeting on 17th March 1949, it was stated that both the Basingstoke Road (Savoy) and Christchurch Gardens substations were still three to four months away from completion, thus delaying the opening of the Whitley Wood route. All the overhead wiring installations south of Whit Pump were, however, stated to be complete and the spur to Stations was expected to be so in the next two to three weeks.

The first trial run to Whitley Wood by a trolleybus is recorded as having taken place on Sunday 13th March 1949 using pre-war AEC trolleybus 120. As it traversed the new wiring, sparks issued from the trolleyheads as it drew its power from the distant Mill Lane substation. To add drama to the occasion, 120 managed to dewire on the return journey, at Buckland Road Junction. On the same day, Karrier trolleybus 160 went to Caversham Bridge; the overhead wiring had been tensioned over the footpath beneath Caversham Road Railway Bridge and the test for height clearance was conducted using the tallest type of trolleybus then in stock, for possible use on what was to become route E (Northumberland Avenue – Caversham Bridge). In the early morning of Friday 18th March 1949, trolleybus 138 went to Whitley Wood on trial, and new trolleybus 141 was seen at Hartland Road on 29th March 1949. As mentioned, the Stations branch wiring extension was still under construction at this time, traction poles being in course of erection in Tudor Road and Station Hill on 14th March 1949, for example. On the same day, Karrier 159 was out on test – but very 'undressed' – for it has always been unusual for a corporation bus or trolleybus to be seen in public in 'ex-body shop condition', with lots of new and unpainted panels. Meanwhile, according to the enthusiast who contributed all of the foregoing, Karrier 161 was being worked on in the body shop.

To avoid the BUTs lying idle, Mr Evans had announced during March 1949 that the first four would enter service on 'main line' routes. So it was that 138 entered service on 21st March 1949 on route A, with 139, 140 and 141 following on 25th March 1949. The entry into service of these four, together with the first two refurbished ex-Huddersfield Karriers (with another one due soon), allowed

A nice study of the rear and offside of AEC Regent II 75 (CRD 864), some five months old, as it waits time at the Whitley Wood terminal stop in Whitley Wood Lane on 6th March 1949. Note that traction poles and trolleybus overhead line have already been installed, trolleybuses eventually being inaugurated along this route on 7th August 1949.

Late W. J. Haynes
© Millane Publishing

179

AEC Regent II 67 (CRD 261) waits time at the Erleigh Road terminal stop at the junction of Addington Road with Cardigan Road on 6th March 1949. The bus has acquired the nearside headlamp that was missing when it was new. Note the trolleybus overhead line, this being at the turn at one end of the ½-mile isolated section erected along Erleigh Road in 1936 for driver training purposes but disused since early 1939.

Late W. J. Haynes
© Millane Publishing

the withdrawal of the first three of the six original lowbridge trolleybuses – Sunbeam MF2A 101, Guy BT 103 and accident-prone Ransomes 105 – all of which were withdrawn on 25th March 1949. Authority to dispose of them was obtained from the Transport Committee at its meeting on 11th May 1949. Surprisingly, however, they were advertised for sale prior to this, on 28th April 1949, through the Municipal Passenger Transport Association and the Public Transport Association. No interest was shown whatsoever, so they were thereafter used as a source of spares, being stored on the newly-acquired site of the proposed depot and workshop facility at Bennet Road. 101, for example, yielded its differential, presumably to keep 106 on the road.

On Thursday 31st March 1949, members of the Transport Committee were given a demonstration of the English Electric Company's system of controlled acceleration as fitted to trolleybus 138. The success of the demonstration, which produced smoother acceleration, resulted in the equipment being ordered for fitting to the remainder of the BUT fleet, at a cost of £50 per vehicle. Not long afterwards, Mr Evans learned that immediate delivery would result in a very much higher price – but if prepared to wait 12–15 months, the equipment could be installed for the quoted price! Thus he decided to postpone the order and, instead, to see how 138 performed in service over an extended period. In the event, the idea was not progressed. It is not known whether the equipment fitted to 138 was actually ordered, or whether it was supplied on a speculative basis; neither is it known when it was eventually removed.

The following day, Friday 1st April 1949, Karrier 159 (VH 6753) entered service. Its destination blinds included **TILEHURST (WESTWOOD RD)**, this destination subsequently appearing on other trolleybuses as **WESTWOOD R^D (TILEHURST)**. The 'reverser' at Tilehurst triangle seems to have been used hitherto only for driver training purposes, as a result of which nothing had previously been included on trolleybus destination blinds for terminating at this location, even in an emergency. Mr Evans had other ideas, as we shall see later.

By 5th April 1949, regular use was being made of the temporarily disused 'side road' wiring as far as Whitley Street for driver training purposes. Once the Whitley trolleybus extensions had been put into use, it became more usual for novices to learn to drive trolleybuses on this part of the network.

Authority was sought, at the Transport Committee meeting of 14th April 1949, for the purchase of up to six miles of grooved cadmium copper trolleybus running wire for normal renewal purposes. The purchase price fluctuated on a day-to-day basis, reflecting the daily price fluctuation on the London metal market. The previous consignment, obtained

The solace of this view of AEC trolleybus 117 (ARD 680) parked in Mill Lane, poles hooked down, facing west at the corner with Letcombe Street, is particularly difficult to appreciate more than half a century later, for the scene has long since been buried under the massive concrete ramp of the Inner Distribution Road. This end of Mill Lane had moments when all was certainly not solace, for it was the departure point, more-or-less every day, of coaches owned by Smith's Luxury Coaches (Reading) Ltd., on various tours, excursions and express services to a number of coastal resorts.

Late W. J. Haynes
© Maiwand Photographic Archive

180

Only six months or so before withdrawal, Guy Arab 28 (BRD 816) pauses outside the former GWR station bound for Staverton Road on 6th March 1949, all the earlier snow having melted to leave plenty of surface water. Note the front destination indicator box rebuilt to Reading's standard form.
Late W. J. Haynes © Millane Publishing

from British Insulated Callenders Cables Ltd. in July 1948, had cost £184 10s 0d per ton. Although the price per ton had now risen to £212 0s 0d per ton, it was expected to fall over the following weeks and Mr Evans would place an order when the price became advantageous. The trolley wire being referred to weighed 0.48 pounds per foot, so a mile of wire thus weighed 1.13 tons.

It will be recalled that in March 1948 a weight limit of 12 tons had been imposed on the bridges in Bridge Street as they required major repair – the country was 'cash-strapped' at the time and the Ministry of Transport was unable to sanction the repair cost. Mr Evans advised the Transport Committee, at its meeting on 14th April 1949, that he had had discussions with the borough surveyor on the point that any fully-laden two-axle double-deck bus could exceed 12 tons, while the recently ordered three-axle trolleybuses could be expected to weigh 14½ tons fully laden. He hoped that, by the time the latter were in service, some of the remedial work to the bridges (now to be phased over three years) would have been completed and the Ministry of Transport might then be persuaded to re-assess the weight limit and give dispensation to the operation over the bridges of large-capacity trolleybuses.

The reader will appreciate that passenger transport operators are extremely unlikely to be able to provide a service which suits everyone without some form of grouse or grumble, or, it has to be said, a carefully thought out suggestion for an improvement. In the 22nd April 1949 issue of the *Berkshire Chronicle* was a letter from an S. W. Foster:

"Sir – May I, through the medium of your columns, call attention to the utter lack of Corporation transport in this area. Briefly, the nearest 'bus route to this district (Park Crescent area – Tilehurst Road) is the Grovelands route from the town centre – and the nearest stop, the corner of Waverley/Tilehurst Roads.

"May I suggest that the 'buses on the Horncastle route be diverted at Liebenrood Road to the corner of Waverley and Tilehurst Roads, thence along Tilehurst Road and down Honey End Lane to the Bath Road again, and the Horncastle. It can here be noted that there is little passenger traffic between Berkeley Avenue and Honey End Lane along this route.

"Another suggestion is that the existing Grovelands route via Waverley Road be diverted to Water Road, thence into Grovelands Road.

Parked in Mill Lane in front of the offices, poles down, utility trolleybus 135 (BRD 800) looks as though it may be a fairly recent repaint – and for a utility trolleybus the paint job is a superb 'mirror finish'. Indeed, the workmanship of the undertaking's coachpainters over the years was second-to-none. There were usually two vehicles at a time in the paint shop for a full internal and external repaint and it took two weeks to complete each vehicle. Everything was brush-painted and nearly all external advertisements were signwritten in flat oil paint before varnishing.

Late W. J. Haynes
© Maiwand Photographic Archive

BUT 9611T trolleybus 146 (DRD 132) emerging from the depot for a test run prior to entering service. Note that it is taxed rather than on trade plates, and that no destination blinds are yet fitted. While we have been unable to identify the conductor, the driver at the rear is Reg Uzell, who later became the undertaking's driving instructor.

© Reading Museum Service (Reading Borough Council); all rights reserved

"Failing the acceptance of these two suggestions, a third means is at hand in supplying the needs of this area, i.e., that either of the Horncastle or Grovelands routes be diverted alternately along Tilehurst Road (one along Water Road, the other down Honey End Lane) as in the order previously stated, thus giving a half-hourly service to the people in this district."

Some months later an alteration to the Grovelands end of motorbus route M was investigated, but it was not until July 1951, outside the scope of this volume, that alternate buses came to be routed via Waverley Road and via Water Road.

At the end of April 1949, it was decided to remove the sliding bulkhead windows on all existing trolleybuses and motorbuses, to prevent conductors talking to drivers whilst the vehicle was moving. The AEC Regent IIs had already been delivered with single-pane bulkhead windows. An exception was that one oil-engined bus would be fitted with a framed window in the bulkhead which could be completely removed when the bus was being used for training purposes. Initially, a Guy Arab is believed to have been selected for this role.

The trolleybus substation at Mill Lane was the only one on the system which had to be continuously manned, because the switchgear was not fitted with any automatic re-closing mechanism. The old power house, in which the rectifier was situated, was at this time serving as temporary accommodation for ambulance crews, including four men currently acting as departmental telephone switchboard operators dealing principally with ambulance service calls. At the Transport Committee meeting on 11th May 1949, Mr Evans reported that he had approached the Hackbridge & Hewittic Electric Co. Ltd., suppliers of the original equipment, who had quoted £500 to provide automatic re-closing equipment, together with an interlock circuit connected up to indicator lights and warning buzzer prominently located in the depot. If installed, the switchboard could be relocated and duties of the four operators re-organised, which would achieve a considerable economy.

In May 1949, in connection with the provision of a second depot and workshop facility at Bennet Road, the Ministry of Works offered three further redundant aircraft hangars. These included an eminently suitable one located in Cambridgeshire which could be dismantled and re-erected. The purchase price was £5,200, the Transport Department being required to remove the building and demolish any unwanted structures to ground level. The offer was accepted by the Transport Committee at a supplementary meeting on 27th May 1949 and a contract for £5,650 for re-erecting the hangar and executing the associated building work was awarded to the Maurice Hill Construction

AEC trolleybus 119 (ARD 682), posing on arrival at Kentwood, heralds another 'first', for it is the first repaint of a trolleybus which dispensed with having an RCT emblem on the front dash panel, with the substitution of a central fleet number instead. It is understood that it returned to service thus on 19th February 1949, a day after Karrier E6 160 entered service. The wasteland on the right was later the site of the Roundabout public house, and is now a retirement home.

Late W. J. Haynes
© Maiwand Photographic Archive

Brand new BUT trolleybus 141 (DRD 127), which had entered service on 25th March 1949, is seen here disembarking passengers at the Bear Inn, Tilehurst, on 1st April. The undertaking had entered a new era – 8ft wide vehicles with platform doors and other innovations such as full depth windscreens and side cab windows for better driver visibility; a wide easily-negotiated staircase with one quarter-turn landing; a new standard of seat frame and upholstery (although the red leather had already been introduced on motorbuses 74–83); and, at 120hp, the most powerful traction motor of any fitted to a Reading trolleybus.

© Late C. Carter

Company. Confirmation that the hangar was being sold to the department was received at the committee meeting on 23rd June 1949. There was still serious overcrowding at Mill Lane depot and at this time upwards of 20 vehicles were still having to be parked in the roadway overnight, notwithstanding that a small garage in Mill Lane belonging to Smith's Luxury Coaches had been rented since the summer of 1948 to house the pool cars. Although this had released space to enable the ambulance and school meals service fleets to remain garaged at Mill Lane depot, Mr Evans had pointed out that, even within the short term, wider and longer buses were going to make the accommodation problem an ongoing one.

Mr Evans further reported at the 15th May 1949 Transport Committee meeting regarding the planned improvements at Mill Lane depot authorised 15 months earlier. the borough surveyor had developed a scheme to extend the depot building over the proposed decking to Tan Lock at an estimated cost of £12,500. It was now necessary to have the committee's authority to proceed, to obtain authority within the council, and then to obtain Ministry of Transport sanction in regard to the complete scheme. The matter was, however, referred back for more information from the transport manager and he supplied a modified scheme at the Transport Committee meeting on 23rd June 1949.

On 25th May 1949, a second Manchester Corporation Transport Crossley motorbus, 2153 (JND 794) was inspected at Mill Lane depot. This was an 8ft wide vehicle, with electrically-operated platform doors, so it gave an opportunity for the transport committee to see for themselves the sort of vehicle that Reading could have on order. It had been agreed by the transport committee, at its meeting on 11th May 1949, to defer a decision to have air-operated platform doors fitted to the twelve Crossley motorbuses presently on order, at a cost of £265 per vehicle (this figure including a revised specification, with the buses also being supplied with air brakes rather than with vacuum brakes). It seems that at this stage the necessary loan sanction for these twelve buses had not yet been obtained and an amended application would have to be made.

As we shall see in due course, however, the motorbus replacement programme did not run to plan. For a start, a letter from The Ministry of Transport dated 10th June 1949 put these decisions into some doubt, as the Ministry, having considered the composition, age and condition of the existing motorbus fleet, was only prepared to agree to a loan sanction for seven vehicles in the financial year 1949/50, with the remaining five deferred until financial year 1950/51. At the Transport Committee meeting on 23rd June 1949, Mr Evans suggested that three vehicles additional to

1936 AEC Regent 54 (RD 8891), outbound at the Mill Lane/Katesgrove Lane stop at the foot of a reconstructed Southampton Street on 25th June 1949, is operating on route H (Emmer Green – Whitley Wood) after trolleybuses had commenced operation to Northumberland Avenue (5th June 1949). L. Cooper, who owned the draper's shop to the right of the picture, was Alf Smith's mother-in-law, Alf Smith being the managing director of Smith's Luxury Coaches (Reading) Ltd., whose large fleet of blue and orange coaches were a familiar sight in the town and, indeed, throughout the south of England.

Late W. J. Haynes © Millane Publishing

Three weeks after the introduction of trolleybuses to Northumberland Avenue, it is quite evident that BUT 143 (DRD 129) is still very new. It is just 'taking off' from the traffic lights (a pleasantly vintage example) at Crown Street/Pell Street to hum up the steeper, narrower section of Southampton Street. Note the novel way in which the rather long (in more ways than one) 'Northumberland Avenue' was squeezed into the blind width on the original sets of destination blinds supplied for these vehicles.

Late W. J. Haynes
© Maiwand Photographic Archive

the seven sanctioned be purchased outright from the department's depreciation fund, which was agreed. Ideally, the quantity of new buses would have been such as to allow their exclusive use on certain, selected routes (because of their platform doors); however, the revised order for ten Crossleys would not allow for this, so Mr Evans decided that they should once again be specified without platform doors, to avoid mixing types on the same route.

Two more BUTs, 142 and 143, entered serviced on 19th May 1949. By this time work on Christchurch Gardens sub-station was virtually complete, so it was decided to commence trolleybus operation between Northumberland Avenue and Caversham Bridge as soon as possible, in advance of trolleybuses being inaugurated to serve Whitley Wood. Erection of the overhead line between Caversham Road and Stations had been completed by the beginning of May 1949, AEC trolleybus 108 being noted on test in this section on 3rd May 1949. A test run over the completed Northumberland Avenue section was made by trolleybus 114 on Wednesday 25th May 1949.

The complete batch of twenty BUT trolleybuses were numbered 138–157 (DRD 124–143) – see Appendices A and B for further information. 157 was fitted with CAV electrically-operated doors instead of the Peters air-operated platform doors fitted to the rest of the batch. This was probably done for experimental purposes (although no documentation survives to explain why); this does, however, presumably account for this vehicle's slightly later entry into service, on 9th August 1949.

The last day of operation of motorbus route N (Hartland Road – Caversham) was Saturday 4th June 1949, using buses 4, 22, 50, 59, 62 and 83. Trolleybus route E (Northumberland Avenue – Caversham Bridge) was introduced the following day, Sunday 5th June 1949. Trolleybus 140 was the first in public service to Northumberland Avenue; also in service on the first day were 139, 141, 143, 145, 147, and 150.

Solely as a result of the survival of a window poster for Whitsun 1949, it is presumed that it was from the same date, 5th June 1949, that the 'main line' trolleybus routes

Corporation buses ran on hire to Thames Valley during the Royal Counties & Hackney Horse Show at Sonning between 22nd and 25th June 1949. When trolleybus route E replaced motorbus route N on 5th June, the displaced motorbuses were retained in service until after this event so that the undertaking's newest buses, AEC Regent IIs 74–83, could be used on hire on the special service (although Leyland Titan 1 (RD 3378) is recorded as also being used). Thames Valley themselves, were, apparently, not so discerning! In this scene at Reading Stations, bus 81 (CRD 870) is setting off for Sonning whilst two sister vehicles are held in the station forecourt.

Late W. J. Haynes © Millane Publishing

became referred to internally as routes A, B and C, the original route D having become absorbed into them (the original route C 'up-and-down-the-bump' had, of course, become defunct). This had the effect of releasing the designation 'route D' for use in identifying the other new trolleybus route to Whitley when it eventually came into operation.

The Royal Counties Agricultural Show was held at Sonning between 22nd and 25th June 1949 and a special service was operated from Stations to the showground by the Thames Valley Traction Company. Reading Corporation Transport loaned eight of their newest buses, AEC Regent IIs 62, 74, 76, 79, 80, 81, 82 and 83, which were fitted with boards showing 'On hire to Thames Valley'. Indeed, they compared very favourably with the stock which Thames Valley provided. They were required at 8.10am on each day, and returned to Mill Lane at around 9.00pm. At the invitation of the mayor, the chairman of the Transport Committee and the transport manager had attended a meeting at the Town Hall on 6th December 1948, which was called with a view to forming a local committee to handle the organisation of the show, and both gentlemen found themselves elected to that committee! As a technicality, an official approach had then to be made to the Transport Committee for authority to hire the department's buses to the Thames Valley Traction Company, as the showground was outside the county borough boundary and thus in Thames Valley's operating area. And, of course, there was that standing order forbidding hire of RCT vehicles to other operators...!

With the loss of eight 'front line' buses from the normal routes to operate the special service, it was decided that the six remaining Leyland Titans, by now in use only as spare vehicles, should be used to make up the service allocation. Two each were allocated to route I (Donkin Hill – Horncastle), route P (Staverton Road – Stations), and route L (Hemdean Road – Berkeley Avenue). Since the withdrawal of motorbus route N earlier in June, the Titans were, in fact, surplus to operating requirements, but even when they had been in daily service, they had for some time only been used at peak periods to run specials and extras. The 'frontline' duties, from 22nd to 25th June, would have been their last appearance *en masse*, and this was, indeed, a fitting swansong. The six buses concerned, 1, 2, 37, 38, 43 and 45, were finally withdrawn from service a few days after the closure of the Royal Counties Agricultural Show, on 30th June 1949, together with AEC Regent 4, which happened to be the last petrol-engined Regent in the fleet. Authority to withdraw and dispose of them had been given at the Transport Committee meeting on 23rd June 1949, after the successful conversion to trolleybus operation of the first of the routes serving Whitley. All seven vehicles were offered for further service in the trade press, and details were also circulated via the Municipal Passenger Transport Association. Inevitably, there was no interest shown by any other undertaking for their continued operation in revenue service. Titan 43 went for further service as staff transport for Huntley & Palmers Ltd. and, for a time, was often seen around Reading in the blue livery of their Associated Deliveries Ltd. subsidiary. No other offers were received and the remaining vehicles were finally taken by two local scrap dealers, the Titans by Tompkins & Smart, of Grazeley Green, and Regent 4 by George Dunaway, of Earley, the sale date for all six being recorded as 15th September 1949. Titan 45 was later to be seen, from the end of October 1949, at Star Motors, Sonning Cutting (although not sold to them).

A note in the surviving records suggests that the lack of interest in these buses was due to the provisions of the recently introduced Town and Country Planning Act, which, it was stated, had *"...definitely spoilt the market for second-hand omnibuses, both double- and single-deck, as most local authorities are becoming very strict on caravan dwellings, and whereas a reasonable price could be obtained 6 months ago, there is (now) little or no market for obsolete vehicles for this purpose"*. Indeed, neither Regent 4 nor any of the Tompkins & Smart Titans appear to have had any subsequent owners; the Titans remained in Tompkins & Smart's yard for some years before being broken up.

Work commenced on Monday 4th July 1949 on the construction of the 'bone-shaped' roundabout at Cemetery Junction using Borough Surveyor's Department direct labour. The first task was the removal of the tram rails, which had given this locality the name by which it is still known. The St. John's coffee stall, which had stood at the end of Kings Road since 1901, had already been relocated to Rupert Street in readiness for the next phase of the works – the adjustments to the line of the existing road kerbs at the perimeter before a start was made on the roundabout itself. By the end of the month one part of the roundabout had been made, which had resulted in a temporary traffic bottleneck, so that all town-bound traffic apart from trolleybuses was diverted along London Road.

A Junior Music Festival on 5th and 6th July 1949 involved the carriage of 1,830 schoolchildren to and from the Town Hall, using up to twelve motorbuses and six trolleybuses on both the outward and return journeys on each of the two days.

Construction of the bone-shaped roundabout at Cemetery Junction, possibly photographed in late July 1949. The trolleybus overhead line has already been adapted. Utility trolleybus 134 (BRD 799) proceeds eastbound through the chaos.

Print from Late H. E. Jordan's collection

Motorbus route L was temporarily diverted circa July 1949 due to sewer construction works in Hemdean Road and eventually, in November, it had to be curtailed while the works progressed along that road. It seems that when work started, initially along Hemdean Road commencing at Church Street, buses were diverted by way of Prospect Street and Chester Street (and subsequently Oxford Street) into Hemdean Road. When the works progressed further along Hemdean Road, buses were diverted via Church Street, Priory Avenue, Priest Hill, Hemdean Rise and Hemdean Hill into Hemdean Road. Once the sewer works had reached Hemdean Hill, the Hemdean Road section of the route had to be temporarily withdrawn and buses turned via Prospect Street and Oxford Street to terminate in Hemdean Road ready to return to town. With effect from 4th December 1949, buses were again able to travel along Hemdean Road as far as the sewer works had progressed and they terminated, again temporarily, at Queen Street, about 150 yards short of Caversham Primary School. We have been unable to discover documentation which would indicate the date of a resumption of the service along the last quarter-mile through to the Hemdean Road terminus, which was at the junction of that road with Hemdean Bottom, Rotherfield Way and Oakley Road. Buses originally terminated by turning right into Rotherfield Way to unload, then reversing across the farm track known as Hemdean Bottom, to a bus stop at the foot of Oakley Road hill to await departure.

Mr Evans presented the department's annual report for the financial year ended 31st March 1949 at the Transport Committee meeting on 21st July 1949. Financially, the undertaking returned an overall profit of £13,389, a shade down on that of the previous year, which had been £14,666. The total increase in income since the fares revision of 2nd November 1947 had been roundly £69,000, which compared rather favourably with the estimate of £64,000, but a continuing downturn in traffic revenue had been detected since December 1948. This had been attributed to the re-introduction of a basic petrol allowance, plus a government fiscal policy designed to restrict personal expenditure. In spite of an increase in revenue on the trolleybuses of £9,735, there was a marginal decrease in profit of £674 and a 6.4% decrease in passengers, by 1,344,114; yet 10,108 more miles had been operated. The motorbuses, on the other hand, had operated an additional 112,316 miles but had carried 796,475 more passengers, an increase of around 3.8%. Although traffic revenue on the motorbuses had increased by £26,431, there was still a small loss amounting to £2,771, compared with a loss of £3,390 the previous year. There had also been, once again, a loss, of £752, in operating the Parcels Express Service. During the financial year, many of the staff working for the department had received better pay and conditions. The prices of petrol and derv had both increased by roundly a halfpenny per gallon, although the cost per mile of tyres on the mileage contract continued to decrease. The trolleybus depot had received its first internal repaint since it was built; after many years, 'camp sheathing' (close sheet piling) to the river frontage had been completed; two sub-stations and the infrastructure to operate trolleybuses south of Whitley Street had been substantially completed; and two-way wiring of the depot connection and the rewiring of Broad Street in both directions had also been carried out. Further, there had been ten new double-deck motorbuses, together with twenty new and ten second-hand trolley-buses, in exchange for the withdrawal and disposal of four time-expired old double-decker motorbuses and six stop-gap nearly-new single-deckers. Two Bedford lorries and a Bedford van had been added to the ancillary fleet. Finally, during the financial year, the department had also obtained 120 replacement TIM ticket machines.

At this time, the Northumberland Avenue section of new trolleybus wiring came into frequent use for trolleybus driver training, Sunbeam MF2A 106 being noted in use for this purpose on 5th July 1949, AEC 108 on 11th July 1949 and AEC 128 on 22nd August 1949. AEC 121 was seen at Northumberland Avenue terminus on 4th November 1949.

Following completion of the Savoy substation, and with the entry into service of BUT trolleybuses 152–156 on 1st August 1949, trolleybus operation was inaugurated on the Whitley Wood – Stations route on Sunday 7th August 1949. This was in advance of its Ministry of Transport inspection – probably permission for this was granted because of Mr Evans' good standing, and because the ministry was busy! The first day of operation was August Bank Holiday Weekend and local residents took the opportunity both to see and to ride on the new service. An interesting feature of this route was the provision of a 'reverser' as a turning facility at Whitley Wood terminus, whereby trolleybuses turned round in much the same manner as the motorbuses that they were replacing. Having pulled across what was then a fairly rural crossroads at the Engineer's Arms, vehicles arriving at the terminus turned by reversing to the left, into Whitley Wood Road, and then drew out into Whitley Wood Lane by making a right-hand turn. Terminal reversing manoeuvres were always supposed to be supervised by the conductor, using a whistle if necessary. Trolleybuses 154 and 143 opened the service that morning, providing a 15-minute head-way, which was stepped up to 7½ minutes in the afternoon. The new service was referred to internally as route D. From the same date, alternate journeys on route E from Northumber-land Avenue became operated to Caversham Bridge or to Stations. Trolleybus 153 was the first to operate from Northumberland Avenue to Stations.

Also from the same date, motorbus route H (Emmer Green – Whitley Wood)

READING CORPORATION TRANSPORT

REVISION OF TROLLEYBUS AND MOTORBUS SERVICES

COMMENCING SUNDAY, 7th AUGUST, 1949

TROLLEYBUS SERVICES

Route "D"—Whitley Wood and Stations	A new service of Trolleybuses will operate between Whitley Wood, St. Mary's Butts and the Railway Stations
Route "E"—Northumberland Ave., Stations & Caversham Bridge	A revised Time-Table will operate between Northumberland Avenue, St. Mary's Butts and Caversham Bridge. A new service of Trolleybuses will operate between Northumberland Avenue and the Railway Stations

MOTORBUS SERVICES

Route "F"—Uplands Road and Shinfield Road	A revised Time-Table will operate
Route "H"—Emmer Green and Whitley Wood	This Service will be discontinued. Facilities are provided from Emmer Green to Friar Street by Motorbus Route "N" and from Railway Stations to Whitley Wood by Trolleybus Route "D".
Route "I"—Donkin Hill & Horncastle	A revised Time-Table will operate.
Route "N"—Emmer Green and Friar Street	A new service of Motorbuses will operate between Emmer Green and Friar Street (Triangle Car Park) via Buckingham Drive, Prospect Street, Reading Bridge, and Blagrave Street in both directions.
Route "P"—Staverton Road and Stations	This service will operate via Northumberland Ave., Whitley St., Silver St., London St., Duke St., Broad St., Queen Victoria Street, and Station Road in both directions.

For Full Details of Time Tables, Routes, Fares and Stages, see Handbills obtainable from Head Office, Mill Lane, Reading; Parcels Office, The Arcade, Broad St., Reading; or from any Inspector or Conductor

Corporation Transport Department,
Mill Lane, Reading
July, 1949

W. J. EVANS, M.I.E.E., M.Inst.T.
Transport Manager and Engineer

Trolleybus operation to Whitley Wood began on Sunday 7th August 1949. Brand new BUT trolleybus 154 (DRD 140) entered service a week earlier, and is seen here on the 'reverser' at Whitley Wood terminus later the same month. Turning at Whitley Wood was akin to motorbus procedure – by pulling forward towards to the Engineer's Arms, reversing to the left, into Whitley Wood Road, then pulling forward to the right, back into Whitley Wood Lane – all without the trolleybooms leaving the overhead line.

Late W. J. Haynes
© Maiwand Photographic Archive

was withdrawn. Its northern section, serving Emmer Green, was replaced by new motorbus route N (Emmer Green – Friar Street Triangle). It ran to a reduced frequency of twelve instead of ten minutes, although with additional journeys superimposed to deal with peak load requirements. In the town centre the service was worked between The Forbury and Friar Street Triangle, in both directions, via Blagrave Street and Friar Street (as per one of the proposals put to the Transport Committee at its meeting on 16th September 1948). It terminated outside the Co-operative Stores on the western side of the junction of West Street with Friar Street (rather than outside Langston's shop as originally considered), then turned via Caversham Road and Lower Thorn Street to load in Friar Street outside the public conveniences at The Triangle car park (which, predictably, caused somebody to write to the local newspaper to complain!). In Emmer Green, the service still terminated at Chalgrove Way (a turning off Kidmore End Road), but became routed via the newly-constructed (and already opened) Buckingham Drive instead of along Peppard Road and past the BBC Monitoring Station at Caversham Park. Route N is recorded as having been opened by AEC Regent II 59. The peak hour superimposed service comprised two extra buses worked in both directions both morning and evening. In the evening peak, the service was further bolstered by two buses running to and turning short at Balmore Drive, presumably to convey workers from the Royal Army Pay Corps headquarters at Balmore House and to pick up homeward-bound workers at the Westfield Road stop from J. Samuel Elliott Ltd.'s joinery works.

Although only a stone's throw away, it will be noted that the new route N did not serve Stations, which certainly failed to impress the Emmer Green residents. There was a tirade of letters, both to the Transport Department and published in the local papers, complaining about the stupidity of the new routing. This was not the Transport Department's fault, however, but rather that of the chief constable of the County Borough of Reading Police, who had been quite insistent that no bus route would be permitted to make the right turn from Station Road into Friar Street. There were, in his opinion, far too many traffic movements in that direction already at that point, and he would only permit a 'straight-through' movement.

Minor timing changes were also made to route F (Uplands Road – Shinfield Road) to give a regular frequency, particularly in the early mornings, in the Caversham area; and to route I (Donkin Hill – Horncastle) to give a regular joint frequency with route M (Erleigh Road – Grovelands) between the town centre and the top of Castle Hill. Route P (Staverton Road – Stations) was given a new terminal point at Stations (in what became known as 'the trolleybus lay-by' on Station Hill). Additionally, as agreed by the Transport Committee at its meeting the previous March, route P was re-routed to avoid duplicating the route of the trolleybuses, now running inbound via Mount Pleasant, Silver Street, London Street, Duke Street, King Street, Broad Street, Queen Victoria Street and Station Road to Stations, and outbound *vice versa* (instead of its previous route inbound via Southampton Street, Bridge Street, St. Mary's Butts, West Street, Friar Street, Greyfriars Road and Station Hill, and outbound via Station Road, Friar Street and West Street to St. Mary's Butts, thence via the reverse of the inbound route).

Motorbus route K (Woodcote Road – Friar Street (GPO)) and route L (Hemdean Road – Berkeley Avenue) both operated to a regular 30-minute frequency. Route F (Uplands Road –

The start of trolleybus operation to Whitley Wood on 7th August 1949 also saw the inauguration of the loop serving Stations. Here, later the same month, two of the new BUTs, 149 (DRD 135) and 146 (DRD 132), are at rest in the lay-by next to the bay platform. This lay-by had been created during widening of Station Hill in 1937-42 and had been used hitherto by Thames Valley Traction Company buses.

Late W. J. Haynes
© Maiwand Photographic Archive

When trolleybus operation to Whitley Wood began, on 7th August 1949, motorbus route H (Emmer Green – Whitley Wood) was altered to run Emmer Green – Friar Street (Triangle car park) as route N. The terminus was in Friar Street due to congestion in Broad Street, but the chief constable of the borough police would not let buses turn right from Station Road into Friar Street; thus, they had to travel via Blagrave Street into Friar Street, omitting Stations – a serious bone of contention with Emmer Green's travelling public! AEC Regent 22 (ARD 13) is seen here heeling round to the left from The Forbury into Blagrave Street bound for Friar Street.

Print from J. R. Whitehead's collection

Shinfield Road) was operated to a 10-minute frequency which was increased to one of 7½ minutes at peak periods but reduced to a 12-minute service after 7.00pm.

The Ministry of Transport inspecting officer, Brigadier Langley, visited Reading on Tuesday 23rd August 1949, to inspect the new trolleybus routes, substations and vehicles. Also present were representatives from the Post Office (in case there were telephone cables present which might fall on the overhead or get fouled by errant trolleybooms), the police and the Borough Surveyor's Department together with the transport manager. Together they boarded 155 to tour the new routes and visit the two new substations. Brigadier Langley made a walking inspection of all junctions, circles and the reverser at Whitley Wood terminus, following which he imposed the usual 5mph speed limit on all overhead junctions. The subject of the St. Mary's Butts turning circle was again aired during Brigadier Langley's inspection, when the test with the parked car, as demonstrated on 3rd January 1949 (see page 177), was repeated. The police objections were reiterated by Inspector Carr and the duration of the experiment (six months) was emphasised. At several loading points along the routes, the Brigadier observed the general reaction of passengers and crews in the operation of folding platform doors on the trolleybuses in service.

Construction of the roundabout at Cemetery Junction was still in progress at this time; the western 'half' had been brought into use on 14th August 1949. Although the new trolleybus overhead layout was not quite ready, Brigadier Langley took the opportunity to see progress to date.

In the afternoon, Brigadier Langley, together with representatives from CAV and Park Royal, inspected the electrically-operated door gear on 157. After testing the door unit, it was agreed that the emergency push button should be replaced by a turncock of the type similar to the Peters equipment on the other vehicles in the batch, and that it should be connected into the battery feed to the motor so that, in an emergency, all that was required was to cut the current and allow the doors to be pushed or pulled open by hand in a similar way to that which was possible with the Peters units. The Brigadier was, however, favourably impressed with the CAV equipment and quite agreeable to the vehicle being kept on test.

On 26th August 1949, the Ministry of Transport relented in regard to the number of new buses it would agree to be funded and allowed for five vehicles in the early months of the following financial year 1950/51. When added to the seven vehicles already agreed for funding in the financial year 1949/50, this restored a full batch of twelve buses. Thus, with twelve Crossleys now due again in 1950, Mr Evans obtained the Transport Committee's agreement, on 8th September 1949, that, following the success of the CAV electric doors fitted experimentally on BUT trolleybus 157, electrically-operated doors should once again be incorporated in the specification for the Crossley motorbuses, at an additional cost of £175 per vehicle (although the price had risen to £185 per vehicle by the time the buses were delivered). Electrically-operated doors were, in fact, lighter in weight and cheaper than the air-operated doors previously specified. Mr Evans had been somewhat impressed that, after 148,000 BUT trolleybus miles, no platform accidents

Traffic on Oxford Road as it was in this view, taken circa spring 1950, is quite tolerable by today's standards! The trolleybus is Sunbeam MF2A 106 (RD 8090), one of the remaining 1936-vintage low-bridge vehicles in its twilight months of service, bound for town and Liverpool Road, as it waits at the Norcot shelter opposite The Pulsometer Engineering Works.

Late W. J. Haynes
© Maiwand Photographic Archive

AEC Regent II 62 (CRD 256), the bus which lost its original body in the depot fire before entering service, in January 1947, is seen here in late August 1949 with its replacement body, standing in Broad Street outside Fifty Shilling Tailors. It shows 'Special' on the front destination blind and is, in all probability, the spare vehicle, held in Broad Street for any untoward eventuality.

Late W. J. Haynes
© Millane Publishing

had occurred. The provision of platform doors on new buses and trolleybuses became the fleet standard thereafter. At the Transport Committee meeting on 15th December 1949, the Crossleys were discussed once again, following the issue of a new Ministry of Transport regulation which permitted an increase in overall length of double-deck buses on two axles to 27 feet. The committee agreed to pay an extra £35 10s 0d per vehicle to build them to the new maximum overall length. The 12-inch length increase permitted the standard dimension between front and rear bulkhead to be retained, which would have to have been reduced on a 26ft long vehicle fitted with doors because, while a minimum platform length had to be maintained, buses fitted with folding doors required additional platform length in order for the doors to fold away.

With the introduction of trolleybuses instead of motorbuses to Whitley Wood, and all the BUTs having entered service, there followed further withdrawals of life-expired motorbuses. This time, pre-war oil-engined AEC Regents began to depart, 8, 9 and 14 being withdrawn on 31st August 1949. Three of the four wartime Guy Arabs (the 'unpopular' Gardner 5LW-engined 6 and 7, together with 6LW-engined 28) were also withdrawn. The fourth Guy Arab, AEC-engined 27, was retained for the time being; it is recorded as having been rebuilt with a standard Reading pattern front destination box and with side and rear boxes also fitted, re-entering service thus on 15th December 1949. A further oil-engined AEC Regent, 26, was withdrawn on 31st December 1949. All these buses were, presumably, selected for withdrawal on the basis that they had non-standard oil engines (AEC 115mm 8.8-litre and Gardner) in a fleet otherwise fitted with AEC 7.7-litre engines. Authority to dispose of the withdrawn buses was given by the Transport Committee in January 1950 and their availability was circulated via the Municipal Passenger Transport Association. This resulted in the Transport Department being approached by Chesterfield Corporation, who wished to buy Guy 28 for spares. That offer was declined, as it was hoped that the vehicle could be sold – at a higher price – as a runner. Other spares were, however, offered to the Derbyshire municipality. Once again, no interest was shown by any other municipal operator for the further use of any of the seven buses; they were advertised for sale by tender on 10th February 1950 and sold on 6th March 1950.

The three Guys went to Beech's Garage, of Hanley, Staffordshire, at £500 each for 6 and 7; and £570 for 28, offers which were later modified to an overall £1,700 for the three on the understanding that Reading Corporation Transport would obtain certificates of fitness on all three vehicles. Bus 7 was still at Mill Lane on 8th April 1950, a month after the others had gone. 6 and 28 were subsequently sold on for further service, to Enterprise Motor Services, of Newport, Isle of Wight, later to become 900 and 901 respectively in the Southern Vectis Omnibus Company fleet

August 1949 in St. Mary's Butts, at the corner with Hosier Street. AEC Regent 51 (RD 8094) was rebuilt at the front following accident damage, and has no cream valance across the front over the windscreen and down the nearside to the front bulkhead. It carries the word 'Relief' on the front destination blind. Note the shops, too – L. Vidcosky, ladies' and gents' tailor, mourning orders executed promptly, next to W. Fossett, tripe dresser and supplier of neatsfoot oil; and Choc Ice Corner ("Okey-Pokey, Choc & Cream Ices")!

Late W. J. Haynes © Millane Publishing

189

When Whitley Wood and Stations became served by trolleybuses on 7th August 1949, route N (Emmer Green – Friar Street (Triangle car park)) was introduced to replace the northern section of route H (Emmer Green – Whitley Wood). Motorbus route P (Staverton Road – Stations) was altered permanently so as not to duplicate the trolleybuses, and given a new terminal point at Stations in the newly acquired bus lay-by ahead of the trolleybuses. A pristine utility Guy Arab 27 (BRD 815) sits biding her time, with front destination box rebuilt to standard Reading type, replacement AEC oil engine and engine side cover open against the nearside front wing.

© A. B. Cross

when Enterprise was taken over. Bus 7 passed to and entered service with Bamber Bridge Motor Services, Preston, and was subsequently re-bodied with a pre-war lowbridge Leyland body.

AEC Regents 8, 9, 14 and 26 were bought by J. C. Thomas, of Wells, Somerset, for an all-in £460. The chassis of 8 was subsequently used by Devon General (via ACV Sales, Southall) to reconstruct another chassis, which was then re-bodied. Devon General were, at that time, rebuilding pre-war single-deck AEC Regal chassis using second-hand double-deck AEC Regent chassis parts and having them bodied with new lightweight double-deck bodies (DR704 (ETT 994), DR706–13 (DUO 317/9-22/7-9) and DR714–8 (DDV 420/1, DDV 446/54/5)), so 26 might have been used for the same purpose as no trace has otherwise been found of the vehicle. The other two, 9 and 14, were sold on for further use, but not as buses: 9 with a Midlands showman and 14 as the basis of a lorry in Essex.

During the autumn of 1949, the departmental car purchased in 1946 was traded in for a replacement. At around the same time, as a result of a suggestion of the transport manager at the Transport Committee meeting of 11th May 1949, the Guy departmental lorry (DP 6373), which had formerly been bus 11, was donated to Reading Technical School, Woodley Aerodrome, Motor Engineering & Maintenance Department after a fruitless attempt to sell it.

The BUTs tended to monopolise the Whitley routes in the early months, although there were exceptions. The only recorded occasion when a utility vehicle ran in service on these routes was on 27th August 1949, when 135 appeared at Whitley Wood, although 136 reached Northumberland Avenue on test runs both in October 1949 and again in 1950. On 1st October 1949, Karrier 158 was noted working Northumberland Avenue – Stations, while on 8th October 1949 it appeared working St. Mary's Butts – Whitley Wood. Thereafter, Karriers appeared quite regularly on the 'side routes'. On 17th December 1949, for example, no less than three of the Whitley Wood route's allocation were Karriers!

The two bridges over Mill Stream and the River Kennet in Bridge Street (between Mill Lane and Simonds' Brewery) were still causing concern in the autumn of 1949. To allow the operation of the new BUT trolleybuses with a full standing load, the borough surveyor had negotiated with the Ministry of Transport for an increase in the laden weight restriction from 12 tons to 13 tons. However, notice was given that the ministry certainly would not allow the three-axle trolleybuses, presently on order, to operate over the bridges with a full load. Load-carrying ability may therefore have been the reason why Karriers were allocated to the 'side routes'. The Karriers weighed only 8 tons 14 cwt 1 qtr unladen and had a seating capacity of 64, compared with the BUTs, which weighed 8 tons 17 cwt 1qtr unladen with a seating capacity of 56. When the Sunbeam three-axle trolley-

For a reason not readily apparent but conceivably due to accident damage, utility trolleybus 134 (BRD 799) had been rebuilt with a straight waistrail to the cab rather than 'dipped' – compare with views of other utility trolleybuses. This rather fine shot is at the outbound Crescent Road stop in Wokingham Road. Note the superb paint finish and the relocation of the front registration number at the bottom of the front dash panel.

Late W. J. Haynes
© Maiwand Photographic Archive

buses on order were subsequently delivered, they had a seating capacity of 68 and an unladen weight of 10 tons 2 cwt 0 qtrs. In spite of the restriction, there were occasions when a Sunbeam three-axle trolleybus was, inadvertently perhaps, allocated to the 'side road', a very early instance being on 31st December 1950, for 177 was ridden upon by a local enthusiast – and duly noted in his diary!

The 'bone-shaped' roundabout at Cemetery Junction came into full use on Sunday 4th September 1949; construction was finally completed in early October 1949. As mentioned previously, the new trolleybus overhead layout was in use well before completion of the roadworks, thus disproving the popular myth that the existence of trolleybus infrastructure obstructed road improvements. The cost to the undertaking of these alterations had been £1,282, but this had resulted in the incorporation of a much-needed turn-back facility at the eastern end of the town. It was decided to make regular weekday peak-hour use of both this and the reverser at Westwood Road, Tilehurst. Both destinations were added to blinds on all trolleybuses from September 1949 and, from 14th November 1949, regularly-operated evening peak-hour trips commenced operation working Cemetery Junction to Westwood Road, Tilehurst at 5.45pm, 5.55pm and 6.05pm (timings westbound from Broad Street). From the same date, however, Huntley & Palmers Factory Specials working to Orts Road (and turning by means of batteries) ceased to operate as such, the Cemetery Junction turn-back facility being used instead.

Ever since it was installed as part of the newly-wired Tilehurst route in 1938, Westwood Road reverser had been used for driver training purposes and little, if anything, else. Significantly, Westwood Road was not included on pre-war or wartime destination blinds, so the facility cannot have been intended for regular turning of service trolleybuses. As five of the six existing trolleybuses (the exception being 101) and the fleet of new AECs on order in 1938 all had traction batteries and could easily turn without wires, a rarely-used reverser would have been difficult to justify unless provided specifically to train and test trolleybus drivers in the reversing ability they had to achieve in order to pass their driving test. The reverser was unusual in that trolleybuses arriving from town turned right into Westwood Road, then reversed out into the major road. In those far-off days, bus (or trolleybus) drivers invariably did not own any form of mechanised transport themselves any grander than a push-bike and took their Ministry of Transport driving test in a bus (or trolleybus) rather than in a car!

On 25th October 1949, there was a fairly sharp increase, for those times, in the price of motor fuels – 2½d per gallon on petrol and 2¼d per gallon on derv fuel oil. This, it was estimated, would cost the department an extra £1,600 per year. However, a certain degree of competition from bulk suppliers became more evident in March 1950, which enabled ¼d per gallon to be shaved off derv and ⅛d per gallon off petrol. The budget, on 19th April 1950, negated these savings, however, with a swingeing increase in the tax on both petrol and derv of ninepence per gallon (a gallon at this time costing between 1s 2d and 1s 6d)!

It was being proposed, at this time, to introduce a traffic scheme whereby Thorn Street became one-way southbound and Cheapside one-way northbound (neither of which affected any bus services), with a clockwise gyratory scheme around The Triangle car park. Lower Thorn Street would become one-way northbound and Caversham Road one-way southbound. If introduced, this would have required a modification to the northbound trolleybus wiring in Caversham Road by re-routing via Friar Street and Lower Thorn Street. Bus and trolleybus stops, including the terminal loading point of the Emmer Green motorbus service (route N), would also have had to be repositioned. At an estimated cost to the Transport Department of £550–£600 to implement, for which there was no budget allowance, it was fortunate, perhaps, that the idea was scrapped.

Revised Sunday timetables were introduced on all trolleybus routes from Sunday 20th November 1949. Effectively, on the 'main line', two routes were operated all day: route A (Wokingham Road – Norcot – Tilehurst) and route C (Liverpool Road – Norcot – Kentwood). This replaced the arrangement whereby Kentwood was linked to Wokingham Road until 2.00pm on Sundays, and Liverpool Road thereafter, as had been introduced on 18th February 1947.

On Thursday 22nd December 1949, the Christmas shopping rush saw short workings on motorbus route F to Cressingham Road and on motorbus route N to Evesham Road, to cope with the extra traffic generated. A fourth ex-Huddersfield Karrier, 162 (VH 6755), entered service on 13th December 1949 and doubtless also helped to move the Christmas shopping crowds. It evidently replaced Leyland TB4 trolleybus 104, another of the six original experimental trolleybuses, as just 18 days later, on 31st December 1949, the latter was taken out of service.

Shortly before withdrawal from service, Leyland TB4 trolleybus 104 (RD 8088) is waiting time at the inbound stop at Kentwood terminus. With 101, 103 and 105 already withdrawn and all twenty new BUT trolleybuses in service, use of 104 and the other two lowbridge trolleybuses remaining in service (102/6) was probably restricted at this stage to use as 'spare' vehicles.

Late W. J. Haynes
© Maiwand Photographic Archive

Above: January 1950. AEC trolleybus 126 (ARD 689) bears down on the photographer, who is standing in the road just west of The Arcade, while 1948-vintage AEC Regent II 78 (CRD 867) loads for Shinfield Road at the stop on the corner of Cross Street and 1936-vintage AEC Regent 48 (RD 8091) departs for Uplands Road at the other end of route F. At the time the view was of a typical workaday Monday – Friday scene in Reading's main shopping street. Through traffic was not too much of a problem and parked vehicles, although often a nuisance, were still not too many at any one time as to become the headache they caused a decade later. *Reading Standard*

Below: New is not necessarily trouble-free! This view, taken in late August 1949, shows brand new BUT trolleybus 153 (DRD 139) being retrieved from a breakdown by the undertaking's 1936-vintage Leyland SQ2 'gearless' tower wagon RD 8892 – it did not carry a fleet number at that stage – at the junction of Caversham Road with Friar Street, on the way back to depot. Stranded vehicles, be they motorbuses or trolleybuses, were rescued by one or other of the department's tower wagons – and, in those days, always towed on a chain! *Late W. J. Haynes © Maiwand Photographic Archive*

21   The Light Brightens

At the last Transport Committee of meeting of 1949, Mr Evans warned that the recruitment of drivers and conductors was becoming increasingly difficult – and that *"...the pre-war type of man ...who had a keen interest in his work, is rapidly disappearing"*. Reading had *"...jobs in excess of the labour available"*. Mr Evans reported that, since 1st April 1949, a total of 103 drivers and conductors had resigned, to be replaced by only 86 trainees, which represented a financial loss to the department in terms of overtime payments and training costs. Shortage of staff was to remain a serious problem throughout the 1950s – and, indeed, it recurred with monotonous regularity at intervals through every remaining decade of the twentieth century!

Every once-in-a-while, local councillors, endeavouring to be seen to be supporting their electorate, try to encourage the professionals that such-and-such a route would be a 'good idea', usually quite ignorant of most of the practicalities of running a bus service. Thus consideration was given, at the Transport Committee meeting on 15th December 1949, to further petitions for a service linking the Donkin Hill area with Caversham 'village', which was seen as an alternative shopping facility to Reading itself. The matter had been brought up earlier in the year, at the Transport Committee meeting on 17th March 1949, when the transport manager was requested to report on the possibility of operating alternate buses from Donkin Hill via Caversham 'village' and Caversham Bridge instead of via Reading Bridge. When he had reported at the following meeting, on 14th April 1949, Mr Evans had been quite unimpressed by the idea, pointing out that it would totally upset the balance of services currently being provided along the George Street corridor, which served factories and residences to a regular timetable. Although it was fair comment that there was no direct connection between Donkin Hill, Briants Avenue and Caversham village, it only required a change of bus at George Street to make that journey.

The cage was evidently rattled quite loudly during a subsequent town council meeting and the matter was 'referred back'. When he reported further to the Transport (Future Policy) Sub-Committee in December 1949, Mr Evans pointed out that claims made in Council that *"...600 houses in Caversham and the Henley Road area, (were) denied access to Thames-Side Promenade, Caversham Court, and other beauty spots in Caversham West"* in fact meant that people were unwilling to walk the 600 yards from George Street/Gosbrook Road. There were also churches and a good many corner shops and the like locally available, while the lack of a doctor's surgery in the Donkin Hill area was the responsibility of the Local Executive Council of the Health Services, not the Transport Department! Mr Evans concluded his December 1949 report with the following vitriolic paragraph:

"The Committee will give serious consideration as to whether they are prepared to give through services without any change of vehicle between any two points within the Borough, or even to provide within reasonable walking distance, a service to any part of the Borough. The Committee may decide that this is part of their policy. If so, I can give you a number of places (in Caversham and in other parts) which would justify priority consideration before any variation is made to the Donkin Hill service. The Committee are also aware that we shall be showing a loss for the present financial year."

Notwithstanding, the matter was referred again to the Transport (Future Policy) Sub-Committee to investigate further. It reported in April 1950 rejecting the idea, although it did suggest, a bit timidly, for fear of incurring Mr Evans' wrath, that it *might* be possible to divert every other bus on route L (Hemdean Road – Berkeley Avenue) via Briants Avenue, Henley Road, Prospect Street and Oxford Street. Mr Evans evidently stuck to his guns, for no such service was entertained. The local politicians on the Transport Committee appeared to be silenced. The route from Donkin Hill continued to run over Reading Bridge but the subject re-appeared in the mid-1950s, when a three-month trial of a cross-Caversham service was introduced after another bout of petitioning – but this service was withdrawn through lack of support!

In July 1949, two petitions had also been received (once again) for a service along Elgar Road, but these, too, were rejected, as it was felt that the new Whitley trolleybus

AEC Regent II 74 (CRD 863), seen here circa early 1950 at the head of the Stations bus lay-by, will shortly depart for Staverton Road. Note the turning circle for the Whitley Wood trolleybus service.

Late W. J. Haynes
© Millane Publishing

193

services, running no real distance away in Southampton Street, might suffer. A special works service already operated morning and evening, of course, serving the CWS printing works in Elgar Road and the CWS preserve works at the Pell Street end of Berkeley Avenue.

With effect from Monday 2nd January 1950, the frequency of route F (Uplands Road – Shinfield Road) was modified, in particular to one of every 12 minutes instead of every 10 minutes after 7.00pm on weekdays; and the frequency of the supplementary service on route I between Donkin Hill and Broad Street was marginally revised.

Co-ordination of the motorbus services to Uplands Road and Woodcote Road was subsequently discussed at the first Transport Committee meetings of 1950. This followed a review of all services in Caversham by the Transport (Future Policy) Sub-Committee, undertaken while investigating the need for a trans-Caversham service to and from Donkin Hill. Mr Evans remained of the opinion that these services could not be combined during the day, but that route F (Shinfield Road – Uplands Road) was adequate in the evenings for the passenger loadings to the whole of Caversham Heights. The users of the Woodcote Road service could see what was coming! There was some orderly protest and a brief reprieve – but the Transport Committee was investigating ways of saving money and, accordingly, from July 1950, as an economy measure to cut out unremunerative mileage, the half-hourly route K (Friar Street GPO – Woodcote Road) was discontinued (Mondays to Saturdays inclusive) after the 7.05pm journey from Friar Street. This provoked two complaints, one from the chairman of Mapledurham Parish Council in the interests of those residents living just over the Oxfordshire boundary *"who looked towards Reading"*. He suggested that there need not be a problem if either (a) Richmond Road (between Woodcote Road and Albert Road/Conisboro' Avenue) was 'made up' (it was at that time a stony, pot-holed track serving only one or two dwellings) or (b) one bus per hour was diverted to Woodcote Road after 7.00pm. This time, however, the complaints were sidelined, in spite of a threat to involve the traffic commissioners.

At the February 1950 Transport Committee meeting, it was the turn of route N, to Emmer Green, to be discussed, it having also been reviewed by the Transport (Future Policy) Sub-Committee in connection with the trans-Caversham deliberations. Requests for a diversion of the route from Buckingham Drive, via Evesham Road and Grove Road, to better serve the newly-built council housing had persisted. Mr Evans, however, was obliged to reject them because of the dangers that would result due to the narrowness, lack of kerbing, open ditches and restricted street lighting along Grove Road. He considered that, particularly in inclement weather, there was a significant risk of a bus going into a ditch and overturning. Indeed, his views had been endorsed by a representative from the traffic commissioners who had inspected the route.

Numerous pleas had been received to re-route inward-running buses from Emmer Green on route N to serve Stations. In reporting to the Transport (Future Policy) Sub-Committee as part of the trans-Caversham investigation, Mr Evans stated that in his opinion *"the new route is satisfactory and I am unable to suggest to the Committee that it be altered"*. Any such request would presumably have been rejected out-of-hand, because of the chief constable's insistence over what he regarded as acceptable and unacceptable vehicle movements at the junction of Station Road and Queen Victoria Street with Friar Street.

The matter was further discussed at the April 1950 Transport Committee meeting, but it was finally decided to make no alteration to existing arrangements. At some stage, the number of peak-hour extra journeys that were superimposed on the basic 12-minute service was increased from two to four in both morning and evening, with an additional evening extra on Thursdays and Fridays only. The evening rush hour Balmore Drive short workings were withdrawn, however, one trip being cut back to run to and from Westfield Road for cater for J. Samuel Elliot Ltd. workers.

Starting in January 1950, the BUT trolleybuses each paid a visit to the paintshop. Presumably, this was when the external livery was enhanced by the extension of the middle cream band above the cab side windows and over the windscreens.

The 1934 Morris 14hp departmental motorcar used by officers and inspectors in the course of their official duties was considered to be long overdue for replacement, and Mr Evans was authorised to order a Morris 8hp motorcar forthwith and to dispose of the old car. At this time, however, there were huge waiting lists for new cars, as the government sought to export as much production as possible in order to pay for essential imports. Indeed, it was a very austere time to be living in Britain. There was 'price control' on most commodities, with Purchase Tax on 'luxury goods'. An increase in personal taxation was having a very profound effect on everyone's individual spending power, to the extent that each and every penny had to be very carefully considered. This was particularly the case when it came to the lower-paid workers, including busmen and the various craftsmen employed at Mill Lane depot, for folk at this level were finding it extremely difficult to meet even the basic cost-of-living. When, for example, economies were effected because the depot canteen started to lose money and simple things, like the price of a cup of tea, were 'put up', sales plummeted to very low levels.

Wintertime is a little gloomy for most people and some inclement weather in early February 1950 caused the department's services on all routes to be hard-pressed, particularly during peak periods. It was not a good time, either, to hold a general election! A Labour government was, however, returned to office but with a much-reduced majority – which put paid to any further nationalisation schemes. Mr Evans, reporting to the Transport Committee at their meeting on 16th February 1950 said *"The problem of handling peak load traffic, both in the morning and evening, is adding appreciably to our operating costs, and it may soon have to be a matter of policy to decide that intending passengers must wait longer for transport at these peak periods. If any members of the Committee can use their influence in other directions, however small, to ease our difficulties at peak times, this will be appreciated"*.

It was not only the peak load traffic on Mondays to Fridays that was a problem. By all accounts the ability to meet the demand for public transport in the borough on Sundays had also become a major problem when we read what 'Chronicler' had to say in 'Reading Week by Week' in the *Berkshire Chronicle* for 31st March 1950:

"Sunday Evening 'Buses – Having of necessity to be out late on Sunday evenings recently, I have heard many adverse comments on Reading's public transport service on this day. I have been unable to do anything but agree when people have said that the 'bus and trolley 'bus service on most, if not all, routes is totally inadequate to meet the needs of the public. The long queues at the various stopping places in

the town provide compelling evidence of the need for an improved service. The situation will assuredly become more acute during the summer, when more people will be out and about. It appears to me that the travelling public on Sunday evenings is as heavy as on Saturdays, and greater than on a Monday. At holiday times normal week-day services are augmented to meet the situation. Why not on Sunday? And would it not be possible to run a later service on Sunday evenings? At present the last 'bus leaves the town centre at the early hour of 10.30pm."

The matter was taken further in a news item in the same newspaper on 2nd June 1950, under the heading *"Sunday Night 'Bus Service – Complaints of its Inadequacy – Changes in the Habits of the People":*

"For some time there has been criticism of the Reading Corporation 'bus service on Sunday nights. One reason appears to be that despite the post-war changes in the habits of the people – Sunday cinema-going is one example – the last 'buses from the town leave at 10.30, an inconveniently early hour in these days. It is particularly inconvenient for people whose homes are on routes served by 15-minute services or services of even less frequency. The position has become aggravated by the longer evenings and the improvement in the weather, resulting in more people being out-of-doors on Sunday nights.

"We have this week received further concrete evidence of the dissatisfaction felt, this time from Emmer Green. Mr. H. R. Willison, of 5, Burnham Rise, Emmer Green, has sent us a copy of a letter written by him to the Transport Manager. In it, he stresses the increasing inadequacy of the Sunday night service to Emmer Green.

"He says that last Sunday night, sixteen passengers, including himself, were left standing at Friar Street because the 'bus was full when it left the town terminus, and it was necessary for him to take a taxi, which he shared with several other people. He adds: 'This happened during a public holiday, when an increase in the normal number of passengers travelling was to be expected'. In view of the above facts and also as your department hold the monopoly of the town's public passenger transport, it is fair to assume that the present state of affairs should have been brought to your notice by your own traffic inspectors.

"The position in Emmer Green is no doubt aggravated by the fact that the Corporation have built a new housing estate there, yet it is understood that 'buses go less frequently than they did."

1939 AEC 661T trolleybus 113 (ARD 676) with 111 (ARD 674) behind, double-parked with motorbus 65 (CRD 259) outside the depot in March 1950. 113 retains its RCT emblem on the front and the running number holders on the cab side it had from new (but which were never used) and the front registration number is still at the bottom of the towing panel (not a good idea when panels could be swapped between vehicles). All of the foregoing will disappear as the W. J. Evans era gathers momentum – 113 and 65 have already lost their triangular AEC badges! Fleet numbers on the nearside front corner – another W. J. Evans touch – were short-lived, eventually replacing the RCT emblem on the front panel.

© *D. A. Jones*

On 6th September 1950 'Chronicler' had this to say in his 'Reading Week by Week' column:

"Last Sunday, in the late afternoon, I spent over twenty minutes waiting for a trolley-'bus. Two came by, but both were full. At that time, many people were going to cinemas or visiting friends and relatives. I'm not suggesting that more transport should be provided on Sunday mornings and in the early afternoon, but the service provided in the late afternoon and evening could be improved. Waiting for 'buses in rainy weather is far from pleasant."

The *Reading Standard* on 13th October 1950 carried the following letter from S. E. Goss, of Shinfield Road:

"May I be permitted to lodge a protest at the Sunday evening bus services in operation on the Shinfield Road route? On a recent Sunday evening a number of people were waiting at the Cressingham Road bus stop at 6 o'clock to board the bus going into town, and I think it is true to say that most of these people were desirous of attending church services. There were upwards of 20 passengers waiting, but, unfortunately, the service bus was full and unable to stop, so that many folk were left behind and possibly arrived late for service. The next bus reached Cressingham Rd. at 6.15. Might I suggest that the Transport Committee of the Corporation give serious thought to providing, say, a single-decker bus at this time, as one can never rely upon catching a bus in time to reach service at the appropriate time.

The same paper, in the issue for on 27th October 1950, carried praise instead, in a letter from 'Elderly Resident':
"May I be permitted, through the medium of your paper, to express my gratitude for the courtesy, patience and kindness received from conductors and conductresses when travelling on Corporation buses? Their assistance is always most willingly rendered."

On 14th October 1949 a plan (No T. 108, see following page) was submitted to the Highways Committee for new cast aluminium timetable cases, which also showed the detail of fastenings to bus stop poles and trolleybus poles. The timetable case was headed with a cast arc which read READING CORPORATION TRANSPORT. It is unknown how many of these cases were manufactured but they were certainly put in place at bus stops at the Stations and in the town centre, and other centres such as Caversham and Tilehurst. Others were placed at the outer termini and at some stops along the inward bus and trolleybus routes in the outer suburbs. These were the first timetable cases to

Very few photographs of Reading's second batch of Bedford OBs, those with Mulliner bodies rather than Duple, seem to have been taken in their very early years. Numbered 68–73 (CRD 591–596) and new in summer 1947, they later became 'maids of all work' and lived a very full life. Bus 70 (CRD 593) is seen here in the depot.

Late L. G. Head © Millane Publishing

be used by RCT and were belated replacements for the time clocks removed during the war. Previously the only written public information was signwritten onto the bus stop flags in the town centre and at Stations, or issued in the timetable booklets. These new timetable cases were painted in municipal dark green, and some of them lasted on the out-of-town stops into the 1970s, with one being sited in the Henley Road passenger shelter well into the 1990s.

There had been more gloom in the spring of 1950 when the government announced its budget. As already mentioned, 9d was put on a gallon of petrol or derv, which was expected to cost the undertaking an extra £5,500 per year, while Purchase Tax of one-third was introduced on commercial vehicles. The undertaking had a Bedford 10/12cwt van on order, still urgently required, which had been sanctioned by the Transport Committee in July 1948 at £325.

Reading had never been over-endowed with passenger shelters; in fact, the provision of shelters was rather poor. A surviving memo dated 6th December 1937 records that there were only ten. However, at the town council meeting on Thursday 7th August 1947 a policy of improvement in the number of bus shelters in the town had been adopted.

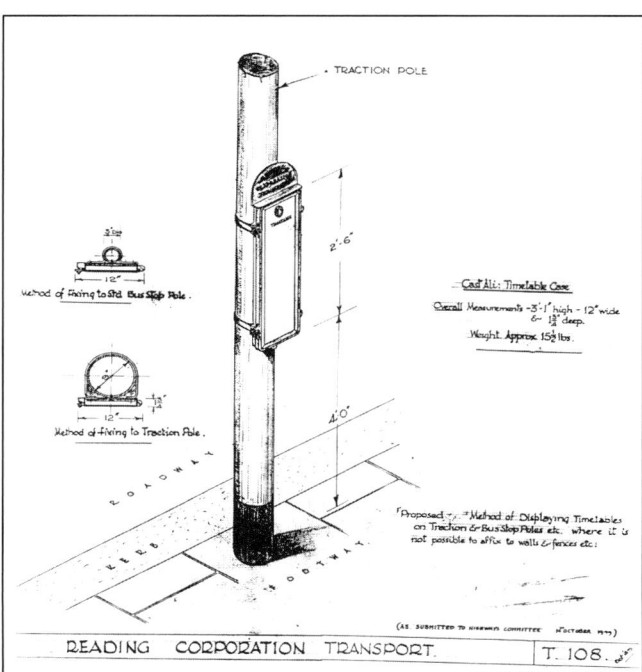

The following week, the *Reading Standard* commented that, at a time when the country was in economic crisis, this was surely not the right time to spend out on bus shelters that hitherto had been done without. At the end of 1948, under an agreement with Messrs William Wynn & Co. Ltd., which included seven year advertising rights, some bus stop shelters were scheduled to be sited in a number of locations. These shelters were distinctive 'bolt together' sectional precast concrete framed structures, 'self-finished' (i.e. plain, undecorated concrete), which, in some locations, lasted into the early 1980s. The first four were erected and in use during the financial year ended 31st March 1949 at the following locations:

Shelter No 1: Caversham Bridge (at the trolleybus terminus loading point)
Shelter No 2: Cemetery Junction (inbound) in Kings Road
Shelter No 3: Callington Rd (inbound) in Northumberland Ave
Shelter No 4: Whitley Street (inbound)

The *Berkshire Chronicle,* in its issue of 15th December 1948, further enlightens us:

"The shelters have a six-ft overhang, compared to the usual four-ft protection, and thus offer better cover from rain. They are made of pre-cast concrete, and should Reading's 'bus queues take a fancy to them, more will be built. All the four should be up by Christmas. Some are 21ft long, making them the biggest 'bus shelters in the town."

By October 1950, however, the arrangements with Wm. Wynn & Co. Ltd., seem to have soured somewhat, possibly because the other six had not materialised but also because the four shelters which had been erected were in no way attractive. Indeed, the owners of the properties adjacent to the one at Caversham Bridge trolleybus terminus would rather have liked the shelter removed and replaced with something else. In an attempt to improve their appearance, they were given a coating of cream paint. The six other shelters scheduled to be erected by Wm. Wynn & Co Ltd. but never built, were as follows:

Shelter No 5: Westfield Road (inbound) in Gosbrook Road
Shelter No 6: Evesham Road (inbound) in Buckingham Drive
Shelter No 7: Lawrence Road (inbound) in Norcot Road
Shelter No 8: Callington Road (inbound) in Basingstoke Rd
Shelter No 9: Grenadier (inbound) in Basingstoke Road
Shelter No 10: Cressingham Road (inbound) in Shinfield Road

Shelter No. 8 was scheduled to replace an earlier type of metal shelter at this location, which was in need of replacement but which, in the event, was retained. The Highways Committee rejected the Transport Committee's proposal to erect Shelter No 6 circa April 1950, the appearance being described as an 'atrocity'! It may be that, as a result, the plans to provide these further six shelters were abandoned.

An appreciation of the dearth of bus shelters in the town will be gained from comments made by Councillor C. R. Evans at a meeting of Caversham Ward Labour Association on Wednesday 5th April 1950, when he said that he was very dissatisfied with the Transport Committee's handling of 'the bus shelter problem'. Only four had been erected in the whole of the town when a good many more were needed, and petitions for their provision at some specific locations had been simply ignored. The shelters, he said, cost the council nothing so he could not understand the complacency of the committee towards such a needed amenity and he was of the opinion that they were both out of touch and sympathy with the travelling public.

Two fairly new shelters sited in the Station Hill lay-by, which became used by the trolleybuses operating on the 'side routes', were handed over to the Transport Department in November 1949 by the Thames Valley Traction Co. Ltd., who had no further use for them, a rental charge of ten shillings a year per shelter payable to British Railways being transferred. These had a red-painted tubular steel framework clad in corrugated asbestos along the back and on the vaulted roof. The framework was quickly repainted Brunswick green because a number of similar red-painted shelters, which were in the vicinity, remained Thames Valley property. The forthcoming transfer failed to escape the attention of 'Chronicler' in his 'Reading Week by Week' column in the *Berkshire Chronicle* for 24th October 1950, with the following comment under 'Tailpiece':

"Isn't it rather curious that Reading Corporation Transport are unable to provide 'bus shelters for passengers at the station, but are not averse to taking over two erected by a private company for the convenience of their passengers."

During 1948, after discussions with the chief constable and the borough surveyor, tubular queue barriers had also been sited at various busy stops in the town centre (and elsewhere in the borough) to control the loadings.

Inconsiderate parking on bus stops was another increasingly common problem, witness 'Chronicler' in his 'Reading Week by Week' column in the *Berkshire Chronicle* for 28th January 1949:

"'Bus Stops and Parking – Is it not time that some action was taken against car and lorry drivers who park their vehicles on 'bus stops? Reading seems to be one of the few towns where such a procedure is allowed. In many other towns of which I know the police take prompt action against offenders. The practice is a danger to other road users and those who desire to board public service vehicles. Only on Thursday I observed a lorry and a car stationary end-to-end right on a stop. This entailed a trolley-'bus pulling up more or less in the centre of the road. Pedestrians had to step out from in front of or behind the parked vehicles in order to reach the trolley-'bus – in itself a dangerous procedure. Some cars following the trolley-'bus turned out to pass, making a third line of traffic, and a danger to vehicles travelling in the opposite direction.

Others pulled up behind the trolley-'bus, making a temporary traffic jam. There is a necessity for 'bus and trolley-'bus stops to be clearly defined in Reading, at any rate at those spots where the passenger traffic is heaviest, and for it to be made an offence to park other vehicles on stops so marked. Less trolley-'bus stops in Broad Street might be necessary to solve the problem."

Nothing was done for over a year. In 1950, it had even become apparent to the powers-that-be that far too much of the available kerb-space, in particular along virtually the whole length of Broad Street, was taken up by bus stops to cater for all the routes operated by Reading Corporation Transport and the Thames Valley Traction Co. Ltd. Initially, this had been due to the huge increase in the numbers of queuing passengers who had had to be catered for during the war. Increasing numbers of private cars in the early post-war years prompted the thoughtless parking of cars on town centre bus stops. The resulting double-parking of buses while loading had already become a problem, because, in turn, it impeded the flow of through traffic.

It was decided that, to free up some of the kerbside for on-street car parking, some 'combining' of certain motorbus stops would have to be adopted, together with the creation of 'bus bays', some of them between 50 and 80 feet long, marked out on the road. Stops in Blagrave Street, Friar Street, Station Road, West Street, Oxford Road, St Mary's Butts, Broad Street and Kings Road were identified as possible sites. At certain stops, particularly in Broad Street, there would have to be a re-introduction of the somewhat unsatisfactory 'two-way queuing' arrangements, which had been used during the war. However, it was proposed that barriers be introduced to protect those passengers who were obliged to queue with their backs to oncoming traffic. It was also suggested that the two stops on the 'main line' trolleybus routes in each direction in Broad Street (the westbound stops outside Wellsteeds and Boots and eastbound outside the Vaudeville and The Arcade) might be reduced to one, either half-way between or by retaining just those outside Boots and the Vaudeville. The sheer size of the queues at each stop at peak times precluded this at the time, although in Mr Evans' opinion there were a number of administrative advantages to having only one stopping point in each direction.

There were also thoughts of providing overtaking loops in the trolleybus overhead wiring at the Broad Street 'main line' stops to facilitate the operation of 'Broad Street Specials' and to allow trolleybuses returning to depot to pass trolleybuses standing in the marked bays. However, all of this was being considered against a background of plans by the borough surveyor to install large floral traffic islands down the centre of Broad Street in order to 'pretty-up' the town centre, all of which was to be paid for as a result of a bequest to the town. However welcome they might have been to enhance the town centre environment, such traffic islands were bound to be somewhat obstructive, given the levels of through traffic and passenger transport requirements in what, at this time, was the main A329 through route! Certainly the possibility of having passing loops in Broad Street surfaced again in July 1951. Broad Street did not get its floral traffic islands; what it did get, later in the 1950s, were double flower baskets mounted at about upper-deck bus window height on each and every traction pole – a definite asset to the town at the time!

The following letter from 'Black Sheep' appeared in the *Berkshire Chronicle* of 18th August 1950:

"Trolley-'Bus Stops: Sir – I see that proposals have been put forward to relieve the traffic congestion in Broad Street by the discontinuance of the trolley-'bus stops at the Arcade and the erection of long "cattle compounds" in the vicinity of the Vaudeville.

"Surely, one of the principal causes for this alleged congestion is the long wait which occurs outside the Vaudeville, presumably for 'bus operators to adjust their time-schedules. This wait could be done outside Broad Street.

"But in any case, the Arcade stop is a tradition itself and serves a useful purpose in gathering the Vaudeville overflow at a place in Broad Street where the pavement is widest. If the plan is carried into effect I foresee a huge pedestrian bottle-neck and a continuous queue of passengers all day long in a new-fangled sheep-pen for we hapless travellers of the regimented era."

Meanwhile, work was progressing in the construction of the new garaging and workshop facility at Bennet Road and, during April 1950, tenders were invited for the construction of 7,000 square yards of *in situ* concrete paving, inspection pits, brickwork and drainage, etc.

From Monday 24th April 1950, some fundamental changes were made in the operation of the 'main line' trolleybus services. The separate identification of a trolleybus route in operation between Liverpool Road and Norcot was withdrawn, the Norcot destination becoming shown only as a short-working of one or other of the 'main line' routes and, in the later months of 1950, an inbound overtaking loop was also provided at Norcot, opposite the Pulsometer Engineering Company's works, in order to allow trolleybuses waiting time under the wires not to have to de-pole. On Mondays to Saturdays, route B (Kentwood – Norcot – Wokingham Road) was altered to operate as route C (Kentwood – Norcot – Liverpool Road) as it already did on Sunday afternoons; the frequency on route A (Wokingham Road – Tilehurst) was increased, in particular to serve the expanding Mayfair housing estate; and route B became simply a short-working of route A which turned at Norcot.

Following a lack of interest shown by the passenger transport industry in any further use for four of the 'experimental' trolleybuses withdrawn in 1949 (Sunbeam MF2A 101; Guy BT 103; Leyland TB4 104; and Ransomes 105); all six, 101–106, were advertised for sale by tender on 8th April 1950. At this time AEC 661T trolleybus 102 and Sunbeam MF2A trolleybus 106 were still in use, but 106 was withdrawn after service on 31st May 1950. Trolleybus 102 was not, in fact, withdrawn until after operation on 31st October 1950. J. C. Lewis, of Maidenhead, successfully tendered for all six vehicles on 29th April 1950, but there were obviously second thoughts by the undertaking about the withdrawal and disposal of 102. A letter to the dealer, dated 1st June 1950, advised that it had been found necessary to retain 102 'for a few more months', due to the postponed delivery of new vehicles; and that 105 would now to be sold without its electrical gear, as this had been presented to Reading Technical School. Upon payment of £210 for the five vehicles, J. C. Lewis collected 101 and 103–106 on 19th June 1950 and subsequently broke them up in his yard in Maidenhead.

As already recounted, it was around this time, too, that 'unused' Karriers 164–166, 168 and 169 (final numbers!) were removed from the yard at Crescent Road to outside storage at the Bennet Road depot site, where they were eventually broken up.

Another disposal at this time was a large stock of tubular steel traction poles which, Mr Evans had declared at the Transport Committee meeting on 10th May 1950, were surplus to requirements as he *"...did not anticipate any large extensions of our trolleybus system within the next few years"*. Evidently, thoughts of extending the trolleybus system over Caversham Bridge into Caversham village, as

BUT trolleybus 140 (DRD 126), southbound in Caversham Road near Stanshawe Road, has gained some cream paint above the side cab windows and over the windscreens, which improves the appearance somewhat. The original destination blinds are evident, however, and the photograph would appear to have been taken circa 1950. Caversham Road railway bridge is in the background on the extreme left and W. M. Paulette's bakery can be seen on the corner of Tudor Road, along which traffic reached the Stations via Station Hill.

Late W. J. Haynes © Millane Publishing

AEC Regent 10 (RD 5361) probably acquired its 'long' radiator at the time its original petrol engine was replaced by an oil engine circa 1946/47. It is seen here parked driverless in St. Mary's Butts, most likely as a spare vehicle, circa summer 1950. Compare this with the view of the same bus on page 175.

© M. Manning

authorised in the Acts of 1914 and 1946, were 'on hold' yet again. It seems that the increasing value of the traction poles in a time of inflation made their sale attractive – especially when balanced against storage costs. At the same time, Mr Evans noted, there was the possibility of using cheaper pre-stressed concrete poles, which could be used experimentally *"...along the accommodation roadway and within the new depot in Basingstoke Road"*. This type of traction pole had been used on the Tolworth Loop in the Kingston district of the London Transport area but, in the event, it did not find favour in Reading.

The greatest number of trolleybuses in service on the Reading system at any one time was 57; this total was achieved when, on 1st June 1950, a fifth Karrier, 163 (VH 6752), ex-Huddersfield 409, entered service, effectively replacing Sunbeam MF2A 106. The fleet then comprised:

AEC 661T	102 and 107–131	=	26
Sunbeam W	132–137	=	6
BUT 9611T	138–157	=	20
Karrier E6	158–160/162/163	=	5

Finances were still tight and, in the undertaking's 1949/50 annual report, Mr Evans warned that *"...the Committee will sooner or later have to consider the problem of either increasing revenue or decreasing costs"*. The department had, in fact, made a trading loss of £1,500 compared to a profit of £13,389 the previous year. Around 395,000 fewer passengers had helped reduce total income by nearly £5,000. It was considered that there had been a drastic change of passenger habit as a result of every taxpayer having to make personal economies resulting from having less to spend because of higher taxation. Certain 'little gems' not recorded anywhere else come to light in annual reports. For example, in the 1949/50 annual report, three Nissen huts were purchased, two of which were erected at Mill Lane depot (in East Yard) as badly-needed storage space – one for timber, the other for tyres. It is also of interest to learn that after twelve years' service and reduced maintenance during the war years, some of the 1938/39-vintage AEC trolleybuses were 'in a very bad state' and may have already been earmarked for withdrawal upon receipt of the new three-axle vehicles. It is also interesting to learn that it was tentatively the intention to obtain 12 further trolleybuses in 1952 and six in 1953 as part of a replacement programme, although this was likely to be postponed two or three years depending on the condition of the existing vehicles.

A scheme was implemented at this time to construct a turning circle at a roundabout in Northumberland Avenue at its junction with Torrington Road, just past South Reading Community Centre, in order to provide a short-working facility on the Northumberland Avenue route. It was erected late in the evenings of 14th and 21st July 1950, with regular use commencing on 7th August 1950, the location being identified as 'Community Centre'. Of the trolleybuses then in stock, this destination was gradually added to the destination blinds of the BUTs although, in the short-term, 'slip boards' were used, propped up in the nearside cab windscreen. The reason for concentrating on equipping just the BUTs with the correct destination was that the utility trolleybuses were about to be withdrawn, the AECs were very rarely in service on the 'side road' anyway, and the Karriers were rarely to be used on the specials which turned here, at least not at this stage of their careers in Reading. It is interesting to note that the destination blinds fitted to the Karriers contained **BUCKLAND RD. CIRCLE** (and also **WANTAGE RD**). Neither location was ever provided with a turning facility in the overhead wiring, and the Karriers were devoid of any battery traction facility – so any thoughts of turning them short at these locations was an impossibility!

At the town council meeting of 1st August 1950, Councillor A. E. Smith, who, it will be recalled, was himself the operator of a large fleet of luxury coaches, made reference to the Transport Committee's annual statement of accounts with a number of rather pertinent observations. Whilst acknowledging that the department had lost £1,500 on the year and that the fleet had been worked extremely hard during the war, there was a lot of leeway to be made up. About £56,000 was owed on the trolleybus installation, comprising the overhead wiring and the new Mill Lane depot facility, while £170,000 was owed on rolling stock, the interest and repayments resulting costing over £11,000 a year. In addition, 12 trolleybuses and 12 motorbuses were on order, at a cost of £126,000 and the suggested programme for more rolling stock was going to cost another £94,000. It had also been agreed to borrow £52,000 to pay for the new premises off Basingstoke Road, for which the full interest costs would be £2,800 per annum. The undertaking was subject to rates payments amounting to £10,000, while the yearly administrative costs of the department had increased from £1,100 in 1942 to a current £9,560. *"Your total interest and repayments this year on rolling stock amounts to £23,000. Next year the cost will be £37,000, and the following year £52,000"*, he warned. *"Next year you look like losing £15,000 and the following year £30,000"*, he added. He considered that the matter called for serious consideration. Fares were already too high and he suggested that they be reduced; increasing them would be counter-productive, as it would drive passengers away and lose them revenue. As there was £74,000 in the reserve fund (it turned out that £24,000 of this was represented by the depreciation fund), he wanted to know why some of it could not be used to pay off outstanding debts and thus avoid having to pay colossal interest charges. If the matter was not given careful consideration, in the not too distant future he could foresee the council having to contribute £20,000 or £30,000 a year in order just to keep the wheels turning – a stern warning if ever there was one!

An interesting experiment commenced on 25th August 1950 involving BUT trolleybus 154, for it re-entered service fitted with fluorescent saloon lighting; although not actually the first, it was one of the earliest vehicles in the United Kingdom to be so equipped. The difference in lighting levels compared with tungsten filament lamps was astonishing, but it was evidently deemed premature to consider having fluorescent saloon lighting fitted to the twelve Sunbeam three-axle trolleybuses, which were 'in build' at that time. Although the lighting equipment was modernised in later years, 154 retained fluorescent saloon lighting for the rest of its life.

The unsatisfactory state of the wood block paving to the roadway at Erleigh Road bus terminus, at the junction of Erleigh Road with Addington Road, which had remained the responsibility of the Transport Department from tramway days, resulted in work being put in hand in September 1950 to remove the wood blocks and level and resurface the area using tarmacadam.

As winter approached, a serious problem was developing over an increasing shortage of drivers and conductors. During the months of June, July and August 1950, no less than 45 men had left the service, a good many of them going to work at the new Ford Motor Company tractor works at Langley where, as unskilled assemblers on a five-day week, their work turned out to be very remunerative. Only 32 replacements (including nine women) had been recruited, so that with a net loss of 13 it was becoming increasingly difficult to find enough staff to work even the timetabled services, especially at peak times.

The *Berkshire Chronicle* carried an intriguing little news item in its 3rd November 1950 issue:

"Passengers push – Some passengers got off and helped pedestrians push a trolley-'bus which broke down at the Cemetery Junction, Reading, last Friday evening. Traffic proceeding to Wokingham was held up for ten minutes and Thames Valley 'buses were diverted along the London Road until the trolley-'bus was pushed out of the way. A fault in the overhead lines was believed to be responsible."

Might this have been an ex-Huddersfield Karrier on a dead section – or something wrong with the Cemetery Junction short-turn facility in the overhead wiring?

Evidently taken sometime during the summer of 1950, AEC 661T trolleybus 102 (RD 8086) was by now the last of the six original trolleybuses, all of which were lowbridge, to remain in passenger service. It is seen here at Liverpool Road terminus prior to a trip to Kentwood on what is now designated as route C.

© M. Manning

22   1950: Moving On

When some of the twelve Sunbeam S7s were ready at Park Royal Coachworks, arrangements were made for their inspection and tilt-testing. On 11th October 1950, 174 was taken to London Transport Executive's bus overhaul works at Aldenham and tilted beyond the legal requirement, the angle of tilt reaching 26° 30' for the chassis and 30° for the body. At Park Royal, 170 was inspected by officials from the undertaking and the Ministry of Transport, in the company of Park Royal's chief inspector, following which some minor adjustments were requested.

Trolleybus 174 had, in fact, been an exhibit at the Commercial Motor Show at Earls Court, London, between 22nd and 30th September 1950, for which purpose it had certain cosmetic refinements, in particular chromium-plated windscreen frames (instead of painted brass). It retained these throughout its life, together with other similarly-treated internal fittings and interior side panelling, which the rest of the batch lacked initially. Meanwhile, 170 was delivered to Reading on 13th October 1950 and 174 was noted at the depot on 20th October 1950.

The new trolleybuses appeared as gigantic vehicles compared with the rest of the fleet (with the possible exception, perhaps, of the Karriers). The bodywork design was not altogether unlike that of the BUTs in appearance, except that the nearside rear upper-deck 'bulge' housing the platform door mechanism had been eliminated and the side destination box moved from high over the platform doors to a position above the rearmost nearside lower-deck saloon window. Most strikingly, front and rear destination boxes were surmounted by a triple-track route number box, all three tracks being turned to a white blank at the end of the blind. It was said that route numbers would be introduced once a substantial proportion of the fleet was equipped to display them, which was expected to be around a decade from this time. In fact, the undertaking did not introduce route numbers until 1964 but, from 1950 on, all new buses were thus equipped.

Delivery of the remainder of the twelve Park Royal-bodied Sunbeam S7 three-axle trolleybuses, 170–181 (ERD 141–152) took place in October and November 1950, and all twelve entered service in November/December 1950. Further details will be found in Appendix A. Concurrently, the twelve Crossley-bodied Crossley DD42/8 motorbuses, 84–95 (ERD 153–164), were also delivered, entering service in November and December. Further details of these will also be found in Appendix A. Numbers 84, 85, 87, 89, 92 and 95 entered service on 1st November 1950 on route I (Donkin Hill – Horncastle). When the remaining Crossleys entered service a month later, they took over operation of route M (Erleigh Road – Grovelands) and route P (Stations – Staverton Road). When new, all was not well with the Crossleys, but that story will have to wait until a subsequent volume is published!

An interesting point derived from a surviving memo is that, having reserved a block of 24 consecutive index numbers with the Reading CBC Motor Taxation Office, originally it was intended that the trolleybuses would carry the registrations eventually carried by the Crossley motorbuses and vice versa. The reason for the trolleybuses originally being allocated ERD 153–164 was, in all probability, to avoid ERD 141–143, because BUT trolleybuses 155–157 were registered DRD 141–143 and there was thus an opportunity for error in identifying vehicles during their lives. It is not apparent, however, as to why the change was made to that which finally resulted, but it is likely that having reserved the 24 index numbers, it was management who decided which batch would be which but the manufacturers were advised 'the wrong way round' or, in actually allocating the numbers at the County Borough of Reading Motor Vehicle Licensing Office, a clerk allocated the batches 'the wrong way round' when preparing the log books. Certainly, from photographic evidence, trolleybus 174 carried ERD 145 at the time it was tilt-tested, while a pre-delivery photograph of Crossley 89 shows it carrying its finally-correct registration ERD 158.

Some minor motorbus timetable modifications were introduced with effect from Monday 6th November 1950. Route I (Donkin Hill – Horncastle) was retimed after 10.07pm; an evening service after 7.05pm was re-introduced on route K (Woodcote Road – Friar Street (GPO)), which ran hourly (which prompts the question as to what the bus might have been doing for the rest of the time, because a round trip on route K took less than half-an-hour); and on Sunday evenings an extra journey was added on route H (Emmer Green – Friar Street Triangle). There were further improvements to route H with effect from 20th November 1950. On Saturdays there was an increased service – every 10 minutes instead of every 12 minutes between 11.00am and 6.00pm – and extras 'as required'; and on Monday to

AEC 661T trolleybus 111 (ARD 674), bound for Norcot, moves onto the Cemetery Junction roundabout after its trip down Wokingham Road from the terminus. In this late afternoon view taken in 1950, note the front fleet number position, between nearside headlamp and foglamp, while the RCT emblem is retained in the centre of the dash panel.

Late W. J. Haynes
© Maiwand Photographic Archive

201

Saturday an earlier first round trip was introduced, departing Emmer Green at 6.30am to connect with trains at 6.45am and 6.50am. Matters still were not right with route H, however, and, at the same time as the foregoing improvements were made, a further petition was received. This asked for (a) restoration of the direct link with Whitley; (b) the restoration of a basic 10-minute frequency; (c) an improved peak hour service; and (d) an even earlier start by weekday buses, to connect with the 6.12am train to Slough and London. These demands will be more properly dealt with in a future volume.

On 10th November 1950, Brigadier Langley again visited Reading, this time to inspect the Sunbeam S7s. Having inspected 178, only recently delivered and yet to enter service, he boarded 174 for a brake test. In order to simulate a fully loaded vehicle, the equivalent weight in bags of ballast was distributed throughout the vehicle and it left the depot with two tons on the upper deck and 1½ on the lower deck, with only six seats on each deck left free for the inspection party. Following this test, the Brigadier, noting that the vehicle had an 'all-metal' body, requested an insulation test on the platform and grab rails to ensure that there was no leakage of electricity. He also went to see the new overhead installations at Norcot and Community Centre and the opportunity was also taken to study proposals for the new Bennet Road depot, then under construction.

As a result of the deliveries of so many new vehicles, there was something of a 'clear-out' of vehicles deemed to be life-expired and/or surplus to requirements.

Dealing first with the trolleybuses, the last remaining 1936 'experimental' trolleybus, AEC 661T 102, was officially withdrawn on 31st October 1950. On the same date, 1938/39 AEC 661T trolleybuses 107–112 were also withdrawn with a view to selling them for further service elsewhere. Indeed, the disposal schedules were actually prepared, but after some discussion at a meeting of the town council on 5th December 1950, the Transport Committee was asked to reconsider its decision. This it did, when it met on 15th December 1950, and 107–112 were 'put into mothballs' instead. At 56 seats, the smaller capacity of the AECs, compared with the 64-seat ex-Huddersfield Karriers and new 68-seat Sunbeam S7s, made them obvious targets for withdrawal and they were stored at Bennet Road with the derelict Huddersfield Karriers and AEC trolleybus 102. All were parked in the open but eventually, in April 1951, 107–112 were moved into the as yet uncompleted depot building.

The six Park Royal-bodied utility Sunbeam W trolleybuses, 132–137, were withdrawn a month later, on 30th November 1950. There had been serious consideration of retaining these vehicles, which were only seven years old, and a report was prepared during August 1950 which looked at the possibility of rebodying the chassis with bodies to the recently increased overall plan dimensions of 8ft wide x 27ft long. This included a detailed examination of the technical issues and chassis modifications necessary to facilitate re-bodying. However, due to the hard ride they gave on Reading's rough roads, it was decided to scrap them. After service on 30th November 1950, they were delicenced, having been advertised for sale on 2nd November 1950, stripped of useful parts and stored at Bennet Road pending disposal. They were removed for breaking, together with 1936 AEC 661T 102, in January 1951, by J. C. Lewis, of Maidenhead. It will be noted that, in effect, the aforementioned trolleybuses were replaced on a one-for-one basis by the twelve new Sunbeam S7s and the last ex-Huddersfield Karrier to be rebuilt, 161 (VH 6759), which entered service on 1st February 1951.

Turning now to the motorbus withdrawals, in the same schedule, dated 2nd November 1950, the sole-remaining utility Guy Arab, the AEC-engined 27, was listed, together with eleven of the oldest remaining pre-war oil-engined AEC Regents (5, 10, 11, 25, 46, 49, 50, 51, 52, 53, 54) so that, in effect, these twelve motorbuses were actually replaced on a one-for-one basis by the Crossleys. In fact, buses 5, 10, 25, 46, 49 and 52 were withdrawn on 31st October 1950 and 11, 27, 50, 51, 53 and 54 were withdrawn on 30th November 1950. Offered for sale by tender in the local papers on 10th November 1950, they were all purchased by Messrs. Beech's Garage, of Hanley, Stoke-on-Trent, for £2,130 the lot, and were collected in batches of four between 18th and 24th December 1950. All twelve of them found re-use at subsequent homes; the final utility motorbus, 27, ended its days first with K & M, Worksop, passing to Major's Coaches of Worksop, before finally moving on to East Midland Motor Services.

It is interesting to note that the foregoing included bus 5, the vehicle on which considerable money must have been spent in having the body rebuilt and re-styled by Vincents of Reading Ltd. in 1946. Also of note is that whilst sister vehicles 11 and 46 were sold out of the fleet, the third of this 1935-vintage trio, 47, re-entered service on 1st November 1950 following an extensive body rebuild, the most noticeable external feature of which, to the casual observer, was an enlargement of the front destination box to what had now become the standard width. If it had not been altered, it would have been the only motorbus left in the fleet with a small pre-1936-sized front destination display. There is no surviving documentation as to why, specifically, 47 was the subject of such an exercise but it would appear to have been an experiment to investigate the cost of maintaining the metal-framed Park Royal bodies of the remaining pre-war AEC Regents over the next few years as an alternative to buying replacement buses at an early date. Equally, there is no apparent reason why bus 48 was selected to be retained – for, together with 47, it was to remain in passenger service for a further six years. Remember, too, that a few months earlier, the undertaking had become a little cash-strapped, soon after it was mooted that six replacement motorbuses would be required in the next two years or so. Alternatively, the experiment may have been conducted with a view to also retaining 11 and 46 (the first buses with metal-framed bodies to be sold) but the cost, as occurred in the London Transport fleet with some metal-bodied STL-class buses stored during the war, proved to be uneconomic. The experiment, however, appears to have paid off in other respects, because no new rolling stock was delivered to the undertaking for five years – until the end of 1955 (entering service in January 1956) – and the last pre-war AEC Regents were not withdrawn until the end of 1958! This rebuild (and doubtless its associated cost) was, on the other hand, undoubtedly responsible for 47's long survival in the Reading fleet, until withdrawal in February 1956. A continuing active life after its disposal from Reading eventually ensured its being obtained for preservation by local enthusiasts.

A bout of winter weather bringing a thin covering of snow and icy road conditions took a hold during the first week of December 1950. This heralded more extensive power cuts in the weeks leading up to the Season of Good Cheer as the cold spell persisted. 'Chronicler', in his usual form in The *Berkshire Chronicle*, acknowledged with thanks and

Instantly recognisable as the only utility to carry an advert on the front above the destination box – and the only one to carry its registration number at the very bottom of the panel – trolleybus 134 (BRD 799) turns into Kings Road from the new 'bone-shaped' roundabout at Cemetery Junction on its way to town and Norcot. This vehicle was rebuilt in October 1945 with a nearside 'square' destination box over the platform and a horizontal waistrail round the cab (instead of retaining the 'dip' at each side where the window depth was increased). The vehicle returned to service following its rebuild on 7th November 1945.

Late W. J. Haynes
© Maiwand Photographic Archive

appreciation the work put in by corporation busmen keeping the wheels turning, usually well up to schedule, in treacherous driving conditions. On the other hand, by all accounts, snow clearance of the borough's roads was very poor – and 'Chronicler' said so!

1950 ended with the purchase of a further 6.6 acres of land adjacent to the Bennet Road depot site from the Highways & Drainage Committee, to allow for future expansion of the facilities, at a cost of £16,500. It also ended with alarm bells ringing and urgent consideration having to be given by the Transport (Future Policy) Sub-Committee to the need for another fares rise because operating costs had increased in excess of anything anticipated. The price of derv had increased yet again, by another farthing a gallon on 14th October 1950, but the main increase in operating costs stemmed from wage awards to virtually every member of staff and associated increases in National Insurance charges.

It was simply not possible to accommodate an 'unexpected' increase in this direction alone of in the region of £20,000 per annum within the parameters of the time. But it is a story which will have to be recounted in detail in a future volume. 1950 had seen the abolition of petrol rationing for private motorists and this freedom, coupled with sufficient cars being permitted by the government to be built for home use (instead of nearly all being exported, as in the early post-war years) produced a growth in private car ownership throughout the 1950s. This, in turn, became a significant factor in the decline in bus traffic thereafter. In many ways, 1950 was the turning point for the bus industry – and for Reading Corporation Transport. The undertaking had already seen the end of large numbers of its over-worked pre-war motorbuses and all of its wartime utility vehicles, with the fleet, both bus and trolleybus, being largely renewed – and its buses and trolleybuses were no longer threatened with nationalisation! As the nation moved out of

The new roundabout at Cemetery Junction gave the undertaking a heaven-sent opportunity to incorporate a trolleybus turn-back facility when the overhead wiring was modified to suit the new road layout. The transport manager was quick to put this to use: regular Monday – Friday peak hour 'extras' were timetabled, turning short at each end of the 'main line' by working Cemetery Junction to Westwood Road, Tilehurst. BUT 9611T trolleybus 141 (DRD 127), working such an extra, is seen here turning at Cemetery Junction for a trip to Westwood Road in the spring of 1950.

Late W. J. Haynes © Maiwand Photographic Archive

the bankruptcy and austerity of the immediate post-war years, it became more affluent and spent its money on cars, televisions and other electrical goods, keeping up with the Jones's, developing a liking for holidays abroad and generally ensuring that it had what had been promised after the Great War but which had never materialised – a utopia – a land fit for heroes. A decade later it was told that it had *"never had it so good..."*. Not, however, for the bus industry, for in retrospect the seeds of decline were being sown by the very same nation from 1950 onwards....

In conclusion, then, what better way is there than setting down in print the sort of town that Reading had become at the time this particular volume is concluded? It so happens that in its edition for Friday, 29th December 1950, the Reading Standard carried a review, as it affected Reading, of a book entitled "*The Marketing Survey of the UK*", published by Business Publications Ltd.:

"Reading, to judge by the new edition of 'The Marketing Survey of the United Kingdom', is a town of civil servants and grocers.

"The number of retail grocers is given as 275, the top figure for all businesses, the town's 172 fully-licensed premises coming a poor second. Tobacconists – there are 148 – come next, followed by confectioners (137) and fruit and greengrocers (130). Stationers and newsagents top the century mark with 113. There are 96 butchers, but only 64 bakers.

"The importance of clothes to a woman is emphasized by the number of women's outfitters. There are 74 against 36 for the mere male. Strangely enough there are only 60 women's hairdressers and beauty shops but 63 men's hairdressers. Meals out should present no problems to local people or visitors, for 92 cafes are open to the general public. Always popular are the fish and chip shops, and these total 49, although there are only 33 fishmongers."

"At the lower end of the scale come sports stores – there are only seven; music shops, four; milk-bars and herbalists, two; and one health food store.

"Of a total of 49,927 men and women employed in the town, 11,005 are engaged on National and Local Government service, the largest number working at any one job. Only 3,574 are employed in the food, drink and tobacco trades, and still fewer – 2,891 – on building and civil engineering. There are 1,507 engaged on the land, and 1,288 in hotels and boarding houses. The printing and paper industry accounts for 1,709, whilst 2,950 work on transport and communications. Other manufacturing industries account for 9,841, and there are even six men engaged in mining.

"To look after our health, there are 61 doctors on the National Health list and 40 dentists, while education is looked after by 577 teachers.

"The population, 97,149 in 1931, is now estimated at 115,500, and although Reading is by no means the most prosperous town in the country – a position held [jointly] by Bournemouth and Hove – its incomes levels index is 104 compared with an average of 100 for the 145 largest cities and towns.

"There are 2,062 television owners, and 41,947 wireless licences taken out annually, whilst 8,771 people keep a dog. The number of private car owners has only increased slightly since 1938. Then the total was 4,901. Now it is 5,197."

In Reading, at the end of 1950, the future for the transport undertaking seemed secure but staff shortages, increasing traffic congestion and falling passenger numbers throughout the next decade would challenge the hopes generated during the early post-war boom years. Looking back, it can be seen that, despite the difficulties, the immediate post-war years, the years of austerity, were the classic days of bus travel, with an unprecedented passenger demand of bus rides for both shopping, entertainment and other leisure activities, and for getting to and from work.

Nationally, those demands were met with a degree of imagination and fortitude by a bus industry grappling with the problems of aged vehicles and the restricted availability and protracted delivery of new vehicles. In that battle, the response by Reading Corporation Transport was similarly imaginative and the Transport Department, in what was still a small provincial town, served its townspeople really well throughout the latter 1940s, the years of austerity, as it had done earlier in the decade, the years of adversity.

Ex-Huddersfield Karrier E6 six-wheeled trolleybus 162 (VH 6755), bound for Kentwood is running over cobbles and tarred-in tram rail in London Road as it approaches the new roundabout at Cemetery Junction. This is the main A4 trunk road from London to Bath and Bristol. Where is all the traffic on this sunny spring evening in 1950?

Late W. J. Haynes
© Maiwand Photographic Archive

Appendix A — Rolling Stock List (Vehicles Acquired 1939–1950)

MOTORBUSES

Fleet No.	Reg'n No.	Chassis Make & Type	Chassis Number	Body Make	Body Layout	Body Number	Date Delivered	Date Into Service	Date Withdrawn
6	BRD 754	Guy Arab	FD.25595	Strachan	UL27/28R	?	17.11.42	14.12.42	31.08.49
7	BRD 755	Guy Arab	FD.25644	Strachan	UL27/28R	?	01.02.43	20.02.43	31.08.49
27	BRD 815	Guy Arab	FD.25897	Strachan	UL27/28R	?	27.05.43	08.07.43	30.11.50
28	BRD 816	Guy Arab	FD.25857	Strachan	UL27/28R	?	21.04.43	02.06.43	31.08.49
12	CDP 231	Bedford OB	OB.17285	Duple	B30F	41982	16.04.46	29.04.46	31.10.48
13	CDP 232	Bedford OB	OB.17210	Duple	B30F	41983	17.04.46	01.05.46	14.10.48
15	CDP 233	Bedford OB	OB.18744	Duple	B30F	41984	18.04.46	01.05.46	14.10.48
16	CDP 234	Bedford OB	OB.19802	Duple	B30F	41985	30.04.46	06.05.46	15.10.48
17	CDP 235	Bedford OB	OB.19808	Duple	B30F	41986	26.04.46	07.05.46	31.10.48
18	CDP 236	Bedford OB	OB.17207	Duple	B30F	41987	01.05.46	08.05.46	31.10.48
58	CRD 252	AEC Regent II	O661.7531	Park Royal	L24/26R	B32474	11.01.47	01.02.47	30.08.61
59	CRD 253	AEC Regent II	O661.7532	Park Royal	L24/26R	B32478	17.01.47	17.02.47	07.08.62
60	CRD 254	AEC Regent II	O661.7533	Park Royal	L24/26R	B32477	16.01.47	01.02.47	31.08.62
61	CRD 255	AEC Regent II	O661.7541	Park Royal	L24/26R	B32475	11.01.47	06.02.47	31.08.62
62	CRD 256	AEC Regent II	O661.7542	Park Royal	L24/26R	B32476	16.01.47	*	*
63	CRD 257	AEC Regent II	O661.7938	Park Royal	L24/26R	B32748	04.02.47	01.03.47	06.09.62
64	CRD 258	AEC Regent II	O661.7939	Park Royal	L24/26R	B32747	30.01.47	06.02.47	30.08.61
65	CRD 259	AEC Regent II	O661.7940	Park Royal	L24/26R	B32746	25.01.47	01.03.47	28.08.62
66	CRD 260	AEC Regent II	O661.7941	Park Royal	L24/26R	B32744	23.01.47	01.02.47	30.08.61
67	CRD 261	AEC Regent II	O661.7942	Park Royal	L24/26R	B32745	25.01.47	01.03.47	25.08.61
68	CRD 591	Bedford OB	OB.50034	Mulliner	B32F	T24	17.05.47	14.06.47	31.10.59
69	CRD 592	Bedford OB	OB.51818	Mulliner	B32F	T46	11.06.47	15.08.47	08.02.60
69	CRD 592	Bedford OB	OB.51818	Mulliner	B29F	T46	§	01.03.62	19.02.64
70	CRD 593	Bedford OB	OB.55229	Mulliner	B32F	T72	17.07.47	05.09.47	31.10.59
71	CRD 594	Bedford OB	OB.56022	Mulliner	B32F	T82	20.08.47	01.11.47	04.09.63
72	CRD 595	Bedford OB	OB.58414	Mulliner	B32F	T102	05.09.47	01.11.47	21.02.63
73	CRD 596	Bedford OB	OB.61684	Mulliner	B32F	T122	03.10.47	06.12.47	31.08.61
62 *	CRD 256	AEC Regent II	O661.7542	Park Royal	L26/26R	B33218	17.09.48	18.09.48	06.09.62
74	CRD 863	AEC Regent II	O661.8086	Park Royal	L26/26R	B33219	c. 25.09.48	01.10.48	28.09.62
75	CRD 864	AEC Regent II	O661.8087	Park Royal	L26/26R	B33220	c. 25.09.48	01.10.48	27.09.62
76	CRD 865	AEC Regent II	O661.8088	Park Royal	L26/26R	B33221	. .48	01.11.48	30.06.64
77	CRD 866	AEC Regent II	O661.8089	Park Royal	L26/26R	B33222	. .48	08.10.48	29.06.64
78	CRD 867	AEC Regent II	O661.8090	Park Royal	L26/26R	B33223	. .48	08.10.48	30.06.64
79	CRD 868	AEC Regent II	O661.8091	Park Royal	L26/26R	B33224	. .48	01.11.48	30.06.64
80	CRD 869	AEC Regent II	O661.8092	Park Royal	L26/26R	B33225	. .48	01.11.48	21.07.64
81	CRD 870	AEC Regent II	O661.8093	Park Royal	L26/26R	B33226	. .48	01.11.48	31.07.64
82	CRD 871	AEC Regent II	O661.8094	Park Royal	L26/26R	B33227	. .48	01.11.48	31.07.64
83	CRD 872	AEC Regent II	O661.8095	Park Royal	L26/26R	B33228	23.10.48	01.11.48	31.07.64
84	ERD 153	Crossley DD42/8	94931	Crossley	L26/26RD	?	14.09.50 ¶	01.11.50	31.01.67
85	ERD 154	Crossley DD42/8	94932	Crossley	L26/26RD	?	14.09.50 ¶	01.11.50	28.08.68
86	ERD 155	Crossley DD42/8	94935	Crossley	L26/26RD	?	26.10.50	01.12.50	14.07.67
87	ERD 156	Crossley DD42/8	94936	Crossley	L26/26RD	?	14.09.50 ¶	01.11.50	28.08.68
88	ERD 157	Crossley DD42/8	94937	Crossley	L26/26RD	?	26.10.50	01.12.50	31.01.67
89	ERD 158	Crossley DD42/8	95301	Crossley	L26/26RD	?	14.09.50 ¶	01.11.50	31.01.67
90	ERD 159	Crossley DD42/8	95302	Crossley	L26/26RD	?	23.10.50	01.12.50	10.01.67
91	ERD 160	Crossley DD42/8	95303	Crossley	L26/26RD	?	26.10.50	01.12.50	26.09.68
92	ERD 161	Crossley DD42/8	95310	Crossley	L26/26RD	?	16.10.50	01.11.50	30.08.68
93	ERD 162	Crossley DD42/8	95311	Crossley	L26/26RD	?	26.10.50	01.12.50	27.09.68
94	ERD 163	Crossley DD42/8	95312	Crossley	L26/26RD	?	18.10.50	01.12.50	30.08.68
95	ERD 164	Crossley DD42/8	95313	Crossley	L26/26RD	?	16.10.50	01.11.50	30.08.68

TROLLEYBUSES

Fleet No.	Reg'n No.	Chassis Make & Type	Chassis Number	Body Make	Body Layout	Body Number	Date Delivered	Date Into Service	Date Withdrawn
107	ARD 670	AEC 661T	661T.268	Park Royal	H30/26R	B5320	14.12.38	17.01.39	21.08.61
108	ARD 671	AEC 661T	661T.269	Park Royal	H30/26R	B5321	19.12.38	17.01.39	11.07.61
109	ARD 672	AEC 661T	661T.270	Park Royal	H30/26R	B5322	06.01.39	18.01.39	23.06.61
110	ARD 673	AEC 661T	661T.271	Park Royal	H30/26R	B5323	16.12.38	19.04.39	16.07.61
111	ARD 674	AEC 661T	661T.272	Park Royal	H30/26R	B5324	28.12.38	16.05.39	05.09.61
112	ARD 675	AEC 661T	661T.273	Park Royal	H30/26R	B5325	17.12.38	21.05.39	04.09.61
113	ARD 676	AEC 661T	661T.274	Park Royal	H30/26R	B5326	31.12.38	21.05.39	14.09.61
114	ARD 677	AEC 661T	661T.275	Park Royal	H30/26R	B5327	12.01.39	21.05.39	14.08.61
115	ARD 678	AEC 661T	661T.276	Park Royal	H30/26R	B5328	17.01.39	21.05.39	30.04.58
116	ARD 679	AEC 661T	661T.277	Park Royal	H30/26R	B5329	25.01.39	21.05.39	30.04.58
117	ARD 680	AEC 661T	661T.278	Park Royal	H30/26R	B5330	04.01.39	21.05.39	30.04.58
118	ARD 681	AEC 661T	661T.279	Park Royal	H30/26R	B5331	13.01.39	21.05.39	30.04.58
119	ARD 682	AEC 661T	661T.280	Park Royal	H30/26R	B5332	28.01.39	21.05.39	26.02.58
120	ARD 683	AEC 661T	661T.281	Park Royal	H30/26R	B5333	07.02.39	21.05.39	29.06.61
121	ARD 684	AEC 661T	661T.282	Park Royal	H30/26R	B5334	17.03.39	21.05.39	21.09.58
122	ARD 685	AEC 661T	661T.283	Park Royal	H30/26R	B5335	25.03.39	21.05.39	21.09.58
123	ARD 686	AEC 661T	661T.284	Park Royal	H30/26R	B5336	31.03.39	21.05.39	21.09.58
124	ARD 687	AEC 661T	661T.285	Park Royal	H30/26R	B5337	24.03.39	21.05.39	21.09.58
125	ARD 688	AEC 661T	661T.286	Park Royal	H30/26R	B5338	18.03.39	21.05.39	21.09.58
126	ARD 689	AEC 661T	661T.287	Park Royal	H30/26R	B5339	15.03.39	21.05.39	27.03.52
127	ARD 690	AEC 661T	661T.288	Park Royal	H30/26R	B5340	01.04.39	21.05.39	22.10.60
128	ARD 691	AEC 661T	661T.289	Park Royal	H30/26R	B5341	18.04.39	21.05.39	31.07.61
129	ARD 692	AEC 661T	661T.290	Park Royal	H30/26R	B5342	22.03.39	21.05.39	28.08.61
130	ARD 693	AEC 661T	661T.291	Park Royal	H30/26R	B5343	12.04.39	21.05.39	27.04.61
131	ARD 694	AEC 661T	661T.292	Park Royal	H30/26R	B5344	16.04.39	21.05.39	19.06.61
132	BRD 797	Sunbeam W	50009W	Park Royal	UH30/26R	B16931	10.03.43	21.04.43	30.11.50
133	BRD 798	Sunbeam W	50010W	Park Royal	UH30/26R	B16932	11.03.43	21.04.43	30.11.50
134	BRD 799	Sunbeam W	50011W	Park Royal	UH30/26R	B16933	29.04.43	03.06.43	30.11.50
135	BRD 800	Sunbeam W	50012W	Park Royal	UH30/26R	B16934	30.04.43	22.06.43	30.11.50
136	BRD 801	Sunbeam W	50014W	Park Royal	UH30/26R	B16936	07.06.43	24.08.43	30.11.50
137	BRD 814	Sunbeam W	50013W	Park Royal	UH30/26R	B16935	08.06.43	04.08.43	30.11.50
138	DRD 124	BUT 9611T	9611T.063	Park Royal	H30/26RD	B33233	05.03.49	21.03.49	15.12.67
139	DRD 125	BUT 9611T	9611T.064	Park Royal	H30/26RD	B33234	05.03.49	25.03.49	15.12.67
140	DRD 126	BUT 9611T	9611T.065	Park Royal	H30/26RD	B33235	09.03.49	25.03.49	15.12.67
141	DRD 127	BUT 9611T	9611T.066	Park Royal	H30/26RD	B33236	16.03.49	25.03.49	11.01.67
142	DRD 128	BUT 9611T	9611T.067	Park Royal	H30/26RD	B33237	19.03.49	19.05.49	05.03.68
143	DRD 129	BUT 9611T	9611T.068	Park Royal	H30/26RD	B33238	19.03.49	19.05.49	05.03.68
144	DRD 130	BUT 9611T	9611T.069	Park Royal	H30/26RD	B33239	19.03.49	01.06.49	03.11.68
145	DRD 131	BUT 9611T	9611T.070	Park Royal	H30/26RD	B33240	20.03.49	01.06.49	17.10.67
146	DRD 132	BUT 9611T	9611T.071	Park Royal	H30/26RD	B33241	22.03.49	01.06.49	15.12.67
147	DRD 133	BUT 9611T	9611T.072	Park Royal	H30/26RD	B33242	04.04.49	01.06.49	01.03.68
148	DRD 134	BUT 9611T	9611T.073	Park Royal	H30/26RD	B33243	20.04.49	01.06.49	04.03.68
149	DRD 135	BUT 9611T	9611T.074	Park Royal	H30/26RD	B33244	30.03.49	01.06.49	13.01.67
150	DRD 136	BUT 9611T	9611T.075	Park Royal	H30/26RD	B33245	07.04.49	01.06.49	01.03.68
151	DRD 137	BUT 9611T	9611T.076	Park Royal	H30/26RD	B33246	30.04.49	01.06.49	30.12.66
152	DRD 138	BUT 9611T	9611T.077	Park Royal	H30/26RD	B33247	13.04.49	01.08.49	20.12.66
153	DRD 139	BUT 9611T	9611T.078	Park Royal	H30/26RD	B33248	05.05.49	01.08.49	31.12.66
154	DRD 140	BUT 9611T	9611T.079	Park Royal	H30/26RD	B33249	21.04.49	01.08.49	16.12.66
155	DRD 141	BUT 9611T	9611T.080	Park Royal	H30/26RD	B33250	28.04.49	01.08.49	01.03.68
156	DRD 142	BUT 9611T	9611T.081	Park Royal	H30/26RD	B33251	10.06.49	01.08.49	14.12.67
157	DRD 143	BUT 9611T	9611T.082	Park Royal	H30/26RD	B33252	21.04.49	09.08.49	09.01.67
158	VH 6757	Karrier E6	54092	Brush	H34/30R	?	25.03.48	18.09.48	31.10.55
159	VH 6753	Karrier E6	54087	Brush	H34/30R	?	08.04.48	01.04.49	31.10.55
160	VH 6751	Karrier E6	54085	Brush	H34/30R	?	19.04.48	18.02.49	31.08.56
161 ¤	VH 6759	Karrier E6	54094	Brush	H34/30R	?	23.06.48	01.02.51	31.12.56
162	VH 6755	Karrier E6	54090	Brush	H34/30R	?	.04.48	13.12.49	31.12.56
163 ¤	VH 6752	Karrier E6	54086	Brush	H34/30R	?	31.05.48	01.06.50	31.12.56
164	VH 6761	Karrier E6	54096	Brush	H34/30R	?	24.05.48	–	–
165 ¤	VH 6760	Karrier E6	54095	Brush	H34/30R	?	21.04.48	–	–
166	VH 6754	Karrier E6	54089	Brush	H34/30R	?	07.06.48	–	–
167 ¤	VH 6750	Karrier E6	54088	Brush	H34/30R	?	19.05.48	–	–
168	VH 6758	Karrier E6	54093	Brush	H34/30R	?	17.06.48	–	–
169 ¤	VH 6756	Karrier E6	54091	Brush	H34/30R	?	17.06.48	–	–

Fleet No.	Reg'n No.	Chassis Make & Type	Chassis Number	Body Make	Body Layout	Body Number	Date Delivered	Date Into Service	Date Withdrawn
170	ERD 141	Sunbeam S7	70032	Park Royal	H38/30RD	B34281	14.10.50	01.11.50	02.11.68
171	ERD 142	Sunbeam S7	70033	Park Royal	H38/30RD	B34282	24.10.50	01.11.50	14.12.67
172	ERD 143	Sunbeam S7	70034	Park Royal	H38/30RD	B34283	24.10.50	01.11.50	02.11.68
173	ERD 144	Sunbeam S7	70035	Park Royal	H38/30RD	B34284	30.10.50	01.11.50	02.11.68
174	ERD 145	Sunbeam S7	70036	Park Royal	H38/30RD	B34285	20.10.50	01.11.50	03.11.68
175	ERD 146	Sunbeam S7	70037	Park Royal	H38/30RD	B34286	31.10.50	01.11.50	02.11.68
176	ERD 147	Sunbeam S7	70038	Park Royal	H38/30RD	B34287	09.11.50	01.12.50	01.11.68
177	ERD 148	Sunbeam S7	70039	Park Royal	H38/30RD	B34288	04.11.50	01.12.50	01.11.68
178	ERD 149	Sunbeam S7	70040	Park Royal	H38/30RD	B34289	08.11.50	01.12.50	03.11.68
179	ERD 150	Sunbeam S7	70041	Park Royal	H38/30RD	B34290	13.11.50	01.12.50	25.10.68
180	ERD 151	Sunbeam S7	70042	Park Royal	H38/30RD	B34291	20.11.50	01.12.50	15.01.68
181	ERD 152	Sunbeam S7	70043	Park Royal	H38/30RD	B34292	20.11.50	01.12.50	03.11.68

Notes:

*　　The original body fitted to motorbus 62 was destroyed by fire whilst in store only two days after delivery. See Appendix B and the historical text for fuller details.

§　　69 was initially sold to the County Borough of Reading Health Committee, but was bought back two years later and re-certified as a PSV.

¶　　Before entering service, these buses had to be returned to Crossley Motors Ltd for rectification work, 85 on 04.10.50 and 84, 87 and 89 on 16.10.50. Bus 85 was 're-delivered' on 16.10.50 and 84, 87 and 89 on 23.10.50.

¤　　On the basis that these ex-Huddersfield Corporation vehicles were allocated consecutive fleet numbers as they were delivered, trolleybuses 161 and 163 are believed to have been originally delivered as 169 and 165 respectively, while unused trolleybuses 165, 167 and 169 had been initially numbered 161, 163 and 167. Numbers were swapped in the interests of having the vehicles which were actually refurbished and entered service in one consecutive block, particularly with regard to (a) selecting the best for refurbishment; and (b) a reduction in the number of vehicles to be refurbished. See Chapter 18 and Appendix B for fuller details.

'Date Into Service' is defined as the day on which the vehicle was used in passenger service for the first time. 'Date Withdrawn' is defined as the day on which the vehicle was used in passenger service for the last time. The dates of entry into service of motorbuses 84–95 and of trolleybuses 161 and 170–181 are included for completeness, albeit that they did not do so until after the end of the period covered by this volume.

Kentwood-bound Sunbeam W utility trolleybus 133 (BRD 798) passes AEC 661T 125 (ARD 688) at Norcot sometime in 1948, by which time 133's rear registration was carried on a metal plate near the bottom of the rear panel instead of being sign-written onto the top nearside corner of the rear platform window. The junction of Oxford Road with Norcot Road was a Y-junction with a small triangular island around which trolleybuses turned when working short to Norcot from town. The Greyhound/Speedway Stadium is behind the trolleybuses.

Late M. J. C. Dare © British Trolleybus Society

Appendix B — Rolling Stock Details (Vehicles Acquired 1939–1950)

This appendix contains a full description of each type of vehicle to have entered service between 1939 and 1949. Types which were in service at the start of this story will be described in a future volume covering the pre-war years, while the Sunbeam S7 trolleybuses and Crossley DD42/8 motorbuses, which entered service as 1950 drew to a close, will also be described in a forthcoming book.

Each description covers the whole of the life of the class, even though in some cases this is well after 1950 when our story ends. While not a perfect solution, this will avoid the need to repeat a class history over two or more volumes, or to split the story between volumes.

MOTORBUSES

6–7 (BRD 754–5) — New 1942/43

Chassis make and type: Guy Arab
Wheelbase: 16ft 3in
Engine: Gardner 5LW five-cylinder 7.0 litres
Gearbox: Four-speed crash
Length: 26ft 0in **Width:** 7ft 6in
Unladen Weight: 6: 7 tons 15 cwt 1 qtr
7: 7 tons 19 cwt 1 qtr
Body make & type: Strachans UL27/28R
Initial cost: £2,256 each
First Registered: 6: 21.11.42 7: 30.01.43

Bodywork Characteristics: These vehicles were of typical austere wartime design to Ministry of Supply specification, having five-bay bodies of timber-framed single-skin construction and steel panelling. Of very box-like appearance, there was a slight rake to the front elevation but the rear was more-or-less perpendicular. The number of opening windows, of the pinch-and-half-drop type, was kept to a minimum, there being two on each side of the upper-deck, in the third and fifth bays from the front, and one per side on the lower-deck, in the third bay. In addition, the front upper-deck windows were divided by a transom, to give inward-opening bottom-hung glazed ventilating windows about 6in deep. Rainshields were fitted over the lower-deck windows and the upper-deck side windows from front to rear, including the rearmost 'corner window', which on these vehicles was more-or-less the same size and shape as the bay windows. The rear emergency door was sheet metal as delivered but was replaced by a glazed type, with a central mullion and rounded ends to the panes, at an early date. The forward-hinged cab door had a square-framed top edge and, initially, the glazed portion was divided into two by a transom which was about the same height as the top of the lower-deck rainshields, so that the top (fixed) pane was quite shallow, and with two very deep sliding panes forming a signalling window. Very soon, probably due to wartime supply difficulties with larger panes, the glazed area was modified by fitting an additional transom, thus dividing the glazed area into three, both lower portions being fitted with sliding glass signalling windows. The glazed part of the cab door and the adjacent offside front cab window were of full-depth, from upper-deck floor level to the waist rail, whilst the front windscreen was shallower by virtue of the bottom edge being higher, slightly raking downwards to the offside to clear the radiator. The roof was single-skin and rather flat and the rear dome was 'angular' rather than beaten to a curved profile. External ventilators were fitted in the roof sides, to the forward part of the second and fourth bays on both sides of the vehicle. One rectangular destination indicator box was fitted, to the front, this being almost square – a very non-standard size and shape as far as the undertaking was concerned. The destination blinds fitted thus had wording on two lines where appropriate. The deep radiator shell was black stove-enamelled, with signwritten registration plate

Quantities of passengers are being disgorged from Guy Arab 7 (BRD 754), which is bound for Grovelands Road, outside the GWR station. The passengers queuing in front of the bus are going in the opposite direction and show a complete lack of interest in the Guy, instead looking quizzically at something which is rounding the corner from Station Road and coming towards them. It will U-turn back towards them, if, indeed, it is the bus for Erleigh Road that they are awaiting. Believed to be early spring 1945. Note the glazed emergency door and the additional transom in the driver's door, both being early modifications made by the department.

Late W. J. Haynes © Millane Publishing

underneath and flanked either side by headlamps. The rear registration number was signwritten (in one line) on the top left-hand corner of the rear platform window. Timber lifeguards were fitted.

External Livery: Delivered in grey primer, they were painted by the undertaking into three-band crimson-and-cream livery before entering service, with the horizontal beading between the crimson and cream bands painted black. 6 was definitely lined-out with a fine cream line along the top edge of the crimson upper- and lower-deck panels; 7 may also have been so treated. Wings, radiator, headlamps, etc., were black and the standard Gill Sans fleet number transfers were affixed to the four usual positions.

Internal Livery: Moquette-covered seats and white Doverite-covered stanchions and rails. White ceilings, crimson side panels and stair risers, black seat rails and varnished wood window surrounds.

Other Notes: The front destination indicator boxes of both buses were changed to the standard Reading pattern, fitted towards the bottom of the front crimson panel. Side and rear boxes were fitted at the same time, that at the side being in the centre of the panel and that at the rear being near the top of the panel. At the same time, a pair of blue identification lights was fitted into the top cream band, immediately below the front upper-deck windows. 6 emerged as such on 13.12.47 and 7 on 20.12.46. 6 (but not 7) seems also to have been fitted with an additional half-drop window in the second bay each side of the lower-deck, which probably took place at the same time as its other alterations. On both buses the rear registration number was transferred to a squareish slightly-inclined plate on the offside rear lower corner, also about the same time. Circa 1947/48, the rainshields of 7 were altered so that they remained over the opening windows only (but still no additional opening windows were provided to the lower-deck) and the bus was also fitted with a sliding window in the front bulkhead behind the driver for driver instruction purposes.

27–28 (BRD 815–6) New 1943

Chassis make and type: Guy Arab
Wheelbase: 16ft 3in
Engine: Gardner 6LW six-cylinder 8.4 litres
Gearbox: Four-speed crash.
Length: 26ft 7½in   **Width:** 7ft 6in
Unladen Weight: 27: 7 tons 19 cwt 3 qtrs
                      28: 8 tons 4 cwt 0 qtrs
Body make & type: Strachans   UL27/28R
Initial cost: £2,385 each
First Registered: 27: 24.05.43   28: 27.04.43

Bodywork Characteristics: As far as is known, these buses were identical to 6 and 7, except that the engine, being longer, caused the bonnet to project somewhat further forward. The front wings were, therefore, swept outwards so that their front edges were brought more forward, towards the front edge of the radiator.

External Livery: As described for 6 and 7, except that by the time they were delivered for painting by the undertaking, cream lining-out had been abandoned.

Internal Livery: As described for 6 and 7, as far as is known.

Other Notes: On 5th June 1943, before entering service, 27 and 28 were noted inside the depot standing side-by-side and both carrying fleet number 28 and registration BRD 816! 27 was fitted with an AEC 7.7 litre engine, running thus from 23rd May 1946 and the Guy name on the radiator top was filed off and replaced by a signwritten 'Reading Transport' in cream on maroon ground. Prior to this the Guy name had been picked out by having a white background and the radiator grille was finished in silver instead of black. 27 ran in an experimental livery (in company with trolleybus 123), which was all-crimson except for horizontal band

All four of Reading's utility Guy motorbuses were specially lined up in the road outside the depot in Mill Lane for this photocall, the two Arab 5LWs at the far end and the two Arab 6LWs nearest the camera (notice the different front wings). For various reasons the photo can be dated to no earlier than autumn 1944 – foglamps, only one headlamp masked, and the Albatross Flour advert on bus 28.

© R. N. Hannay

mouldings which were picked out in cream, but retaining black wings, etc., this taking place during 1946 and possibly commencing at the same time as receiving its AEC engine. It was subsequently repainted back into standard livery. The front destination boxes of both buses were altered to the standard Reading pattern and side and rear boxes added, as described for 6 and 7, and it would also appear that an additional half-drop opening window was fitted on both sides of the lower deck in the second bay from the front at the same time, 27 emerging so finished on 15.12.49 and 28 on 15.04.47. The rear registration numbers were re-positioned on a squareish slightly-inclined plate on the rear lower offside corner, as described for 6 and 7, also about the same time, and 28 received a pair of blue identification lights in the top cream band immediately below the front upper-deck windows. Note the very late date on which 27 was dealt with, as it was withdrawn a year later – indeed, the foregoing refinements took place after the other three Guy Arabs had been withdrawn! However, 27 never received blue identification lights.

12, 13, 15–18 (CDP 231–6) New 1946

Chassis make and type: Bedford OB
Wheelbase: 14ft 6in
Engine: Bedford KMO six-cylinder petrol, 3.519 litres
Gearbox: Four-speed crash
Length: 24ft 0in **Width:** 7ft 6in
Unladen Weight: 3 tons 6 cwt 2 qtrs
Body make & type: Duple B30F
Initial cost: £1,048 10s each
First Registered: 12: 17.04.46   16: 03.05.46
13: 01.05.46   17: 03.05.46
15: 26.04.46   18: 03.05.46

Bodywork Characteristics: These vehicles had Duple's standard service bus bodies of four bay construction, with the last three bays fitted with opening windows on the offside and the last two on the nearside. The front nearside bay was fitted with a door, which slid rearwards along the outside of the vehicle on operation of a lever by the driver. A hinged emergency door was fitted to the centre of the rear. Rainshields were fitted the full length over the saloon windows along both sides. The windscreens and front destination box had bright metal frames/trimming and a bright metal front bumper bar was also fitted. The offside front windscreen was divided by a transom to give a 6in deep fixed light to the top of the screen, whilst the remainder was hinged to open outwards. No rear destination indicator box was fitted. Timber lifeguards. Bright metal wheel trims to front wheels. Pressed aluminium front registration plate mounted to the offside of the radiator, above the bumper.

External Livery: All crimson but with the horizontal waist rail moulding under the windows all round the sides and rear of the bus picked out in cream, together with the moulding from the front corner windows of each side, up and across the top of the windows at cant rail level and down the rearmost side corner windows, to join the waist rail moulding. Black wings. There was a noticeable similarity, therefore, to the experimental livery applied to Guy motorbus 27 and AEC trolleybus 123 at the time these buses were delivered.

Internal Livery: White ceilings. Crimson lower panels and brown-varnished window surrounds. Rexene-covered seating with no top grab rail.

Other Notes: These buses were supplied by Great Western Motors Ltd, Reading, the local Vauxhall and Bedford dealers. Re-seated to B28F soon after delivery, possibly to comply with a post-war re-tightening of Ministry of Transport certificate of fitness standards. It is confirmed that this batch had no twin seat forward of the entrance on delivery, and it is thought that the rearmost seats on each side were changed to single seats. Hired during the summer of 1947 to Smith's Luxury Coaches (Reading) Ltd at weekends. Having been ordered as 'stop gaps' when new double-deckers were in short supply, these vehicles were sold back to Great Western Motors Ltd. in November 1948, at a profit, and 18 was put into the showroom window in Station Road. It is believed to have had only about 52,000 miles on the clock at this time.

Duple-bodied Bedford OB 17 (CDP 235) 'waits time' in the purpose-built terminal lay-by in Berkeley Avenue before returning to Hemdean Road on route L, circa 1947.
Late W. J. Haynes © Millane Publishing

Note: From this point a new policy of motorbus fleet numbering began, following on from the highest-numbered bus in the fleet (57) up to 100 and then starting again from 1. This remained in effect until 1968, when vehicles became numbered by type.

58–67 (CRD 252–261)   New 1947

Chassis make and type: AEC Regent II
Wheelbase: 16ft 6in
Engine: AEC A173 six-cylinder diesel, 7.7 litres
Gearbox: Four-speed crash
Length: 26ft 0ins   **Width:** 7ft 6ins
Unladen Weight: 6 tons 18 cwt 3 qtrs
Body make & type: Park Royal L24/26R
Initial cost: The Transport Committee minutes quote an estimated cost of £2,670 each but this was stated as subject to fluctuation at the time of delivery.

Delivered:

Fleet No.	Chassis to Mill Lane for Storage	Chassis Sent to Bodybuilder	Completed Bus Received	First Registered
58	16.11.45	13.02.46	11.01.47	29.01.47
59	09.11.45	.02.46	17.01.47	31.01.47
60	09.11.45	.02.46	16.01.47	29.01.47
61	13.11.45	.02.46	11.01.47	01.02.47
62	13.11.45	.02.46	16.01.47	17.09.48
63	10.08.46	07.11.46	04.02.47	27.02.47
64	10.08.46	06.11.46	30.01.47	27.02.47
65	09.08.46	05.11.46	25.01.47	01.03.47
66	10.08.46	02.11.46	23.01.47	29.01.47
67	23.08.46	04.11.46.	25.01.47	27.02.47

Bodywork Characteristics: The design and construction of the semi-austerity five-bay body of lowbridge layout, in composite single-skin construction, appears to have been unique to Reading – yet at a time when standardisation was important to maximise output. The front elevation was gently raked and the rear was upright as far as the emergency door, curving from there to merge with the rear roof dome. All side and rear window pans had radiused corners at top and bottom, and all lower-deck bay windows except the rearmost were divided near the top by a narrow transom, above which were fitted a pair of sliding windows per bay, supplied with a rubber-buffered chromium plated knob. The front upper-deck windows were radiused at the bottom corners only and, near the top, were divided by a transom, above which were fitted bottom-hung inward-opening louvre windows. The rear emergency door was divided by a central mullion and all corners of both panes were radiused. No rainshields were fitted over the windows on either deck. The offside front driver's cab window and the front bulkhead windows (which were much higher at their bottom edges than the waist rail) were radiused on all corners. The driver's cab was provided with a sliding door, the glazing to which was divided by a narrow transom, below which were fitted two sliding panes as a signalling window. The windscreen was not radiused and was in two parts, divided horizontally near the bottom, with a tapering fixed pane to over the radiator and the top pane top-hung to open. The front destination box was positioned in the centre of the panel. This batch <u>never</u> acquired a pair of blue identification lamps immediately below the front upper-deck windows. The rear destination indicator was fitted immediately over the rear lower-deck platform window and that at the side was positioned slightly lower than the centre of the panel over the platform and was provided with a rainshield over. The roof was of single-skin construction with projecting hoops externally. Tubular lifeguards were fitted and mud-flaps were only fitted to the front mudguards. No front wheel rings were ever fitted and, although there is photographic evidence that when new these vehicles had step rings, they do not appear to have been retained for very long. The front wings were dished over the dumb-irons to meet the radiator. The bonnet sides and top were louvred. Horn located above the offside headlamp.

External Livery: As originally delivered the batch was painted in three different styles, all a departure from the hitherto standard livery of crimson with three cream bands

A relatively new AEC Regent II 60 (CRD 254) crossing Caversham Bridge on 'a journey to town, thence Shinfield Road'. Actually, the view is posed – for a photo for use in the Silver Lining Savings Exhibition, held at the Town Hall in February 1948.

© Late C. E. May

(see photos on page 137). 58–61 were crimson with cream window surrounds and all the equivalent areas, to both sides and the front but not to any of the rear. The metal panel on the rear of the offside, aft of the saloon windows, was divided diagonally to the rear corner, the lower 'triangle' being cream. Wings and horizontal beading were black. 63 and 66 (possibly 62 also) were crimson with the window surround area cream, including the rear corner pillars of the upper-deck, with black wings and horizontal beading. 64, 65 and 67 were similar but the rear upper-deck pillars were crimson. It was this livery which became adopted as standard; the other buses appear to have retained their experimental liveries until their first scheduled repaint. In all cases the rear bulkhead window surround on the platform was crimson. Fleet numbers were applied to the usual four locations, though for most of their life the batch had a smaller signwritten fleetnumber at the rear, in the centre, just under the rear platform window, to allow room for an advertisement below. Prior to delivery, 66 (at least) carried an external livery more akin to that of 64, 65 and 67 but with the panels between the upper-deck floor level and the top of the lower-deck windows in crimson instead of cream and with the nearside fleet number at the front bulkhead rather than the rear bulkhead. The front registration number was carried centrally at upper-deck floor level rather than at the bottom of the radiator. All would appear to have been Mr Little's preferences, which Mr Evans changed before delivery. Towards the end of their lives, 62, 66 and 67 had received standard-sized rear fleet numbers. Initially, however, the nearside fleet number appeared both ends of the bus – presumably as an experiment.

Internal Livery: Ceilings were white and the lower panels dark blue. Window surrounds were originally cream Rexene but at later repaints became a simulated wood-grain finish. At their last repaint most became a yellow ochre colour, but 59 and 61 (at least) reverted to cream at their last repaint. The platform and stairs area was crimson. Seats had no top grab rails but were straight-topped and finished in blue leather. On the lower-deck the seating was conventional, but on the upper-deck every alternate seat was a three-seater instead of the usual four (i.e. from front to back 4-3-4-3-4-3-3) to allow circulating room. At a time when seating capacity was very important this was a rather strange choice to unnecessarily 'lose' two seats. Upper-deck saloon lighting was by exposed lamps, the sockets for which were mounted on a continuous panel mounted inclined along the sides of the roof. Stanchions and rails were covered in black Doverite. The floors were linoleum-covered and fitted with metal strips to the gangways and stairs. The platform was fitted with wood battens running across the width of the bus.

Other Notes: On Saturday 18th January 1947, a fire occurred at Mill Lane depot in the machine shop, where several of the batch were being stored between delivery and entry into service. Unfortunately, 62 was so badly damaged that it had to be sent back to Park Royal for a new body. Repairs effected to the chassis cost £333 2s 5d and the cost of rebodying was £2,347 10s 0d, both costs being met by an insurance claim. 62 was re-delivered on 17.09.48, entering service on 18.09.48 carrying a body identical in all respects to the second batch of AEC Regent IIs, 74–83, and the reader is referred to that section (see pages 213/4) for further details. It is remarkable, of course, that the bus entered service the day following delivery – in those days, RCT would spend a few days quality-checking a bus first – but that is what surviving records indicate! The new Park Royal body number was B33218. 58 was fitted with a blind inside the cab to the offside front bulkhead window; this window was altered in 1958/59 for driver instruction. 59 ran for some years with a 'short' pre-1938 radiator, being again fitted with a standard post-war one on 06.02.62, some months prior to withdrawal.

68–73 (CRD 591–6)   New 1947

Chassis make and type: Bedford OB
Wheelbase: 14ft 6in
Engine: Bedford KMO six-cylinder petrol, 3.519 litres
Gearbox: Four-speed crash
Length: 24ft 0in   **Width:**   7ft 6in
Unladen Weight: 3 tons 11 cwt 0 qtrs
Body make & type: Mulliner B32F (operated as B31F when on stage carriage work)
Initial cost: £1,267 each.
First Registered: 68: 06.06.47   71: 01.11.47
                       69: .08.47   72: 01.11.47
                       70: 06.09.47   73: 29.11.47

Bodywork Characteristics: Although built by a different bodybuilder, these vehicles were markedly similar to the Duple-bodied Bedford OBs of 1946 (see page 210), the only obvious difference being that a rear destination box was provided. Windscreens, destination box surrounds etc. were not bright metal, however, and the front registration plate was signwritten, hung in the centre under the radiator.

External Livery: Crimson, with the areas to the side windows painted cream with black beading. Black wings.

Internal Livery: White ceilings and crimson lower panels. Two centrally-placed roof ventilators. Seats of red leather on tubular frames, having no top grab rail, and set on a plinth above gangway level. One long, black Doverite-covered handrail fixed slightly off-centre along the length of the saloon ceiling, towards the offside. Square-shaped opaque fluted glass lamp covers. Two bell pushes per side.

Other Notes: The batch had its seating reduced to 29 in 1950, possibly to comply with the post-war re-tightening of Ministry of Transport certificate of fitness standards. As 29-seaters, there was a single inward-facing seat, fixed at the very back, on the offside. Down-seating from 32 probably involved removal of a pair and substituting the afore-mentioned single seat in this rearward position and removing the pair forward of the entrance. Reversing lights were fitted at a late stage in their life, consisting of what appeared to be a standard sidelight mounted high on the rear offside corner pillar. At some time, the rear fleet number was transferred from the centre of the rear emergency door to the offside rear, over the registration number. They tended to be 'maids of all work', being used to pioneer several new routes in the 1950s, on reliefs, tours of the town, school duties, on civic duties and the collection of ballot boxes from the various polling stations at local and general elections. 69 was delicensed on 05.10.59 (probably on expiry of its certificate of fitness) and officially transferred to the Health Department on 08.02.60 (although it may have been used by that department from as early as November 1959). It retained its Transport Department livery and fleet number, and continued to be garaged at Mill Lane, fitted with a 'Private' blind exposure. It was handed back to the Transport Department in February 1962, when the Health Department purchased a Bedford minibus, and was refurbished, recertified and re-entered passenger service on 01.03.62. It continued to work until 19.02.64, latterly on driver instruction, and was used for a farewell tour by the Reading Transport Society on Sunday 16th February 1964, to mark the passing of the last petrol-engined PSV in service with the department. It was then used solely as a driver training vehicle, its seating being reduced to 2! It later fell into disuse, got very tatty and weather-beaten, and was eventually sold. 73, either from new or subsequently, had the nearside windscreen divided to match the offside, the lower pane remaining fixed, and a painted aluminium cowl fitted over the top pane.

74–83 (CRD 863–872) New 1948

Chassis make and type: AEC Regent II
Wheelbase: 16ft 6in
Engine: AEC A173 six cylinder diesel, 7.7 litres.
Gearbox: Four-speed crash
Length: 26ft 0ins **Width:** 7ft 6ins
Unladen Weight: 6 tons 18 cwt 3 qtrs
Body make & type: Park Royal L26/26R
Initial cost: £3,638 each
Delivered:

Fleet No.	Chassis to Mill Lane for Storage	Chassis Sent to Bodybuilder	Completed Bus Received	First Registered
74	19.03.47	May/Jun 48	c 25.09.48	01.10.48
75	16.04.47	May/Jun 48	c 25.09.48	01.10.48
76	16.04.47	May/Jun 48	. .48	21.10.48
77	26.02.47	May/Jun 48	. .48	07.10.48
78	13.05.47	May/Jun 48	. .48	07.10.48
79	13.05.47	May/Jun 48	. .48	25.10.48
80	04.06.47	May/Jun 48	. .48	25.10.48
81	04.06.47	May/Jun 48	. .48	25.10.48
82	. .47	May/Jun 48	. .48	21.10.48
83	. .47	May/Jun 48	23.10.48	25.10.48

Note: 62 in its re-bodied form was identical to this batch.

A copy of a surviving letter from the undertaking to Park Royal indicates that *"one chassis would be dispatched from Reading on Tuesday, 25th May 1948; one chassis on 1st June 1948; two chassis on 8th June 1948; and two chassis on each Tuesday following until all are delivered".* Surviving correspondence suggests that, after the chassis of bus 62 was repaired by AEC following destruction by fire of its original body, it was returned to Reading for storage pending bodying and, thus, there were 11 chassis to be dispatched to Park Royal for bodying. Completed vehicles were delivered during late September and through most of October 1948.

Bodywork Characteristics: This second batch of AEC Regent IIs was of five-bay all-metal double-skin construction and of lowbridge layout. In overall appearance these vehicles were lowbridge versions of a standard Park Royal design supplied to other provincial undertakings around this time. The front elevation was gently raked and the rear was upright as far as the rear emergency door, curving from there to merge with the rear roof dome. The side and upper-deck front windows had radiused corners at the bottom only. The rear lower-deck platform window, the front offside cab window and the centrally-divided rear emergency door were radiused on all corners. There was a greater degree of curve on the foremost lower corner of the cab window. The first four bays on both sides of the upper-deck and bays two and four of the lower-deck were fitted with half-drop windows of the 'pinch' type. The front upper-deck windows were fixed panes. Rainshields were fitted over the upper-deck windows along the sides and across the front, and also over the lower-saloon windows. Long, narrow front bulkhead windows were fitted, radiused at the lower corners and with the bottom edge somewhat higher than waist rail level. That on the nearside was a half-drop. A sliding door was provided to the driver's cab, similar to that fitted to 58–67, as was the windscreen, which differed only in that the bottom edge of the opening part was framed and painted. The front and rear destination boxes were in similar positions to 58–67, but that at the side was

Already a couple of years old by the time this picture was taken, on 25th June 1949, Mulliner-bodied Bedford OB 69 (CRD 592) is seen here westbound in Broad Street opposite the Vaudeville Cinema. The Cadena Café was famous for its smell of fresh-ground coffee wafting around this part of Broad Street and Reed & Sons Ltd, outfitters who specialised in school clothes, were just as famous for having their advert on the front of most of the corporation's pre-war AEC motorbuses (such as the bus following). Burton, of course, was just famous! The constable is a member of the Reading Borough Police, later to become absorbed in the Thames Valley Constabulary.
Late W. J. Haynes © Millane Publishing

positioned immediately over the rearmost nearside lower-deck bay window. A pair of blue identification lamps was fitted just below the front upper-deck windows. The roof was of single-skin construction with projecting hoops externally. Tubular life-guards were fitted and mudflaps to both front and rear mudguards. The front wings were dished over the dumb-irons, in a similar fashion to 58–67, to meet the radiator. The bonnet top and sides were louvred. Horn located above the offside headlamp.

External Livery: Crimson, with the window surround areas cream, lined on the beading in black, the rear upper deck corner pillars remaining crimson. Black wings etc. Fleet numbers in the standard positions, those on the rear elevation signwritten to reduced size as for 58–67 to allow an advertisement to be carried below. Ribbed aluminium unpainted panel below driver's door and below the fuel filler on the offside.

Internal Livery: White ceilings, crimson lower panels, stairs and platform and lower halves of the window surrounds. The top half of the window mullions was cream mottled metal, which only became repainted later in life. The head to the windows all round the upper-deck was dark wood-grain finish. Seats were covered in red leather on Deans tubular frames with top grab rail. Stanchions and rails covered in black Doverite. Floors covered in linoleum with metal strips to gangways and stairs. Wood battens to platform fixed across the bus. Upper-deck lighting fitted on inclined panels as for 58–67.

Other Notes: Always considered rather handsome vehicles, and always maintained in pristine condition, even when withdrawn these vehicles did not look fit for scrapping. 83 had numerically the last chassis number for the O661 Regent series which had commenced in 1929. Indeed, this batch was originally intended to be the Regent III model, but Regent II production was extended by AEC to accommodate this batch to avoid a perceived delay in delivery, as recounted in the historical narrative. 82 ran for its final years with a 'short' pre-1938 radiator. 80–83 acquired a new set of destination blinds in the late summer of 1953, which had thicker lettering and introduced for the first time for some years the tapered two-line exposure with **GROVELANDS VIA WATER ROAD** and **GROVELANDS VIA WAVERLEY ROAD**:

> GROVELANDS VIA WAVERLEY RD
> GROVELANDS VIA WATER ROAD

An exposure which was included but, as far as is known, never used was **HIGHMOOR ROAD**. **EVESHAM ROAD** and **CRESSINGHAM ROAD** were also included from new. 83 was used for an enthusiasts' tour on 6th March 1949, when new, and again on 26th July 1964 when the Reading Transport Society ran her on a farewell tour, these being the last 7ft 6ins wide buses in the fleet and the last with open rear platforms.

Driverless (while he nips off to the subterranean toilets and the conductor gets the tea-can re-filled), AEC Regent II 76 (CRD 865) waits at Stations circa late August 1949, when the bus was nearly a year old. This vehicle was one of the less severely-styled second batch of Regent IIs, new in autumn 1948.

Late W. J. Haynes © Millane Publishing

TROLLEYBUSES

107–131 (ARD 670–694) New 1938/39

Chassis make and type: AEC 661T
Wheelbase: 16ft 3in
Motor: English Electric type 406/3E (80hp) series-wound (equipped for battery traction)
Brakes: English Electric series dynamic rheostatic and Westinghouse air on brake pedal
Length: 26ft 0in **Width:** 7ft 6in
Unladen weight: 7 tons 7 cwts 0 qtrs
Body make & type: Park Royal H30/26R
Initial cost: £2,187 each
First Registered: 107/8: .01.39 109/10: .03.39
  111–31 .05.39

Bodywork Characteristics: Metal-framed body of five-bay highbridge construction. All upper-deck bay windows and front windows opening. All bay windows on lower deck opening except last bay. Both windscreens opening. Cab door windows on both sides with curved top. Front destination box of large single-track type immediately above centre cream band. Rear destination box in centre cream band immediately over the lower-deck rear window. Large, almost square, side destination box over the rear platform entrance originally displaying an ultimate destination and four or five 'via' points. On the introduction of wartime destination names on 3rd August 1940, the 'via' indications were discontinued and never reinstated.

Front elevation of body curved gently rearwards; a pair of white lamps was fitted just below the front upper-deck windows. A holder for 'running number' plates was provided at the immediate front offside (per London Transport practice), but this was never used in Reading. Rear elevation curved gently under at bottom. Rounded roof, quarter-turn stairs. Wings, including those at the rear, were of moulded rubber. When new, these vehicles were fitted with a small crimson painted board hinged up and held by a turnbuckle catch over the platform on which was sign-written in cream the words 'BUS FULL'. Presumably it was intended that these should be used in appropriate circumstances but they never appear to have been used. It is not known when they were removed.

External Livery: Crimson, relieved with three cream bands, edged in black to waist rails below windows of both decks and at upper-deck floor level. Black wings, crimson wheel centres. Delivered lined-out in cream on crimson panels and crimson on bottom and centre cream bands. The upper cream band was not so lined. Plain fleet numbers were originally located beneath the bottom cream band on the offside behind the front bulkhead, on the nearside by the platform and on the rear beneath the registration plate (which was situated in the cream band immediately underneath the rear platform window). There was no fleet number on the front of the vehicle originally, although the centre dash panel carried the RCT emblem in gold.

Internal Livery: Ceilings white. Brown leathercloth covering to panels and bulkheads. Window surrounds were also originally brown leathercloth-covered, but were later painted and varnished to simulate dark wood finish. Moquette-covered tubular-framed seats with no top grab rail. The Royd No. 2 moquette was of one design on 107–119 and of a different design on 120–131. Platform and stairs crimson. Black Doverite plastic-covered stanchions

Photographed at the Three Tuns before turning, AEC 661T trolleybus 129 (ARD 692), with both headlamps masked to conform with blackout regulations, and in 'lined out' livery, depicts the condition of these vehicles circa April/May 1942, about halfway through the war. These vehicles bore the brunt of massive increases in wartime loadings on the town's trolleybuses; in spite of this, some of the 25 – including this one – put in over 22 years of active service.

Late W. J. Haynes © Maiwand Photographic Archive

An atmospheric wartime view circa April/May 1942 at the Three Tuns. AEC trolleybus 123 (ARD 686), in 'lined-out' livery, with the wartime embellishments of white rear bumper and, indeed, the bottom part of the platform centre stanchion. Note also the wartime destination displays and white rings round the traction pole. The picture was, in fact, posed for the camera: witness the position of the trolleybus relative to the usual loading point, and the crew (including conductress) on the platform. It depicts Edgar Jordan's wife, Lillian, and pram containing their first offspring. Edgar Jordan, much later the Reading tramways historian, was Inspector 'Tim' Jordan's son.   *Late W. J. Haynes © Maiwand Photographic Archive*

and grab rails. Metal tread strips to linoleum-covered floors. 'Chocolate block' rubber covering to platform.

Other Notes: 107 and 108 were first used on 17th January 1939, followed a day later by 109. All three vehicles were used on the Erleigh Road training section for a time, in order to accelerate trolleybus driver training. When the section of line between Norcot Road and Tilehurst became available for driver training in April 1939, 110 was also put to use from 19th April and 111 from 10th May 1939. All other vehicles were put into service when the main line opened for revenue service on 21st May 1939.

Lining-out was omitted from the mid-war years, disappearing gradually as vehicles were repainted. Fleet numbers were subsequently applied to the front of the vehicles, commencing with 113 on 13th March 1948, the number being positioned towards the bottom of the nearside dash panel, just above the fog lamp. Commencing a year later, the RCT emblem in the centre dash panel was replaced by the fleet number on repaint, the first trolleybus to re-enter service without the emblem being 119 on 19th February 1949. The rear registration number originally comprised raised numerals under a glass panel in the position referred to above. This was removed and replaced with a signwritten square metal plate on the offside of the rear lower panel, commencing with 113 in December 1945. In order to accommodate an advertisement on the lower rear panel, the cream fleet number at the top of same was repositioned onto the cream band where the registration plate had been, the transfer being hand-painted over in crimson. The original panes of blue-tinted glass in the front lower-deck bulkhead window behind the driver were replaced by plain glass, that behind the driver being painted brown in later years rather than being fitted with a blind. The front upper-deck opening windows were replaced by fixed panes on all vehicles except 108 and 116–119. The rear two-tier bumpers were removed in 1955 as a result of complaints from crews that they suffered an electric shock when taking the trolley retriever pole from the tube under a 'live' vehicle.

123 was experimentally repainted in an 'all-crimson' livery without cream bands, but with the band mouldings picked out in cream, and ran in this condition from 7th June 1946 until 23rd November 1946 (not quite six months) before being returned to normal livery.

On 31st October 1950, 107–112 were withdrawn from service, the intention being to sell them. Following a request from the town council to reconsider the matter, the Transport Committee decided to store 107–112 indefinitely at Bennet Road. On 27th March 1952, 126 overturned on the Kentwood section of Oxford Road, following which it was withdrawn on discovery that the chassis was twisted; it was taken to Bennet Road and stored. On 4th April 1952, 112 was removed from store at Bennet Road to replace it and, after a thorough overhaul, returned to service on 17th December 1952. When the ex-Huddersfield Karriers were beginning to show signs of their age and, in order to obtain a comparison of cost of renovating the Karriers or the AECs in store, 108 was taken to Mill Lane in 1954 and given a thorough body overhaul but without some of the modifications made to others in the batch still in service. On completion of the work, 108 was returned to store.

Subsequently it was decided to extensively overhaul the other stored AECs (107/109–111) and use them, together with 108, as replacements for the Karriers. Thus as each AEC became available, a Karrier was with-drawn from service.

107:	ex-store	22.06.55	re-entered service	01.11.55
108:	ex-store	24.09.55	re-entered service	01.11.55
109:	ex-store	?	re-entered service	13.08.56
110:	ex-store	06.09.55	re-entered service	01.07.57
111:	ex-store	27.08.56	re-entered service	01.11.57

As a result of 108's previous body overhaul and the fact that it did not receive some of the modifications as applied to others in the batch, it ran until withdrawal in 1961 retaining opening front windows on the upper-deck. It also retained its original front dash layout, in which the panel below the windscreen was divided vertically between the windscreen central pillar and the top of the removable towing panel, instead of being rebuilt with a full-width panel divided horizontally immediately above the towing panel.

Reduced demand for public transport in the late 1950s caused a reduction in the size of the fleet. 119 was withdrawn after an accident in Kings Road on 26th February 1958 and 115–118 were subsequently withdrawn on 30th April 1958. 115/6/8/9 were sold for breaking in June 1958, followed by 126 (which had been stored at Bennet Road since overturning in 1952) a month later. On 21st September 1958, 121–125 were also withdrawn and were sold for scrap in October 1958. 117 meanwhile was, for some unknown reason, retained until October 1959 before disposal.

The remaining 14 vehicles were replaced by 12 new Sunbeam F4A trolleybuses in 1961. As each of the AECs was withdrawn, the motor was salvaged before the vehicle was disposed of for breaking, so that six of the new Sunbeam F4As could be fitted with these motors as a cost-saving measure, with others held as spares to keep the new vehicles in operation for some years to come.

Although the first F4A did not enter service until June 1961, a start was made withdrawing the remaining 14 AECs in December 1960, commencing with 127 (which had sustained accident damage). On 14th September 1961 the last, 113, was finally withdrawn. It was, in fact, the last pre-war passenger vehicle to be operated by the department, and was secured for preservation by the Reading Transport Society (now the British Trolleybus Society). It is now restored and fully operational at the Trolleybus Museum at Sandtoft, in Lincolnshire.

132–137 (BRD 797–801/814) New 1943

Chassis make and type: Sunbeam W
Wheelbase: 16ft 3in
Motor: English Electric type-409A (l00hp) series-wound (equipped for battery traction)
Brakes: Series dynamic rheostatic and Westinghouse air on brake pedal
Length: 26ft 0in   **Width:** 7ft 6in
Unladen weight: 7 tons 18 cwt 0 qtrs
Body make & type: Park Royal UH30/26R
Initial cost: £3,095 each
First Registered:
132: 10.04.43   135: 08.05.43
133 10.04.43   136: 15.06.43
134: 03.05.43   137: 01.07.43

Bodywork Characteristics: Timber-framed single-skin five-bay body, of highbridge 'utility' wartime design, originally with two opening windows per side on the upper-

Photographed on Wednesday afternoon, 1st September 1943, there is no traffic apart from the two trolleybuses. Sunbeam W 132 (BRD 797), which is only just over four months old, leads 1939-vintage AEC 113 (ARD 676) as they decant their passengers at the Three Tuns before turning. In the days of strict economy in the mid-war period, it is interesting that the utility vehicles were equipped with fog lamps which could not be used! Note the air raid shelter direction sign and the white hoops round the traction pole that could do with a repaint.
Late W. J. Haynes © Maiwand Photographic Archive

deck and one per side on the lower-deck. The front windows of the upper-deck were fitted at the top with inward-opening ventilator hoppers. The bottom edges of the cab side windows were raked slightly downwards towards the front to give a deeper windscreen. Only the offside windscreen opened. Doors to both sides of cab. The front destination box was of the large single-track type, fitted immediately over the windscreen. There were no side or rear destination boxes. The rear upper-deck emergency door was originally panelled in metal instead of being glazed. Angular rear dome to roof. Rear elevation gently raked up to roof and front elevation slightly curved to roof. Slight 'V' in front dome. Sunbeam badge (later removed) in lower cream band under centre windscreen mullion.

External Livery: Crimson with three cream bands, but centre cream band not carried round top of windscreen. These vehicles were delivered painted in grey primer, the undertaking painting them into fleet lively before entering service. They did not receive lined-out livery as this was being phased out about the time they were delivered. The circular RCT motif, used exclusively on trolleybuses, was located on the front dash panel from new. Front fleet numbers were applied on the bottom nearside corner of the front dash panel, over the fog lamp, in the late 1940s.

Internal Livery: Ceilings white-painted. Crimson side panels and bulkheads and varnished wood surrounds to windows. White Doverite plastic-covered stanchions and grab rails. Moquette seating was supplied from new, a luxury not afforded to utility vehicles being delivered elsewhere at this time.

Other Notes: These vehicles were purchased essentially to cope with increased traffic on the 'main line' generated by the vast numbers of evacuees to Reading during the war. This batch was, in fact, the first series of trolleybuses to be constructed to full utility specification, for reasons recounted in the historical text. In 1945, 134 underwent a rebuild, which resulted in a 'square'-type side destination box being fitted over the platform, although no rear box was fitted. The windscreen was also reduced in depth as a result of the cab waistrail being rebuilt horizontally, so that the cab side windows were level with the bottom edge of the saloon windows. The upper-deck rear emergency door was replaced by one having rounded ends to the panes and with no rain gutter. On completion, 134 reappeared in service on 7th November 1945. It was also the only Reading utility trolleybus to receive an advert above the front destination box and to have the front registration number at the bottom of the removable towing panel rather than the top.

The rear registration number was originally painted on the top nearside corner of the rear platform window but in 1946/47 this was replaced by a slightly-inclined 'squareish' signwritten metal plate on the offside of the rear panel. In the same period, 133 had the offside front lower-deck bulkhead window behind the driver painted over. 133/4/5/7 received small blue identification lights on the front below the upper-deck windows in the cream band. All had their upper-deck rear emergency windows glazed by 1947 – possibly considerably earlier.

138–157 (DRD 124–143)　　　　New 1949

Chassis make and type: BUT 9611T
Wheelbase: 16ft 4in
Motor: English Electric type-410/3B (120hp) series-wound (equipped for battery traction)
Brakes: Series dynamic rheostatic and Westinghouse air on brake pedal
Length: 26ft 0in　　**Width:** 8ft 0in
Unladen Weight: 8 tons 17 cwt 1 qtr
Body make & type: Park Royal H30/26RD
Initial cost: £5,309 each
First Registered:
138: 19.03.49	148: 26.05.49
139: 24.03.49	149: 26.05.49
140: 24.03.49	150: 26.05.49
141: 24.03.49	151: 26.05.49
142: 18.05.49	152: 28.07.49
143: 18.05.49	153: 28.07.49
144: 26.05.49	154: 28.07.49
145: 26.05.49	155: 28.07.49
146: 26.05.49	156: 28.07.49
147: 26.05.49	157: 28.07.49

Bodywork Characteristics: All-metal body of five-bay construction with first four opening bay windows per side on upper-deck and first three per side on lower-deck. Driver's cab windscreen and side windows full height and depth to give all-round visibility. These were the first vehicles owned by the undertaking to be 8ft wide and fitted with folding platform doors. The front destination screen was of the large single-track type, in the centre of the panel, in a projecting box. The rear destination screen was situated immediately below the top cream band, giving room for advertisements on the panel below. The side destination screen was over the entrance, also immediately below the top cream band. The side destination box was operated from the upper-deck rear seat. Two steps up to the platform. There was a slight bulge over the doorway to accommodate the door mechanism. More upright but still raking front, compared with earlier trolley vehicles, merging into a rounded roof. Small blue identification lights on the front below the upper-deck windows (the last batch of vehicles to be fitted with this feature). The rear elevation was perpendicular to the bottom of the upper-deck emergency door, where it curved to merge into the rear roof dome.

External Livery: Generally as described for 132–137, although the lower cream band did not extend across the front of the vehicle due to the depth of the cab windows.

Internal Livery: Ceilings white. Crimson lower panels. Cream mottled metal upper part to window surrounds and crimson lower half, both of which only became repainted later in life. Crimson stairs and platform areas. Wood grain varnish finish to woodwork trim. Black Doverite plastic-covered stanchions and grab rails. 'Chocolate block' rubber-covered platform and step. Metal strips on linoleum to saloon floors. Deans tubular steel-framed seats, with bright metal top hand-grab rails, upholstered in red leather and filled with foam rubber, similar to those fitted to motorbuses 74–83.

Other Notes: These vehicles were delivered in 1949 for the Northumberland Avenue and Whitley Wood routes, which were due for conversion to trolleybus operation that year, although they were soon to be seen over the whole trolleybus system. They were the first 8ft-wide passenger

Right and below: *A glimpse of the future – BUT 9611T trolleybus 144 (DRD 130) shows its sleek, modern lines in these Park Royal Vehicles Ltd pre-delivery photographs, part of a series of which these are representative. The bus is constructed to the newly-approved 8-foot width and is fitted with platform doors and a safety staircase. Deep windscreens provide the driver with excellent visibility, while the 120hp motor provides plenty of power!*

© British Commercial Vehicle Museum

vehicles to enter service in the Home Counties, and among the first in the country to have driver-operated platform doors. The Transport Manager, Mr W. J. Evans, designed many of the new safety features incorporated into the vehicles. Basing his design on the 1939 AEC trolleybuses (107–131), the front windscreens were made deeper to afford better driver visibility and the rear platform was designed to be on the same level as the lower-saloon floor, although this resulted in a higher initial climb for passengers from ground level. The stairs were wider for easier negotiation, and platform doors were fitted to reduce platform accidents. A door interlock was provided, linked to the power pedal, so that ordinarily the vehicle could not move with the doors open (although it was possible to override this facility should the need arise). When new, 157 differed from the remainder in that it had CAV electrically-operated doors, whereas the others had Peters compressed air doors. 155 and 156 (originally at least) had Peters air brakes instead of Westinghouse. Before entering service, 138 had had controlled acceleration equipment installed by the English Electric Company, enabling the trolleybus to accelerate more smoothly. English Electric offered to fit this device to all the BUTs for approximately £50 per vehicle. A demonstration was arranged for 31st March 1949 for members of the Transport Committee. All were appreciative of the benefits and, at its meeting on 11th May 1949, the Committee authorised the necessary expenditure to equip all 20 BUTs. Not long afterwards, Mr Evans learned that immediate delivery would result in a very much higher price but, if prepared to wait 12–15 months, the equipment could be installed for the quoted price. Thus he decided to postpone the order and instead, to see how 138 performed in service over an extended period. In the event, Mr Evans did not pursue the idea; it is not known when the automatic acceleration equipment was eventually removed from trolleybus 138. 144 was used for official photographs which appeared in various transport journals at the time. When it was only six months old, it was decorated for Road Safety Week, carrying a white board over its front dome advertising the event. BUT 154 was temporarily taken out of service in July 1950 to have a GEC traction motor fitted, together with trial GEC control equipment incorporating a modified scheme of rheostatic braking. A feature of this equipment was that the motor shunt field current varied continuously during the braking period, reaching a very high value corresponding to about 10,000 amps/square inch at standstill. A relay was incorporated, to switch off the shunt just before the bus came to rest, in order to prevent overheating of the shunt field should the driver hold the brake pedal down for the duration of service stops. A variety of tests were conducted by GEC, who were trying to develop further this type of braking. Fluorescent lighting was also installed to this bus, making the interior considerably brighter at night-time and reducing the glare that the standard filament lamps produced. This part of the experiment was carried out on behalf of GEC in collaboration with Mr Evans and CAV who, between them, had developed a new method of operating hot cathode fluorescent tubes. This was replaced in May 1959 by a more modern system developed by Philips. 154 was re-motored with a GEC type WT269F traction motor of 95 hp in

September 1959, which it retained until withdrawal; whilst so fitted, it had 'limited regeneration' (believed to have been a means whereby only part of the energy of braking is converted into electricity and fed back into the line, the remainder being dissipated via resistances). In the mid-1950s, as an economy measure when passenger levels were depleted, trolleybuses 142 and 144 alternated with 147 and 151 for a year in store; this went on for about five years. In 1959, the undertaking obtained Ministry of Transport approval to increase the seating capacity of all 20 vehicles from 56 to 59 by adding an extra bench seat at the rear of the upper deck. At the same time, the opportunity was taken to modify the rear, downward-opening upper-deck emergency window by rebuilding with a 12in-wide mullion to provide a platform on which staff could stand to carry out repair work to the booms and trolleyheads. 154 was the first to be treated, re-entering service on 1st May 1959. A year later, the 12in mullion was made about 3in wider on 154 only. Below are the dates of re-entry into service for each vehicle following completion of this work:

154: 01.05.59	153: 01.05.60	155: 01.04.61
140: 01.06.59	148: 01.07.60	144: 01.09.61
150: 01.07.59	149: 01.08.60	157: 01.10.61
139: 01.09.59	142: 01.09.60	143: 01.11.61
156: 01.10.59	145: 01.12.60	138: 01.01.62
141: 01.01.60	147: 01.01.61	152: 01.03.62
146: 01.03.60	151: 01.03.61	

From 1963, the BUTs tended to be used more for peak hour duties only, rather than on all-day service, mainly due to the fact that both types of Sunbeams (the 1950 S7s and the 1961 F4As) had a larger seating capacity. During the phased abandonment of the trolleybus system, it was the BUTs that bore the brunt of withdrawals as routes closed. In January 1967, as a result of the Whitley Wood route being abandoned, 141, 145, 149, 151, 152, 153, 154 and 157 were withdrawn whilst, due to abandonment of the Northumberland Avenue route in December 1967, the end was spelled out for 138, 139, 140, 146 and 156. When the Kentwood/Armour Hill route was abandoned in March 1968, trolleybuses 142, 143, 147, 148, 150 and 155 were withdrawn, leaving 144 as the sole survivor. 144's future was quite safe by now, as it had been earmarked for preservation, and it remained in service until 27th September 1968. It was then taken to the new Bennet Road workshops (which were on a different site to the Bennet Road premises mentioned elsewhere in this book) to receive a special repaint in preparation for it to run as Reading's last trolleybus. After final abandonment of the system, on 3rd November 1968, 144 was subsequently taken to its new home, a small private museum in Belton, Lincolnshire. It returned to Reading in 1976 to take part in the Transport Department's 75th Anniversary celebrations. It has been a permanent resident at the Trolleybus Museum at Sandtoft since 2006, following the death of owner M. J. C. Dare the previous year.

BUT trolleybus 149 (DRD 135) loading in St. Mary's Butts on 25th June 1949, three weeks after inauguration of the trolleybus route serving Northumberland Avenue. Note the obvious newness of the vehicle (including the lack of adverts), the high position of the rear destination box and the novel way of condensing 'Northumberland Avenue'. The rear fleet number is now positioned not in the centre of the rear lower-deck emergency door but in the dead centre of the whole width of the back of the vehicle, so that part is on the emergency door and the rest is on the adjacent rear panel!

Late W. J. Haynes © Maiwand Photographic Archive

158–169 (ex-Huddersfield) New 1934
(VH 6757/53/51/59/55/52/61/60/ 54/50/58/56)

Chassis make and type: Karrier E6
Wheelbase: 16ft 10⅝ in
Motor: Metropolitan Vickers type-201 (80hp) compound-wound
Brakes: Originally regenerative on power pedal and rheostatic and air on brake pedal. Regenerative braking facility subsequently disconnected (before entering service in Reading in the case of 161–3).
Length: 30ft 0in **Width:** 7ft 6in
Unladen Weight: 8 tons 14 cwt 1 qtr
Body make & type: Brush H34/30R (body numbers unknown)
Initial cost: £228 each, when new to Huddersfield.

It is virtually certain that all the Karriers were allocated their <u>original</u> Reading fleet numbers in the order in which they arrived in Reading – see the re-numbering theory recounted in Chapter 18, which has not been repeated here in the interests of saving space.

Bodywork Characteristics: Timber-framed body of seven-bay construction, with three 'pinch'-type opening windows per side per deck. Three windows to the front upper-deck. Bottom edge of cab windows on same level as bottom edge of saloon windows. Top edge slightly higher than top edge of saloon windows. Offside windscreen opening. Rainshields to upper-deck bay and rear corner D-windows. Front elevation raked to full height, but front dash panel protruded 3 or 4 inches, and extreme front was about 12in forward of front wings. When delivered to Reading these vehicles had a 'Mae West'-type panel at the front, but this was altered to a plain panel during rebuilding. High ground clearance. Roof was flat on top. Trolleybooms somewhat short, with consequential splattering of graphite grease from the overhead over the rear of the vehicle. Radio interference suppressors on roof visible under timber cover. Two steps up to platform. Retriever pole housed along nearside through orifice in rear bulkhead. Destination indicators of those which entered Reading service were changed from Huddersfield Corporation layout to a small single-track type, that at the front being just above the centre cream band. The rear destination indicator was situated just below the top cream band and that at the side just above the platform entrance.

External Livery: Basically standard trolleybus livery, as detailed earlier. Front fleet number was located under nearside headlamp on 158, with RCT motif in centre of dash panel. 160, the second vehicle in this batch to enter service (on 18th February 1949) was the first trolleybus to be outshopped without the RCT motif, the fleet number being repositioned in its place, a practice continued on all trolleybuses thereafter.

Internal Livery: White ceiling. Dark wood stain to panels and window frames. Moquette-covered seats with no top grab rails. Crimson to platform and stairs area.

Other Notes: These vehicles had been delivered to Huddersfield Corporation in November 1934 as their Nos. 7–18, being Huddersfield's first production batch of trolleybuses, 1–6 having been experimental vehicles. 8 and 10 (later Reading 160 and 159 respectively) entered service a few days earlier than the others, the rest entering service on either 11th or 12th November 1934, when they took over from Huddersfield's trams on the Lindley and Outlane

The first ex-Huddersfield six-wheeler Karrier to be outshopped ready for service was trolleybus 158 (VH 6757), seen here in all its glory outside the department's offices, in a condition in which the undertaking could be justly proud.

© Reading Museum Service (Reading Borough Council); all rights reserved

DETAILS OF SERVICE WITH HUDDERSFIELD

1934 No.	1942 No.	Reg'n No.	Into Service	Out of Service	Left Hud'field	Left Sunbeam
7	407	VH 6750	12.11.34	28.02.48	. .	19.05.48
8	408	VH 6751	08.11.34	28.02.48	07.04.48	19.04.48
9	409	VH 6752	11.11.34	25.03.48	. .	31.05.48
10	410	VH 6753	05.11.34	25.03.48	. .	08.04.48
11	411	VH 6754	12.11.34	28.02.48	. .	07.06.48
12	412	VH 6755	12.11.34	28.02.48	26.04.48	.04.48
13	413	VH 6756	11.11.34	31.05.48	09.06.48	17.06.48
14	414	VH 6757	12.11.34	28.02.48	24.03.48	25.03.48
15	415	VH 6758	11.11.34	31.05.48	. .	17.06.48
16	416	VH 6759	11.11.34	31.05.48	. .	.06.48
17	417	VH 6760	12.11.34	28.02.48	13.04.48	21.04.48
18	418	VH 6761	11.11.34	28.02.48	. .	24.05.48

DETAILS OF SERVICE WITH READING

Rdg No.	Into Service	Out of Service	Initial Disposal	Taken Away
167	n/a	n/a	Dismantled Mill Lane	04.52
160	18.02.49	31.08.56	H. Remblance, Stepney	01.57
163	01.06.50	31.12.56	H. Remblance, Stepney	01.57
159	01.04.49	31.10.55	H. Remblance, Stepney	01.57
166	n/a	n/a	Dismantled Bennet Rd	04.52
162	13.12.49	31.12.56	H. Remblance, Stepney	01.57
169	n/a	n/a	Dismantled Bennet Rd	04.52
158	18.09.48	31.10.55	H. Remblance, Stepney	01.57
168	n/a	n/a	Dismantled Bennet Rd	09.51
161	01.02.51	31.12.56	H. Remblance, Stepney	01.57
165	n/a	n/a	Dismantled Bennet Rd	04.52
164	n/a	n/a	Dismantled Bennet Rd	04.52

to Waterloo services. On 4th October 1938, 12 (later Reading 162), en route to Outlane, was buffeted by high winds, resulting in the vehicle running out of control and overturning onto its nearside. Fortunately, there were only two passengers on board and their injuries were of a minor nature. The subsequent investigation attributed the incident to a faulty air compressor, which the driver had already reported as defective.

These vehicles operated in regular service in Huddersfield until 11th July 1941, subsequently being relegated to peak-hour extra duties, due to the fact that more modern trolleybuses were being delivered which were fitted with run-back and coasting brakes to cope more safely with the steep hills encountered on the Huddersfield system. Such features rendered 7–18 non-standard and, as such, they were kept away from routes with steep gradients. In 1942, these vehicles were renumbered 407–418. Age and non-standard equipment led to thoughts about replacing them so, in the mid-1940s, an order was placed for 32 new trolleybuses to replace all non-standard trolleybuses in the Huddersfield fleet. At that time, the Reading undertaking was having problems coping with the post-war demand for public transport. Thus, a search for second-hand vehicles began. The Huddersfield Karriers had just come onto the market and, as they were the best of what few second-hand vehicles were available at the time, Reading decided to purchase them at a cost of £200 each.

The first to arrive in Reading was ex-Huddersfield 414 (VH 6757), on 25th March 1948, the others following until the last arrived in June 1948. Fleet numbers were chalked on, presumably allocated in their order of arrival in Reading. The original intention was to give each vehicle an overhaul and place it in service quickly but, on closer inspection, it was realised that the timber-framed bodies had deteriorated more than had been anticipated. The number of vehicles it was planned to refurbish was soon reduced to ten and subsequently to six.

Of those which did enter Reading service, each was extensively rebuilt by the undertaking, taking about six months per vehicle. When taken in for rebuild, each vehicle was first stripped down mechanically and electrically and the parts overhauled. After the chassis was cleaned and silver-painted, the vehicle moved to the body shop, where the body was completely rebuilt using the original structure where possible. Although the original design was followed in principle, several new features were incorporated. The most noticeable change was at the front, where the dash panel was redesigned and a detachable towing panel provided. In consequence, the headlights were repositioned nearer to the side of the vehicle. As modified, the dash had a less fussy appearance than the original, which had featured a central 'Mae West' panel which gave the impression that it replaced a motorbus radiator. These vehicles were not fitted with the blue or white identity lights carried by most other Reading double-deck vehicles at this time. During the rebuilding, the Huddersfield route number boxes mounted above the ultimate destination boxes were removed from front and rear although, surprisingly, no improvement was made to the size of the ultimate destination display, which was very small and difficult to read from ground level. Neither was any opening made in the cab ceiling to enable the driver to observe what the front blind was showing, so that at each terminus it was necessary for the conductor to stand in front of the vehicle to inform the driver when the correct destination was showing. 158 (VH 6757) was the first to enter service, on 18th September 1949, with the other five following gradually at extended intervals, until the last, 161 (VH 6759), entered service on 1st February 1951.

The six that were not used were temporarily stored at a corporation-owned yard in Crescent Road (off Wokingham Road), where they remained until early 1950. Five of them, 164–166/168/169, were then taken to the site where Bennet Road depot was being built at the time, although 167 was taken to Mill Lane and dumped in East Yard. Of the six unused Karriers, 168 was dismantled in September 1951, the remainder being dismantled in May 1952.

Crews were certainly not appreciative of these vehicles, two of the main drawbacks being that they did not have a battery traction facility and also that they had high-tension lighting circuits, which meant that the lighting flickered when the vehicle passed under 'dead' sections of overhead. This caused annoyance to conductors when collecting fares during the hours of darkness.

The Karriers served Reading well for over six years and, when withdrawn, these vehicles were at least 21 years old. They were replaced in service by five AEC 661T trolleybuses (107–111), which had been in store at Bennet Road depot since November 1950, each of which was extensively overhauled. As each AEC became ready to re-enter service, a Karrier was withdrawn. 158 and 159 were withdrawn on 31st October 1955, 160 on 31st August 1956 and 161–163 on 31st December 1956. All were stored at Bennet Road upon withdrawal until sold for scrap in January 1957.

Appendix C   Subsequent Disposals of Vehicles

This appendix contains the disposal records and subsequent history of each vehicle to have entered service between 1939 and 1949. Vehicles which were already in service at the start of this story will be described in a future volume covering the pre-war years, while the Sunbeam S7 trolleybuses and Crossley DD42/8 motorbuses, which entered service as 1950 drew to a close, will also be described in a forthcoming book.

The information in this appendix has been derived from a number of sources over a period in excess of fifty years, including the undertaking's files and local motor taxation records, local enthusiasts' observations and, not least, those records maintained by the PSV Circle, to which due acknowledgement is made. The latter published their *PK18: Fleet History of Reading Transport Ltd and its Predecessors* in February 2012 and the following closely accords with their records.

MOTORBUSES

6	BRD 754	Remained delicenced at Mill Lane after withdrawal (09.49) until sold (10.03.50) to Beech's Garage (Hanley) Ltd., (dealer), Hope Street, Hanley, Staffs; Sold to M. J. Wavell (Enterprise Motor Services), Newport, Isle of Wight (03.50 to 06.51), passing to Southern Vectis Omnibus Co. (900). Re-numbered 700 (c 10.55) and withdrawn (11.55); to AMCC (dealer), Stratford, London, E15 (01.56); R. J. Bleanch, 3 Station Road, Hetton le Hole, Co. Durham (.56); withdrawn (.60) and presumed broken up.
7	BRD 755	Remained delicenced at Mill Lane after withdrawal (09.49) until sold (04.50) to Beech's Garage (Hanley) Ltd., (dealer), Hope Street, Hanley, Staffs; sold to Bamber Bridge Motor Services Ltd. (4), Preston, Lancs (12.50 to 07.53), then rebodied with a 1935 Leyland L27/28R body from a Leyland TD1 (ATD 596), running as such 07.53 to 10.55; then to G. A. Leak (Paramount Coachways), 8 Linnett Street, Preston, Lancs (.55 to 08.56); sold to AAP (breaker), Dukinfield, Manchester (08.56) and presumed broken up.
27	BRD 815	Remained delicenced at Mill Lane after withdrawal until sold (18.12.50) to Beech's Garage (Hanley) Ltd., (dealer), Hope Street, Hanley, Staffs; sold to K. and M. (Hauliers) Ltd (K and M Coaches), Nottingham (No.9) (02.51) to (12.53); Major's Coaches Ltd., Worksop, Notts (12.53) to (18.09.55), passing to East Midland Motor Services Ltd. (D32) and withdrawn (11.55); F. Cowley (dealer), Salford, Lancs (12.55). Any further afterlife and final disposal unknown (registration void by 12.58).
28	BRD 816	Remained delicenced at Mill Lane after withdrawal (09.49) until sold (10.03.50) to Beech's Garage (Hanley) Ltd., (dealer), Hope Street, Hanley, Staffs; M. J. Wavell (Enterprise Motor Services), Newport, Isle of Wight (03.50) to (06.51), passing to Southern Vectis Omnibus Co. (901). Re-numbered 701 (c 10.55) and withdrawn (11.55); AMCC, (dealer), Stratford, London E15 (12.55); J. P. Williamson, Gauldry, Fife, (.56) to (.); Autodrome Engineers, Audenshaw, Manchester (04.57) to (.58); Don Everall (Commercial Vehicles) Ltd, (dealer), Wolverhampton, Staffs (.58) and broken up (03.59).
12	CDP 231	Great Western Motors Ltd., (dealer), Reading, Berks (11.48); H. Kimber and H. Brewer (Ockendon Coaches), South Ockendon, Grays, Essex (05.49) to (04.55); Scott Hale (contractor), Globe Road, Hornchurch, Essex as staff transport (04.57) to (c. 07.62); W. Redfern, (dealer), Barking, Essex (by 07.63) and used as an office. Any further afterlife and final disposal unknown.
13	CDP 232	Great Western Motors Ltd. (dealer), Reading, Berks (11.48); Anderton, Oxford (.49) to (.); H. H. & J. Say, Gloucester (08.50) to (12.51); W. G. Richards, Moylgrove, Pembrokeshire (12.51) to (.); O. Williams, Cardigan (01.58) to (07.58); Knox (contractor), Bristol (03.60). Birmingham Coach Sales (dealer) (12.62); last licensed as a lorry. Any further afterlife and final disposal unknown.
15	CDP 233	Great Western Motors Ltd. (dealer), Reading, Berks (11.48); G. H. Dix, Freeland, Eynesham, Oxon (.49) to (.); A. W. Robinson (Rydale Motors), Pickering, N. Yorks (07.49) then Mrs D. Robinson (Rydale Motors), Pickering, N. Yorks (03.52), passing to Rydale Motors Ltd., Pickering, N. Yorks (05.58) and withdrawn (11.60); Edward Larkin, 14 Erskine Road, Hartlepool (05.65) as a mobile shop. Any further afterlife and final disposal unknown.
16	CDP 234	Great Western Motors Ltd. (dealer), Reading, Berks (11.48); J. & G. Browning, Box, Wilts (01.49) and to G. Browning, Box, Wilts (.51) to (08.57); E. Mortimer & Son Ltd. (contractor), 15 Argyle Street, Weston, Bath, Somerset as staff transport (04.58) to (09.59) and sold (12.63); noted derelict in yard of Bath Plant Hire (Mortimer), Weston, Bath, Somerset (05.65). Any further afterlife and final disposal unknown.
17	CDP 235	Great Western Motors Ltd. (dealer), Reading, Berks (11.48); C. H. Stout (Valentine Coaches), Shalbourne, Wilts (06.49) to (01.63); C. Homer, 4 Verwood Road, Leigh, Andover, Hants (04.64); noted with an unidentified owner at Gosport, Hants (02.65). Any further afterlife and final disposal unknown.
18	CDP 236	Great Western Motors Ltd. (dealer), Reading, Berks (11.48); A. G. Varney, Buckingham (07.49) to (04.62); sold to private owners Price and Fairbanks, Stevenage, Herts (04.62), converted to mobile caravan and intended for use to convey owners and their families overland to New Zealand, leaving Stevenage (05.62). Last licensed to Anthony John Price, 1 Longmeadow, Stevenage, Herts (05.62) and apparently scrapped.
58	CRD 252	Remained delicenced at Mill Lane until sold (06.09.61) to CDS Trading Co. Ltd., (dealer), 272 London Road, Wallington, Surrey, passing to Lansdowne Coaches, (dealer), London E11 (and appeared in a photograph in an advertisement in the *Daily Telegraph* (17.02.62) for the People's League for the Defence of Freedom). Any afterlife and final disposal unknown.

59	CRD 253	Remained delicenced at Mill Lane until sold (09.62) to J. C. Thomas, (dealer), South Street, Wells, Somerset, passing to R. Irvine (Tiger Coaches) (dealer), Dews Hill Garage, Salsburgh, Motherwell, Lanark by (05.63); A. & C. McLennan, Spittalfield, Perth (06.63) to (c 03.67) (fitted with platform doors (08.63)); believed sold (c 07.68) to students, initially at St. Andrew's University, Edinburgh; converted to mobile caravan and used (still in A. & C. McLennan livery) on sundry Continental touring holidays and seen passing north through Reading (c.08.68); UK registration declared void (02.74); last noted derelict outside a used car yard in Zottegem, Belgium (04.81). Any further afterlife and final disposal unknown.
60	CRD 254	Remained delicenced at Mill Lane until sold (11.09.62) to J. C. Thomas, (dealer), South Street, Wells, Somerset, passing to R. Irvine (Tiger Coaches) (dealer), Dews Hill Garage, Salsburgh, Motherwell, Lanark by (10.62). Observed used by unidentified Scottish fruit farmer as pickers' transport (20.10.62), being driven on general use trade plate 062 V. Atholl Homes (contractor), 29 Park Circus, Glasgow as staff transport (10.62) to (05.64). Any further afterlife and final disposal unknown.
61	CRD 255	Remained delicenced at Mill Lane until sold (11.09.62) to J. C. Thomas, (dealer), South Street, Wells, Somerset, passing to R. Irvine (Tiger Coaches) (dealer), Dews Hill Garage, Salsburgh, Motherwell, Lanark by (10.62); Garner's Buses, Bridge of Weir, Renfrew (16), (c 10.62) to (12.64); Davis (breaker), Glasgow (01.65) and broken up.
62	CRD 256	Remained delicenced at Mill Lane until sold (20.09.62) to R. Irvine (Tiger Coaches) (dealers), Dews Hill Garage, Salsburgh, Motherwell, Lanark; Garner's Buses, Bridge of Weir, Renfrew (15) (.62) to (12.64); Davis (breaker), Glasgow (01. 65) and broken up (04.65).
63	CRD 257	Remained delicenced at Mill Lane until sold (20.09.62) to R. Irvine (Tiger Coaches) (dealer), Dews Hill Garage, Salsburgh, Motherwell, Lanark. Atholl Homes (contractor), 29 Park Circus, Glasgow as staff transport (10.62) to (03.64). Any further afterlife and final disposal unknown.
64	CRD 258	Sold (01.09.62) to O. J. Hambridge (Hambridge Coaches), 1 Lyne Road, Kidlington, Oxon and withdrawn (12.64); P. J. Bennett (dealer), Dedworth, Berks (12.64), being kept at Newtall Garage, Dorchester, Oxon (03.65) before being moved to Dedworth. Subsequent afterlife not recorded until Autospares, (breaker), Bingley, W. Yorks (11.67) and broken up.
65	CRD 259	Remained delicenced at Mill Lane until sold (09.62) to J. C. Thomas (dealer), South Street, Wells, Somerset, passing to R. Irvine (Tiger Coaches) (dealer), Dews Hill Garage, Salsburgh, Motherwell, Lanark by (05.63); A. & C. McLennan, Spittalfield, Perth (05.63) to (09.65) (fitted with platform doors (c 05.63)); W. Heath, Fordoun Flying Club, Laurencekirk, Kincardineshire as an airfield control tower/messroom (.68) to (03.75); acquired for preservation (29.03.75) by P. A. Whitehead, Reading.
66	CRD 260	Remained delicenced at Mill Lane until sold (06.09.61) to CDS Trading Co. Ltd, 272 London Road, Wallington, Surrey, passing to Lansdowne Coaches (dealer), London E11 (and appeared in a photograph in an advertisement in the *Daily Telegraph* (17.02.62) for the People's League for the Defence of Freedom). Any afterlife and final disposal unknown.
67	CRD 261	Remained delicenced at Mill Lane until sold (06.09.61) to CDS Trading Co. Ltd, 272 London Road, Wallington, Surrey, passing to Lansdowne Coaches (dealer), London E11 (and appeared in a photograph in an advertisement in the *Daily Telegraph* (17.02.62) for the People's League for the Defence of Freedom). Any afterlife and final disposal unknown.
68	CRD 591	Remained delicenced at Mill Lane until sold (10.59) to J. C. Thomas (dealer), South Street, Wells, Somerset; reported in Somerset (12.59), owner unknown. Any subsequent afterlife and final disposal unknown.
69	CRD 592	Initially withdrawn from passenger service (05.10.59), passing to County Borough of Reading Health Department (02.60) (retaining bus livery and fleet numbers and garaged at Mill Lane) until (02.62). Returned to Transport Department ownership (02.62) and overhauled, re-certified and resumed PSV duties until expiry of certificate of fitness (19.02.64). Retained for driver instruction (with two seats), ultimately falling into disuse (c.08.64) and parked for some months in East Yard. Sold (03.12.65) to P. J. Bennett (dealer), Dedworth, Berks; R. A. Trussler, 81 Grenfell Road, Maidenhead, Berks (12.65) to (08.69) as a mobile shop and subsequently noted in Twyford, Berks (12.65) and Windsor, Berks (.68). Any subsequent afterlife and final disposal unknown.
70	CRD 593	Remained delicenced at Mill Lane until sold (12.59) to W. L. Thurgood (Coachbuilders) Ltd., Ware, Herts; F. A. Jones, 75 Tanfield Grove, Corby, Northants (c .60) to (09.62) as a mobile shop. Any subsequent afterlife and final disposal unknown.
71	CRD 594	Remained delicenced at Mill Lane until sold (08.10.63) to H. C. Goodman (Heating) Ltd., Caversham Road, Reading, Berks as staff transport until sold (08.65) to K. Johnson & Son (greengrocers), 60, Chagford Road, Reading, Berks as a mobile shop; withdrawn (08.68) but still owned to (04.69) at least.
72	CRD 595	Remained delicenced at Mill Lane until sold (09.04.63) to R. Irvine (Tiger Coaches) (dealer), Dews Hill Garage, Salsburgh, Motherwell, Lanark; J. B. Bennett (Glasgow) Ltd, 26 Market Street, Kilsyth, Stirling (contractor) and used in Motherwell, Lanark as staff transport (.63) to (05.64); Sold back to R. Irvine (Tiger Coaches) (dealer), Dews Hill Garage, Salsburgh, Motherwell, Lanark (05.65) and broken up.
73	CRD 596	Remained delicenced at Mill Lane stripped of useful parts and seating reduced to 20, until sold (04.05.62) to P. J. Bennett (dealer and breaker), 'Chez Nous', Holyport Road, Holyport, Berks; R. A. Trussler, 81 Grenfell Road, Maidenhead, Berks (10.62) to (11.65) as a mobile shop in the Maidenhead/Ascot/Fifield area. Any subsequent afterlife and final disposal unknown.

74	CRD 863	Remained delicenced at Mill Lane until sold (04.12.62) to R. Irvine (Tiger Coaches) (dealer), Salsburgh, Motherwell, Lanark; J. B. Bennett Ltd. (contractor), Banton Mill, Banton, Kilsyth, Stirling (c .63) to (06.65) and used as staff transport in connection with Cumbernauld New Town development. Any subsequent afterlife and final disposal unknown.
75	CRD 864	Remained delicenced at Mill Lane until sold (04.12.62) to R. Irvine (Tiger Coaches) (dealer), Dews Hill Garage, Salsburgh, Motherwell, Lanark; H. (later Barbara) McEwan, 8-14 Cross Street, Lennoxtown, Stirling (by 07.63) to (by 04.66). Any subsequent afterlife and final disposal unknown.
76	CRD 865	Remained delicenced at Mill Lane until sold (22.07.64) to P. J. Bennett (dealer and breaker), 'Chez Nous', Holyport Road, Holyport, Berks, being stored at Dedworth, Berks. Intended to be sold to students for an overland journey to India sponsored by Guinness, leaving (29.08.64) but sale was not effected. Transferred for storage at Newtall Garage, Dorchester, Oxon, then believed purchased by Hughes, Winnersh, Berks and sent for auction to Southern Counties Car Auctions, Frimley, being seen passing through Reading (13.03.65); presumably did not reach its reserve and seen westbound in Oxford Road, Reading (29.04.65) possibly bound for Dorchester. Any subsequent afterlife and final disposal unknown.
77	CRD 866	Remained delicenced at Mill Lane until sold (22.07.64) to P. J. Bennett (dealer and breaker), 'Chez Nous', Holyport Road, Holyport, Berks, being stored at Dedworth, Berks; C. Margo (Margo's Coaches), 20A Lower Addiscombe Road, Croydon, Surrey (08.64) to (01.66), operated in Reading C. T. livery. To an unidentified dealer (03.66). Any subsequent afterlife and final disposal unknown.
78	CRD 867	Remained delicenced at Mill Lane until sold (22.07.64) to P. J. Bennett (dealer and breaker), 'Chez Nous', Holyport Road, Holyport, Berks, being stored at Dedworth, Berks; C. H. Holmes (Rye Hill Park Coaches), Peckham, London SE15 (09.64) to (03.66) and used on school contract work, operated in Reading C. T. livery. Sold to an unknown dealer, possibly back to P. J. Bennett (dealer and breaker), 'Chez Nous', Holyport Road, Holyport, Berks (.66); Gordon Adams (Mobile Print), Old Windsor, Berks, as a mobile printing workshop still in Reading C. T. livery but minus seats (.66) to (.66); Bruce Bishop (Scrap Metals) Ltd., Slough, Bucks (01.67) and scrapped piecemeal over an extended period but gone by (04.69).
79	CRD 868	Remained delicenced at Mill Lane until sold (23.07.64) to R. Irvine (Tiger Coaches) (dealer), Dews Hill Garage, Salsburgh, Motherwell, Lanark (being driven away on general use trade plate 963 V); J. & M. Harris, 140 Castlemilk Drive, Glasgow 55 (08.64) to (04.66); unidentified bus breaker, Barnsley, S. Yorks (04.66) and broken up.
80	CRD 869	Remained delicenced at Mill Lane until sold (23.07.64) to R. Irvine (Tiger Coaches) (dealers), Dews Hill Garage, Salsburgh, Motherwell, Lanark (being driven away on general use trade plate, believed to have been 688 V); J. & M. Harris, 140 Castlemilk Drive, Glasgow 55 (08.64) to (04.66); unidentified bus breaker, Barnsley, S. Yorks (04.66) and broken up.
81	CRD 870	Remained delicenced at Mill Lane until sold (04 or 05.08.64) to P. J. Bennett (dealer and breaker), 'Chez Nous', Holyport Road, Holyport, Berks, being stored at Dedworth, Berks; C. Margo (Margo's Coaches), 20A Lower Addiscombe Road, Croydon, Surrey (08.64) to (01.65), operated in Reading C. T. livery. To an unidentified dealer (03.66). Any subsequent afterlife and final disposal unknown.
82	CRD 871	Remained delicenced at Mill Lane until sold (04 or 05.08.64) to P. J. Bennett (dealer and breaker), 'Chez Nous', Holyport Road, Holyport, Berks, being stored at Dedworth, Berks. Transferred for storage at Newtall Garage, Dorchester, Oxon, and sent on approval to O. J. Hambridge (Hambridge Coaches) Kidlington, Oxon but returned. Then believed purchased by Hughes, Winnersh, Berks and sent for auction to Southern Counties Car Auctions, Frimley, being seen passing through Reading (13.03.65); presumably did not reach its reserve and seen westbound in Oxford Road, Reading (29.04.65) possibly bound for Dorchester. Any subsequent afterlife and final disposal unknown.
83	CRD 872	Remained delicenced at Mill Lane until sold (04 or 05.08.64) to P. J. Bennett (dealer and breaker), 'Chez Nous', Holyport Road, Holyport, Berks, being stored at Dedworth, Berks; Transferred for storage at Newtall Garage, Dorchester, Oxon; O. J. Hambridge (Hambridge Coaches), Kidlington, Oxon (12.64) to (08.66), operated in Reading C. T. livery; Passenger Vehicle Sales (dealer), Upminster, Essex (01.67); PVS Contracts (71), Upminster, Essex (01.67) but not operated, being sold to J. Bone (breaker), Highwood, Chelmsford, Essex (02.67) and broken up.

TROLLEYBUSES

107	ARD 670	Remained delicenced at Mill Lane after stripping of useful parts until sold (25.08.61) to P. J. Bennett (breaker), 'Chez Nous', Holyport Road, Holyport, Berks and broken up.
108	ARD 671	Remained delicenced at Mill Lane after stripping of useful parts until sold (14.07.61) to C. Stanley (breaker), Sindlesham, Berks and broken up.
109	ARD 672	Remained delicenced at Mill Lane after stripping of useful parts until sold (28.06.61) to C. Stanley (breaker), Sindlesham, Berks and broken up.
110	ARD 673	Remained delicenced at Mill Lane after stripping of useful parts until sold (19.07.61) to P. J. Bennett (breaker), 'Chez Nous', Holyport Road, Holyport, Berks and broken up.
111	ARD 674	Remained delicenced at Mill Lane after stripping of useful parts until sold (08.09.61) to P. J. Bennett (breaker), 'Chez Nous', Holyport Road, Holyport, Berks and broken up.
112	ARD 675	Remained delicenced at Mill Lane after stripping of useful parts until sold (11.09.61) to P. J. Bennett (breaker), 'Chez Nous', Holyport Road, Holyport, Berks and broken up.

113	ARD 676	Delicenced after service on 14.09.61, motor removed as part of contract of sale (for use in a new trolleybus). Vehicle minus motor sold to Reading Transport Society (15.09.61) for preservation.
114	ARD 677	Remained delicenced at Mill Lane after stripping of useful parts until sold (17.08.61) to P. J. Bennett (breaker), 'Chez Nous', Holyport Road, Holyport, Berks and broken up.
115	ARD 678	Remained delicenced at Mill Lane after stripping of useful parts until sold (06.58) to J. Thompson (breaker), Cardiff and broken up.
116	ARD 679	Remained delicenced at Mill Lane after stripping of useful parts until sold 06.58) to J. Thompson (breaker), Cardiff and broken up.
117	ARD 680	Remained delicenced at Mill Lane after stripping of useful parts until sold (10.59) to J. Thompson (breaker), Cardiff and broken up.
118	ARD 681	Remained delicenced at Mill Lane after stripping of useful parts until sold (06.58) to J. Thompson (breaker), Cardiff and broken up.
119	ARD 682	Remained delicenced at Mill Lane after stripping of useful parts until sold (06.58) to J. Thompson (breaker), Cardiff and broken up.
120	ARD 683	Remained delicenced at Mill Lane after stripping of useful parts until sold (04.07.61) to C. Stanley (breaker), Sindlesham, Berks and broken up.
121	ARD 684	Remained delicenced at Mill Lane after stripping of useful parts until sold (10.58) to J. Thompson (breaker), Cardiff and broken up.
122	ARD 685	Remained delicenced at Mill Lane after stripping of useful parts until sold (10.58) to J. Thompson (breaker), Cardiff and broken up.
123	ARD 686	Remained delicenced at Mill Lane after stripping of useful parts until sold (10.58) to J. Thompson (breaker), Cardiff and broken up.
124	ARD 687	Remained delicenced at Mill Lane after stripping of useful parts until sold (10.58) to J. Thompson (breaker), Cardiff and broken up.
125	ARD 688	Remained delicenced at Mill Lane after stripping of useful parts until sold (10.58) to J. Thompson (breaker), Cardiff and broken up.
126	ARD 689	Towed to Mill Lane after overturning (27.03.52); delicenced and stripped of useful parts after deciding to scrap; transferred to Bennet Road and remained in store until sold, partly cannibalised (07.58) to J. Thompson (breaker), Cardiff and broken up
127	ARD 690	Withdrawn as a result of an accident (22.10.60); remained delicenced at Mill Lane after stripping of useful parts until sold (19.05.61) to C. Stanley (breaker), Sindlesham, Berks and broken up.
128	ARD 691	Remained delicenced at Mill Lane after stripping of useful parts until sold (05.08.61) to P. J. Bennett (breaker), 'Chez Nous', Holyport Road, Holyport, Berks and broken up.
129	ARD 692	Remained delicenced at Mill Lane after stripping of useful parts until sold (02.09.61) to P. J. Bennett (breaker), 'Chez Nous', Holyport Road, Holyport, Berks and broken up.
130	ARD 693	Withdrawn as a result of an accident (27.04.61); remained delicenced at Mill Lane after stripping of useful parts until sold (19.05.61) to C. Stanley (breaker), Sindlesham, Berks and broken up.
131	ARD 694	Remained delicenced at Mill Lane after stripping of useful parts until sold (21.06.61) to C. Stanley (breaker), Sindlesham, Berks and broken up.
132	BRD 797	Delicenced and useful parts removed; parked at premises at Bennet Road (11.50) until sold (01.51) to J. C. Lewis (breaker), Maidenhead and broken up.
133	BRD 798	Delicenced and useful parts removed; parked at premises at Bennet Road (11.50) until sold (01.51) to J. C. Lewis (breaker), Maidenhead and broken up. Registration declared void (by 11.53).
134	BRD 799	Delicenced and useful parts removed; parked at premises at Bennet Road (11.50) until sold (01.51) to J. C. Lewis (breaker), Maidenhead and broken up. Registration declared void (by 11.53).
135	BRD 800	Delicenced and useful parts removed; parked at premises at Bennet Road (11.50) until sold (01.51) to J. C. Lewis (breaker), Maidenhead and broken up.
136	BRD 801	Delicenced and useful parts removed; parked at premises at Bennet Road (11.50) until sold (01.51) to J. C. Lewis (breaker), Maidenhead and broken up.
137	BRD 814	Delicenced and useful parts removed; parked at premises at Bennet Road (11.50) until sold (01.51) to J. C. Lewis (breaker), Maidenhead and broken up.
138	DRD 124	Remained delicenced at Mill Lane after stripping of useful parts until sold (17.01.68) to P. J. Webber (breaker), Chalvey, Slough and broken up by Warren and Webber (breakers), Chalvey, Slough.
139	DRD 125	Remained delicenced at Mill Lane after stripping of useful parts until sold (12.01.68) to P. J. Webber (breaker), Chalvey, Slough and broken up by Warren and Webber (breakers), Chalvey, Slough.
140	DRD 126	Remained delicenced at Mill Lane after stripping of useful parts until sold (18.01.68) to P. J. Webber (breaker), Chalvey, Slough and broken up by Warren and Webber (breakers), Chalvey, Slough.
141	DRD 127	Remained delicenced at Mill Lane after stripping of useful parts until sold (19.01.67) to P. J. Bennett, Holyport, Berks but broken up in one of two yards in Chalvey, Slough also used by Warren and Webber.

142	DRD 128	Remained delicenced at Mill Lane after stripping of useful parts until sold (14.03.68) to P. J. Webber (breaker), Chalvey, Slough and broken up by Warren and Webber (breakers), Chalvey, Slough.
143	DRD 129	Remained delicenced at Mill Lane after stripping of useful parts until sold (08.03.68) to P. J. Webber (breaker), Chalvey, Slough and broken up by Warren and Webber (breakers), Chalvey, Slough.
144	DRD 130	Remained delicenced at Mill Lane until sold (23.11.68) to M. J. C. Dare, Reading for preservation at Westgate Trolleybus Museum, Belton, Lincs; passing to The Trolleybus Museum at Sandtoft (12.05) for continued preservation.
145	DRD 131	Remained delicenced at Mill Lane after stripping of useful parts until sold (24.01.67) to P. J. Bennett, Holyport, Berks but broken up in one of two yards in Chalvey, Slough also used by Warren and Webber.
146	DRD 132	Remained delicenced at Mill Lane after stripping of useful parts until sold (16.01.68) to P. J. Webber (breaker), Chalvey, Slough and broken up by Warren and Webber (breakers), Chalvey, Slough.
147	DRD 133	Remained delicenced at Mill Lane after stripping of useful parts until sold (11.03.68) to P. J. Webber (breaker), Chalvey, Slough and broken up by Warren and Webber (breakers), Chalvey, Slough.
148	DRD 134	Remained delicenced at Mill Lane after stripping of useful parts until sold (14.03.68) to P. J. Webber (breaker), Chalvey, Slough and broken up by Warren and Webber (breakers), Chalvey, Slough.
149	DRD 135	Remained delicenced at Mill Lane after stripping of useful parts until sold (23.01.67) to P. J. Bennett, Holyport, Berks but broken up in one of two yards in Chalvey, Slough also used by Warren and Webber.
150	DRD 136	Remained delicenced at Mill Lane after stripping of useful parts until sold (11.03.68) to P. J. Webber (breaker), Chalvey, Slough and broken up by Warren and Webber (breakers), Chalvey, Slough.
151	DRD 137	Remained delicenced at Mill Lane after stripping of useful parts until sold (14.01.67) to P. J. Bennett, Holyport, Berks but broken up in one of two yards in Chalvey, Slough also used by Warren and Webber.
152	DRD 138	Remained delicenced at Mill Lane after stripping of useful parts until sold (10.01.67) to P. J. Bennett, Holyport, Berks but broken up in one of two yards in Chalvey, Slough also used by Warren and Webber.
153	DRD 139	Remained delicenced at Mill Lane after stripping of useful parts until sold (13.01.67) to P. J. Bennett, Holyport, Berks but broken up in one of two yards in Chalvey, Slough also used by Warren and Webber.
154	DRD 140	Remained delicenced at Mill Lane after stripping of useful parts until sold (03.01.67) to P. J. Bennett, Holyport, Berks but broken up in one of two yards in Chalvey, Slough also used by Warren and Webber.
155	DRD 141	Remained delicenced at Mill Lane after stripping of useful parts until sold (15.03.68) to P. J. Webber (breaker), Chalvey, Slough and broken up by Warren and Webber (breakers), Chalvey, Slough.
156	DRD 142	Remained delicenced at Mill Lane after stripping of useful parts until sold (17.01.68) to P. J. Webber (breaker), Chalvey, Slough and broken up by Warren and Webber (breakers), Chalvey, Slough.
157	DRD 143	Remained delicenced at Mill Lane after stripping of useful parts until sold (21.01.67) to P. J. Bennett, Holyport, Berks but broken up in one of two yards in Chalvey, Slough also used by Warren and Webber.
158	VH 6757	Delicenced and stripped of useful parts; stored at Bennet Road (11.55) until sold (01.57) to H. Remblance (breaker), Stepney, London, E14 and broken up.
159	VH 6753	Delicenced and stripped of useful parts; stored at Bennet Road (11.55) until sold (01.57) to H. Remblance (breaker), Stepney, London, E14 and broken up.
160	VH 6751	Delicenced and stripped of useful parts; stored at Bennet Road (09.56) until sold (01.57) to H. Remblance (breaker), Stepney, London, E14 and broken up.
161	VH 6759	Delicenced and stripped of useful parts; stored at Bennet Road (01.57) until sold (01.57) to H. Remblance (breaker), Stepney, London, E14 and broken up.
162	VH 6755	Delicenced and stripped of useful parts; stored at Bennet Road (01.57) until sold (01.57) to H. Remblance (breaker), Stepney, London, E14 and broken up.
163	VH 6752	Delicenced and stripped of useful parts; stored at Bennet Road (01.57) until sold (01.57) to H. Remblance (breaker), Stepney, London, E14 and broken up.
164	VH 6761	Delivered to Mill Lane, stripped of useful parts and removed to yard at Crescent Road, Reading (.48) and left until (c. 06.50) whence removed to Bennet Road and left derelict until dismantled and burnt (04.52).
165	VH 6760	Delivered to Mill Lane, stripped of useful parts and removed to yard at Crescent Road, Reading (.48) and left until (c. 06.50) whence removed to Bennet Road and left derelict until dismantled and burnt (04.52).
166	VH 6754	Delivered to Mill Lane, stripped of useful parts and removed to yard at Crescent Road, Reading (.48) and left until (c. 06.50) whence removed to Bennet Road and left derelict until dismantled and burnt (04.52).
167	VH 6750	Delivered to Mill Lane, stripped of useful parts and removed to yard at Crescent Road, Reading (.48) and left until (c. 06.50) whence removed to Mill Lane and dumped derelict in East Yard until dismantled (04.52).
168	VH 6758	Delivered to Mill Lane, stripped of useful parts and removed to yard at Crescent Road, Reading (.48) and left until (c. 06.50) whence removed to Bennet Road and left derelict until dismantled (24.09.51).
169	VH 6756	Delivered to Mill Lane, stripped of useful parts and removed to yard at Crescent Road, Reading (.48) and left until (c. 06.50) whence removed to Bennet Road and left derelict until dismantled and burnt (04.52).

Appendix D — Summary of Route Developments 1939–1950

The routes and services in operation as our story begins in early 1939 are described on pages 12/13. Alterations to and expansions of these routes and services during the period covered by this volume are summarised in chronological order below. See also maps on page 33 and inside front and back covers.

21.05.39 **Introduction of trolleybuses on 'main line':** Tramway replacement trolleybus services introduced, running beyond the extent of the tramway system, also covering existing motorbus services, as follows:

Trolleybus route A   Three Tuns – Norcot Road Junction – Tilehurst
Trolleybus route B   Three Tuns – Norcot Road Junction
Trolleybus route D   London Road – Norcot Road Junction

As a result, motorbus route G discontinued and Blagrave Hospital Special curtailed at Park Hospital. Motorbus route J cut back from Three Tuns to operate Roebuck – Erleigh Road (via Oxford Road) but motorbus route M (Grovelands Road – Stations (via Tilehurst Road)) extended from Stations via motorbus route J to Erleigh Road and thence via Crescent Road and Wokingham Road to Wokingham Road tram terminus to compensate. Sunday morning motorbus route A (Roebuck – Three Tuns) had already been discontinued from 14.05.39.

WAR DECLARED

03.09.39 **Minor modification to network of services:** Co-incidental to declaration of war, motorbus route M cut back from Wokingham Road tram terminus to Erleigh Road to operate as Grovelands Road – Erleigh Road.

25.09.39. **Reduction in service due to petrol rationing introduced on 23.09.39:** Route K (Woodcote Road – Broad Street) and route L (Hemdean Road – Berkeley Avenue) reduced to morning peak (7.00 – 9.30am) and evening peak (5.00 – 7.30pm) operation only (Mon – Sat); route J (Roebuck – Erleigh Road) cut back to operate a shuttle Roebuck – Norcot Road Junction only (Mon – Sat) but route M (Erleigh Road – Grovelands Road) frequency increased to compensate; Mon – Fri off-peak morning and afternoon operation of all other motorbus routes reduced. Due to evening 'black-out slow-running' conditions, all evening motorbus timetables altered to suit. Evening operation of trolleybus route D (Norcot Road Junction – London Road) withdrawn and every third vehicle on route A from Tilehurst diverted to London Road instead of Three Tuns. A new (reduced) Saturday motorbus timetable was also introduced.

01.10.39 **Reduction in service due to petrol rationing introduced on 23.09.39:** Sunday operation of route K (Woodcote Road – Broad Street) and route L (Hemdean Road – Berkeley Avenue) withdrawn. Sunday operation of route M (Erleigh Road – Grovelands Road) cut back to operate Grovelands Road – Stations only (with a last departure from Broad Street 10.30pm); route J (Roebuck – Erleigh Road (via Oxford Road))(Suns) truncated to operate Norcot Road Junction – Roebuck. Other Sunday last motorbus departures from Broad Street brought forward, to 10.45pm (routes F, H and I) and 10.50pm (route N). Last trolleybus departures from Broad Street (routes A, B and D) remained unaltered.

01.10.39 **Originally intended end of British Summer Time 1939 – now postponed to 19.11.39.**

02.10.39 **Reduction in service due to petrol rationing introduced on 23.09.39:** Last departure on route M from Stations for Erleigh Road 10.42pm; last route J Roebuck shuttle departed Norcot Road Junction 10.45pm.

Circa 10.39 **Modification for 'blackout slow running':** Evening operation of trolleybus route D (Norcot Road Junction – London Road) again modified for 'blackout slow running', possibly daily, by reverting almost to original, but being operated as Three Tuns – Norcot Road Junction instead of London Road – Norcot Road Junction (i.e. the running of every third journey from Tilehurst to London Road instead of Three Tuns was abandoned).

19.11.39. **End of extended British Summer Time 1939.**

20.11.39. **Trolleybus and motorbus last departures advanced:** Daily last motorbus and trolleybus departures from Broad Street brought forward to 10.12pm (route M to Grovelands Road); 10.20pm (route I and route M to Erleigh Road); 10.24pm (route D); and 10.30pm (routes A, B, F, H and N) although, on Saturdays only, the last departure on route I was also 10.30pm. The last route J Roebuck shuttle was advertised to depart Grovelands Road (not Norcot Road Junction) at 10.40pm. In general, until this time, last buses had departed the town centre at 11.00pm (10.30pm on Sundays).

25.02.40 **Onset of British Summer Time 1940** (not returning to Greenwich Mean Time until 07.10.45).

06.03.40 **Defence Regulations instruct time to be advanced to TWO hours ahead of Greenwich Mean Time to give 'Double Summer Time'.**

06.03.40 **Trolleybus last departures retarded:** Co-incidental with the onset of Double Summer Time, last trolleybuses from Broad Street (routes A, B and D) revert to 11.00pm.

27.04.40 **De-congestion of Broad Street – Minor motorbus route extension – motorbus last departures advanced:** Route K terminus at Broad Street (Vaudeville) moved to St. Mary's Butts (the inward route from

Stations being via Station Road, Friar Street and West Street and the outward routing remaining unchanged, via Broad Street, Queen Victoria Street and Station Road). Route N terminus at Broad Street (The Arcade) moved to King Street with no change to route. Also, on completion of road works to improve the junction of Berkeley Avenue with Bath Road, the Berkeley Avenue terminus of route L moved from Littlecote Drive to a new location 300 yards westwards, to a purpose-made turning bay on the approach to that junction. Last motorbus departures from Broad Street revert (Mon – Sat) to 11.00pm (except Berkeley Avenue 10.07pm; Grovelands Road 10.40pm; Erleigh Road and Horncastle 10.50pm); and Sun 10.45pm (except Grovelands Road, Erleigh Road and Lower Caversham 10.40pm). Last departure Pond House for Roebuck 11.15pm (Mon – Sat) and 11.00pm (Sun).

03.08.40 **New destination names introduced to confuse any possible enemy invaders:**

TILEHURST	became	BEAR INN	CAVERSHAM HEIGHTS	became	UPLANDS ROAD
CAVERSHAM	became	PROMENADE	LOWER WHITLEY	became	WOOD LANE JUNC.
WHITLEY STREET	became	WHIT-PUMP	EMMER GREEN	became	CHALGROVE WAY
LONDON ROAD	became	LIVERPOOL ROAD	LOWER CAVERSHAM	became	DONKIN HILL
SHINFIELD ROAD	became	MERRY MAIDENS	NORCOT ROAD JUNCTION	became	NORCOT JUNC.

26.08.40 **School special contract service for Reading Education Committee:** From junction of Cressingham Road with Northumberland Avenue, via Long Barn Lane, Basingstoke Road, Christchurch Road, Kendrick Road, London Road and Sidmouth Street, to junction of Queens Road with Sidmouth Street. Inward journeys at 8.55am and 1.35pm; outward journeys at 12.00 noon and 4.20pm. Operated mainly for use by evacuee schoolchildren from South Lambeth Road Schools.

Circa 09.40 **End of Double Summer Time 1940 – leaving time still ONE hour in advance of GMT.**

04.11.40 **Service improvements – retarded motorbus last departures:** Various improved daytime, evening peak hour and early evening services on motorbus routes F, I and N. Motorbus route J (in operation latterly as a shuttle over the Roebuck – Grovelands Road (Pond House) section) reinstated most of the day (daily) as a full Roebuck – Stations (via Oxford Road) service, to avoid transfer to/from already over-full trolleybuses on routes A, B and D – but in late evenings it continued to operate as a Roebuck – Pond House shuttle. Motorbus route H experimentally extended from Chalgrove Way to Courtenay Drive. Lunchtime peak operation re-instated on motorbus routes K and L. Motorbus last departures from Broad Street retarded to 10.15pm (except Berkeley Avenue 10.07pm and last departure Pond House for Roebuck 10.15pm). Trolleybus last departures from Broad Street remained 11.00pm.

07.11.40 **Service improvements sequel:** Motorbus route H Courtenay Drive extension reverted to Chalgrove Way (after just 3 days!) due to timekeeping problems.

c. 12.12.40 **Service improvement:** Morning, afternoon and early evening off-peak operation of motorbus route K (Woodcote Road – St. Mary's Butts) reinstated (Mon – Sat).

18.12.40 to 24.12.40 **Hired motorcoaches with drivers supplied by Smith's Coaches** (but with Reading Corporation Transport conductors) substituted on trolleybus route C on 18.12.40 to 21.12.40, 23.12.40 and 24.12.40, 10.00 am – 8.00pm (i.e. NOT on Sunday, 22nd December 1940). This was done to release the trolleybuses for operation on the overcrowded trolleybus routes A, B and D.

25.12.40 **Operation on Christmas Day:** The first Christmas Day since early tramway days on which a public service operated. Four workmen's specials were also operated for Huntley, Boorne & Stevens at 7.00am from London Street, to Lower Whitley, Lower Caversham, Tilehurst and Three Tuns, in addition to war workers' specials.

04.05.41 **Onset of Double Summer Time 1941.**

c. 06.41 **Modification:** To avoid a blackout accident, no motorbus route H relief journeys for Wood Lane Junc to operate beyond the Grenadier and school journeys to terminate at the Grenadier instead of Wood Lane Junc.

28.07.41 **Fuel conservation measures:** Motorbus route J (Roebuck – Stations) withdrawn entirely (Suns), also on Mon – Fri morning off-peaks (9.20am – 11.40am) when a shuttle service Pond House – Roebuck substituted; Weekday morning and afternoon off-peak journeys also cancelled on motorbus route K (Woodcote Road – St. Mary's Butts) and motorbus route L (Hemdean Road – Berkeley Avenue), both thus operating morning, lunchtime and evening peaks only.

10.08.41 **End of Double Summer Time 1941 – leaving time still ONE hour in advance of GMT.**

06.10.41 **Fuel conservation measures:** Daily motorbus last departures from Broad Street advanced to 9.30pm; Trolleybus last departures remain as 11.00pm (Mon – Sat) and 10.45pm (Sun).

05.04.42 **Onset of Double Summer Time 1942.**

06.04.42 **Protective fares:** 'Protective fares' charged within the borough by the Thames Valley Traction Co. Ltd. abandoned for rest of war – inward journeys only.

09.08.42 **End of Double Summer Time 1942 – leaving time still ONE hour in advance of GMT.**

01.10.42	**Fuel and rubber conservation measures:** Numerous stopping places abolished – see Appendix E (page 236).
04.01.43	**Fuel and rubber conservation measures:** All Sunday morning services, motorbus <u>and</u> trolleybus, withdrawn, services on all routes commencing 1.00pm; motorbus last departures from Broad Street advanced to 9.00pm (daily); last trolleybus departures from Broad Street advanced to 9.30pm (Mon – Sat) and 9.00pm (Sun). Stations – Erleigh Road section of route J believed 'officially' terminated as part of these changes.
04.04.43	**Onset of Double Summer Time 1943.**
c. 19.04.43	**Fuel and rubber conservation measures:** Minor cuts in off-peak Mon – Fri daytime service on trolleybus route D (Liverpool Road – Norcot Junc).
c. 04.43 (?)	**Special war workers' services:** Sunday morning special workmen's motorbus services for war workers ('temporary services') introduced on <u>seven</u> routes. Details have not survived.
08.07.43	**Service modifications:** Motorbus route H (Chalgrove Way – Wood Lane Junc) major timetable alterations due to extended running times. Motorbus route J (Stations – Roebuck (via Oxford Road)) minimum 3d. protective fare introduced on outward journeys as far as Reading West Station. Motorbus route K (St. Mary's Butts – Woodcote Road) double-decked and re-routed via St. Anne's Road, Priest Hill, The Mount, Albert Road and Highmoor Road to Woodcote Road, and vice versa.
18.07.43	**Service modifications:** Resulting from the need to allow adequate rest periods for crews working the late shift the previous day, Sunday operation of all trolleybus and motorbus services altered to start/finish 30 minutes later than hitherto, i.e. starting at 1.30pm instead of 1.00pm; finishing at 9.30pm instead of 9.00pm.
15.08.43	**End of Double Summer Time 1943 – leaving time ONE hour in advance of GMT.**
c. 09.43	**Service modifications:** Motorbus route K (St. Mary's Butts – Woodcote Road) two trips per day reinstated on the old route via St. Peter's Hill to serve St. Peter's Hill School, operated by single-deckers.
c. 10.43	**Service modifications:** Motorbus route K terminus altered from St. Mary's Butts to Friar Street (GPO), running from Stations via Blagrave Street and returning via Friar Street and Station Road.
02.04.44	**Onset of Double Summer Time 1944.**
03.04.44	**Improved fuel availability:** Mon – Fri frequency improved on motorbus route I (Donkin Hill – Horncastle) from alternate 15/20 mins to regular 15 mins; Sunday services increased from 20 mins to 15 mins on motorbus route F (Uplands Road – Merry Maidens), motorbus route H (Chalgrove Way – Wood Lane Junc) and motorbus route I (Donkin Hill – Horncastle).
31.07.44	**Trolleybus network extension:** Trolleybus route D extended from Norcot Junc to Kentwood (Daily); Motorbus route J (Stations – Roebuck (via Oxford Road)) (Mon – Sat except Mon – Fri morning off-peaks) and Pond House – Roebuck (Mon – Fri morning off-peak shuttle) withdrawn.
c. 08.44	**Special war workers' services:** Pond House – Roebuck motorbus shuttle service re-introduced as an early Sunday morning war workers' 'temporary service'.
03.09.44	**Special war workers' services:** Three journeys on early Sunday morning workers' motorbus service (known as a 'temporary service') from Bear Inn replaced by an equivalent trolleybus service from Kentwood to Norcot Junction, designed to meet workmen's trolleybus specials from Bear Inn. Presumably the motorbus-operated Pond House – Roebuck 'temporary service' was withdrawn as a result.
17.09.44	**End of Double Summer Time 1944 – leaving time ONE hour in advance of GMT.**
c. 10.44	**Service modification:** Motorbus route J (Pond House – Roebuck) shuttle service re-introduced (Mon – Sat morning and evening peak hours only (7.00am to 8.40am and 5.00pm to 7.40pm) in response to petition.
06.11.44	**Improved fuel availability:** Motorbus last journeys from Broad Street extended to 10.00pm instead of 9.00pm (Mon – Sat); trolleybus last journeys from Broad Street extended to 10.00pm instead of 9.30pm (Mon – Sat); motorbuses and trolleybuses last journeys from Broad Street on Sundays remained at 9.30pm; route K (Woodcote Road – Friar Street (GPO)) <u>possibly</u> strengthened to operate throughout the day (Mon – Sat).

MR J. M. CALDER RETIRES – MR W. M. LITTLE TAKES OVER

01.04.45	**Onset of Double Summer Time 1945.**
16.04.45	**Service modification:** Motorbus route J (Pond House – Roebuck) Mon – Sat peak hour shuttle withdrawn due to lack of support.
25.06.45	**Improved fuel availability:** Departures of last buses and trolleybuses Mon – Sat from Broad Street was revised to 11.00pm instead of 10.00pm but, due to an acute staff shortage, it was not possible to extend this to Sundays and Sunday operation continued to be from 1.30pm to 9.30pm.
15.07.45	**End of Double Summer Time 1945 – leaving time ONE hour in advance of GMT.**

RETURN TO PEACE

12.08.45	**Improved service:** Times of Sunday morning workmen's motorbus services between Broad Street and Wood Lane Junction, Donkin Hill and Chalgrove Way varied. Outward route to Wood Lane Junc. via Duke Street, London Street, Silver Street, Mount Pleasant, Whitley Street, Basingstoke Road, Buckland Road, Northumberland Avenue, Hartland Road, Basingstoke Road and Whitley Wood Lane. Inbound route was the reverse of the above to Whitley Street, then Southampton Street, Bridge Street and St. Mary's Butts.
07.10.45	**End of British Summer Time 1945 – time reverting to GMT.**
c. 11.45	**Service modification:** Trolleybus routes A, B and D revised, becoming:

Trolleybus route A Three Tuns – Norcot Junction – Bear Inn
Trolleybus route B Three Tuns – Norcot Junction – Kentwood
Trolleybus route D Liverpool Road – Norcot Junction

c. 12.45	**Service modification:** Motorbus route K (Friar Street (GPO) – Woodcote Road) school journeys operated via St. Peter's Hill withdrawn.
11.01.46	**Emergency diversion – road collapse in eastern Broad Street (south side):** Road surface in Broad Street opposite The Arcade collapsed, resulting in westbound trolleybuses on routes A, B and D having to be diverted via Duke Street, London Street, Mill Lane, Bridge Street and St. Mary's Butts, which required vehicles to de-pole and battery across the entrance to the main depot as there was no through wiring provided at that time**.** Diversion believed to have lasted 2 – 3 days. Motorbuses, meanwhile, are understood to have operated through Broad Street as best they could, a window-bill dated 15th January 1946 indicating that it may prove necessary at short notice to alter (a) the routeing of omnibuses through Broad Street; and (b) the positioning of stopping places in Broad Street.
18.02.46	**Motorbus routes modified to operate permanently along duo-directional corridors:** Route F (Merry Maidens – Uplands Road) diverted inwards from Merry Maidens via London Street, Duke Street and King Street to Broad Street (reverse of outward journey) in lieu of via Crown Street, Southampton Street, Bridge Street and St. Mary's Butts. Route N from Callington Road OR Staverton Road re-routed from Whitley Street to run directly via Southampton Street and Bridge Street to St. Mary's Butts (i.e. now omitting Silver Street and Crown Street). Route N now terminated in St. Mary's Butts, as opposed to King Street, and turned via Oxford Road, Cheapside, Friar Street and West Street, returning south via the reverse of the inbound route. Route H (Wood Lane Junc – Chalgrove Way) also diverted via Southampton Street and Bridge Street to St. Mary's Butts, then Broad Street, Queen Victoria Street, Station Road and Stations, returning via the reverse of the foregoing (in lieu of London Street, Duke Street, King Street and Broad Street and *vice versa*). Route I (Horncastle – Donkin Hill) and route L (Berkeley Avenue – Hemdean Road) diverted permanently in both directions via St. Mary's Butts to Broad Street in lieu of via Gun Street and Minster Street. These changes eliminated buses from Gun Street and Minster Street for regular licensed operation, a situation that was to prevail until the town centre pedestrianisation projects of the mid-1990s – although these streets were used from time to time for buses on diversion, not least during the various tram rail removal and road reconstruction works of 1946/47 described below.
19.03.46 to 01.04.46.	**Road reconstruction in Oxford Road temporarily closing Cheapside:** The terminal turning loop of route N temporarily revised via West Street and Friar Street, then turning around The Triangle car park via Caversham Road and Lower Thorn Street and returning to St. Mary's Butts via Friar Street and West Street.
08.04.46	**Road reconstruction in Broad Street and King Street (north side):** Westbound 'main line' trolleybuses on routes A, B and D temporarily re-routed as before via Duke Street, London Street, Mill Lane, Bridge Street and St. Mary's Butts, which required vehicles to de-pole and battery across the entrance to the main depot as there was no through wiring provided at that time. Motorbuses on route F (to Uplands Road) and route M (to Stations) diverted via High Street, Market Place and Friar Street to Station Road, stopping opposite the GPO at the Woodcote Road stop. Motorbuses on route I (to Horncastle), route L (to Berkeley Avenue) and route M (to Grovelands Road) diverted between Station Road and St. Mary's Butts via Friar Street and West Street, stopping in Friar Street east of Greyfriars Road, instead of via Queen Victoria Street and Broad Street. All routes serving Broad Street <u>eastbound</u> remained unchanged. Queen Victoria Street, which was closed as part of the Broad Street (north side) re-construction, was re-opened from 29th May 1946. We believe that while it was closed, motorbuses northbound on route H (to Chalgrove Way), route I (to Donkin Hill) and route L (to Hemdean Road) left Broad Street via Cross Street and Friar Street to gain Station Road. Broad Street was re-opened to two-way traffic on 31st May 1946 and duo-directional public transport returned to Broad Street on Monday, 3rd June 1946 – see below.
14.04.46	**Onset of British Summer Time 1946.**
12.05.46	**Service improvements:** The Callington Road branch <u>only</u> of route N was extended from St. Mary's Butts to Promenade via West Street, Friar Street and Caversham Road and with a much improved frequency but trolleybus route C (Whit-Pump – Promenade) was reduced to peak hours only, effectively becoming a 'short-working' facility to the aforementioned extended route N. This facilitated the release of trolleybuses for service on 'main line' trolleybus routes A, B and D during the daytime. Improved frequencies also introduced on route

H (Wood Lane Junc – Chalgrove Way) (15 mins to 10 mins), route I (Horncastle – Donkin Hill) (15/20 mins to 15 mins) and route M (Erleigh Road – Grovelands Road) (15/30 mins to 15 mins). Last buses from town centre on Sundays became 10.30pm instead of 9.30pm.

03.06.46 **Road reconstruction of West Street junction and Duke Street junction:** West Street and Duke Street were closed to through traffic. Trolleybus operation of routes A, B and D reverted to the normal routeing westbound through Broad Street instead of being diverted via Duke Street, Mill Lane, Bridge Street and St. Mary's Butts. Trolleybus operation of route C (Whit-Pump – Promenade) was suspended completely *"until the completion of the reconstruction"* and operated instead by motorbuses; also additional relief motorbuses operated over route N between Whitley Street and Promenade. Due to the closure of West Street, routes C and N were diverted between St. Mary's Butts and Caversham Road via Oxford Road and Cheapside instead of West Street and Friar Street. Also due to the closure of West Street, route M was diverted in both directions between Greyfriars Road and St. Mary's Butts via Friar Street, Cheapside and Oxford Road and route O, the factory special from Staverton Road to Huntley & Palmers, was run into St. Mary's Butts, where it U-turned to run to Watlington Street via Bridge Street, Mill Lane, London Street and Queens Road. The closure of Duke Street caused motorbus route F (Merry Maidens – Uplands Road) and route M (Erleigh Road – Grovelands Road) to be operated between Broad Street and London Street via Minster Street, Gun Street, Bridge Street and Mill Lane <u>in both directions</u> (!). Motorbus route H (Chalgrove Way – Wood Lane Junc.), motorbus route I (Horncastle – Donkin Hill) and motorbus route L (Berkeley Avenue – Hemdean Road) all reverted to their normal routeing through the town centre. Note also that trolleybuses operating routes A, B and D were put to considerable inconvenience when running into and out of depot, having to run to Norcot Junction in order to enter Broad Street for Three Tuns and Liverpool Road and having to run to Three Tuns and return to Broad Street in order to run in to depot via St. Mary's Butts and Bridge Street – notwithstanding the fact that all trolleybuses (apart from 101) were fitted with battery traction facilities! Sufficient reconstruction work was completed on or by 22nd June 1946 to enable a partial reversion to normal.

25.06.46 **Road reconstruction of Broad Street at West Street Junction and King Street at Duke Street Junction:** Motorbus route F (Shinfield Road – Uplands Road) and route M (Grovelands Road – Erleigh Road) reverted to 'normal' routeing between Broad Street and London Street, (so presumably at Duke Street Junction half the roadway was closed at a time) but in view of work starting in St. Mary's Butts, initially at the West Street end, route M was temporarily split to operate Erleigh Road – Stations and St. Mary's Butts – Grovelands Road, passengers on the Grovelands Road section bound for Stations being advised to change buses in Castle Street on to route I, which was specially timed to meet. Trolleybus route C (Whit-Pump – Promenade), latterly motorbus-operated, was temporarily suspended entirely but the Staverton Road operation of route N remained unaffected and continued to terminate in St. Mary's Butts. The Callington Road – Promenade service was split to operate Callington Road – St. Mary's Butts (where it also turned), whilst the other section was operated Promenade – West Street, terminating/picking-up on the <u>east</u> side of West Street and returning to Promenade via Oxford Road and Cheapside. Route H (Wood Lane Junc – Chalgrove Way), route I (Horncastle – Donkin Hill), and route L (Berkeley Avenue – Hemdean Road) became diverted between St. Mary's Butts and Broad Street via Gun Street and Minster Street <u>in both directions</u>, stopping in Broad Street at The Arcade and opposite Cross Street. Motorbus routes M and N returned to normal on Wednesday 10th July 1946 and the remainder (routes H, I and L) the following day, <u>together with the reinstatement of trolleybuses on route C (Whit-Pump – Promenade)</u>, which in itself suggests that the reconstruction of the northbound dual carriageway section of St. Mary's Butts had been completed but not the southbound carriageway or the junction of Castle Street, Bridge Street and Gun Street with St. Mary's Butts. An additional Kentwood stop was also provided in Broad Street opposite The Arcade from the same date.

There then appears to have been a respite of roundly four months before any more town centre road reconstruction work took place.

06.10.46 **End of British Summer Time 1946.**

.11.46 **Road reconstruction of St. Mary's Butts, Bridge Street and 'lower' Southampton Street:** A window poster dated 4th November 1946 announced that in the event of a necessity to operate a one way traffic scheme, buses proceeding towards town would keep to their normal route, while buses leaving town would be diverted for part of their journey via Duke Street, with a main town centre boarding point in Broad Street near The Arcade.

MR W. M. LITTLE RESIGNS – MR W. J. EVANS TAKES OVER

09.01.47 **Service improvement:** We assume that the outstanding reconstruction in St. Mary's Butts (i.e. the southbound carriageway of the dual carriageway section) then took place, followed by the Castle Street, Bridge Street, Gun Street, St. Mary's Butts intersection. Thus, the Staverton Road section of route N was extended from St. Mary's Butts to Stations and re-designated as route P, (obviating the need for a terminus in St. Mary's Butts), running inwards from St. Mary's Butts via West Street, Friar Street, Greyfriars Road, and Station Hill and <u>nominally</u> outwards via Station Road, Friar Street and West Street to St. Mary's Butts. At the same time, the route was also diverted to operate via Christchurch Gardens and Northumberland Avenue in lieu of via Basingstoke Road and Buckland Road. However, while work proceeded with reconstructing the southbound carriageway of St. Mary's Butts, trolleybus route C (Whit-Pump – Promenade) would have been suspended again and motorbus route H (Chalgrove Way – Wood Lane Junc), motorbus route I (Donkin Hill – Horncastle), motorbus route L (Hemdean Road – Berkeley Avenue), motorbus route M (Erleigh Road – Grovelands Road), motorbus route

	N (Promenade – Callington Road), and motorbus route P (Stations – Staverton Road) became diverted <u>outbound</u> via Broad Street, Minster Street and Gun Street to Bridge Street and thence Southampton Street.
12.01.47	**Road reconstruction of Bridge Street and 'lower' Southampton Street:** Initially, the work involved just Bridge Street, for which purpose a one-way traffic scheme northbound was implemented between Mill Lane and Gun Street. Specifically due to the road reconstruction, trolleybus route C (Whit-Pump – Promenade) was therefore *"discontinued until further notice"*. The <u>outbound</u> routeing of motorbus route H (Chalgrove Way – Wood Lane Junc), motorbus route N (Promenade – Callington Road), motorbus route P (Stations – Staverton Road) and motorbus route L (Hemdean Road – Berkeley Avenue) was changed from operating <u>outbound</u> via Minster Street, Gun Street, Bridge Street and Southampton Street, to being routed via Broad Street, King Street, Duke Street and London Street, routes H, N and P continuing via Silver Street and Mount Pleasant to Whitley Street and route L via Crown Street and Pell Street to regain its route into and along Berkeley Avenue. Inbound routeings of all <u>these</u> routes remained unaltered but with the inbound routeing of route L (Berkeley Avenue – Hemdean Road) reverting to normal via St. Mary's Butts to Broad Street instead of the diversion via Gun Street and Minster Street.
02.02.47	**Sunday service improvements:** Minor alterations (improvements) made to motorbus route F (Merry Maidens – Uplands Road), motorbus route M (Erleigh Road – Grovelands Road) and motorbus route N (Callington Road – Promenade).
03.02.47	**Service improvements:** Minor alterations (improvements) made (Mon – Fri after 7.00pm) to motorbus route H (Chalgrove Way – Wood Lane Junc).
18.02.47	**Service reduction:** Monday – Friday off-peak frequency reduced on 'main line' trolleybus route A (Three Tuns – Bear Inn), route B (Three Tuns – Kentwood) and route D (Liverpool Road – Norcot Junction) 9.00am to 12 noon and 7.00pm to 11.00pm, presumably due to an acute shortage of trolleybuses. No alteration to Saturday timetable. A seemingly new arrangement of the 'main line' trolleybus services was introduced <u>on Sundays</u>, viz.

Between 9.00am and 2.00pm:	Route A	Three Tuns – Bear Inn	every 20 mins
	Route B	Three Tuns – Kentwood	every 20 mins
From 2.00pm:	Route A	Three Tuns – Bear Inn	every 6 mins
	Route D	Liverpool Road – Kentwood	every 12 mins

c. 03.47	**Road reconstruction in Bridge Street and 'lower' Southampton Street:** Route L (Berkeley Avenue – Hemdean Road) <u>believed</u> to have had its <u>outbound</u> temporary routeing changed from via Duke Street, London Street, Crown Street and Pell Street to Berkeley Avenue, to via Duke Street, London Street, Mill Lane and across Southampton Street to its normal routeing via Katesgrove Lane; while at the same time its normal <u>inbound</u> routeing to Broad Street via Katesgrove Lane, Bridge Street and St. Mary's Butts was changed to a temporary routeing from Katesgrove Lane, across Southampton Street, Mill Lane, London Street, Duke Street and King Street to Broad Street.
16.03.47	**Onset of British Summer Time 1947.**
13.04.47	**Double Summer Time 1947 begins** (re-introduced by the Attlee government).
13.04.47	**Destination names revised as follows:**

MERRY MAIDENS	reverted to	**SHINFIELD ROAD**	**THREE TUNS**	became	**WOKINGHAM ROAD**
CHALGROVE WAY	reverted to	**EMMER GREEN**	**PROMENADE**	reverted to	**CAVERSHAM**
WOOD LANE JUNC.	became	**WHITLEY WOOD**	**WHIT-PUMP**	reverted to	**WHITLEY STREET**
BEAR INN	reverted to	**TILEHURST**	**GROVELANDS RD**	became	**GROVELANDS**
NORCOT JUNC.	became	**NORCOT**			

14.04.47	**Improved service:** Motorbus route P (Stations – Staverton Road) frequency increased to 20 mins (Mon–Sat).
05.05.47	**Road reconstruction in 'upper' Southampton Street: also introduction of a 'public anti-confusion' loop:** That part of Southampton Street between Whitley Street and Crown Street was closed completely for reconstruction while similar work was still taking place in 'lower' Southampton Street and Bridge Street, for which a one-way traffic scheme northbound only was in operation; and at this stage it would also appear that one carriageway, possibly southbound, in St. Mary's Butts, was closed. This phase resulted in trolleybus route C (Whitley Street – Caversham) being reinstated but operated 'temporarily' as a peak-hour motorbus route, with buses bound for Whit-Pump being diverted from West Street into Broad Street via the same routeing as that currently being taken by diverted motorbus route N here following. Due to some unforeseen and continuing bridge works in Bridge Street, which resulted in the bridge being closed to southbound traffic until the end of November 1947, the <u>outward</u> routeing of motorbus routes H, N and P (together with the motorbuses working trolleybus route C) continued to be from Broad Street via Duke Street and London Street, thence via Silver Street and Mount Pleasant. Inbound, trolleybus route C (Whit-Pump – Promenade) (temporarily operated by motorbuses), motorbus route N (Callington Road – Caversham) and motorbus route P (Staverton Road – Stations) were all diverted from Whitley Street via Mount Pleasant, Silver Street and Crown Street, to rejoin their normal inbound routeing via 'lower' Southampton Street and Bridge Street into St. Mary's Butts. In connection with 'public anti-confusion' measures (as described in the historical text), motor-

bus route F (Shinfield Road – Uplands Road), motorbus route H (Whitley Wood – Emmer Green) and motorbus route M (Erleigh Road – Grovelands) were diverted inwards from London Street via Mill Lane, Bridge Street and St. Mary's Butts, with route F proceeding into Broad Street and route M proceeding to Stations via West Street and Greyfriars Road.

. .47 **Road reconstruction in 'lower' Southampton Street at Katesgrove Lane:** Motorbus route L (Hemdean Road – Berkeley Avenue) became temporarily diverted via Southampton Street and Pell Street in both directions in lieu of via Katesgrove Lane during lifting of tram track in Southampton Street in the vicinity of Mill Lane and Katesgrove Lane. It was subsequently decided to retain this as permanent – see entry for 29.03.48.

05.07.47 **Special late-night services:** Operated from Stations to various parts of the town on seven routes, meeting trains from Henley Royal Regatta. No other details have survived!

.08.47 **Reconstruction of Whitley Street:** southbound traffic temporarily diverted from Mount Pleasant via Highgrove Street and Christchurch Road (exact dates not known).

10.08.47 **End of Double Summer Time 1947 (and finally) – reverting to British Summer Time.**

18.08.47 **Road reconstruction in 'upper' Southampton Street:** Upon completion of the northbound carriageway (i.e. downhill), inbound motorbuses operating trolleybus route C (Whitley Street – Caversham), motorbus route H (Whitley Wood – Emmer Green), motorbus route N (Callington Road – Caversham) and motorbus route P (Staverton Road – Stations) became operated into town from Whitley Street via the whole length of Southampton Street, Bridge Street and St.Mary's Butts but with the outward routeing remaining unaltered, viz., continuing to operate to Whitley Street via Duke Street, London Street, Silver Street and Mount Pleasant.

29.09.47 **Ending of 'public anti-confusion' loop:** Following completion of reconstruction of the lower section of Southampton Street and Bridge Street, motorbus route F (Shinfield Road – Uplands Road) and motorbus route M (Erleigh Road – Grovelands) were restored to normal routeing via London Street and Duke Street in both directions, instead of operating inwards via London Street, Mill Lane, Bridge Street and St. Mary's Butts.

c. 10–11.47 **Roadworks:** Roundabout being constructed at the Basingstoke Road end of Whitley Street.

02.11.47 **End of British Summer Time 1947 – reverting to GMT.**

02.11.47 **Service improvement:** Motorbus route N extended from Callington Road, further along Northumberland Avenue, to Hartland Road, although peak hour short-workings to Callington Road were still provided.

01.01.48 **Protective fares:** Reinstatement of 'protective fares' charged within the borough by the Thames Valley Traction Co. Ltd. (abandoned for the duration of the war on inward journeys only).

14.03.48 **Onset of British Summer Time 1948.**

29.03.48 **Road reconstruction in 'upper' Southampton Street:** Upon completion of the southbound carriageway (i.e. up the hill), motorbus route H (Whitley Wood – Emmer Green), motorbus route N (Hartland Road – Caversham) and motorbus route P (Staverton Road – Stations) were restored to normal outbound routeing via Bridge Street and the whole of Southampton Street to Whitley Street, (route H from Broad Street and routes N and P from West Street). The temporary diversion of motorbus route L (Hemdean Road – Berkeley Avenue) routed from Broad Street via St. Mary's Butts, Bridge Street, Southampton Street and Pell Street to Berkeley Avenue (instead of via Southampton Street and Katesgrove Lane to Berkeley Avenue) became permanent – because the route became permanently double-decked and Katesgrove Lane was deemed unsuitable for double-deck operation. It has not been possible to establish exactly when route C was withdrawn for good but it may well have been with effect from this date, as it does not feature in the details given in the window poster referring to these changes but does most certainly when the changes of 18th August 1947 were being similarly advertised.

26.04.48 **Service improvement:** Improved evening frequencies on motorbus route F (Shinfield Road – Uplands Road), motorbus route H (Whitley Wood – Emmer Green), motorbus route K (Woodcote Road – Friar Street (GPO)), motorbus route L (Berkeley Avenue – Hemdean Road), motorbus route N (Hartland Road – Caversham) and motorbus route P (Staverton Road – Stations). The frequency on the supplementary operation of route I (Broad Street – Donkin Hill) was also improved on weekday evenings and on Sunday afternoons.

12.06.48 **Service improvement:** Saturday short-working extras provided on motorbus route H (Emmer Green – Whitley Wood) between Stations and Basingstoke Road/Hartland Road junction.

31.10.48 **End of British Summer Time 1948 – reverting to GMT.**

03.04.49 **Onset of British Summer Time 1949.**

05.06.49 **Extension of trolleybus system and consequent alteration to existing motorbus routes:** New trolleybus route E (Caversham Bridge – St. Mary's Butts – Northumberland Avenue) introduced, resulting in motorbus route N (Caversham – Hartland Road) being withdrawn. It would also appear that trolleybus route D (Liverpool Road – Kentwood) was re-designated route C with effect from this date to clear the way for route D to be allocated to the imminent new trolleybus route from Stations and St. Mary's Butts to serve Whitley Wood.

22–25.06.49	**Special service:** Thames Valley Traction Co. Ltd. operated a special service between Reading Stations and the Royal Counties Agricultural Show ground at Sonning, for which the undertaking hired eight of its new(ish) AEC Regent IIs.
. 07.49	**Road works:** Motorbus route L (Hemdean Road – Berkeley Avenue) temporarily terminated in Hemdean Road at Oxford Street during sewer works along Hemdean Road towards the Hemdean Road terminus.
07.08.49	**Extension of trolleybus system and consequent alteration to existing motorbus routes:** Trolleybus route D (Stations – St. Mary's Butts – Whitley Wood) inaugurated, being an extension of the original trolleybus service from Whitley Street, together with a spur from Caversham Road to Stations; trolleybus route E also altered, to operate alternate journeys from Northumberland Avenue to Stations and to Caversham Bridge. Motorbus route H (Emmer Green – Whitley Wood) cut back, that section of route H between the town centre and Whitley Wood being withdrawn, and the remainder re-designated route N and re-routed to operate Emmer Green – Friar Street (The Triangle), being routed from Emmer Green via Vastern Road, Blagrave Street and Friar Street (setting down outside the Co-operative Stores) and turning empty via Caversham Road and Lower Thorn Street to terminate at The Triangle car park (at the site of the present Chatham Street Inner Distribution Road interchange roundabout), returning by the same route. In Emmer Green, buses commenced using the newly-constructed Buckingham Drive instead of what now became Old Peppard Road past BBC Caversham Park – but continued to terminate in Kidmore End Road at Chalgrove Way. So as not to operate in direct competition with trolleybus route D, motorbus route P (Staverton Road – Stations) was diverted to run permanently via Silver Street, London Street, Duke Street, King Street, Broad Street, Queen Victoria Street and Station Road to Stations (and vice versa) in lieu of via Southampton Street, Bridge Street, St. Mary's Butts, West Street, Friar Street, Greyfriars Road and Station Hill, returning via Station Road, Friar Street and West Street to St. Mary's Butts. Route F (Shinfield Road – Uplands Road) and route I (Donkin Hill – Horncastle) were also the subject of some minor timing changes.
c. .10.49	**End of British Summer Time 1949 – reverting to GMT.**
14.11.49	**New 'bone-shaped' roundabout at Cemetery Junction:** Upon the roundabout being brought into use, together with a new trolleybus overhead layout which incorporated a 'turn-back' facility for vehicles arriving from the town centre, three weekday afternoon 'rush-hour extra' journeys were introduced on trolleybus route A, operating Cemetery Junction – Westwood Road, Tilehurst. From this date, battery turns at Orts Road by trolleybuses working factory extras to Huntley & Palmers ceased.
20.11.49	**Service improvement:** Revised <u>Sunday</u> timetable introduced on all trolleybus routes. On the 'main line' instead of there being a change in the pattern of services from 2.00pm, all-day operation was introduced, as follows: Trolleybus route A Wokingham Road – Norcot – Tilehurst Trolleybus route C Liverpool Road – Norcot – Kentwood
04.12.49	**Road works:** Temporary termination of motorbus route L (Hemdean Road – Berkeley Avenue) in Hemdean Road at Oxford Street ceased and buses terminated instead (until further notice) in Hemdean Road at Queen Street (near Hemdean Road schools).
02.01.50	**Improved service:** Modified frequency (including every 12 mins after 7.00pm) on route F (Shinfield Road – Uplands Road) and on the supplementary service operating on route I between Broad Street and Donkin Hill.
c. .04.50	**British Summer Time 1950 begins.**
24.04.50	**Service modification:** Trolleybus operation on the 'main line' modified so that Norcot became only a short-working facility from Wokingham Road. The new arrangements thus became: Trolleybus route A Wokingham Road – Norcot – Tilehurst Trolleybus route B Wokingham Road – Norcot Trolleybus route C Liverpool Road – Norcot – Kentwood **Revised service:** Evening operation of motorbus route K (Woodcote Road – Friar Street (GPO)) withdrawn after the 7.05pm journey from Friar Street (GPO).
07.08.50	**Improved service:** Short-working facility at Community Centre brought into use on trolleybus route E.
c. .10.50	**End of British Summer Time 1950 – reverting to GMT.**
06.11.50	**Modified evening service:** Motorbus route I (Donkin Hill – Horncastle) retimed after 10.07pm on Mon – Sat; Evening operation of motorbus route K (Friar Street (GPO) – Woodcote Road) reintroduced, operating hourly after 7.05pm on Mon – Sat; Motorbus route N (Friar Street (The Triangle) – Emmer Green) extra journey on Sunday evenings.
20.11.50	**Improved service:** Motorbus route N (Friar Street (The Triangle) – Emmer Green) given an improved Saturday service.

Appendix E   The Thirty-Nine Stops

The proposed alterations to effect a reduction in the number of intermediate bus stops with a view to saving tyre rubber, brake and clutch linings (on motorbuses) and fuel by reducing the number of stopping points along a route to no more than four per mile, which were required to be submitted to the regional transport commissioner for approval, were listed in a memo dated 14th September 1942, as follows:

Route J (Roebuck – Grovelands Road)
1. Remove bus stops inwards and outwards on lamp post 2292, about 150 yards west of Carlisle Road.
2. Remove stops inwards and outwards at Carlisle Road.
3. New stop to be fixed approximately half-way between items 1 and 2.
4. Remove stops inwards and outwards at Cranbourne Gardens.
5. Remove stops inwards and outwards at Bramshaw Road.

Route F (Uplands Road – Merry Maidens)
6. Remove stops inwards and outwards near the south end of Albert Road.
7. Remove stops inwards and outwards on lamp post M.V.252 in Christchurch Road, between Cintra Avenue and The Mount.
8. Remove stops inwards and outwards from lamp post 1947 in Shinfield Road, about 150 yards north of Cressingham Road.

Route M (Grovelands Road – Erleigh Road)
9. Remove stops inwards and outwards on lamp post 567 in Waverley Road, about 50 yards west of Wantage Road.
10. Remove stop, inwards only, at the junction of London Road and Kendrick Road.
11. Remove fare stage in London Road at Sidmouth Street.
12. Fare stage removed from Item 11 to be re-fitted on traction pole near the entrance to Kendrick Girls' School, approximately 26 yards west of item 11.
13. Outward stop position at the bottom of Craven Road to be moved approximately 50 yards towards Erleigh Road.
14. Inward stop position to be removed from Craven Road to approximately 40 yards up Erleigh Road, on traction pole No. E84.
15. Remove stops inwards and outwards at Reading School entrance in Erleigh Road.
16. Remove stops inwards and outwards at Denmark Road in Erleigh Road.

Route I (Donkin Hill – Horncastle)
17. Remove the Fare Stage position at Southcote Lane in Bath Road approximately 100 yards eastwards (near the first house past the Railway Bridge).
18. Remove stops inwards and outwards in Bath Road near Berkeley Avenue.
19. Remove bus stops inwards and outwards at the Waterworks, Bath Road.
20. Remove stops inwards and outwards at Downshire Square, in Bath Road.
21. Remove stops inwards and outwards at house 'Dunedin' in Bath Road.
22. Remove stops inwards and outwards at Field Road in Castle Hill.
23. Remove fare stage position, inwards and outwards, from near Almshouses in Castle Street, to west side of Coley Street.
24. Remove bus stops inwards and outwards at Boarded Lane in Castle Street.
25. Remove bus stops inwards and outwards in Vastern Road near the junction with Forbury Road.
26. Move Fare Stage position from Kings Meadow Road/Vastern Road, to under the southernmost Railway Bridge of the Great Western Railway bridges crossing Vastern Road.
27. Remove stops inwards and outwards from Queens Road/George Street.
28. Remove fare stage position outwards only, from the junction of Washington Road/Gosbrook Road, to near the junction of Kings Road/George Street. (This same Fare Stage will also serve 'H' route, and displace the fare stage in Gosbrook Road at the west side of the junction with George Street.)
29. Move bus stops inwards and outwards, from the east side of St. John's Road, to the west side of St. John's Road.
30. Remove bus stops inwards and outwards half way along Briants Avenue.
31. Move bus stops inwards and outwards from the south end of Donkin Hill to the north end of Briants Avenue.
32. Remove stop outwards at the north end of Donkin Hill.
33. Remove stop inwards in Henley Road, near the junction of Anglefields Road.
34. Remove stop outwards in Henley Road near the junction of Rossendale Road.

Trolley Vehicle Route C (Whit-Pump – Promenade)
35. Remove stops inwards and outwards in St. Mary's Butts, near the Coffee Stall.
36. Remove stops inwards and outwards in Caversham Road, near Vastern Road.
37. Remove stops inwards and outwards in Caversham Road, near York Road.
38. New stops to replace Items 36 and 37 – Outward stop to be on traction pole C65, near the junction of Swansea Road, and inward stop to be on pole C64 near the junction of Brigham Road.

Route F (Uplands Road – Merry Maidens)
39. The Vastern Road stop which has previously been identical with the stop at Vastern Road for TV Route 'C', will be separated from it (Item 38) and the new stop position will be on the next pole – pole C62.

Appendix F   Tickets

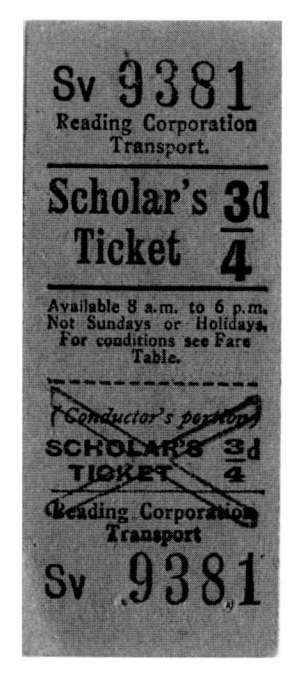

The tickets used by Reading Corporation Transport during the period covered by this book were of three different types. Printed, pre-paid tickets (left) were sold, often at a discount, e.g. to workmen, scholars etc. They were printed on thin coloured card, with different colours for different categories/values of ticket, and generally carried advertising on the reverse.

The TIM (Ticket Issuing Machines Ltd) (bottom left) was printed by the machine onto a blank roll of thin paper – usually white, although coloured tickets were issued occasionally for special purposes. The first TIM machines came into use in tramway days, and the last ones were phased out of general use in October 1986.

A pre-production trial of the new Bell Punch Ultimate system (below) took place in 1948, as described on page 154. This system issued square tickets on thick paper, with a range of four values for the trial (five or six when put into production), each having its own identifying colour. The ticket machine printed onto the ticket details of the journey taken and the type of fare paid. Fare values for which no individual ticket was available could be recorded by the issue of a combination of lower-value tickets. The trials in Reading used a test batch of tickets printed with the words '**BLANK CORPN.**'!

AEC Regent 9 (RD 5132) – an early 'oiler' – seen outside the depot in 1943. These views certainly convey an impression of a very hard-worked corporation motorbus at a rare moment off from its usual toils – mostly overloaded – as if contemplating its next brutal spell in service. The approaching gent in the left-hand image is thought to be Jimmy Calder, the transport manager. The rear view shows the classic lines of mid-1930s coachbuilding, evocative advert and features like the spring steel bumper bar (white-painted for the wartime blackout, as was the bottom of the platform stanchion).

Both Late W. J. Haynes © Millane Publishing

Index

Absenteeism 50, 64, 68/9, 91
Accidents 30, 42, 55, 86, 112, 116, 145/6, 164, 177, 216/7
platform 63, 116, 145, 169, 172
AEC 661T, delivery (main batch) 21
experimental (102) 70, 198, 202
leaf spring failures 37/8
specification etc 206, 215-7
temporary withdrawal 202, 216/7
withdrawal/disposal 217, 225/6
AEC Regal 4 .... 19, 38
AEC Regent, conversion to diesel 117, 120/1
delivery 15
refurbishment of No. 5 .... 117, 120/1
withdrawal 185, 189/90, 202
AEC Regent II, ... 136/7
destruction of No. 62 by fire 134/5, 141, 160, 205, 207, 212/3
orders/delivery 115, 117, 120, 125, 134, 136, 141, 160
specification etc 205, 207, 211-4
withdrawal/disposal 223-5
AEC Regent III, provisional order for 123, 125
Air raids 30, 43, 48, 69, 72
instructions to bus crews 45, 69
Air Raid Precautions 15, 17, 19, 72, 95
Air raid shelters 15, 25, 31, 34, 105
Ambulance service 17, 27, 72, 117, 134, 138, 145, 155, 178, 182/3
Ambulances, inter-hospital 17-19, 25-27, 29, 43, 54, 116
Anti-blast netting 31
Army specials 59, 106
Austerity era, definition of 96

Batteries, traction 21, 22, 69, 102, 110, 170, 172, 177, 179, 191, 199, 235
BBC, transport for 57
Bedford OB 123
delivery 118/9, 123, 143/4
hire to Smith's Coaches 144, 210
specification etc. 205, 207, 210, 212/3
withdrawal/disposal 161, 207, 223/4
Bennet Road depot 143, 155/6, 170/1, 180, 182, 198, 202/3
Blackout 30/1, 228/9
cessation of 87, 89, 96
exercises 19, 26/7
markings on buses 31, 42, 53, 65-67, 114
slow running 30, 99, 228
Borough boundary, extension of services beyond 62, 151
Bridge Street bridges 113, 131/2, 181, 190
British Summer Time 37, 100, 145, 228, 231-5, 230
'Bus Moving' indicators 35
Bus stop flags 36, 41, 63, 141-3
Bus stops, re-siting/elimination 39, 61, 64, 102, 147, 197, 229, 236
BUT 9611T, controlled acceleration equipment 180, 219
delivery 178/9
entry into service 179, 184, 186
fluorescent lighting 200, 219
orders 120, 145, 160
specification etc 145/6, 206, 218-20
withdrawal/disposal 226/7

Calder, James McLennan (Manager, 1920-45) 87, 90-2
Caversham, proposed trolleybus extensions in 107/8
Caversham Road railway bridges 64, 99/100, 146, 155, 179
Celebration of Victory Day 110/1
Cemetery Junction, remodelling of 148, 185, 188, 191, 203, 235
Christmas Day, bus services on 46/7, 68, 76, 89, 175, 229
Civil Defence Scheme 15
Conductresses 49-51, 59, 64, 68, 92, 112/3, 127, 144, 200, 216
Controlled acceleration equipment 180, 219
Co-ordination Agreement, proposed 61/2
Crescent Road yard 170, 198
Crossley DD42/8 .... 146, 165/6, 183/4, 188/9, 201/2, 205, 207, 240

Decontamination of vehicles 15, 34
Depots .... see *Bennet Road, Mill Lane*
Destination Blinds 22/3, 41, 136, 141/2, 157/8, 180, 199, 214
Dewirements 31, 158
Direction of Labour 49, 50, 68, 96, 113
Discount tickets/tokens 107, 127, 147
Dispersal of fleet (precaution against air raids) 15, 27, 54/5, 79
Double Summer Time 39, 61, 72, 77, 87, 99/100, 145, 228-30, 233/4
Driver training 99, 180, 182, 186, 191, 209, 213, 216
Drivers, hire from Smith's Coaches 38, 46, 48
Duty codes 55

Education Committee, school meals vans 116, 155, 183
Emergency Committee for Civil Defence 18, 30
Emmer Green, proposed trolleybus extension to 108
Erleigh Road trolleybus line 107, 216
Evacuation, civilian 15, 28/9, 35, 40/1, 43/4, 48, 89, 95, 229
government/commercial 29, 44, 57, 73
Evans, William John (Manager, 1946-67) 123, 125/6
Exercises, military/civil defence .... cover, 2, 19, 26/7, 48, 52, 63

Factory Specials 22, 59, 106, 127, 129, 138, 172/3, 191, 235
'Fairy lights' 147/8
Fares 22, 127, 147, 203
minimum 73, 125, 230
pre-collection of 63
protective (Thames Valley) 45, 61, 130, 165, 229, 234
stage structure 107, 127, 147
uncollected 51
See also *Discount, Pre-paid, Scholars' and Workmen's fares/tickets*
Fire at Mill Lane Depot, 18th January 1947 .... 129, 134/5
Fire watching 48, 87
Fleet, dispersal (precaution against air raids) 15, 27, 54/5, 79
summary as at 01 May 1939 .... 16/7
vehicles acquired 1939–1950 205-227
Flooding 2, 138-140, 159
Fluorescent lighting (trolleybus 154) 200, 219
Fog 100/1, 147/8, 164, 177
Football services 13, 47, 89, 134, 148, 157, 167 173-5
Freezing weather 38, 54, 91, 133/4, 138, 202/3
Fuel rationing/shortages 32, 34, 37, 52, 61, 64, 68, 72/3, 229/30
end of 76, 89, 100, 230
Future Policy Sub-Committee 10, 62, 102, 107/8, 127, 151, 153, 156, 193/4, 203

Gas, producer 64
Gas warfare and 'gas chamber buses' 15/32 .... 15, 17/8, 25/6, 38/9
Greenwich Mean Time 45, 100, 145, 228-31, 234/5
Guy Arab, delivery 80-82
engine replacement (AEC) 121
rebuilds 158, 189/90, 209/10
route allocation 80, 153
specification etc. 205, 208-10
withdrawal/disposal 189, 202, 223
Guy B, hire to London Transport 118
perimeter seating 53/4
reconditioning 14/5
use as inter-hospital ambulances 17-19, 25-27, 29, 43, 54, 116
use as 'mobile gas chambers' 17/8, 25/6
use for Road Safety Week promotion 112/3
withdrawal 15, 17, 116, 118, 120, 123, 138
Guy BA, withdrawal 15
Guy BT 103 .... 70, 180, 198
Guy CX, withdrawal 15
Guy FCX, perimeter seating 54
use as 'luggage vans' 28/9, 43
use as mobile enquiry offices 38, 54
use as 'mobile gas chambers' 38/9
use for 'War Week' promotions 39, 54, 75
withdrawal/disposal 18, 23, 26, 49, 75, 116

Headlamp masking 30/1, 42, 84, 89
Headlamps, nearside, removal of 127, 136
Home Guard 34, 41, 52, 63, 87, 93, 110
Horse buses 9
Horse trams 9
Hospital services 13, 22, 59, 173
Housing estates 10, 40, 95, 108
Housing shortage, post-war 96, 132/3, 147, 152, 159
Huddersfield Corporation .... see *Karrier E6*

Identity lights (blue or white) 7, 30, 156, 158, 209-11, 214/5, 218, 222
Inspectors, female 50, 127
'Invisible Lighting System' 31

Johannesburg Sunbeams 51/2

Karrier E6 .... 154/5, 160, 167-72, 177, 179, 198, 202, 206/7, 221/2, 227
Kentwood, extension of trolleybuses to 73, 83-5, 108

Last buses, time of 37, 39, 46, 52, 64, 68, 72, 89, 100, 109, 195, 228-30
Leyland TB4 104 .... 71, 191, 198
Leyland Titan 36 (open-staircase) 47, 115, 161, 174/5
Leyland Titans, condition of 75, 94, 115
withdrawal 115, 123, 157, 161, 177, 185
Little, William Morison (Manager, 1945-46) 91
Livery, description of 7
experiments & revisions 119-122, 124, 136/7, 146, 150, 209-12, 216
loss of RCT emblem from 170, 177/8, 182, 216

Loans of vehicles to other undertakings	48, 118, 144, 184/5, 210, 235
Local Defence Volunteers	see *Home Guard*
London Transport, hire of Guy B to	118
Lorries, departmental	116, 159, 190
Loudspeakers on buses	35
Management	13, 100
Manchester Corporation, inspection of Crossleys	145, 165/6, 183
McGuirk, Driver J. E.	110
Mill Lane depot,	146/7, 150
air raid shelter	15, 34
boiler house	55, 143
camouflage measures	34, 142
canteen	62/3, 97
construction	23
East Garage	2, 138, 154, 167
East Yard	171, 199
fire, 18th January 1947	129, 134/5
fuel supply system	15, 43, 55/6
Middle Garage	178
overhead shop	86
power station/substation	15, 41
Tan Lock, decking over of	129, 130, 156, 183
telephone repeater station	46
trolleybus wiring layout	157
'war effort' manufacturing operations at	44, 48, 64
workshops	34, 55, 86, 97, 154, 156
Minimum fares	73, 125, 230
Motorbuses, inauguration	9
Nationalisation	95, 136, 151/2, 178, 194
Northumb'd Ave, trolleybus ext'n	40, 108/9, 145, 156/7, 163/4, 179, 184, 234
Paint comparison tests	172
Parcels Express Service	23, 25, 38, 48, 63, 74, 76, 83, 97, 100, 111, 130, 186
Place names	7
Platform accidents	63, 116, 145, 169, 172
Platform doors	145/6, 153, 165, 183/4, 188/9, 219
Police Emergency Bus	44
Power cuts/failures	21, 100, 132/3, 138, 159, 202
Pre-fabricated housing	96, 159
Pre-paid fares	77, 107, 127, 147
Producer gas	64
Protective fares, Thames Valley	45, 61, 130, 165, 229, 234
Queue barriers	96, 197/8
Queue conductors	63, 174
Queue Regulators	40
Queuing	39/40, 47, 62, 96, 102, 104, 143, 197/8
Radio interference suppressors	71, 163
Ransomes 105	55, 71, 116, 180, 198
Rates relief	178
RCT emblem	170, 177/8, 182, 215/6, 218, 221
Reading, early closing day in	11
origins & history	9
population	9/10, 44, 61, 204
Reading Stations, extension of trolleybuses to	146, 148, 179, 187
road re-modelling	23/4, 49, 73, 146
Reading West station specials	55, 57-9
Reading Tramways Company	9
Regenerative braking	6, 172, 220
Requisitioning of buses	38, 49, 79
Reverser, Westwood Road	22, 180, 191
Reverser, Whitley Wood Lane	186-8
Road Safety Week	112/3, 146/7, 219
Roadblocks	42, 60
Roads, postwar reconstruction	101/2 104-6, 109-11, 113, 128/9, 131/2, 185/6, 200, 231-5
Roebuck, proposed trolleybus extension to	40, 108
Royal Ordnance Factory specials	57-9
Scholars' tickets/passes	107, 127, 147
Schools services	13, 43/4, 59, 74, 101, 106/7, 127/8, 174, 229
Secondhand vehicles, search for	51, 149, 154
Services, extension beyond borough boundary	62, 151
post-war re-routing	104/5, 131/2, 231-5
route maps	33, inside front & back covers
summary as at May 1939	12/3
Shelters, passenger	56, 61, 72, 176, 196/7
Silver Lining Savings Exhibition	150, 153, 211
Smith's Coaches	27, 29, 38, 180, 183
hire of drivers from	38, 46, 48
hire of vehicles from	43, 46, 106/7, 148, 173/4, 229
hire of vehicles to	144, 210
storage of RCT vehicles by	54
Special services, commercial/industrial/military/school/sports	57-9, 173-5
Stadium specials	13, 89, 174
Staff Athletic & Social Club	93
Staff buses	59
Staff, photographs of	50, 87, 90, 92, 97, 110, 112/3, 126, 144
Staff serving in Armed Forces	48, 62, 96
Staff shortages	38, 48-51, 76, 193, 200
Staircases	145/6
Standing passengers	32, 37, 53/4, 56, 63, 155
Statistics: mileage	10, 37/8, 52, 63, 74, 83, 100, 111, 125, 130, 186
passengers	5, 9/10, 37/8, 44, 52, 63, 74, 83, 100, 111, 125, 130, 155, 186, 199
revenue	10, 38, 52, 100, 111, 127, 130, 147, 155/6, 178, 186, 199
Stations	see *Reading Stations*
Street furniture, visibility of	30/1, 36, 63
Street lighting	11, 25, 87, 99, 101, 133
Strike, workshop staff	155, 167
Substations	15, 37, 48, 144/5, 154, 163, 182, 184
Sunbeam F4A	217
Sunbeam MF2A 101/6	70/1, 180, 198
Sunbeam S7	146, 149, 164/5, 190/1, 200-2, 207, 240
Sunbeam W	80/1, 202, 206, 217/8, 226
Sunday morning services	64, 68, 89, 109, 230
Tea van service	63, 74
Termini, renaming of	41, 136, 141, 229, 233
Thames Valley Traction Co	24, 29, 61/2, 64, 84, 118, 130, 132, 151, 153, 158, 187, 197
hire of buses from	174
hire of buses to	184/5, 235
Tickets	128, 237
See also *Discount, Pre-paid, Scholars' and Workmen's fares/tickets*
Ticket machines, Bell Punch Ultimate	154, 237
TIM	37, 52, 154, 237
Timeclocks	15, 35, 45
Timetables	20, 62, 195/6
Tours	159/60, 178/9
Tower wagons	116, 192
Traction batteries	21/2, 69, 102, 170, 172, 177, 179, 191, 199, 235
Traffic Regulator's hut	61, 165/6
Tram rail, removal	25, 34/5, 42, 52/3, 98, 101/2, 104-6, 113, 131/2, 154, 185
use for road blocks	42
Tramways, abandonment	10, 21
electrification	9
horse	9
Trolleybuses: general info	6
Caversham/Emmer Green extensions (proposed)	107/8
Erleigh Road training line	107
inauguration	10
Johannesburg Sunbeams	51/2
Kentwood extension	73, 83-5, 108
'main line', inauguration	20-3
Northumberland Ave extension	40, 108/9, 145, 163/4, 179, 184, 234
'original six'	17, 21, 70/1, 198
overtaking loop, Norcot	198, 202
Roebuck extension (proposed)	40, 108
Stations extension	146, 148, 179, 187
tours	159/60
town centre loop (proposed)	156
Whitley service, suspension	91, 109-11, 131
Whitley Wood extension	40, 108/9, 145, 154, 163-5, 179, 186/7, 235
Turning circle, Bear Inn	22
Cemetery Junction	148, 185, 188, 191, 203, 235
Community Centre	199
Norcot Junction	22
Northumberland Avenue	156/7, 199, 202
St. Mary's Butts	161/2, 177, 188
Three Tuns	22, 149
Whitley Street	164
Turning loop, Liverpool Road	22
Tyres	64, 72, 130, 186
Uncollected fare boxes	51
Unfrozen buses, definition of	79
Utility buses, definition of	79
Vans & cars, departmental	68, 74, 91, 100, 116, 125, 134, 159, 190, 194, 196
Vastern Road railway bridges	21, 107/8, 138, 146
VE Day	92/3
VE2 Day	93, 95, 100
VJ Day	95
Welfare Officer	64, 68
Whitley trolleybus service, suspension of	91, 109-11, 131
Whitley Wood, trolleybus ext'n to	40, 108/9, 145, 154, 163-5, 179, 186/7, 235
Windows, anti-blast precautions	31, 43, 46
Women, employment of	49-51, 59, 64, 68/9, 103, 112/3, 127, 144, 200, 216
Workmen's fares/tickets	58, 77, 107, 127/8, 147, 177
Works services	46/7, 57-9, 68, 76/7, 85/6, 91, 96, 127, 138, 194, 229/30, 235

A New Era Beckons...

Above: *A pre-delivery photograph of bus 89 (ERD 158), a Crossley-bodied Crossley DD42/8, which took up service immediately after the period covered by this book. One of a batch of twelve '8-footers', these were the first motor-buses to be received which were fitted with platform doors.*   ACV Limited